Praise for *Special Providence*

"Brilliant . . . thought-provoking . . . Walter Russell Mead, a prolific and engaging writer, has produced a history of American foreign policy turning upon American ideas and practices since the days of the Founders. At its core is a myth-breaking proposition that the U.S. has been actively, and mostly successfully, involved in the world economically and diplomatically since the early days of the Republic. American isolationism, the author argues, is a myth propagated to rally public opinion for engagement in the early days of the Cold War."

—*The Washington Monthly*

"A stunning achievement. At a time of crisis, Mead's book forces the reader to rethink the central ideas that have guided American foreign policy in the past and are likely to shape its future."

—James Chace, author of *The Secretary of State Who Created the American World*

"In his ambitious and important new book, Walter Russell Mead offers a provocative and highly original way of looking at American foreign policy, one that moves far beyond the conventional wisdom of 'realists vs. idealists.' His insights linking the grand sweep of American history to our present world situation are particularly valuable. I recommend this book to anyone who is interested in America's role in our increasingly complex world."

—Richard C. Holbrooke, author of *To End a War*

"Exceedingly interesting . . . a treasure trove for modern-day policy-makers seeking historical justifications for their positions . . ."

—James P. Rubin, *The New Republic*

"A fresh and well-written introduction to American foreign policy traditions."

—*Foreign Affairs*

"To understand U.S. foreign policy, it is necessary to understand the United States. Nobody understands either better than Walter Russell Mead. This book is destined to join the small list of classics that explain America to the world and to Americans themselves."

—Michael E. Lind, author of *Vietnam, The Necessary War*

"This important book—high-spirited, eloquent, and imaginative—could well change the way we think about America's relations with the world."

—Ronald Steel, author of *Temptations of a Superpower*

"This ingenious and provocative account of American foreign policy's past is a splendid introduction to its future."

—Michael Mandelbaum, author of *The Dawn of Peace in Europe*

"Few people writing on U.S. foreign policy are as brilliant and original as Walter Russell Mead. In *Special Providence* he shatters old diplomatic theories and historical assumptions with a creative vengeance. The result is a brave, landmark study that cannot be ignored."

—Douglas Brinkley, author of *Rise to Globalism: American Foreign Policy Since 1938*

American
Foreign Policy
and How
It Changed
the World

SPECIAL PROVIDENCE

Walter Russell Mead

Routledge
Taylor & Francis Group

NEW YORK AND LONDON

Published in 2002 by
Routledge
29 West 35th Street
New York, NY 10001
www.routledge-ny.com

Published in Great Britain
Routledge
11 New Fetter Lane
London EC4P 4EE
www.routledge.co.uk

Routledge is an imprint of the Taylor & Francis Group.
Printed in the United States of America on acid-free paper.

10 9 8 7 6 5

Library of Congress Cataloging-in-Publication Data

Mead, Walter Russell.
    Special Providence : American foreign policy and how it changed the world / Walter
Russell Mead.
        p. cm.
    Originally published: New York : Knopf, 2001.
    "A Century Foundation book."
    Includes bibliographical references and index.
    ISBN 0-415-93536-9 (pbk. : alk. paper)
    1. United States—Foreign relations. 2. United States—Foreign relations—Philosophy. I.
Title.

E183.7 .M47156 2002
327.73—dc21
                                                                                2002026704

To my teachers, and especially to Bruce Cooper,

Robert Parker, Acosta Nichols, Richard Irons,

Richard Brodhead, and Leslie Gelb

God has a special providence for fools, drunks,
and the United States of America.

—ATTRIBUTED TO OTTO VON BISMARCK

Contents

Foreword

Since the end of the Cold War, scholars of foreign policy have been seeking a way to describe the new architecture of American foreign policy. Certain that something profound has happened, they have engaged in a wide-ranging search for the new "grail" of understanding— some overarching synthesis that would explain the central themes and goals of U.S. policy for the twenty-first century. There are a number of significant obstacles to achieving success in this quest. Not least is the fact that, given the relatively short time since the end of the standoff between the West and the Soviet bloc, there is good reason to be cautious about the durability of any particular definition of current global political issues.

The past dozen years have been full of surprises, starting with the collapse of the Soviet Union and extending, most recently, to the sudden, perhaps significant, opening of North Korea. One might expect, therefore, that this constantly shifting landscape would compel restraint when it comes to sweeping generalizations about both the present and the future. But, to the contrary, there has been a steady stream of published opinion outlining new "grand strategies" for the United States in the post–Cold War era. Without belittling the quality of the best of these works, it is fair to say that, as of this writing, we still await the definitive analysis of U.S. policies toward the world at this early moment in a new century.

This is not to say that, because of the remarkable alterations in world politics, fresh insight into the nation's goals and missions is impossible. In fact, as this book by Walter Mead, author and senior fellow for U.S. Foreign Policy at the Council on Foreign Relations, suggests, in the right hands the broad questions of American policy are susceptible to both enhanced clarity and deeper understanding. Mead's basic assertion is straightforward. He contends that, although the United States does have enormous additional room in which to maneuver in the twenty-first century, it scarcely has a blank slate on which to write a new foreign policy. He perceives certain fundamental characteristics or themes in our stance toward international questions, themes that, he argues, remain as powerful today as they have been in the past. Mead is persuasive when he asserts that one of the best ways to comprehend our current choices and determine possible responses is to reflect upon the abiding strains in our foreign policies over the past two hundred years. In other words, Mead uses American history as a lens for sharpening our perceptions about the present and the future. He explains the way in which American foreign policy has always echoed deeply held and lasting notions about both the outside world and our national interests.

Surveying the record of American diplomacy, Mead posits four principal schools of thought, identifying them with four great individual Americans—Hamilton, Jefferson, Jackson, and Wilson. He emphasizes, of course, that the balance among the clusters of views represented by these four schools has shifted over time, usually in response to changes in the world. Still, Mead convincingly contends that the sharper our understanding of these four approaches, the better we will grasp American reactions to past and future foreign policy challenges. Moreover, our flexibility, as represented by the shifting influence of each school, has, in Mead's view, been a continuing source of strength for us. And, whether one is in complete agreement with him or not, Mead's work is certain to provoke fresh thinking about America's current and future foreign policy debates.

Through this book and others, The Century Foundation is attempting to contribute to the reexamination of American foreign policy that has been taking place since the end of the Cold War. Our efforts in this area began with a firsthand report on the events leading to the collapse of the Berlin Wall: Elizabeth Pond's report, *After the Wall*, which was followed a few years later by her full-length study for us, *Beyond the Wall*. In the early post–Cold War years, we also published Richard Ullman's *Securing Europe*, James Chace's *The Consequences of Peace*, Jonathan Dean's *Ending Europe's Wars*, Michael Mandelbaum's *The Dawn of Peace in Europe*, John Gerard Ruggie's *Winning the Peace: America and World Order in a New Era*, and Steven Burg's *War or Peace? Nationalism, Democracy, and American Foreign Policy in Post-Communist Europe*. We also supported numerous analyses of America's foreign policy toward nations in other parts of the world, its trade relations, its arms and intelligence policies, and its relations with the United Nations. Our most recent publications looking at this critical issue include Edward Luck's *Mixed Messages: American Politics and International Organizations,* Leon V. Sigal's *Hang Separately: Cooperative Security between the United States and Russia,* and a volume edited by Morton Abramowitz, *Turkey's Transformation and American Policy.* In addition, we have a number of ongoing examinations of current American foreign policy–making: a search for a new foundation for U.S. foreign policy by Michael Mandelbaum, a number of books and papers examining U.S. foreign policy toward Asia, and forthcoming books by David Calleo, Henry Nau, and Gregory Treverton.

Ultimately, any important new work about foreign affairs must come to terms not only with the end of the Cold War but also with the accelerated pace of change in the modern era. If the task of writing in this area thus seems more daunting than it has in the recent past, perhaps that is only because we are more aware of the certainty of unpredictable change. In this context especially, Walter Mead's approach to policy questions is particularly useful. His perspective helps to remind us of who we are and who we have been. This way of thinking may well be our most reliable guide to answering another important question: What should we do next? On behalf of The Century Foundation, I congratulate him on the completion of this thoughtful book.

Richard C. Leone, President, The Century Foundation
March 2001

Introduction

This is a book about how and why American foreign policy works. In little more than two hundred years, the United States has grown from a handful of settlements on the Atlantic seaboard to become the most powerful country in the history of the world. Both foreigners and Americans themselves take this remarkable development for granted. Throughout the U.S. rise to world power, most observers have believed that the country did not care very much about foreign policy and was not very good at it. Even today in the United States, most policy-makers and pundits think that foreign policy played only a very marginal role in American life before World War II, and that there is very little to be gained by studying the historical records of our past.

When Richard C. Leone and The Century Foundation commissioned me to write a book about American foreign policy at the end of the Cold War, I found myself increasingly drawn to question this conventional wisdom. I wondered if American success in the rough-and-tumble contest of nations wasn't due just to dumb luck, the special providence for drunks, fools, and the United States of America that Bismarck believed watched over us. I also wondered if the American foreign policy system had a logic of its own, a different logic from the one that governed the foreign policy of the traditional great powers of Europe.

Two discrepancies led me to ask these questions. First, there was the odd fact that while much conventional discussion of foreign policy assumes at least tacitly that democracy is at best an irrelevance and at worst a serious obstacle in foreign affairs, in the twentieth century democratic states were generally more successful in foreign policy than either monarchies or dictatorships. The clearest examples come from Germany and Japan. Under nondemocratic regimes, both Germany and Japan followed risky, aggressive foreign policies that ultimately brought them to misery and ruin. Starting under much less favorable external circumstances after World War II, democratic German and Japanese governments made their countries rich, peaceful, and respected. Was it possible that something about democracy actually improves the ability of governments to conduct their foreign affairs?

Second, I could not escape the fact that the two most recent great powers in world history were what Europeans still sometimes refer to as "Anglo-Saxon" powers: Great Britain and the United States. Besides having a large number of cultural similarities, these two countries have historically looked at the world in a different way than have most of the European countries. The British Empire was, and the United States is, concerned not just with the balance of power in one particular corner of the world but with the evolution of what we today call "world order." A worldwide system of trade and finance made both Britain and the United States rich; those riches were what gave them the power to project the military force that ensured the stability of their international systems. Both Britain and the United States spent less time thinking about the traditional military security preoccupations of European power diplomacy and more time thinking about money and trade. "A nation of shopkeepers!" Napoleon scoffed about Britain—but the shopkeepers got him in the end.

Could it be that the British shopkeepers and American democrats know something about foreign policy that Napoleon and Bismarck didn't?

These questions led me to the study of the history of American foreign policy. What I found has changed the way I look at that subject, and at American politics, today.

For one thing, I found that foreign policy has played a much more important role in American politics throughout our history than I expected. Our contemporary battles over the North American Free Trade Area (NAFTA) and the World Trade Organization (WTO) are the latest installments in a long line of American political contests over trade issues. Long before World War II or even World War I, foreign policy questions were deciding American elections, reshaping American politics, and driving the growth of the American economy.

I also found that American thinking about foreign policy has been relatively stable over the centuries. The arguments over foreign policy in George Washington's administration—and some of the bitterest political battles Washington engaged in were over foreign policy—are clearly related to the debates of our own time.

Americans through the centuries seem to have had four basic ways of looking at foreign policy, which have reflected contrasting and sometimes complementary ways of looking at domestic policy as well. *Hamiltonians* regard a strong alliance between the national government and big business as the key both to domestic stability and to effective action abroad, and they have long focused on the nation's need to be integrated into the global economy on favorable terms. *Wilsonians* believe that the United States has both a moral obligation and an important national interest in spreading American democratic and social values throughout the world, creating a peaceful international community that accepts the rule of law. *Jeffersonians* hold that American foreign policy should be less concerned about spreading democracy abroad than about safeguarding it at home; they have historically been skeptical about Hamiltonian and Wilsonian policies that involve the United States with unsavory allies abroad or that increase the risks of war. Finally, a large populist school I call *Jacksonian* believes that the most important goal of the U.S. government in both foreign and domestic policy should be the physical security and the economic well-being of the American people. "Don't Tread on Me!" warned the rattlesnake on the Revolutionary battle flag; Jacksonians believe that the United States should not seek out foreign quarrels, but when other nations start wars with the United States, Jacksonian opinion agrees with Gen. Douglas MacArthur that "There is no substitute for victory."

These four schools have shaped the American foreign policy debate from the eighteenth century to the twenty-first. They are as important under George W. Bush as they were under George Washington and from everything that I can see, American foreign policy will continue to emerge from their collisions and debates far into the future.

While this book is an attempt to explain the U.S. rise to world power, it is not intended as yet another paean to what some seem to see as America's Manifest Destiny to rule the world. The long economic boom of the 1990s spawned some triumphalist literature about the American way of capitalism and the growth of American power. This book is not a part of that literature; it ends on a cautionary, not a triumphalist, note. After each of the three great wars of the twentieth century—the two world wars and the Cold War—many voices in America proclaimed an "end to history." With the powers of evil defeated, the United States and its allies, some argued each time, would go on in the postwar period to build a new world order of justice, peace, and democracy.

History, alas, has a way of hanging on. More than a decade after the Cold War, it now seems clear that the twenty-first century is bringing the United States new challenges and new problems. Not all countries will become democratic; not all democratic countries will agree with the United States about how the world should be run. Foreign policy will not become a field of dreams; our choices will sometimes be painful ones, and together with new opportunities and adventures this century may well bring new wars and new problems that are even worse than those of the bloody century just past.

But if this book is not triumphalist, it is optimistic. American foreign policy will not bring history to an end, but it has done a remarkably good job of enabling the United States to flourish as history goes on. I do not know how long the present moment of American supremacy will last, or if the world is due for a second American century. I am not even sure that another century of American global hegemony is what the American people should hope for. But the long and successful record of this country's unique—and uniquely complex—foreign policy system gives me solid grounds for believing that whatever else happens in the world, our foreign policy tradition offers the American people real hope for a prosperous and democratic future.

Walter Russell Mead
July 2001

SPECIAL
PROVIDENCE

Chapter One

THE AMERICAN
FOREIGN POLICY
TRADITION

L ord Bryce, a British statesman who served as Britain's ambassador to the United States from 1907 to 1913, once wrote that the
role of foreign policy in American life could be described the way travelers described snakes in Ireland: "There are no snakes in Ireland."[1]

That at the turn of the twentieth century the United States had no
foreign policy worth noting was a view that, in retrospect, many Americans would come to share. How such a view arose is somewhat mysterious. Americans of 1900 thought they had an active, indeed a global,
foreign policy. The Spanish-American War had only recently ended, and
American forces were still in the midst of a bitter war against guerrilla
freedom fighters in the Philippines. It was a time, in fact, when many
Americans were struck by a sense that the United States was coming of
age. "Th' simple home-lovin' maiden that our fathers knew has disappeared," said Mr. Dooley in 1902, "an' in her place we find a Columbya,
gintlemen, with machurer charms, a knowledge iv Euro-peen customs
an' not averse to a cigareet."[2]

In 1895 one of America's many successful but largely forgotten secretaries of state, Richard Olney, had forced the British to back down in a
boundary dispute between British Guiana (now Guyana) and Venezuela.
"Today the United States," stated Olney, "is practically sovereign on this
continent, and its fiat is law upon the subjects to which it confines its

interposition."[3] Not content with forcing the British to acknowledge their secondary status in the Western Hemisphere, the United States was exerting increasing influence in Asia. It was Secretary of State John Hay who proclaimed the Open Door policy toward China, and, rather surprisingly, the other great powers accepted American opposition to further partition of a weak Chinese empire. Under Lord Bryce's friend Theodore Roosevelt, the United States would humiliate Britain three times in the Western Hemisphere: First, the Hay-Pauncefote Treaty of 1900 saw Britain give up its long-standing insistence on equal rights in any Central American canal. When the Senate rejected this agreement as too generous to Britain, the unhappy Lord Pauncefote, Britain's ambassador to the United States, had to concede even more Isthmian rights and put his name to a second and even more humiliating agreement with Hay. The third humiliation came when Britain, increasingly anxious not to offend the United States at a time when tensions were growing with Germany, agreed to settle a boundary dispute between Alaska and Canada on American terms.

The energetic Roosevelt's foreign policy did not stop with these successes. He would send the famous "White Fleet" of the U.S. Navy on a round-the-world tour to demonstrate the nation's new and modern battle fleet; arbitrate the Russo-Japanese War; send delegates to the 1906 Algeciras Conference in Spain, convened to settle differences among the European powers over Morocco; and generally demonstrate a level of diplomatic activity entirely incommensurate with the number of Hibernian snakes.

The closing years of the nineteenth century and the opening years of the twentieth saw American politics roiled by a series of foreign policy debates. Should Hawaii, Cuba, the Philippines, or Puerto Rico be annexed, and if so, on what terms? Should the United States continue to participate in its de facto currency union with Britain (the gold standard), or not? How high should tariffs on foreign goods be—should the United States confine itself to a "revenue tariff" set at levels to support the country's budgetary needs, or should it continue or even increase the practice of protective tariffs?

Lord Bryce knew all this very well, but he had reasons for making the statement he did. Like many British diplomats of his day, he wanted the United States to remain part of the British international system, a world order that was in 1900 almost as elaborate as, and in some respects even more interdependent and integrated than, the American world order that exists today.

There was, he conceded, one diplomatic representative the United States did require, however. The Americans could fire the rest of their ambassadors and not notice any real difference, he said, but the United States did need to keep its ambassador at the Court of St. James.

This change would have been a great deal more beneficial to Great Britain than to the United States, but the good lord had a point. In 1900 Great Britain was at the center of a global empire and financial system, a system that in many respects included the United States. On the occasion of Queen Victoria's Diamond Jubilee in 1897, often considered the high-water mark of British power and prestige, the *New York Times* was moved to acknowledge this fact. "We are part," said the *Times* in words that were no doubt very welcome to Lord Bryce, "and a great part, of the Greater Britain which seems so plainly destined to dominate the planet."[4]

In a certain sense the *Times* was right. One hundred years ago the economic, military, and political destiny of the United States was wrapped up in its relationship with Great Britain. The Pax Britannica shaped the international environment in which the United States operated.

In the last analysis Lord Bryce's comment was less an informed observation about American history and foreign policy than it was a hopeful statement about the durability of the British Empire. It was a prayer, not a fact. Bryce hoped that Britain could continue to manage the European balance of power on its own, with little more than the passive American participation it had enjoyed since the proclamation of the Monroe Doctrine. The British statesmen of his day hoped that if they offered the United States a "free hand" in the Western Hemisphere, and supported the Open Door policy in China, the United States would not contest Britain's desire to shape the destinies of the rest of the world.

That Lord Bryce would have discounted and minimized the importance of foreign policy in the United States does not startle; that so many important American writers and thinkers would join him in a wholesale dismissal of the country's foreign policy traditions is more surprising. Indeed, one of the most remarkable features about American foreign policy today is the ignorance of and contempt for the national foreign policy tradition on the part of so many thoughtful people here and abroad. Most countries are guided in large part by traditional foreign policies that change only slowly. The British have sought a balance of power in Europe since the fifteenth century and the rise of the Tudors. The French have been concerned with German land power and British or American economic and commercial power for almost as long. Under both the czars and the commissars, Russia sought to expand to the south and the west. Those concerns still shape the foreign policy of today's weakened Russia as it struggles to retain control of the Caucasus, project influence into the Balkans, and prevent the absorption of the Baltic states and Ukraine into NATO.

Only in the United States can there be found a wholesale and casual dismissal of the continuities that have shaped our foreign policy in the past. "America's journey through international politics," wrote Henry Kissinger, "has been a triumph of faith over experience. . . . Torn between nostalgia for a pristine past and yearning for a perfect future, American thought has oscillated between isolationism and commitment."[5]

At the suggestion of columnist Joseph Alsop, the extremely intelligent George Shultz acquired a collection of books about American diplomacy when he became secretary of state, but nowhere in his 1,138-page record of more than six years' service does he mention anything he learned from them. [6] The 672 fascinating pages of James A. Baker III's memoirs of his distinguished service as secretary of state are, with the exception of a passing mention of Theodore Roosevelt's 1903 intervention in Panama, similarly devoid of references to the activities of American diplomats or statesmen before World War II.[7]

For Richard Nixon, American history seemed to begin and end with the Cold War. American history before 1945 remained a fuzzy blank to him; even in his final book he could call the United States "the only great power without a history of imperialistic claims on neighboring countries"[8]—a characterization that would surprise such neighboring countries as Mexico, Canada, and Cuba (and such countries as France and Spain that lost significant territories to American ambition) as much as it would surprise such expansionist American presidents as Thomas Jefferson, Andrew Jackson, James Knox Polk, James Buchanan, Ulysses Simpson Grant, and Theodore Roosevelt.[9] Other than warning about the dangers of isolationism and offering panegyrics on American virtues, Nixon was largely contemptuous of or silent about the traditional aims, methods, and views of American foreign policy, although he frequently and respectfully referred to the foreign policy traditions of other countries with which he had had to deal.

The tendency to reduce the American foreign policy tradition to a legacy of moralism and isolationism can also be found among the Democratic statesmen who have attempted to guide American foreign policy in the last twenty years. Some, like Jimmy Carter, have embraced the moralism while rejecting the isolationism; others share the Republican contempt for both. The copious and learned books of Zbigniew Brzezinski show few signs of close familiarity with the history of American foreign policy or with the achievements of his predecessors, much less a sense of the traditional strategies and goals that guided their work. Similarly, the memoirs of former secretary of defense Robert McNamara and former secretary of state Dean Rusk rarely touch on American foreign policy before 1941. When former secretary of state Warren Christopher selected and published the most important speeches of his tenure in office, the collected documents contained only one reference to the diplomatic activity of any American before FDR, and that was to what Christopher sees as the failures of Woodrow Wilson's efforts vis-à-vis the League of Nations and human rights.[10]

The deep lack of interest in the history of American foreign policy is not confined to high officials. The overwhelming majority of their talented and hardworking colleagues in think tanks, universities, the national media, and government departments that are concerned with developing, carrying out, reporting, and reflecting on the foreign policy of the United States do not know very much about the history of American foreign policy before World War II, do not particularly want to learn more than they already know, and cannot think what practical purpose a deeper knowledge of American foreign policy history might serve.

This lack of knowledge and curiosity about the history of American foreign policy contrasts with what is in general a passion for historical learning among our foreign policy intellectuals. The history of American foreign policy from Pearl Harbor forward is well known and well studied. Lives of such statesmen as Dean Acheson, the Bundy brothers, and Harry Truman—sometimes long and detailed biographies running to several large volumes—find respectable audiences, as do the memoirs of living American statesmen. Foreign policy analysts and journalists are also reasonably well versed in the domestic side of American history and, particularly since the end of the Cold War, the American foreign policy establishment justly prides itself on its knowledge of the histories and cultures of the many peoples and nations with which American foreign policy has had to deal. It is only the history of our foreign policy before World War II that lies buried in obscurity.

The widespread indifference to and disdain for that history is, at least on the face of things, somewhat surprising. The United States has had a remarkably successful history in international relations. After a rocky start, the young American republic quickly established itself as a force to be reckoned with. The Revolutionaries shrewdly exploited the tensions in European politics to build a coalition against Great Britain. Artful diplomatic pressure and the judicious application of incentives and threats enabled the United States to emerge from the Napoleonic Wars with the richest spoils of any nation—the Louisiana Purchase rose on the ruins of Napoleon's hopes for a New World empire. During the subsequent decades, American diplomacy managed to outmanuever Great Britain and the Continental powers on a number of occasions, annexing Florida, extending its boundary to the Pacific, opening Japan to world commerce, thwarting British efforts to consolidate the independence of Texas, and conquering the Southwest from Mexico despite the reservations of the European powers.

During the Civil War, deft American diplomacy defeated repeated efforts by powerful elements in both France and Britain to intervene on behalf of Confederate independence. The United States demonstrated a sure diplomatic touch during the conflict, prudently giving in over the seizure of Confederate commissioners from a British ship in the *Trent* affair, but firmly forcing a reluctant Great Britain to observe the principles of neutrality and to pay compensation for their violation in the controversies over Confederate ships built by British firms.

Within a generation after the Civil War, the United States became a recognized world power while establishing an unchallenged hegemony in the Western Hemisphere. As to American intervention in World War I, it was a failure only compared to the lofty goals Wilson set for himself. The United States failed to end war forever and to establish a universal democratic system—challenging goals, to say the least—but otherwise it did very well. With fewer casualties than any other great power, and fewer forces on the ground in Europe, the United States had a disproportionately influential role in shaping the peace. Monarchical government in Europe disappeared as a result of the war: Since 1918 Europe has been a continent of republics, and the great thrones and royal houses that once mocked the United States and its democratic pretensions have vanished from the earth.

Fashionable though it has long been to scorn the Treaty of Versailles, and flawed though that instrument undoubtedly was, one must note that Wilson's principles survived the eclipse of the Versailles system and that they still guide European politics today: self-determination, democratic government, collective security, international law, and a league of nations. Wilson may not have gotten everything he wanted at Versailles, and his treaty was never ratified by the Senate, but his vision and his diplomacy, for better or worse, set the tone for the twentieth century. France, Germany, Italy, and Britain may have sneered at Wilson, but every one of these powers today conducts its European policy along Wilsonian lines. What was once dismissed as visionary is now accepted as fundamental. This was no mean achievement, and no European statesman of the twentieth century has had as lasting, as benign, or as widespread an influence.

Even in the short term, the statesmen who sneered at Wilson did no better than he did. The leaders of France, Britain, and Italy—Georges Clemenceau, David Lloyd George, and Vittorio Orlando—did not do very well at Versailles; none of them gained anything of real or lasting value by the peace. The United States was the only true winner of World War I, as it had been the real winner of the Napoleonic conflicts of the previous century.

World War I made the United States the world's greatest financial power, crushed Germany—economically, America's most dangerous rival—and reduced both Britain and France to a status where neither country could mount an effective opposition to American designs anywhere in the world. In the aftermath of the war Britain conceded to the United States something it had withheld from all its rivals in two centuries of warfare: Britain accepted the United States as co-monarch of the seas, formally recognizing the right of the United States to maintain a navy equal to its own. Wilson and Warren Harding succeeded where Napoleon and Wilhelm II had failed, and they did it without a war with Great Britain. An American diplomacy that asserted American interests while emphasizing the community of values between the two principal English-speaking nations induced Great Britain to accept peacefully what no previous rival had extracted by force.[11]

The result of World War II was more of the same. The United States entered the war later than any other great power, lost less blood in the fighting, and realized greater gains from the settlement than any other combatant. Churchill defended the British Empire against Hitler and Hirohito, but he was no match for Franklin D. Roosevelt. Stalin gained hegemony over the wasted landscapes of Europe's devastated east, but the United States secured an unchallenged position of leadership in a bloc of countries that included the richest, most dynamic, and most intellectually advanced societies in the world.

Since that time, the United States has made mistakes, but overall its diplomacy has been remarkably successful. The United States not only won the Cold War, it diffused its language, culture, and products worldwide—the American dollar became the international medium of finance; the American language became the lingua franca of world business; American popular culture and American consumer products dominated world media and world markets. The United States is not only the sole global power, its values inform a global consensus, and it dominates to an unprecedented degree the formation of the first truly global civilization our planet has known.

Despite all this, foreign policy commentators and practitioners alike hold that the United States, in order to succeed in foreign policy, must abandon its naive "oscillation between idealism and isolationism" and embrace the mature, sophisticated, worldly approach of European statesmen. They have succeeded at foreign policy, critics say, and we have repeatedly failed.

Nobody, however, seems to ask a basic question: Which European country has had a more "sophisticated" and successful foreign policy than the United States in the twentieth century or, indeed, ever?

Kissinger points to Klemens von Metternich, but the great Austrian prince outlived his own system and saw it collapse in 1848. Great Britain marched into the twentieth century like a lion but limped out like a palsied lamb, retaining only the energy to bleat that the brash and clumsy Americans ought to defer to its superior wisdom, experience, and realism in foreign affairs. As Dean Acheson said once, Britain had lost an empire and had not found a role; far from solving this problem, British statesmen since Harold Macmillan have failed either to establish British leadership within the European Union or to find a great-power role for Britain outside Europe.

France achieved little in the twentieth century, or indeed since the death of Talleyrand, that the United States ought to emulate. Since Napoleon III brought the disaster of the Franco-Prussian War on himself, French foreign policy has known many defeats and pyrrhic victories, but few real successes. In 1918 France recovered Alsace and Lorraine, but only at the cost of a war that bled it white and destroyed forever its standing as a military power of the first rank. France's interwar policy was never coherent or feasible; the Little Entente in east central Europe was a fiasco, and France's collapse in 1940 still casts a shadow over its standing in Europe and the world. Charles de Gaulle, unquestionably the greatest French foreign policy leader of the twentieth century, is chiefly celebrated for his courage in liquidating the disastrous struggle to maintain a colonial regime in Algeria. Over the other failures, betrayals, brutalities, futilities, and disasters of French statesmen in Indochina, and in North and West Africa after World War II, let friendship and gratitude for the legacy of Lafayette cast their veils of discretion. France's European policy under François Mitterrand ended with reluctant acquiescence in German unification and a growing recognition that the century-long effort to defend France's historic position as the leading political power in Europe had failed. This is not a record for American statesmen to emulate.

Farther east, the record is darker. Should the United States imitate the "realism" of the Soviet Union and borrow the policy of the losing power in the Cold War? Or should we look to the policy of the Romanovs, which brought their empire crashing down into chaos and ruin?

If we return to Germany, we see that the delicate structures of Bismarck collapsed, that the aggressiveness of Kaiser Wilhelm II led to disaster, and that Hitler's drive for domination culminated in national catastrophe. Japan's efforts to model its foreign policy after those of European states produced a similar debacle in Asia. It was only when Germany and Japan began to take lessons from the fecklessly idealistic United States—an emphasis on commerce rather than militarism, a disinclination to spend unnecessary money on their armed forces, a dedication to the construction of international systems of security and law—that these two countries began to succeed. Similarly, the greatest success story in modern Europe, the development of the EU, originated in economic cooperation demanded by the United States in return for Marshall Plan aid, and Jean Monnet, the architect of the union, found his inspiration and guidance on the western side of the Atlantic.

Compared, in sum, with the dismal record of the other great powers, American foreign policy—with a handful of exceptions, most notably Vietnam—looks reasonably good. Cast morality aside for the moment. From a purely practical standpoint, no European power, with the possible exceptions of Switzerland, Sweden, and Vatican City, has done better than the United States in the twentieth century; most have done much, much worse. It may be that we have lessons to learn; what is not so certain is that Europe is the place we must look for our teachers.

Not only has American foreign policy been more successful than the conventional wisdom acknowledges, it has played a much more central role throughout American history than many Americans believe. The leading statesmen of the United States often devoted more of their attention to foreign policy questions before and during the Civil War than they did during the twentieth-century Cold War. Indeed, of the first nine presidents of the United States, six had previously served as secretary of state, and seven as ministers abroad. Four of the first twelve—Washington, Jackson, William Henry Harrison, and Zachary Taylor—won fame for commanding American troops in the field, fame that was in each case the most important single factor in their gaining the presidency. Six of the fifteen American presidents who served before Lincoln had been *both* secretary of state and minister to Great Britain; a seventh, Jefferson, had been secretary of state and minister to France; and an eighth, John Adams, had been minister to both Britain and France.

The greatest minds and the most powerful politicians in the United States were eager to serve as secretary of state in the nineteenth century. Only the presidency itself stood higher in precedence, in power, and in political visibility. Success in foreign policy was considered one of the strongest possible qualifications for a presidential candidate, and such great leaders as Henry Clay, John Calhoun, and Daniel Webster distinguished themselves in this office. Throughout the nineteenth century the American diplomatic and consular service included some of the greatest names in politics and letters. Writers like Washington Irving, George Bancroft, Nathaniel Hawthorne, John Lothrop Motley, and George Washington Williams[12] represented their country abroad; in 1902 the political cartoonist Thomas Nast served as a United States consul in Ecuador. Formidable political figures, including William Seward, Charles Francis Adams, James G. Blaine, and John Hay, regarded their diplomatic service as the peak of their careers.

It was no accident that so many American political leaders devoted so much attention to foreign policy in the so-called isolationist period. The prosperity and happiness of the average American family were visibly

Presidential Experience in Foreign Affairs

	Secretary of State	Other Cabinet Level, Military, or Diplomatic Post	Chief U.S. Representative to Great Britain	Chief U.S. Representative to Other Great Powers	Commanded U.S. Forces in War as a general
1789 to Civil War					
George Washington					✓
John Adams		✓	✓	✓	
Thomas Jefferson	✓	✓		✓	
James Madison	✓				
James Monroe	✓	✓	✓	✓	
John Quincy Adams	✓	✓	✓	✓	
Andrew Jackson					✓
Martin Van Buren	✓		✓		
William Henry Harrison*				✓	✓
John Tyler					
James Knox Polk					
Zachary Taylor					✓
Millard Fillmore					
Franklin Pierce					✓
James Buchanan	✓		✓	✓	
World War I to 2001					
Woodrow Wilson					
Warren G. Harding					
Calvin Coolidge					
Herbert Hoover†					
Franklin D. Roosevelt‡					
Harry S Truman					
Dwight D. Eisenhower	✓				✓
John F. Kennedy					
Lyndon B. Johnson					
Richard M. Nixon					
Gerald Ford					
Jimmy Carter					
Ronald Reagan					
George Bush		✓		✓	
Bill Clinton					
George W. Bush					

*U.S. minister to Colombia (under Simón Bolívar's presidency)
†Director of war relief in Europe, secretary of commerce
‡Assistant secretary of the navy

tied to international affairs, and the connection was lost neither on the voters nor on those who hoped to win their support for office.

Statistics for the period are inexact, but the evidence suggests that the U.S. economy was at least as dependent on foreign trade in 1790 as it was two hundred years later.[13] Economically the United States was more dependent on the rest of the world in the nineteenth century than it was during much of the Cold War. From 1948 to 1957, foreign trade accounted, on average, for 7.3 percent of the GNP; from 1869 to 1893, for 13.4 percent.[14]

This trade was not simply a concern of seaboard towns: Agricultural exports streamed from American farms to European markets. Between 1802 and 1860 cotton exports rose from a value of $5 million a year to $192 million a year; between 1866 and 1900 those same cotton exports had an average annual value of $213 million. The proportion of the vital cotton crop exported to British manufacturers rose as high as 64 percent.[15] Wheat exports, which were negligible before the Civil War, had jumped to a century-high value of $191 million by 1880, and averaged $88 million per year between then and the end of the century.[16] Between 1850 and 1900 agricultural products made up between 73 and 83 percent of all exports from the United States[17] at a time when up to half of the American population worked in farming.[18]

Access to foreign markets was a requirement for American farmers in remote settlements. So much so that most prominent American political leaders believed that control of New Orleans and its port was essential, not merely to national happiness, but to unity. While Davy Crockett and Daniel Boone roamed the Appalachian wilds, informed opinion in the United States and abroad held that the Middle West would not remain in a federal union that could not provide its inhabitants with safe access to international markets. The volunteer backwoodsmen who followed Andrew Jackson to New Orleans knew why that city was fundamentally important to American prosperity and union, and they grasped the importance of the battle they fought there.

Their children and grandchildren never forgot their dependence on foreign customers and on the means of transporting their produce to market. American farmers were utterly dependent on export markets for their wheat, corn, tobacco, and cotton. The cash income of a family on the Illinois plains depended on the conditions of the European wheat market. As Rep. Sidney Breese remarked on the floor of Congress in 1846, "Illinois wants a market for her agricultural productions. She wants the market of the world. Ten counties of that State could supply all the home market."[19] As the bestselling pamphleteer William H. "Coin" Harvey pointed out, the interest rates farmers paid on their loans, and the freight rates they paid the railroads that carried their produce, were also determined to a large extent by conditions in London. Once a farming community had passed the initial pioneering stage of subsistence agriculture and began to sell its surplus produce, it entered the world market. And once that community developed banks and sought to borrow money for public or private improvements, it encountered an international system of credit and trade that in some ways was more closely integrated in the nineteenth century than it is today.

The nineteenth century was no time of arcadian isolation from the rigors of the world market. Time after time, American domestic prosperity was threatened or ruined by financial storms that originated overseas. Ron Chernow reports in his book *The House of Morgan* that a member of Congress groused in 1833 that "the barometer of the American stock market hangs up at the stock exchange in London."[20] He was not wrong. The European depression that followed the Napoleonic Wars spread to the United States. The panic of 1837 had its origins in London.[21] The panic of 1857 began after the Crimean War when troubles in France spread to London money markets, and from there to New York.[22] After the successful permanent laying of the transatlantic cable in 1866, information from London financial markets traveled to Wall Street and the rest of the country at telegraph speed. For the rest of the century the American economy remained vulnerable to shocks caused by collapses and crashes on international financial markets. The panic of 1893, for example, was caused by the collapse of the Argentine loan market and its effects on British banks.[23]

Foreign investment played a greater role in American prosperity during the nineteenth century than it does now. The United States had to borrow the money for the Louisiana Purchase from the Dutch, and during Jefferson's presidency foreigners are believed to have held more than half the national debt. "No man," said Sen. John Taylor of South Carolina during an 1811 debate over bank policy, "who has attentively considered the rise, progress, and growth of these States, from their first colonization to the present period, can deny that foreign capital, ay, British capital, has been the pap on which we first fed; the strong aliment which supported and stimulated our exertions and industry, even to the present day."[24]

Foreign money dug the canals, built the railroads, and settled much of the West. One-third of the investment for the great American canals came from overseas; foreigners poured between $2.5 billion and $3 billion into American railroads, and by the early 1880s foreign cattle barons owned more than twenty million acres of the American West.²⁵ The largest shareholder when the New York Central Railroad was formed in 1853 was Benjamin Ingham, a British-born investor who held dual citizenship in the United Kingdom and the Kingdom of the Two Sicilies.²⁶ Other pre–Civil War British investors in American railroads included William Makepeace Thackeray, Josiah Wedgwood, and Manchester School thinker and politician Richard Cobden.²⁷ Like many Englishmen, the distinguished essayist and clergyman Sydney Smith had an unhappy experience with his American investments. After a number of American states, including Pennsylvania, defaulted on their bonds following the panic of 1837, he wrote: "I never meet a Pennsylvanian at a London dinner without feeling a disposition to seize and divide him; to allot his beaver to one sufferer and his coat to another; and to appropriate his pocket-handkerchief to the orphan, and to comfort the widow with his silver watch, Broadway rings, and the London Guide, which he always carries in his pockets . . . he has no more right to eat with honest people than a leper has to sit with clean men."²⁸

Those foreign investors had political power in the United States, and Americans resented it but could do little about it. Not that they didn't try. Jackson's message announcing his veto of the renewal of the charter for the Bank of the United States cited as a prime reason for his opposition the windfall profits to the non-American investors who controlled so much of the bank's stock.²⁹ Sixty years later the Populist Party platform called for the expropriation of farmlands owned by aliens.³⁰ Discriminatory legislation against foreigners proliferated in the late nineteenth century, with twelve states passing laws restricting foreign ownership of land.³¹

Anger against British control was not restricted to the populist West. In 1884 the New York–based *Banker's Magazine* looked forward to the happy day "when not a single good American security is owned abroad and when the United States shall cease to be an exploiting ground for European bankers and money lenders. The tribute paid to foreigners is . . . odious."³² Charles Francis Adams, son of the Charles Francis Adams who represented the United States in Britain during the Civil War, and brother of Henry, compared British investment in the United States with the rapacious tactics and devastating consequences of the

British investment in India.33 In 1885 the *New York Times* called for congressional action: "We believe that the building up of great estates by Englishmen should be prevented."34

The great banks of the Anglo-American establishment like the House of Morgan controlled the nation's money supply and had the power of life and death over most businesses. Populist agitators lambasted the "Money Trust"; the noted author, lecturer, and political crusader Mary Lease attacked the pro–gold standard president Grover Cleveland as an agent of "Jewish bankers and British gold."35 Like third-world politicians who complain today about the International Monetary Fund (IMF), American politicians could make little headway against the entrenched power of foreign investors in the American economy.36 As many populists suspected, some of this was due to bribes paid to American politicians by representatives of British interests. Daniel Webster, for example, accepted a payment of nine hundred pounds from the British banking firm Baring, to help push Maryland to resume payments to British creditors.37

Like it or not, the United States was inextricably bound up in the British economic system. And, though the absence of historical polling data makes the statement impossible to prove, the average American in 1845 or 1895 appears to have been at least as aware of the links between domestic prosperity and the international economy as his or her counterpart is today, and perhaps more so.

Politically the first 140 years or so of American independence were not a quiet time in American foreign relations. Virtually every presidential administration from Washington's to Wilson's sent American forces abroad or faced one or more war crises with a great European power. During the Napoleonic Wars, of course, the United States fought an undeclared naval war with France and both declared and undeclared wars with Great Britain. These wars and their consequences—including Jefferson's embargo, which banned all trade between the United States and Europe—had immense repercussions on domestic society. The embargo was perhaps the most painful economic shock the United States ever experienced.38

The federal union almost broke up over the War of 1812, and then British troops sacked Washington and attacked Baltimore and New Orleans. The consequences were not limited to the battlefield; American foreign trade fell by 90 percent between 1807 and 1814 as the British navy blockaded the coast of the United States. The resulting collapse in

DANIEL IN THE LION'S DEN

Unlike Jackson, politicians like the Hamiltonian Daniel Webster who were seen as "soft on Great Britain" often came under attack when they made concessions to other countries. In this 1852 cartoon, Webster, then Secretary of State, is shown getting soused in the den of the British lion, with the cartoonist suggesting that, just as Webster had allegedly sacrificed American interests in Britain's favor in the Clayton-Bulwer Treaty, he would now take too soft a line in a round of negotiations over the offshore fishing rights of Americans.

Frank Bellew. Library of Congress, Prints and Photographs Division, LC-USZ62-34224

the prices of tobacco, cotton, and other agricultural products drove uncounted Americans to the brink of bankruptcy.

Until well after the Civil War the United States was in a permanent war atmosphere, in which either it or its European negotiating partners were continually threatening war, levying sanctions, and issuing threatening orders to their armed forces. The objects of these threats were not limited to the Western Hemisphere; American fighting forces were found in every ocean and on every continent during this time of isolation and innocence.

Great Britain, as the only global power of the day, was the country with which the United States most often came closest to war. From the end of the War of 1812 to the Venezuela boundary crisis of 1895, there was scarcely an administration or a decade in which the United States and Great Britain did not face a crisis or war scare in their tense and turbulent relations.[39]

While the conventional wisdom of the Cold War era holds that the American people had little to fear from warfare during the nineteenth century, that is not the way Americans thought at the time. During the Revolution, British troops occupied every major city in the colonies, and did not abandon New York until well after the defeat at Yorktown. Throughout the nineteenth century both military planners and public opinion wrestled with the possibility of foreign invasion, and especially of attacks on American cities.

From 1816 through the end of the century, boards of engineers and naval authorities would develop plans for coastal fortifications, but faced widespread skepticism that fortifications of any type could prevent modern navies from taking and burning American cities. A million men "armed with a profusion of every appliance of a modern first class army and intrenched (sic) about New York City could not protect it from capture and destruction or contribution by even a second-rate European naval power," wrote Henry P. Wells in an 1886 article in *Harper's* magazine.[40] A substantial portion of American defense spending went for coastal fortification during the century, with physical results that can still be seen in the impressive forts found along the Gulf and Atlantic coasts of the United States, but the great forts were unable to prevent broad apprehension about the consequences of war. Confidence in the system further declined after the Civil War experience, where forts like Moultrie, Sumter, and Fisher fell to northern attack.

The following generation drew the appropriate conclusions. The United States was, wrote U. S. Grant in 1885, "without the power to resist an invasion by the fleets of fourth-rate European powers. . . . We should have a good navy, and our sea-coast defences should be put in the finest possible condition."[41]

"Our wealthy seacoast cities lie at the mercy of any hostile fleet," said naval engineer officer Eugene Griffin in an 1888 article in the influential *North American Review*.[42] During the Spanish-American War, a great panic swept the American East as rumors spread that the Spanish fleet was steaming north to wreak havoc on the defenseless metropolitan areas of the coast.

In important respects the nineteenth-century debate over coastal defenses paralleled the twentieth-century debates over missile defense. In both cases proponents argued that saving even one of the nation's cities from otherwise certain destruction in war would justify the cost of any defense system; opponents of both National Missile Defense (NMD) and coastal defense argued not that the threat was illusory—it was blatant and gross—but that the strategic defense concept was fundamentally flawed, and that the available technology was insufficient to provide the desired results.

The economic consequences of a war with Great Britain were also clearly visible to every banker, farmer, trader, and consumer of industrial goods. New England's opposition to the War of 1812 grew out of this awareness. As the crisis-ridden nineteenth century continued, an understanding of the consequences of war penetrated into the consciousness of editorial boards and politicians. War with Great Britain would have meant the instant disruption of every branch of American business. The stock markets would have crashed. Most banks would have failed instantly. Crop prices would have dropped precipitously. All trade with the rest of the world would have been interrupted by a British blockade. The prospect of invasion either from the coast or Canada would have cast a dark shadow over every business and home in the country; few American households would have escaped the consequences of war before a single shot was fired, a single city burned to the ground.

Given that background, one should not underestimate the importance of the stormy state of Anglo-American relations during the era. A whole series of questions agitated the relations between the two Atlantic powers, keeping them continually at or near the boiling point. Under President Martin Van Buren, American support of Irish and Canadian rebels against British rule in Canada brought the two countries within a hairbreadth of war.

The boundary between the United States and what became Canada was another fertile source of quarrels. A dispute over the boundary between Maine and New Brunswick was a major issue in the presidential election of 1840 and led to the "Aroostock War," in which both the United States and Britain rushed troops to the remote area under dispute.

At the same time the British government was actively intriguing to bring the newly independent Republic of Texas within its sphere of influence. American fears of British designs played a large part in the American decision to annex the Lone Star Republic and helped launch the Mexican War.[43]

ULTIMATUM ON THE OREGON QUESTION

Far from being isolated and ignorant about the wider world, nineteenth-century Americans often followed foreign affairs with close attention. This 1846 cartoon presents an argument that Britain's domestic problems were so dire that the United States could afford to ignore British threats and press for more territory in Oregon. As Queen Victoria warns the Americans to "Beware how you rouse the British Lion!," her threat is undercut by the evident reluctance of the lion to stir unless the government agrees to "Unloose my chains and fill my belly!"—that is, to agree to radicals' demands for domestic political reforms and better economic conditions. The cartoonist portrays Russia and France (represented respectively by their then-rulers, Czar Nicholas I and King Louis-Philippe) as wishing either to stay neutral or to support the United States in any clash over Oregon. The Irish leader Daniel O'Connell tells Victoria that without political concessions to Irish demands there will be no Irish soldiers for her army. *Edward Williams Clay. Library of Congress, Prints and Photographs Division, LC-USZ62-7722*

Besides Texas the major issue in the election of 1844 was the Oregon boundary issue, with "Fifty-four Forty or Fight!" the slogan of those who wished to fight a war with Great Britain over conflicting claims to what is now British Columbia.

THE PENDING CONFLICT

While most Americans today think of the Civil War as largely a domestic contest in which foreign countries and foreign policy were irrelevant, the attitude of foreign countries toward the Confederacy was one of the crucial questions of the war. In this 1863 American cartoon, Britain and France—both of which came close to recognizing the Confederacy and to demanding that the Union accept their intervention to negotiate a settlement to the war—are seen as supporting Jefferson Davis, who is trampling on the American flag and wielding a club labeled "Pirate Alabama" (a reference to the Confederate warship *Alabama,* built in "neutral" British ports, which attacked Union shipping until it was destroyed by the U.S.S. *Kearsarge* off the coast of France in June 1864).

Library of Congress, Prints and Photographs Division, LC-USZ62-42025

The 1850s saw another rash of crises between the two countries. Southerners hoped to establish new slave states in Cuba and Nicaragua. The British were extending their control along the coasts of Central America in the hopes of controlling communication between the Atlantic and the Pacific. British efforts to search ships under the American flag in the effort to suppress the Atlantic slave trade also caused crises; closer to home, so did the British refusal to return slaves on American ships driven into British-controlled harbors.

The Civil War, of course, saw the United States and Britain approach the brink of war. Only narrowly was war averted when the British negligently allowed Confederate commerce raiders to fit out in British ports. For years after the war, American and British diplomats would rattle their sabers in negotiations over compensation for damages inflicted by Confederate ships like the *Alabama*.44

Relations between the United States and Great Britain did not decisively improve until the final decade of the nineteenth century, when Britain's fears of such rising European powers as Russia and Germany led it to adopt a more conciliatory, even cringing, tone in its dealings with the United States.

The United States also had a troubled relationship with Spain. A long and not particularly edifying diplomatic campaign of threats, baseless claims, bribery, and intimidation resulted in the Spanish cession of Florida to the United States by 1819. The United States made known its hostility to any attempt by Spain to reestablish its rule over its lost South American colonies, and instability in Cuba brought the United States and Spain to sword's points several times before it finally erupted in the Spanish-American War. Between freelance attacks by private American citizens known as filibusters, violation of American neutrality laws in support of Cuban rebels, and diplomatic maneuvers like the Ostend Manifesto, American policy toward Spain was marked by aggressive designs and disregard for international law, until William McKinley put a final end to four centuries of Spanish power in the Western Hemisphere and the Pacific.

Although France and the United States had fewer points of contact after Napoleon gave up his dreams of North American empire and sold Louisiana to Jefferson, the relations between Paris and Washington were also rocky at times in the nineteenth century. The United States and France skirted armed conflict during Jackson's administration when he sent a naval expedition to back up his threats after France failed to honor agreements relating to compensation for American shipping losses during the Napoleonic Wars. Both during and after the Civil War, the United States and France were regularly engaged in harassing and threatening each other. Napoleon III openly sought the breakup of the United States and the independence of the South; his attempt to establish a puppet emperor in Mexico while the United States was distracted by the Civil War was the grossest and most dangerous challenge the Monroe Doctrine ever faced. French troops were not withdrawn from Mexico until Gen. Ulysses S. Grant, almost immediately after Appomattox, dispatched Gen. Philip Sheridan to the Rio Grande with victorious Civil War troops.[45] (After being abandoned by his French patrons, the "Emperor" Maximilian perished before a Mexican firing squad in 1867.)

The United States was also heavily involved with Latin America. As early as 1832, the United States sent a fleet to the Falkland Islands to reduce an Argentine garrison that had harassed American shipping. The Mexican War was, of course, the greatest example of American intervention, but by the Civil War, American forces had seen action in Haiti (1799, 1800, 1817–21), Tripoli (1815), the Marquesas Islands (1813–14), Spanish Florida (1806–10, 1812, 1813, 1814, 1816–18, 1817), what is now the Dominican Republic (1800), Curacao (1800), the Galápagos Islands (1813), Cuba (1822), Puerto Rico (1824), Argentina (1833, 1852, 1853), and Peru (1835–36).[46] Between the Civil War and the Spanish-American War, marines were sent to Cuba, Uruguay, Argentina, Chile, Colombia, and Haiti.[47]

During the recurring great-power crises of the nineteenth century, serious statesmen constantly saw war as possible, probable, or even inevitable. Public opinion agreed, and international crises were accompanied by violent waves of popular agitation. Americans in the nineteenth century were no strangers to newspapers with war-scare headlines. Foreign policy issues loomed large in elections. Administrations were constantly aware that the American people would not permit their government to look weak or to appease foreign governments. Often, indeed usually, the American government was more pacifistic and isolationist than public opinion. At several points in the nineteenth century, the popular pressure for war against Britain and France was almost overwhelming. Furthermore popular opinion often pressed the American government to involve itself more directly in European affairs. Such agitation was particularly strong concerning the Greek war for independence, the Hungarian revolution of Louis Kossuth, and the Fenian rising of Irish immigrants against British rule in Canada, but these were far from the only times when significant parts of the American population wanted to see American arms used to vindicate American principles or interests in far-flung corners of the world.

Statesmen did what they could to dampen the popular fervor. The dying General Grant added a concluding section to his *Memoirs* that consisted largely of recommendations for American defense and foreign policy in the years to come. Much of the conclusion was devoted to an attempt to soften popular resentment against Britain for its conduct during the Civil War and to make the case for a permanent, natural alliance between the two English-speaking powers.[48]

In addition to these diplomatic and military contretemps with great European powers and its hemispheric neighbors, the American government in the nineteenth century took an active role in opening up Asia and Africa to trade. As American whalers and merchants spread out across the world in search of profits and whale oil, diplomats and naval forces followed. Sometimes these visits were peaceful. By the time of the Civil War the United States government had sent official missions to Vietnam, Thailand, the Ottoman Empire, China, Sumatra, Burma, and Japan.[49]

Sometimes American presidents dispatched more than diplomats. The U.S. Marines had already ventured "from the halls of Montezuma to the shores of Tripoli" by the Civil War. The marine hymn could in fact have said more; by 1860 the marines had already been far to the west and south of Mexico as well as to the east and north of Libya. Jefferson's dispatch to Tripoli and Algiers of a punitive mission against the Barbary pirates was the first but by no means the last such expedition sent out by American presidents. The village of Quallah Battoo on the coast of Sumatra was shelled and burned by an American force sent by Jackson; the visit was repeated when the inhabitants continued obdurate in their disrespect for the flag. In 1843 American marines fought with villagers in coastal Liberia after Comm. Matthew Perry was attacked; the marines returned to Liberia in 1860 to protect American lives and property.

In 1843 American marines landed in Guangzhou (Canton) to protect Americans from Chinese mobs. They returned thirteen years later and defeated five thousand Chinese troops in a pitched battle. A permanent marine presence would guard American traders and diplomats in China and participate—under foreign commanders—with European forces in the suppression of the Boxer Rebellion in 1900.

China and Sumatra were not the only places in Asia in which American forces were engaged in conflict during the "virginal isolation" of the nineteenth century. In 1871 marines retaliated for a Korean attack on an American ship and a diplomat by seizing two forts in a punitive expedition. Commodore Perry's orders directed him to shell Japan if the mikado refused his request for trade and diplomatic relations. In 1863, at the height of the Civil War, American forces landed in Japan and what is now Panama.[50] By 1900 American forces were established throughout the South Pacific, and the United States had weathered a serious international crisis with Germany over the control of Samoa.[51]

The U.S. Navy has maintained a global presence much longer than most Americans realize. The permanent Mediterranean squadron was established in 1815 to keep the Barbary pirates in check. In 1822 the United States established its West Indian and Pacific squadrons, the latter charged with protecting American whalers and commercial interests in South America and the South Sea islands. In 1826 this was followed by a Brazil or South Atlantic squadron, with the East India squadron following in 1835 and the African squadron established off the west coast of Africa in 1843. In other words, during the period of American innocence and isolation, the United States had forces stationed on or near every major continent in the world; its navy was active in virtually every ocean, its troops saw combat on virtually every continent, and its foreign relations were in a perpetual state of crisis and turmoil.

The importance of foreign policy in American politics was even greater than this list would indicate. Foreign policy and domestic politics were inextricably mixed throughout American history. The question of American independence was, of course, an issue of foreign relations, and the formation of the French alliance was the key to the successful conclusion of the Revolutionary War. It is no exaggeration to say that we owe the Constitution to the requirements of foreign affairs. After the Revolution, the inability of the Continental Congress to manage foreign relations under the Articles of Confederation was the first and foremost reason put forward by the supporters of the new Constitution in the great national debate over ratification. The balance of power between federal and state authorities in the new Constitution was determined in large part by the need for a national government strong enough to conduct an effective foreign policy. "My idea is that we should be made one nation in every case concerning foreign affairs, and separate ones in what is merely domestic," wrote Jefferson in 1787.[52] The jealous friends of states' rights concluded that it was better to establish a strong central government among the ex-colonies than to face the wiles and pressures of European empires as a feeble and divided confederation.

This proved to be wise. Foreign policy questions dominated the administrations of Washington and Adams: The Jay Treaty; the XYZ Affair, involving scandalous revelations about French attempts to extract bribes from American diplomats; the continued British presence in the Old Northwest; the undeclared war with France; the Genet Affair, the question of whether the United States should "tilt" toward Britain, France, or neither—these were the great issues of late-eighteenth-century American politics.

The nineteenth century saw more of the same. Even after the conclusion of the Napoleonic Wars, when international relations in general assumed a less dramatic cast, foreign policy questions remained at the heart of American politics. There were four great issues in nineteenth-century American politics: slavery, westward expansion, the tariff, and monetary policy. Of these only slavery was a purely domestic issue, but it should be noted that foreign policy issues were absolutely critical to the course of the Civil War in which the slavery controversy climaxed. Secretary of State William Seward planned for a time to cut short the Civil War by provoking a war with the European powers that would rally the North and South to a joint effort. European intervention was the strategic goal of the Confederacy throughout, and the battle for foreign public opinion was for a reluctant Lincoln a decisive consideration in favor of his issuing the Emancipation Proclamation. "To proclaim emancipation would secure the sympathy of Europe and the whole civilized world. . . . No other step would be so potent to prevent foreign intervention," wrote Lincoln in 1862.[53]

Of the remaining great issues, westward expansion was obviously a foreign policy issue; the tariff question then as now had both domestic and foreign policy implications, and the debate over whether to keep the gold standard or to permit the free coinage of silver was fundamentally a question about the relation of the American economy to the British-dominated international system. As William Jennings Bryan said in the concluding peroration of his "Cross of Gold" speech, "It is the issue of 1776 over again. . . . instead of having a gold standard because England has, we will restore bimetallism, and then let England have bimetallism because the United States has it."[54]

Despite the long record of vigorous U.S. activity and intense interest in the world beyond its shores, despite the enormous impact foreign policy has had on domestic politics throughout U.S. history, and despite its unparalleled record of success in international affairs, the United States continues to enjoy both at home and abroad a kind of hayseed image when it comes to foreign policy, that of an innocent barefoot boy unaccustomed to the wiles and ways of the sharp international operators. Yet time after time it has been this innocent who has taken the pot— perhaps after spreading his cards on the table, scratching under his overalls, and naively inquiring if his full house beats the other fellow's two pairs.

The more I study the history of American foreign policy, the more deeply convinced I become that our national foreign policy tradition has much to teach us. We don't just draw lucky cards; we also play the game well. Over two hundred years we have developed our own unique style, which suits us. Certainly it has enabled us to become the richest and most powerful nation in the history of the world.

Given that the world is becoming a more interdependent place, and given that both the dangers and the opportunities of international engagement are rapidly rising, it seems reasonable to suppose that the skillful conduct of foreign policy will be at least as important to the happiness and security of the American people in the future as it has been so far.

It is not only the American people whose happiness and security will be greatly affected by the quality of American foreign policy in coming years. The United States has become the central power in a worldwide system of finance, communications, and trade. Any disruption of that system will unleash enormous economic distress around the world. And despite the many imperfections and injustices that exist in the present international system, poor people in developing countries will be likely to suffer worst from any major disruptions.

Managing both the political and the economic dimensions of this global system—while never forgetting the importance of the American and allied military power that stands as the ultimate safeguard of the towering edifice of global society—is an enormous and demanding task that only becomes more challenging as the global system continues to develop and grow. American leaders will have to work cooperatively with allied and associated countries around the world while preserving the foundations of American power. They must deter other countries from challenging the basic institutions and features of the global system and, if new challengers like the Soviet Union should rise up, be ready to defeat them. At the same time they must see that the world system works for other countries as well as for the United States; for the United States to be prosperous and secure they must ensure that developed and developing countries alike find it easier to reach their national goals by working within the global system than by trying to tear it down.

My reading in the history of American foreign policy tells me that there are real reasons to hope that Americans will rise to the dizzying and daunting challenges of the twenty-first century. But I have also become aware of the degree to which our national ignorance of our own past successes impoverishes our foreign policy process today. Our elites and our policy-makers would benefit from a richer, deeper understanding of the principles and goals of their predecessors. More important, a stronger, surer grasp of the important principles of the history of American foreign policy will enable the American public better to evaluate and compare the proposals and policies of contending candidates and political parties. The end result will be greater public support for better policies. It is the hope of that outcome that led me to write this book.

Chapter Two

THE
KALEIDOSCOPE OF
AMERICAN
FOREIGN POLICY

The preceding chapter posed a challenging question: Why, with a record so active and glorious, is American foreign policy held in such low esteem? Why do distinguished observers and practitioners alike so routinely ignore and/or disparage the foreign policy traditions of a country that has risen so rapidly and even easily to a power and preeminence unexampled in history?

The mystery only deepens when we examine the content of the criticisms so widely leveled against American foreign policy, past and present. Instead of a clear and consistent indictment, what we get is a barrage of mutually incompatible charges: that American foreign policy is too naive, too calculating, too openhanded, too violent, too isolationist, too universalist, too unilateral, too multilateral, too moralistic, too immoral.

One large group of distinguished critics attributes purported U.S. failings in foreign policy to the excessive influence of democratic public opinion on the process. Walter Lippmann, for example, has written that "They [the people] have compelled the government, which usually knew what would have been wiser, or was necessary, or was more expedient, to be too late with too little, or too long with too much, too pacifist in peace and too bellicose in war, too neutralist or appeasing in negotiation or too intransigent."[1]

For some, the primary danger is that uneducated public opinion will lead the United States into an aggressive, unilateral foreign policy. In this view, populist influence in foreign policy, magnified by demagogues, poses a serious and chronic threat. According to former president Carter, Ronald Reagan's rabble-rousing opposition to the Panama Canal Treaty ("We built it, we paid for it, it's ours and we should tell Torrijos and company that we are going to keep it!") was popular *because* Reagan presented the issue "simplistically."[2] In Carter's view, mature, enlightened statesmen, with their sensible programs for multilateral cooperation, are too frequently checked and hindered by the blind passions of an ignorant populace, whipped up into frenzies by unscrupulous politicians. The public is a savage beast; we rouse it at our peril.

Others agree that American popular opinion is dangerous and uninformed, but worry that the consequence will be, not hotheaded aggression, but timid and retiring isolationism. Writing in 1994, *New York Times* columnist Anthony Lewis attributed the lack of public support for President Bill Clinton's Haiti policy to "a general public disinclination to send American forces anywhere abroad," and cited a danger of populist "neo-isolationism."[3]

Another school of thought blames the appalling ignorance of American public opinion for the prevalence of wishy-washy idealism in our foreign policy. In a 1994 speech given at the Malaysian Strategic Research Centre, Henry Kissinger pointed to the profound ignorance of the American people as a cause for our flawed approach to foreign policy. He noted that during the Reagan administration a poll found that 30 percent of the respondents identified Norway as the country where the contras were fighting.[4] To this historic or traditional American ignorance, Kissinger charged, we have now added a new layer. The current generation, being raised on television rather than books, has learned to form "impressions" rather than to have "ideas."[5] The result of our ignorance is a foreign policy that rejects the tried-and-true method of maintaining the balance of power to base itself on "a belief that you [can] solve problems by a missionary activity"—spreading democracy.[6]

Others don't blame the populace at all. Lippmann, they say, is wrong: The popular instincts are sound; it is the elites who are to blame for our failures. For social critic Eric Alterman, a more democratic and populist foreign policy would be a better foreign policy.[7] A large group of critics join him in blaming the elites for our many and manifest foreign policy sins. Perhaps the harshest critic is Christian Coalition founder Pat Robertson, who argues that the American foreign policy elite, principally directed from the inner core of the Council on Foreign Relations, flirts with a satanic conspiracy to pave the way for the Antichrist.[8] MIT linguistics professor Noam Chomsky has a somewhat more benign view, but still argues that "[t]op advisory and decision-making positions relating to international affairs are heavily concentrated in the hands of representatives of major corporations, banks, investment firms, the few law firms that cater to corporate interests, and the technocratic and policy-oriented intellectuals who do the bidding of those who own and manage the basic institutions of the domestic society. . . ."[9] While the elite does not actually make blood sacrifices to Satan or consciously pave the way for the Antichrist, its values and priorities, Chomsky says, are clear: "American aid and diplomatic support increase as human rights violations increase, at least in the Third World. Extensive violations of human rights (torture, forced reduction of living standards for much of the population, police-sponsored death squads, destruction of representative institutions or of independent unions, etc.) are directly correlated with U.S. government support."[10]

By comparison, the critique by AFL-CIO president (and Council on Foreign Relations member) John Sweeney is relatively mild. "As corporations and banks have forged the rules of the global marketplace—codifying its rules in agreements like NAFTA and institutions like the World Trade Organization—they protected property, but left people at risk. Multinational companies escaped labor, consumer and environmental regulation."[11] Investment is everything, people are nothing in the elite-driven, economically oriented world of American foreign policy.

It is a brutal picture, but others have criticized the elite for different reasons. Observers like Richard Nixon, Irving Kristol, and Ronald Reagan agreed that an elite dominates the American foreign policy process and excludes the silent majority of the American people, but they identified a very different elite than do Robertson, Chomsky, and Sweeney. For these critics a wobbly-kneed, spineless, and effete elite is too weak, too confused, and too decadent to protect basic American national interests, much less to worship Satan or murder charismatic human rights leaders in developing lands. In Nixon's immortal prose, a group of "pinstriped, pantywaist pinkos" in the State Department and graduates of "Dean Acheson's Cowardly College of Communist Containment" betrayed the national interest.[12] Kristol identifies their basic mistake: an illusion that we are moving toward an eventual "world community." "In such a world," he writes, "foreign policy—the defense of one's national interests—would cease to exist, having been completely replaced by a diplomacy aiming to reconcile the interests of all. Our State Department acts most of the time as if that world were already at hand, as if diplomacy were no longer the handmaiden of foreign policy but its master."[13]

Other critics of the American elite have managed to combine these two views. The elite is both ruthless and spineless: ruthless in pursuit of narrow economic interests, spineless in its failure to stand up for the national interest and the interests of individual American workers. That is the position of columnist and perennial presidential candidate Pat Buchanan.

Abroad, there are also different views both of the state of American society and of the nature of our foreign policy. Some, like Malaysian prime minister Muhammad Mahathir, say we are a decadent society that poisons the world with our vile and degraded popular culture; our decline is inevitable and already far advanced.[14] Others see us as a dynamic force for change that poses a danger to other ways of life precisely because of the energy and growth we display.[15] Former Soviet president Mikhail Gorbachev warned that our hasty acts, our unilateralism, and our blustering adventurism threaten to create horrible chaos and pose a danger to all right-minded nations.

Another view holds that American isolationism is the greatest danger the world faces. At any moment we could pick up our marbles and go home, leaving both Europe and Asia to find their own balance. And still another holds that we have created such a strong and subtle hegemony that it is the difficult duty of every nation on earth to resist us. "France does not know it," its late president Mitterrand once said, "but we are at war with America. Yes, a permanent war, a vital war, a war without death. Yes, they are very hard, the Americans, they are voracious, they want undivided power over the world."[16]

The criticisms of American policy are so various and vociferous that they remind one of G. K. Chesterton's observations about the attacks on Christianity in his day. Noting that some critics attacked the church because it was hostile to women, while others despised it because only women went to its services; that some accused it of a hatred of pleasure and promotion of a life-hating asceticism, while others attacked the luxuriant corruption of its high clergy; that some attacked it for promoting a weak-minded pacifism, while others attacked its implacable crusading spirit of intolerance, he began to wonder whether a religion that was wrong in so many incompatible ways might be as miraculous and unexpected as one that was, in fact, true.

In the case of American foreign policy, we must observe that it is at least possible that there is a method to its madness. The rise of American power has been consistent, striking, sustained over the long term, and accomplished at an astonishingly low cost considering the size and range of the power the country has amassed. If we did not have the historical record before us, we should no doubt conclude that a nation with an approach to foreign policy so vociferously if inconsistently attacked by so many critics could not be a very great power for very long. As it is, we face the fascinating paradox that the foreign policy traditions, practices, and institutions of the world's most successful country encounter a near-universal yet strangely incoherent contempt.

Let us not submit to the tyranny of facts. Success alone should not drive us to conclude that American foreign policy has often been brilliant—after all, it could be great luck or, as our ancestors would have put it, the blessings of Providence or God's will that the country has been so successful. Prince Otto von Bismarck appears to have thought so; near the end of his long life the great statesman is said to have despaired of explaining the country's success and, throwing up his hands, pronounced the famous observation attributed to him concerning drunks, children, and the United States of America.[17] The United States, on such a view, is the Mr. Magoo of the world community. But what seems indisputable is that, whether due to luck, skill, or the Providence of God, the record of American foreign policy is overall a successful one, that Mr. Magoo has thus far come through life in good shape.

Not Worth a Continental?

One major reason why American foreign policy gets so little respect is that it violates so many of the expectations that various analysts and observers bring to the subject. A surprising number of people today still share a set of conventional views about what foreign policy should be and how it should work that have little to do with the contemporary world. This strangely fossilized conventional wisdom is not just Eurocentric; it is what can be called Continentalist. That is, the conventional wisdom does not simply assume that the foreign policy experience and practices of European states in their heyday define what international life "really" is; it focuses only on the approaches and ideas emanating from the Continental powers of nineteenth-century Europe (especially Prussia, France, and Austria) and ignores the many distinctive features that marked the foreign policy experience of Britain during that century and the United States today. Indeed, many conventional critics of American foreign policy find certain strains of nineteenth-century British foreign policy (notably the liberal, values-driven foreign policy of Prime Minister William Gladstone) almost as vulgar and appalling as they find American foreign policy today.

Continental realism, as this approach to foreign policy can be called, remains extremely influential in academe and in what Alterman calls the punditocracy; unfortunately it adheres to a set of assumptions—some conscious, some less so—about foreign policy that make it almost impossible to understand what American foreign policy is or how and why it works.

Continental realism is not just the belief that "realism" rather than "idealism" is the most appropriate ideological framework within which to understand and to pursue the diplomatic life of nations. Realism, the belief that countries are driven by interests and the quest for power in international relations rather than ideals and benevolence, is widespread among Anglo-Americans as well as Continentals. In fact, many Continental Europeans have felt over the years that when it comes to putting the principles (so to speak) of realism into practice, the hypocritical and greedy Anglo-Americans have far outdone their Continental rivals.

But in addition to the belief that international relations are on at least some levels an amoral struggle of all against all, Continental realism also features some distinctive beliefs about the way states are organized, the nature of the interests they pursue, and the kind of policy processes that lead to success. These assumptions simply do not apply to American reality, and attempting to understand American history and policy in their light leads only to one error after another. It is like using a map of Oregon to plan a road trip in Georgia; there is no way to avoid getting lost.

Those who assume that effective foreign policy must be made today in the ways the great powers of Continental Europe made it in the nineteenth century, and that the aims of effective foreign policy must always and everywhere be restricted to the kinds of goals that a Metternich or a Bismarck would recognize and support, think that the ideal foreign policy looks in a sense like a nineteenth-century realist painting. American foreign policy is, however, more like a kaleidoscope, whose images, patterns, and colors alter rapidly and apparently at random. The assumptions of Continental realism cannot yield a coherent view of either the strengths or the weaknesses of the American method of foreign policy. The result, as we have seen, is less a coherent and thoughtful critique than a heartfelt but incoherent and uncomprehending rejection, something more like the response of conventionally trained critics of realist art to the early Impressionists than a sober assessment of the American way of power.

There are three principal areas in which the differences between the American and Continental contexts block Continentally oriented observers from fully understanding the American approach.

First, there is the problem of economics. For statesmen like Metternich and Bismarck, and those in their tradition, politics is everything in foreign policy; economics is, at best, an afterthought. In the Anglo-American tradition economic issues are vital: It is economic success that creates the financial basis for national power. Continental powers dueled over Europe like scorpions in a bottle; the British and the Americans took advantage of this continental preoccupation to build the international economic power that brought both of the English-speaking powers to global hegemony.

This was, of course, in part due to luck and not skill. Britain had the Channel, and the United States had the Atlantic; both of these powers were outside the bottle with the other scorpions and so enjoyed the freedom to think about other things. Nevertheless, that freedom gave British and American strategic thought a different cast from Continental approaches, and without understanding the special character of the Anglo-American synthesis of the economic and political elements of international power politics, it is not possible to understand what British or American foreign policy is all about.

Later I will look more carefully at the intellectual structure of what could be called American realism in contrast to the Continental variety, but one point needs to be raised here. For most of American history the immediate objects of foreign policy have been economic questions. From a Continentalist perspective, worrying about tariffs, monetary coordination, and trading rights hardly looks like foreign policy at all. "I don't give a shit about the value of the *lira*!" the Continentalist Nixon said to his staff.[18]

For Continentalists, economic policy is not the high and challenging business of the state. For American realists, getting economic policy right is the true grand strategy of the state; if we have the money we will somehow find the ships and men. If one looks at American foreign policy through the Continentalist perspective and assumes that the economic issues are minor and that only "high politics" counts, it looks as if the United States has had, compared to the Continental powers at any rate, relatively little involvement in foreign policy from the end of the War of 1812 into the twentieth century. And until the Cold War Americans seem only episodically involved in foreign policy, alternating brief periods of activism with long stretches of isolation. Only restoring economic policy to the realm of "high politics" allows us to understand why American statesmen and public opinion were so deeply involved in foreign policy for much of our history.

The second distortion that weakens the ability of those wearing the spectacles of Continental realism to see the true nature of American foreign policy has to do with scale. Continental realists are Eurocentric, and see the European continent as the main theater of world politics. For at least three hundred years the Anglo-Americans have dissented. In eighteenth-century British politics, the "blue water" Tories mostly favored leaving Europe to its own devices while the British navy and British merchant shipping strengthened the British Empire around the world. The dismal battles of the scorpions in their tiny European bottle was a distraction from the real business of Britain, said the Tories. Have a strong-enough navy to, as it were, cork the bottle so that none of the scorpions could crawl out, and Britain would be secure.

The Whigs disagreed. The Tories, they said, were right to hold that the true path to world power lay outside Europe; nevertheless it was a mistake to ignore Europe entirely. Britain needed to maintain the capacity to intervene in the Continental wars, to prevent any scorpion from devouring the rest and growing strong enough to push the cork out of the way and climb out of the bottle.

Continental powers and statesmen did not ignore the wider world, but the grim battle among scorpions they could never escape forced their attention and resources time and again away from the wider world and back to the dismal battlefields of Europe. For the Continental powers, European politics was a matter of life and death; world politics was a luxury.

Americans have ultimately reached a conclusion not too dissimilar from the Whig view of Europe. The old continent is too important to ignore, but it is far from being the only fish, or even the most interesting fish, in the sea. Asia and Latin America have therefore received a major share of American attention and concern; whereas an economically oriented foreign policy focusing on the third world seems to many Continentalists to be unworthy of serious consideration.

As early as the time of the Stuarts, Anglo-American strategic thought grappled with questions of world order. As maritime trading peoples, the British and the Americans were busy weaving webs of trade and investment covering whole continents and seas. Elihu Yale, the trader from colonial Connecticut whose success with the East India Company funded the bequest that gave his name to Yale College, was already part of a global economy. Maintaining the security of that global system was the concern of the London merchants and financial magnates of the day, as well as of the king's ministers. The eighteenth-century mob that dumped East Indian tea into Boston Harbor was protesting in part against the economic policies by which the British government of the day sought to further what would now be called globalization under British hegemony.[19]

Call it empire, hegemony, world order, or globalization, the question of global economic integration under British or American auspices and the political strategies that advance this great process have been at or near the center of both American and British foreign and domestic politics for centuries. Frederick the Great thought about how to snatch Silesia from Maria Theresa; Alexander Hamilton thought about how to integrate the infant American economy into the British world system on the best possible terms.

From the standpoint of Frederick the Great and the many foreign policy observers who still (often unconsciously) share the basic features of his worldview, what Hamilton was doing was not real foreign policy at all—it was something vulgar and mercantile. Frederick may have had a point, but of course it was Hamilton rather than Frederick who laid the foundations of world power.

Finally, Continental realism has a third set of assumptions about foreign policy processes that simply makes it impossible for those consciously or unconsciously under its influence to think coherently about American foreign policy. These assumptions include a whole series of ideas about the nature of political power, the role of the state in society, and the strengths and weaknesses of democracy.

From the standpoint of Continental realism, American foreign policy and, for that matter, the whole American government look wrong. Massachusetts congressman Fisher Ames put his finger on the problem in a speech he made to the House of Representatives in 1795: "A monarchy is a merchantman which sails well, but will sometimes strike on a rock, and go to the bottom; a republic is a raft which will never sink, but then your feet are always in the water."[20] Because the raft of American foreign policy lacks all the features that Continental realists look for in a vessel, they consistently fail to grasp the raft's capabilities.

To begin with, Continental realists believe in what we might call the "auteur" theory of foreign policy. Like film critics who see films as the personal creation of a single hand—usually that of the director—so Continental realists believe that the best foreign policy is the product of a single great master: a Bismarck, a Talleyrand, a Metternich, or a Kissinger.

The great genius labors, essentially alone, at something like a vast, complex, and multidimensional game of chess. A pawn is advanced here, a rook sacrificed there; here a feint, there an advance, there a strategic retreat that tempts the opponent to lose everything by advancing too far. Sometimes this great man works as the servant of another master of the foreign policy universe. (That, at any rate, is how Nixon saw his relationship with Kissinger.) More often, however, he stands alone in confrontation with rivals, bureaucratic obstacles, and uninformed superiors. The immature Kaiser Wilhelm II "dropped the pilot" when he forced Bismarck's resignation; Talleyrand stepped aside when he was convinced that Napoleon's excessive ambition could lead only to disaster.

This is, of course, a nineteenth-century Romantic vision of the foreign minister as a dark Byronic hero: Brooding, silent, and bearing vast responsibilities, he is excused from the normal restraints of morality in the service of his titanic, earth-altering vision. (If Kissinger can be believed on the subject, the similarity between foreign ministers and Byronic heroes also extends into the boudoir.)

It is very clear that the American political system is not geared to creating a smooth path for such characters. Bismarck loathed and despised the Reichstag and dealt with it as little as possible; a would-be American Bismarck must not only spend endless hours testifying in detail before sometimes hostile panels, but everywhere he turns he finds constitutional mandates that force him to obtain congressional or senatorial approval before proceeding. Had Richelieu, Bismarck, or Metternich been born in the United States, it is unlikely that any of them would have had the patience or political skills to become, or long to remain, secretary of state. (Talleyrand, however, might have done very well.) In any case American foreign policy is usually a group effort—like a product of the old Hollywood studio system, rather than the independent production of a lone auteur. (Sadly, the American secretary of state often occupies a position in the foreign policy world more like that of a Hollywood writer than a director.)

Even if a Metternich- or Richelieu-class grand master managed to climb the greasy pole of American politics to become secretary of state, under the best of circumstances his or her tenure would be short. Bismarck served nine years as prime minister of Prussia before serving nineteen years as chancellor of Imperial Germany; Metternich served Austria for thirty-nine.[21] The American presidency often changes hands every four years and must change every eight; only under unusual circumstances will a long-serving secretary of state receive an invitation to continue serving under a new president. More frequently, presidents change secretaries of state once or more during a four-year term; since 1789 the United States has had forty-three presidents and sixty-five secretaries of state.

Short tenure, moreover, would be the least of the obstacles confronting a would-be American Bismarck. Beyond the opposition and harassment of several committees in two houses of Congress, along with the annoyance of suffering the vanity and interpositions of committee chairs, a secretary of state soon discovers that the State Department has no monopoly even in the executive branch over the formation of foreign policy. There is also the small shadow bureaucracy of the National Security Council—weak in institutional resources but powerful in its proximity to the president—and the wider world of competing cabinet departments, each with its own foreign policy. The Pentagon maintains extensive contacts with foreign governments and militaries, and it has strong views on overall American foreign policy. When the Defense Department disagrees with the State Department on a policy matter, it does not quietly fold its tents and steal away repentantly into the night; it argues forcefully for its own position or simply continues to conduct its policy without reference to the views of Foggy Bottom.

Beyond the Pentagon there are the intelligence agencies, each with its own set of views and priorities, and each well-equipped to conduct substantial activities without oversight or coordination with State. The U.S. Trade Representative has cabinet rank and holds an office with a separate mandate over a broad and sometimes ill-defined zone of trade and economic policy. Other agencies, too, have their own international contacts and agendas, and the State Department itself is no monolith, but rather a chaotic zone of bureaucratic conflict. Offices established by congressional mandate are often more accountable to their congressional patrons than to their nominal superiors in the State Department; in any case the career staff at the State Department knows that secretaries come and go, but Congress is forever.

While this wild and exuberant bureaucratic growth reached its full luxuriant profusion only late in the twentieth century, the pattern of divided authority, short tenure, and internal rivalry in the executive branch is a very old one in the United States, and it has been frustrating presidents and secretaries of state since George Washington tried to resolve the squabbles between Hamilton at Treasury and Jefferson at State in the 1790s.

That American foreign policy is rarely the product of a single, deliberative mastermind only begins to delineate the difference between the American article and the European ideal. The American foreign policy process violates basic Continental ideas about foreign policy in other important ways. The first is the constitutional process, a process designed to create a clunky, shuddering machine that lunges forward in fits and starts, one that is always divided against itself, with half the government almost always investigating the dirty laundry of the other. If that were not enough, the Constitution is designed to highlight the influence of local and parochial interests in the foreign policy process. From a Continental point of view, this is the opposite of the way foreign policy should work, and many make the not unnatural assumption that a process so ghastly cannot possibly succeed.

The division of authority between the executive and legislative branches of government makes for a slow, uncertain, and often ridiculous process of public debate. Obscure but long-serving legislators reach important policy-making positions through the power of seniority. As chairmen of the Senate Foreign Relations Committee, men like Idaho's senator William Borah (1923–33) or North Carolina's Jesse Helms (1995–2001) care very little for international public opinion or the niceties of diplomatic discourse. What is unthinkable to the international community—the United States refusing to join the League of Nations in 1919 and, more recently, refusing to pay UN dues—is politics as usual for these senatorial barons. To be deplored by foreign ambassadors, lamented by the Council on Foreign Relations, and despised by international civil servants at the International Monetary Fund (IMF), the World Bank, and the United Nations only strengthens the appeal of many American politicians back home.

There is another problem. The debate over foreign policy in the United States often gives substantial weight to the kind of voices that are deemed eccentric or dangerous in many parts of the world. The American voices who want to put the enforcement of human rights on the front burner of the international diplomatic agenda, those who do not want their sons and daughters sent abroad except to defend the United States from direct attack, those who want an end to the secretive bureaucracies and enormous military and intelligence budgets of what Cold War critics have called the "National Security State"[22] and those who worry that the EU may prefigure the kingdom of the Antichrist, all embrace approaches to foreign policy that differ radically from the more conventional views held in the chancelleries of our NATO allies.

The United States is not unique in having idealistic and/or populist voices in its foreign policy—think of the Catholic zeal of Hapsburg Spain, the antipopery of British popular feeling under the Stuarts, or the anti-German *revanchisme* of French popular opinion after 1871—but the particular mix, power, and composition of these voices is our own.

Unconventional voices are strong in part because while the interests and values of the commercial classes along the eastern seaboard have historically had similarities to the views of similar elites in Europe, the United States has always included many regions with different views and priorities in foreign policy. Suspicion of both elite interests and strong government ran deep in the early years of the Republic; the Constitution was deliberately loaded with provisions that were emphatically calculated to make it difficult for the government to take strong, active, and swift action in international politics, and the distribution of power among the states ensures that each regional voice will receive due weight in the American political process.

The Senate, apportioning its votes equally among the fifty states, makes certain that the full regional diversity of the United States will be faithfully reflected in the conduct of its foreign policy. Since the United States is one of the world's most regionally diverse societies, the decentralizing effect of the Senate on American foreign policy is marked. The thickly populated, overwhelmingly industrial states of the Northeast and the Middle Atlantic regions and the isolated, lightly populated states of the Rocky Mountains and the southwestern deserts have different foreign policy interests. What is good for Texas, historically a low-wage state with an economy oriented toward the production of raw materials and farm commodities, is very often bad for Massachusetts, a higher-wage state that consumes what Texas produces. In the 1970s the soaring price of oil created a boom in Texas and a bust in Massachusetts. "Drive 75 and Freeze a Yankee!" exulted bumper stickers in the Oil Patch. Ten years later, oil prices slumped; Massachusetts enjoyed what its politicians called an economic "miracle," while Texas languished in a near-depression.

The states also differ on the regions of the world that are most important to them. Texas inevitably looks to Mexico; opportunities for trade and problems of immigration involve Texan interests like no other questions in foreign policy. Michigan looks to Canada. California is interested in Mexico and fascinated by the Pacific Rim. Culturally, geographically, and economically, Europe is a long way from Los Angeles. Oregon and Washington are riveted by Japan, and consider Mexico to be a minor concern. Outside the confines of Wall Street, New York cares less about Japan and more about Europe. Florida is more concerned with Cuba than with any other country, and with Latin America generally to the near-exclusion of other concerns. The South and the agricultural Midwest think of the rest of the world largely as potential markets for their agricultural products. The industrial Midwest sees sources of competition as well as potential markets everywhere.

The strange arithmetic of the Senate ensures that alternative and regional views of the national interest will be well represented in the process. In 1998 more than 50 percent of total American exports came from seven states accounting for only fourteen out of the one hundred seats in the Senate. Twenty-six states, however, commanding a majority in the Senate, were responsible for a combined total of less than 10 percent of American exports. Under these circumstances, it is not surprising that the politics of trade policy should sometimes take strange directions.

Voting patterns founded on these regional realities have often shaped American foreign policy in the past. At the outbreak of World War I, the Midwest was dominated by opponents of United States participation; New England favored intervention. Mothers in Nebraska did not want their sons to die in what they felt was a war to safeguard the right of Anglo-American bankers to travel unmolested on luxury liners to England. New Englanders felt that the protection of American shipping and European trade was a vital interest that could not be neglected. This was a reversal of earlier debates in American history, when New England had been more pacifistic. New England had little sympathy for American expansion in the Pacific, and its delegation opposed the annexations of Hawaii and the Philippines. The latter was ratified by a single vote, with the New England senators voting heavily against. New England had also opposed the War of 1812, the annexation of Texas, and the Mexican War. ("Are you not large and unwieldy enough already? Have you not Indians enough to expel from the land of their fathers' sepulchre?" John Quincy Adams—the former president, now a congressman— asked the South and the West during a debate in the House on the annexation of Texas.[23] The answer was in both cases emphatically no.)

The South had been consistently annexationist and aggressive. As noted earlier, before the Civil War Southerners looked to Texas, Central America, and Cuba for more slave states; afterward they continued to hope that American expansion in the region would benefit their impoverished area. Southern values had always led many young men to pursue military careers; the economic devastation of the Civil War and the social prestige of its veterans made military careers even more attractive to subsequent generations and—after service in the national army once more became accepted in southern society at the time of the Spanish-American War—established a distinctive regional ethos of military service and combative patriotism that continues to influence southern and, therefore, national politics. The long tenure in office of southern representatives in both houses of Congress gave southern states unparalleled opportunities to endow themselves with military bases; this network deepened the region's already fiercely patriotic pride.

From the standpoint of Continental realism, the presence of regional and congressional voices in the American foreign policy process is only part of the problem. Behind this reality is an even deeper problem, one that not only Continental realists but many observers schooled in history and political science regard as an absolutely critical deficiency in the American system: its democratic nature.

The ink was hardly dry on the Constitution when American society began a process of transformation from the elite federal republic envisioned by most of its founders toward a much more democratic national state. The American people insisted on having a much louder voice in foreign policy than some of the founders thought wise; as a result foreign policy was shaped in part by democratic values, interests, and aspirations through both the nineteenth and the twentieth century.

In the opinion of many observers both foreign and domestic, that is not a good thing. Until very recently few sensible people have ever believed in the ability of democracies to conduct their foreign affairs in a moderate, firm, constructive, and farsighted fashion.

We often forget today just how revolutionary the American experiment has been. This attempt at democracy on a continental scale has always inspired misgivings; nothing so broad in scope had ever been tried before, and the previous, smaller experiments mostly came to grief. The first political scientists had watched in horror while the Athenian democracy embarked on an adventurous foreign policy, vacillated in the conduct of the resulting war, played politics with the military command, and entrusted the fate of the city-state to an unprincipled and unbalanced adventurer. "The fairest of names, but the worst of realities—mob rule," said Polybius of democracy. "[M]ore cruel than wars or tyrants," was the verdict of Seneca, who, as the tutor of Nero and an acquaintance of Caligula, had ample opportunity to assess the problems of tyranny up close.[24]

Subsequent centuries saw the consequences of democratic government in city-states throughout the Mediterranean in antiquity, and again in Italy during the Renaissance; it was not an inspiring performance. The French Revolution, and to a lesser degree the American Revolution, did not, at first, change many minds.

The first three American presidents were all convinced that foreign entanglements could wreck the young republic—though they differed over which entanglements might pose the greatest danger. Washington and John Adams believed that the friends of France were intent on a Jacobin-style revolution in the United States, accompanied by an ideologically motivated war in support of the French Revolution. Jefferson, for his part, believed that Washington, with a sinister pro-British faction at his back, was willing to support a coup if necessary to get the pro-British Jay Treaty through the Senate. These fears arose partly out of the weakness and instability that characterized the young republic, but more fundamentally, even in Jefferson's case, out of a belief that democratic states were in general less able than others to manage their foreign relations.

Other friends of the Republic agreed. "I do not hesitate to say," wrote Alexis de Tocqueville, "that it is especially in the conduct of their foreign relations that democracies appear to me decidedly inferior to other governments. . . . Foreign politics demand scarcely any of those qualities which are peculiar to a democracy; they require, on the contrary, the perfect use of almost all those in which it is deficient."[25]

At the time of the American Revolution, there was something like an intellectual consensus on the type of government necessary to conduct an active and successful foreign policy: an aristocracy. Aristocrats had the leisure to travel abroad and to study the history and languages required for diplomacy. They took the long view of their country's interests; they were prepared to undertake policies whose benefits might not mature for many years. Aristocrats were eager to win fame through distinguished service to the state; they were well versed in the traditional interests of their country and of its relations with its various neighbors and rivals. The aristocracy of an entire nation formed a body that was small enough to be reached and persuaded by the counsels of reason but large enough to resist the passions of a small faction. While the aristocracy might oppress its fellow citizens through discriminatory domestic laws, in dealings with foreign countries it would represent the interests of the nation as a whole.

Monarchies shared some of these advantages. Kings knew diplomatic history and were educated to understand the basic interests of their nation. They were aware of their long-term dynastic interests and were more concerned than any of their subjects with the honor and the safety of the nation. On the other hand, as historians and politicians have had ample opportunity to note, the private quarrels and passions of monarchs had played a large and often unfortunate role in European history. The War of the Spanish Succession around the turn of the eighteenth century, to take one example, cannot be explained without an understanding of the personal character and ambitions of Louis XIV of France. George III's personality played some role both in driving the colonists to rebel and in dragging out hostilities.

Nonetheless, the people, it was commonly believed, were a worse ruler than any king when it came to foreign policy. Kings might be emotional and fickle, but they were models of constancy compared to the mob. In 1830 Benjamin Disraeli rose in the House of Commons to attack the idea of democracy.

If you establish a democracy, you must in due time reap the fruits of a democracy. You will in due season have great impatience of the public burdens, combined in due season with great increase of the public expenditures. You will in due season have wars entered into from passion and not from reason. You will in due season find your property is less valuable and your freedom less complete.[26]

Deficit spending and military adventures comprised the conventional verdict on democracy not only of Disraeli's time but of almost all generations from the Homeric age into the twenty-first century. In this view, Ronald Reagan's combination of big budget deficits with large military budgets and a forceful foreign policy represents the penultimate form of democracy, to be followed in due course by an even more unscrupulous demagogue who wins the votes of an ignorant populace by catering to their prejudices, and uses the powers so gained to make himself a dictator.

The widespread view of our times that democracies don't get into aggressive wars was not accepted by our predecessors. The growth of democracy in the United States and Europe went hand in hand with an enormous increase in bellicosity in international relations. As we have seen, it had been only with difficulty that American and British statesmen managed to keep inflamed popular opinion from pushing their nations into wars over the Oregon boundary in the 1840s and the *Trent* affair in 1861.[27] An irresistible tide of popular opinion drew the hesitant William McKinley into the Spanish-American War. Public opinion in all the major European countries greeted the outbreak of war in 1914 with enthusiasm, and at every great diplomatic crisis in the fifty years from the Civil War to World War I, in all the more-or-less democratically ruled countries, it consistently favored the more warlike course, and those who worked for international compromise risked their political lives.

If American opinion was less warlike than European opinion in 1914, the next six years could serve as a textbook case for the vacillation and emotionalism against which critics of democracy had warned. American feeling swung from pacifism in 1914 to bloodthirsty ferocity three years later. In 1916 the American people reelected Woodrow Wilson because he had kept them out of war; a year later, they were renaming sauerkraut "liberty cabbage" so as not to give aid and comfort to "the Hun." In 1918 they were ready to fight in the trenches to establish democracy and peace worldwide; by 1920 they wanted nothing more than to forget the horrors of war and the responsibilities of peace in a headlong return to "normalcy."

This was not just an American flaw. Every European democracy was vindictive and warlike in 1919 when cooler heads supported a moderate peace; all the democracies were pacifistic fifteen years later, when firmness would have been useful against Hitler. In 1938 popular opinion everywhere, and especially in the United States, could not be bothered to note the real threat to peace posed by Hitler's Germany. In 1950 the American people could be stampeded into hysteria over the largely imaginary menace of Stalin's short-term plans for world conquest.

It is not just that democracies are excitable and fickle. Democratic theory holds that the people are capable of giving wise judgments about domestic politics because each person is most capable of determining which candidate or measure best serves his or her interests. But it is much less clear that citizens are informed about the vital issues in foreign policy. Kissinger's statistic about contras in Norway does not stand alone. Articles and surveys regularly appear with dismal statistics, like the Cold War poll that indicated that 50 percent of Americans couldn't find Britain, France, or Japan on a map.[28]

Even the warmest advocates of democracy hesitate to suggest that the mass of the American people are well read in world history, that they understand the role of international institutions, or that they grasp the history and purposes of American diplomacy, let alone those of other nations. It is improbable that the electorate has any conscious clear sense of long-term national policy or interests, and it clearly does not demand thoughtful debate on foreign affairs from its political representatives.

The ignorance that hampers the formation of enlightened public opinion on foreign policy questions is not simply a matter of factual and historical ignorance. There is a moral gap as well between the experience of the citizens of a democracy and the conditions of their state. In the language of classic political theory, the citizens of a democratic state live in an environment shaped by a reasonably beneficent Lockean social contract. Economic life may be competitive, but individual citizens in a healthy democracy live in a society imbued with a healthy social and moral consensus. Most of the people obey most of the laws most of the time. Most of the laws are agreeable to most of the feelings of most of the people; the laws of a democracy must reflect in some way, however imperfectly, the moral sense of the national community.

Sovereign states do not—at least not yet and perhaps not ever—live in a Lockean world. The state is in a Hobbesian state of nature, and until and unless the world's quarreling nation-states form a real social compact and equip an international agent with the means to enforce its terms on the recalcitrant, international relations will inhabit a different moral atmosphere from that of the interpersonal relationships of most private citizens. This lends a curious moral air to international diplomacy, one far removed from the morality and habits of thought that make for a healthy domestic society. Since the Peace of Westphalia in 1648, European states have existed in a moral vacuum—the cynical pragmatism of the *cuius regio*. This is the war of each against all, one in which promises are made to be broken and in which Machiavelli reigns as patron saint.

This does not mean, as self-consciously Nietzschean hyperrealists sometimes think, that nations *always* behave treacherously. All things being equal, it is generally better for states to keep their promises and to be perceived, as often as possible, as upholders of international law and pillars of righteousness. As in civil life, the most successful participants do not advertise their transgressions. They are not generally found among motorcycle gangs; they do not tattoo skulls on their biceps; they do not boast of their will to power and their criminal records. Instead they wear pinstripes, join the Episcopal Church, and hire lawyers and accountants to ensure that their business practices, whatever can be said from a moral point of view, remain—if only by a whisker—on the right side of the law. If they or their corporations should be caught in some illegal or disgraceful act, they hire more lawyers and flacks to put the best light possible on whatever has occurred. Successful governments do likewise; the bombast of aggression and the rhetoric of conquest are the marks of an amateur out of his depth.

Anyone can be immoral, but the accomplished amorality of diplomacy is more difficult to acquire. As a habit of mind it is generally confined to elites, partly because its possession usually leads to successful careers. Again, Continentalists are not wrong to observe a tendency in democratic states for public opinion to oscillate between a naive belief that the international world is simply a larger version of the domestic arena, a space that can and should be run on the same principles as the local church or at least the neighborhood hardware store, and a disillusioned conviction that there are no principles, not even any pragmatic ones, in international life. In other words, democracies tend either to rise above or sink below the morality appropriate to the international scene. A democracy can, so to speak, easily have too many drinks and then pay a sordid call on a prostitute; it is much harder for a democracy to maintain a cultivated mistress in a fashionable apartment. Unfortunately it is precisely this latter attitude of stylish and accomplished amorality that has historically worked well for diplomats.

But the inability of citizens to judge, or act wisely on, foreign policy matters does not result simply from a lack of intellectual background and moral education. Diplomacy has always been a secret art; its most inspired practitioners have loved the darkness and fled the light. Free and open debate is essential for the health of a democracy, but in matters of foreign policy the most important truths are often the ones nobody states.

This secrecy provides an environment in which corruption and treason can flourish. Foreign states can and do seek influence among the citizens of other states. They subsidize publications and journalists; they award contracts; they open the doors to business opportunities; they endow academic chairs; and they contribute to charitable foundations. Much of this activity is perfectly legal, and—by building international friendships and establishing human ties among the citizens of different states—it makes an important contribution to world peace. The givers expect nothing specific in return. But some of this activity is intended to induce foreign citizens to undertake specific acts, to influence legislation, to win special favors, or to influence defense policy.

In a democratic republic, where the responsibility for policy is so diffuse that, as in the case of the House and the Senate, many individuals can influence the outcome of a policy, it is perfectly possible for foreign agents, by bribes and other favors, to induce representatives to be responsive to considerations other than the interests of their constituents or even of their country. Unfortunately the secrecy that surrounds diplomacy, added to the comparative ignorance of democratic voters about the subject, ensures that the more foreign policy comes to dominate the political agenda, the less well democracy can work.

This is one reason why the Founding Fathers were so pessimistic about the ability of the United States to succeed in foreign policy. "Our form of government," said John Adams in 1809, "inestimable as it is, exposes us, more than any other, to the insidious intrigues and pestilent influence of foreign nations."[29] Washington, whose bitterest political battles were fought over foreign relations, agreed. He worried that foreigners would suborn and corrupt the democratic process. "Against the insidious wiles of foreign influence," he said in words that would not be welcomed by the lobbyists and Beltway bandits who now infest the city that bears his name, Americans must be eternally vigilant, since "history and experience prove that foreign influence is one of the most baneful foes of Republican government."[30]

Europe's suspicion of the influence of democracy on foreign policy was more than political-science theory. Foreign policy has historically been seen in most countries as the area in which the power of the state has reigned supreme, and within the state the most power over foreign policy has usually gone to the most centralized and mighty organs of state. Nobody in modern Europe doubted that foreign policy was the preserve of the central authorities as opposed to that of regional units in a federation. Foreign policy was the area in which Europe's monarchs clung most tenaciously to their historic powers against the demands of parliamentarians. The Hapsburgs and the Hohenzollerns never gave up their personal control over foreign policy; even the kings and queens of Britain preserved more power here than they did in domestic affairs. George III was largely responsible for Britain's American policy up to and during the American Revolution. Prince Albert played an important role in British diplomacy until his involvement in the *Trent* crisis, shortly before his death. In the twentieth century Edward VII's personal diplomacy helped bring about the Anglo-French rapprochement in the run up to World War I, and George V's refusal to shake hands with the Bolshevik murderers of his relatives Czar Nicholas II, Empress Alexandra, and their son and four daughters, delayed British recognition of Bolshevik Russia. Even today, foreign policy is the most jealously guarded and privileged aspect of state power through much of the world. Most democratic governments have more power to keep secrets in foreign policy than they do in domestic affairs, and there is an almost universal feeling among European governments that foreign policy should be, as far as possible, insulated from the turmoil of democratic politics.

The framers of the Constitution were well aware of this view, and of the reasons for it, and the division of powers in the Constitution reflects this conventional European belief. In foreign policy, the federal government is supreme, with no powers reserved to the states. Within the federal government, power is concentrated in the executive branch. The president has more power in foreign policy, and in the related domain of military affairs, than in any other areas. The Senate can give him advice, and his treaties and ambassadorial appointments require its consent. The House of Representatives—until the twentieth century, the only branch of the federal government elected by direct popular vote—has even less power; its role is limited to voting appropriations and declarations of war. The power of judicial review over foreign policy decisions is also severely limited; treaties are expressly declared "the supreme law of the land"—courts must interpret and enforce them, but only under very narrow and restricted circumstances can the Supreme Court alter or declare unconstitutional a properly ratified treaty. (And state governments have no role at all in this process.)

By the standards of American politics, this is as close as the federal government gets to a carte blanche. The foreign policy provisions of the Constitution jibe closely with Alexander Hamilton's ideas about the distribution of power among the branches: He wished for a strong executive, an advisory senate, and a weak popular assembly possessing only a negative power of the purse. When foreign policy gets beyond negotiations and moves into actual war, generations of experience have shown that in fact the powers of the federal government, and especially of the executive branch, grow even greater.

And yet, while all this has perhaps slightly constricted the force of democratic debate in American foreign policy, the fact remains that we are more used to seeing American presidents following public opinion than leading it. When it comes time to make major foreign policy decisions, domestic political advisers have a prominent place at the table and, in many cases, a decisive voice. To many observers, American and foreign alike, that is a bad thing and makes it that much harder for presidents and secretaries of state to make good foreign policy.

Finally, statesmen and political scientists attuned to the values and history of continental statesmanship have another problem—it might be called a "boundary problem"—in grasping the reality of American foreign policy. Classical analysis of foreign policy makes many assumptions about what states are and how they relate to their societies. Most of these analyses are rooted in the experience of European states over many centuries, and they tend both to heighten the distinctions between state and private activities abroad and to marginalize the importance of private interactions. What nations do is foreign policy; what civil society and business do is not, though in some cases these activities may influence the foreign policy of the state.

These assumptions and conclusions don't work as well in the American as in the European context. While the American state resembles European states in some ways, in others it follows a logic of its own. Throughout American history the distinction between state and society has been blurrier than in Europe, and fewer of the key activities of American society have been led or carried out by the state.

This is as true in foreign policy as in many other aspects of national life. In European history states tended to monopolize or control many aspects of the way in which one society interacted with others. Even international business was closely connected with states in early modern and medieval Europe. Commercial republics like Venice and Genoa saw extremely tight links between government and commerce. In Holland and Britain, much international commerce was carried out by organizations like the Dutch and British East India Companies, which combined aspects of both government and business. The missionary activities of many European states were also closely linked to their national policy. The role of Catholic missionaries in Spanish, Portuguese, and French colonial ventures is typical of the way in which many activities we would now categorize as those of civil society and nonstate actors were once directed by, or at least coordinated with the policy of, the state.

Without that kind of historical experience, American merchants and missionaries have acted with more independence from the state, though both groups have been willing to call for state support when they thought they needed and could get it. It is not wrong to speak of a foreign policy of the American people, one that is not always identical to the policy of the American state but that is not always completely separate from it either. The movement of both missionaries and merchants into Hawaii was independent of the state, yet in some ways it expressed the policy of the United States toward that kingdom better than official declarations did. More than once popular policy has run ahead of the state and ultimately forced the state—sometimes reluctantly—to support it. The movement by American pioneers into Texas, their subsequent rebellion against Mexico, and the process by which Texas was ultimately brought into the Union show this phenomenon at work. The United States government was directly involved only in the final annexation, but the expansion into Texas—as well as the similar and continuing expansion into Indian lands guaranteed by treaties—shows that a consistent popular "foreign policy" was at work throughout the period.

While it is still possible to distinguish between what the government adopts as policy and what other actors do on their own, many activities that would have been directed by states in other parts of the world were carried out by civil society in the United States. Foreign policy studies that compare state activities in Europe with state activities in the United States tend to underestimate the degree, and in some cases misjudge the direction and effect, of the broad engagement of the United States with the rest of the world.

The many different failures of the American state to live up to Continental models of what states should look like point to a basic difference between the American and European processes that Continentally oriented observers cannot help but interpret as an American weakness. American foreign policy does not proceed out of a single, unified worldview. There are vital differences over the definition of national interests, even at the heart of the American foreign policy process.

American foreign policy rests on a balance of contrasting, competing voices and values—it is a symphony, or tries to be, rather than a solo. It often seems that this chaotic condition cannot be the basis for sound, long-term policy. But history teaches something different. The United States was consumed by controversy over foreign policy from 1949 to 1989, a period when every fundamental element of that policy came into question. Yet through it all the United States adhered to a central strategic goal. It contained the Soviet Union and brought about the collapse of the European communist system without fighting a nuclear war. At virtually every point during the Cold War, American foreign policy looked like a mess. Idealists and realists struggled over possession of the policy; demagogues pulled the country one way or another, the military-industrial complex still another; ethnic lobbies distorted overall foreign policy; the country did things it oughtn't to have done, such as allowing United Fruit to dictate policy over Guatemala in 1954, and it left undone things it ought to have done, like normalizing relations with China before 1973. It was possible—even easy—to write books denouncing the failures, inconsistencies, incongruities, and irregularities in American foreign policy. Our European friends missed no opportunity to snipe at our policies from the sidelines and, God knows, they had plenty to snipe at.

And yet.

When all is said and done, the United States stuck to its policy of containment. It built the NATO alliance, the largest (and longest-lasting) intimate security partnership among sovereign states in modern history. It built a system of international trade wider and freer than anything that had ever existed. It presided over an international system that saw the dismantling of European empires affecting 40 percent of the earth's surface and without the outbreak of any general war. It developed security doctrines to keep in check the unprecedented destructive power of nuclear weapons, and it managed a conflicted relationship with a rival nuclear power without disaster for forty years.

How and why the United States broke all the training rules but won all the prizes was one of the most fascinating and important stories of the twentieth century; learning how to repeat that success in this even more challenging century is the most important single task facing the American people today.

Chapter Three

CHANGING THE
PARADIGMS

Foreigners, and especially Europeans, might naturally rely on the assumptions of Continental realism, unsatisfactory as they may be, to analyze American foreign policy. But we are still left with a deeper mystery: Why do so many American citizens, statesmen, and scholars find their own tradition so wanting? Many of the bitterest critics of American foreign policy process are American citizens; some have held high office in the American government. What possible cause can there be for what appears to be an amnesia pandemic depriving so many American foreign policy leaders of any real knowledge of, or interest in, the foreign policy traditions of the American state? How and why have the assumptions of Continental realism gained such dominance in the bureaucracies and universities of the latest and greatest of the anglophone global hegemonies?

It is tempting to say that American policy-makers ignore the lessons of American history because Americans are one of the least historical-minded peoples in the world, tending to agree with Henry Ford's claim that "[H]istory is more or less bunk." However, indifferent to history as many Americans may be, in everything having to do with political life they are, compared with most Europeans, almost fanatically tradition-minded. No European polity has anything like the American love affair with the Constitution. The French do not honor and venerate the leaders of their Revolution as Americans venerate our Founding Fathers. Many Americans, perhaps most, consider the Declaration of Independence, the

Constitution, and the Bill of Rights to be something like sacred scripture: revelations of eternal principles, valid for all time. The Constitution is widely and justly accepted as a distillation of political wisdom and a still-living guide for contemporary conduct. The Bill of Rights and the Declaration of Independence are venerated as timeless expressions of principles summoning us to realize their noble ideals. We do not generally ask whether these documents are adequate for our purposes; the Bill of Rights and the Declaration judge us, we do not judge them.

The profound and extraordinary traditionalism of Americans extends into other fields. Our law courts still follow the precedents of Supreme Court Chief Justices John Marshall and John Jay; our military academies honor the courage and teach the tactics of our Revolutionary and Civil War heroes.

It is only our diplomats and our foreign policy thinkers who find little to inspire them in the record of our past. The position of the United States in world politics has changed strikingly from generation to generation and even decade to decade, and this naturally tends to obscure the underlying continuities in our diplomatic tradition and cause each generation to feel that it is meeting historical tests for the first time. Precisely because the ascent of the United States from a weak confederacy to a world empire was so rapid, it is understandable that Americans are forever discounting the relevance of their grandparents' and even their parents' experiences and ideas. The generation of 1895, which forced Britain to acknowledge American hegemony in the Western Hemisphere, could hardly sympathize with the generation of 1860, which trembled in fear lest Britain intervene in the Civil War. The generation of 1860, similarly, could scarcely imagine the world of 1825, in which the United States was an almost insignificant part of the global political system.

Perhaps, but this line of argument proves too much. It takes us back to Ford. If the foreign policy of the eighteenth century has little to teach contemporary diplomats, why should the campaigns of Washington, Sherman, and Lee have anything to teach our generals today? Why should the political institutions of the eighteenth century—formed in such a different world for such a different people—still guide us today? What relevance do legal precedents involving footbridges and the regulations affecting the branches of now-defunct national banks have for contemporary lawyers, engaged as they are in high-stakes battles over types of property that did not even exist when Marshall pondered the legal theories of the Maryland bench?

Moreover, at a time still—just—within living memory, American attitudes toward our traditional foreign policy were similar to public attitudes toward other time-honored and -tested elements of national life. As late as the 1930s, the Monroe Doctrine was not a historical curiosity but a living and active principle whose terms were frequently invoked by statesmen to justify their policies in the same way that Reagan or Madeleine Albright might have referred to "the lessons of Munich" in defending a particular stand overseas. Washington's Farewell Address was still memorized by schoolchildren and recited on ceremonial occasions; Washington's warnings about "entangling alliances," and his enunciation of principles for American diplomacy, enjoyed the same popular veneration as Jefferson's sentiments in the Declaration of Independence. Hamilton's American System—industrial protection to protect "sunrise industries" and American wages—was firmly and widely believed to be the last word in political economy.

Indeed, during the Cold War and into the present, the attitudes of American policy-makers and opinion leaders on foreign policy remain largely shaped by a reaction against the uncritical veneration of historic American stands. So powerful were these older historical traditions that their hold on the American public imagination posed the greatest single obstacle to the generation of statesmen charged with the development of an American foreign policy for the 1940s. The Monroe Doctrine, understood to oppose United States involvement in Europe, and Washington's Farewell Address, understood to oppose participation in partnerships of any kind, were potent sources of opposition to United States entry into World War II and the subsequent creation of the Cold War security system. Hamilton's theory of protectionism, however applicable it may have been when the United States was a relatively minor participant in a global trading system shaped in mercantilist London, was a poor guide for an American generation that needed to replace Britain as the center of an international trading system based on free trade.

Unfortunately, the public imagination of the time had been captured by a peculiarly literal-minded and unhelpful simplification of a complex tradition. This simplification combined ideas about foreign policy that had long been held by much of public opinion with other, more recent ideas generally traceable to widespread American disillusionment with the results of World War I.

In fact the United States in the 1920s and 1930s lay under the spell of a historical myth—call it the myth of virtuous isolation. It was in fact a profoundly antihistorical myth, based on the premise that the wise Founding Fathers had once and for all laid down the road on which American foreign policy should travel. Abstracted from any historical context, a "literal" reading of Washington's Farewell Address was used to argue against any American alliances with foreign powers under any circumstances whatever. The Monroe Doctrine was similarly read as mandating as a first principle of statecraft that the United States would prohibit any foreign power from meddling in the Western Hemisphere, while keeping its own nose out of the East.

This myth presented itself as the eternal and unchanging creed of the American people through the generations. It was the foreign policy equivalent of the Bill of Rights: the one true faith, handed down from on high. The United States prospered when we honored it; when we strayed from its precepts, and worshipped false idols, we suffered. Woodrow Wilson broke the sacred laws that George Washington and James Monroe had brought down from Sinai and led the country into a European war; as a result the United States fought an expensive and brutal war for the benefit of bloodstained and treacherous empires like Britain, whose cruel, unprincipled elites were only too happy to exploit the naïveté of their American "allies."

Like all powerful myths, the myth of virtuous isolation contained more than a kernel of truth; like all myths, it also contained other things. As a historical reaction to World War I, growing in large part from disappointment with the postwar conduct of the Western Powers, the critique of the Allies was not without merit. Britain, for example, for so long the great apostle of fiscal regularity and the enemy of repudiation— a country for the sake of whose bondholders two generations of American farmers were subjected to painful and unpopular tight-money policies so that United States debts from the Civil War could be paid, in gold, to the uttermost farthing—found the resources to maintain a large navy, harass Gandhi's freedom movement, and bomb Kurdish rebels in Iraq but pleaded poverty when it came to repaying its war debts to the American taxpayer. After 1919 the belief grew rapidly that the Western Allies, in cahoots with the New York bankers who loaned billions to the belligerents and for whom an Allied defeat would have meant ruin, had snookered the United States into what turned out to be simply a savage conflict between two bands of imperialist robbers.

These views, though hardly a full and fair account of World War I, were not wholly implausible on their face, and commanded widespread assent in the postwar United States. Nostalgic for a past that had never existed, eager to turn their backs on the depressing spectacle of European scorpions grappling in their bottle, Americans bought the myth of virtuous isolation. As the storm clouds gathered again over the world in the 1930s, and the Roosevelt administration girded its loins to lead the nation into a second global conflict, the debunking of this myth was an urgent priority. Similarly, for those preparing the ground for U.S. participation in the Cold War, the myth of virtuous isolation was the greatest obstacle to the policies they wished to urge on the nation.

The debunkers had a difficult, counterintuitive case to make. Isolation, virtuous or not, was appealing in the dangerous world of the twentieth century. Harding had evoked this nostalgia by calling for a return to "normalcy" after the First World War, and its restoration is what many Americans believed they had sacrificed and fought for in the Second. Wartime propaganda had reinforced this expectation. Fascism and Japanese militarism had been the cause of the war; now those evil ideologies had been crushed. The world's free peoples—the brave Russians; the rapidly developing democratic Chinese; the plucky British; and the long-suffering French—were now in control and, many Americans expected, the necessity of American intervention would fade away.

It was the sad duty of the American government in the 1940s to persuade the nation that this was not so. There was not much time for this task; the winter of 1947 brought the United States face-to-face with one of the most perilous situations in modern European history. Europe's economies had not only failed to recover from the devastation of war, but much of the Continent appeared to be sinking deeper into a depression whose end could not be foreseen. "Europe is steadily deteriorating . . . ," wrote Under Secretary for Economic Affairs Will Clayton in May of that year. "Millions of people in the cities are slowly starving. . . . Without further prompt and substantial aid from the United States, economic, social and political disintegration will overwhelm Europe."[1]

Well-organized Communist parties in Italy and France appeared to be gaining strength at the expense of the fragile democratic forces. Meanwhile, Britain's economic and military power, long sagging, was beginning to crumble; the United States would have to face the new postwar world without a single powerful ally. President Truman, already performing poorly in the polls, faced an uphill battle for election in his own right; the congressional elections of 1946 saw a stunning collapse of the once-secure Democratic majorities in both houses.

These were the unpromising circumstances in which the great debate on postwar American foreign policy had to be launched some fifty years ago, and the response of the American foreign policy establishment was to create what, without prejudice, we can call the myth of the Cold War. As historian Michael Kammen reminds us in his book *Mystic Chords of Memory*, myths are not intrinsically bad. They are even necessary; they are condensations of historical traditions and received ideas that form a useful shorthand for debate. Democratic society depends on myths; without such a convenient historical shorthand that compresses and simplifies extremely complex historical events and political questions into ideas and images that nonspecialists can understand and use, democratic debate would simply disappear.

Like most myths, the myth of the Cold War was a mixture of fact, interpretation, and fiction; it was intended to meet the needs of the nation at a specific point in time, and it implies no disrespect for an old myth or for those who put it together to suggest that, with the passing of time, the old myth may have lost its utility.

There were two main elements in what became the myth—or, to use a less evocative but perhaps less invidious term, the paradigm—of the Cold War. One was a myth about Them; the other was a myth about Us. The myth about Them—that communism was a united global force engaged in a determined, aggressive crusade to impose its vicious ideology in every corner of the globe—was never very accurate, and hampered thoughtful American foreign policy–makers throughout the Cold War. The myth was politically useful in that it mobilized American public opinion for the struggle. Dean Acheson conjured up the image of a communist tide flowing throughout the Middle East to persuade leading congressmen to support aid to Greece and Turkey, but he knew at the time that he was being, as he would later say, "clearer than truth."[2] The notion of a monolithic communism was politically mischievous because it effectively prevented American public opinion from understanding the Cold War in any coherent or sensible way. Without this myth the United States might never have stumbled into the Vietnam War; on the other hand, without it we might never have summoned up the national will to fight the Cold War for forty years. Fortunately, the collapse of communism has now largely robbed this myth of its power to harm.

The Cold War myth about the United States was less obviously inaccurate than the myth about communism; unfortunately this myth still helps shape American foreign policy discussions today and, unless its influence is countered, it will wreak a great deal of mischief in the post–Cold War era.

Essentially, the Cold War myth about the United States was born of desperation. The difference between the apparent content of traditional American policy—isolationist and protectionist—and the demands of the Cold War era for an interventionist and free-trade policy was so great that little effort was wasted in attempting to look for links between the old and new foreign policies.

In the heat of political debate there was no time and little inclination for subtle hairsplitting about the nature of American foreign policy in past generations. It was idle to say that the Monroe Doctrine and the special relationship with Great Britain constituted a sophisticated and successful American participation in the global balance of power. It was too late to replace popular, totemistic veneration for Washington's Farewell Address with a deeper understanding and appreciation for the historical circumstances surrounding the speech and an exegesis of the subtle—and still relevant—ideas that it contained. Too much political oratory, too many history books, had been dedicated to propagating the now-rigidified myth of virtuous isolationism. A handful of foreign policy intellectuals—including Walter Lippmann—tried to reinterpret the received wisdom. The Monroe Doctrine, wrote Lippmann, wasn't isolationist: It was a tacit agreement between the United States and Great Britain to maintain the balance of power.[3] But the policy-makers and practical statesmen could not afford to plunge into these dangerous cross-currents. "There was no 'unwritten agreement,'" Franklin Roosevelt flatly said in the same fireside chat in which he also declared that the United States would become the "arsenal of democracy."[4]

Like Roosevelt, the Cold Warriors instinctively and probably correctly felt they were better off emphasizing the discontinuities between old and new American policy. As they labored to counter the influence of the myth of virtuous isolation, Roosevelt and his Cold War successors ended by throwing up their hands. The old myth was too strong; it could be buried, but it could not be revised. So what they said instead was that isolation had been the right foreign policy in its day, but that its day was over. True, said the Cold Warriors, the American diplomatic history of the nineteenth century was largely a blank. Except for westward expansion, the United States essentially had no foreign policy from the proclamation of the Monroe Doctrine in 1823 until McKinley's war with Spain. America's traditional isolation was the result of the weakness of the United States, the power and presence of the British navy, and the undeveloped state of technology in the nineteenth century. During this period the American people knew little and cared less about foreign affairs. Isolated from the rest of the world, Americans developed strange and unrealistic ideas about how the world worked. But now the world had changed, and the old ideas didn't work anymore.

The United States was like a girl educated in a strict convent, said the Cold Warriors; once it stepped out into the world, its past experience was of very little use in dealing with its new surroundings and situation. The American people, in Kissinger's words, had been "brought up in the belief that peace is the normal condition among nations, that there is no difference between personal and public morality, and that America was safely insulated from the upheavals affecting the rest of the world."[5]

This "conventual" school goes on to say that it was because of this historical inexperience that the United States adopted idealistic foreign policy goals during World War I, and also through inexperience that the United States took refuge in isolationism after its repudiation of the Treaty of Versailles. Never having had a foreign policy before, the United States was simply unprepared to face the world into which it emerged in the twentieth century.

In what the Cold Warriors never tired of calling that "complex" and "sophisticated" world, the old verities of a rural era had to be discarded. The world had shrunk, and American power had grown. The United States could no longer sit peaceably disarmed, shielded from foreign conflicts by the mighty oceans on its shores. By the time the United States itself was physically attacked, it would be too late to win another war. It was therefore necessary to build and maintain peacetime alliances of just the kind against which President Washington had so trenchantly warned.

Nor could the United States safely indulge its moralistic illusions. The dreams of sanctity proper to a young girl in the convent had to be discarded in the hurlyburly of the real world. If the United States wanted omelets, it would have to break eggs. According to the myth of the Cold War, because the United States was so uniquely virtuous and virginal, this lesson came hard. The innocent decency of the American people kept rebelling at the distasteful but necessary measures of amoral realpolitik recommended by Kissinger and his colleagues.

In essence the early Cold Warriors ended by posing the foreign policy questions of the day in terms of the need for the United States to cast off a heritage, once useful and beloved, now inappropriate and burdensome. "When I was a child, I spake as a child, I understood as a child, I thought as a child," Saint Paul told the Corinthians. "But when I became a man," he continued, "I put away childish things."[6] The Cold Warriors urged their fellow Americans to do the same thing.

It worked. The early Cold Warriors buried the myth of virtuous isolation—or, more accurately, they embalmed it and laid it to rest underneath the new myth of the U.S. coming of age. Their view is, in a simplified form, the respectable history of American foreign policy that many of us dimly remember from our high school and college days. It represents a vision so familiar that people take it for granted. It is the intellectual background to much of the punditry that one hears and reads in the contemporary media. It is the basis for the thinking of much of the American foreign policy establishment. Unfortunately it is a poor foundation for the choices that the nation must make in the coming years.

Like most historical myths, the Cold War myth is a mixture of helpful and harmful ideas. Much of what it says is lucid analysis that remains essential to any reasoned approach to American foreign policy today. After 1945 the United States clearly did need to take a more active role in international politics than it ever had before. Historically the United States had been a free rider in the British world system. From 1945 it would assume the privileges and shoulder the costs of global hegemony on its own. Some of the most hallowed concepts in the American foreign policy tradition had to be discarded or revised. Permanent neutrality was no longer an option. It was indeed too late to start planning for national security when an enemy nation had already upset the European balance of power. In trade policy the United States would, in the post-British era, have to open its markets to the goods of other nations if it sought market access in return.

On these and many other points, the Cold War myth was a useful basis for national discussion and national policy. But, like every historical myth, its usefulness had limits. Now, at the end of the Cold War, the Cold War myth has become a positive obstacle to reasoned discussion about the future foreign policy of the United States. We need to reconnect with the national foreign policy tradition that the Cold Warriors relegated to the background.

On one level the myth of the Cold War was a historical travesty. The United States was not a hermit kingdom before the Cold War. And it wasn't, as the Cold War myth seemed to imply, Emperor Hirohito who "opened up" a reluctant United States by bombing Pearl Harbor; it was President Millard Fillmore who sent Comm. Matthew Perry ten thousand miles to open up Japan in March 1852—and he, and the political community around him, had solid reasons for sending the long-suffering commodore on this wearying and dangerous voyage. As we have already seen, the American statesmen of the eighteenth and nineteenth centuries had compiled a distinguished record in international relations, and the politics of foreign policy had been intimately linked to the great party struggles of American history. Furthermore, along with Great Britain, the United States espoused a distinctive approach to world politics which had consistently produced better results than the realpolitik of the old continent.

No one knew all this better than the generation of American statesmen who laid the foundations of the postwar world in the 1940s and constructed the new myth. The American leaders of that generation were steeped in the traditions of American foreign policy and of Anglo-American realism. Most if not all of them had read Rear Adm. Alfred Thayer Mahan's works on sea power in early youth. Theodore Roosevelt's global politics had electrified them—and left his cousin Franklin with a lifelong desire to emulate and surpass his achievements. A working knowledge of British history was one of the chief subjects of liberal education in those days, and anyone occupying senior government or business positions in the 1940s had extensive firsthand experience of the British Empire and its "special relationship" with the Americans. Men like Roosevelt and Acheson—not to mention Eisenhower, John Foster Dulles, and George C. Marshall—grew up in a world in which their British counterparts were at once their rivals and their only real peers. But time was short, and the need was urgent; the early Cold Warriors did what they could with what they had, and they successfully built strong popular support for forty years of Cold War and laid the foundation for the ultimate American victory over perhaps the most destructive and dangerous tyranny in the history of mankind.

At the same time, however, their success in relegating American traditions of statesmanship to the ash heap of history had unintended consequences. In particular, closing the door on the American past opened the door to another set of historical traditions and strategic thought: the ideas, values, and unconscious assumptions of Continental realism. Paradoxically, even as the United States moved to defeat the latest and most dangerous of the Continental realist empires, and even as Western

Europe and Japan saw their fortunes improve as they adopted elements of traditional American foreign policy, the foreign policy ideas of the Soviet Union, Wilhelmine Prussia, and Metternich's Austria would rise to power in the United States.

Continental Realism and the Cold War

The world of the Cold War was propitious for the European strategic ideas that wafted into the United States in the second half of the twentieth century. The international environment faced by the United States during the Cold War looked in many ways like the world faced by Bismarck and Metternich. The competition between the United States and the Soviet Union could easily be construed as a twentieth-century analog of the old struggles for the mastery of Europe. True, the competition was on a global scale, rather than the local scale of European politics, but time and distance had shrunk. The United States and the Soviet Union were in many ways back to the scorpions-in-a-bottle struggle of European politics.

Moreover the economic dimensions of the U.S.–Soviet competition, while basic and ultimately decisive, tended to disappear from view for long periods of time. In reality, with the Western European and Japanese economic revivals of the 1950s—a success made possible largely by the world economic order initiatives of American foreign policy in the 1940s—the Soviet Union's threat to the West sharply diminished. Money trumped Marx; communism had little appeal in an increasingly affluent West.

Economics again visibly drove international politics in the waning years of Soviet power. The Communist regime ultimately crumbled as its increasing economic shortcomings, including its ability to match Western technological advances, undermined the legitimacy of its social order even in the eyes of the Communist elite and increasingly put the costs of military parity with the United States out of reach.

These decisive economic developments occupied the center of policymakers' attention only in the opening and closing phases of the Cold War. During the long middle passages of the forty-year rivalry, attention largely focused on the military and political aspects of the rivalry, and for these questions, Continental realism seemed to provide an adequate intellectual and political framework.

Meanwhile, other factors largely unrelated to the U.S.-USSR rivalry helped make Continental realism look more plausible in the United States by concealing the economic context of traditional American policy from both elite and mass audiences. This process began with the shift in the U.S. international position from debtor to creditor status early in the twentieth century, gained force with the breakdown of the Britain-based international system of finance and trade between 1914 and the Great Depression, and climaxed after World War II.

The status of the United States as a debtor, capital-importing nation was one of the great determining features of its existence during the late eighteenth and through the nineteenth century. Virtually every American business and household was kept constantly aware of its connection to and dependence on the international financial system; and attitudes toward Britain and toward the external world generally were shaped to a significant degree by the effects of this dependency and the resentment and multiple inconveniences it caused.

All that changed in the twentieth century. During World War I, Britain became thoroughly and massively indebted to the United States, and proved to be a notably less punctilious debtor than the United States had been. By the time the Depression was in full swing, Britain had in essence defaulted on its $4 billion official war debt to the United States.[7]

This default caused substantial American ill feeling, but the more profound consequence of the change in financial fortunes in the twentieth century was a change in American psychology and politics. Foreign investors were no longer seen as powerful, unaccountable forces shaping the American economy as they pleased regardless of the consequences for ordinary American farmers, workers, and small businessmen. The Federal Reserve System was now in charge of American interest rates; Britain had nothing to do with it.

Few events show the growing independence of American financial markets from Europe more clearly than do the very different reactions on Wall Street to the outbreaks of the two world wars in 1914 and 1939. On July 31, 1914, trading on Wall Street stopped with the outbreak of hostilities and did not resume fully for eight months.[8] Twenty-five years later, when Europeans rushed off to the slaughterhouses again, neither the outbreak of hostilities nor even the fall of France closed the New York Stock Exchange for a single second. During the Cold War, American financial markets were even more independent of European developments.

Given that both the Depression and World War II further disrupted the fabric of international trade and investment already badly damaged by World War I, the early years of the Cold War saw the economic interdependence of the United States with the rest of the world sink to its lowest point.

It has now been more than a century since the United States faced what was once a common feature of economic life: a deep and destructive recession caused by high interest rates demanded by exacting foreign creditors. Although Americans have become more aware of the influence of the international economy on their own prosperity than they were between 1945 and the economic firestorms of the early 1970s, we still do not follow the news on foreign markets with the sense of helpless dependency that our ancestors often knew. Only OPEC's ability to disrupt the American economy through oil-price shocks today gives us a faint sense of the overwhelming, frustrating, and apparently arbitrary power that foreigners once had over the living standards of ordinary Americans.

Financial independence changed the way Americans thought about foreign policy. As the foreign dimension of economic policy debates diminished in the twentieth century, so too did broad public understanding of Americans' former dependence on the conditions of international markets. As this understanding was lost, foreign policy became disconnected from important domestic political battles in the present, but also imaginatively in the past. Educated opinion remembered Bryan's declamation against crucifixion on a "cross of gold" but forgot his linkage of the issue to the power of Britain and the question of America's policy toward it.

Foreign competition as well as foreign creditors largely disappeared after World War II. During most of the Cold War the United States faced no serious economic competitors, much less true rivals, anywhere in the world. Germany and Japan lay in ruins; Britain's once-mighty empire was gone; and unlike other great-power rivals in the past, the Soviet Union never posed an international commercial or financial challenge. Until the 1970s, when German and especially Japanese technology threatened to challenge the American lead in key industries, American corporations were better managed, better capitalized, and better equipped than almost all their rivals. The old economic order, in which a large number of leading economies of roughly equivalent size and technological sophistication competed in markets around the world, seemed lost forever.

All these forces acting together contributed to a sea change in the way many Americans looked at foreign policy. Without contemporary experience of the consequences of international economic interdependence, many Americans came to believe that international economic policy neither was nor should be nor, indeed, ever had been a central concern of foreign policy. They came, in other words, to share the outlook of Continental realism on the relative unimportance of economic issues in international affairs.

Once the American people had forgotten the way that international economic forces had once driven domestic politics, the myth of virginal isolation entombed within the myth of the Cold War looked very plausible. Once economic issues drop out of the history of American foreign policy, foreign policy diminishes from a major obsession of nineteenth-century American politics into an occasional hobby. Judging only by the importance of political and military issues, American involvement in world affairs throughout the nineteenth century looked, without too much squinting, to be just as episodic and marginal as the myth of the Cold War said it was.

The immediacy and the horribly vivid nature of the security threats of the Cold War era also reinforced the idea that a virginal, isolated United States had come of age in a dangerous world. The looming menace of the Soviet Union, still wrapped in the prestige of the Red Army's militarily decisive contest against Nazi Germany and bolstered by a growing nuclear capacity, and the ominous rumblings from Communist China were new kinds of threats for Americans, as was the experience of leading the fight for world order as opposed to fighting in Britain's shadow. The United States had moved from being one great power among many in the relatively benign climate of the Pax Britannica to a position of global hegemony at a time of profound international political crisis and under the unprecedented shadow of thermonuclear war. James Buchanan and Grover Cleveland had never faced anything like *this*.

Other factors also contributed to the rise of Continental realism in the United States during the Cold War. From the Great Depression through World War II and the Cold War, the federal government steadily became larger, more powerful, and more secretive. Within the burgeoning government, power flowed away from Congress toward what became known as the imperial presidency. A culture of security clearances and classified data grew up in what had once been the most open capital in the world, and presidents of the United States, who once traveled virtually without pomp, now never left home without a contingent of bodyguards that would have embarrassed a Caesar. The United States government was, in other words, looking more and more like the old imperial states of Continental Europe. And, at least as far as the concentration of power in the executive went, most foreign policy professionals thought this was a good idea. Congress, a theoretically coequal branch of government whose role in foreign policy had been designed by the Founding Fathers, was considered an interfering busybody by the diplomats of the new dispensation. The fuddy-duddy Founders in their isolation had, argued the Cold Warriors, signally failed to design a Constitution suitable for a great power.

The domestic legislation of the Founding Fathers also came to look outdated as the precepts of Continental realism tightened their grip in the Cold War years. Sen. Joseph McCarthy was only the most extreme voice of a large chorus claiming that the harsh realities of the international scene made traditional American concepts of civil liberties obsolete.

Partly because Senator McCarthy and others so grossly overreacted in the 1950s, scoffing at the hysterics of anticommunism became a favorite sport of American intellectuals, with many inspiring reflections on the courage of those who refused, often at considerable personal and professional cost, to "name names" or otherwise cooperate with various congressional and state investigations. This is all very well, and the abuses were real, but one must also remember that the communist movement was one of the great horrors of world history, responsible for untold suffering and uncountable millions of deaths. Furthermore, although historians have not yet and may not ever work out the numerical proportions, a significant number of American Communists did in fact do everything in their power to assist the foreign policy of the Soviet Union.

"Anti-anticommunists" noted that many members of Communist parties in the United States and elsewhere were good-hearted social idealists motivated more by genuine passion for racial and social justice than by any desire to build Stalinist police states. This was true, and from the standpoint of evaluating the intentions and motives of many honest American Communists, it should not be forgotten.

Nevertheless, the capacity of communist ideology to capture some of the finest minds and keenest consciences of the day made communism more frightening, dangerous, and disgusting, not less; the ability to pervert the good makes a bad thing worse.

Even so, the idea that mere membership in a political party, however poisonous or misguided, could bar an American citizen from certain professions or expose citizens to loss of civil employment or the threat of criminal prosecution was a novel and repulsive innovation foreign to every sentiment of the Bill of Rights. For many Cold Warriors, however, an expansive concept of civil liberties was one of the illusions that a virginal Columbia had picked up in her convent; now that we had come of age we would have to narrow our concepts of liberty at the same time that we strengthened our state.

Social and cultural factors also pushed the United States toward Continental realism. The old, Anglocentric WASP establishment that had long led the nation's foreign policy lost much of its power and influence during the Cold War years, and the new establishment that rose in its place lacked both the intuitive grasp of the Anglo-American tradition and the personal history of contact with British leaders that had shaped the old elite. Some of this shift reflected the growing egalitarianism of American life, as descendants of turn-of-the-century immigrants rapidly climbed social and professional ladders in the post–World War II climate of opportunity. Some reflected the changes in the structure of American financial and corporate leadership as power moved from a handful of firms based mostly on Wall Street and as rival regional financial and corporate power centers gained strength in the decades following World War II. Mass access to higher education in the 1950s created new cohorts of academics and foreign policy professionals whose personal backgrounds owed little to England, and whose university education drew less and less from traditional British ideas of liberal education.

The Cold War years were also the years of accelerating British decline. When the sun never set on the British Empire, its policies and its history commanded the fascinated attention and respect of envious Americans. The dingy, dull, and declining Britain of the Cold War possessed few such attractions for rising American generations, and as the memories of British greatness faded, Americans rarely thought any longer of British foreign policy as a source of inspiration.

As Britain's sun set, the Russian star rose. Stalin's diplomacy had been a model of Continental cynicism and guile; his contemptuous dismissal of papal power—"Oho! The Pope! How many divisions has *he* got?"[9]—could serve as a succinct summary of the strategic thinking of Continental realism. The Stalinist state—secretive, centralized, able to command and concentrate the full resources of its society in the service of international ambitions, and accountable to no public opinion—was, from a Continental perspective, one of the most admirably equipped scorpions ever to scrabble against the glass walls of the European bottle.

No one appreciated the great-power political capabilities of the Soviet state better than the American diplomats and policy makers who had to oppose it. It was a short step from a healthy respect for Soviet power to the conclusion that the United States needed to imitate Soviet strategic thinking; increasing numbers of American policy makers found themselves taking that step as the Cold War dragged on.

The shift from traditional American approaches to foreign policy to Continental realism was gradual and slow. Men like George I. Kennan, Dean Acheson, Walter Lippmann, and Averell Harriman helped ensure that the values and priorities of the old approaches continued to inform the foreign policy process through the 1960s. The influence of Continental realism in American foreign policy did not peak until the Nixon and Ford administrations, when, as national security adviser and secretary of state, Henry Kissinger placed American foreign policy on solidly Continental grounds.

The Nixon and Ford administrations represented the zenith of Continental realism's influence in American foreign policy. International life was seen as a morals-free zone. On the one hand, the United States would support any distasteful regime, bar none, in the interests of strengthening our global posture against the Soviet Union. Some who attacked this idea bitterly when it was applied to regimes like Augusto Pinochet's in Chile applauded it when it led to the opening toward China and Nicolae Ceausescu's independent-minded if bizarre and tyrannical Romania. As conservatives noted at the time, however, the Nixon-Kissinger approach also took the moral element out of the U.S.-Soviet rivalry. It was as if the United States and the Soviet Union were two great powers like Prussia and Austria, and could reach a détente based on common interests while setting aside their philosophical differences, just as Catholic Austria and Protestant Prussia had done.

From the standpoint of personal morality, it needs to be emphasized, there is nothing in the record to suggest that Nixon and Kissinger weren't acting on the basis of sincere conviction and an honest desire to promote the peace and happiness of the human race. The darkness was in their worldview rather than in their personal characters; they were conservative statesmen trying to safeguard the interests entrusted to them in a dangerous and hostile world.

Given this worldview, the Vietnam War was neither a moral crusade for the administration nor a moral disaster. It was a practical problem to be addressed in a pragmatic way. The United States would lose prestige if it withdrew too precipitately or was seen to "lose" the war; at the same time, it didn't matter much who would be running Vietnam in ten years' time.

Economic issues scarcely existed for the administration. For an economically focused foreign policy, the slow erosion of the Bretton Woods system of fixed exchange rates based on the American dollar would have been seen as the primary threat to United States interests and the health of the anti-Soviet coalition in 1969—a threat far greater than anything Ho Chi Minh could ever assemble in the far-off jungles of Indochina. Under the Bretton Woods system established during the 1940s, the U.S. Federal Reserve System was the de facto central bank for all the market economies; the United States could effectively control the monetary policies of all its allies, and it generally did so in the interest of the domestic American economy—often to the irritation of its partners. Had traditionally oriented American diplomats like Alexander Hamilton, Andrew Mellon, or Henry Morgenthau been directing policy, American foreign policy in the Nixon years would have focused on either strengthening Bretton Woods or mitigating the consequences of its fall. The solemn and oft-repeated U.S. pledges to our key Cold War allies and trading partners to redeem paper dollars in gold at a fixed price of thirty-five dollars an ounce would have far outweighed any promises to Saigon. For the Nixon administration this perspective seems to have been too farfetched to be seriously considered, much less adopted as the basis for American policy.

The methods of Nixon's foreign policy were as Continental as the substance. Congress was frozen out of foreign policy as much as possible, and the administration attempted to withhold vital information about military and intelligence operations from the legislators responsible for funding them. Within the executive branch, power was concentrated to an unprecedented degree, as normal bureaucratic channels and departments were ignored. A small network of officials operated the "real" foreign policy of the United States; Nixon's concept of foreign policy required the personal direction of a single guiding mind—an auteur rather than a studio.

The Nixon administration was not without its successes. The opening to Beijing changed the global balance of power, making U.S. victory in the Cold War more likely while reducing the chances of a direct U.S.-Soviet confrontation along the way. The strategic arms limitation agreement also brought a welcome stability to relations between the two superpowers. Nonetheless, what the administration's Continentalist approach to foreign policy principally produced was a series of major train wrecks. Putting Vietnam ahead of Bretton Woods led directly to the two costliest failures of the Cold War. The final inglorious end to the American effort in Vietnam could not have been more humiliating had it been scripted in the Kremlin; the bitterness engendered by the prolongation of the war had not faded from American politics by the end of the century and posed one of the most serious obstacles to Nixon's successors as they sought to continue the Cold War. Similarly the economic consequences of the collapse of Bretton Woods and the hastily improvised way in which they were handled inflicted lasting damage on the American economy and on U.S. relations with both Western Europe and Japan. Nixon and Kissinger succeeded where Charles de Gaulle had failed: On the subject of monetary policy they united Europe against the United States. From the collapse of the Bretton Woods system to the present day, Europeans have buried all their differences, however bitter, and cooperated to win greater monetary independence from Washington in good times and bad. The consequences of the chaotic collapse of the system spread farther. The inflationary waves set off by the currency crash led to the oil price shocks and the economic stagflation of the 1970s, which had massive consequences for private investors and for national economies all over the world, undermining governments, exacerbating social conflicts, and setting the stage for such further problems as the third-world debt crisis of the 1980s.

The same Nixon years that saw the low-water mark of American fortunes in the Cold War also witnessed the high-water mark of the conscious influence of Continental realism in American foreign policy. Since that time we have seen an anomalous and ultimately incompatible pair of developments. At the level of policy, American foreign policy has been rapidly and steadily moving away from Continental realism and back toward traditional American and Anglo-American priorities and concerns. At the level of theory, however, much of the analysis of American foreign policy remains locked in the concepts and myths of Continental realism and the Cold War.

After the Nixon and Ford years the return to traditional American foreign policy concerns was swift; the dismal state of the global system in the 1970s and the breakdown of domestic political consensus over foreign policy compelled both Carter and Reagan to address urgent, unmistakable priorities. Both the liberal Democrats who came to power with President Jimmy Carter and the conservative Republicans who came in with Ronald Reagan four years later moved decisively away from the Nixon and Kissinger approach.

The decade of economic turmoil and inflation that followed the catastrophically mismanaged demise of the Bretton Woods system forced policy makers back to the economic table as they scrambled to repair the damage to the Western economic order that Nixon had unwittingly caused. Ultimately the success of the American economy specifically and the international economy in general would inflict more damage on Asian communism than the Vietnam War ever did, and convince Soviet president Mikhail Gorbachev that radical political and economic reform was the only option open to his country.

While Carter and Reagan disagreed on many issues, both agreed that a strong human rights policy was a crucial element in an effective Cold War strategy for the United States. Carter willingly, and Reagan at first reluctantly but with increasing confidence and enthusiasm, withdrew American patronage from the dictatorial third-world regimes that Nixon's diplomacy had hailed as key allies. Pinochet's dictatorship in Chile, whose bloody seizure of power was supported by the Nixon administration, was isolated and placed under sanctions by Reagan. The South African apartheid regime, which Nixon supported in its failed war against Cuban troops and Soviet-backed guerrillas in Angola, was progressively isolated under the Reagan administration. Ferdinand Marcos of the Philippines, lionized by Nixon, lived to see Reagan throw his prestige behind the 1986 "People Power" revolution of Corazon Aquino. American backing for human rights would also play a key role in the decline and fall of the Soviet Empire. Lech Wałesa, Andrei Sakharov, and John Paul II had no more divisions than Pius XII; they turned out, however, to have enough.

Carter and Reagan came by very different roads to the conclusion that the Cold War struggle with the Soviet Union required a moral dimension. Here it was Reagan whose instinctive approach to international politics found the transition easy and natural. Steeped in the anticommunism of the American right, Reagan had chafed as Nixon and Kissinger attempted to manage U.S.–Soviet relations on the basis of realpolitik. That communism was an evil was not only one of Reagan's strongest personal convictions; reminding Americans of its evils, was, he correctly believed, a way to strengthen the resolve of Americans and their allies around the world for what proved to be the last act in the long battle.

For Carter, making anticommunism a centerpiece of foreign policy was more difficult and distasteful, especially at a time when the reaction against the Vietnam War had made anticommunism even less fashionable than usual in his party. Nevertheless, by the end of Carter's presidency, a combination of ideological opposition to communism based on the USSR's abysmal human rights record and a principled opposition to what was interpreted as Soviet aggression in Afghanistan had driven the administration back toward moral anticommunism as an organizing principle of American foreign policy. Morality and economics were back as driving forces in American policy; and in the end they did what amoral geopolitics could never do: defeated the Soviet Union while strengthening the international order whose protection the United States had inherited from Britain.

With the end of the Cold War, the traditional themes of Anglo-American foreign policy returned to center stage. The disappearance of the overwhelming threat and challenge once posed by the Soviet Union left the United States facing the same kinds of questions Great Britain had faced in the nineteenth century—and which had faced the post–World War II American statesmen who created the conditions for European and Japanese recovery in the 1940s. President George H. Bush's call for "a new world order" and President Bill Clinton's call for the expansion of free markets and free governments make clear that questions of economic order and human freedom had clearly been placed in the limelight.

But if Continental realism had in practice been abandoned by a generation of American policy makers, in the intellectual realm it had been neither rejected nor refuted. The United States was moving in the patterns of its traditional foreign policy concerns, but still under the spell of the Cold War myth. Our pre-1945 history and traditions of foreign policy were, so we believed, worthless. Our method of government was profoundly unsuited to the challenges of foreign policy. Our national instincts were wrong. Anglo-American statesmanship had triumphed over yet another Continental realist empire, but we did not yet know what we had done, or how.

The American statesman who has made the most successful attempt to abandon Continental realism and base American foreign policy on traditional Anglo-American ideas is Henry Kissinger, the man who as Secretary of State carried American foreign policy farthest in a Continental direction. The enormous success of the Helsinki Accords—negotiated but at the time not highly valued by Kissinger—encouraged him to assign greater weight to human rights issues in the formulation of policy. Most recently, in his 2001 book *Does America Need a Foreign Policy?*, Kissinger places economic issues at the core of U.S. foreign policy and looks to great American leaders like John Quincy Adams for inspiration and ideas. Indeed, like many of our great strategic thinkers, Kissinger finds himself in what I will describe later as the Jeffersonian school of American foreign policy.

Kissinger's path holds lessons for us all. Americans need to recover intellectually what our practical diplomacy—and a few statesmen like Kissinger—have already rediscovered. We need to become aware of our foreign policy traditions and history and learn to appreciate our strengths and make allowances for our weaknesses.

What we really need is a myth for the twenty-first century which condenses those historical experiences and realities that are relevant to the conditions we face in the new world slowly taking shape around us. That myth will help Americans to reconnect with the pre–Cold War past, identify and celebrate the qualities in American ideology and politics that have contributed to the nation's remarkable success, and, it is to be hoped, create a useful framework for public debate over the policy choices that the United States faces in the decades ahead.

A Myth for the Twenty-first Century

To suggest that we need a new paradigm for American foreign policy is not to say that we need to throw out the old one completely, or that we should mindlessly congratulate ourselves on our mental superiority over our grandparents. After all, the Cold War paradigm got us through the Cold War, and that was no mean achievement. If the United States faced an international emergency today on the scale of the crisis it faced after World War II, it is far from certain that we could field a team to match George Marshall, Harry Truman, George Kennan, and Dean Acheson.

Nevertheless, we need a new intellectual approach to foreign policy that is less attuned to the siren songs of Continental realism and that takes greater heed of the questions and interests that actually drive the

American foreign policy process. In particular we need an approach to foreign policy that highlights issues that were discounted by Cold War–era thinking but that increasingly preoccupy us today: economics, the problems of international order building or globalization, and the relationship of democracy and foreign policy.

Economics, morality, and democracy are three things that Continental realism largely seeks to banish from the realm of high international politics. They are and inevitably will be central concerns of American foreign policy far into the future, and Americans need an approach that, without neglecting or mishandling security issues, can comfortably deal with the central issues of our day.

Without this kind of new—or, rather, old—thinking, American policy makers will have increasing difficulty winning domestic support. Our external situation at the end of the Cold War once again has many similarities with the international position of the United States in the nineteenth century. For one thing we are a debtor nation again, with domestic interest rates and economic conditions to some degree dependent on the perceptions and the actions of foreign investors. Our financial markets are much more exposed to developments overseas than they were fifty years ago—here, too, the position of the United States today is in some ways more like our position in 1890 than in 1950. At the same time tens of millions of Americans now experience something that their nineteenth-century ancestors understood well, but that those of the twentieth century tended to forget: Their livelihoods depend both on the ability of their employers to meet foreign competition, and on world market prices for the goods Americans produce—prices that are often moved by events that take place overseas.

The changes in the country's relationship to the international economy are already raising the temperature of the foreign policy debate. Economic issues don't just involve policy elites; they affect the interest of every family in the country. NAFTA was one of the most passionately argued issues in American life during a period in the 1990s. The contemporary debates over tariffs are stirring up some of the same kind of passion that tariff issues did in the nineteenth century; it is likely, as the effects of the U.S. international deficit become more apparent, that debates over interest rates and over questions relating to the financial integration of the United States with the rest of the world will also grow more impassioned and more central to our national political life.

Other major foreign policy issues will also require a mindset more like that of the the traditional Anglo-American approach. The price of energy and the security of the national energy supply will be a prominent foreign policy concern in which security and economic issues, and domestic and foreign policy issues, will be inextricably linked. Relations with other great economic powers—the EU, Japan, and, increasingly, China—will require integrated approaches to economic and security questions.

The question of rogue states is another issue that takes policy makers back to older patterns in Anglo-American history. From hill tribes in Afghanistan to Islamic extremists in Sudan and hostile nationalists in Iraq, British policy makers and military leaders faced many of the same problems their American successors are looking at today. The necessary balancing act between living up to ideals and standards that provide legitimacy to the world order on the one hand and on the other acting decisively and effectively in defense of one's core interests will be a major problem for American diplomacy in the years ahead, as it was for British diplomacy one hundred years ago.

In the pages that follow I will attempt to depict a new paradigm, a new way of thinking about American foreign policy, that I hope can assist policy makers, opinion leaders, and the general public opinion that ultimately controls American foreign policy and sets its limits.

Myths need to be clear—clearer than truth, as Acheson said—and no myth is incontrovertible; generalizations have exceptions; and the more sweeping the generalizations the more numerous and more significant the exceptions. A picture of American foreign policy that stresses the continuities since 1789 will inevitably do less than full justice to the many and significant differences that also exist. But small facts should not be allowed to obstruct our purpose; the United States needs as accurate, comprehensive, and clear a myth as we can make.

What I see as the most promising potential new paradigm or myth for American foreign policy depends on four basic ideas. The first of these has already been presented: the idea that foreign policy, understood as including questions of the relationship of the American economy to the international economic system, has been a central concern of American politics throughout our history.

The second idea is that the basic shape of American foreign policy throughout American history has been determined by the nation's interest in the international, largely maritime trading and financial order that over the last few centuries has gradually spread over the earth and integrated the economies of many nations and continents. What we now call globalization—the growth of an international economic system—is one of the most important historical developments of the last five centuries. Indeed, the colonization of what became the United States was an episode in this long process.

For most of American history the global economic order was centered on Great Britain, and therefore our key national dependency on and concern about this order implied a close if sometimes conflicted relationship with Great Britain. This British-based international system affected both the political and economic interests of the United States. Economically we were concerned to have opportunities for our trade and to control the impact on our domestic order of the international economic system. Politically the United States always had to think about whether Britain would wield the power of its global system in ways that would benefit us, or at least not impose unacceptable risks and costs. In the worst case Americans had to think about what to do if a clash of interests with Great Britain led to war. (Contingency planning for a war against the British Empire was an important activity for American military strategists well into the twentieth century.) Increasingly, as British power declined, the United States had to think about whether Britain could maintain this system, and what the United States should do if and when Britain failed.

Although the word *globalization* is new, and although the process has accelerated and deepened in recent years, globalization has been the most important fact of world history during the entire history of the United States. Because of our geographical situation and the commercial and enterprising nature of American society, globalization has been at the heart of American strategic thinking and policy making for virtually all of our history.

The history of American foreign policy divides into four eras based on our changing relationship to Great Britain and the emerging global order. The first era, lasting from 1776 to 1823, saw the United States win its political independence from the British Empire, and then immediately begin to work out the question of its relations with the British economic system and imperial power. Both Britain and the United States had to grapple with questions about the relationship. On the British side: Should the mother country try to strangle the infant Union, or was

Britain better off with a strong and stable trading partner? From the American side, another set of questions had to be addressed. Was the United States better off undermining Britain by forming alliances with strong Continental powers, or was it wiser policy to side with British attempts to maintain a balance of power in Europe? Should we have stood ready to help Britain keep the continental scorpions stuffed in their bottle, or would it have been safer to help one of the scorpions out, thus ensuring that Britain never had the leisure or resources to turn on the United States?

Opinion in both countries seesawed on these issues, but ultimately each side reached a consensus. The British acknowledged that Britain was better off trading with the United States than adding the dangers and expenses of an anti-American foreign policy to all the worries of maintaining a balance of power in Europe and building a growing global system. The United States for its part decided that having Britannia rule the waves was better than letting the rest of the scorpions out of the bottle. For its own selfish reasons, Britain would do its best to keep the European empires bottled up in Europe. The United States decided that it would not only not stab Britain in the back, but it also hinted that, if one of the scorpions got too strong, the United States as an absolutely last resort might come to Britain's assistance and help keep the bottle firmly corked.

We can and should say now what policy makers knew but lacked the time to say earlier in the century. Franklin Roosevelt was technically right that the Monroe Doctrine was not so formal or clear even as an "unwritten agreement." But Walter Lippmann was also right to say that there was a tacit understanding. The myth of isolation was wrong. The Monroe Doctrine was not only not isolationist, it was anti-isolationist. It amounted to the recognition that American safety depended on the balance of power in Europe. With that doctrine's promulgation, the first era in American foreign policy came to a close. The strategic principles of the Monroe Doctrine have continued without interruption to shape American foreign policy from that day to this. American interventions in the world wars as well as the Cold War were not a series of revolutionary departures from Monroe's statecraft; they were examples of the same thinking that led Monroe to proclaim it. Just as Monroe and his talented secretary of state, John Quincy Adams, were prepared in the last analysis to help Britain prevent the French or the Spanish from reestablishing dynastic empires in the Americas in 1823, twentieth-century American presidents were prepared to step in to keep Germany and the Soviet Union from overturning the European power balance and spreading their power through the rest of the world. If another antidemocratic power should threaten to unite all Europe under its dominion tomorrow, we would step in and resist it again. We would do the same thing in Asia, and for the same reason. Our policies have changed over the decades and centuries to reflect changing circumstances; our basic strategic posture has not changed since 1823.

The second era in American foreign policy lasted from 1823 through 1914. During this time the United States existed in a Britain-centered global order. Britain's power, and therefore the world order, were secure during most of these years. There was no need to think about helping to prop up the system; Britain seemed perfectly capable of handling that on its own. Instead the United States concentrated on getting the best deal for itself within the British system, while staying on guard against the danger that Britain might be tempted by its strength to crush or divide it. The Republic wanted to ensure that the economic structure of the emerging and developing economic system would be favorable to both its long- and its short-term economic development. The United States believed that over time American power and influence within the British system would grow, and looked forward to the day when it would surpass Great Britain as what today is called a global superpower.

The uneasy balance between the two powers was largely in Britain's favor early in the period. The Union victory in the Civil War marked the beginning of a period when the United States moved steadily toward equality, and more, with Britain, increasingly asserting influence over Britain's global policies as Britain's awareness grew of its dependence on good relations with the United States. Perhaps the 1871 Treaty of Washington marked the true turning point: It provided for international arbitration of all outstanding issues between the two nations, and under it the United States was ultimately awarded $15.5 million for damage to Union shipping during the Civil War by British-built Confederate raiders. It was the first treaty between the two nations that clearly favored the American side.

During this period the United States first began to think seriously about its future when and if the Pax Britannica ended. One response was American imperialism; if Britain fell, it would be necessary for the United States to follow a more active world strategy. The acquisition of bases and coaling stations (fuel depots to allow the coal-fired navies of the day to project power in distant waters) throughout the Pacific was part of

THE BRITISH LION DISARMED

The *Alabama* is the focus of this 1868 cartoon by Thomas Nast, the most famous American cartoonist of his day. America, shown as Columbia, is clipping the claws of the British lion with a set of scissors labeled "Alabama Claims"; the cartoon celebrates Britain's being forced to compensate American interests for damages caused by Confederate commerce raiders which the British illegally allowed to be built in their ports. British concessions in the *Alabama* dispute marked a new equality in Anglo-American relations. *Thomas Nast. Library of Congress, Prints and Photographs Division,* Harper's Weekly, *August 1, 1868, page 488*

a process by which American policy makers prepared for the end of the Pax Britannica.

The third era of American foreign policy encompassed the two world wars and saw the rapid decline and fall of the British world system. In the years between 1914 and 1947 the United States was forced to wrestle again with some of the basic strategic questions it had examined in the first, pre-Monroe era. With the old mother country visibly in decline, should the United States supplement British power as it waned, propping up Britain as it propped up the global order? Should the United States instead stand back and let the world order look after itself? Or should the United States replace Great Britain as the gyroscope of world order, with all the political, military, and economic costs, benefits, and responsibilities that role would entail?

Between the start of World War I and the winter of 1947, the United States experimented with all of these approaches. Slowly it became unpleasantly apparent that there was no middle way: The United States had to choose between filling Britain's old role in its own way or living in a world in which no power took responsibility for the kind of world order in which we had always existed. This was no choice at all.

The third era in the history of American foreign policy ended with the decision that opened the fourth, in which we still live. In 1947 as in 1823, Americans concluded that the national interest required a strong maritime power able to uphold the balance of power in Europe and to maintain an international economic and political order in the rest of the world. By 1947 that power could no longer be Great Britain; it would have to be the United States. Atlas shrugged, and the United States would shoulder the sky. Since World War II, that choice has been and remains the cornerstone of American foreign policy. The Cold War, large though it loomed at the time, and vital as it was to win, was less of a milestone in American history than many assume. The real decision, whose implications and consequences are still with us today, was to take on Britain's old role. The Cold War was an incident in American foreign policy, not an epoch, and its end left the United States with essentially the same set of responsibilities, interests, and tasks that we had when it began.

The third element in a new paradigm has to do with the importance of democracy in American success. Contrary to conventional views about the unsuitability of democratic societies for success in foreign policy, the tumult of the American foreign policy process, and especially its grounding in democratic society, has on the whole been beneficial over time. The democratic process has provided a method for aligning the policy of the country with its interests that is superior to anything that individual statesmen, however gifted, could accomplish.

The United States achieves its success in foreign policy through a process very different from the classic Continental model. Instead of a brooding great genius producing our national strategy in splendid isolation, somehow a policy—or even a group of sometimes conflicting and sometimes complementary minipolicies—emerges from the jostling and jumbling of political interests, politicians' egos, economic and ethnic lobbies, regional voting blocs, and random noise that make up the American political process. In other words, American foreign policy emerges in much the same way its domestic policy does: from the democratic political process

The foreign policy pie gets divided in the same way that domestic lobbies exert policy influence based on their political strength, their institutional position, and the priority they set on particular policy outcomes. An industry group gets preferential treatment for its foreign trade interests in much the same way it gets favorable treatment in the tax code. An impassioned and well-financed ethnic lobby can enjoy enormous influence over a particular, narrowly defined segment of American foreign policy in much the same way that single-issue lobby groups gain influence in domestic policy. The squeaking wheel gets the grease, and by the time all the goodies are handed out, almost everybody gets something.

That is democracy in action in our foreign, as well as in our domestic, policy. Yet, over the long sweep of history, it appears that the United States has followed policies that progressively made it richer, stronger, and safer than other countries using more conventional and respectable methods. How did this happen?

The basic answer is, of course, the same one that is often given to explain why the democratic process works in domestic policy: The final result more or less accurately reflects the wishes of the interest groups and individuals who compose a given society. If the results of the process displease a substantial portion of the public, that dissatisfaction will become an increasingly powerful political force that pulls policy back in a direction that reduces dissatisfaction. The system is stable because it is homeostatic; although social interest groups perceive themselves as engaged in a constant struggle, the net effect of all those struggles is to keep society constantly seeking the point at which dissatisfaction is minimized.

None of this is to say that such results are always or even often fair; for historical and economic reasons, the United States has many groups whose political strength is not commensurate with their numbers. This is true in foreign as well as in domestic policy . Some relatively small ethnic groups are well organized, and their lobbies are well funded; other groups may be larger in absolute number but weaker in political influence. There are approximately four times as many Mexican Americans as Jewish Americans in the United States,[10] but Mexico does not (yet) receive four times the attention, aid, and support Israel does. Nevertheless, to the degree that Mexicans, Jews, Turks, Greeks, Arabs, Irish, Italians, Poles, and many others organize themselves and devote resources to shaping American foreign policy toward their respective old countries, the political process takes note of their strength and provides them at least a modicum of satisfaction.

There is another advantage to the democratic nature of the American process that has come into play during the Cold War. It is because politics drives foreign policy that the United States has been able to continue to follow an economically oriented, order-building foreign policy despite the influence of Continental realism among foreign policy intellectuals. Our officials may think that missile payloads and strategic competition are more intellectually interesting than free trade and free international capital flows, but political pressure forces them to respond to economic issues. Similarly political leaders may secretly think that morals have no proper place in international politics, but to avow this viewpoint openly and to act on it would be political suicide.

Given that the foreign policy process in the United States arrives at solutions and compromises that more or less satisfy the various groups who want something from American foreign policy, we must still ask why the results of the domestic process match conditions in the outside world—why the policy that pleases American interest groups should somehow over the long run also work relatively effectively outside the country. If a special providence is at work in American affairs, guiding the country to continuing success, it is surely at work here: Somehow the jangling and perpetual jostling and quarrels of our domestic interest groups work themselves out to mandate policies that turn out to be practical.

It doesn't always end this way. There are examples of countries whose domestic political processes generate foreign policies backed by a strong national consensus that lead to disaster. France marched enthusiastically against Prussia in 1870, as virtually every interest group in society cheered Napoleon III into what proved to be a catastrophic war. Nor do we have to look overseas for such miscarriages. The protectionist Hawley-Smoot Tariff, now widely blamed for deepening the depression, was broadly popular at the time; polls showed consistent support for the Vietnam War until the Tet offensive of 1968. But we do not need to show that the American foreign policy process is infallible; we merely seek to understand why it works as well as it has.

What seems to happen in the United States is that there is a set of deeply rooted approaches to foreign policy that informs the democratic process and ensures that most of the time the country ends up adopting policies that advance its basic interests. These approaches—call them schools—appear very early in American history, and while they have each evolved in response to changes in the international order and in American society, they have also remained identifiable over the centuries. Thus our debates as well as our concerns have much in common across generations, and many of the ideas and alternatives present in contemporary discussions would have been familiar to American politicians and thinkers throughout our history.

These schools operate on many different levels. They reflect deepseated regional, economic, social, and class interests; they embody visions for domestic as well as foreign policy; they express moral and political values as well as socioeconomic and political interests.

All four schools are deeply rooted in the American experience. To some degree one can trace their roots to the four folkways that historian David Hackett Fischer identifies in colonial America, where the cultural, ideological, and political differences among the colonists appear to have arisen from the differences in the regional cultures out of which they emerged in the British Isles.[11]

The four schools are not blood types with every individual typed by one and only one label; it is rare for statesmen or ordinary citizens to be wholly wrapped up in the ideas and values of just one of the schools. Most Americans combine different elements of different schools in their makeup.

I have named the four schools after four figures in American history. Alexander Hamilton's name has been given to the school of foreign policy that sees the first task of the American government as promoting the health of American enterprise at home and abroad. Hamiltonians have historically attempted to ensure that the United States government supported the rights of American merchants and investors and have been quick to understand the importance of the British world order for American interests. Hamiltonians have generally supported cooperation with Britain and, when the British Empire fell, were among the earliest and strongest backers of the idea that the United States should take up the British burden. A partial list of prominent Hamiltonians in American history would include Henry Clay; Daniel Webster; John Hay; Theodore Roosevelt; Henry Cabot Lodge Sr., who opposed Woodrow Wilson over the Treaty of Versailles; Dean Acheson; and the senior George Bush.

The second school includes those who believe that the United States has both a moral and a practical duty to spread its values through the world. This school is called the Wilsonian school for obvious reasons, although there were Wilsonians long before Woodrow Wilson was born. More interested in the legal and moral aspects of world order than in the economic agenda supported by Hamiltonians, Wilsonians typically believe that American interests require that other countries accept basic American values and conduct both their foreign and domestic affairs accordingly. This school has much deeper roots farther back in American history than is sometimes recognized; American foreign policy in many parts of the world has been heavily influenced by the activities and lobbying of American missionaries.

A third school that has often opposed Hamiltonian policy has typically seen the preservation of American democracy in a dangerous world as the most pressing and vital interest of the American people. It has consistently looked for the least costly and dangerous method of defending American independence while counseling against attempts to impose American values on other countries. This school has included some of the most distinguished and elegant strategic thinkers in American history—men like John Quincy Adams and George Kennan—as well as passionate and proud democratic isolationists like the historian Charles Beard and the novelist and political essayist Gore Vidal. While Walter Lippmann's complicated intellectual makeup, combined with a long and active career, prevent him from being assigned to only one school, his concern for "solvency" in foreign relations and his desire to achieve American strategic goals at the lowest possible risk and cost place him at least partly in this camp. I have called this the Jeffersonian school. While Jefferson's own foreign policy often deviated from orthodox Jeffersonian principles, on balance his deepest concerns about American destiny and liberty resonate better with this school than with any other.

The final school is named for Andrew Jackson, not so much a tribute to the personal views or the foreign policy record of the nation's seventh president as a recognition of the enormous populist appeal that enabled him to electrify and transform American politics. The Jacksonian school represents a deeply embedded, widely spread populist and popular culture of honor, independence, courage, and military pride among the American people. Arizona senator John McCain appeals to Jacksonian sentiment; so did World War II generals George S. Patton Jr. and MacArthur. One measure of Jacksonian influence in American politics is the degree to which successful generals become formidable political figures. The list stretches from Washington, Jackson, and William Henry Harrison (the Old Tippecanoe who defeated Tecumseh and his Indian confederation at the 1811 Battle of Tippecanoe and ran successfully against Martin Van Buren in 1840) through Mexican War heroes Zachary Taylor and Franklin Pierce and Civil War generals Grant, Rutherford B. Hayes, and James Garfield. All told, ten former generals have become president of the United States; and several other presidents, including Theodore Roosevelt, John Fitzgerald Kennedy, and the elder George Bush, were mightily assisted in their careers by heroic war records. Jacksonian attitudes and ideas have played and still do play an immense role in shaping the American debate over foreign policy.

While the interest groups, regions, and to some degree the economic interests that each school reflects have remained more or less constant through the generations, the policy proposals and priorities of the four schools have developed over time in response to historical, social, and economic changes both within the United States and beyond its borders. In the early twentieth century all four schools were severely tested by the problems posed by the decline of the British Empire. Yet within a generation all four had made an adjustment. The commerce- and finance-based Hamiltonians dropped their historic support for protection and supported free trade as a necessary economic policy for a hegemonic power. Jeffersonians modified their historic aversion to great-power politics to provide critical support for the Cold War. Wilsonians linked their vision of a universal moral order on earth to the concrete needs of the American hegemony. Jacksonians provided forty years of broad, and unwavering popular support for the bloody and dangerous Cold War.

I will soon describe each of these visions or schools in greater detail, show how each has evolved in response to changes in American society and the world, and outline the strengths and challenges that each school faces after the turn of the twenty-first century. I will also look more carefully at how they relate to one another— how they form coalitions and how each of them has played a role in the foreign policy controversies of the recent past.

It is not my intent to "prove" from documents or other sources that these visions existed throughout American history, or that they gave rise to schools of thought or to self-conscious political movements. Nor do I intend to build a fully fortified and elaborated theory of state action and foreign relations that can easily accommodate the four-school theory as a "case study."

My goal instead is to show how the "four schools" idea can help us think more clearly about American foreign policy. Thinking of American foreign policy in this way helps me to understand and even, on occasion, to predict the reactions of American politicians and public opinion to changing international circumstances. It has deepened and clarified my understanding of the relationships between domestic politics and the politics of foreign policy. It has helped me focus on the continuities in the American foreign policy tradition, to see the history of American foreign policy as more of a unified whole and less as a sequence of unrelated episodes. It helps me to distinguish between problems that are relatively easy for the American political system to address, and those problems for which the American system may not be able to develop an effective response. It has helped sharpen my ideas about what the aims of American foreign policy should be in the future, even as it has deepened my understanding of what has been attempted and accomplished in the past.

Naming the four schools for historical figures was a difficult choice, but seemed ultimately the best one available. Serious historians cringe, and rightly so, at the wholesale abuses entailed by this practice. To speak of "Wilsonians" who lived and died one hundred years before Wilson proclaimed his Fourteen Points violates every canon of historiographical responsibility. Worse, each of the four men whose names I appropriated for one of these schools had a distinguished and varied career. The Hamilton of 1801 did not have the same views that he held in 1776. So too, notoriously, did the mercurial and elusive Jefferson develop and vary his views during his fifty years in the public eye. On what grounds can one abstract from a long career a set of principles that define the essence of a contribution?

Moreover, as the schools evolved over the decades and centuries, they sometimes moved away from some of the key views of the "founder." The school I call Hamiltonian followed in the master's protectionist footsteps for almost 150 years after his death, but by the end of World War II, the leading figures of American business either had embraced or were just about to embrace the doctrine of free trade. For these Hamiltonians, as I call them, the economic interest of American capitalism was of the essence; the specific means by which these interests could be advanced was a secondary question that depended on circumstances. Would Hamilton have agreed? Does it matter that the question can never be answered?

Jackson's historical image has been bedeviled and clouded by precisely the same confusion my use of his name for the populist school compounds and supports. Many of Jackson's followers were unreflective, uneducated populists. Jackson himself was a subtle, sophisticated, and in many ways surprisingly modern statesman.

What Jackson loses by my method, Wilson gains. Among other, more admirable traits, Wilson unfortunately was afflicted with a despicable racism; he imposed Jim Crow segregation on the District of Columbia and gave a special White House showing of *The Birth of a Nation*, D. W. Griffith's apologia for the Ku Klux Klan. He also rejected the Japanese request to include a declaration on racial equality in the Treaty of Versailles. To put this man's name on a school of thought that has spearheaded the drive against racism at home and imperialism abroad is a stretch.

Peccavi. Yet the other alternative, to borrow abstract nouns from political science or intellectual history to label the schools, would be equally irresponsible and even less honest. Terms like *idealist, realist, populist,* and *libertarian* look much less ambiguous than the names of historical figures, but the appearance of clarity is deceiving. No one was a "realist" in the modern sense in the eighteenth century; the term as we use it today refers to a series of historical experiences and intellectual debates that didn't exist then. To call nineteenth-century Wilsonians "idealists" is just as anachronistic as to call them Wilsonians; the pseudo-precision of the abstract term lends an unjustifiable air of political-science authority to the discussion that the softer, less precise "Wilsonian" doesn't carry. To call Jeffersonians "libertarians" or Jacksonians "populists" similarly would create at least as many confusions as the labels I have chosen. The four schools as I see them are definite and distinct entities, but they change over time, they mix and blur, and, most important, they are part of political history rather than the history of ideas. They are movements and communities of interest and feeling rather than abstract principles. They are churches rather than creeds.

In the end, it seemed better to give the schools names that frankly admit and even advertise their tentative and inexact character while evoking the great themes and stirring stories that make up the history of American foreign policy. We are, after all, used to a certain imprecision in these historical terms. Karl Marx once famously remarked that he was not a Marxist. Many observers have noted the sometimes sharp distinction between Freud and some of the Freudians, and differences between Christ and the Christians have sometimes been pointed out.

There is another confession I ought to make. I have written this book as though the four schools were the only important forces affecting the politics of American foreign policy. That is of course not true.

In the contemporary world, American politics includes a great many elements that do not fit easily within this or any elegant simplification. Ethnic lobbies, ethics lobbies (like those who want the United States either to support or oppose abortion rights for women in developing countries), economic lobbies, ideological lobbies, and many other interest groups are constantly tugging at American foreign policy.

I see the schools as different from the lobbies; schools ultimately reflect a broad strategic concept of the national interest, while lobbies are more concerned with specific policy outcomes on a narrow range of issues. Even so, the four schools I have singled out are not the only entities to promote a distinct vision for American foreign policy as a whole.

One example, now defunct, comes to us from the past. We might call it the Davisonian school, after the American secretary of war who ultimately became the first and only president of the Confederacy. Jefferson Davis and his allies believed that the first and almost the only duty of the United States government was to promote the security and therefore the extension of slavery. Tariff policy, territorial expansion, relations with Britain: For Davisonians the question always came back to preserving their "peculiar institution." Loyalty to slavery eventually overcame both their common sense and their loyalty to the United States; Davisonians ended up, literally, as a school of treason as they rushed to meet their doom. Yet at one time they competed for power in American politics on at least equal terms with the four schools that remain.

Other small schools or sects survive. Marxist social thought in particular has produced a number of schools that have usually been numerically small, but sometimes politically or intellectually important.

However, I believe that the Hamiltonian, Wilsonian, Jeffersonian, and Jacksonian movements are unique in that they have existed more or less continuously from the eighteenth century through the beginning of the twenty-first, and that although each of them has experienced some vicissitudes of fortune, all of them have had a demonstrable and significant impact on American foreign policy debates in all the great eras of American history.

Of course none of the schools is monolithic. Among Wilsonians there are at least two major groups. Right Wilsonians believe that the United States as it exists today has generally fulfilled the dreams of the Founding

Fathers. We do not need to reform ourselves at home; we can and should attempt to spread the values and practices of American society as they currently exist through the world. Many neoconservatives fall into this camp. Radical Wilsonians believe that the United States is far from living up to the true values of the nation. We must simultaneously act to reform ourselves while we seek to reform others. Right Wilsonians may disagree with Hamiltonians over priorities and policies in specific cases, but in general right Wilsonians see few problems with the existing financial and corporate structure of the United States and believe that part of the value system we should be exporting includes the American way of business. Radical Wilsonians could not disagree more, believing that American and multinational corporations and everything they stand for are among the chief obstacles to the spread of true values both at home and abroad.

My discussion of the Hamiltonian tradition largely deals with only one of several such currents in Hamiltonian thought. I have omitted an account of, among others, the southern branch of the Hamiltonian school. The southern Hamiltonians include early Federalist leaders like George Washington as well as men like John C. Calhoun before his defection to Davisonianism and Cordell Hull, secretary of state under Franklin Roosevelt. Southern Hamiltonians agreed with northern Hamiltonians that national economic development was the key to national power, but they did not confuse national development with the sectional interest of New England or the financial interest of Wall Street. One of the great tragedies of Southern history is that most Southerners followed Calhoun out of Hamiltonianism into the wilderness of Davisonian futility. After the Civil War, Southern unionists slowly began to rebuild the tradition that called for free trade, military spending in the interests of both military strength and national economic development, and federal spending on public works and infrastructure projects. The rebirth of southern Hamiltonianism was one of the most important developments of the twentieth century, and southern Hamiltonians have repeatedly supplied the key congressional support for active American foreign policy.

Beyond clearly recognizable subgroups like these, it is also possible to divide the schools into purists and synthesizers. As an example, some synthesizing Hamiltonians take their ideas of the benevolence of commerce and the importance of international law so far into the empyrean that they approach a fusion with some of the pragmatic Wilsonians. Herbert Hoover was one such man.

One might also divide all the schools into "high flyers" and "low flyers." The high flyers in every school are eager to put the school's doctrines into systematic shape and to press the logic of the school's vision to its farthest conclusions; low flyers tend to concentrate more on particular issues. High-flying Wilsonians look for grand programs of international law and world federalism; lower-flying Wilsonians might be more interested in specific environmental or feminist programs or ideas.

These are only some of the more prominent subgroups in the schools. American politics is like a large sheet of paper covered with millions of tiny iron filings. It seems to me that many of these filings line up in interesting patterns, patterns that lead me to hypothesize the existence of four powerful magnets lying under the paper. But not all the filings fall into neatly patterned lines. Some of them are outside the effective power of my hypothetical magnets; some of the filings are under the influence of more than one magnet. Some have become magnetized themselves and formed little clumps that exercise their own influence on the surrounding space. Some lie where the competing forces of different magnets cancel each other out. And then, because my filings are only a metaphor and we are actually talking about people and political groups rather than inert metal, some of the objects on the paper ignore the magnets hypothetical or otherwise, and get up and walk around on their own.

Readers will have to judge for themselves whether enough of the filings line up with enough of the magnets enough of the time to make this theory useful, but whatever the merits of the "four schools" theory of American foreign policy, at least it helps explain why the critics of American foreign policy attack from so many, and from such incompatible, directions. If we think of American foreign policy as the product of four different schools of thought, with different schools and combinations of schools in charge to varying degrees at different moments in time, the contradictory criticism is easy to understand. Whenever one school is in the captain's chair, the other three schools will be discontented, and a babble of competing, contradictory criticism will be heard. There will, however, be one more domestic note of discord. Since American foreign policy is usually a compromise, the purists of the dominant school—and purists are often the most active and eloquent of writers and also for some reason often end up with chips on their shoulders and time on their hands—will also be dissatisfied. Each of the four schools will look back at the record and find that American foreign policy has rarely if ever lived up to the vision that animates its views. Add to this cauldron of perpetual discontent and recrimination the critiques from Continental realists in the United States and abroad, and we need no longer wonder why the raft of state is surrounded by howls, imprecations, and warnings of imminent shipwreck as it mushes unsinkably if not very stylishly through the waves.

American foreign policy is complex at its core. At any given moment it is more likely to be the product of a wide and diffuse coalition rather than of a single unitary vision. American foreign policy is at least as complicated to fathom as the elephant was for the proverbial blind men; the tusks are sharp, the tail is skittish, the ears flap, the trunk picks pockets, the feet tread heedlessly on smaller creatures, the breath smells of peanuts, and the creature as a whole is bulky and hard to move—but moves rapidly and violently if endangered, and sometimes merely if it is alarmed by a mouse with a beard, a cigar, and a Spanish accent. But also like an elephant, American foreign policy generally gets what it wants.

Perhaps the success is because of these different characteristics and qualities rather than in spite of them. Alternating among four different approaches, each capable of combining with and complementing the others, American foreign policy benefits from both flexibility in the short term and, in the long run, strong continuities of purpose. If the four schools are rooted in and speak for different interests—regional, economic, cultural, social—in the United States, their competition for political influence provides an environment within which the national interest can be more or less defined and expressed. The rising or falling strength of the different schools in the foreign policy discourse generally reflects the rising or falling importance of the special interests for which each school speaks.

From this perspective it appears that over time the competition of the four schools for influence yields a foreign policy that is better than the product of a single individual mind, however great—just as the operation of market forces over time tends to produce an outcome that is superior to the results of any single plan, however wise. The representative nature of American political society means that there is at least a rough equivalence between the political strength of the given schools and their weight in the nation—and the invisible hand takes care of the rest.

Historians may or may not conclude that the four-schools approach can be sustained by the historical record; political scientists may or may not find that it can be reconciled with an intellectually coherent theory of domestic or international politics. But whatever its drawbacks, this approach to American foreign policy does at least explain why a democratic republic with a notoriously erratic and undisciplined foreign policy process has nevertheless found its way, through many generations and in many varieties of circumstance, to foreign policies that have consistently advanced the country toward greater power and wealth than any other power in the history of the world. Perhaps it can help us think constructively about the challenges to come in a time likely to be more dangerous and complicated than anything in the millennium that preceded it.

I am not quite out of the confessional mode. There is one more admission to make: I am not proposing this paradigm simply because it looks like a viable intellectual solution to some otherwise vexing questions about how American foreign policy works. There is a motive to my mythos, and like those who developed and publicized the myth of virtuous isolation and the myth of the Cold War, I have a political purpose for the paradigm I propose.

Recovering a sense of the connection of contemporary American foreign policy with the achievements and traditions of our predecessors is not just a matter of intellectual good housekeeping. Infusing our public debates on foreign policy with a greater awareness of the long-term nature of our national interests and our ways of conceptualizing and realizing those interests will make life easier and better for American citizens in general, and also for that group of American citizens called to public service in the field of foreign affairs.

In particular it is important to link the foreign policy debates of the passing day to the great principles that have shaped our national life from the beginning. The traditionalism of the American people, the way Americans venerate the core founding documents, Founding Fathers, and founding principles of the state, is one of the most powerful forces in the United States. The power of these traditions paradoxically grows as the difference in times and circumstances between the original thirteen colonies and the current imperial Republic increases.

This respect for national tradition is one of our strongest and most valuable national traits. It is based on two different elements: an admiration for the founding principles based on the degree to which the enlightened ideas of the Revolutionary era still commend themselves to the American mind, and a sober historical recognition that under their guidance the American Republic has enjoyed a far happier political and material existence than any other commonwealth of comparable size in the history of the world.

"[A]ll experience hath shewn," as Jefferson wrote in the Declaration of Independence, "that mankind are more disposed to suffer, while evils are sufferable, than to right themselves by abolishing the forms to which they are accustomed." Jefferson did not know, but we do, what happens when for more than two centuries a form of government and set of governing principles to which the people are accustomed have proved to be a font of blessing and an ark of security. The people become passionately attached to these principles and those forms, and they will make any sacrifice to hold them fast.

In the decades to come the United States of America will need this kind of support for its foreign policy. In this new century the traditional concerns of the American people—world order with all that that implies, and the military strength and political will to defend it—will be as critical as ever.

The great political debates in the United States over what kind of order to build, and how to build and defend it, will be complex and many sided. The resources needed for successful policy will inevitably sometimes be great; the sacrifices of blood, treasure, and comfort may be even more formidable than anything exacted in American history to date.

For American foreign policy to have the best chance of bringing about the free, prosperous, and peaceful world that Americans—together with the citizens of most other nations in the world—want, American public opinion will need a framework of debate and decision making that it trusts. If possible our foreign policy should be able to command the same loyalty and depth of understanding that our domestic political structures enjoy.

In the context of American politics, the most likely way to achieve this goal will be to cultivate an informed public opinion that understands the big sweeping picture of American foreign policy through history, that can follow debates based on analogy from British as well as American experience, and that can trace the foreign policy of the moment back to the core founding insights and approaches that have guided the country from the beginning.

Reconnecting with the past will not close down discussion and debate over foreign policy, nor will it brand dissent from American foreign policy as disloyalty to the American nation. Rather, deeper public understanding of the very rich and varied traditions of American statesmanship and debate will legitimate differences over priorities and values in American foreign policy. If after all there is one lesson that American history seems unambiguously to teach, it is that a wide and free debate is the best means to assure the prosperity, the destiny, the liberty, and the safety of the American people.

Chapter Four

THE SERPENT AND
THE DOVE

The Hamiltonian Way

66 "Be ye," Christ told his disciples, "wise as serpents, and innocent as doves." This, like so much of the advice in the Bible, is both eminently sensible and damned hard to follow. The craft of Machiavelli is an uncomfortable guest in the bosom of Saint Francis.

In foreign policy the meaning of this injunction is relatively clear: Statesmen should pursue their goals with the sinuous pragmatism of the wily serpent, yet their purposes ought to be as humane and peaceable as those that legend attributes to the dove.

In American foreign policy, the serpents and the doves seem generally to be mingled. The tendency to divide our statesmen into realistic serpents and idealistic doves often misses the balance between the two qualities that our best statesmen maintain and that to some degree is intrinsic to American realism. Many who look at the Hamiltonian tradition of statesmanship and see its commercial orientation, its absence of illusions about the frailties of human nature, and its willingness to consider such morally painful ideas as the balance of power and the use of force in international relations, identify the Hamiltonian tradition with the—presumably—realistic and unsentimental philosophy of the snake. When one considers, on the other hand, the Wilsonians' professed faith in human nature, the strong commitment to human rights, and the persistent dream of a world of nation-states united by their devotion to the ideas of liberty and their detestation of war, there is a tendency to identify the Wilsonian cause with the emblem of the dove.

Neither school is really that simple. Beneath the Hamiltonian pinstripes beats the heart of a romantic dreamer; while the high ideals of the Wilsonian can conceal a sober and, at times, even a mean-spirited calculation of national, ethnic, and factional interest. Both schools of American foreign policy are hard for the untutored to read; both endlessly confuse foreign observers; both deal with ideas and visions that do not fit the traditional concerns and assumptions of European politics in the world of Richelieu and Metternich.

Of the two schools, the Hamiltonian may be the more deceptive. Unwary European diplomats in the company of Hamiltonian thinkers like Henry Cabot Lodge Sr. or the elder George Bush may think that they are dealing with men who inhabit the same intellectual universe that they do: Hamiltonians speak the language of Continental realism. Phrases like "the national interest" and "the balance of power" are often on their tongues. Speaking very broadly, as a group they often either come from or work for the class of people in the United States who most resemble the upper classes of European society; they have read the same books as their European counterparts, studied the same subjects at school, heard (if musically inclined) the same operas, and hold similar opinions on many subjects.

From the earliest years of the Republic, Hamiltonians have instinctively felt that the intellectual process through which the United States would develop its foreign policy was essentially the same process any state would employ: It would consider its interests, take stock of its strengths and its weaknesses, and develop a policy that would safeguard those interests within the limits of its resources. This similar intellectual process has led—or misled—many observers to confuse the Hamiltonian foreign policy tradition with Continental realism. In fact, traditional Hamiltonian thought on foreign policy is as different in its way from the European mainstream as Wilsonian thought.

This is not because Hamiltonians embrace a fundamentally different view of human nature than do Continental foreign policy realists. When it comes to human weaknesses and foibles, Hamiltonian thought is unblinking. Unlike so many eighteenth-century political reformers, the American Founding Fathers were notoriously convinced that humankind was quarrelsome and greedy; that, as the psalmist tells us, the human heart is wicked above all things. They did not expect a spirit of generosity and fair play to guide the councils of foreign countries any more than they expected the American political process to be a series of enlightened debates among dispassionate philosopher-kings. In foreign policy as in domestic, the Hamiltonians looked to interest as the guide to conduct.

Yet, when the Hamiltonians came to consider the foreign policy interests of the United States, they came up with a radically different list of interests than those drawn up in most of the chancelleries of Europe. European powers were surrounded by jealous and powerful rivals, and their relations alternated between war and armed truce. European states were forced to understand their interests primarily in military terms.

Great Britain, on the other hand, the country whose situation most resembled that of the United States, was an island nation in a relatively isolated corner of Europe. As we have seen, Britain had only one thing to fear from the Continent: that a single power would come to dominate the rest and then harness the combined economic forces of Europe to build a navy that could invade Britain and an economic system that could ruin it.

As a result the British developed a strategic doctrine that was different from the views of its Continental neighbors. British security could be safeguarded by specializing in the construction of an invincible navy and by defending the balance of power in Continental Europe, while British prosperity could be enhanced by developing a global trading system. The financial resources created by its trade enabled Britain to subsidize its temporary Continental allies and to keep its armed forces, especially the navy, up to strength.

Great Britain was a "normal" European country, but it was one with a singularly favorable geopolitical position—a position its diplomats and traders sought to exploit to the fullest. The British state was also different from the Continental states. By the eighteenth century the British royal family and its attendant aristocracy were quite different from their counterparts in Continental Europe. William III, Mary II, Anne, and, even more, the upstart Hanoverians held their thrones by parliamentary decree and lacked the prestige and so-called divine right of the Hapsburgs or the Bourbons; the old British aristocracy had been largely killed off in the Wars of the Roses and the Civil War, and the new aristocracy was primarily a commercial rather than a military caste, continually refreshed by the scions of new fortunes allying themselves with older bloodlines. The British state was more intimately and more extensively connected with British society than were the other European states with theirs. The Anglican Church, originating in the tangled amatory propensities of Henry VIII, was a pragmatic and flexible institution by comparison with both its Protestant and Catholic rivals on the European mainland; even its own bishops were less firmly united in doctrine than in their belief that all good Englishmen ought to belong to the national church. By comparison with other European nations, Great Britain lacked a state that existed over and above civil society and that presumed to rule it by divine right.

Both socially and in terms of its foreign policy interests, the United States might be called the "Britain of Britain." Compared with its Continental neighbors, Britain was a loose society governed by pragmatism; the United States took this logic several steps farther. Britain's monarchy existed by the grace of Parliament; the United States would be a republic. Britain had a weak state church; the United States disestablished religion. Britain was an island trading nation protected by the Channel; the United States was a continental trading nation protected by the Atlantic.

As Hamiltonians worked out their ideas concerning American foreign policy, they found themselves—naturally and inevitably under the circumstances—looking at Britain as a model. But they went beyond their model. The United States was farther from Europe than Britain was, and even less exposed to the jealousies of rival powers. Its territories were larger, its population would eventually be greater than any of the European powers', and it faced no prospect of equally powerful neighbors. The United States in the long run would be almost as large and at least as powerful as Russia; with three thousand miles instead of thirty separating it from the nearest great power, the United States would be safer than Britain from any Continental power.

British policy was more commercial and less militaristic than Continental policies; American policy could and would be more commercial still. Indeed, the importance of trade would determine the Hamiltonian definitions of U.S. security interests. If the United States was isolated from European armies, it was also potentially isolated from European trade. The weakest point of the United States was its sea link across the Atlantic to Europe. Access to trade with the rest of the world would clearly be a paramount American interest. It was an interruption of trade, rather than the loss of territory to rivals, that would most worry American foreign policy intellectuals through the first 150 years of national independence.

A foreign policy that was fundamentally commercial changed the nature of the American relationship with other powers. Security policy has historically been played like a zero-sum game. If Austria became more secure vis-à-vis France, France was then less secure vis-à-vis Austria. There might be occasional happy exceptions to this dismal rule, but in general a policy of military competition inevitably involves states in conflict. Their interests cannot all be served to the same degree, and every political settlement will leave some power or group of powers unhappy and restlessly intriguing for change.

The zero-sum game of military rivalry played an enormous role in European power politics, and the prospects for cooperation among participants in such a game are not good. Today's temporary ally is tomorrow's mortal foe.

Commercial relations do not work in the same way. In commercial transactions it is possible to have both a satisfied buyer and a satisfied seller. Furthermore, economic prosperity is not a zero-sum game. If Austria becomes richer, it can buy more goods from France, and this will make France richer. Increases in human productivity are beneficial to all. War, on the other hand, would hurt the economic interests of both nations, interrupting their trade, diverting their resources from productive to military uses, and increasing taxation in both countries.

Unlike Lenin, who saw capitalism as the leading cause of international warfare, Hamiltonians see commerce as, potentially, a cause of peace. The expansion of trade, and the substitution of the win-win strategy of commerce for the zero-sum game of war, would become important Hamiltonian aims in the twentieth century. This intoxicating vision of a win-win world order based on international law often led Hamiltonians to sound almost Wilsonian in their hopes for the future state of mankind; but from the beginning, the open-ended quality of the Hamiltonian worldview meant that Hamiltonians saw the United States as responding to a different historical logic from the one that dominated Europe.

Hamiltonians would be much more hospitable to the instruments of warfare—above all, to navies, but also to a professional standing army—than American politicians who worried about the political consequences of professional armed forces, but the traditional foreign policy of the United States assigned military matters a significantly smaller role than was common in Europe. If American relations with Europe were to be primarily commercial, then—even taking the darkest view of human selfishness—it seemed that American relations with Europe were not doomed to exist on the same low level as the relations of the European powers with one another. As long as Continental Europe kept its nose out of the business of the Western Hemisphere, the United States could look forward to relations that were at least open to outcomes that satisfied both sides.

The gloomy psychology of Continental diplomacy and the inevitable militarization of its policy in part proceeded from, and in part reinforced, the militaristic bias of the Continental states. The American state and diplomatic service took on a different coloring. As we shall see, Jeffersonians and Jacksonians were revolted by the idea of an elite diplomatic service; Hamiltonians had no such objections in principle, but the nature and purposes of the state and the foreign service would be different in a commercial republic from those of a state in a military monarchy. Thus European states were heavily informed and penetrated by an ethos that was not only elitist and aristocratic but frankly and proudly military. The princes, chancellors, ministers, and ambassadors of nineteenth-century Europe, to say nothing of its generals and officers, were frequently descended from warrior aristocracies. Until the eighteenth century it was not uncommon for Europe's monarchs to command their troops in the field; as late as 1743, George II of Britain appeared in person to oppose the French at the Battle of Dettingen. Militaristic Prussia, in which the needs of the army drove the evolution of the state, was an extreme example, but with every great Continental power of early modern Europe the history of the state was to some degree the history of its armed forces, and the state was less involved in civilian affairs and proportionately more involved in military matters than now. Once again Britain, though fully committed to the cultivation and projection of military force, was the least militaristic of the great powers, and once again Hamiltonians, without repudiating British and even Continental ideas about the nature of humankind and the competition of states, came to very different practical conclusions about what needed to be done.

In the Hamiltonian view, the American state needed to have a competent military, but the state itself was civilian. American diplomats generally spent more time dealing with trade, and far less time dealing with military matters or other matters of state, than their foreign colleagues did. Hamiltonian opinion, in general, thought this was a blessing.

A consciousness that geography promised a glorious destiny for the United States was another factor that made Hamiltonian diplomacy sunnier than the European variety. During most of American history, geography and demography united to proclaim that, all things being equal, the mere passage of time would make the United States increasingly richer, more powerful, and better respected in the world community. In the darkest days of the first tumultuous decades of independence, and again in the depths of the Civil War, American diplomats operating in the Hamiltonian tradition could console themselves with the thought that their worst difficulties were temporary—that if the United States could survive, it was destined to thrive. This was an assurance that few European diplomats outside Russia, secure in its vast territories and population, could share; other countries faced perennial and perpetual threats to their status as great powers or even to their independence. For the United States, fears about independence and unity were intermittent and emerged only at times of great crisis.

The result was an approach to diplomacy that, while it sprang from and operated within the traditional framework of European diplomacy, was less defensive and more optimistic. It started from the same premises but moved to very different conclusions. Hamiltonians did not have to believe that the United States must either conquer or be conquered in its international relations; they could and did believe that the United States, without neglecting its military forces, was able to seek constructive compromises of mutual benefit in its dealings with foreign powers. "Realistic" as it may have been in a formal sense, at the practical level Hamiltonian foreign policy was a radical innovation in the world of great-power diplomacy.

The Hamiltonian Tradition of the National Interest

Operating on the intellectual basis of what (to distinguish it from its darker Continental cousin) can be called American realism, Hamiltonian thinkers and politicians gradually developed distinctive definitions of American national interests, and on the strategies best adopted to secure them. Although the body of doctrine has grown and developed over the centuries, Hamiltonian thought also shows a substantial degree of continuity.

One of the earliest and most important of these interests, one that occupied the minds of the American colonists even before the Revolution, is what can be called the freedom of the seas. In its narrowest sense this involves the freedom of American citizens, American goods, and American ships to travel wherever they wish in the world in the interests of peaceful trade. No sea, no ocean, no strait should be closed to American ships. Piracy must be suppressed, and foreign nations must abide by international law in their treatment of neutral shipping during war.

Freedom of the seas in even this narrow sense remains the single point on which American interests are most likely to come into conflict with those of other powers. Thomas Jefferson, no Hamiltonian and one of the most pacific presidents in American history, sent expeditions to fight the Barbary pirates, who were seizing American ships. To protect this freedom we fought undeclared naval wars with both Britain and France and, of course, the War of 1812 during the Napoleonic Wars in Europe, as both sides sought to restrict the trade of neutral nations with their enemies.

The interest in safeguarding American commerce had grown even stronger by the time of the Civil War. "It would be superfluous in me," Charles Francis Adams, Lincoln's minister to Great Britain during the Civil War, reminded the British prime minister, Lord Palmerston, as a series of Confederate ships prepared to leave British harbors to attack Union shipping, "to point out to your Lordship that this is war."[1] At the height of the Civil War, when victory was anything but certain, the North believed that its maritime interests were important enough to force it to take on the world's greatest military power.

The twentieth century saw a continuation and even an expansion in the importance of this principle. In World War I shipping questions caused us to quarrel seriously with Britain and ultimately to enter the war against Germany. In World War II we were already fighting an undeclared naval war with Germany in the North Atlantic when Japan attacked Pearl Harbor. Interference with shipping led President Gerald R. Ford—when the Vietnam syndrome was at its peak—to launch a rescue attempt when Cambodians captured an American ship in 1975. The North Korean seizure of the USS *Pueblo* in 1968 created a serious international crisis.[2] President Reagan sent American ships into the Persian Gulf to protect neutral shipping during the Iran-Iraq war and confronted Libya with the threat of war when that country tried to bar American ships from crossing its "line of death" in international waters. In 1996 President Clinton sent the Seventh Fleet into the Taiwan Straits to assert the right of free passage during Chinese missile tests aimed at intimidating Taiwan. There is little doubt that future presidents will respond to similar challenges with similarly strong measures.

Freedom of the skies supplements this value in the twenty-first century. The United States takes the lead in fighting against hijacking and other threats to peaceful legal commercial travel in the skies. Geography still makes the United States more dependent on safe and quick intercontinental transportation of goods and people than most other countries and, in true Hamiltonian fashion, the United States considers interference with this right of passage to be a direct and immediate threat to its vital interests, and it reserves the right to respond with the most vigorous diplomatic measures—and, when necessary, the use of force. No other principle has played such a major role in our diplomatic history; infringing on our freedom to travel by sea and air remains the fastest way for foreign powers to start a war with the United States. While the United States welcomes the cooperation of international organizations and other countries in efforts to curb interference with free traffic by air and sea, in practice it remains prepared to act unilaterally and, if necessary, in the teeth of international opinion.

The freedom of the seas is related to the second great national interest as understood by Hamiltonian opinion. It is not enough for our ships and goods to have free passage through international waters; American cargoes must have the same rights and privileges as the cargoes of other nations at the harbors for which they are bound. An open door for American goods is as important as an open ocean for American ships.

American diplomacy has consistently concerned itself with opening markets ever since the Revolutionary War. The first official foreign mission of the colonies was the mission of Benjamin Franklin to the court of Louis XVI. British armies were occupying American cities; British fleets controlled the coasts; but the first treaty that the new nation signed was not just about a military alliance. It was also a trade treaty: France and the United States granted each other "most favored nation" status, and American goods were to be admitted to French markets with as few obstacles as possible.

The quest for an open door for American goods also brought the United States into conflict with the European powers' efforts to maintain exclusive trade privileges within their colonial empires. For most of American history the European powers controlled large colonial empires in both hemispheres. Often, though not always, the imperial powers sought special trading rights for themselves in their colonies, and restricted or even prohibited foreigners from trading or investing in them. The American colonists had resented this system when Great Britain imposed it on the thirteen colonies; they continued to resent the attempts by

Britain, France, the Netherlands, Portugal, and Spain to limit the right of American ships to trade with their overseas colonies after the Revolution.

This long-standing theme in American foreign policy could still make its presence felt in the twenty-first century. The "banana war" between the United States and the EU that vexed transatlantic relations during the Clinton administration represented American opposition to ways in which the EU discriminated in favor of exports from former European colonies in the Caribbean (and the European companies that controlled their export trade) against "dollar bananas," grown in countries like Ecuador and Guatemala and distributed by U.S.-based firms.

The attempt to open the doors of the colonial empires was a major thrust of American policy in the early decades of independence, and success in this endeavor played an important role in American economic development. Not that American diplomats could claim all the credit, however. The collapse of the Spanish and Portuguese empires in the New World, France's abandonment of its imperial ambitions in the Western Hemisphere, and the triumph of free trade principles in British politics meant that the first half of the nineteenth century was a time in which American access to world markets increased dramatically.

Given these successes, the open door diminished as an element in American foreign policy until the end of the nineteenth century witnessed a new worldwide scramble for colonies and economic advantages by the European powers. The United States was not greatly exercised about the partition of Africa, but the extension of European influence on the Pacific Rim presented a much more serious problem. Hamiltonians believed that the United States could not accept an exclusive colonial partition of China. The United States consistently opposed European schemes to divide China into spheres of influence, and pursued a long-term strategy to acquire bases in the Pacific to ensure that European nations, either singly or in combination, could never extend the exclusive colonial system to a country whose trade, Hamiltonians firmly believed, was vital to the future of the nation.

This policy should not be confused with the kind of principled anti-imperialism to be found among Jeffersonians. As in the cases of Hawaii, the Panama Canal, and the Philippines, Hamiltonian thinkers and politicians were perfectly capable of behaving as imperialistically as any European power when they believed that the national interest required it. But they were not gratuitously imperialistic. Unlike many of the Europeans, they did not seek to plant the national flag wherever they could. "I have about the same desire to annex [the Dominican Republic]," said Teddy Roosevelt, "as a gorged boa constrictor might have to swallow a porcupine wrong-end-to."[3]

When the imperialistic mania was at its height, and the idea of an open door for trade began to look utopian in a world increasingly divided into quarreling empires, Hamiltonians wanted to make certain that the United States got its fair share. Hamiltonian brains briefly teemed with schemes to annex everything from Canada and Baja California to the unclaimed bits of Africa, but this fit soon passed. The basic view that dominated Hamiltonian opinion through most of our history was that the United States had few territorial ambitions beyond what became the forty-eight contiguous states and the central and northern Pacific, but that we wanted very much to enjoy open commercial relations with all the world.

This did not necessarily mean that we wanted the rest of the world to enjoy open commercial relations with us. It was clearly in the national interest of the United States to open foreign markets to American-made goods; it was much less clear to Hamiltonian manufacturers and bankers that it was in the national interest to allow foreign goods to trade freely in the United States. It was certainly not in the sectional interest of the northeastern states, or in the class interest of Hamiltonian manufacturers. The zenith of Hamiltonian power in the United States lasted from Abraham Lincoln's election to the outbreak of the Great Depression; of the seventeen presidential elections held between Lincoln's nomination in 1860 and Hoover's defeat in 1932, the Republicans won all but four. This was also the period in which American tariffs were at the highest levels in our history.

During most of that time, most British statesman believed that free trade benefited Great Britain even if other countries did not reciprocate. It was Britain's willingness to allow American goods reasonably free access to its market without reciprocation that allowed the United States a free ride in terms of international trade. When Britain responded to the Smoot-Hawley Tariff in the United States by raising reciprocal tariffs against American goods, the game was up.

The weight of Hamiltonian opinion gradually shifted from protectionism toward free trade as the lesson of reciprocity sank in. In the aftermath of World War II, Hamiltonian opinion would shift even further, ultimately reaching the old British view that free trade would benefit the American economy even if other countries failed to open their markets in return. Although Hamiltonian trade policy has changed its methods over the centuries, the central idea—that national prosperity through an appropriate trade regime is the responsibility of the federal government—has never changed. Hamiltonians have never believed in using tariffs simply as a revenue tax, raising or lowering tariffs in line with the fiscal needs of the government. For Hamiltonians tariffs and trade policy have always been a political levy, used to shape national economic development.

Another interest, which played a sporadic but sometimes vital role in the Hamiltonian view of the national interest, was a variation of the open door. Periodically in modern history there have been strategically necessary materials only available from a handful of countries. What oil is today, rubber was yesterday. Other, rarer materials are needed for military manufacturing; since the nineteenth century the United States has conducted its foreign policy with one eye on the necessity of maintaining its access to supplies of these materials. Any country or group of countries that found itself with a monopoly in some key material and that then attempted to use this monopoly against the United States would soon find itself the object of vigorous countermeasures. The vital role of oil and energy policy in shaping American foreign policy and military strategy today points to the continuing importance of these considerations in our policy.

Freedom of the seas leads to the open door for goods, which in turn leads to satisfaction of another American interest, equally vital from a Hamiltonian point of view: the need for a free flow of money between the world's principal trading nations. Unless dollars, pounds, and francs can be freely exchanged for one another in some predictable way, and unless traders and investors can freely move money from one country to another, the advantages of trade would be largely lost.

The implications of this for both foreign and domestic policy are incalculably large. Keeping the world's money markets integrated involves accepting important restraints on domestic policy. Governments must, for example, engage in sound fiscal and monetary policies if their currencies are to be useful mediums for international transactions. Countries cannot borrow excessively, nor must they depreciate the value of their money by printing too much of it. These considerations do not merely require fiscal restraint on the part of governments; they demand the establishment of institutions that can function as central banks and as honest arbiters in controversies between citizens and noncitizens. There must be an authority to ensure that currencies keep their value and to guarantee liquidity for international capital transactions. Courts must treat noncitizens on a level with citizens when it comes to the enforcement of commercial contracts.

These considerations have been central to Hamiltonian thinking since the eighteenth century—since the era of the Articles of Confederation. The need for the United States to maintain sound public finance was one of the reasons that Hamilton and his associates favored the establishment of a constitution and a strong national government. The assumption of the public debt and the establishment of the First Bank of the United States were the direct and immediate causes of the first great fight between the parties that became known as Hamiltonians and Jeffersonians during the Washington administration. The need to honor and enforce debts owed to British subjects in American state and national courts was part of the wrenching debate over the Jay Treaty with Great Britain, one of the first full-scale battles over foreign policy in American history.

From 1789 until World War I the need for a sound international medium of exchange was felt primarily in the formation of Hamiltonian domestic policy. The fights over the First and Second Banks of the United States were critical battles before the Civil War; the controversies over greenbacks and free silver did much to shape domestic politics in the following half century. For Hamiltonians, the importance of these battles lay only partly in domestic questions over prices and inflation. An unstable dollar against the pound would curtail the flow of British investment, which remained crucial to American economic expansion until the twentieth century. The gold standard, attacked by Bryan as a "cross of gold" on which evil bankers wished to crucify mankind, was for Hamiltonians the necessary instrument of international—and therefore, of national—business. Moderate Hamiltonians repeatedly proclaimed their readiness to consider silver coinage if Britain and the other leading countries would agree, but no agreement on this point was ever forthcoming. Foreign and domestic policy were inextricably mixed; great domestic battles had foreign policy implications and vice versa.

The shift in financial power away from Great Britain and toward the United States in the early decades of the twentieth century meant that the continuing Hamiltonian concern for a stable international financial system would thenceforward involve a more active international role for the United States. Throughout the "isolationist" 1920s, the Federal

Reserve Bank cooperated closely with the central banks of Britain, Germany, and France. While the United States declined to join the League of Nations or the World Court, and while Hamiltonian politicians running for office declaimed the virtues of isolationism, American officials became intimately involved in the intricacies of European financial reconstruction. The end of World War II would see an even greater increase in Hamiltonian activism in search of international financial stability, and, with the end of the Cold War, the preservation of an orderly international system that promoted free flows of capital would emerge as a keystone of American foreign policy.

Hamiltonians and the Pacific

The American traders and merchants who were the earliest supporters of Hamiltonian policies and principles in American foreign policy had been interested in the possibilities of the Pacific from early in the colonial era. Arthur Power Dudden's book *The American Pacific* recounts a story of strong interest in the possibilities of the Pacific trade as early as the Washington administration; this trade would play, and still plays, a major role in Hamiltonian thinking about the American national interest. As early as the seventeenth century, Boston merchants were showing an interest in the China trade, and an American colonist sailed the Pacific with Captain Cook.

After independence it was not long before Americans began to appear in Pacific ports. The first ship to reach China under an American flag sailed from New York on George Washington's fifty-second birthday, less than a year after Britain recognized American independence. By 1800 more than a hundred American ships had sailed from Guangzhou, and the possibilities of the Pacific trade were looking very bright. "There is no better advice to be given to the merchants of the United States," wrote John Adams in 1785, "than to push their commerce to the East Indies as far and as fast as it will go."[4]

The trade deficit with China also appeared very early, as did political struggles in the United States about how to deal with it. The Chinese notoriously did not want to buy Western goods. American merchants tried to solve this in some of the then usual ways, including the sale of opium shipped from Smyrna (now Izmir) on the west coast of Turkey. As early as the 1840s, the Far Eastern trade of the United States was raising the sorts of moral and economic questions we are familiar with today. On the one hand, mercantile opinion favored trade without regard for moral and social considerations. American missionaries for their part loathed the opium trade. They supported the efforts of the Chinese government to suppress it, and their American supporters attacked the cynicism of merchants whose love of profit recognized no limits.

American commercial activity in the Pacific soared. Much of this was at the expense of marine mammals. Sealers and fur trappers combed islands and bays from southern Chile to the Arctic Ocean; at the peak of the Pacific whaling industry, more than six hundred American ships cruised its waterways in search of spermaceti, whale oil, and baleen. By the middle of the nineteenth century, the Hawaiian islands were already part of an American sphere of influence; missionaries, whalers, merchants, and plantation owners were steadily changing the nature of island society and making the archipelago a base for American influence and trade.

The Hamiltonian and mercantile tradition in American foreign policy has always regarded Pacific trade as a natural and necessary part of American commerce, and the protection and furthering of that commerce has been a constant theme in Hamiltonian diplomacy and activity throughout American history. This has not been simply a history of trade; the American military presence in the Pacific dates back to the War of 1812.

For almost all of that history, Hamiltonian thinking about American policy in the Far East was guided by principles that changed very little until the cataclysm that swept through Asia in the 1940s. Even then the changes were superficial; American thinking about the Far East today is visibly descended from the views of men like Adams and Perry.

Trade—and, later, investment—were the paramount considerations in relations with Asia, and the political and military involvement of the American government was always to be closely related to these goals. Freedom of the seas and the open door had special applications in Asia. Freedom of the seas clearly implies such things as humane treatment of shipwrecked sailors and the suppression of piracy. As early as the 1830s American naval ships regularly patrolled Far Eastern waters in the service of both these interests. A national policy of establishing commercial agreements with Asian governments also dates from this era. Asian markets were to be opened to American goods at gunpoint if need be; in the relations between Perry and the reluctant Japanese one can perhaps see the first signs of what would become a traditional trade problem in the relations of the two nations as the Japanese attempt to keep imports out and the Americans attempt to open Japanese markets.

These policies involved the United States very early in a complex relationship with both Asian and European governments. Briefly stated, the United States generally sided with European governments when the issues involved the rights of foreigners to trade and the security of foreigners in Asian countries. On the other hand the United States generally opposed the partition and colonization of Asian countries by European powers, especially in the case of China.

As Japan outstripped its neighbors in industrial development, it began to seek equal treatment with European powers and to establish a sphere of influence in China and elsewhere similar to those created by European countries—and by the United States in its own neighborhood. The United States vehemently opposed this, not only because a Japanese empire would lead to violations of the open door and, possibly, set off a colonial scramble in China similar to the partition of Africa, but also because a strong Japan seemed to pose a long-term threat to the security of Hawaii and the American west coast.

Since that time the United States has generally favored a balance-of-power policy in Asia, supporting the weaker powers against the stronger in the hope of preventing the rise of any power that could dominate the others. Until 1945 Japan was that power, and the United States consistently opposed its ambitions. After the Communist victory in China, it was China, in alliance with the Soviet Union, that seemed to be the aspiring hegemon. American policy, still bent on its traditional Asian goals, switched sides and supported a war-weakened Japan against a newly vigorous China. It is at least imaginable that new changes in the Asian balance of power will see the United States make new changes in its alliances, but it is likely that for the foreseeable future, concern for the balance of power in Asia will remain a key factor in American policy.

The Special Relationship

Although Hamiltonian thinking about American foreign policy was rooted in the British foreign policy tradition, there was one extremely important difference between the situations of the United States and the United Kingdom. That difference was the United Kingdom itself. No power has dominated American foreign policy thinking as Britain has done; the national preoccupation with the Soviet Union during the Cold War was neither as intense or as focused as the national concern with Great Britain during most of our history.

Britain was an inescapable fact for our ancestors. American traders and missionaries in the farthest-flung corners of the globe alternately competed against and cooperated with their British counterparts. British finance dominated American commerce, and its tentacles extended even into remote agricultural and mining communities. From the invention of the telegraph until the development of radio, Great Britain controlled the world's systems of communication. For decades its industrial technology was without rival or peer. Its mighty fleets were the only foreign force capable of attacking the United States at home. Great Britain was to the nineteenth century something like what the United States became to the twentieth; the United States in the nineteenth century was something akin to what Brazil is today. The existence of an economically powerful, potentially hostile superpower—a power that alternated between friendly support for the United States and designs against its independence and prosperity—was the great fact of American foreign policy for almost 150 years after the Revolution, just as its disappearance is the great fact with which we must live today.

Britain has occupied a special, central place in Hamiltonian thinking since the Federalist period. At every crisis in American foreign policy from the Treaty of Paris, which established our independence, to the Kosovo war, Hamiltonians have seen Great Britain as the key to a successful American policy, and they have done their best—in early times with little cooperation from pigheaded and shortsighted British diplomacy—to preserve close relations between the two great English-speaking nations.

This policy is not simply the product of sentimental Anglophilia. In terms of power politics the United States and Great Britain have a special relationship that goes beyond their common language, heritage, and democratic values. If the inhabitants of the British Isles had spoken Japanese and practiced Zoroastrianism under the direction of an absolute monarch, Hamiltonians would still have built a close relationship with Britain. This does not mean, however, that the common heritage means nothing to the two countries. American businessmen in the nineteenth century, and their British counterparts in the twentieth, benefited enormously from sharing the language and the legal system of the world's hegemonic power.

It was partly a matter of trade. As a market for American goods and as a source for manufactured goods, the importance of Great Britain to the young republic is impossible to exaggerate. In 1790 the United Kingdom absorbed 35 percent of America's total exports; one hundred years later that proportion had risen to 52.2 percent.[5] Great Britain remained the largest single purchaser of American exports until 1946,[6] when it was overtaken by Canada. (If the British Empire had held together, it would today incomparably be the most important economic partner of the United States. To Canadian and British trade flows, add those with the Gulf states, Nigeria, Hong Kong, Singapore, Australia, and New Zealand. The British Empire would be our most important source of oil, and would far surpass Mexico as a trading partner and Japan as a source of capital.)

Beyond this the United States and Great Britain enjoyed a financial relationship that grew steadily closer during the nineteenth century. The United States became increasingly important as a source of raw materials and foodstuffs for Britain, as a safety valve for immigration from Ireland, and as an outlet for foreign investment.

The growing importance of British investment in the United States created a strong pro-American party in Britain and a strong pro-British party in the United States, contributing in turn to the continuance of good relations and further improving the climate for economic cooperation. Thus two members of the influential Baring family of British bankers married members of Philadelphia's prominent Bingham family in the late eighteenth century. The House of Baring became the American government's most important foreign banker, arranging the financial transactions that paid for the Louisiana Purchase and continuing to handle American financial affairs in Great Britain during the War of 1812. The Barings invested heavily in the United States, purchasing more than one million acres of Maine land; in 1840 it would be the 1st Lord Ashburton, born Alexander Baring, who worked out a compromise settlement over the boundary between Maine and New Brunswick with Daniel Webster.

After the crisis of 1837, in which nine American states defaulted on their debts, it was again the House of Baring that helped the offenders resume regular payments, and that helped persuade nervous British investors that American markets were once again sound investments.

The most important banking firm in the United States was the House of Morgan, a fully transatlantic institution, with its principal offices in

London for much of the nineteenth century. Morgan examined American borrowers carefully for creditworthiness before placing their securities in the London market, and by placing Morgan partners as directors of client firms, the house maintained a strict and conservative watch over the financial practices of American companies in the interest of lenders. For a generation the House of Morgan served as the de facto central bank of the United States. It rescued the dollar during the gold panic of 1893 and prevented a massive financial collapse in the wake of the panic of 1907. In 1913 its place was taken by the Federal Reserve Bank, which continued Morgan's tradition of close collaboration with the Bank of England until the Nixon administration.

These relationships were critical both to Hamiltonian domestic and foreign policy throughout American history, but bilateral finance and trade were not the only elements in Hamiltonian thinking about Anglo-American relations. From a defensive standpoint, from 1783 to World War I, Great Britain had the power to make war on the United States. If the British navy supported the United States, however, no European country was strong enough to cross the Atlantic with a fleet that could inflict serious damage. During all this time a good relationship with Great Britain meant that no other European power could trouble the United States at home. At the same time Canada served as a hostage for British behavior in North America. If Britain used its naval superiority to threaten the American coast, the United States by the middle of the nineteenth century had the resources to conquer Canada by land. The result was a balance of power between the two English-speaking countries that was distinctly favorable to the United States and grew more so as time went by.

The Anglo-American connection also drew strength from the two countries' common interests in Europe. Both Britain and the United States had an overwhelming interest in the balance of power in Europe. As long as the European nations were divided among themselves, no European superpower could contest Britain's power at sea, and therefore no new threats could arise against the United States. This was of course the foundation of the Monroe Doctrine, and it was the interest that drew the United States toward intervention on Britain's side in both world wars and in the Cold War.

This special relationship meant that the United States could have an extraordinarily simple and cheap national defense policy in the nineteenth century. For Hamiltonians in those years, American security policy was a simple matter, and something Lord Bryce could understand: Stay strong enough to ensure that Britain respected American rights, and otherwise, stay out of European politics.

As long as Britain was strong, the United States could pursue this policy at a low cost. Beyond the needs of the western frontier, the United States required only a navy, and for much of the nineteenth century, even this was largely neglected, with no terrible results. This system worked best for the United States before the Civil War. At that time only Britain and Russia were significant powers beyond the confines of Europe. The Dutch and Portuguese empires in Africa and Asia were of little concern or interest to the United States, the Germans had no colonies, and the French were concerned only with the Mediterranean.

The external situation began to change late in the nineteenth century, and Hamiltonian thinking evolved along with it. First France and then Germany established the foundations of global empires. The French, who very much wanted the Confederacy to succeed, used the Civil War to revive the old scheme of installing a European prince on an American throne, briefly establishing the unfortunate Hapsburg archduke Maximilian in Mexico City. This adventure ended in disaster, but French soldiers and sailors moved into Asia and the South Pacific. More ominously, Germany established itself in Africa and China; one alleged motive for the American annexation of the Philippines was to prevent the kaiser from taking the islands.[7] Worse still from the American perspective, German immigration and German trade were beginning to establish the Germans as rivals to the British in the southern cone of Latin America. The scorpions were scrambling out of the bottle, and the British no longer seemed able to keep them contained.

As the nineteenth century drew to its close, Hamiltonians began to worry seriously about international relations. Two nightmare scenarios troubled military planners and gave publicists ammunition for increased campaigns to enlarge the armed forces. On the one hand Germany might succeed in overturning the balance of power in Europe, and become so powerful by land and sea that the United States would have to fight a long, hard struggle against it. Germany had already made it clear that it had naval ambitions; it wanted to be a world power, not a European power. A Germany triumphant in Europe would be a formidable and expansionist rival.

There was another, even more frightening possibility, however. Britain's quest for new foreign policy options as its relative power declined might take it away from its special relationship with the United States. Before World War I, Britain was working to build an Anglo-Japanese naval alliance. The United States worried that Britain and Japan would agree to divide up China between themselves, and the United States would be helpless to prevent it. In the long run this would create the American nightmare of a strong Japan that could attack the Philippines, Hawaii, and ultimately the west coast. The worst-case American scenario at the time was that Britain could form an alliance with Germany in Europe, along with Japan in Asia. This gang of three could then divide up the old world among themselves any way they wished. In *Philip Dru: Administrator*, the odd, best-selling novel by Woodrow Wilson's closest Washington friend and confidant, Colonel Edward M. House, exactly this nightmare came to pass.

Hamiltonian Policy in the Twentieth Century

Despite these dangers Hamiltonians were in an expansive and confident mood at the dawn of the twentieth century. The declining power of Britain increased British dependence on its special relationship with the United States. Britain grew increasingly deferential to American views about the Western Hemisphere. British decline also afforded new scope as well as new necessity for the United States to act as a global power, propping Britain up while reaping increased commercial and political benefits from the special relationship.

These two trends in Hamiltonian thinking pointed to the same place: the Isthmus of Panama, where an American railroad had connected the Atlantic and the Pacific since the days of the California gold rush.

The creation and the control of an Isthmian canal offered immense advantages to the nation able to achieve them. Most Americans today have very hazy ideas about the facts of maritime geography. This is partly because of the dominance of air travel, and partly because the Panama Canal has revised maritime geography so far in our favor. Without the Panama Canal, San Francisco is closer by sea to London than it is to New York. (Brazil juts so far out into the Atlantic that ships bound from New York for Cape Horn must sail far to the east. Ships from western Europe actually have a more direct and shorter route.) Without the canal, boats in Britain were better positioned to reach China and California than were those on the east coast of the United States. With it the United States

DEFENCE OF THE CALIFORNIA BANK

This cartoon appeared early in 1849 and shows how Americans under-stood the relationship between international politics and domestic events. The rulers of Britain, Russia, France, and Spain are shown as attempting to take California—newly interesting because of the Gold Rush—from the United States. Zachary Taylor (shown as an eagle) responds, "Retreat you poor D[evil]s! nor a squabble engender. For our Gold unto you we will never surrender." To the tune of "O Susanna!," Victoria sings, "Oh, Dear Albert [her Prince Consort], don't you cry for me. I'm off to California with my shovel on my knee." American fears for the security of California were not at all far-fetched. Neither the transcontinental railroad nor the Panama Canal then existed, and the west coast of the United States was easier to reach by sea from Europe than from Boston or New York.

S. Lee Perkins. Library of Congress, Prints and Photographs Division, LC-USZ62-7212

would be able to maximize the advantages of what would become a cen-tral location between the two coasts of the great Eurasian supercontinent.

Given the stakes, and given the element of rivalry that always infused the special relationship, it is not surprising that Britain and the United States struggled for years to control the canal, or at least to deny control to each other. In the first phase of the rivalry, Britain was stronger, and British agents staked out claims to the Caribbean coast of Nicaragua, then believed to be the most promising starting point for a canal. But

THE EUROPEAN PLAN

In this 1880 illustration, Thomas Nast draws a connection between
stingy congressional defense appropriations (represented by the poster
of the U.S. army portrayed as a skeleton) and the plans or efforts of
Britain and France to build a canal through Panama without American
leadership or even participation. Nast calls South America the "Southern States" and the line of the proposed canal the "Mason-Dixon Line."
This was not a call for the United States to annex South America;
rather, it was a reminder to American readers both of the Franco-
British desire to split up the United States during the Civil War and of
the vital importance of the whole Western Hemisphere to U.S. security.
Thomas Nast. Library of Congress, Prints and Photographs Division, Harper's Weekly,
March 13, 1880, page 161

the growing power of the United States forced the British to recognize that a canal without the consent and cooperation of the Americans
would be impossible. In the Clayton-Bulwer Treaty of 1850, both sides
acknowledged a standoff and agreed that neither would build a canal
without the other. This was the agreement that Teddy Roosevelt had the
great satisfaction of scuppering when the Hay-Pauncefote Treaty of 1901
recognized that the United States could dig, administer, and fortify a
canal without British participation.

At the time of its construction, the Panama Canal was able to accommodate the largest ships in the world. This meant that the American navy enjoyed enormous advantages compared with the navies of other powers and could project power into both the Atlantic and Pacific Oceans much more easily—and cheaply—than any other state. Combined with the growing population on the Pacific coast and a string of outposts and bases across the Pacific, the canal gave the United States a guaranteed advantage in the coming competition to benefit from the possibilities of trade with what would one day come to be called the Pacific Rim.

Yet these triumphs in Panama and elsewhere did not make the United States more secure. The same relative decline of British power that enabled Uncle Sam to treat John Bull so unceremoniously in the New World had consequences in the Old. There Germany was the rising power. German scientists were developing new technologies faster than the British; German industrialists were developing new methods and products that the British could not match; German merchants were driving the British from market after market around the world.

Germany's new prominence in the world went beyond economics: Germany was developing armed forces that, potentially, could dominate Europe. Even worse, Germany sought new colonies and dependencies abroad. German merchants appeared in China; German agents staked claims in Africa; German bankers appeared in Latin America. Worse still: Germans read the works on the importance of sea power by the American rear admiral Alfred Thayer Mahan; Germany decided that neither its colonies nor its trade could be secure unless it had a navy that rivaled Britain's.

In another troubling sign, the extremely rapid growth of Japanese power indicated that world history was moving into a new phase. For two centuries, European nations had enjoyed such technological and commercial advantages that non-European peoples had scarcely been able to figure in world politics. The comforting notion had spread through European civilization that the causes of this superiority were racial: that yellow, brown, and black human beings were simply incapable of mastering the technological secrets of white civilization.

Japan's defeat of Russia at the dawn of the twentieth century signaled the definitive defeat of such racial theories. The European nations and their daughter states around the world would have to come to terms with the moral, political, and economic claims of nonwhite peoples as these groups mastered Western technologies and sought redress of their many grievances.

The emergence of non-European power centers also changed the dynamic of the global power system. The powerlessness of the non-European peoples had been a critical element contributing to the British supremacy of the eighteenth and nineteenth centuries. It reduced the strategic problem of British foreign policy to the maintenance of the balance of power in Europe. With this in hand, British power would be undisputed around the world.

The first power to challenge that idea was the United States itself, and the first task of British diplomacy after the defeat of Napoleon was the establishment of a solid relationship with the new nation. But the rise of Japan was more challenging. The Pacific Rim was so distant from Europe that even a relatively weak Japan by European standards would be a significant factor in the local power equation. Furthermore it was not as simple for Britain to reach an accommodation with Japan as with the United States. Not only were British and Japanese societies more different than was the case for Britain and the United States; conciliating Japan created problems for the British relationship with the Americans.

Japanese ambitions in Asia were conventional by the standards of the era: The Japanese wanted a colonial empire like those of the other great powers, and China was the place where they could get it. Any lasting British arrangement with Japan would have to concede Japan a free hand in significant parts of China. Japan wanted a relationship with Britain that would parallel Britain's relationship with the United States. Just as the British gave the Americans a relatively free hand in the Americas, the Japanese wanted a free hand in Asia—a goal Japanese statesmen described by saying that they wanted an Asian version of the Monroe Doctrine. But any attempt to reach such an arrangement brought British policy into direct collision with the American insistence on the open door. The British concept for Asia involved an old-fashioned understanding with Japan; the American concept involved a new kind of arrangement with China, where the United States had both commercial and sentimental interests.

The British never solved this problem. With the costs of maintaining the European power balance escalating drastically, Britain could no longer achieve military domination of the Far East at an acceptable cost. Britain could not contain a hostile Japan indefinitely, but no other powers in the Far East were capable of balancing Japan. China was too weak and divided; Russia under the czars was unable to play a major role after its humiliating defeat; the United States, unwilling to see Britain reach an arrangement with Japan, was equally unwilling to give Britain the kind of active support and material assistance that an anti-Japanese policy would have required. The British dithered helplessly in this situation until World War II, when the Japanese dealt British power a blow in East Asia from which it never recovered.

The rise of the nonwhite peoples in what had once been a stable British maritime trading world was the background noise to the fall of the British Empire. At times, as in India, independence movements posed direct political threats to British rule. But all the time and everywhere, the rising power and assertiveness of nonwhite peoples, whether colonial subjects or not, increased the burden of Britain's global role. The non-European world was no longer passive and impotent. It was no longer a European balance of power that Britain had to maintain, but a global one. This feat was beyond the capacities of Britain's statesmen; the cost was too high for Britain's economy to bear; and, ultimately, the military resources required to sustain it were beyond Britain's ability to assemble.

This process was still in its early stages in the years before World War I, but the implications for American foreign policy were clearly revolutionary, and the dim shadows of all the responsibilities that Washington assumed later in the century were already visible to the discerning. The Panama Canal would make it possible for the United States to assume a more active role in international politics; the decline of the British Empire would make that role necessary.

If Europe's rivalries were once again to spill out into other continents, the United States would once again have to worry about the rights of neutral shipping, and it would need a navy that could vindicate those rights around the world. Naval considerations were only the beginning of the vast implications of British weakness for the American armed forces. If Britain could no longer provide the security shield that gave the Monroe Doctrine its meaning, the United States would have to make good the deficit. There was more. The hopes of the China trade—and the fears about what it would mean to be shut out of it—imposed immense new military burdens on the United States. The signs of a breakup in the European order were the signs of a new and more difficult era in American foreign policy, and Hamiltonians began to read the foreign news with increasing interest and to embark on a major program of naval rearmament.

The close of the nineteenth century and the opening of the twentieth found the United States involved in an increasingly active global foreign policy under the leadership of self-described Hamiltonians like Teddy

Roosevelt and Henry Cabot Lodge. The war with Spain and the occupation of the Philippines was the most dramatic sign of a newly energetic policy. But the Spanish-American War was not alone. In an act difficult to reconcile with the Monroe Doctrine or any concept of isolation, the United States participated with five European nations in a campaign against the Boxer rebels in China. Under Roosevelt the United States not only helped Russia and Japan negotiate a peace settlement to end their war, it participated in what John Quincy Adams would have called a congress of European powers to settle a dispute between Germany and France over their respective rights in North Africa.

For Hamiltonians, the United States had been irrevocably committed to a global foreign policy throughout its history. The First World War stirred Hamiltonian ideas of intervention and solidarity with Britain that had been prominent under Washington. Hamiltonian opinion favored intervention against France and for England in the 1790s; its views had not changed in 1914. From the moment the British declared war on Germany, Hamiltonian opinion favored intervention on the British side. While Wilson urged strict neutrality, the sons of Hamiltonian bankers and industrialists rushed to France and Canada, not to flee the draft but to volunteer for duty against Germany in such special combat units as the Lafayette Escadrille.

Between the Declaration of Independence and American entry into World War I, 141 years intervened. During much of that time Hamiltonian ideas about foreign policy helped guide the United States. Under Hamiltonian leadership, the United States had defined its interests in global terms, articulated them on the basis of its national interests realistically defined and advanced them through a diplomacy that was neither isolationist, unrealistically idealistic, nor amateurish. No diplomacy is always successful; no nation ever gets everything it wants, and no statesman avoids the occasional blunder. But by any meaningful standard, American foreign policy was extraordinarily successful until World War I, and the intellectual and political foundations laid down in those days still serve us well today.

Atlas Shrugs

The fall of the British Empire was the most important event in international politics in the twentieth century, and in the whole history of American foreign policy. The great international conflicts of the twentieth century—the two world wars and the Cold War—can be grouped together as the wars of the British succession, as Germany, Japan, the Soviet Union, and the United States scrambled to inherit the British mantle.

From this perspective the United States had three great achievements to its credit in the twentieth century: assisting in the dismantling of the decaying fabric of the old empire, seeing off the challenges from Germany, Japan, and the Soviet Union, and building a new international order to support the American system that replaced Great Britain as what Colonel House called "the gyroscope of world order."

During this century of rapid international change and great danger, Hamiltonian ideas informed many of the key decisions the United States made. Accustomed to thinking on a global scale, familiar with the economic and political institutions that undergirded the British Empire, Hamiltonians were quick to grasp the implications for American interests of British decline, and they understood how to build a new hegemony as the old one collapsed.

The dismantling of the British Empire transformed the context in which American foreign policy was made and thought about. Before 1945 the world order was more or less a given, to which American statesmen reacted in various ways. Since then it has been in large part both the creation and the responsibility of American statesmen. On the one hand the United States has had to get along without John Bull's assistance. As a result foreign policy has been more burdensome and dangerous since 1945. On the other hand, America had the opportunity to shape the world in accordance with its own interests and values.

The consequences of the fall of the British Empire for American politics and policy were so profound that they have led many to see an unbridgeable chasm between American foreign policy before and after Britain's fall. This is the reality behind the myth of the American coming of age—that after 1945 American foreign policy makers entered a new world.

But, though obviously true to a certain extent, focusing too exclusively on the differences between the new and old worlds blinds us to the important continuities linking the eras. Furthermore, it ignores the extent to which the dismantling of the British Empire was something that, at least partially, Americans did—and did on purpose. Robert Skidelsky subtitled the third volume of his magnificent biography of John Maynard Keynes *Battling for Britain,* in reference to Keynes's efforts to salvage some remnant of British power from the resolute American efforts to use the opportunity of World War II to destroy it. Skidelsky goes so far as to say that the United States had three principal war aims in World War II: the defeat of Japan, the defeat of Germany, and the defeat of Great Britain. The last is only slightly hyperbolical.

For the Hamiltonians, the fall of the British Empire did not mean a change of ideology. Their approach to the new situation was guided by their old constellation of ideas and values. They were realists in their views of human nature and of the relationships between states, but they were American realists. They instinctively thought in the terms and values of Anglo-American strategic and economic categories. Freedom of the seas, the open door, and an international legal and financial order that permitted the broadest possible global trade in capital and goods would remain Hamiltonian goals even as the British Empire tumbled in ruins.

The optimism that lies at the heart of American realism was clearly revealed by the Hamiltonian approach to the need for a new, United States–based world system. Committed to the view that an economically oriented international system can circumvent the zero-sum problem that condemns purely security-based systems to the endless rounds of dreary war and revisionism prophesied by Continental realists, Hamiltonian policy makers in the United States looked to base their postwar system to an unprecedented degree on the free consent of member nations. With the European empires, even Britain's, visibly crumbling, the Hamiltonians made no effort to replace the Union Jack with the Stars and Stripes above government offices in the developing world. Hamiltonians would favor strong military forces to protect vital American interests, and as the Soviet challenge grew deadlier they helped mobilize American opinion for the long and bitter Cold War. But absent a direct threat from the Soviet Union, Hamiltonians from 1945 on visualized and sought to build a global economic system that rested primarily on the free participation of independent states.

It is such initiatives that confound those who would like to divide American statesmen into realists and idealists, serpents and doves. Operating on their understanding of the nation's commercial and strategic interests, Hamiltonians not only designed but set about implementing a visionary plan for a world order of free states accepting common international law. Germany and Japan would be readmitted to full participation in the global trading order; the newly independent countries of the developing world would assume equal status in it as well.

Those who denounce (or, in the case of Continental realists, admire) Hamiltonians for their presumed hard-nosed, realistic approach to promoting the national interest have misunderstood the synthesis of principles and interests that does so much to define the Hamiltonian mind. Business is the highest form of philanthropy; commerce is the fastest road to world peace. Others may scoff at that view, and attack what they see as the conscious hypocrisy of the Hamiltonian foreign policy establishment. Yet that belief is sincerely held and deeply felt. Whether one agrees with it or not, it is impossible to understand the motives and the actions of Hamiltonian policy makers without understanding the psychological and intellectual influence of this conviction.

Even as Hamiltonians sought to fulfill their traditional goals in the new circumstances that followed the fall of the British Empire, they understood that the new international situation would require bold changes in time-honored American strategies. To adjust to new circumstances, Hamiltonians would change their policy approach in three important ways after World War II. Those adjustments, largely complete by 1950, continue to shape American foreign policy today.

The most important change came in the policy toward Britain. From 1789 to 1941, Hamiltonians generally believed that America's place was at Britain's side. From 1941 to the present, they have believed that Britain's place is at America's. American intervention in World War I was in many ways shaped to support Great Britain's international position. This was as true in finance as it was in politics; once the United States entered the war, the British government received official credit from the United States on very favorable terms. In particular American authorities extended balance-of-payments assistance without requiring the British government to call in privately held dollar-denominated or gold-backed securities from British companies and citizens.

Those terms became even more favorable when Britain first made repayment contingent on receipt of German reparations and then repudiated its war debt outright. While diligent Allied propaganda during World War II trumpeted the disinterested nature of such provisions as Lend-Lease, in reality the United States adopted a far harsher economic approach to British wealth after 1939. This time the British were forced to divest themselves of a substantial portion of their foreign holdings, offering enormous opportunities for American capital to acquire those assets under wartime conditions. Despite the best efforts of Lord Keynes, the United States picked the imperial carcass very clean during the war, so clean that Britain—for more than a century the richest country in the world—had to ration basic foodstuffs and heating supplies into the early 1950s. For more than a decade British citizens were unable to exchange pounds for dollars freely and in unlimited quantities. Thanks in part to American policy, Britain's recovery from victory in World War II was slower and less dramatic than the German and Japanese recoveries from defeat.

The loss of much of two centuries of foreign investment in six years of war was a staggering blow. The fatal blow was the determined American insistence that Britain would have to give up the right to construct an imperial preference system of tariffs after the war. This was the open door with a vengeance; Britain would have the cost of governing its increasingly restless colonies, but it would be unable to derive any benefit from its possessions. Moreover, without a preferential system, it stood no chance of integrating the "white dominions" (Canada, New Zealand, Australia) into a wider Westminster system. All these countries could and did move from the British into the American orbit.

Hamiltonians felt that the United States had ended its years in Britain's shadow. Having learned everything our mother had to teach, it was time to put the old lady on the shelf. The day Hamiltonians had looked forward to since colonial times—when the island empire would yield pride of place to the continent—had arrived. The end—world order—remained the same, but the old means were dispensed with. Henceforward the Americans would build a world order on their own, relegating Britain to the position of sidekick.

The cool deliberation with which the Americans picked the bones of the Empire during the war was a signal illustration of the interplay of serpent and dove. No reptilian brain could have dealt as unsentimentally with an old friend as Franklin Roosevelt and the Treasury Department dealt with Churchill's government. On the other hand, the Americans dismantled the British Empire without fighting a war against it, and in fact while defending it against other, much more brutal enemies. Indeed, the knowledge that American supremacy would be more moral and easier to bear than a German yoke played a major role in the British decision to reject Hitler's peace offers and to throw everything into a struggle to the death. After all, British thinking went, the goal of the Americans was not a German- or Japanese-style empire but a commonwealth of independent states under American hegemony. It was a policy that so neatly combined the values of Machiavelli and Saint Francis that one could scarcely discern the dividing line between the reptile and the bird of peace.

The Hamiltonians' grandfathers had been content to be free riders as long as British hegemony was stable. As the British system began to weaken, their fathers supported it. The Hamiltonians of the middle of the twentieth century replaced it, and as they did so, they made two major changes in longstanding American foreign policy. One change concerned security policy; the other, economics.

In security matters, Hamiltonians became committed to American alliances with foreign countries. This caused no great intellectual or moral problems for Hamiltonians; they had always taken Washington's Farewell Address as pragmatic counsel rather than holy writ. Hamiltonian opinion had in any case always been keenly aware of the tacit alliance with Britain, dating back to 1823, and had understood in both 1914 and 1939 that the tacit alliance had to become overt.

Nor had Hamiltonians opposed a military alliance with Britain and even France after World War I. The story of the interventionist-isolationist controversy has become so confused in historical memory that most Americans have only a very distorted idea of what the fight over the ratification of the Treaty of Versailles was really about. Hamiltonian opinion, embraced by such dedicated opponents of Wilson as Henry Cabot Lodge (a self-described Hamiltonian and author of an admiring biography of the master), was willing to accept the treaty with modifications that satisfied congressional scruples on various points and that, while divesting the League of Nations of the supranational authority that Wilson wanted, would have left it roughly as strong as the United Nations is today. The debate between Lodge and Wilson was not over whether the United States should join the League of Nations but what that league should be like. The third group in that debate, led by Senator Borah, were the genuine isolationists, but they were small in number and, if Wilson and the Hamiltonians could have agreed on a compromise, the United States would have joined the League and ratified the Versailles treaty by a comfortable majority.

After World War II, Hamiltonian opinion would support a worldwide web of security treaties, both collective and bilateral, with the object both of containing the Soviet Union and of replacing the British Empire with a global security structure incorporating the newly independent nations of the former European empires.

The final, and more wrenching, major change concerned trade policy. As a longtime free rider in the British system, American industry had enjoyed a century of domestic protection and global markets by the outbreak of the Second World War. From the 1828 "Tariff of Abominations" (the object of South Carolina's nullificatory wrath) to the McKinley Tariff, raising tariffs to new levels in 1890, and the notorious Smoot-Hawley Tariff of 1930, Hamiltonian economic policy dovetailed with sectional interests to saddle (or, in Lodge's view, to bless) the United States with an elaborate and, on the whole, ever rising system of industrial tariffs. Originally intended to ensure that the United States built a manufacturing economy rather than remaining trapped in the colonial role of providing raw materials for British industry, industrial protection became less important as American industry achieved first technological parity and then in many cases a substantial technological lead. By the end of World War II, when much of the world's industrial plant was bombed out, and American companies had unique and unchallenged access to the only fully functioning capital market in the world, the old system of industrial protection served no general American interest.

In fact protection undermined American interests. Other countries needed to run trade surpluses with the United States to acquire the dollars they needed for food and reconstruction. To rebuild Europe, to keep Japan alive, and generally to build a functioning world order, Hamiltonians had to relinquish one of their oldest and most cherished instruments of policy. They did so with the swiftness of both calculation and action that generally characterizes this school, and from the late 1940s to the present, the Hamiltonians have been the strongest supporters of free trade.

This has been a very brief account of an active and determined party in American life. The heart of the Federalist, Whig, and Republican Parties, Hamiltonian politicians and statesmen, many consciously professing to follow Hamilton's policies and ideas, have done much to shape American foreign policy over the last two centuries. Since the end of the Cold War, Hamiltonian ideas have clearly helped shape security and trade policy, and one may safely assume that the feathered serpent—or the cold-blooded dove—of Hamiltonian calculation will continue to play a major strategic role in formulating American foreign policy long into the future.

Chapter Five

THE
CONNECTICUT
YANKEE IN THE
COURT OF
KING ARTHUR

Wilsonianism and Its Mission

Another Logic

In 1912, senators from states like South Dakota and Iowa found themselves deluged by mail from angry constituents. From one small community after another, the letters carried the same message: Stop the China Railway Loan.

The senators, most of whom had passed their lives in happy ignorance of Chinese railroad financing, sent their assistants to the library shelves to research the issue. With China's finances reeling following years of civil and international war, a group of European governments had helped put together a bond-issue package to bail out China's railroads and support new construction and badly needed repairs.

What mysterious force was responsible for U.S. farm communities and elderly widows knowing about, let alone protesting, this measure? The answer to that question was the missionaries.

Since early in the nineteenth century there had been a substantial worldwide presence of American missionaries. Beginning in 1806 with a handful of Massachusetts seminary students who asked God to guide their lives as they took shelter by a haystack from a sudden thunderstorm, tens of thousands of missionaries proceeded out of the United States to the four corners of the earth, determined to relieve the world's peoples of the burdens of superstition, paganism, feudalism, and ignorance; to combat exploitation of the poor; to promote democracy, public health, and literacy; to reform the world's sexual mores; and to end the oppression of women overseas.

This vast popular movement, stronger than ever today, knew no boundaries of race, sex, or denomination. African American missionaries were among the early colonists in Liberia; within a generation of the abolition of slavery, African American churches in the south as well as the north were supporting a network of missionaries bringing the light of Christ to the home of their ancestors. At a time when women were denied the vote, relegated to secondary roles in religious life, and barred from access to most professional schools, one generation after another of pioneering American women gained medical, theological, and other training to serve all over the world. Women established and led forty-one mission boards, actively sending missionaries abroad. By 1890 women constituted 60 percent of American missionaries serving abroad, and by 1900 there were more than three million women actively participating in denominational societies.[1]

The politicians deluged with mail about the Chinese railway proposal quickly learned what was happening. Sun Yat-sen, a Chinese Christian educated in missionary schools, had just established a republican government in China with strong support from the missionary community. Sun's movement seemed to fulfill the fondest hopes of three generations of American missionaries in China and their millions of American supporters: A Christian Chinese, educated and trained in American spiritual and democratic values, had overthrown China's rotten feudal government and was proceeding to regenerate that vast and ancient land. That is exactly what the missionaries had planned—that is why they labored to convert the Chinese to Christianity; that is why they established and supported thirteen colleges and a medical school in China; that is why for generations they had been helping the best and most promising young Chinese study in the United States. It was the firm purpose of the American missionaries to make China an advanced, Christian, and democratic country, and when Sun Yat-sen took power, those missionaries were convinced that the destined hour was at hand.

With Chinese democracy dawning, the missionary world was outraged that greedy capitalists should take advantage of the temporary difficulties of the new regime to impose onerous conditions on the loan. Now was the time to treat China with generosity, to help this forward-looking democratic regime. American policy certainly could and should lead the way. The missionaries, generally sent out from and supported by small groups of American churches in rural as well as in urban areas, wrote to their friends and supporters denouncing the loan and urging them to protest to Congress. The good church people complied, and the halls of Congress soon echoed to anti–railway loan rhetoric.

In the end the missionaries got their way. U.S. opposition killed the original railway proposal, and a new agreement, more favorable to China, was drawn up.

This is but one example of a second school at work in the American foreign policy process, a school that often favors what some misleadingly call an "idealist" foreign policy. For convenience we can call this school Wilsonian, but the label should not blind us. Wilsonians were actively shaping American foreign policy long before Wilson moved to Washington, and the ideas that underlie this Wilsonian school are more deeply rooted in the national character and more directly related to the national interest than might appear at first glance.

While Wilsonianism has unique characteristics drawn from American culture and history, the phenomenon of a great power linking its destiny to the spread of a particular ideology is not unique to the United States. Athens and Sparta looked for allies, respectively, among the democratic and aristocratic parties of the Greek city-states of their era. The spread of Hellenic civilization was an object of policy for Alexander the Great and his successors; the Christian emperors of Rome and Byzantium and the Muslim caliphs of Damascus and Baghdad believed that faith could, would, and should follow the flag, so to speak.

As the Cross and the Crescent slugged it out in the Near and Middle East, the powers of Western Europe also consciously sought—and generally found—ideological rationales for their political ambitions. England, Holland, Sweden, and the Lutheran princes of Germany were Protestant powers; the Hapsburg dominions were proudly Catholic. The cynical power politics of eighteenth-century Europe, in which "enlightened" despots agreed on all major philosophical and religious questions, disputing only the possession of various pieces of turf, was an exception to the general rule that the wars of great powers have spiritual or at least ideological importance. The French Revolution put an end to that unnatural state, and from the war of the First Coalition against the French Revolution to the present day, competition among powers has usually been linked to a competition among ideas.

The particular set of ideas with which the United States has been most closely associated, and the cultural stratum from which they chiefly proceed, is closely linked to those that informed our predecessor at the apex of world power. In the nineteenth century, indeed, British commentators often remarked on the instructive difference between the selfless altruism of British Liberal foreign policy and the gratingly self-seeking activities of their Yankee cousins. The twists and turns of the "nonconformist conscience" of Liberal Britain—so named because of its roots among the heirs of the Puritans and Dissenters of British history—were by turns sources of amusement and frustration for continental statesmen. British Liberals fought against the pragmatic tilt toward the Ottoman Empire that British imperial interests seemed to require, arguing that Ottoman atrocities in the Balkans demanded what we would now call a "human rights" response from the world's hegemonic power. It was the British who abolished slavery and put the British navy to work suppressing the slave trade in Africa and the surrounding seas; British Liberals defied American opinion and risked an international crisis rather than return fugitive slaves who reached British soil. It was Britain whose emissaries trekked the wilds of Africa and sent punitive expeditions to put down the slave trade; Britons summoned the powers of Europe to squelch ethnic conflict and terrorism in the Balkans, suppressed the thuggee cult of ritual murder in India, and ended the practice of suttee, in which high-caste Hindu widows were expected to commit suicide by leaping onto their husband's funeral pyres.

British Liberal opinion continued to support what, in an American context, we would call Wilsonian policies up through the fall of the British Empire and into modern times. When Wilson tried to impose a Wilsonian peace at the end of World War I, his strongest foreign allies were found in the British Liberal Party, and the most savage attacks on the shortcomings of the Versailles treaty were penned by John Maynard Keynes, the towering intellect of British Liberal thought in the twentieth century.

Disgruntled Conservatives, overlooking the worldwide rise in con-

ABE LINCOLN'S LAST CARD; OR, ROUGE-ET-NOIR

The shared heritage of the "nonconformist conscience" in the U.S. and
Britain has not always brought the two countries closer together. As
this 1862 *Punch* magazine cartoon by Sir John Tenniel (the most
famous British political cartoonist of his time, chiefly remembered
today as the illustrator of Lewis Carroll's *Alice in Wonderland*) reminds
us, many idealistic Britons sympathized with the Confederacy, believing that Southern whites should have the right of self-determination.
The Emancipation Proclamation is shown here as the last, desperate
throw of a losing gambler (playing against Jefferson Davis).
Sir John Tenniel. Library of Congress, Prints and Photographs Division, LC-USZ62-1973

sciousness and nationalism among the Empire's third world subjects, and
ignoring the impact of the rise of other industrial powers on Britain's
relative economic and military power, went so far as to blame Liberal
wimpishness for the fall of the Empire. Churchill, for one, was convinced
that a show of determination would have crushed Gandhi's movement
and cemented Britain's hold over the Indian subcontinent.

The Empire is gone, but the British Liberal conscience is still on display today. Prime Minister Tony Blair was the sole strong and unconditional advocate of the use of ground troops in the 1999 war between
Yugoslavia and NATO. More broadly the new Labour government he has

built is an attempt to reconstruct the old Liberal party and tradition on the ruins of British socialism, and should Blair's movement succeed we can look to a revived and invigorated British Liberal voice calling for "idealistic" policies on every subject from Third World debt relief to minority rights. True to their traditions, Blair's New Labour liberals sought to ban foxhunting but declared an open season on human rights violators, holding Chile's former dictator, General Pinochet. Under house arrest for seventeen months in Britain, Pinochet was released on March 2, 2000, after the UK decided on grounds of the General's poor health not to extradite him.

The nonconformist conscience migrated into other former British colonies besides the United States. In a 1966 essay, "Canada: 'Stern Daughter of the Voice of God,' " former secretary of state Dean Acheson chided Canadian statesmen for what he called a "moralistic" rather than a "moral" foreign policy: a policy that, in his view, could be said to value omelets too cheaply and eggs too high. No one familiar with political debates in Australia and New Zealand will miss the common note of nonconformist moralizing; it was also heard among the English-speaking whites in South Africa who opposed apartheid.

Far from being uniquely American, or uniquely confined to the twentieth century, the prevalence of this common streak—morality, say its friends; moralism, say its critics—in the offshoots of the British Empire is one of the chief marks by which other countries define what they somewhat anachronistically continue to call a common "Anglo-Saxon" tradition of statesmanship. Europeans, Indians, Chinese, Africans, and Latin Americans have also noticed something about this tradition that tends to escape notice in the "Anglo-Saxon" world: that the espousal of these high ideals has not prevented the successive rise of two English-speaking empires to global hegemony. The Anglo-Saxon conscience may be sensitive and easily excited, they say, yet it is also flexible, and generally manages to concentrate its outrage on those aspects of the world's evils that threaten to thwart some interesting project of an Anglo-Saxon state.

The Anglo-Saxons may be as innocent as doves, note our neighbors and critics, but that has singularly not interfered with our ability to be as cunning as serpents.

Our concern here is not with the nonconformist conscience across the "Anglo-Saxon" world, or with its more distant cousins found throughout the Protestant, Germanic-language-speaking peoples of northern Europe, but with its specific history and meaning in the United States. Rooted originally in the separatist piety of Puritan New England, and nurtured in the long, cool afterglow of Yankee Calvinism in decline, the Wilsonian subculture has exercised a continuous and powerful influence inside and outside government from the eighteenth century onward. Despite its long historical record in the United States and abroad, this streak of the national character continues to make both foreign and American analysts uncomfortable. The Hamiltonian school of foreign policy is a well-known, comfortable presence in international relations. It is familiar, if often misunderstood. Much more problematic from the standpoint of conventional diplomacy is the Wilsonian streak in the national character: a view that insists that the United States has the right and the duty to change the rest of the world's behavior, and that the United States can and should concern itself not only with the way other countries conduct their international affairs, but with their domestic policies as well.

The venom and ridicule that realists in Britain and elsewhere have poured and continue to pour on the Wilsonian approach to foreign policy is both startling and strange. Ever since the first Washington administration, when, especially before the Reign of Terror, a substantial force in American politics believed that the duty and interest of the United States required it to join revolutionary France in a general war against the monarchical states, the Wilsonian impulse has been treated with the kind of hostility with which Ahab and Jezebel greeted the sermons of Elijah, or with which Herodias heard the preaching of John the Baptist.

Indeed, it was Wilson's head on a platter that Sigmund Freud sought to serve up when, with American diplomat William C. Bullitt, he penned the most venomous portrait extant in psychoanalytic literature, a "psychobiography" of Wilson. Henry Kissinger's warnings against moralism in American foreign policy are a recent and relatively mild example of this genre. Even so thoughtful and generous a historian as the Pulitzer Prize–winning Walter McDonough has singled out the "global meliorist" Wilsonian tradition as an illegitimate interloper in the otherwise stately procession of American foreign policy.

And yet, as with so many biblical prophets, the sons build a tomb for the visionaries their fathers had killed. We have already noted that Europe has come to accept the prophet that it scorned, and that every European state west of the old Soviet Union now conducts its policy along recognizably Wilsonian lines. Ronald Reagan, who came to office preaching a realist gospel and denouncing the liberal wimpery of the Carter foreign policy, made the international support of human rights a cornerstone of his own administration. Even the archrealist Kissinger himself now takes pride in the Helsinki Accords, which realists once dismissed or condemned.

The Missionary Tradition

From the end of the Cold War to the end of the Clinton administration, Wilsonianism battled with Hamiltonianism to be the dominant force in American foreign policy. Much of the contemporary fighting over foreign policy—as, for example, with respect to China—reflects a conflict between the Hamiltonian quest to build a global commercial order and the Wilsonian view that that order must also be based on principles of democratic government and the protection of human rights. And just as contemporary Hamiltonian politics emerge from a long historical development, so too the forces seeking to give a Wilsonian shape to American foreign policy today have deep roots in American history, and have developed their ideas through many generations of experience and reflection.

When most students of foreign policy, whether American or foreign, think about American idealism in action, they think about acts of statecraft by politicians. They think of Wilson at Versailles or Bill Clinton sending marines to Haiti. But just as the story of American commercial relations with the rest of the world is only in part, and indeed in very small part, the story of governments interacting with other governments, so *a fortiori* is the story of Wilsonianism a story of popular action. Wilsonianism represents to a large degree part of a consistent and centuries-old foreign policy of the American people, something related to, and both influenced by and influencing, the foreign policy of the American government, but still something to be understood on its own terms and in its own way.

The story of American missionary activity—a story by no means confined to the actions of religious missionaries of any or even of all denominations, but encompassing the work of countless Americans in religious work, medical work, relief work, and political activism of various kinds throughout the world—is part of the "lost history" of American foreign policy. It has played a much larger role in the relationship of the United

States to the world, in that of the world to the United States, and in the growing sense of a world community than is generally recognized. Yet the missionary endeavor, one of the greatest and most sustained efforts ever made by large numbers of the American people in any field, and one with vast consequences for this century, is in intellectual eclipse. Feminist historians are mining its rich ores for the sake of uncovering the role women played in this venture. Some African American historians, likewise, are looking into the ways in which grassroots African American church communities were able to plan and sustain an international program even before the abolition of slavery. There have been strong surveys of missionary activity in particular countries such as a 1974 study of Chinese missions edited by John K. Fairbanks. Daniel J. Boorstin's *The Democratic Experience* recognizes the centrality of the missionary experience for understanding the American engagement with the world. But in general, mission history has lost the importance it once had in the field—when, for example, the great historian of American missions, Kenneth Scott Latourette, served as president of the American Historical Association in 1948.

An eclipse this dark of a subject this important requires explanation, and there are several reasons why so few contemporary historians turn their attention to this vital subject. The general indifference to nineteenth-century American foreign policy plays a role. Eurocentric historians ignore mission history because it deals primarily with events in what are now developing countries. Elite-oriented historians of foreign policy pass over what was always primarily a grassroots movement. Historians sympathetic to the aspirations of the developing world find the subject inherently distasteful: From a certain angle missions appear as a particularly odious variety of cultural imperialism, one with close links to political and economic imperialism. Additionally, until very recently many mainstream postwar American historians have largely discounted the importance of religious matters in American history. Partly for methodological reasons and partly for cultural and ideological ones, those historians have concentrated on secular topics. Missionary history—complex, crossing denominational and geographical boundaries, with its original documents often scattered in obscure denominational archives—has been even more seriously neglected. Furthermore, the missionary enterprise is distinctly unfashionable in the multicultural world of the contemporary campus. The contemplation of a prolonged American attempt to export Christian values and beliefs to the developing world was inherently distasteful to the fin-de-siècle liberal mind. Exporting values to unenlightened parts of the world—Africa, Alabama, China—remains a central concern of American liberals today, but it makes people uncomfortable to see the same dogmatic certainties and missionary impulses that were prevalent among their grandparents used to spread such different values and beliefs. At some point the contemplation of such historical disparities might lead one to question the comfortable ethical and political certainties of enlightened opinion today—and this is not an enterprise to be recommended to young academics with careers to build.

Conservative Christian scholars who might be expected to celebrate and therefore study mission history also have problems with the subject. Although the denominations that still maintain active missionary programs do study "missiology," their interest lies in training future missionaries and developing more successful ways to preach the Gospel. Real mission history poses problems for evangelicals and other conservative Christians. The modern ecumenical movement, like many of the pioneering figures of liberal theology, emerged from the missionary world. A dispassionate study of the American missionary record would probably conclude that the multicultural and relativistic thinking so characteristic of the United States today owes much of its social power to the unexpected consequences of American missions abroad.

If a full account of the American missionary movement is beyond us here, even a quick sketch will suffice to indicate its central importance in the development of American foreign policy and of the subcultures that shape and sustain it. After the famous 1806 Haystack Prayer Meeting outside Williams College, in which a group of students vowed to dedicate their lives to foreign missions, a small trickle—soon to become a mighty flood—of missionaries left the United States for service abroad. Adoniram Judson and his wife stopped briefly in India before reaching Burma (now Myanmar). By 1819, Mrs. Judson found that, while the women of Burma showed distressingly little interest in the Gospel of Christ, they were extremely eager to learn to read and to sew, and that both they and their menfolk were desperate for information about the wider world.[2]

As the extraordinary religious revivals known as the Second and Third Great Awakenings of the early nineteenth century deepened the element of religious fervor in American culture, the number of young people seeking careers in foreign missions grew rapidly. But since every denomination kept its own records in its own way, and some of the most missionary-minded denominations (like the Baptists) eschewed the kinds of hierarchical organization beyond the congregational level that promotes record-keeping, good estimates of the number of missionaries and mission-related personnel are hard to make. One listing counts about five thousand American Protestant missionaries abroad in 1900, with the number increasing to more than nine thousand by 1915.[3]

These numbers are surely incomplete. They are restricted to full-time religious workers and do not count the instructors serving in missionary schools and colleges abroad, medical personnel, or agricultural and other technical specialists supplementing mission efforts. The wives of male missionaries also generally worked in medical, educational, and religious endeavors but were not always counted as mission workers. In addition, a significant number of American missionaries came from outside the ranks of Protestant churches. Such indigenous American religious movements as the Seventh-Day Adventists and the Latter-day Saints have long had an active presence in international missions.

The number of Protestant mission workers would increase throughout the twentieth century, reaching approximately fifty-two thousand missionaries by the end of the 1970s. Catholic, Pentecostal, Adventist, and Latter-day Saints missionaries would increase even more rapidly during the twentieth century; by the start of the twenty-first it appears that something on the order of one hundred thousand Americans were serving religious missions abroad.[4] Fourteen thousand Utah residents were estimated to have been omitted by the 2000 Census because they were serving tours of duty as missionaries abroad—a number large enough to cost Utah an additional seat in the House of Representatives.

If we add to these numbers other Americans involved in secular service overseas—working with nongovernmental organizations dealing with refugees, development, medical services, and such agencies as the Peace Corps—we see that the fire kindled at the Haystack Meeting has spread to all the corners of the world, and that the effort to spread what Americans in each generation have identified as the key features of the American way of life to the rest of the world is a powerful, long-established, and growing force in our society.

The larger mission boards functioned in some ways as the first multinational corporations in American history. Receiving contributions in dollars, they dispensed funds all over the world. They employed local inhabitants, established networks of schools and colleges, ran demonstration farms, and set up printing presses—sometimes in alphabets designed by the missionaries for previously analphabetic cultures. By 2000 one missionary organization, the Wycliffe Bible Translators, had translated at least part of the scriptures into 1,571 languages.[5] By 2001, the United Bible Societies had published copies of the scriptures in 2,261 different languages and dialects;[6] the Gideons—known to most Americans as the source of the Bibles found in hotel and motel rooms across the country—had distributed, gratis, nearly one billion copies of at least the New Testament in eighty languages and 175 countries around the world.[7]

The missionary presses published Bibles and other inspirational literature; they also published scientific, medical, agricultural, and historical works, often giving local inhabitants their first systematic exposure to the ideas and the background of the Western world. The digests of political, historical, cultural, and economic information that were prepared by missionaries and compiled by mission boards, into what sometimes evolved into annual or biannual publications, were the most comprehensive collections of information on the non-Western world that the nineteenth-century public could find. Diplomats moving to a new posting and businessmen seeking new markets turned to the missionary world as their best source of information. Dictionaries and grammars prepared by missionaries were often the best or the only sources available for language study.

It would be a mistake, however, to think of the missionaries as nothing more than psalm-singing fishers of souls. From the early days, when Ann Hasseltine Judson found herself introducing literacy to the women of Burma and Reverend Judson was teaching Western technologies to Burmese men, the missionary movement has done much more than build churches and sing hymns. Indeed, much of what we now regard as left-wing secular idealism has its roots in the missions, just as such schools as Harvard, Princeton, and Yale began as religious colleges before evolving into the secular universities we know today.

The transition from full-time religious missionary to doctor, nurse, or agronomist was easy to make. The missionaries inevitably found themselves dealing with a wide range of problems in the countries to which they moved. Very early on, missionaries found that, in order for them to be effective, they had to do more than preach the Gospel. Foreign languages had to be learned, and in some cases alphabets developed for them, so that the Scriptures could be read in the new language. But the problems were greater: How to attract the heathen to the church? The obvious answers sprang to mind, especially because they were hallowed by Christ's own instructions: Feed the hungry, educate the children, treat the sick.

Religious missionaries, however zealous for souls, could not be blind to the other needs of those among whom they lived. Ignorance, lack of sanitation, the oppression of women, disease—these also had to be dealt with, partly as evils in and of themselves that the missionaries felt obliged to combat, and partly because opposition to them would draw souls to Christ's message.

And very quickly the missionaries' task grew more complex. Social injustice was the greatest evil found in many parts of the earth. Feudal bondage systems offended the missionary heart as much as Arthurian England's feudalism offended Twain's Connecticut Yankee. How could a Christian brother or sister stand silent in the face of such injustice, especially when, as in Korea, the feudal nobility were the fiercest foes of Christianity and used their power to keep the humble poor from attending church?

And then there was the problem of the nonmissionary presence of the West. Unscrupulous traders, lascivious sailors, and rapacious imperialists were constant sources of danger to the peoples of the non-Western world. Great civilizations and empires like the Ottoman Empire and China were hard pressed to cope. Many tribal peoples were utterly overwhelmed; some would not survive the nineteenth century, and others would lose touch with their own cultures without finding a way to approach the new cultures and technology of the West. Missionaries, who often saw themselves as the allies of the non-Western peoples among whom they lived, had complex relationships with all these forces. Thus missionaries generally opposed the opium trade in China and certain aspects of Western economic imperialism, but welcomed the presence of Western troops when their lives and property were endangered. Individual missionaries, of course, had outlooks ranging from wholehearted support for business to suspicion of any endeavors that diverted the attention of their flocks from the Cross. In virtually all cases, however, missionaries saw themselves as filling an intermediary role—attempting to protect their congregations from the depredations of unscrupulous Westerners, while also serving as avenues through which Western values, ideas, and techniques could penetrate local cultures.

American missionaries played an important role in stabilizing and policing the behavior of American businessmen and others overseas. Women serving as independent professionals or wives of accredited missionaries were often the only women of European stock in a particular city or area; they set a social and moral tone for respectable expatriates, while the missionary community generally considered itself responsible for the care of the souls of Americans overseas. American merchants, who of course often saw no contradiction between their economic activities and their spiritual values, were included in church and missionary activities. Missionaries played a role in the spread of such institutions as Rotary International and the YMCA.

Improved educational opportunity often struck the missionaries as an important weapon. Offering education to bright young people would give missionaries an opportunity to mold the impressionable minds of a new generation of leaders and would win them the goodwill of the parents. Education would expose the young people to the nineteenth-century synthesis of faith, science, morality, and political economy that the missionaries themselves believed to be the last word in human affairs. The development of education became one of the hallmarks of American Christian missions. Even today, some of the most famous and prestigious institutions of learning in the Middle East are missionary foundations, including Robert College in Turkey and the American University of Beirut. Before 1949 the American missionary network in China supported many of that country's strongest and most outward-looking universities, as well as a large program promoting Chinese study in the United States. The missionary colleges and universities recruited scholars from the United States in many fields besides religious studies, and many of these campuses became the nurseries of the political movements that would shape the struggle of the non-Western world for political and cultural independence in the twentieth and twenty-first centuries.

The missionary movement played a major role in the development of international civil society. It can be difficult for Americans today, used to the bitter alienation that now exists between organizations like the National Organization for Women (NOW), for example, and much of the conservative Catholic and evangelical communities, to appreciate the close historical link between many of today's secular civil society organizations and the missionary movement. There was a time when the supple hands of a Woodrow Wilson could thump together the two tubs that more recently have been thumped separately by Pat Robertson and Hillary Clinton. In those days an aggressively proselytizing and self-confident Protestantism was the home and natural ally of the feminist, prohibitionist, peace, and antitobacco movements. Some glimpse of that earlier era can still be seen in the way that right- and left-wing groups attack such countries as China for a poor human rights record, and for the way the wars on smoking and drugs bring diverse communities together in a coalition not altogether dissimilar from the large social movement for Prohibition.

The very concept of a global civil society comes to us out of the missionary movement; apart from a handful of isolated intellectuals, no one before the missionaries ever thought that the world's cultures and societies had or could have enough in common to make a common global society feasible or desirable. Certainly before the missionaries no large group of people set out to build just such a world. The concept that "backward" countries could and should develop into Western-style industrial democracies grew up among missionaries, and missionary relief and development organizations like World Vision and Catholic Relief Services remain at the forefront of development efforts. The idea that governments in the Western world had a positive duty to support the development of poor countries through financial aid and other forms of assistance similarly comes out of the missionary world. Most contemporary international organizations that provide relief from natural disasters, shelter refugees, train medical practitioners for poor countries, or perform other important services on an international basis can trace their origin either to missionary organizations or to the missionary milieu.

The missionary movement indeed deserves far more credit for promoting the idea of a global human community than it often receives. At a time when advanced opinion in the western world was increasingly susceptible to theories of eugenics, "scientific racism" and social Darwinism, missionaries, sometimes acting on the basis of a literal reading of Genesis, stoutly maintained that human beings of all races and nations were descended from common ancestors, shared a common and universal heritage, and were all possessed of equal and inalienable rights.

In any case we can see that in the secular as well as in the religious branches of the missionary movement there has been a concerted, two-centuries-old attempt by an important segment of the American people to transform the world and to bring about a social, economic, medical, and religious revolution. This group has believed that it is the responsibility of their government to support this effort, and while they have never fully succeeded in converting the U.S. government into an entirely eleemosynary organization, they have had and continue to have a substantial amount of success in influencing and shaping the foreign policy of the United States.

Those who saw an American duty to remake the world in its image spent the nineteenth century seeking action from the United States government on three different levels. On the first level came the demand for an active role by the American government in giving American missionaries the right of entry into other countries, providing them with legal protection once there, protecting their property, and, ultimately, as converts were made, protecting the Christian minority against private pogroms or government discrimination and/or persecution.

At this level the missionaries enjoyed a substantial degree of success. Arguing that the American citizen spreading the word of God deserved at least the same degree of support from his home government that an American merchant shipping opium could expect, missionaries rapidly established the principle that the United States government would use its good offices wherever possible in the interest of missionary endeavors. Early treaties with China, Japan, Siam (now Thailand) and the Ottoman Empire gave American missionaries the right to take up residence, hold property, and proselytize without persecution. Missionaries, like other foreigners, sought and usually received extraterritorial status in non-European countries. Exempt from the laws of the land in which they lived, they were subject only to the jurisdiction of their own country's officials.

As the missionary movement grew, and grew more successful, missionaries and their allies moved to a second level of political activism. It became increasingly important to protect the lives, property, and other interests of American missionaries, and the effort to do so consumed more of the energy and time of the American diplomatic community. The breakdown of order, and the subsequent destruction of missionary property in countries like China, involved the United States government in forceful negotiations to obtain compensation. The threat to missionary and Chinese convert lives at the time of the Boxer Rebellion helped build the American domestic consensus for participation in the five-nation force that marched to the relief of the foreign contingent in Beijing. Afterward, however, missionary opinion led the United States to dissociate itself from the extortionate demands for compensation that the European governments made to the defeated Chinese. Perhaps the missionaries' most dramatic success in persuading the U.S. government to make the protection of missionary property a chief diplomatic goal came in 1917, when they persuaded Wilson not to declare war on the Ottoman Empire, an ally of Germany in World War I. To declare war, they told the White House, would mean the closure of the enormous missionary-owned educational system and possibly the confiscation of property. It would certainly have left the Christian minorities of that empire without any international protection at a time of bloody communal violence.

Wilson agreed. The United States never declared war on the Ottomans, and the missionaries kept their schools.

On the third and highest level of activity, missionaries sought to persuade the U.S. government to use its influence to promote what would now be called a human rights agenda in the developing world. In some countries, even the very modestly sized native Christian communities that appeared in the nineteenth century alarmed local authorities and traditional religious communities. The introduction of Western-style printing presses and the development of increased written literature on sensitive political, cultural, and economic subjects further troubled the officials of some countries. Attempts to suppress the new Christian congregations—in Korea, in the Ottoman Empire, in China—met with stiff diplomatic resistance from the United States, and it was under the auspices of the missionary movement that American diplomats began to make a regular practice of negotiating with foreign governments to reduce human rights violations.

The formation of Western-style colleges and universities, with American norms of free academic discourse, was also an issue of concern, as was access by women students to educational opportunity. On the island now known as Sri Lanka, missionaries had to overcome local beliefs that it was "disgraceful" for young women to learn to read or to be seen in schools. Unwanted girl children adopted by compassionate missionaries were in some cases the only young women allowed to participate in educational programs.[8]

Missionaries also sought to shape American policy toward individual countries to promote their chances for peaceful, independent modernization. Wilsonians sought to control American policy toward countries like China, Siam, Hawaii, and the Ottoman Empire, not merely to protect their property but also to improve the chances that these and other countries would develop in what Wilsonians considered to be promising directions. The results were sometimes very mixed, but the intent was always clear: The missionaries and their friends believed that American foreign policy should support the social and political objectives of the missionary movement.

One conspicuous example of missionaries playing a major, and controversial, role was in shaping American policy toward the then Kingdom of Hawaii. The archipelago's location had always made it a matter of concern to the United States government; possession of Pearl Harbor was in many ways the key to the control of the most important sea lanes of the Pacific. Denial of Hawaii to other countries was essential to keeping the west coast of the United States secure against attack. As American missionaries and their converts became increasingly influential, the U.S. government was increasingly lobbied—usually with substantial if not total success—to support missionary-backed "reforms" aimed at weakening the institution of the traditional monarchy and making Hawaii more of a democracy. That these reforms accelerated the decline of traditional Hawaiian society and made the country more vulnerable to American annexation did not trouble the missionaries unduly; then as now, Wilsonians do not grow excessively sentimental about "cultural differences" when those are used to legitimate nondemocratic forms of government.

The first treaties between the United States government and both China and Siam were largely the work of missionaries, and missionaries were valued advisers to the Siamese government during its long and ultimately successful attempts to fend off European imperialists.

Missionaries and their allies also exerted considerable influence over both public opinion and American foreign policy with respect both to great powers like Russia and Japan and to much of what, in the twentieth century, would become known as the third world. An open letter to Belgium's odious King Leopold II written by George Washington Williams, a well-respected African American foreign correspondent with strong links to the missionary community, helped fan the worldwide storm of outrage against the brutality taking place in the Congo Free State. Williams was attacked by a Belgian newspaper as "an unbalanced negro," but his writings helped force Leopold to give up his personal control over the Congo Free State.[9] In explaining his decision to annex the Philippines, President McKinley relied on missionary rather than mercantile logic when he told the American people that they had an obligation to "Christianize" the (Catholic) Filipinos.[10] Japan's concessions to the missionaries, allowing them to operate schools and preach freely in Korea, helped reconcile American opinion to Japan's brutal occupation of that country, while it was missionary accounts of Japan's brutality in China that decisively turned American opinion against Japanese expansion in Asia, setting the stage for the Pacific phase of World War II. After the war General MacArthur's reconstruction of Japan was essentially an implementation of the missionary program at the point of bayonets. The traditional ruler gave up his claim to divinity; freedom of religion was established; feudalism was abolished and land distributed to the peasants; women were emancipated; a Western, democratic system of government was introduced; freedom of the press was granted; trade unions were legalized, and war was outlawed. Without the long missionary experience Americans would have had neither the chutzpah or the know-how that characterized the occupation in Japan, a foreign policy venture that despite all the attendant controversy is generally considered one of the most important and successful initiatives in American history.

Although the American Jewish community did not share the proselytizing zeal of its Christian neighbors, American Jews engaged in a substantial program of overseas relief and aid for Jews abroad and, often in association with Christian missionaries and philanthropists, began to exert influence in nineteenth-century American politics to ensure that the United States placed its diplomatic weight behind efforts to protect Jewish communities abroad from persecution. Shortly after the Civil War, when the newly independent Romanians began to celebrate their independence from Ottoman oppression by persecuting Romanian Jews, the Hayes administration sent an American Jew, Eugene Schuyler, to serve as consul in Romania with special instructions to support Romanian Jews. American diplomats also regularly protested the mistreatment of Russian Jews. American revulsion at Russian anti-Semitism and absolute rule was one of the powerful arguments advanced against U.S. intervention on the side of the Allies in World War I; as it happened, the United States entered the war only after the February revolution forced Nicholas II's abdication and an end to the feudal tsarist regime.

Beyond the influence they exercised on American policy toward particular countries, the missionary community and their friends, supporters, and others who shared their values back in the United States also sought to develop broad concepts for American foreign policy in general: a grand strategic vision for the exercise of American power. As the British Empire declined and the United States moved toward replacing the British world order with one of its own, the missionary or Wilsonian vision had enormous impact in shaping the architecture of American hegemony. We will return to an analysis of this strategic vision and its impact on the construction of the United States–led world order, but we need first to round out the picture of nineteenth-century Wilsonianism by examining the impact that the missionary movement and the assorted philanthropical, spiritual, and political movements associated with it had on the United States and the world.

How the Missionaries Changed the World

Although the missionaries exerted a considerable influence over government policy, their major impact was outside government: the creation of institutions, relationships, and cultural and social realities in the United States and foreign civil society, along with other changes that resulted from missionary activity.

In many ways, the missionary movement has had more impact inside the United States than beyond its frontiers. First, through most of American history, missionaries and their offspring have served as a gateway between the mass of the American people and people abroad. While traders, travelers, government officials, sailors, journalists, consultants (like the ex-Confederate generals who advised the Egyptian government on military modernization after the Civil War), and government officials have long maintained a significant American presence around the world, missionaries and mission-related personnel were, for much of our history, the chief bridge between Americans and the non-European countries in which the majority of the world's population lives.

In particular the missionaries built personal connections between ordinary people in the United States and abroad. Although the exact structure varied from denomination to denomination, and although mission-related schools and colleges were structured differently from direct missions, the entire missionary endeavor rested on voluntary support and contributions by grassroots Americans. Missionaries were sent out by a local congregation or by a group of congregations in the same geographic area, and the personnel were often young women or men who had grown up in the communities that now undertook their support. Missionaries corresponded regularly with their home congregations and periodically returned on leave to visit friends and family and to renew their supporters' enthusiasm and commitment. Millions of Americans who never visited a foreign country in their lives felt intimately connected to a women's literacy program in China, a secondary school in Armenia, a Bible college in the Balkans, or simply a local congregation building a church in Polynesia. Some missionary accounts became bestselling books, combining exotic details of foreign cultures with inspiring narratives of faith. Visits by local missionaries or nationally well-known mission figures were high points in the local year.

The mission movement was an early point of entry for women, African Americans, and Catholics into direct contact and experience in foreign affairs. Because professional education was open to women who were accredited to foreign missionary boards, many of the brightest and most ambitious women of the post–Civil War generations made their careers overseas. To some degree the mission movement was the lever that cracked open the doors of professional education to women; it was manifestly absurd to admit female students to professional schools only on condition that they leave the country immediately on graduation.

Missions were also egalitarian and democratic in that they brought Americans into direct contact with the external world regardless of geography and class. Poor rural communities supported foreign missions and received letters and visits from abroad; as politicians discovered when their mailboxes filled with protests over the Chinese railway loan, many American citizens who were not part of the foreign policy or economic elite of their day cared very deeply about events overseas.

Another important domestic consequence of the missionary movement was the internationalization of the American university. The idea of the college as a mission field goes back at least to Rev. Eleazar Wheelock's 1769 foundation of Dartmouth for the education of Indians along Christian principles; but by the middle of the nineteenth century, missionaries were regularly sending promising young people from abroad back to the United States for a college education. For many American students, the mission students were the first foreigners they met. Over the years, that they met under circumstances of equality in which all the power and prestige of the local religious and educational establishment supported courteous and friendly treatment of the foreigner had a major impact on many thousands of college students. In some cases mission students were the only members of non-European racial groups permitted to attend colleges.

The first Chinese student admitted to higher education in the United States was Yung Wing, enrolled at Yale in 1850.[11] By 1999 an estimated thirty-one thousand students from mainland China and Taiwan were enrolled in higher education in the United States.[12] The effects on American and Chinese history of this long and growing exchange have already been dramatic, and promise to reverberate and develop through many years to come.

This was only one of many ways in which the missionary movement contributed to the slow erosion of popular American prejudices and hatreds. The cause of interracial adoptions, for example, was enthusiastically supported by Nobel Prize–winning novelist (and missionary daughter) Pearl S. Buck. Having grown up in China among the Chinese, she simply did not share the racial prejudices that so distorted American life in her time. During the Korean War she joined the missionary community in urging Americans of European descent to adopt Korean war orphans—only a generation after laws were passed banning "Oriental" immigration into the United States, and a decade after many Japanese Americans were forced into internment camps for the duration of World War II.

Buck was by no means alone. Missionaries may have gone out to the field with prejudices of various kinds, which some of them may never have dropped, but for many the mission experience utterly changed their view of the world. As local churches developed in mission countries, missionaries increasingly had to learn to work first with and then under local church authority. With a handful of exceptions, most missionary salaries were too low to allow the missionaries to live in the remote splendor of the businessmen and government officials who went out from the West to govern Africa and Asia during the colonial eras. Their friends, neighbors, and professional associates were increasingly drawn from the countries where they lived; their children's playmates were "natives," and, through their ties to the alumni of mission colleges, their friends included leaders in the emerging nationalist movements of the colonial world. Patronizing and prejudiced as many missionaries undoubtedly were, the mission field was the first place in which large numbers of well-educated Americans learned to work as equals with people from other cultural backgrounds, and just as the mission boards had been among the first multinational corporations in American history, so too were they the first American organizations that systematically moved to place locals in positions of leadership.

That the United States was prepared for world leadership after World

War II is largely a result of the missionary movement. Missionary kids, fluent from childhood in foreign languages and at home in foreign cultures, were invaluable assets for American forces during the war, and after it for occupation and diplomatic missions and as key staffers in the vast international expansion of American business. According to one recent survey, roughly 50 percent of "foreign culture experts" during World War II were missionary offspring.[13] This was particularly crucial at a time when the European empires were collapsing across the third world, which is precisely where the American missions were located.

The process by which the "backwash" from a missionary movement changes the home culture is still under way today. Catholic missions and missionary orders in Central and Latin America have done much to sensitize American society to the values and concerns of those societies. The energetic and phenomenally successful mission work of the Latter-day Saints has made Utah one of the most cosmopolitan states in the Union. This geographically isolated state is increasingly involved in trade and other international relationships, thanks to the exchanges and contacts brought about by the Mormon missionary effort. With young Mormons expected to serve two years in the mission field, and with many foreign converts coming to Salt Lake City to study in its hallowed halls and sacred cloisters, Utah is surprisingly rich in dynamic young people who are fluent in a foreign language—and who have friends and connections abroad. The June 9, 1978, decision by Mormon spiritual authorities to admit black men to the full Mormon priesthood clearly reflected missionary experience, and it parallels the steps by which many other American church communities have moved beyond the racism embedded in popular culture.

Finally the presence of American and other Western missionaries abroad inspired a "missionary reflux," accelerating the penetration of American society by non-Western and Islamic religious ideas. Missionary endeavors to translate the sacred writings of other faiths into English may have been for purposes of arming Westerners for religious controversy with the heathens, but the ideas of those texts quickly found a place in American thought. Emerson and Thoreau read Hindu scriptures, and their thought, and the development of American intellectual life, was deeply influenced by these ideas.

More recently the United States has increasingly become the scene of conscious missionary efforts by such traditionally nonmissionary faiths as Hinduism and Buddhism, as well as by Muslims. These efforts, plus immigration, have fostered the development of significant and growing bodies of non-Christian, non-Jewish religious believers in the United States, and the ideas and values of these religious traditions have disseminated widely into American life.

Thus, whatever their original intentions may have been, the missionaries helped open the door to non-Christian ideas in American culture. The result, in making the American public more respectful and tolerant of, and more informed about, non-Western traditions, has enormously increased the ability of the American people to play a constructive part in the development of a global civilization.

The missionary movement and the allied and assorted movements of philanthropic internationalism beginning in the nineteenth century also wrought substantial changes in the world beyond America's borders. Mission churches were planted that over time grew to have great influence in the politics and cultures of many countries; an international civil society took root along with the beginnings of global movements for peace, disarmament, arbitration, and human rights. American missionaries and philanthropists were not the only actors in this drama. Missionaries proceeded outward from much of Europe during the era. Britain in particular was home to a vibrant missionary movement and, particularly in the first half of the nineteenth century, was the unquestioned world center of the abolition and peace movements. Nevertheless, as time wore on, American missionaries, backed by the religious fervor and philanthropic bent of the American people as well as by the material riches of American society, moved toward center stage, and the British retreated into a supporting role. Since the late nineteenth century the percentage of American missionaries among Protestant missionaries world-wide has steadily grown.

Although it would be a serious mistake to measure the influence of the missionary movement by looking solely at its success in planting churches, the missionaries enjoyed a broad though not universal success in spreading their faith, and the churches they planted have in some cases gone on to play important roles in the history of many non-Western countries. South Korea is a case in point. Christianity was essentially unknown in Korea two hundred years ago. By 1995 33 percent of the population was Protestant, another 7 percent was Catholic, and a large additional number belonged to unique Korean syncretistic churches, combining Christian and traditional Korean beliefs.[14] This group included the well-known and controversial Unification Church, led by Rev. Sun Myung Moon. For most of the twentieth century, the churches and their members played major political roles. Under the Japanese occupation, mission schools were among the few avenues open to Koreans wishing to escape the Japanese-dominated educational system, and the churches were reservoirs of Korean nationalism. During and after the Korean War the churches and the foreign missions were important in the construction and stabilization of the South Korean state, while the Christian churches played a leading role in the democracy movement that ultimately brought the South Korean military dictatorship to an end. Of the first two Korean presidents elected democratically the first, Kim Young Sam, was Protestant, and the second, Kim Dae Jung, was Catholic.

Although the demographic consequences of the missionary effort in China were not as dramatic, the long-term consequences of mission activity in China may be even more dramatic than in Korea. The tradition of Chinese students coming to American universities began under missionary auspices, and the continuing flood of Chinese students into American universities following the normalization of relations has once again resulted in the exposure of, ultimately, hundreds of thousands of China's best and brightest to a wide range of American ideas and influences.

The overseas Chinese, among whom missionaries and Chinese churches continued to work after 1949, have joined Christian churches in rates that approach conversion rates in Korea (14 percent in Singapore,[15] somewhat higher in Indonesia, the United States, and Vietnam, and substantially higher in the Philippines). This is not a universal trend: Only 3.6 percent of Taiwan's people are now Christian, and this figure includes non-Chinese tribal groups. In Hong Kong and Thailand the percentage is similarly low.[16] All in all, it appears that something between fifty and one hundred million people of Chinese descent around the world profess one or another form of Christian faith, a number equal to or higher than the total population of Britain or France and substantially larger than the total population of the United States at the time the American churches inaugurated their missionary program to China.[17] It is quite possible that in this century these communities will have great impact on the religious and cultural climate not only of Southeast Asia, but of China itself and the entire world. Anecdotal evidence suggests that despite (perhaps because of) Communist persecution of Christian communities in China, both Protestant and Catholic churches are experiencing extraordinary growth, with a large number of conversions registered in the official, state-tolerated churches, and perhaps even more explosive growth among the unregistered Protestant and Catholic congregations.[18] Given the general disillusionment with communist ideology, the social upheavals associated with industrialization, and the decline of traditional Chinese beliefs since 1949, and given the religious fervor in significant elements of the overseas Chinese community, this century may well witness another sustained round of Christian missionary activity in China, this time spearheaded by Chinese leaders and Chinese churches and paid for with overseas Chinese money.

In Latin America old, cherished dreams of the missionaries may also be coming true, and in the process reshaping social and political realities. Guatemala and other countries may have Protestant majorities. In Brazil, Chile and elsewhere Evangelical and Pentecostal communities have experienced remarkable growth. Anecdotal evidence suggests that a major Protestant religious revival is also taking place in Cuba. This growth is transforming society in some areas of Latin America, and not merely in rural areas populated by indigenous minorities as was once largely the case, but in major urban centers as well. The astounding spread of Protestant Christianity among Hispanics in the United States will provide an increasingly wealthy and influential base of support for missionary efforts in the future. It appears likely that this century will see Latin America become a religiously mixed region, and the five centuries of identification of Latin American society with Catholicism will come to an end—with enormous implications for the political, social, and economic future of the Western Hemisphere.

American Catholic missionaries have also had a significant impact abroad. Once a mission field for foreign Catholic priests, the United States has become one of the most important sources of Catholicism's international strength. Both Catholic and Protestant missionaries from the United States have played a major role in the dramatic expansion of Christianity in Africa, an expansion that has continued and even accelerated after the end of colonial rule. As in the Philippines, Korea, and Taiwan, local Christians and their churches played important roles in democracy movements throughout Africa. Anglican archbishop Desmond Tutu is only the best known of a galaxy of African Christians who continue to struggle for African versions of Western democratic institutions. It is likely that without Christian missionaries, Islam would ultimately have replaced polytheism throughout Africa; the spread of

Christianity there has genuine world-historical importance. The vibrant Catholicism of many Africans seems likely to prove a major element in the continuing strength of the Roman Catholic Church in the third millennium. Meanwhile, church organizations continue to play leading roles in providing relief for the victims of Africa's wars and catastrophes, and any progress toward stable democratic rule in much of Africa will be to a very large extent the child of the churches planted by the missionaries in the colonial era.

However great its religious impact has been, the key to appreciating the importance of the missionary movement in American foreign policy lies in understanding its nonreligious impact. A good example is in the former lands of the Ottoman Empire. Basically coterminous with the modern Middle East plus much of southeastern Europe, this region was the object of the first great missionary endeavor of the American missionary movement, antedating the major push in China by fifty years. Here the religious objectives of the American missionaries—the conversion of the Muslims of the Ottoman Empire to Christianity—were almost entirely frustrated. Furthermore, the method they chose—uplifting the Christian minorities of the empire both spiritually and materially—ended in the ruin of some of the world's most ancient Christian communities. The ultimate historical judgment on the American missionary record in the Middle East may be that the missionaries accomplished in one century what Islam failed to do in thirteen: eliminating Christianity as a living religion in much of the Middle East.

Yet, even though they failed to reach their religious goals, the missionaries changed the Middle East in ways that still endure.

Once the first missionaries realized that the region's Muslims were largely uninterested in the Christian message, they changed tactics. The American missionaries turned to the ancient Christian minorities of the empire, including communities of people who had survived under Muslim rule almost since the lifetime of the Prophet: Armenians, Syrians, Lebanese, the Nestorean and Chaldean Christians of Iran and Mesopotamia, the Copts of Egypt, and the considerable minority of Palestinian Arabs, who, one thousand years after the Muslim conquest, still chose to remain in the communion of their fathers. Additionally, because much of the Balkans was then still under Ottoman rule, the Greeks, Bulgarians, Macedonians, and others became objects of American Christian mission solicitude.

The Christianity of these ancient communions was very different from the American Protestantism of the era. Differences in dogma among the mostly Orthodox and Oriental traditions of the Eastern churches and American Evangelicalism were only part of the difference. Without the discipline of the Roman communion or the active lay leadership of the Protestant world, and condemned to second-class citizenship under the Ottoman system, the Christian communities of the Middle East were in a condition that the earnest missionaries found shocking—reminiscent, to those earnest disciples of Jonathan Edwards and Timothy Dwight, of the worst eras of stagnation, barbarism, and corruption in the Dark Ages of the West. The Scriptures and divine worship were often in tongues as indecipherable to the clergy as to the people. Both the laity and the clergy were in a degraded state, suffering from formalism, simony, apathy, illiteracy. No wonder, said the missionary strategists, that the Muslims show no interest in the religion of Christ. These Christian communities give them nothing to emulate or respect. The missionaries therefore decided to begin the conversion of the Ottoman world by reawakening the Christian communities.

The missionaries launched movements of national revival among the minorities of the Near East. Over time they enjoyed signal success. Printing presses published both practical and spiritual works in the contemporary languages of the minorities. Boarding schools and colleges were founded for both girls and boys. Bright students received scholarships to study in the United States.

Gradually this made an impact, both religious and otherwise. In some cases Protestant Christian communities seceded from the jurisdiction of the traditional authorities; in others the new influences were accommodated without an open break. Partly because European and Western influence was simultaneously on the rise in the Muslim world, Christianity ceased to be a social and economic disadvantage. Christian children educated in missionary schools spoke Western languages, understood Western concepts, and soon came to benefit from extensive business and social networks. As Ottoman minorities like the Greeks and the Serbs struggled for and gained independence in the European portion of the empire, Christian minorities grew increasingly discontented elsewhere.

The Muslim majority watched all this, and was inspired both to emulate the success of the minority by attending Western and even missionary schools, and to develop a national consciousness of its own. Turkish and Arab students flocked to American (as well as European) colleges in the region, where social and secular revolutionary ideas spread. Both

Turkish nationalism and Arab nationalism owe a great deal to the educational labors of the missionaries, but neither Turks nor Arabs embraced their religious ideals. The Christian minorities, long tolerated in the Muslim world under the enlightened precepts of the Holy Koran, were no longer seen as tame minorities. They were bearers of disturbing Western influence and, as Western pressure on the crumbling Ottoman and Arab worlds increased, they were seen as the conscious agents of foreign imperial powers.

As tensions rose, and continued to rise through the late nineteenth century and into contemporary times, increasing numbers of Christians in the Middle East took advantage of their familiarity with the Western world to emigrate—in many cases, to the United States. The proportion of Christians among the Arab population of Palestine has fallen by more than two-thirds since 1914.[19]

This is a religious failure on a grand scale, but the impact of the missionary presence on the secular and political scene in the Middle East has been profound, with consequences that will be unfolding for many years. Missionary educated intellectuals played a major role in the development of Arab nationalism; even today Palestinian Christians play a much larger role in the politics of Palestine than their numbers would justify. The continuing attraction of Western ideas, divorced from Christian theology, remains fundamental and profound; witness the democracy movement in contemporary Iran and the continuing discussions in the Islamic world about the proper role of women.

While American missionaries were not the only Western influence in the Middle East, until the 1940s the American missionary presence was unique in that it was relatively disinterested. Until the end of World War II Britain and France were the leading Western imperial powers in the region, and the United States had no bases and only modest investments. The result was a Middle Eastern sympathy for the United States that has still not entirely disappeared. Arab nationalists looked to the United States as a friendly, anti-imperial power until relatively recently; even as late as the Suez crisis of 1956, the United States took the Arab side against a coalition of Britain, Israel, and France. Turkey still sees the United States as a sympathetic power, as do the Armenians and the Georgians.

Liberal democracy, in power almost nowhere in the Middle East, is a force with which the Middle East's rulers must nevertheless contend. A liberal, modernizing strain of Islam, developed by Muslim thinkers earlier in the century and modeled, in some cases directly, on the steps Christian theology took to accommodate modern developments in science and politics, remains the leading ideological opponent of the fundamentalist movements that appear to be running out of steam in much of the Middle East. Here too, in Muslim rather than in Christian form, some of the core ideological concepts that the missionaries preached more than a hundred years ago are likely to play important roles in this century.

The secular contributions of the missionary movement may, on a global scale, ultimately have more impact than do their religious achievements. Liberal democracy has, officially at least, become the ruling ideology in southern, southeastern and most of northeastern Asia. China, Vietnam, Myanmar, and North Korea remain socialist with varying degrees of conviction and success, but none of these societies look as if they will be setting the ideological agenda for the future. In most of Africa, liberal democracy has no serious ideological rival; it haunts the chancelleries of the Muslim Middle East and duels with the recidivist national fascisms of the Balkan Peninsula.

Supporting this worldwide movement toward humane and liberal democracy is a host of civil society movements for human rights, protection of journalists, the defense of ethnic and religious minorities, women's rights, justice for refugees, disarmament, and other liberal causes. In many cases there are direct institutional links between these organizations and the missionary churches. In many others the links are cultural, ideological or personal. In some cases, like the Korean democracy movement, these movements are in large part based in churches. In others, as with the large network of farmer-based, nongovernmental organizations (NGOs) in Thailand, missionaries, church-related development organizations, and foundations support indigenous, non-Christian movements. Throughout the third world, international movements against such evils as child labor, female circumcision, and debt peonage carry on the missionary tradition in the circumstances of the present.

In all its forms this global movement, controlled from no single center and focused on no single object, owes much to the missionaries, American and otherwise, who gave their lives to spread what they believed to be the linked messages of Christian faith and democratic government in the non-European regions of the world. It is only natural that Wilsonians seek as vigorously now to align American foreign policy with the goals of this great international movement as they did in the past.

Much of the history of this century will consist of the efforts of Wilsonians in the United States and their allies and kindred spirits abroad to realize the vision of universal brotherhood and peace.

Wilsonian Grand Strategy

Just as Hamiltonians developed a set of basic ideas about how to define and defend the national interests, Wilsonians through American history have worked from a basic set of ideas about American foreign policy. And while Wilsonian foreign policy concepts contain much that realists find hard to swallow, the core strategic ideas of the Wilsonian community are neither as impractical nor as contradictory as their critics often allege. Their logic is powerful; the Wilsonian approach to national security has much to recommend it, and the Wilsonian element in our foreign policy has made substantial contributions to the growth of the nation's power.

The first principle of Wilsonian foreign policy is that democracies make better and more reliable partners than monarchies and tyrannies. Far from naive, this perspective rests on a sophisticated understanding of political dynamics. Nonrepresentational governments are unreliable partners for several reasons. We can start by citing royal caprice. In 1756, Louis XV was widely believed to have gone to war with Frederick the Great to avenge himself for a series of insults that the Prussian monarch permitted himself at the expense of the French king's *maîtresse en titre*. (Frederick, for example, named the dog that shared his bed "Pompadour.")[20] To this add succession politics: In Hanoverian England, the Prince of Wales was almost always at political odds with the King. A power whose policy can change with a death or a marriage is hardly the most reliable of friends. Again, Frederick the Great's career is instructive: His throne was saved at the hour of defeat when the Russian czarina Elizabeth was replaced by her weak and Prussophile heir, Peter. This was the "miracle of the House of Brandenburg" that Josef Goebbels thought of when he heard of Franklin Roosevelt's death, and rushed excitedly to tell the Führer the news. But as Hitler and Goebbels discovered, democratic governments are less prone to rapid reversals than are autocratic systems.

This is only the surface of the argument. Nonrepresentative polities are unstable not simply because their rulers can be erratic. They are unreliable precisely because public opinion is imperfectly reflected in the government. Governments can adopt and pursue policies that have no backing in society. Those policies can last until the government falls in chaos and confusion, to be replaced, perhaps, by a regime that lurches equally uncertainly in another unsuitable direction. There is nothing abstract about this argument. The monarchs of Europe were constantly wobbling on their thrones in the nineteenth century; when revolutionaries didn't bring them down, assassins shot them. Policies in democracies are less likely to diverge from what is politically popular, and when democratic governments fall there is less danger of an overshoot in another direction. Democratic policies are pulled toward the center and toward a rational concept of interest, argue Wilsonians; that makes them more predictable and more likely to keep promises once made. Wilsonians think of monarchical, oligarchic, and tyrannical states as resembling pyramids balanced on their noses; democracies are like pyramids standing on their bases. The first kind are much more likely to move violently and massively in unpredictable ways.

In particular, democracy guards against one of the most dangerous forms of misrepresentation and misgovernance: the domination of the state by a military elite. Such military states may, and frequently do, prefer war to peace; war consolidates military authority and ensures military control over resources. It is only civilians who benefit from peace and only democracy, say Wilsonians, ensures that the millions who seek peace can control the thousands who want war. To put it in a nutshell: Tyrants give power to generals; democracies give it to moms.

Furthermore over time democracies are likely to move toward increasing degrees of moral and political agreement. Mass-led societies are more like one another than societies directed by individuals or small classes. This homogeneity leads to increasing degrees of agreement over the proper constitution and rules of international society; democracies are more likely to agree than are aristocratic or monarchical states.

Democracies are also reliable because they tend to prosper. Successful capitalism depends on the rule of law, and democratic governments more than any others are likely over time to develop fair and effective legal systems. At the same time, because voters reward politicians whose policies lead to economic growth and punish those deemed responsible for recessions, democratic states over time can be expected to move increasingly toward effective economic policy.

Finally, these advantages tend to increase over time as democracies grow more stable, more part of an order. Wilsonians look—with some justice—to the evolution of the Atlantic community in the twentieth century as a vindication of these theories. War among these societies was commonplace before they became democracies. Now war among them is almost unthinkable, and they have all grown very rich.

As a corollary to their support of democracy around the world, Wilsonians—again under missionary influence—became determined opponents of colonialism. The British *raj* was evidently not democratic; the less enlightened rule of other colonial empires was even less tolerable. Wilsonian opinion, which had flirted briefly with the imperialist option at the turn of the twentieth century, soon joined the chorus calling for the United States to give up its own colonies.

Wilsonian beliefs lead to the principle that the support of democracy abroad is not only a moral duty for the United States but a practical imperative as well. This belief first appeared in American politics at the time of the French Revolution, and it reappeared with every great European revolutionary movement of the nineteenth century. What we would now call Wilsonian voices called for intervention in the Latin American, Greek, Polish, Hungarian, and Cuban wars for independence. In 1848–49 the navy went so far as to pick up republican refugees after the collapse of the Roman republic. Wilsonians supported American interventions in Hawaiian politics as that kingdom slowly died, but Wilsonians were unable to trigger American armed intervention in a foreign war for independence until the intervention in Cuba in 1898. In the twentieth century growing American power gave more scope for Wilsonian interventions, and American forces engaged in "democratic" and "humanitarian" interventions with increasing regularity.

An important factor in the growth of Wilsonian determination to spread democracy was the startling success of American post–World War II policy in Germany, Italy, and Japan. Although all these countries had tried parliamentary systems in the past, none of these former Axis powers had ever known real stability under democratic rule. The experiments in democratic governance that began after World War II started under very unfavorable circumstances. All the countries had been devastated by the war; Italy was divided between an energetic and militant Communist Party and a somewhat obscurantist Christian right. Initially, very few politicians in Japan sincerely supported the American democratic experiment. In Germany, where most historians blamed the collapse of the Weimar Republic on the consequences of the harsh Treaty of

Versailles, the new democracy began life under far more adverse conditions than those of Weimar. Germany lost vastly more territory in 1945 than in 1919; its economy was far more bitterly disrupted, and its entire social order had been twisted and distorted by twelve years of Nazi rule.

Yet in all three cases, democratic governments put down roots, and all three countries became reliable American allies during the Cold War and after. These were hard cases; if democracy could take root in what had been Nazi Germany it could surely flourish anywhere.

The more sustained interventions for democracy, involving methods short of force, that characterized missionary activity in the nineteenth century also increased and accelerated in the twentieth. Organizations such as Radio Free Europe and Voice of America in the Cold War, and the National Endowment for Democracy, supported nonviolent efforts to spread democratic ideas and solidify democratic policies abroad. The vast network of nongovernmental prodemocracy organizations continues to ask for and to receive consular and diplomatic support from the United States in many places around the world, much as the missionaries did. The work of transforming the world on democratic lines goes on.

After the promotion of democracy, the next object of Wilsonian strategic thought is the prevention of war. Always brutal and destructive, war under modern conditions, say Wilsonians, is becoming unbearable and potentially risks the extermination of the human race. The modern antiwar movement dates back to the 1820s and 1830s, when evangelical Christian groups summoned a series of peace congresses to look for ways and means to end the scourge of war. As improved methods of communications, combined with a growing destructive power in arms, brought the shocking spectacle of modern war in all its horror closer to civilian readers, the antiwar movement gained strength, quickly moving in three complementary directions. The peace congress movement has continued under different institutional forms through the present day, convening international gatherings of activists to develop proposals for a peaceful world, and seeking through student exchanges and institutional ties across national boundaries to build a network of activists and organizations in many countries determined to stop war. The second branch of the movement sought to reduce the horrors of warfare by imposing codes of conduct on it and by limiting the production, distribution, and use of arms. This program led to the formation of the

International Red Cross and the Geneva Convention, and ultimately to such measures as contemporary treaties to ban land mines, to prevent the enlistment of children younger than sixteen in military forces, and to establish an international criminal court. The third branch of the modern peace movement seeks to prevent war by developing alternatives to it: forums to which nations can take disputes instead of fighting it out, and international organizations for collective security. This third approach led to the development, first, of bilateral arbitration treaties and, later, to the League of Nations, the World Court and the United Nations.

The original leadership in these peace movements was European, but American Wilsonians participated early on and sought, often successfully, to get U.S. government support for these ventures. After a national grassroots campaign spearheaded by Civil War heroine Clara Barton, President Chester A. Arthur brought the United States into the Red Cross system in 1881, and with his support Congress ratified the Geneva Convention in 1882. As the United States moved to the center of the world stage, Wilsonians sought, and still seek, to put the growing muscle of the United States behind the world peace movement. Where they can, Wilsonians want the United States to take the lead in this movement; when the United States lags, when it fails to sign the land mine treaty or falls behind in its UN dues, Wilsonians take on themselves the task of bringing the United States into compliance with what they hope will develop into a genuinely Wilsonian international order.

The Consequences of Wilsonian Politics

Judging from the low esteem in which some observers hold it, one might think that Wilsonianism is a major drag on American foreign policy. While there are problems, and we will examine them, it is important to understand the many ways in which the presence of Wilsonian tendencies in American foreign policy provides great benefits.

The first great benefit has nothing directly to do with our foreign policy but has nevertheless been of enormous value in that area. Despite Wilson's own sorry record on race, the Wilsonian idea that the American Revolution is incomplete, that the United States has a duty to fight until the equal rights of all are acknowledged and respected has had major consequences in American history. In particular it has provided an ideological and moral bridge that allows minorities, immigrant groups, and others to feel a strong patriotism and loyalty to a country that oftentimes has been very reluctant to grant them their rights. Frederick Douglass felt—justly, from a Wilsonian standpoint—that he was the "real" American, while the racists and slaveholders around him were defective Americans. The "real" America was on Douglass's side, even as the defective and incomplete America of daily life trampled on his sensibilities and violated his rights at every turn.

Immigrants have looked, and still do look, at the Wilsonian idea of America and have found it to be something they could love and strive for in the face of discrimination and hardship. At the same time Wilsonian doctrine sends a message to nonminorities that they have a patriotic duty to make room for the immigrants, to welcome them into the community, and to struggle against the national heritage of racism. In peace and war this tradition brings the United States many blessings, without it this would be a much weaker and unhappier country.

Beyond the inestimable blessing of making the United States a more inclusive, welcoming, and united country, Wilsonian politics has conferred another great benefit on American foreign policy by aligning it with the major movements of contemporary history. There have been two fundamental movements in international society over the last two centuries: the spread of democracy, and the rise to independence and development of increasing portions of the non-European world. Some powers have stood in the way of these processes, and they paid a ruinous price. Thanks largely to pressure from the Wilsonian school, the United States has generally supported these trends, and reaped corresponding rewards.

The Wilsonian presence has also provided a strong base of popular support for an active, engaged American foreign policy, often enough for policies that serve Hamiltonian ends. As it happens a strong common set of concerns draws Wilsonians and Hamiltonians together. Although it is true that they often quarrel and fight—China policy being one venerable example, the struggle between Wilson and Lodge over the shape of the League of Nations another—the two schools are often able to work together on the set of interests and values they have in common.

After all, both schools of thought look to a stable world order as the ultimate, best-case outcome of their activities. The Hamiltonian hope that there will be a worldwide trading and investment system based on international law and enforced by honest, transparent judiciaries in many states—with a World Court perhaps in the background when national justice seems more biased than august—closely parallels much of the Wilsonian agenda.

Despite their yearning for peace, Wilsonians have often joined Hamiltonians in supporting, if necessary, war against states that make war on the international order. Hamiltonians may snicker when Wilsonians talk about war to make the world safe for democracy—and Wilsonians groan at the thought of Hamiltonians wanting to make the world safe for plutocracy—but in practice the targets of Wilsonian and Hamiltonian wrath are often the same. Hamiltonians may think the crime is principally an assault on the balance of power. Wilsonians see it as an attack on international law, or as the violation of neutrality. But since aspiring hegemons generally do have to trample on such inconveniences, the result is that just when American merchants need them most, American missionaries have often been ready to troop to the colors.

When it came to European colonial empires in the third world, Wilsonian idealism and Hamiltonian realism dictated the same course. Barring exceptional circumstances (such as the communist threat in French Indochina), Wilsonians believed that the United States should work by all peaceful means to undermine the colonial system. Wilsonian opposition to colonialism was more consistent and inflexible than the nuanced Hamiltonian approach. Nevertheless, over the long sweep of history the two schools of thought supported American policies that limited the extension of the colonial system and undermined it where possible.

China policy over the last 150 years illustrates how the conflicting but also complementary perspectives of Hamiltonians and Wilsonians combined to shape policy. Even as missionaries battled merchants, lobbying to outlaw the opium trade that merchants saw as commercially necessary, both groups saw the need for the United States to oppose the partition of China while ensuring that American nationals benefited from all the concessions that the European powers were able to extract. Merchants wanted aggressive consular protection backed up by an effective naval presence for commercial reasons; missionaries wanted the same kind of protection for their own more spiritual goals. Both merchants and missionaries wanted, and still want, to see China establish a reliable, independent judiciary to provide both Chinese citizens and American investors with all the protections of the law. Working together, Hamiltonians and Wilsonians kept Washington focused on China policy; and certainly on Taiwan, and possibly ultimately on the mainland, Chinese society may well evolve in the broad general direction that both American schools would prefer.

Wilsonianism benefits American foreign policy in another important way. Since most great powers have guiding ideologies, it is a good thing that Wilsonianism is particularly well-suited for winning friends and influencing people abroad.

To begin with Wilsonianism is a universal, not a particular, ideal. That is, no races, individuals, countries, or cultures are in principle excluded from the Wilsonian vision of a world of peaceful democracies treating one another with respect.

This counts. In the British Empire foreigners were always seen as inferior, and the darker and less British-acting they were, the more inferior. When foreign peoples were brought into the British Empire, it was as subject peoples. This was a time bomb; Indians, among others, either had to abandon their self-respect or fight for their freedom.

In the American hegemony, by contrast, all nations and all peoples are assumed to be, or at least capable of becoming, equal. Not that all Wilsonians have subscribed to the equality of races. But unlike British imperial ideology, Wilsonianism has proved capable of evolving, and has generally been a force for the recognition of equality both within and beyond the United States. International law as imagined by Wilsonians will protect poor and weak countries as well as the rich and the strong. A fully Wilsonian system would replace might with right in the judgment seat of nations. This is an intoxicating vision, to which Ecuadorians and Ethiopians can subscribe as well as Americans, and it is a great advantage for the United States.

Wilsonian universalism also extends to classes. Everyone, rich or poor, is welcome to the shelter of the Wilsonian revival tent. Not all ideological movements have been so broad minded. Besides the lamentable economic strategies and tyrannical government structures that bolshevism built, and that hobbled its struggle for world domination, bolshevism was also at war with the most powerful and articulate elements in international society: the ruling bourgeois class of the capitalist countries and the petty bourgeois who dominate intellectual, journalistic, and cultural life. While bolshevism claimed individual converts from both classes, societies had to undergo wrenching revolutions and complete economic and social change to join the bolshevik camp. The deepest religious feelings of the common people had to be opposed; the basic interests of the elites had to be powerfully rooted out.

Wilsonianism doesn't have to work that hard to conquer. Emperors and kings can hang on to their thrones if they will share their power.

Despite the fears of past generations, experience in the United States and elsewhere shows the rich that their goods are safe in democratic societies—perhaps safer, since transparent legal systems erect more safeguards between the individual and state power. Whole societies can be, and have been, converted to Wilsonian values.

Furthermore the Wilsonian ideal is nonsectarian. That is, while it historically emerged from Christianity—and from Protestant, low-church Christianity at that—the Wilsonian ideal of a community of states all run on democratic lines is one that can actually be adopted by states and cultures that are neither Protestant nor even Christian. Democracy can be an ideal for Argentines, Indians and Japanese; it can also be one for Iranians, many of whom hope to see their Islamic republic incorporate more features of the Wilsonian program while maintaining its Islamic character.

For the United States to be seen as the main international supporter and avatar of so effective and seductive an ideology is clearly a major advantage in international affairs. It ensures that to some degree the most active, intelligent, and forward-looking elements in many other countries regard the United States sympathetically. While they can and do oppose American designs in particular cases, on the whole broad sectors of the active and progressive classes in foreign countries will be more likely to tolerate and even support American influence and power, and they will be slow to see anything but benefits from closer relations with the United States.

Even those governments like China's, which remain anti-Wilsonian, are haunted by the power and attraction of Wilsonian ideals. Not every generation of Chinese students will build models of the Statue of Liberty on Tienanmen Square, but many of China's best and brightest will continue to see Wilsonian ideas both domestically and in international society as the most beneficial means to China's own growth and development. The United States does not need a Comintern to spread its ideas and build political allies in the rest of the world; the natural appeal of Wilsonian ideas to the contemporary mind does that job without our help.

Another way in which Wilsonianism works to build support for the United States will be felt more in this century than in the last: the position of the United States as the most visible and powerful example of a country that believes in equal rights for women. There is every reason to believe that this will be the century of the woman, with the rise of

women to equal power and rights one of the most fundamental developments all over the world. U.S. feminism is perhaps the quality that Continental realism would consider its least useful asset from a foreign policy
point of view; in reality, however, our successful and dynamic feminist
movement, together with our advocacy of equal rights for women in
international politics, will help keep the United States on the right side
of history and make us powerful friends and allies among emerging leadership groups around the world.

An additional benefit provided by the Wilsonian school is one that
ought to make Wilsonians uneasy. In effect, the power of Wilsonian ideas
in American foreign policy is pervasive but not universal. Tell it not in
Gath, publish it not in the streets of Askelon, but the United States does
not always conduct its foreign policy on Wilsonian lines. Again, this did
not start with the world wars or with the Cold War, nor has it ended.
Saudi Arabia is one of the least Wilsonian places on the face of the earth,
but the United States can and does support its royal family. The United
States steadfastly supported the very undemocratic regime of Indonesia's
seven-term president Suharto, only withdrawing that support when his
power was obviously disintegrating.

I won't unsettle readers by heaping up unpleasant examples; a quick
glance through an atlas or a good newspaper should provide ample food
for thought. How fortunate it is, then, that a foreign policy that is and
perhaps must sometimes be so—well, so *morally challenged*—should be so
radiantly garbed in ideals so sublime. How useful it is that so many people around the world see Wilsonian ideals as defining the norm of American foreign policy, and interpret its other aspects as unfortunate and
temporary deviations from it.

In effect the very strength and sincerity of the Wilsonian school
allows the United States to do something that democratic societies cannot easily do consciously: to play the suave and accomplished hypocrite.
Wilsonians proclaim noble principles and sincerely plan to apply
them—but then, alas, they sometimes lose policy battles. The Clinton
administration extended most favored nation status to China despite that
country's un-Wilsonian approach to human rights. The United States
fell far behind in its UN dues, despite the fervent lobbying of its Wilsonian friends.

Yet if Wilsonians are disappointed by defeats like this, they are not
discouraged. They see their job as moving U.S. policy step by step
toward an ideal; they know that progress will be halting and slow, and

that at times there will be considerable backsliding. None of this affects their sincere (and therefore often convincing) declarations to foreigners about the enduring principles of American foreign policy, or their bedrock convictions about the superior morality and social organization of the United States. No mere and ugly fact can deface an image so sublime; no sin cannot be overcome by grace; no temporary weakness or failing can overthrow the right, the duty, and the destiny of the United States to spread its democratic revolution to the ends of the earth.

Far from sneering at Wilsonianism and its acolytes, realists should thank God that they exist. Annoying as Wilsonian moralists can be at times, on the whole they have done much to strengthen the hands of American foreign policy makers.

With all these advantages, Wilsonianism clearly brings great strengths to American foreign policy, but its critics are correct that the Wilsonian program involves the United States in difficulties and dangers. First and foremost it sets a high bar for American foreign policy success. The global triumph of democracy and the rule of law are ambitious goals, and they necessarily involve the United States in perpetual quarrels with a number of nondemocratic countries, some of which are quite powerful and important.

The very high and ambitious nature of these goals also makes strategic thinking difficult in a Wilsonian context. Given that we can't achieve the complete Wilsonian program everywhere on earth this week, where should we start? What evils shall we let fester as we prioritize other causes? How much repression of Turkish Kurds shall we tolerate to facilitate our efforts to force Saddam Hussein to treat Iraqi Kurds better? Do we ignore female circumcision in Somalia while we concentrate on judicial reform in that country? How many Chechens can Russian president Vladimir Putin kill before we withdraw support for his regime, and how many more kills does he get if we become convinced that the only alternative to a Putin government is a Communist restoration?

More positively, how exactly does one build a peaceful, stable, just, and democratic world? The fragmentation of the Wilsonian world into thousands of nongovernmental groups—many formed to advocate single issues—and its divisions along religious and ideological lines make all questions of strategic choice extremely difficult for politicians working in a Wilsonian context.

Wilsonian policy also involves contemporary American foreign policy in a difficult contradiction. On the one hand, as global hegemon, the United States is by definition a status quo power. But to the extent that we are exporting Wilsonian values, we are a revisionist one as well. Many Wilsonians want to redraw the world's maps—to make Tibet an independent state, for example.

Wilsonians also want to make changes within international boundaries. They want dictatorial regimes to yield power to democratic opponents, peacefully if possible, through violent struggle if there is no other way. Thanks to Wilsonian strength in the American foreign policy process, Congress provides substantial sums of money for propaganda and other activities aimed at hastening the happy day of democratic transitions.

Both of these goals—boundary changes and regime changes—pose great challenges for other countries. It is not always clear how the United States will resolve the struggles between the conservative and radical trends in its foreign policy with respect to any given country or question. This naturally unsettles other states, both potential targets of our revolutionary diplomacy and other countries that will inevitably find their interests affected by American initiatives. European investors and their governments worry that the United States will impose sanctions on European companies that trade with regimes the United States seeks to isolate; a country like Turkey or Jordan must worry when the United States uses its power at the United Nations to force it to close its borders with an important trading partner.

All this gives the United States government one painful headache after another. Wilsonian lobbies demanding strong action against countries that persecute dissidents, permit the genital mutilation of women, suppress trade unions, hunt whales, eat dogs, oppress national minorities, or otherwise offend the moral sensitivities of some organized American constituency create constant demands for government action. This unfortunately decreases the comfort level of other countries with American power and increases their concern that too much American power endangers their vital interests.

Yet for students of American foreign policy the question of whether Wilsonianism is a good or a bad thing is an idle one. Wilsonianism, with all its virtues and its defects, is a real thing. It is deeply, probably ineradicably, rooted in American culture and history, and those who hope to shape the country's foreign policy must come to terms with it one way or another.

Chapter Six

"VINDICATOR ONLY OF HER OWN"

The Jeffersonian Tradition

The Hamiltonian and Wilsonian approaches to American foreign policy, however controversial they may sometimes be, are relatively well understood. Though in some ways alien and in others offensive to the classical approaches of European diplomacy, over time they have become familiar enough to be easily comprehensible. Furthermore, throughout the twentieth century, other countries to a greater or lesser extent appropriated elements of Hamiltonian and Wilsonian political thought to their own circumstances. This is not difficult to do. The universalism of Wilsonian logic gives it international resonance and popularity. The commercial interest in most countries is strong enough to create some domestic analog of Hamiltonian politics, and the commercial advantages that flow to countries supporting or at least participating in a United States–led international Hamiltonian order are substantial enough to create significant interest groups in most countries that endorse Hamiltonian proposals for reasons of their own.

The Jeffersonian and Jacksonian schools, however, which more directly spring from idiosyncratic elements of American (or Anglo-American) culture, remain less well known, less well liked, and much less well understood. This is natural. Hamiltonian and Wilsonian values are universal, and both Hamiltonians and Wilsonians want the United States both to build an international order and to make domestic concessions and changes for the sake of that order. They believe in reciprocity; if they want the world to become more like the United States, they also want the United States to accommodate better to the rest of the world.

Jeffersonians and Jacksonians would be happy if the rest of the world became more like the United States, though they don't find this likely. They resist, however, any thought of the United States becoming more like the rest of the world. If the United States makes even such trivial concessions to international order as adopting the metric system, it will be because of Hamiltonian and Wilsonian efforts. In very different ways Jeffersonians and Jacksonians believe that the specific cultural, social, and political heritage of the United States is a precious treasure to be conserved, defended, and passed on to future generations; they celebrate what they see as the unique, and uniquely valuable, elements of American life and believe that the object of foreign policy should be to defend those values at home rather than to extend them abroad.

Since the end of the Cold War, the concerns and values of Hamiltonians and Wilsonians have been at the center of the formation of American foreign policy. Under both the first Bush and the Clinton presidency, the construction of a global trading system and the extension of democracy were the central themes of American foreign policy.

To many observers in the United States and abroad, the widespread opposition in the United States to this post–Cold War consensus is both distasteful and difficult to understand. Puzzlingly, the Jeffersonian-Jacksonian opposition to mainstream American foreign policy cuts oddly across ideological and political lines. The AFL-CIO and liberal activists like Ralph Nader joined with arch-conservative Pat Buchanan and quirky populists like Ross Perot in attacking free trade initiatives like the World Trade Organization treaties and the treaties that established NAFTA. Neo-Marxists joined with neoconservatives to oppose American involvement in humanitarian interventions in the former Yugoslavia; Noam Chomsky[1] manned the barricades with Richard Perle to keep our boys out of Kosovo.

The conventional distinctions between isolationist and interventionist, realist and idealist, hawks and doves, and even populist and elitist approaches don't adequately describe the opposition to the dominant post–Cold War foreign policy; nor do they help us understand the poten-

Democracy works best, they say, when the people elect thoughtful, experienced legislators and magistrates who make policy and write laws better than the uninstructed public could do on its own. Property is a minority interest. The demagogues who flatter public opinion, and the unscrupulous politicians who will say or do anything to gain office, may please the people, but they will undermine the security of property and therefore ultimately the stability of the government and the happiness of society. For Jeffersonians big business is a necessary evil to be tolerated for the sake of democracy; for Hamiltonians democracy in some of its forms can be a necessary but dangerous evil.

The disagreement over the proper strength and role of the federal government is similar. Hamiltonians (and Wilsonians) see a strong central government as the indispensable guarantor of national freedom. Jeffersonians have generally seen a strong central government as, at best, a necessary evil and, at worst, as the most dangerous enemy of freedom. Hamiltonians believe that if the Jeffersonians would stop trying to interfere, the United States would be better governed than other states, but still very much a state among states. Jeffersonians believe, passionately, that the United States should be something better and different. Hamiltonians believe that a well-ordered, well-administered state provides good government to the people. Jeffersonians believe that the people should govern themselves as simply and directly as possible.

Perhaps most profoundly, Hamiltonians believe that the Revolution was a good thing, but that it is over. Like Wilsonians, Jeffersonians believe that the American Revolution continues. One believes that the United States is a country that has had a revolution; the other believes that America is a revolutionary country. Jeffersonians generally believe that the United States has a long way to go before it achieves the Revolutionary goals of 1776. It is one thing to say that all men are created equal; it is another to build a society that fully embodies this great truth. In more than two centuries of struggle and reflection, Jeffersonians have expanded their understanding of their ideas and expanded their application. Jefferson could write the Declaration of Independence and own slaves; the ideas that he unleashed have gone beyond him. As long as women suffer discrimination, as long as racial and ethnic minorities are excluded from full participation in the political and economic life of the nation, as long as lesbians and gays suffer discrimination based on sexual preference, today's Jeffersonians tell us, the great promises of the Revolution remain unfulfilled.

Even as Jeffersonians labor to extend and fulfill their vast and sweeping vision of that Revolution, they are constantly involved in a bitter struggle against counterrevolutionaries, those who would deny the rights promised in the Declaration of Independence or infringe on the liberties guaranteed by the Bill of Rights. By a logical process obvious and clear to themselves, though sometimes difficult for others to follow, Jeffersonians have convinced themselves that the right of exotic dancers to bare their breasts in bars is guaranteed by the Constitution, as are the rights both to produce and to consume pornography. The temple of liberty is always under siege. Here a Mississippi school board wants children to recite the Lord's Prayer at the start of the school day; there a prosecutor wants to introduce improperly obtained evidence into a criminal trial. Over there a university board of trustees is trying to fire a professor for expounding questionable ideas, and a police chief is refusing a marching permit to a group of American Nazis who want to commemorate Hitler's birthday by marching through a neighborhood populated by Holocaust survivors. In all these cases Jeffersonians will be found (not always enthusiastically) at what they take to be the barricades of freedom.

Government is not the only force from which the Revolutionary legacy must be defended. Since Jefferson tried to persuade Washington to veto the act establishing a charter for the First Bank of the United States, Jeffersonians have worried about the ability of large economic concentrations to infringe on popular liberty. Active in the resistance to the wave of corporate mergers toward the end of the nineteenth century, Jeffersonians overcame their suspicion of federal power to support antitrust legislation. In the contemporary world Jeffersonians like Ralph Nader continue to seek limits on the political power of economic concentrations.

Although the 1960s and 1970s left many Americans with the impression that the civil liberties movement was primarily an aspect of the Left, Jeffersonianism (like most American political movements) cannot so easily be fitted into categories drawn from European political battles. The libertarian movement is an expression of Jeffersonian thought. Organizations like the libertarian Cato Institute advocate limited government and individual civil liberties, and attack the nexus of close relationships and mutual support between large corporations and big government in both foreign and domestic policy. One of the most important developments in American society since the end of the Cold War has been the progressive rebirth of Jeffersonian activism among legal circles on the Right, with movements growing to strengthen the rights of private property against government regulation, and to revive the limits on federal power vis-à-vis the states. That "right" Jeffersonians and "left" Jeffersonians come together on foreign policy issues—that, for example, the Cato Institute supports a limited-objective foreign policy and opposes humanitarian interventions—indicates the strength and continuing vitality of Jeffersonian thought in foreign policy.

In the long sweep of history, neither the Jeffersonians nor the Hamiltonians have had everything their own way. Hamiltonians have had the satisfaction of watching the growth of federal power, the establishment of a professional military and civil public service, and of two centuries of trade and financial policy organized largely in ways that generally accord with the interests of the leading business interests of the day. Jeffersonians, on the other hand, have seen suffrage extended progressively to all adult men, to women, and to racial minorities. The Bill of Rights has preserved individual liberty despite the growing strength of the federal government.

The Defense of Liberty

The Jeffersonian view of the United States as a revolutionary nation with a revolutionary mission runs deep. The Jeffersonian party looks at the American Revolution with something of the same emotion with which good Bolsheviks once viewed Lenin's October revolution. In Jeffersonian eyes, the American Revolution was more than a break with a blundering king and a usurping Parliament; it was the start of a new era in the world.

The original Jeffersonians were steeped in the rich tradition of English and Scottish dissent. They often saw the American Revolution as the latest—sometimes as a secular—step in the British Reformation, and they saw themselves as Cromwellian Roundheads attempting to complete that Reformation against the opposition of the Hamiltonian Cavaliers. The emancipation of the British people from the medieval superstition of the Roman Catholic Church and (so Puritans charged) the only slightly less superstitious patchwork of the Church of England had been the program of the radical church reformers in England and Scotland. Just as the halfhearted official reformers in England had lopped off the pope but otherwise retained the panoply of papistry—bishops, sacraments, divine-right monarchy—so the halfhearted Hamiltonians wanted to get rid of the king of England but set up a social order in the United States that would be as much like the old British version as possible.

The Jeffersonians believed themselves to be the political and intellectual vanguard of the common man, the heirs and the completers of the long British struggle for liberty. For Jeffersonians parasitism, whether of church or state, was the great enemy of the common people. "Their spiritual fetters were forged by subtilty {sic} working upon superstition,"[2] as John Quincy Adams said of the British people. Popes and bishops used the artful wiles of priestcraft to beguile the people into supporting their luxurious lifestyles. Government officials and insiders set up a parallel operation in civil life. Aristocrats and courtiers told the people that the mysteries of government were too complex for them to comprehend; they deliberately mystified the inherently straightforward art of government into a byzantine labyrinth in which the honest farmer would be too confused to perceive the larceny of his goods and betrayal of his interests by the effete drones who dedicated themselves to defrauding and confusing him.

The unique circumstances of the American Revolution—the long, popular seasoning in the British struggle for liberty, the agricultural character of the population, the absence of nearby enemies requiring permanent national mobilization for war—offered Americans a rare, perhaps unique, opportunity to try to start over: to build a system of liberty on the purest revolutionary principles. To capitalize on that rare and precious opportunity to build a free country was the highest aim of Jeffersonian domestic policy; to preserve that sanctuary and that Revolution has been and remains the highest aim of Jeffersonian statecraft in international relations.

This defensive spirit is very far from the international revolutionary fervor of the Wilsonian current in American life. Wilsonians could be called the Trotskyites of the American Revolution; they believe that the security and success of the Revolution at home demands its universal extension through the world. Jeffersonians take the Stalinist point of view: Building democracy in one country is enough challenge for them, and they are both skeptical about the prospects for revolutionary victories abroad and concerned about the dangers to the domestic Revolution that might result from excessive entanglements in foreign quarrels. Wilsonians are reasonably confident that the Revolutionary legacy in the United States is secure from internal dangers. They also believe that the United States, without too much blood or gold, can spread democracy around the world. The tide of history is running with American democracy, Wilsonians believe: The American Revolution is sweeping the world.

Jeffersonians have a very different view. They believe that democracy is a fragile plant—difficult to grow, harder to propagate. Looking back at the long struggle in Britain—the Magna Carta, the Reformation, the Civil War, the Glorious Revolution, enemies from within and without, usurpations of kings, intrigues of bishops, invasions and Jacobite risings—then the struggles of the American Revolution with its treasons and disasters, the nation's chief cities in flames or in enemy hands—Jeffersonians could not be so sanguine about the possibilities for defending democracy at home, much less extending it abroad.

In the decades following the American Revolution, there was ample evidence to justify Jeffersonian forebodings about the difficulty of establishing democracy abroad. The French Revolution, originally greeted with hope and support by Jefferson and others, quickly degenerated into bloodshed and tyranny. The wars of liberation in South America set up one bloody shambles after another; neither life nor property was safe in most of that region, and a legacy of misrule was established that lingers in some countries to this day. It was a disillusionment comparable to what many idealists felt more recently as one newly independent African democracy after another collapsed into chaos and tyranny following decolonization in the 1960s. Experiences like these have created an enduring sense among Jeffersonians that the United States could better serve the cause of universal democracy by setting an example rather than by imposing a model.

But democracy was not merely difficult to propagate abroad, it was difficult to defend at home. The gutters of history, ancient and modern, were strewn with the wreckage of democracies. The Thirty Tyrants overthrew the democracy of Athens; Julius Caesar established an empire in Rome. Mobs debased, oligarchies perverted, dukes and princes overthrew republican governments in the city-states of early modern Italy. Almost everywhere in Europe absolute monarchs suppressed traditional institutions like parliaments and assemblies.

Liberty could not even trust her friends. Cromwell set up civil and ecclesiastical powers more arbitrary than those he had suppressed; Napoleon directed the energies of France more thoroughly in the service of his personal ambitions than had any Louis.

The Hebrew Scriptures revealed the distressing truth that not even the chosen people could maintain their liberties. In the days of the judges, "[E]very man in Israel did what was right in his own eyes." But that wasn't enough for them: "Give us a king," the people said to Samuel.

As God asked, Samuel did his best to warn them: If I choose a king for you, he told the clamorous assembly, "He will take the best of your fields and vineyards and olive orchards and give them to his servants. He will take the tenth of your grain and of your vineyards and give it to his officers and to his servants. He will take your menservants and maidservants, and the best of your cattle and your asses, and put them to his work. He will take the tenth of your flocks, and you shall be his slaves. And in that day you will cry out because of your king, whom you have chosen for yourselves; but the Lord will not answer you that day."[3]

The first Israel had lost its liberty to a centralizing, tax-gathering, bureaucracy-building state. What guarantee could be given for the second?

Liberty is infinitely precious, and almost as infinitely fragile; that is the core belief of the Jeffersonian movement. In this it differs from all the other major political forces in American life. Hamiltonians believe that commercial development can secure the blessings of free government; Jeffersonians note that in one democracy after another, great commercial interests have subverted the political process to its destruction, and that the ambitious rich man can be the greatest danger to a democratic system. Wilsonians believe that the force of progress and enlightenment is moving mankind toward a reign of peace and reason; Jeffersonians believe that history goes backward as well as forward, and that ambition and the lust for wealth are too deeply embedded in human nature to be easily harnessed by just and rational laws. Jacksonians, as we shall see, believe that the deep, good heart of the American people will instinctively repel any threat to their cherished democracy; Jeffersonians know too well the degree to which an unchecked, unbridled popular passion can endanger the very democracy that it wants to protect.

Jeffersonians therefore find themselves in an odd and difficult position. They believe, perhaps more than anyone else, that democracy is the best possible form of government, but they constitute the only major American school that believes history is not necessarily on the side of the American experiment.

Jeffersonian Foreign Policy Doctrine

From this sense of democracy as uniquely precious but achingly vulnerable has developed the Jeffersonian approach to foreign policy. The Jeffersonian mind does not scan the foreign policy horizon in a search for opportunities; rather, it mostly sees threats.

This hasn't always been true. The early Jeffersonians had objectives, mostly territorial: Chiefly they wanted control of the Gulf Coast from Florida to the mouth of the Mississippi, which many of them believed also required the possession of Cuba. The Louisiana Purchase and the annexation of Florida largely satisfied the Jeffersonian hunger for land. Jeffersonians like John Quincy Adams opposed the annexation of Texas, counseled caution in the Oregon controversy with Britain, and bitterly denounced the Mexican War. Wilsonians and Hamiltonians together plotted the overthrow of the Hawaiian monarchy and U.S. annexation of that land and people; Jeffersonians wanted to leave the Hawaiians alone. Jeffersonians like Mark Twain denounced the war that established American rule in the Philippines with the kind of fierce invective their successors would hurl at the planners of the Vietnam War. Few things were clearer to the Jeffersonians than that the growth of the American republic into an intercontinental empire was a bad business all around.

Once the United States had achieved a reasonably clear title to most of the key real estate on the Jeffersonian shopping list, there was little more, concretely, to be gained from an activist foreign policy. Jeffersonians certainly found little to tempt them in the ambitious plans periodically put forward by Hamiltonians and Wilsonians for global systems. The worldwide commercial system the Hamiltonians wanted would reinforce precisely the commercial elite that Jeffersonians deeply feared at home. It was a bad thing, not a good one. Endlessly involving American arms, credit, honor, and prestige in attempts to spread democracy to ungrateful and incapable republics in South America or, worse, intervening in Balkan wars between the Ottoman sultans and their rebellious Christian subjects seemed to involve risks, including conflicts with other powers and building up a strong military-industrial complex in the United States, dependent on the public treasury and addicted to war.

There are two basic kinds of danger to liberty that might arise from developments in foreign policy: There are those things that foreign countries may do to us that threaten our liberties directly; there are also, perhaps more dangerous, the things we may do to ourselves as we seek to defend ourselves against others, or even as we seek to advance our values abroad. In the first group fall the obvious, notorious dangers of foreign policy: Foreign countries might invade, devastate, occupy, and finally conquer the United States. Using threats or bribes, they could suborn the government or corrupt politicians and bend the United States to their will. They could so infringe on the rights of American citizens abroad—the impressment of seamen, the confiscation of property, piracy, extortion, mistreatment of diplomats—that the American government would have no alternative but war.

These were real and alarming enough—particularly in the era of Napoleon—but they were far from the most insidious dangers Jeffersonians saw lurking in the world of foreign affairs. What they feared most was not successful foreign invasions of the United States. Distance, the sea, and the American victory in the Revolution all counseled courage in the face of that danger. Rather, they feared what the effort of continually resisting invasion, or participating in foreign politics, would do to American democracy. Victory, even universal global hegemony, would be a hollow prize.

"She well knows," John Quincy Adams said, speaking of the United States,

> that by once enlisting under other banners than her own, were they even the banners of foreign independence, she would involve herself, beyond the power of extrication, in all the wars of interest and intrigue, of individual avarice, envy, and ambition, which assume the colors and usurp the standard of freedom. . . . She might become the dictatress of the world: she would be no longer the ruler of her own spirit.[4]

Senator Borah, the Jeffersonian chairman of the Senate Foreign Relations Committee who drove Hamiltonians and Wilsonians almost to despair with his resourceful opposition to the League of Nations, echoed Adams's thoughts almost a hundred years later when he rose on the Senate floor to make a last attempt to block ratification of the Versailles Treaty, including U.S. membership in the League of Nations: "When you shall have committed this Republic to a scheme of world control based upon force . . . you will have soon destroyed the atmosphere of freedom, of confidence in the self-governing capacity of the masses, in which alone a democracy may thrive. . . . And what shall it profit us as a Nation if we shall go forth to the domination of the earth and share with others the glory of world control and lose that fine sense of confidence in the people, the soul of democracy?"[5] Like Adams, Borah believed that excessive intervention in the Hobbesian world of international politics would corrupt and undermine the Lockean, democratic order that the American people had established at home.

These dangers that the Jeffersonians foresaw from the beginning and sought to ward off were, to a large extent, unavoidable. The world intrudes on us whether we like it or not. Enlightened Jeffersonians have always therefore known that real isolation is impossible; the task of foreign policy as they see it is to manage the unavoidable American involvement in the world with the least possible risk and cost. Unlike the other major schools, the Jeffersonians are always braced to choose among evils. Government itself is a necessary evil to the Jeffersonian mind. The same thing is true about foreign policy: We would be much better off if we didn't have to have one at all. As it is, Jeffersonians believe, we will bear what we must while avoiding what we may. Since we must have a foreign policy of some kind, let us find one that does the least possible damage to our democratic institutions.

Some might call this an isolationist attitude, and isolation has always been an attractive alternative to the Jeffersonian mind, but we should recognize that it proceeds not out of an ignorant and ostrichlike sense of the nation's indestructibility, but rather out of a keen, aching, and even morbid sensitivity about the exquisite vulnerability of the American experiment to the consequences of developments overseas.

The Avoidance of War

War was the first and greatest evil Jeffersonians sought to avoid. Jefferson genuinely hated and feared it, "as much a punishment to the punisher as to the sufferer."[6] War was not detestable only because of the casualties it caused or the hatreds it fomented but also because it threatened to undermine American democracy at home. Frequent participation in major international wars would, the early Jeffersonians believed, pose—win or lose—a major threat to American liberties. Wars cost money, piling up debts that concentrated power in the central government and forced most of the population to labor and pay taxes to support the minority that owned the government bonds issued to cover the debt; wars built up a concentrated economic and political machinery dependent on government funds, addicted to secrecy, and with a permanent interest in discovering ever new dangers abroad; they also made the development of strong standing armies and navies inevitable, a development that, historically, has often been fatal to republican liberty.

Though Jeffersonian thinking about the economic dangers of war has changed somewhat over the years, the core ideas remain similar. During the eighteenth and nineteenth centuries, Jeffersonians hated and feared the national debt with a passion that today is difficult for even the most dedicated "debt hawks" to appreciate. In addition to all the arguments that are still brought forward by those who wish to cut the federal deficit (the burden for future generations, the "crowding out" by federal spending of private investment, the danger of inflation), the early Jeffersonians brought forward a political argument as well. The national debt was a danger to democracy because it divided the citizens into two classes—taxpayers and interest collectors. In American circumstances that generally meant that the products and income of farmers were taxed to provide a stream of income for merchants, capitalists, and others with ready cash to invest. The hallmark of Jefferson's administration through 1807 had been his success in paying down the debt. When he assumed office, the debt stood at $83 million; by 1807 it was $69 million;[7] had it not been for the Louisiana Purchase, it would have stood at $54 million.

In 1809, as yet another war crisis with Britain loomed on the horizon, Jefferson advised his friend James Monroe, the new secretary of state, to do everything possible to avoid war: "If we go to war now, I fear we may renounce forever the hope of seeing an end of our national debt. If we can keep at peace eight years longer, our income, liberated from debt, will be adequate to any war, without new taxes or loans, and our position and increasing strength put us *hors d'insulte* from any nation."[8]

The prospect of debts resulting from wars horrified generations of orators. After the Civil War, President Andrew Johnson lamented that the cost incurred in the war to free the slaves would reduce millions of Northerners to debt peonage for generations.[9]

"We are going to pile up a debt that the toiling masses that shall come many generations after us will have to pay," said Nebraska senator George W. Norris in a speech against Wilson's proposed 1917 declaration of war against Germany. "Unborn millions will bend their backs in toil in order to pay for the terrible step we are now about to take."[10]

For Jeffersonians there were two key goals in domestic politics. Merchants and bankers had to be prevented from setting up a monetary aristocracy as antidemocratic as the blood aristocracies of Europe, and the central government had to be prevented from growing so powerful that it threatened the freedoms and rights of the states and citizens alike.

Those goals were related, and one of the most important connections was the national debt. Debt strengthened the mercantile classes, and government spending made possible by that debt strengthened the central government. What Jefferson and the Jeffersonians feared would happen next was simple: The creditor class would use its wealth to gain effective control of an ever more powerful government. Almost two hundred years before Eisenhower's warning along similar lines, Jeffersonians feared the growth of a military-industrial-financial complex. The more the government spent, the larger and stronger the class of military contractors and other dependents would be. The deeper into debt the government went, the larger and stronger would be the class of creditors, insisting that the government use its monopoly of force and its taxing authority to extract resources from the mass of the people to pay off the creditor class.

The other reason Jefferson hated war was that it led the state to build up its armed forces. Such buildups were often associated with deficit spending and therefore with increases in the national debt, and they also put force in the hands of the central government. Much of this feeling originally came out of reflection on the long struggle between the British Parliament and the House of Stuart. The efforts of the Stuart kings to build a Continental-style absolute monarchy in Britain often turned on the question of standing armies; once the king had an irresistible standing army he could overawe Parliament and do exactly as he pleased.

War requires secrecy, and it strengthens the executive against the legislature, thought Jeffersonians, and they were right. Today's imperial presidency is the offspring of fifty years of crisis and of hot and cold war between 1939 and 1989. In 1935 the U.S. armed forces consisted of 251,799 people in uniform and 147,188[11] civilian employees. The total budget of the Army and Navy Departments was $924 million.[12] There was no independent national intelligence operation. The United States kept informed about foreign countries through its regular diplomatic service, which employed 4,471[13] people. The total State Department budget was $16 million.[14] Sixty years later the total intelligence budget was classified—that fact in itself a horror for Jeffersonian democrats. The Pentagon employed 3.25 million people, including both civilians and those in uniform.[15] The number of intelligence employees was also classified information and unavailable to the general public, but reliable estimates indicated that between 70,000 and 80,000 people were employed from a total budget of about $27 billion.[16] An estimated 15 million[17] classified documents rested in government vaults, unavailable for citizens' inspection. The costs from the last sixty years of crisis and war have seen the national debt rise from $40.4 billion[18] (with annual interest payments of $1 billion) in 1939 to peak at $5.5 trillion early in the Clinton administration (with annual interest payments of $362 billion).[19]

The United States won most of the wars fought in these years, but the government and the people were much farther apart at the end of the experience than they were at the beginning. It was not only misguided militia members stockpiling canned goods and reading up on secret government missions in fearful black helicopters who distrusted the government; tens of millions of otherwise perfectly sensible Americans believed in vast government conspiracies and coverups regarding everything from the Kennedy assassination to alleged contacts with aliens. The corrosive effects of secrecy on public trust and democratic government are an important reason why Jeffersonians are led so reluctantly even into just wars.

For most of American history Jeffersonian opinion has seen war as a last and very undesirable resort. Instinctively Jeffersonians are slow to react to provocations. Secretary of State Cyrus Vance's refusal to resort to force during the Iranian hostage crisis of 1979–80 parallels Jefferson's resolute determination to avoid intervention in the Napoleonic Wars despite provocations from both Britain and France. This was the policy that another Jeffersonian, William Jennings Bryan, hoped to follow with respect to German provocations during World War I.

When it becomes politically or morally impossible to ignore provocations, or to respond to them with nothing more than verbal protests, Jeffersonians will still not turn to war. They see economic sanctions, for example, as far preferable. Not only do sanctions not embroil the country in alliances and debt, but they strike at the very commercial interests that Jeffersonians wish to contain at home. From the days of Jefferson's economic sanctions intended to force Britain and France to recognize American rights to the attempts to use economic sanctions as a tool to improve human rights conditions in contemporary China, Jeffersonian opinion has been quick to disrupt commerce to serve national political objectives and slow to resort to outright war.

Wilsonians hate war, too, but for different reasons. The Wilsonian hatred of war stands more on humanitarian than on political grounds. As we know, Wilsonians do not share the Jeffersonian fear of central authority. Nevertheless, from the nineteenth century through the Cold War, Jeffersonians worked with Wilsonians to make wars less likely or less horrible through legal means. They looked to arms limits, disarmament agreements, and strict rules of war as ways to achieve these goals—and, if possible, to reduce the costs of defense in times of peace. Beginning after the Civil War, Jeffersonians sought to induce foreign countries to enter into arbitration agreements with the United States and one another, pledging to submit their differences to peaceful arbitration and accepting cooling-off periods before resorting to hostilities.

That war should be the last resort of policy remains a primary pillar of Jeffersonian thought today. After negotiation has failed, after arbitration has been unsuccessful, after sanctions have had no effect—you can still go to war if you must. Even then, however, Jeffersonians would prefer a gradual approach to war: Turn the thermostat up a little at a time; try to get your results with the least possible application of force.

The Constitutional Conduct of Foreign Policy

If the avoidance of war is the first principle of Jeffersonian statesmanship, the second is the constitutional conduct of foreign policy. Here Jeffersonians often stand alone; the other three schools are willing and ready to lay the sacred scrolls aside when the cannons thunder, or even when they threaten to thunder. "Silent enim leges inter arma," Cicero told a Roman jury in 52 B.C.: The law shuts up when weapons speak.[20]

Hamiltonians like Dean Acheson have roundly and frankly cursed the Constitution with its intricate framework of toils and snares, the opportunities it gives for recalcitrant senators to gum up the works of the executive machine. Wilsonians, too, when their blood is up because of some pestilential foreign evildoer, are able to emancipate themselves from an excessive reverence for constitutional norms. Few of them, for example, sought to apply the War Powers Act in the Yugoslav war of 1999. As for Jacksonians, it was Andrew Jackson who said, when, in 1832, the Supreme Court overturned the Indian Removal Act, "John Marshall has made his decision; now let him enforce it."[21]

Not only do Jeffersonians actually value what so many regard as the odious constitutional restrictions on executive power, they would sometimes even like to see them tightened. Throughout American history they have sought to defend congressional power and dignity in foreign affairs. In the fights over the League of Nations, the UN Charter, and the treaty that founded NATO, Jeffersonians insisted on language that affirmed that no treaty could bind the United States to send troops abroad for war without congressional consent. The War Powers Act of 1973, requiring congressional consent when American troops are placed in harm's way and the bane of every president since Richard Nixon, was a classically Jeffersonian measure in attempting to assert congressional control over American involvement in foreign conflicts.

The concept of government secrecy is deeply inimical to Jeffersonian ideas. Efforts to control the CIA, to declassify as many secret documents as quickly as possible, and to subject intelligence and military institutions to constant and intensive congressional oversight within a framework of law proceed directly from Jeffersonian values.

Opposition to fast-track authority—a system by which recent presidents have negotiated broad multilateral trade agreements under congressional rules that allow a vote on the entire final package, rather than rules that would allow either house to pick the deals apart—also reflects Jeffersonian concerns about the integrity of congressional authority. Supporters of the fast track decry the way the traditional procedure allows individual representatives and senators to conduct horse trading, erect procedural obstacles, and distinguish themselves by all the tricks that our legislators have developed through more than two centuries of parliamentary manuevers. To Jeffersonians, giving a powerful voice in trade negotiations to the representatives of each state and section is a good thing, not a bad one. If this annoys our trading partners, it's probably because they know that the constitutional process improves our chances of getting a better deal. In any case Jeffersonians don't feel the same sense of urgency about concluding ever new and improved trade agreements that drives Hamiltonians from one round of trade talks to the next.

Frustrated Hamiltonians roar that in fact opposition to fast-track comes from special interests that just want protection. Jeffersonians shrug; they are well aware that the U.S. government system is one that proceeds more by personal interests than principles. They see nothing wrong with cooperating with South Carolina textile mill owners one week and Oregon timber cutters the next. The constitutional system has lasted this long, they believe, precisely because there are many competing interests in this country that do not want to give up their right to be heard and to shape policy, even foreign policy. To the Jeffersonian mind this is not a disagreeable and possibly dangerous defect in our system; it is one of the glories and strengths of that system, and they aim to defend it.

Economy of Interests

In 1806, President Thomas Jefferson wrote a congratulatory letter to Alexander I on his accession to the Russian throne. "It will be among the latest and most soothing comforts of my life," wrote the author of the Declaration of Independence to the most autocratic ruler on earth, "to have seen advanced to the government of so extensive a portion of the earth, and at so early a period of his life, a sovereign whose ruling passion is the advancement of the happiness and prosperity of his people; and not of his own people only, but who can extend his eye and his good will to a distant and infant nation, unoffending in its course, unambitious in its views."[22]

Flowery compliments to an autocrat? Uriah Heepish comments about the humble rank of the United States in the family of nations? "[U]noffending in [our] course, unambitious in [our] views"?

This is not the tone of William B. Travis crying out "Give 'em hell!" from the ramparts of the Alamo; this is not the "I have not yet begun to fight" spirit of John Paul Jones or the spirit that moved Gen. Anthony C. McAuliffe to reply "Nuts!" to the German demand that he surrender his outnumbered and surrounded forces in the Battle of the Bulge.

It is, however, the classical and unmistakable tone of Jeffersonian diplomacy. Speak softly, and carry the smallest possible stick; Jeffersonians believe that is the best method for avoiding unnecessary war. Define your interests as narrowly as possible, and you will have the fewest possible grounds for quarrels with others.

Hamiltonians argue that American commercial interests provide justification for interventions abroad. Jeffersonians disagree. "No, it wouldn't be much thrill to die for Du Pont in Brazil," replied the unwilling young soldier in a 1941 antiwar version of "Billy Boy," as sung by the Almanac Singers, an influential folk ensemble.[23]

In a speech that was widely quoted by Jeffersonian opponents of the Vietnam War (and was more recently reprised by Gore Vidal), a Jeffersonian who had somehow surmounted the handicap of being named Smedley Butler to reach the rank of general in the Marine Corps summed up a career of military intervention in the interest, as he saw it, of American business. "I spent most of my time being a high-class muscleman for Big Business, for Wall Street and for the bankers. . . . In short, I was a racketeer, a gangster for capitalism. . . . I helped make Mexico . . . safe for American oil interests in 1914 . . . made Haiti and Cuba a decent place for the National City Bank boys to collect revenue in."[24]

If the broad commercial interests asserted by Hamiltonians and the Hamiltonian willingness to sacrifice constitutional niceties and parochial interests to the construction of an international trade system seem excessive and dangerous to Jeffersonians, the even more universal moral interests and duties asserted by Wilsonians horrify them. Arguing with China over self-determination in Tibet, demanding free elections in Kosovo, or opposing ethnic murder in Rwanda look, to the Wilsonian mind, like simple and self-evident cases in which the American national interest in an orderly world coincides with the country's moral duty. The Jeffersonian view on this subject was stated by John Quincy Adams in 1821: "Wherever the standard of freedom and independence has been or shall be unfurled, there will her [America's] heart, her benedictions and her prayers be. But she goes not abroad in search of monsters to destroy. She is the well-wisher to the freedom and independence of all. She is the champion and vindicator only of her own."[25]

This view is not based on cowardice or moral indifference. It rests in the Jeffersonian belief that excessive involvements overseas can compromise our democratic standards at home. Governing foreign peoples—in the Philippines at the beginning of the twentieth century, in the former Yugoslavia at its end—undermines American democratic institutions and values, say the Jeffersonians. We shall find ourselves mixed in with corrupt and unworthy allies; today we help the Afghan mujahideen by arming and training them against the Soviet Union, and tomorrow they turn those weapons against us and become a thorn in our flesh throughout the Middle East. We protect the Albanians in Kosovo from Serb "ethnic cleansers," only to behold the Albanians using their new freedom to drive their Serbian enemies from their homes in turn.

More often than Hamiltonians and Wilsonians, Jeffersonians believe that the best policy for the United States is to let well enough alone. Jeffersonians see the risks and costs of intervention as so high that only real threats to the nation's existence justify such adventures. They are critical of others' claims that the national interest is endangered by particular crises. Wilsonians argued for intervention in Yugoslavia on the analogy of the West's failure to deter Hitler. Jeffersonians replied that there is a substantial difference between Hitler's Germany and Milosevic's Yugoslavia, that Yugoslavia has far less ability to disturb the general European equilibrium and threaten vital American interests.

Jeffersonians use the same skepticism to ask where the nation's true security perimeter is to be found. Particularly with the end of the Cold War, they often question American troop commitments in Europe and the Far East. Is it really in the national interest, they ask, for the United States to be at the center of negotiations between the South Koreans, the North Koreans, the Japanese, and the Chinese over North Korea's development of a missile program?

This is essentially the argument that Jeffersonian opponents of a large and intrusive federal government make in domestic policy. Is a given federal program or regulation really necessary? Will the benefits truly outweigh the costs? Do we in any case want to see the federal government growing continually larger and more powerful?

Jeffersonian skepticism about the merits of an active foreign policy has libertarian roots, and more than any of the other schools, Jeffersonians have consistently tried to ensure that the same anti-big-government logic that is so often so powerful in domestic politics be extended to the conduct of the nation's foreign policy.

Economy of Means

Having defined American interests as narrowly as possible, Jeffersonians then seek to serve them as economically as possible. This is partly about money. A dollar not spent on the military or diplomatic establishments is a dollar not taxed from American citizens, a dollar not devoted to the projects of a centralizing government, and a dollar that can't be spent by the dominant political party on corrupt contracts and sweetheart deals that cement its hold on power. Jeffersonian politicians want to see defense and diplomatic expenses kept low, and they want State Department and military accounts carefully kept and regularly scrutinized.

But Jeffersonian parsimony is about more than saving taxpayer money. Jeffersonians have imposed qualitative as well as quantitative restrictions on U.S. military and diplomatic establishments.

Once Jeffersonians conceded that a standing army and a defensive navy were necessary, they did their best to keep both of these institutions as humble and as close to the people as possible. Professional career soldiers in the federal service were suspect; military academies even more so. In 1830 Congressman Davy Crockett of Tennessee denounced the U.S. Military Academy at West Point, noting that its graduates were "too delicate" for military service, unlike the hardy sons of the western soil. Was the academy being properly managed, Crockett asked: "I want to know if it has been managed for the benefit of the noble and wealthy of the country, or for the poor and orphan."[26] West Point, thundered the future Massachusetts senator and Reconstruction heavyweight Charles Sumner in 1845, was "a seminary of idleness and vice."[27] For some time it was unclear that the dangerous institution would survive. Ulysses Grant, who went to West Point only because his father forced him to, eagerly followed congressional discussions of a proposal to close the institution during his plebe year. But after a close and bitter debate the proposal was defeated, and after an abortive attempt to get himself expelled, Grant resigned himself to the prospect of a military career.[28]

The populist disdain still felt for "career politicians" was at one time also extended to career soldiers, with the added worry that career soldiers (knowing no trade but war, dependent on their political masters for employment and advancement) would be at best advocates of warlike policies and at worst the willing tools of any central government wishing to subvert popular liberties.

Thus Jeffersonians opposed the establishment of a peacetime standing army. Then they opposed the establishment of West Point. With West Point a fact of life, they did their best to keep it on short commons (with notoriously stingy appropriations) and, by giving the power of appointment to representatives and senators, did their best to ensure congressional control over this dangerous institution. Finally Jeffersonians supported militias and, later, the various National Guard formations as alternatives and supplements to a professional standing army.

Their approach to the navy was even more draconian. Jeffersonians wanted naval appropriations kept to the absolute minimum. There was nothing so likely to get the United States involved in foreign quarrels as a blue-water navy. The larger the navy the more pressure there would be on the United States to defend various commercial and humanitarian "interests" in far-off lands, and the mere presence of American forces in foreign ports made confrontations more likely. In 1872 an American vessel in the port of Smyrna came close to firing on an Austro-Hungarian vessel in a controversy over the imprisonment of a Hungarian citizen who had declared his intention of becoming an American citizen.[29] Why, asked Jeffersonians, should questions of war and peace be left to cocky naval commanders in distant lands? Keep the ships home, and there will be fewer fights.

Jeffersonians developed theories of coastal defense and coastal fortification to divert spending from blue-water-navy vessels to coastal barges and forts. More than once in the nineteenth century, the chronically underfunded navy declined to levels well below the minimum needed for combat effectiveness even against second-rate naval powers.

Today, the Jeffersonian approach to foreign policy looks to cut military costs to the lowest possible level, and aims to ensure civilian control over military and intelligence institutions. Contemporary pressure for the declassification of as many Cold War documents as possible, and for new restrictions on the ability of bureaucrats to classify government papers as secret, reflects the traditional Jeffersonian attempt to keep the military and intelligence communities open, accountable, and weak.

Diplomats can be as deadly as ships, and the State Department, too, has had to endure hostile scrutiny from tightfisted Jeffersonians. The thought of bewigged, bejeweled, and bepowdered American diplomatic fops mincing across ballroom floors with their European colleagues inspires a visceral revulsion in the honest Jeffersonian mind, akin to the one that overcomes readers when the pigs in *Animal Farm* dress up like humans to have dinner with the neighboring farmers.

Jeffersonians consistently act to ensure that American diplomats do not forget the important distinction between a virtuous republic and decadent monarchies and dictatorships. From 1778 to 1893, U.S. emissaries to foreign lands went by the title of "minister" rather than "ambassador," because of a widespread view that an ambassador was, and could only be, the personal representative of one monarch to another.[30] In 1854 Secretary of State William L. Marcy issued orders that no ministers of the United States could dress in court uniforms of any kind. Embarrassed American diplomats wore ordinary evening dress to glittering European court receptions and were occasionally mistaken for butlers.[31]

American diplomats were well aware of the political perils that lay in the practices of European courts. At times they obeyed the dictates of court etiquette, but took pains not to advertise this fact back home. Thus when George III, mad and blind, finally died in 1820, the diplomatic corps made a collective decision to dress their servants in mourning. Richard Rush, the American minister to Britain at the time, went along with the decision but chose to pay the cost out of his own pocket rather than submit mourning expenses for George III to congressional scrutiny.[32] This was surely wise.

At other times, as in 1828, when U.S. minister James Barbour created a stir by refusing to kiss the hand of the queen of Portugal at a reception, the Americans preferred to scandalize their diplomatic colleagues rather than offend against republican principles back home.[33]

To ensure that American diplomats abroad remembered their republican roots, Jeffersonians limited their number and were anything but extravagant in making provision for them. As late as 1916 the entire budget for the Department of State, including janitorial staff in its Washington headquarters, came to $6 million.[34] And the tradition of relative meanness in diplomatic budgets continues. In 1999 Philip Lader, the American ambassador to Britain, had a salary about half that of Britain's ambassador to the United States. Congressional refusal to allocate an adequate representation allowance is one reason why many of the most prominent U.S. diplomatic posts are reserved for wealthy campaign contributors who can pay the costs of wining and dining foreign elites out of their own pockets. Such congressional penny-pinching on the diplomatic budget was widely blamed for leaving American embassies in Africa dangerously exposed to terrorist attacks like those that killed 223 people at the embassies in Kenya and Tanzania in 1998.[35] At a time of critical economic negotiations with China, when the Chinese trade surplus with the United States was one of the leading issues in American foreign policy, the staff of the economic section of the U.S. Embassy in Beijing did not even have a fax machine, much less the computers and software needed to monitor developments there.[36]

Yet Jeffersonians are unwilling to cut the diplomats off completely. True, secret discussions and decisions among a champagne-drinking elite in foreign ballrooms are hardly the Jeffersonians' preferred method for the settlement of great issues of state. On the other hand Jeffersonians agree strongly with Winston Churchill that "to jaw-jaw is better than to war-war." An effective diplomacy can be an effective means of staving off worse evils, and from Jefferson forward some of America's most effective ballroom mincers have been Jeffersonian democrats.

Jeffersonian Strategic Ideas

Based on their core values and ideas about the national interest, Jeffersonians have put forward a variety of suggestions for American grand strategy. As circumstances have changed, Jeffersonian strategic concepts have changed, but as in the case of Hamiltonian and Wilsonian ideas, Jeffersonian approaches to American foreign policy continually seek to advance a core set of interests and values from one generation to the next.

In all of the four major eras of American foreign policy (1789–1823, 1823–1914, 1914–1947, 1947–present), Jeffersonians have attempted to shape the American strategic response. In the first, tumultuous era, Jeffersonians proposed balancing France's dominant power in Europe against Britain's too-threatening power on the seas. They reversed course following the War of 1812, and Jeffersonian strategic concepts largely dominated American grand strategy in the decades following the proclamation of the Monroe Doctrine.

As British power declined, Jeffersonians opposed attempts to enlist the United States in the support of the British world system, resisting entry into World War I and opposing United States membership in the League of Nations. Jeffersonians played a significant role in shaping American foreign policy between the two world wars and were largely responsible for inventing and popularizing the myth of virtuous isolation to justify their strategic ideas. Badly damaged by the failure of American foreign policy between 1919 and 1939 to stabilize world politics, during the Cold War Jeffersonians were generally relegated to a secondary position in foreign policy debates until the Vietnam War revived interest in a foreign policy of limits.

Intellectually the first era of American foreign policy remains in some ways the most interesting, and the strategic concepts advanced at that time were more radical than any seen since. In particular, while Hamiltonians steadfastly believed that the only real policy for the United States was some kind of alliance with Great Britain, Jefferson and others asked whether, instead of siding with Britain to balance any aspiring hegemon on the continent of Europe, we should balance with Napoleon against Britain? Britain, after all, was the most dangerous power in the world to American interests. The British fleet was the mightiest military force that could be brought into action against the United States. It was British merchants and traders who, armed with the mother country's backing and their superior access to London finance, competed with American interests around the world. Two land powers, one in Europe and one in North America, would limit Britain's pretensions; at the same time, British sea power would keep the continental European powers safely on their own side of the ocean.

At various times during his presidency, Jefferson flirted with both alternatives. He came closest to an alliance with Britain when Napoleon forced a weak Spanish government to return the Louisiana Territory (which France had ceded to Spain in 1767) to France. A French presence in New Orleans, Jefferson wrote to Robert R. Livingston,[37] then American minister to France, would force the Americans to "marry ourselves" to the British fleet and nation. At other times British provocations, especially to American shipping, grew so outrageous that it was difficult to craft a response short of war.

While puzzling over these alternatives, Jefferson in his diplomacy concentrated on keeping the United States out of the Napoleonic Wars and, hopefully, on luring Britain and France into a bidding war for American support.

It worked, sort of. Neither Britain nor France offered the United States the assurances it wanted for freedom of the seas, but France sold us Louisiana and Britain recognized the transfer. In the long run the peaceful acquisition of 828,000 square miles comprising some of the most fertile soil in the world far outweighed any temporary problems with the impressment of seamen and the seizure of cargoes.[38]

Some of his diplomatic moves were more successful than others—the Louisiana Purchase is considered one of the great strokes in American, or indeed, world history; the embargo prohibiting all American trade with Europe was seen even at the time to be a dismal failure—but in success or in failure, Jefferson stood by his core principles: Almost anything is better than war, and the first duty of the government is to protect liberty rather than commerce.

The Monroe System

This period of strategic uncertainty came to an end under the presidency of James Monroe, as he struck up what Jefferson, in a congratulatory letter written from Monticello, called a "cordial friendship with England." The rapprochement with Britain that the Monroe system entailed was, Jefferson agreed, the best possible policy for the United States. "Great Britain," he wrote, "is the nation which can do us the most harm of any one, or all on earth; and with her on our side we need not fear the whole world."[39] Although the United States and Britain would move repeatedly to the brink of war in the next seventy years, neither country ever broke with the logic of the arrangement proposed by British foreign secretary George Canning and shrewdly modified by Secretary of State John Quincy Adams.

Later Jeffersonian mythmakers would recast the Monroe Doctrine as a unilateral American declaration of principled isolation from European affairs, but as those who developed the idea well knew, the doctrine in fact represented the U.S. answer to the strategic dilemma of its first fifty years. Given basic British respect for American interests and territorial integrity (an attitude enforced by Britain's fears of political isolation by a combination of conservative Continental states, and strengthened by British appreciation for the fighting qualities occasionally exhibited by American forces in the War of 1812), the United States would no longer hesitate. It was better to come to an arrangement that would strengthen Britain on the seas than to support the efforts of Continental powers to limit British power.

The rationale for this step was clear in 1823, and only became clearer as the United States grew steadily stronger through the nineteenth century. If Britain ever weakened, the Continental powers would have been only too eager to take advantage of Latin America's prevailing anarchy and weakness to intervene and carve new empires for themselves in the New World. The fear of European dynastic adventures in Latin America was anything but fanciful. The Portuguese royal house of Braganza maintained a grip on Brazil until the overthrow of the emperor Dom Pedro II in 1889. France, Spain, Prussia, Russia, and Austria supported a Bourbon restoration after the Congress of Vienna. Spain did not recognize the independence of Peru until 1879. Most of the Latin American states were so weak and so badly governed during much of this time that without foreign protection they would have faced great difficulties defending their independence.

For all its arrogance and ambition, Britain was, Jefferson, Adams, and Monroe agreed, a safer partner than any of the Continental states could be. Although many of the obstacles persisted that had caused Jefferson in the 1790s to gag at the Hamilton-Jay policy of an understanding with Britain, by 1823 an understanding with the mother country was the least bad option. Let a British rather than an American fleet police the waters of Latin America against the powers of Europe. Let Britain guarantee the independence of Latin republics, with tacit American support. Preserving its freedom of action, the United States could enjoy most of the benefits of a full-fledged alliance with Britain, while leaving Britain, for reasons dictated by its own interests, to pay almost all of the cost.

With this great step decided, and with the strategic relationship between the two countries more or less determined, Jeffersonian politics in the nineteenth century did its best to palliate the costs of the new policy while extracting every possible ounce of benefit.

From a Jeffersonian point of view, the chief defect of the new policy

"A BRUTAL ASSAULT"

This illustration from "Coin's Financial School," the most important populist economic tract of the 1890s, shows the continuing Jeffersonian unease about participation in the British-dominated international financial system of the time. As a sinister John Bull (the standard symbol for Great Britain) throttles the fair maid Prosperity, her hero, Silver, is prevented from coming to the rescue. Jeffersonians believed that British capital and its American hirelings represented a permanent danger to the interests of American farmers.

Library of Congress, Rare Books Division, HG 529.H33 1894

was that it forced the United States several steps along the path of economic and political development supported by Hamilton. The end of the Napoleonic Wars and the new relationship with Britain opened many doors to American trade, strengthening the seaboard commercial interests against the Jeffersonian farmers and artisans. "The spirit of manufacture has taken deep root among us, and its foundations are laid in too great expense to be abandoned," Jefferson acknowledged as early as

1809.[40] Jeffersonian Republicans introduced and carried the chartering of the Second Bank of the United States; if we were to proceed closely with Britain we needed a national financial system suitable for a commercial and maritime power. At the same time leading Jeffersonians found themselves endorsing protective tariffs and internal improvements distressingly similar to those originally proposed by Hamilton. At a time of British technological and financial superiority, a system of protective tariffs was the only way to ensure that the United States would not sink utterly into the role of a provider of raw materials for the British industrial machine, and an outlet for its finished products. In the last analysis the lesser evil was the development of a domestic manufacturing sector; the greater evil was to remain a permanent appendage to the British dynamo.

Throughout the nineteenth century, right up to the free silver fight under William Jennings Bryan, Jeffersonians would try to limit the scope of these concessions and preserve as much monetary independence from Britain as possible. It might be necessary to operate within the British international order, but one could still test the limits. At the same time, Jeffersonians did their best to limit the tariff to the level genuinely needed to foster "infant industries," and to prevent the system from becoming a form of permanent entitlement for influential industrialists.

On the other hand, the great advantage of the Monroe system, from the Jeffersonian point of view, at least, was the degree to which it freed the United States from the distasteful necessity of maintaining large military forces. The nineteenth century saw Jeffersonians trying with a great deal of consistency and a reasonable amount of success to hold the level of American forces at the absolute minimum required.

In the decade preceding the Civil War, the United States had 27,958[41] men under arms, compared to 293,224[42] for Great Britain, 390,000 for France, 350,000 for Austria, 220,000 for Prussia, and 550,000[43] for Russia. Although American military strength rose to unprecedented levels during the Civil War, the demobilization afterward was thorough and swift. In 1877, the year in which federal troops were finally removed from the South, army enrollment had fallen back to 34,094.[44] In 1881 the U.S. Navy was widely believed to be inferior to the naval forces of Chile.[45] An important element in this program of minimum military force was the demilitarization of the United States–Canada frontier. Thanks to understandings with Britain, beginning in 1817 with the Rush-Bagot Convention, demilitarizing the Great Lakes,[46] the frontier was one of the most lightly fortified major borders in the world even at a time when American-British relations were still crisis-prone.

In a sense Jeffersonians built a strategic relationship with Great Britain that had some interesting structural similarities with the balance the United States reached with the Soviet Union during the Cold War. Britain, a potentially hostile global superpower, had the option at any time of devastating American cities with its navy, and of throwing American financial markets into chaos and collapse through its control of the international credit system. On the other hand the Americans could withhold needed imports of cotton and wheat, and the loss of access to the American market meant ruin for many of Britain's major industrial companies. British banks were also so dependent on their loans and securities in the United States that financial disruptions on the American market would have brought London down. In addition, as many British strategists recognized as early as the Civil War, any military conflict between the two powers might begin with British attacks on the major American cities; it would involve a catastrophic economic upheaval in both countries before its probable ending in the American conquest of Canada, and possibly in the loss of the British possessions in the West Indies as well.

Thus the two powers were in a situation of mutual deterrence—either could inflict unacceptable damage on the other, but only at the cost of accepting similar damage itself. In the nineteenth century as in the Cold War, Jeffersonians wanted to maintain this deterrence at the lowest possible cost. That meant nuclear arms limitations and other agreements with the Soviet Union in the Cold War; during the nineteenth century it meant, above all, the demilitarization of the American-Canadian frontier.

This frontier, including the Alaska boundary, stretches for 5,525 miles. In the early twentieth century, France maintained a regular army, not counting reserves, of 540,000 troops to defend the 280 miles[47] of frontier it shared with Germany: 1,928 soldiers for every mile of frontier. At even one-tenth of this ratio, the United States would have had to maintain a standing army of more than a million men to fortify its land frontier with the British Empire. As it was, the United States was able to defend its boundaries against the British threat with approximately 1 percent of the manpower-to-mile ratio forced on France.[48] Diplomacy had succeeded in maintaining deterrence with disarmament.

The Jeffersonian diplomats of the 1820s charted a course for the United States that enabled it to win the greatest possible security dividends at the lowest political and military cost. For three generations the Monroe system met basic American security needs while allowing the American people to escape much of the cost of great-power politics. Unfortunately, as British power began to weaken, American statesmen were forced to move beyond the Monroe system. From a Jeffersonian point of view nothing since has worked as well. There is something to be said for this view. The United States spent very little on defense in 1900 but was very secure. One hundred years later we spend far more than any country in the world on defense, and are no more secure than we were.

The Great Dilemma

Although Jeffersonians were traditionally far more suspicious of the British than were either Wilsonians or Hamiltonians, the decline and fall of the British Empire presented Jeffersonians with more serious challenges than the ones faced by those global schools. Accustomed to seeing foreign policy as a kind of field of dreams, both Hamiltonians and Wilsonians made a relatively easy transition from cooperating with Britain to replacing it.

No such easy option existed for Jeffersonians. An American effort to set up a global system to replace Great Britain is, on the face of things, a very bad choice from a Jeffersonian point of view. A global hegemon leads a hard and busy life. Are the tribes revolting in Kabul? Is a coup brewing in Manila? Is piracy on the upswing in the South China Sea? Are Arabs bombing Israelis (or vice versa) in the Holy Land?

A global hegemon must determine if any of the thousands of crises that occur in any random decade pose a threat to the hegemonic order. Moreover, even if the hegemon decides that, this time, the revolt of this particular tribal group in this particular sector of the hinterlands of Kabul does not require an armed response, forces must still be maintained in reserve that are capable of acting in Afghanistan, Korea, Somalia, or Taiwan.

Meanwhile, to the capital of a global hegemon come the representatives of every power on earth, many armed with the means of bribery. (Herod, Jugurtha, Mithridates, Cleopatra—all went to Rome or sent their plenipotentiaries.) Once there the visitors seek by fair means or foul to win hegemonic backing for their various schemes. Bribing the press, bribing politicians, offering lucrative contracts to powerful companies in order to win their support for their lobbies—no expense, no craft, is too much when it comes to influencing the policy of a hegemonic power.

Moreover, the capital of a hegemon is invariably a place of secrets, many of them dirty. There are secret agreements with allies, the secrets of military planning, the secrets of a vast and active intelligence community and a web of agents. Many of the hegemon's allies are not particularly nice. In most of this sad world's bloody struggles, both sides are crooked, both drenched in blood, and neither attached to the cause of liberty, virtue, or anything else that goes beyond personal and clan ambition. Inevitably the hegemon enters into arrangements with murderers and thugs; inevitably the hegemon seeks to make its allies more effective at murder and thuggery than their opponents. Hegemonic agents and officials first wink at, then connive at, then foment and encourage murder.

This is no Jerusalem, no "City upon a Hill." This is Babylon; it is Nineveh. It is the Augean stables, not an honest republic. Jeffersonians saw nothing attractive in the prospect of the United States replacing Great Britain as the world's hegemonic power.

Jeffersonians therefore spent much of the first half of the twentieth century looking for ways to avoid this crown of thorns. Jeffersonians were the last of the major schools to accept the necessity of American participation in the two world wars and the Cold War; during the Cold War they were the least convinced of the necessity or the utility of the struggle.

Jeffersonians in the twentieth century had mixed political fortunes. In the short term the aftermath of World War I resulted in a groundswell of support for Jeffersonian ideas. Opponents of American participation in the war had consistently pointed to the dubious role played by Wall Street and New York banks in the gradual movement toward war. "We have loaned many hundreds of millions of dollars to the allies in this controversy," Senator Norris told the Senate in 1917, adapting to new conditions the old arguments that Jeffersonians had used against the Hamiltonian merchants who wanted an alliance with Britain in the Napoleonic Wars. Citing the banks and the munitions contractors "who would expect to make millions more if our country can be drawn into the catastrophe," Norris frankly blamed Wall Street for bribing newspapers and waging a sophisticated and well-financed campaign to drag the United States into a horrible, pointless, immoral war.

"Their object in having war and preparing for war is to make money.

Human suffering and the sacrifice of human life are necessary, but Wall Street considers only the dollars and cents," said Norris. As a result of this propaganda, he passionately warned, "Millions of our brethren must shed their lifeblood, millions of broken-hearted women must weep, millions of children must suffer with cold, and millions of babes must die from hunger, and all because we want to preserve the commercial right of American citizens to deliver munitions of war to belligerent nations."[49]

Norris failed to sway his colleagues, who voted by 82 to 6[50] for the declaration of war against Germany, but the aftermath of the war convinced many Americans that he had been right all along. The Bolshevik publication of the secret treaties among the Allies revealed the selfish purposes that lay behind British and French professions of democratic idealism. The naked display of British imperialism after the war—including the violent suppression of independence protests in India and the bloody extension of British rule in the Middle East and over the former German colonies in Africa—further soured American opinion of the postwar Allies, as did the harsh, shortsighted, and vindictive French policy toward Germany in the immediate postwar era.

The final blow came after the depression gravely undermined American respect for business leaders and the famous 1934 Nye hearings in Congress, conducted by Senator Gerald Nye of North Dakota, substantiated many of Norris's claims about the corrupt and hidden influence of New York banks in building political support for U.S. entry into the war. With Britain and France defaulting on their war debts to the United States while finding plenty of money to oppress their colonial subjects, American opinion turned against further cooperation with its wartime allies.

This feeling resulted in the Neutrality Acts of 1935 and 1936, which prevented American banks from lending money to belligerent nations and took other steps to curtail Hamiltonian efforts to involve the United States in future European wars.[51] Behind the acts stood a powerful American consensus that the United States had been snookered into participation in World War I by a combination of Hamiltonian bankers and European imperialists. The lessons of history, Americans believed, counseled against participation in future conflicts of this kind.

The rise of fascism did not, at first, disturb this consensus. In assessing the events of those years, however, it is important to understand that, at least in the beginning, it was historical sophistication and knowledge of the world that informed the Jeffersonian reluctance to take an active role in resisting Hitler. At least until Neville Chamberlain's Munich folly in 1938, Jeffersonians hoped and believed that France and Britain could contain a greatly weakened Germany, and that disarmament agreements could limit the ability of Japan and other revisionist powers to challenge the existing world order. Unfortunately the abject failure of the British and French governments to stop Hitler created an untenable situation in Europe, while Japan proved more aggressive, and China more feeble, than informed American opinion had supposed.

The failure of Britain and France to take effective action against Hitler in the 1930s was in no way the fault of the United States. Military experts almost unanimously agree that until the cession of the strategic Sudetenland in the Munich accords, a show of resistance from Britain and France would quickly and easily have forced Germany to back down and led to a military coup against Hitler.

Jeffersonians, accustomed from the Revolution forward to think of both Britain and France as effective and aggressive imperial powers, failed to understand the degree to which World War I had destroyed the moral capacity of both countries to act like great powers. Their assessment was wrong, but it was not foolish or naive. (Such charges could more properly be leveled at U.S. policy in the Pacific, where the widespread American tendency to overestimate the ability of China to defend itself against Japanese aggression was rooted in Wilsonian rather than Jeffersonian illusions.)

Jeffersonians and many others hoped and believed until much too late that the international balance of power would take care of itself without direct American intervention. Surely, they reasoned, Britain and France would crush Hitler before he became a real danger to them. Once that point was passed, they assumed again, with all of history and reason on their side, that Britain and France would swallow their ideological hatred of the Soviet Union to make common cause against revisionist Germany. After all, Catholic France had made an alliance with the Turks against Catholic Austria.

Sadly and ironically the Jeffersonians were undone by their faith that the European powers would recognize and act on their own self-interest. They could not believe that the historic great powers of the modern world would sit passively by and watch the destruction of the European power balance on which they depended.

Jeffersonians could and did argue rationally, up until the summer of 1939, that a coalition of European powers pursuing their own best interests could stop Germany without American help. It was only after the

Soviet-German alliance of 1939 that war was inevitable; only after Hitler's blitzkrieg victory over France in May and June 1940 was it inescapably clear that vital American interests would sooner or later require U.S. participation in the European war.

Unfortunately a great many Jeffersonians continued to make the case against United States participation in the war long after a dispassionate study of the strategic realities would have shown that the time had come to prepare, urgently, for war. Distinguished and brilliant Jeffersonians like the historians Charles and Mary Beard, whose earlier work had masterfully summarized two centuries of Jeffersonian thought and exposed the connections between arms sales, bank loans, and American entry into World War I, did lasting damage to their reputations by persisting too long in opposition to American entry into World War II. Even in 1947 Charles Beard was obsessively trying to prove that Roosevelt had deceived the American people into a course that inexorably led to an unnecessary war.

The Jeffersonian party was badly damaged by its persistent and ill-timed isolationism in the run up to the war. Jeffersonians found themselves once more on the wrong side of history, politically speaking, after war, when they either opposed the Cold War outright or argued for a less muscular American response to Soviet behavior.

Other factors combined to reduce Jeffersonian influence to historic lows in the middle of the twentieth century. As the school most opposed to a strong and centralized federal government, Jeffersonian political power was deeply shaken by a series of events that convinced most mid-century Americans, left and right, that the problems of the twentieth century demanded a much stronger federal government than the country had tolerated in the past.

The economic distress of the depression led first to a vast expansion of the role of the federal government, as the New Deal provided economic leadership and emergency assistance to millions of Americans who were otherwise without hope. The acceptance of deficit spending as a routine tool to stimulate the economy undermined one of the basic doctrines of Jeffersonian political economy. A large government deficit was seen as a method of transferring money from the rich to the middle class. By 1950 few Americans doubted that the economic realities demanded a strong and active federal government.

The growth of the power and size of private corporations was an additional factor leading many Americans to find new merit in the growth of federal power. States were helpless to regulate large corporations; the safety and liberty of individual Americans seemed as threatened if not more so by unaccountable private power than by politicians who in the last analysis were subject to at least some kind of democratic controls.

Conservatives who opposed the New Deal state and economic regulations found their own reasons to support a vast increase in the federal government as a result of the Cold War. The life-and-death struggle with the Soviet Union, the vast expenses of money and the large standing military forces required by the struggle convinced most conservatives that the federal government had to outgrow its traditional size.

Other developments of the period also undermined the strength of Jeffersonian politics in the United States. The middle of the twentieth century was the high-water mark of the administrative state, a time when the American people and their elected representatives increasingly felt that crucial decisions should be left to experts and professionals. The development of antibiotics and the conquest of terrifying diseases like tuberculosis, syphilis, and polio gave scientific medicine enormous prestige. Scientists and engineers created new miracles like television and scourges like nuclear weapons.

Given these new and powerful technologies, it seemed reasonable that the average citizen needed to defer to expert opinion. Traditionally Jeffersonians had denounced elites as parasites who deceived public opinion into believing that government was too complicated for anyone but "experts" to understand and administer. The claims of those parasites to necessary special knowledge had not been true in 1800, and American democracy had put power into the hands of ordinary people.

But what if those claims had become true by 1950? What if the questions of modern life really *were* too difficult and complicated for ordinary people to judge?

A final blow came with the civil rights movement of the 1960s. Classic Jeffersonian thought always saw the federal government as the threat to liberty; state and local governments were closer to the people and less likely to abuse their power. But the civil rights movement put this conviction to the test. What if states and local governments used their power to deny citizens their constitutional rights? Wasn't it the duty of the federal government to assert the power of the federal Constitution in defiance of state discrimination? And shouldn't all true friends of liberty stand with the federal government against the usurping states?

All these developments powerfully reinforced the central anti-

Jeffersonian myth of the Cold War era: that America's democratic values both at home and abroad were the truths of a simple, bygone age. In the complex, sophisticated world of the middle of the twentieth century, the American people needed to discover the maturity to part with their Jeffersonian ideals.

Under all these pressures Jeffersonian thought went into eclipse and came close to disappearing as one of the four main influences on American foreign policy, and in domestic policy as well. Nevertheless, Jeffersonian ideals were too deeply entrenched in American life to vanish completely. Unpopular though their ideas sometimes became, Jeffersonians continued to do their best to shape American policy through what for them were often the dark days of the mid-twentieth century.

In foreign policy the residual strength of Jeffersonian opinion made itself felt in opposition to or, at most, in very critical support of the Cold War. Even in decline, schools are not monoliths. People with Jeffersonian backgrounds had different views during the Cold War. Unlike the small group in the United States who in principle supported socialist revolutions in the developing world, and the even smaller number of Americans who consciously supported the Soviet Union, Jeffersonians generally adopted one of a number of positions.

A minority of the Jeffersonian minority, shifting in size but always of intellectual importance, believed that the entire effort of the Cold War was unnecessary. Arguments in support of this position changed during the forty years of confrontation but often included the assertion that the Soviet Union was a defensive, not an offensive, power. United States policy was forcing it into hostility; if we relaxed and made the Soviet Union feel more secure, international tension would diminish.

Another, typically Jeffersonian argument brought forward during the Cold War maintained that the European balance of power could regulate itself effectively without so much American participation. Whatever the USSR's intentions might be, once Western Europe had stabilized after the war, the Soviets were no longer capable of dominating Europe. The Soviet Union was too backward and its internal tensions too great, while the Western Europeans had no interest in undergoing a Soviet revolution.

As the focus of the Cold War competition shifted to the developing world, Jeffersonians (with occasional Wilsonian support) argued that American strategy was counterproductive. By allying itself with corrupt tyrannical regimes in the interests of anticommunism, the United States actually strengthened the forces it sought to oppose. Disgusted by the corruption, incompetence, and greed of kleptocratic but pro-Washington dictators, many of the brightest and most idealistic of the rising generation of the developing world were drawn toward the communists—just as idealistic Europeans had been drawn, temporarily, toward the communists during the antifascist struggles of the 1930s. Many of the revolutions we were opposing, argued some Jeffersonian critics, actually deserved to win. We were betraying our own professed commitment to human rights and democratic institutions, and sullying ourselves by becoming the accomplices—indeed, in some cases the trainers and enablers—of murderers, torturers, and thieves.

More moderate Jeffersonian opinion was influenced by these arguments, but not so far as to dissent from the Cold War effort completely. Rather, moderate Jeffersonians looked for ways to minimize the cost of what they saw as a necessary struggle (necessary, some thought, because of Soviet intransigence; necessary, others believed, because of the strength of pro–Cold War opinion in the United States).

Desperate for alternatives to what was seen as an excessively risky, dangerous, and expensive Cold War strategy, Jeffersonians looked for cheaper ways to contain the Soviet Union than a worldwide coalition financed and led by the United States. Many supported a positive response to the 1950s peace feelers from the Soviet Union, proposing a settlement on the basis of a neutralized, permanently disarmed Germany.

Perhaps the most often mentioned alternative strategy was to identify and exploit divisions within the Communist bloc. Arguing that Mao, Ho Chi Minh, and others were, like Tito, more profoundly nationalist than they were pro-Soviet, Jeffersonians urged the early recognition of China, and proposed that the United States try harder to detach China, Vietnam, Romania, and other countries from the Soviet Union. Treating these countries with unremitting hostility would only drive them further into the Soviet embrace, strengthening rather than undermining the opposing bloc.

Another Jeffersonian response to the Cold War was to argue the logic of arms control. If America's strategic goal was deterrence and a balance of armaments, there was nothing to be lost and a great deal to be gained—money saved, military-industrial complex weakened, perhaps a lessened chance for nuclear war—and nothing to be lost by reaching a strategic balance at the lowest possible level of arms.

In keeping with their traditional ideas and priorities, Jeffersonians did their best to limit the tendency of the Cold War climate to curb civil liberties. Jeffersonians generally opposed what they saw as the excessive and demagogic efforts to root out communists and left-wing sympathizers from the government, universities, pulpits, and media. They led the charge against laws that made membership in the American Communist Party illegal and defended the right of Communists and Communist sympathizers to speak freely.

From a Jeffersonian perspective there were times—many times—in the Cold War when American liberty was less endangered by the machinations of its Communist enemies than by the ham-fisted and repressive tactics of its alleged friends.

While Jeffersonian voices were generally in the minority during the Cold War era, they were not without influence in the formation of American foreign policy. When arch-hawk Richard Nixon began the rapprochement with Communist China, Jeffersonian ideas about the conduct of the Cold War had clearly reached the mainstream. Nixon's approach to détente with the Soviet Union—minimizing ideological conflicts with a dangerous great power in order to reduce the costs and risks of American foreign policy—is something that Jefferson himself might have tried. Certainly Nixon's determination to take human rights off the agenda in working out arms control agreements with Leonid Brezhnev recalls Jefferson's humble and unctuous letter to Alexander I.

During the 1980s the Reagan administration tacitly acknowledged the merit of Jeffersonian arguments against a too-close association with criminal regimes in the name of anticommunism when it withdrew American support from the apartheid regime in South Africa and the Marcos dictatorship in the Philippines. Jeffersonian logic on disarmament was also widely accepted; every president from Kennedy through Reagan engaged in serious efforts to limit the development and spread of nuclear weapons.

After two decades in which the Jeffersonian ideas and language of limited American involvement in the world and limiting the exercise of U.S. power were distinctly out of fashion, they enjoyed a revival as the Vietnam War reminded many Americans of the case against the arrogance of power and the imperial presidency that grew up after a generation of Cold War and crisis. With Walter Lippmann, one of the chief coauthors of Wilson's Fourteen Points, writing one Jeffersonian column after another attacking imperial hubris in Vietnam, and William Fulbright of Arkansas thundering against "the arrogance of power" on the

Senate floor, the Jeffersonian ideas that animated the despised isolationists of the 1940s returned to the center of American foreign policy
debate.

From the 1970s onward, the tide began to turn back in favor of Jeffersonian ideas. The disappointments and defeats of the Vietnam
War, and the revelations of government deceit published in the Pentagon
Papers and blaring in the daily headlines during the Watergate scandal,
revived popular distrust of the federal government.

The resurrection of Jeffersonian influence in foreign policy was
assisted by the partial reversal in the late twentieth century of the centralizing, professionalizing trends of the century's middle years. The
nuclear power accident at the Three Mile Island plant contributed to an
ongoing revival of skepticism about turning important social decisions
over to scientists and experts. A mass rebellion against medical authority
saw millions of Americans second-guessing their doctors and the medical
establishment, "taking control of their own treatment," and returning to
old ideals of self-reliance.

Libertarianism also revived as an economic doctrine. The regulated
commercial oligarchies and monopolies, such as the three major television networks and AT&T, that were the pride of the midcentury American establishment were derided as inefficient dinosaurs. Central control,
it was suddenly discovered, hindered innovation and fostered mediocrity.
Deregulation became the watchword in regulatory policy; the American
economics profession rediscovered the wonders of freedom.

A similar reevaluation took place in government. After years of cen-
tralization, policy-makers began to find new virtues in state government.
Beginning with the Nixon administration, Washington began to return
revenue and power to state governments. By the 1990s even the Supreme
Court had rediscovered federalism, issuing a series of decisions limiting
the legislative powers of the national government.

Other developments in American society in the closing years of the
twentieth century also pointed to a Jeffersonian renaissance. Jeffersonians
and Wilsonians share a passion for freedom, but they have very different
ways of securing it. It is a difference of approach that can be traced back
to the seventeenth century, when the Puritans drove freethinkers like
Roger Williams and Anne Hutchinson from Massachusetts. Wilsonians
share the Puritan view that the godly have the right and the duty to

enforce conformity with good principles on the weaker members of society. They see the state as the appropriate entity to enforce God's law.

Late-twentieth-century American society appeared to be moving from a Puritan and Wilsonian era into a libertarian and Jeffersonian period. The late 1960s began a period in which the American people were moving from asserting the importance of social and sexual conformity to asserting their right to live in their own way without permission or restraint from authority of any kind.

While American politics is a big, muddy river with many eddies and countercurrents, it appears that on the whole society continues to move away from supporting government efforts to control personal choices and behaviors. The best marker might be the war on drugs, perhaps the most sustained effort of our times by government at all levels to regulate personal behavior. In the closing years of the 1990s an interesting backlash appeared to be developing against efforts to control drugs by blanket prohibitions, long sentences, and enforcement tactics that infringed classic Jeffersonian concepts of civil liberties. The rising popularity of a family of approaches known as "harm reduction" as alternatives to the war on drugs show Jeffersonian ideas once again at work. The prospect that American money and, worse, troops might find themselves associated with dubious paramilitary organizations in a twilight struggle against drug dealers and their guerrilla allies is a classic nightmare for Jeffersonians. The potential impact on the morale and even the morality of American armed forces of prolonged involvement in messy, brutal, and inevitably corrupt drug interdictions mixed with civil wars in foreign countries makes Jeffersonians shudder. Efforts to change United States domestic policy to avoid the dangers of a shooting war on drugs abroad reflect the deepest Jeffersonian strategic and political values.

In any case, the recovery from its midcentury eclipse of the Jeffersonian approach, bolstered by a revived interest in libertarian economics and decentralized government, now seems well positioned to continue.

The Strengths and Weaknesses of the Jeffersonian Tradition

Like the other schools we have examined, the Jeffersonian approach to foreign policy has both advantages and disadvantages. At times, as in the years 1939–41, Jeffersonian ideas would have led the United States into a major disaster. At other times, as in the long period during which the Monroe system gave a basic strategic direction to American foreign policy that was notably successful, Jeffersonian ideas have been responsible for policies that brought many years of peace and stability to the United States at a very low cost.

To some degree analyzing the strengths and weaknesses of the Jeffersonian contribution to American foreign policy is an intrinsically partisan process that yields no universally accepted answers. Hamiltonians would criticize Jeffersonian timidity and constitutional fetishism, say, on the issue of fast-track, as endangering major trade opportunities for the United States. Wilsonians might denounce the Jeffersonian reluctance to support humanitarian interventions in Somalia and Rwanda and argue that the resulting weakness in American foreign policy resulted in major losses for American prestige.

Jeffersonians simply disagree, arguing that the democracy they defend is more valuable than the opportunities they lose.

There are, however, a number of areas in which the positive contributions of the Jeffersonian approach to foreign policy are indisputable. As one example, the Jeffersonian emphasis on maintaining and extending the power of democracy in American life plays a major role in keeping the political system healthy and in conserving what trust remains between the rulers and the ruled in the contemporary United States. Legitimacy in mass democracy is a fragile thing; the power of Jeffersonian ideas about democracy is one of the primary supports enjoyed by our form of government. Furthermore the long Jeffersonian struggle against central authority may have won only limited victories against Hamiltonian and Wilsonian centralizers, but those victories are important and will be more so in the future. As the sheer size of the American population grows, maintaining the health and autonomy of state and local governments will become steadily more important. The less power individual citizens can hope to exercise at the national level, the more important it is that serious questions can be debated and resolved at the state and local levels, where the average person can still be a participant in democracy rather than simply a spectator.

Another major contribution is that Jeffersonian ideas have produced and continue to produce some of the most brilliant thinkers and scholars in the field of American foreign policy. Whether one looks at Jefferson himself, John Quincy Adams, or, more recently, figures like George Kennan and (in some phases of his long and varied career) Walter Lippmann, it is striking how many of our most brilliant foreign policy intellectuals have been shaped in large part by Jeffersonian concerns.

The Jeffersonian mind-set, eager to understand foreign states and conditions, but also eager to leave them as they are, is peculiarly conducive to the intellectual formation of brilliant regional students. Of the four schools Jeffersonians are most often moved by a disinterested appreciation and respect for foreign cultures. Jeffersonians are less eager to make sales than Hamiltonians are, and less preoccupied with either secular or religious proselytization than Wilsonians are—but they are interested in understanding foreign cultures and peoples on their own terms. Very often Jeffersonian regional specialists have talked policy makers out of what would have proved rash and ill-founded initiatives and found ways of achieving important American objectives with less friction and trouble than we might otherwise face.

The greatest advantage the country derives from the Jeffersonian tradition emerges out of the Jeffersonian desire to define the national interest as tightly as possible and then to develop the most elegant possible strategy for securing that interest. It is a tradition that adds intellectual rigor and, often, great practical value to the foreign policy debate. It is arguably the natural home for American grand strategy. The combination of a realistic grasp of the problems of the external world with a passionate desire to secure the nation's vital interest at the lowest possible cost may be the mind-set best suited to conceive and promulgate national strategic initiatives.

Furthermore, the Jeffersonian tradition supplies something occasionally lacking in the other three schools: a critical tradition that seeks systematically to investigate, and in some cases controvert, the claims made by proponents of Hamiltonian and Wilsonian activism. If nothing else, Jeffersonian skepticism keeps Wilsonians and Hamiltonians on their toes, forcing them to think through their policies more thoroughly than they otherwise might, and to be able to defend their programs in public debate.

Paradoxically, Jeffersonian pacifism and skepticism tend to unite American opinion once war has finally come. In the case of World War II, the large and well-organized isolationist movement came out openly in support of the war effort after Pearl Harbor. With one exception (Montana representative Jeannette Rankin, the first woman elected to Congress [1916], who also voted against America's entry into World War I), the eloquent congressional and senatorial critics of intervention voted for the declaration of war on Japan. The existence and visibility of a high-powered antiwar lobby can mobilize public opinion for war: If even these people think we have to fight, then maybe war is really inevitable.

The Jeffersonian approach to foreign policy has one other advantage: Every vehicle should have at least one reverse gear, and Jeffersonianism often provides exactly that. When the United States needs to lower its international profile for some reason—as, for example, in the immediate aftermath of the Vietnam defeat in the 1970s—Jeffersonian ideas and values allow us to approach the problem in a positive, thoughtful way. Rather than recoiling after a humiliating defeat, the United States was recovering its traditional values, abandoning the arrogance of power, returning to a more constitutional approach to foreign policy, and scaling back the imperial presidency. From a Jeffersonian perspective, these are all good things. We don't do them simply because a loss of prestige compels us to draw in our horns. Rather we do them because we now have an opportunity to introduce some overdue reforms. If the long flow of this century should bring about conditions in which the United States can no longer design and uphold a world order, but must adjust to the designs and plans of others, it will be the Jeffersonian strain in American foreign policy thinking that will come forward with strategies that allow us to make the best of it, to accommodate to changing international conditions while as far as possible preserving our domestic institutions and values.

Chapter Seven

TIGER, TIGER, BURNING BRIGHT

The School of Andrew Jackson

When the stars threw down their spears,
And water'd heaven with their tears,
Did he smile his work to see?
Did he who made the Lamb make thee?

—William Blake, "The Tiger"

Riding the Tiger

In the last five months of World War II, American bombing raids killed more than 900,000 Japanese civilians, not counting the casualties from the atomic strikes against Hiroshima and Nagasaki.[1] This is more than twice the total number of combat deaths (441,513) the United States has suffered in all its foreign wars combined.[2] The nuclear attacks on Hiroshima and Nagasaki in August 1945 caused an estimated 127,150 additional deaths,[3] 28.7 percent of the total American war dead in 225 years of foreign wars and more than the combat deaths suffered by American forces in any foreign war except World War II itself.

On the night of March 9–10, 1945, 234 Superfortresses dropped

1,167 tons of incendiary bombs over downtown Tokyo; 83,793 Japanese bodies were found in the charred remains, a number greater than the 80,942 combat fatalities the United States sustained in the Korean and Vietnamese wars combined.[4]

Some charge that racial antipathy gave a unique ferocity to American war tactics in the Pacific theater. Hardly. It appears that more German civilians died in the three-night-long Anglo-American firebombing of Dresden than American soldiers died in World War I; military historian Michael Clodfelter observes that at the time the Dresden raids constituted the largest slaughter of civilians by military forces in one place at one time since the campaigns of Genghis Khan.[5]

It isn't fashionable to say so, but the United States of America is the most dangerous military power in the history of the world. Since World War II, the United States has continued to employ devastating force against both civil and military targets. Out of a prewar population of 9.49 million, an estimated 1 million (North) Korean civilians are believed to have died as the result of the actions of American forces during the 1950–53 conflict there.[6] Almost 34,000 American soldiers were killed during the conflict, meaning that U.S. forces killed approximately 30 North Korean civilians for every American soldier who died.

The United States dropped almost three times as much explosive tonnage in the Vietnam War as it used in World War II.[7] The conditions of that unhappy conflict make civilian casualties difficult to estimate, but some 365,000 Vietnamese civilians are believed to have died as a result of the war during the period of American involvement.[8] That is a ratio of 8 Vietnamese civilian deaths for every American killed in the war.[9]

The ratio of civilian to combat deaths in these two wars surpasses the ratio observed in Germany's eastern theater of operations in World War II. German forces are estimated to have suffered slightly more than 2 million combat deaths in the war against the Soviet Union, and to have been directly responsible for approximately 10 million (Soviet) civilian deaths,[10] with a ratio on the order of 5 Soviet civilian deaths for every German soldier killed. Whatever the validity of Clausewitz's admonition that casualty reports are never accurate, seldom truthful, and in most cases deliberately falsified, these numbers are too striking to ignore.

They do not, of course, suggest a moral parallel between the behavior of German and Japanese aggressors and American forces seeking to defeat the aggressors in the shortest possible time. Furthermore German and Japanese forces used the indiscriminate murder of civilians as a routine police tool in occupied territory, and wholesale massacres of civilians often accompanied German and Japanese advances into new territory. The deliberate extermination of Jewish, Polish, and Soviet civilians by German forces in areas under their control has no significant parallel on the American side. In neither the Atlantic nor the Pacific theater of World War II did American troops perpetrate atrocities comparable to those committed by Soviet soldiers during their advance into Germany. The days-long orgy (in December 1937) of murder, looting, and torture by Japanese forces that has been called the Rape of Nanking had no parallel on the American side. Nor, of course, did Americans engage in atrocities in any way comparable to the Holocaust or to Japanese mistreatment of civilians who fell under the Rising Sun.

Both German and Japanese forces killed American civilians when the opportunity presented itself. German U-boats killed between fifty and one hundred American merchant marines before the formal declaration of war.[11] If Hitler's V-1 or V-2 rockets had been capable of reaching the United States, he certainly would have used them for that purpose. Sixty-eight civilians died in the unprovoked Japanese attack on Pearl Harbor.[12] Unable to launch conventional air strikes against the American mainland, the Japanese sent off rice-paper balloons, glued together by schoolgirls, that carried bombs across the Pacific on the jet stream. Some exploded in the forests of the Pacific Northwest, setting forest fires; one killed five picnicking Sunday school students and their teacher.[13]

In the struggles against communist expansion during the Cold War, the evils the Americans opposed were also worse than the ones they inflicted. Tens of millions more innocent civilians in communist nations were murdered by their own governments in peacetime than ever died as the result of American attempts to stop communism's spread. War, even brutal war, was more merciful than communist rule.

Nevertheless, the American war record should make us think. An observer who thought of American foreign policy only in terms of the commercial realism of the Hamiltonians, the crusading moralism of Wilsonian transcendentalists and the supple pacifism of the principled but slippery Jeffersonians would be at a loss to account for American ruthlessness at war. One might well look at the American military record and ask William Blake's question in "The Tiger": "Did he who made the Lamb make thee?"

Clearly some way of thinking beyond the three schools we have so far reviewed must be at work. We are not simply a people of merchants, missionaries, and constitutional lawyers.

Those who prefer to believe that the present global hegemony of the United States emerged through a process of "immaculate conception" avert their eyes from many distressing moments in the American ascension. Yet students of American power cannot ignore one of the chief elements in American success: The United States over its history has consistently summoned the will and the means to compel its enemies to yield to its demands. Attacks on civilian targets and the infliction of heavy casualties on enemy civilians have consistently played a vital part in American war strategies.

Through the long sweep of American history there have been many occasions when public opinion, or at least an important part of it, got ahead of the politicians in Washington in demanding war. Many of the Indian wars were caused less by Indian aggression than by movements of frontier populations hungry for land and willing to provoke and fight wars with Indian tribes under Washington's protection—contrary to both the policy and the wishes of the national government. The War of 1812 came about largely because populist so-called War Hawk politicians in the South and Middle West wanted it. As noted earlier, Lincoln just barely managed to prevent a war with Britain over the *Trent* affair during the Civil War; outraged, hawkish public opinion made it difficult for him to find an acceptable face-saving solution to the problem. More recently, Presidents Kennedy, Johnson, and Nixon were all haunted by fears that pulling out of the Vietnam War would trigger a popular backlash; without the popular pressure for this most unpopular of wars, it is likely that the American involvement in Vietnam would have been less deep and more quickly ended. As radio stations blared out "Bomb Iran" to the tune of the Beach Boys' hit song "Barbara Ann," Jimmy Carter struggled for months to keep the United States out of a war with Iran over the 1979–80 hostage crisis, before dispatching an ill-fated rescue mission.

Once wars begin, a significant element of American public opinion supports waging them at the highest possible level of intensity. The devastating tactics of the wars against the Indians, General Sherman's campaign of 1864–65, the unprecedented aerial bombardments of World War II, culminating in the greatest single acts of violence ever perpetrated by human beings—the atomic attacks on Hiroshima and Nagasaki—were all broadly popular in the United States. During both the Korean and Vietnam wars, presidents came under intense pressure not only from military leaders but also from public opinion to hit the enemy with all available forces in all available places. Generally, throughout the Cold

War a hawkish, or more hawkish, stance was the path of least resistance in American politics. Politicians who advocated negotiated compromises with the Soviet enemy were labeled as "appeasers" and paid a heavy political price.

During the Cold War, European diplomats spent much of their energy and time trying to restrain their American ally's disconcerting tendency to confront the Soviets at every opportunity. Churchill tried to persuade Eisenhower to negotiate seriously with Stalin's successors over Germany; Konrad Adenauer and Charles de Gaulle, no slouches themselves in the anticommunist department, could never understand the American failure to recognize Mao's government in China. The Europeans usually wrung their hands or sniped during the long, sad Vietnam War, deploring America's unthinking hawkishness.

The Korean and Vietnamese wars lost public support in part because of political decisions not to risk the consequences (including those in European opinion) of all-out war, not necessarily stopping short of the use of nuclear weapons. Until late in the Vietnam War, American public opinion was generally more exercised over Washington's failure to apply all available force to Vietnam than it was over the necessity for the war altogether. The riskiest decision George H. Bush took in the Gulf War wasn't the decision to send ground forces into Iraq; it was to stop short of the occupation of Baghdad and the capture and trial of Saddam Hussein. Despite the continuing presence of the "Vietnam syndrome," interventions by Presidents Reagan and Bush in Grenada and Panama were widely supported by American public opinion.

It is often remarked that the American people are more religious than their allies in Western Europe. But it is also and equally true that they are more military-minded. Currently the American people support without complaint the highest military budgets in the world and the largest peacetime military budgets in world history. In 1999 the United States spent nearly as much on defense as its NATO allies, South Korea, Japan, Russia, China, and the Persian Gulf states participating in the Gulf Cooperation Council (GCC) combined.[14] In response to widespread public concern about a decline in military preparedness, both parties supported substantial increases in military spending in the years to come.

And Americans don't merely pay for these forces, they use them. Since the end of the Vietnam War, regarded by some as opening a new era of reluctance in the exercise of American power, the United States has deployed combat forces or used deadly force—in addition to Iran, Grenada, Panama, and Iraq—over or in Cambodia, Lebanon, Libya, Saudi

Arabia, Kuwait, Turkey, Somalia, Haiti, Bosnia, Sudan, Afghanistan, the South China Sea, Liberia, Macedonia, Albania, and Yugoslavia. This is a record no other country matches or even comes close to matching.

It is also generally conceded that, with the exception of a handful of elite units in the British forces and a few others, American troops have a stronger "warrior culture" than their counterparts in NATO and Japan—in other words, than in the armed forces of other developed countries. Indeed, of all the NATO countries north and west of Turkey and Greece, only Great Britain has anything like the American "war lobby" that springs up in times of national crisis, a political force that under certain circumstances demands war, supports the use of force, and urges political leaders to stop wasting time with negotiations, sanctions, and UN Security Council meetings in order to attack the enemy with all possible strength.

Why is it that American public opinion is sometimes so quick, and sometimes so slow, to support armed intervention abroad? What are the provocations that can energize public opinion (at least some of it) for war? How, if at all, is this war lobby related to the other elements of American public opinion on issues of foreign policy? The key to that warlike disposition, and to other important features of American foreign policy, is found in the fourth and last of the great schools, the "Jacksonian school," so named here in honor of the seventh president of the United States.

The School of Andrew Jackson

It is a tribute to the general historical amnesia about American politics between the War of 1812 and the Civil War that Andrew Jackson is not more widely counted among the greatest of American presidents. The victor in the Battle of New Orleans—even if it took place after the formal end of the war, perhaps the most decisive battle in the shaping of the modern world between Trafalgar and Stalingrad—Jackson laid the foundations of American politics for most of the nineteenth century, and his influence is still felt today. With the ever-ready help of the wily Albany political boss Martin Van Buren, he took American politics from the era of silk stockings into that of the smoke-filled room; every political party since his presidency has drawn on the symbolism, the institutions, and the instruments of power that Jackson pioneered.

More than that, he brought the American people into the political arena. Restricted state franchises with high property qualifications meant that in 1820 many American states set higher property qualifications for voters than British boroughs did for elections of members of Parliament. From Jackson's presidency onward, universal male—and now, universal adult—suffrage has been the basis of American politics and political values.

His political movement, or, more accurately, the community of political feeling that he wielded into an instrument of power, remains in many ways the most important in American politics. Largely though not exclusively Democratic through the Truman administration (a tradition commemorated in the annual Jefferson-Jackson Day dinners that are still the high points on Democratic Party calendars in many cities and states), the shift of Jacksonian America toward the Republican Party under Nixon is the most important political change in American life since World War II, and the future of Jacksonian political allegiance is one of the keys to the politics of this century.

For all this influence, the Jacksonian school gets very little political respect and is more frequently deplored than comprehended by both American and foreign intellectuals and foreign policy scholars. That is too bad; the dynamics of American foreign policy remain indecipherably opaque without an understanding of this vital force.

Suspicious of untrammeled federal power, skeptical about the prospects for domestic and foreign do-gooding (welfare at home, foreign aid abroad), opposed to federal taxes but obstinately fond of federal programs seen as primarily helping the middle class (Social Security, Medicare, mortgage interest subsidies), Jacksonians constitute a large political interest. In some ways Jacksonians resemble the Jeffersonians, with whom their political fortunes were linked for so many decades. Like Jeffersonians, Jacksonians are profoundly suspicious of elites. They generally prefer a loose federal structure with as much power as possible retained by states and local governments. But the differences between the two movements run very deep, so deep that during the Cold War, members of the two schools were on opposite sides of most important foreign policy questions. To use the language of the Vietnam era, a time when Jeffersonians and Jacksonians were literally fighting in the streets over foreign policy, the Jeffersonians were the most dovish current in mainstream political thought during the Cold War, while the Jacksonians were the most consistently hawkish.

One way to grasp the difference between the two schools is to recognize that both Jeffersonians and Jacksonians are civil libertarians, passionately attached to the Constitution and especially to the Bill of Rights, and deeply committed to preserving the liberties of ordinary Americans. But while the Jeffersonians are most profoundly devoted to the First Amendment, protecting the freedom of speech and prohibiting a federal establishment of religion, Jacksonians see the Second Amendment and the right to bear arms as the citadel of liberty. To oversimplify, Jeffersonians join the American Civil Liberties Union (ACLU); Jacksonians join the National Rifle Association (NRA). In so doing, both are convinced that they are standing at the barricades of freedom.

Both Jeffersonians and Jacksonians can overcome their fear of federal power in the interest of regulating big business, but otherwise they differ sharply on the issues that justify federal activism. Jeffersonians are sometimes reluctantly willing to suspend their suspicion of federal power when it is used in defense of liberty at home—to write and enforce sweeping civil rights laws, for example. Jacksonians find these policies to be intrusive and objectionable interferences beyond the proper sphere of federal action, but see nothing wrong in federal activism against crime, even at the cost of constitutional niceties that are dear to Jeffersonian hearts.

For foreigners and for some Americans, the Jacksonian school is the least impressive of the four. It is the most deplored abroad, the most denounced at home. Jacksonian chairs of the Senate Foreign Relations Committee are the despair of high-minded people everywhere as they hold up American adherence to the anti-global-warming Kyoto protocols, starve the UN and the IMF, cut foreign aid, and ban the use of American funds for population control programs abroad. When the other three schools talk about the problems of American foreign policy, the persistence and power of the Jacksonian school are high on their list.

While some of the despair may be overstated and perhaps a reflection of different class interests and values, it is true that Jacksonians often figure as the most obstructionist of the schools, the least likely to support Wilsonian initiatives for a better world, the least able to understand Jeffersonian calls for patient diplomacy in difficult situations, or the least willing to accept Hamiltonian trade strategies. Yet without Jacksonians the United States would be a much weaker power, and the other schools would soon feel their absence more strongly than they now bemoan their political views.

Perhaps Jacksonian politics are so poorly understood because Jacksonianism is less an intellectual or political movement than it is an expression of the social, cultural, and religious values of a large portion of the American public. Jacksonianism is doubly obscure because it happens to be rooted in one of the portions of the public least represented in the media and the professoriat. Jacksonian America is a folk community with a strong sense of common values and common destiny, periodically led by intellectually brilliant men like Jackson himself. It is neither an ideology nor a self-conscious movement with a clear historical direction or political table of organization. Nevertheless, Jacksonian America has produced, and looks likely to continue to produce, one political leader and movement after another, and it is likely to continue to enjoy major influence over both foreign and domestic policy in the United States in the foreseeable future.

The Jacksonian Folk Community

It is not fashionable today to think of the American nation as a folk community bound together by deep cultural and ethnic ties. Believers in a multicultural United States attack this idea from one direction, but conservatives too have a tendency to talk about the United States as a nation based on ideology rather than ethnicity. Former British prime minister Margaret Thatcher, among others, has said that the United States is unique because it is based on an idea rather than, like other nations, on a community of national experience. The continuing and growing vitality of the Jacksonian tradition is, for better or worse, living proof that she is at least partly wrong.

It is certainly true that not all Americans feel themselves to be part of a folk community that is Christian (if not Protestant) in religious background, if not always practice; European in origin—but largely without strong ties to a specific country other than the United States—and self-identified with American society from the colonial era until today. Many Americans do not qualify, and do not want to qualify, for membership in such a community of feeling and culture. Many other Americans do, however, and living as they do in communities where the overwhelming majority of their friends and associates share that sense of identification, they naturally if perhaps unreflectively assume that this ex-European, Christian, but above all American "folk" is a nation, like the French, the English, or the Greeks.

If Jeffersonianism is the book ideology of the United States, Jacksonian populism is its folk ideology. Historically American populism is based less on the ideas of the Enlightenment than on the community values and sense of identity among the British colonizers who settled this country before the Revolution. In particular, as one learns from the work of historian David Hackett Fischer, what we are calling Jacksonian populism can originally be identified with a subgroup among these settlers, the so-called Scotch-Irish who settled the backcountry regions of the Carolinas and Virginia and who went on to settle much of the Old West—which would become West Virginia, Kentucky, parts of Indiana and Illinois—and the south and south central states of Tennessee, Missouri, Alabama, Mississippi, and Texas. Jacksonian populism today has moved beyond its original ethnic and geographical limits. Like country music, another product of Jacksonian culture, Jacksonian politics and folk feeling have become a basic element in American consciousness that can be found from one end of the country to the other.

The Scotch-Irish were a hardy and warlike people, with a culture and outlook formed by centuries of bitter warfare before they came to the United States. Fischer shows how, trapped on the frontier between England and Scotland, or planted as Protestant colonies in the hostile soil of Ireland, this culture was shaped through centuries of constant bloody war. The American Revolution, the War of 1812, and generations of savage frontier conflict in the United States reproduced these conditions in the New World. The Civil War, fought with particular ferocity in the border states, renewed the cultural heritage of war. Since that time each American generation has been baptized by fire—in the Spanish-American War, the two world wars, in Korea, Indochina, and the Persian Gulf, new generations of American Jacksonians rallied to the colors.

The Great Assimilation

Although the role of what we are calling Jacksonians in the nineteenth-century United States is clear, many twentieth-century observers made what once seemed a reasonable assumption that Jacksonian values and politics were dying out. These observers were both surprised and discomfited when Ronald Reagan's political success showed that Jacksonianism had done more than survive; it was, and is, thriving.

What has happened is that Jacksonian culture, values, and self-identification have spread beyond their original ethnic limits. In the 1920s and the 1930s, the highland, border tradition in American life was widely seen to be dying out, ethnically, culturally, and politically. Part of this was due to the economic and demographic collapse of the traditional home of Jacksonian America, the family farm. At the same time, mass immigration from eastern and southern Europe had tilted the ethnic balance of the American population ever farther from its colonial mix. New England Yankees were a vanishing species, limited to the hills of New Hampshire and Vermont, while the cities and plains of Connecticut, Massachusetts, and Rhode Island filled with Irishmen, Italians, Portuguese, and Greeks. The great cities of the United States were increasingly peopled by Catholics, members of the Orthodox churches, and Jews, all professing in one way or another communitarian social values very much at odds with the individualism of traditional Anglo-Saxon and Anglo-Celtic culture.

As Hiram W. Evans, the surprisingly articulate imperial wizard of the Ku Klux Klan, wrote in 1926, the old-stock American of his time had become "a stranger in large parts of the land his fathers gave him. Moreover, he is a most unwelcome stranger, one much spit upon, and one to whom even the right to have his own opinions and to work for his own interests is now denied with jeers and revilings. 'We must Americanize the Americans,' a distinguished immigrant said recently."[15]

Protestantism itself was losing its edge. The modernist critique of the Bible found acceptance in one mainline denomination after another; Episcopal, Presbyterian, Methodist, and Lutheran seminaries accepted critical, post-Darwinian readings of Scripture; self-described fundamentalists fought a slow but, apparently, losing rearguard action against the modernist forces. The new mainline Protestantism was a tolerant, even a namby-pamby religion; the wealthiest and most influential Protestant families seemed to drift from orthodoxy into ever more ethereal and ultimately ever fainter religious ideas and convictions.

The old nativist spirit, anti-immigrant, anti–modern art, and apparently anti–twentieth century, still had some bite—KKK crosses flamed across the Midwest as well as the South during the 1920s—but it all looked like the death throes of an outdated worldview. There weren't many mourners; much of H. L. Mencken's career was based on exposing and mocking the limitations of what we are calling Jacksonian America.

Most progressive, right-thinking American intellectuals in mid-century believed that the future of American populism lay in a social democratic movement based on urban immigrants. Social activists like Woody Guthrie consciously sought to use cultural forms like folk songs to ease the transition from the old individualistic folk world to the collective new one that they believed was the wave of the future; they celebrated unions and other strange, European ideas in down-home country twangs so that, in the bitter words of Ku Kluxer Evans, "There is a steady flood of alien ideas being spread over the country, always carefully disguised as American."[16]

What came next surprised almost everyone. The tables turned, and Evans's Americans "Americanized" the immigrants rather than the other way round. In what is still a largely unheralded triumph of the melting pot, the northern immigrants gradually assimilated the values of Jacksonian individualism. Ties to the countries of emigration steadily weakened; second, third, and fourth generations showed increasing tendencies to marry out of the group.

Outwardly most immigrant groups completed an apparent assimilation to American material culture within a couple of generations of their arrival. A second type of assimilation—an inward assimilation to, and adaptation of, the core cultural and psychological structure of the native population—took longer, but third-, fourth-, and fifth-generation immigrant families were increasingly Americanized on the inside as well as without.

This process should not be understood as a simple one of consciously or even unconsciously copying or adopting the beliefs and behavior patterns of the nativist population. Some of this no doubt occurred as part of the general hunger to assimilate, but many—perhaps most—of the cultural changes within the immigrant communities had to do with the consequences of their members' exposure to the economic and social realities of American life. Neither church nor synagogue nor the community of elders had any legal powers over individuals in the United States. Each successive generation of immigrants had more opportunity to escape the constraints of the ethnic community, and the economic rewards of moving into the mainstream were high.

Physically the old neighborhoods broke up after World War II. The northern industrial working class moved into the suburbs, along with the refugees from the dying American family farm, to form a new populist mix. As increasing numbers of the descendants of immigrants moved into the Jacksonian Sun Belt, the pace of assimilation grew.

Meanwhile the descendants of Jacksonian farmers had also arrived in the suburbs. In some cases, as in the great migration to the booming automobile factories in Michigan, white southerners moved north, to rub elbows with more recent immigrants from Europe. In others, Okies and their successors journeyed to the promised land of California, where, with Jewish, Catholic, and Eastern Orthodox refugees from cold climates and limited upward mobility, they built a new version of traditional American popular culture and politics. The suburban homeowner with his or her federally subsidized mortgage replaced the homesteading farmer (on free federal land) as the central pillar of American populism. Richard Nixon, with his two-pronged appeal to white southerners and the "Joe Six-pack" voters of the north, was the first national politician to recognize the power of this newly energized current in American life.

Urban, immigrant America may have softened some of the rough edges of Jacksonian America, but the descendants of the great wave of European immigration sound more Anglo-American from decade to decade. Rugged frontier individualism has proved to be contagious; each generation descended from the great turn-of-the-century immigration has been more Jacksonian than its predecessor. The social and economic solidarity so characteristic of European peasant communities has been overmastered by the individualism of the frontier. The descendants of European working-class Marxists now quote Adam Smith; Joe Six-pack thinks of the welfare state as an expensive burden, not part of the natural moral order. (Mary Six-pack, like Jane Doe, has her doubts.) Intellectuals have made this transition as thoroughly as anyone else. The children and grandchildren of trade unionists and Trotskyists now talk about the importance of liberal society and free markets; in the intellectual pilgrimage of Irving Kristol, what is usually a multigenerational process has been compressed into a single, brilliant career.

The result is that Jacksonian values look set to continue to play a key role in American life. Ronald Reagan owed much of his popularity and success to his ability to connect with Jacksonian values. Ross Perot, Jesse Ventura, George Wallace, Pat Buchanan, and John McCain in different ways and to different degrees, have managed to tap into the power of the populist energy that Old Hickory rode into the White House.

The new Jacksonianism is no longer rural and exclusively nativist. Frontier Jacksonianism may have taken the homesteading farmer and the log cabin as its emblems; today's crabgrass Jacksonianism sees the homeowner on his modest suburban lawn as the hero of the American story. The crabgrass Jacksonian may wear green on St. Patrick's Day; he or she might go to a Catholic church and never listen to country music (though, increasingly, he or she probably does). But the crabgrass Jacksonian doesn't just believe, she knows that she is as good an American as anybody else, that she is entitled to her rights from church and state, that she pulls her own weight and expects others to do the same. That homeowner will be heard from. In both domestic and foreign policy, this century will be profoundly influenced by the values and concerns of Jacksonian America.

Jacksonian Values

To understand how crabgrass Jacksonianism is shaping and will shape American foreign policy we must begin with another unfashionable concept: honor.

Although few Americans today use this anachronistic word, honor remains a core value for tens of millions of middle-class Americans. The unacknowledged code of honor that shapes so much of American behavior and aspiration today is a recognizable descendant of the frontier codes of honor of early Jacksonian America. The appeal of this code is one of the reasons that Jacksonian values have spread to so many people outside the original ethnic and social nexus in which they were formed.

The first principle of this code is self-reliance. Real Americans, many Americans feel, are people who make their own way in the world. They may get a helping hand from friends and family, but they hold and keep their places in the world through honest work. They don't slide by on welfare, and they don't rely on inherited wealth or connections. Those who for whatever reason don't work and are therefore poor, or those who don't need to work because of family money, are viewed with suspicion. Those who meet the economic and moral tests belong to the broad middle class, the broad folk community of working people whom Jacksonians believe to be the heart, soul, and spine of the American nation. Earning and keeping a place in this community on the basis of honest work is the first principle of Jacksonian honor, and it remains a serious insult to say, or even to imply, that some member of the American middle class isn't pulling his or her weight in the world.

Jacksonian honor must be acknowledged by the outside world. One is entitled to, and demands, the appropriate respect: recognition of rights and just claims, acknowledgment of one's personal dignity. Many people in the United States will still fight, sometimes with weapons, when they feel they have not been treated with the proper respect. But even among the less violent, Americans stand on their dignity and rights. Managers whose style seems demeaning to their subordinates, teachers who humiliate their students, politicians who condescend to their constituents—all will pay a price for their temerity. Conversely, those who are careful to respect the individual dignity of their subordinates, and can demonstrate a rational basis for their authority—knowledge, talent, experience—will enjoy loyalty and respect in return. Jacksonian Americans are skeptical of authority, but once it is acknowledged as legitimate, the honor code demands that authority, too, receive its due respect.

Economic success, when clearly due to hard work, is also respected. Jacksonians believe that everyone should have an equal start, but Jacksonian society does not insist that all its members end up in the same place. There have been times in American history—such as the late nineteenth century and to a lesser extent during the depression—when popular resentment against the perceived injustices of the American economic order led to strong political movements against what Theodore Roosevelt once called the "malefactors of great wealth."[17] Those periods, however, have been exceptions, and popular resentment of the rich remained milder and less politically effective in the United States than in Europe. Generally, when Jacksonians believe that the rules of the game are reasonably fair, they believe that winners deserve the respect and admiration of the rest.

Respect is also due age. Those who know Jacksonian America only through its very inexact representations in the media think of the United States as a youth-obsessed, age-neglecting society. In fact Jacksonian America honors age. Jackson was sixty-one when he was elected president for the first time; Reagan was sixty-nine.[18] Movie stars often lose their appeal with age; but those whose appeal stems from their ability to portray and embody Jacksonian values—like Jimmy Stewart and John Wayne—only become more revered. Jacksonians may not always, or even very often, obey their parents and the elderly, but they care for them. Social Security and the whole vast network of programs to create a dignified retirement for older Americans was put in place by a society that was demographically much younger than the United States is today. There is perhaps no point on which the American political consensus is broader today than that this network be maintained at all costs, and even expanded where possible. The widespread American networks of senior citizen discounts for everything from movie tickets to airline fares are completely uncontroversial. A failure to give older people their proper due would be an inexcusable breach of the code.

The second principle of the code of honor is equality. Among those members of the folk community who do pull their weight, there is an absolute equality of dignity and right. No one else has a right to tell the self-reliant Jacksonian what to say, do, or think. Any infringement of equality will be met with defiance and resistance. The Jacksonian is, and insists on remaining, independent of church, state, social hierarchy, political parties, and labor unions. Jacksonians may choose to accept the authority of a leader or movement or faith, but they will never accept an imposed authority, or any implication that one member of the middle-class American community is better than any other member in good standing. The young are independent of the old: "Free, white and twenty-one" is an old Jacksonian expression; the color line has softened, but otherwise the sentiment is as true as it ever was.

The third principle is individualism. Given the freedom to think and live as one pleases, Jacksonian America offers every individual the opportunity to seek satisfaction and salvation through whatever means the individual finds helpful. The Jacksonian does not just have a right to self-fulfillment, he or she has a duty to seek it. The insistence on independent judgment goes far back in American history. Jacksonians and their Scotch-Irish ancestors first revolted from the Catholic Church, then the Church of England, then the hierarchical Protestant denominations like Methodism and Presbyterianism. The revolt from established denominations continues today.

A concern for self-improvement, not necessarily related to orthodox religious faith, is another hallmark of the Jacksonian quest for individual fulfillment. In 1862 nineteen-year-old Sarah Morgan, living in Baton Rouge as it was about to be shelled by Federal gunboats, earnestly confided to her diary that her "lack of self esteem" was a problem she needed to deal with.[19]

In 1827, Mrs. Fanny Trollope, the mother of novelist Anthony Trollope, was forced by her husband's debts to leave her native Britain and come to the United States, where she spent two years. Next to her revulsion at the twin American habits of chewing tobacco in public places and missing spittoons with the finished product, she most despised the social and religious heterodoxy of American revivalists, the dressing habits and independent ways of American servants, and the passion for equality she found everywhere she looked.

"The theory of equality," Mrs. Trollope observed, "may be very daintily discussed by English gentlemen in a London dining-room, when the servant, having placed a fresh bottle of cool wine on the table, respectfully shuts the door, and leaves them to their walnuts and their wisdom; but it will be found less palatable when it presents itself in the shape of a hard, greasy paw, and is claimed in accents that breathe less of freedom than of onions and whiskey. Strong, indeed, must be the love of equality in an English breast if it can survive a tour through the Union."[20]

In Jacksonian America, everyone must find his or her own way. Each individual must choose a faith, or no faith, and a code of conduct based on conscience and reason. No one has the right to tell anybody else what to think or believe, and the Jacksonian feels perfectly free to strike off in an entirely new religious direction. "I sincerely believe," wrote Mrs. Trollope, "that if a fire-worshipper, or an Indian Brahmin, were to come to the United States, prepared to preach and pray in English, he would not be long without a 'very respectable congregation.' "[21] She didn't know the half of it.

Yet despite this individualism, the Jacksonian code also mandates acceptance of certain social mores and principles. Loyalty to family, raising children "right," sexual decency (usually identified with heterosexual monogamy, which can be serial), and honesty within the community are virtues that commend themselves to the Jacksonian spirit. Children of both sexes can be wild; both women and men must be strong. Corporal punishment is customary and common; Jacksonians find objections to this time-honored and (they feel) effective method of discipline outlandish and absurd. Although women should be more discreet, both sexes can sow wild oats before marriage; after it, to enjoy the esteem of their community, a couple must be seen to put their children's welfare ahead of personal gratification.

The fourth pillar in the Jacksonian honor code struck Mrs. Trollope and others as more dishonorable than honorable; nevertheless it persists. Let us call it financial esprit. While the Jacksonian believes in hard work, he or she also believes that credit is a right and that money, especially borrowed money, is less a sacred trust than a means for self-discovery and expression. Although previous generations lacked the faculties for consumer credit that Americans enjoyed at the end of the twentieth century, many Americans have always assumed that they have a right to spend money on their appearance, on purchases that affirm their status. The strict Jacksonian code of honor does not enjoin what others see as financial probity. What it rather enjoins is a daring and entrepreneurial spirit.

Credit is seen, to some degree, as less an obligation than an opportunity. Jacksonians have always supported loose monetary policy and looser bankruptcy laws. In earlier times, before national credit agencies made one's past impossible to escape, the mobility of Americans allowed a certain freedom from bad luck and bad decisions. In today's world easy credit and easy bankruptcy provide similar escape valves. In any case the Jacksonian spirit is not the sober, penurious spirit of the humble, gray-garbed Quaker. Flash and dash are admired, not censured.

Finally, courage is the crowning and indispensable part of the code. Jacksonians must be ready to defend their honor in great things and small. Americans believe that they ought to stick up for what they believe and insist on their rights and dignity. In the nineteenth century, Jacksonian Americans fought serious duels after aristocrats in Europe had given them up, and Americans today remain far more likely than Europeans to settle personal quarrels with extreme and even deadly violence.

Jacksonian America's love affair with weapons is, of course, the despair of the rest of the country. Jacksonian culture values firearms and the freedom to own and use them. The right to bear arms is a mark of civic and social equality. For men and many women, owning and knowing how to care for firearms is an important part of life. Jacksonians are armed for defense: defense of the home and person against robbers, defense against usurpations of the federal government, and defense of the United States against its enemies. In one war after another Jacksonians have flocked to the colors; independent soldiers and difficult to discipline, they have demonstrated magnificent fighting qualities in every corner of the world. Jacksonian America views military service as a sacred duty; when Hamiltonians, Wilsonians, and Jeffersonians dodged the draft as in Vietnam or purchased exemptions and substitutes in earlier wars, Jacksonians soldiered on, if sometimes bitterly and resentfully. Failure to defend the country in its hour of need is to the Jacksonian mind evidence of at best distorted values and more probably contemptible cowardice. An honorable person is ready to kill or to die for family and flag.

Jacksonian society draws an important distinction between those who belong to the folk community and those who do not. Within the folk community, among those bound by the code and capable of discharging their responsibilities under it, Jacksonians are bound together in a social compact; outside that compact is chaos and darkness. The criminal who commits what, in the Jacksonian code, constitute unforgivable sins (cold-blooded murder, rape, the murder or sexual abuse of a child, the murder or attempted murder of a peace officer) can justly be killed by the victims' families or colleagues, or by society at large—with or without the formalities of law. In many parts of the United States, juries will rarely if ever convict police, whatever the charge, nor will they condemn revenge killers in particularly outrageous cases. The right of the citizen to defend family and property with deadly force is a sacred one as well. Unlike most of the rest of the Western world, Jacksonian America widely accepts the routine use of deadly force to prevent crimes against property and has no hesitation about the death penalty against minors convicted of capital crimes. Death to the enemies of the community! It is a legacy from colonial times, confirmed by the experience of two centuries of American life, and one of the most deeply ingrained instincts in the Jacksonian world.

The absolute and even brutal distinction drawn between the members of the community and outsiders has had massive implications in American life. Through most of American history the Jacksonian community was one from which many Americans were automatically and absolutely excluded: Indians, Mexicans, Asians, African Americans, obvious sexual deviants, and recent immigrants of non-Protestant heritage have all felt the sting. Through most of American history in most of the country, the law has been helpless to protect such people from economic oppression, social discrimination, and mob violence, including widespread lynchings. Legislators would not enact laws; if they did, sheriffs would not arrest, prosecutors would not try, juries would not convict.

This tells us something very important: Through most of American history and to a large extent even today, equal rights emerge from and depend on this popular culture of equality and honor rather than flow out of abstract principles or written documents. The many social and legal disabilities still suffered in practice by unpopular minorities demonstrate that the courts and the statute books even today enjoy only a limited ability to protect equal rights in the teeth of popular feeling and culture.

Even so, Jacksonian values play a major role in African American culture. If anything, the role of Jacksonian values in African American life has increased with the increasing presence of African Americans in all military ranks.

The often-blighted inner-city social landscape has in some cases re-created the atmosphere and practices of American frontier life. In many ways the gang culture of some inner cities resembles the social atmosphere of the Jacksonian South, as well as the hard-drinking, womanizing, violent male culture of the Mississippi in the days of Davy Crockett and, a generation later, Mark Twain. Bragging about one's physical and sexual prowess, the willingness to avenge disrespect with deadly force, a touchy insistence that one is as good as anybody else—Billy the Kid would have been right at home.

Dr. Martin Luther King, Jr., who like many African Americans grew up surrounded by and immersed in Jacksonian culture, showed enormous sensitivity to these realities even as he set about working to overthrow some of the habits, practices, and beliefs most deeply rooted in that culture. King and his followers exhibited exemplary personal courage. Their rhetoric was deeply rooted in Protestant Christianity. The rights they asked for were precisely those that Jacksonian America values most for itself, though they scrupulously avoided the violent tactics that would have triggered an unstoppable Jacksonian response. King elicited bloody and violent resistance from Jacksonian America, but he touched it as well, and the bulk of both northern and southern Jacksonian opinion is steadily, if not always rapidly, moving to recognize the right of people of all colors and backgrounds who live under the honor code to be considered members of the community and entitled to its respect and protection.

This new and hopefully growing feeling of respect and tolerance emphatically does not extend to those, minorities or not, who are not seen as code-honoring Americans. Those who violate or reject the code—criminals, irresponsible parents, drug addicts—have not benefited from the softening of the Jacksonian color line. Social policy and feeling about these groups hardened even as code-honoring minorities have seen a significant and continuing improvement in their position.

Jacksonian Politics

As in the case of the other schools, Jacksonian foreign policy is related to Jacksonian values and goals in domestic policy. For Jacksonians the prime goal of the American people is neither the commercial and industrial policy sought by Hamiltonians, the administrative excellence in support of moral values that Wilsonians seek, or Jeffersonian liberty.

Jacksonians believe that the government should do everything in its power to promote the well-being—political, moral, and economic—of the folk community. Any means are permissible in the service of this end as long as the means themselves don't violate the moral feelings, or infringe on the freedoms, that Jacksonians believe are essential in their daily lives.

Jacksonians are instinctively democratic and populist. Hamiltonians mistrust democracy; Wilsonians don't approve of the political rough-and-tumble; Jeffersonians support democracy in principle but remain concerned that tyrannical majorities can overrule minority rights. Jacksonians believe that the political and moral instincts of the American people are sound and can be trusted. They don't need education and guidance from cultural elites. They don't need administrative or constitutional safeguards on the will of the majority. In the Jacksonian view the civil liberties and restrictions in the Constitution exist primarily to defend the majority from the schemes and machinations of elite minorities. For minorities to use constitutional provisions to check the will of the majority is an unconscionable abuse of process, like a criminal getting a conviction reversed on a technicality. If the people want prayer in the schools, emergency economic legislation during a depression, the death penalty, limits on free speech by subversives, or the quarantine of a suspect ethnic minority in wartime, then the judiciary has no business overruling laws voted in by proper majorities.

The simpler and more direct the process of government, the more confident are Jacksonians that it will produce good results. Referendums work better than legislative processes. In general, while the three other schools welcome the representative character of our democracy because they believe that representatives, with greater experience, greater leisure, and a broader view of the issues can perform legislative and policy-making functions better than the average citizens, Jacksonians tend to see representative, rather than direct, institutions as necessary evils.

This gives Jacksonians a somewhat different approach to government than those of the other schools. Jacksonians, more than suspicious of governments and elites, simply assume that governments have corruption and inefficiency the way picnics have ants. Every administration will be corrupt; every Congress and legislature will be, to some extent, the plaything of lobbyists. Career politicians are inherently untrustworthy; if it spends its life buzzing around the outhouse, it's probably a fly.

This can make Jacksonian polities much more tolerant of corruption in practice than, say, Wilsonians. Wilsonians see corruption as the mortal enemy of sound administration and fair judging. Jacksonians see it as human nature and, within certain ill-defined boundaries of reason and moderation, an inevitable by-product of government, even good government.

This Jacksonian attitude toward politics has roots in both wings of today's North-South Jacksonian coalition. It was Jackson who introduced the principle of rotation in office—the spoils system, to its enemies—into the federal service. Southern populist governments, not excluding the Long dynasty in Louisiana, were famously corrupt. So too were the urban political machines that represented northern immigrants. Tammany Hall voters were as one with white supremacist South Carolina Senator "Pitchfork" Ben Tilman's southern populist allies on this one. Corruption is inevitable, so let's make it work for us rather than for our enemies.

It is perversion rather than corruption that most troubles Jacksonians. Instead of trying, however ineptly, to serve the people, have the politicians turned the government against the people? Are they serving large commercial interests, weird ideological pressure groups, people who are not members of the folk community or, worst case, are they by either ineptitude or wickedness serving hostile foreign interests? In the past Jacksonians asked: Are they keeping interest rates high to enrich foreign bankers? Are they giving all our industrial markets to the Japanese? Are they allowing communists to steal our nuclear secrets and hand them to the Soviets and the Chinese? Are they fecklessly frittering away huge sums of money on worthless foreign aid programs that transfer billions to corrupt foreign leaders? Are they giving the Panama Canal to a tinhorn dictator?

Jacksonians tolerate a certain amount of perversion, but when governmental perversion becomes unbearable, they look to a popular hero to restore government to its proper functions. It was in this capacity that Jackson was elected to the presidency; the role has since been reprised by any number of politicians on both the local and national stages. Recent decades have seen Reagan master the role, while Perot, Ventura, Wallace, Buchanan, and McCain have auditioned for it. The Jacksonian hero dares to say what the people feel and defies the entrenched elites. "I welcome their hatred," said Franklin Roosevelt, one of many American patricians who won the trust of the Jacksonian masses. The hero may make mistakes but will command the unswerving loyalty of Jacksonian America so long as his heart is perceived to be in the right place. It is not absolutely necessary to be a military hero, but it helps.

When it comes to big government, Jeffersonians worry more about the military than about anything else. For Jacksonians, spending money on the military is one of the best things government can do. Yes, the Pentagon is inefficient and contractors are stealing the government blind, but by definition the work that the Defense Department does in defending the nation is a service to the Jacksonian middle class. Yes, the Pentagon should spend its money more carefully, but let's not throw the baby out with the bathwater. Jacksonian opinion is much more sensitive to allegations of waste and mismanagement in programs that Jacksonians don't set much store by—welfare abusers in limousines and foreign aid swindles generate more anger among many Jacksonians than do stories of six-hundred-dollar hammers at the Pentagon.

The profoundly populist worldview of Jacksonians contributes to one of the most important elements of their politics: the belief that while problems are complicated, solutions are simple. False idols are many; the true God is one.

Jacksonians believe that Gordian knots are there to be cut. In public controversies the side that is always giving you reasons why something can't be done, and endlessly telling you that the popular view isn't sufficiently "subtle," "complex," "sophisticated," or "nuanced"—that is the side that doesn't want you to know what it is doing, and is not to be trusted. Alexander Hamilton had a million good reasons for establishing the national debt. Philadelphia banker and Jackson antagonist Nicholas Biddle had a million reasons why we couldn't break up the Bank of the United States. Jimmy Carter had a million reasons why he couldn't bomb Iran, and a million more why we had to give away the Panama Canal. George H. Bush had a million good reasons for raising taxes, and for cutting short his offensive in the Gulf War before overthrowing Saddam. Clinton had a million good reasons for lying about his marital fidelity.

If politicians have honest intentions, they will tell you straight out what they plan to do. If it's a good idea, you will like it as soon as they explain the whole package. "Complex," when applied either to policies or to situations, is, for Jacksonians, a negative term. Reagan brilliantly exploited this; as in the case of Jackson, Reagan's own intuitive approach to the world led him to beliefs and policies that appealed to Jacksonian opinion right from the start.

The movement to impose term limits on representatives and senators reflects basic Jacksonian thinking: Washington makes bad decisions because decision makers have become too remote from the people. Term limits will ensure that fresh blood from the hinterlands will keep Washington more honest, and the knowledge that they have to go back home after one or two terms will keep more representatives on their toes.

Economic Policy

Jacksonians also have strong convictions on economic policy. If the purpose of government is to serve the folk community (generally referred to in American politics as "the American middle class"), then the purpose of economic policy ought to be to improve the economic position of the middle class. Deficit spending and a large national debt are bad things, but failure to meet the economic needs of the middle class is substantially worse.

From the Washington administration onward, the political passions and energies of Jacksonians have been concentrated on economic policy issues, with the steadfast goal of turning the government into an instrument for enriching the folk. This does not mean, as it does for Hamiltonians, enriching the elite, although Jacksonians don't begrudge letting the elite get a taste if the middle class is treated with appropriate respect.

The first two political shocks experienced by Jacksonians under the Constitution were the excise tax on whiskey and the speculative windfalls that accrued when the new government redeemed depreciated currency at par and assumed the state debts. In an age of bad roads and small markets, whiskey was the one product of the rural, small-farmer, hog-and-corn economy that commanded a market price worth the cost of transportation. Using surplus corn to make whiskey was a chief source of cash income for small farmers; the federal excise tax on it was seen as discriminatory and unjust and led to armed rebellion.

Worse, word soon spread that the tax revenue was needed to pay holders of state and federal paper. Unsophisticated Jacksonian war veterans, paid in depreciated dollars, had long since disposed of what they believed to be near-worthless paper. Federal politicians had informed their friends back home of the impending fiscal measures, allowing well-connected speculators to reap rewards that by right should have gone to Revolutionary War veterans. Anger at these and similar measures brought

Jefferson to power as an anticentralizing, antidebt candidate, and the lasting disenchantment of the people with Hamiltonian financial shenanigans is one of the keys to understanding the politics of the nineteenth century. The moonshiner up in the hills keeping the "revenuers" at bay with his weapons remained a popular character in American folklore for centuries.

Jacksonians, however, in Hamilton's day and later, were less concerned that the government was spending money than that it was taking Jacksonian money and giving it to others. When it came to expenditures that benefited small farmers, Jacksonian opinion was more understanding. One of the great political footballs of the first two-thirds of the nineteenth century was the question of land sales, the price at which federal land would be made available. Jacksonians wanted cheap, even free giveaways of farm-size plots of federal land. This goal was ultimately achieved with the passage of the Homestead Act of 1862. Allocation of federal land at below-market prices, or free of charge, made a substantial hole in the federal books, yet Jacksonian opinion felt little anxiety about it.

Similarly, while Jeffersonians tried to keep military forces small, and to avoid incessant, perhaps occasionally even unjust wars against Native American tribes, Jacksonians wanted an aggressive federal presence and role in managing the Indian presence, and in removing the Indians from particular districts as the tide of folk settlement moved on. Representatives from western states also worked to get substantial cash payments to compensate farmers for war damage in the Indian conflict zones. These claims could be as inflated as pain-and-suffering awards in today's product-liability cases; Jacksonians thought that paying them was part of the function of government.

Another early boondoggle for Jacksonians was the vast and fecund swamp of Civil War pension claims. Ultimately the ever-expanding and -loosening criteria, not to mention special congressional pensions voted to those who couldn't qualify under existing rules, allowed virtually any politically active white male in the Union states to collect a cash pension for life. Mark Twain (who wrote about Jacksonians but was himself a staunch Jeffersonian) mocked and denounced it, budget hawks like Grover Cleveland tried to rein it in, but the great pension machine moved serenely on.

During the twentieth century the U.S. Treasury continued and accelerated the transfer of public funds to private ownership under constant pressure by ever more sophisticated Jacksonian politicians. The history of the Veterans Administration is a great testimonial to the power of this political force. The politics of such issues as Agent Orange and Gulf War syndrome, and the progressive extension of benefits to larger classes of veterans and quasi-veterans, recapitulates the history of the Civil War pension program. This is yet another example of the continuities in American politics from generation to generation. The vast federal subsidies for home ownership were the twentieth-century counterparts to the Homestead Act. These subsidies go far beyond the generous mortgage interest and property-tax-deductibility provisions of the tax code. Starting with the New Deal, bank regulation, Federal Reserve policy, and the structure of the credit markets have been frequently used by the federal government to improve the affordability of housing.

In addition to housing programs, the Social Security system—adopted after a classic campaign of Jacksonian political activism for the Townsend Plan, a depression-era proposal calling for regular monthly payments to elderly Americans as a form of economic stimulus—represents a massive commitment of federal resources to the middle class. Medicare—and especially the loophole that allows many families to charge off elder relatives' medical costs to the government while keeping hold of their home equity and other resources—is another immensely popular and astronomically expensive program that in essence represents a massive transfer of government resources into private, mostly middle-class hands.

Even as the social safety network for poor Americans was being dismantled in the 1990s, and even as Jeffersonian, Wilsonian, and even Hamiltonian politicians and citizens worried about the growth of federal deficits and the expansion and proliferation of middle-class entitlements, an important new class of entitlement was springing up: tax credits and school vouchers for families with children. It is likely that such supports will grow, along with programs to reduce the burden of college tuition for the middle class; middle-class entitlements are overwhelmingly popular with voters.

Jacksonian Foreign Policy

Those who like to cast American foreign policy as an unhealthy mix of ignorance, isolationism, and irresponsibly trigger-happy cowboy diplomacy are often thinking of the Jacksonian tradition. Jacksonian populism, which, according to such students of American public opinion as Michael Lind, remains the most widespread political philosophy among the American population at large, is stronger among the mass of ordinary people than it is among the elite. It is more strongly entrenched in the heartland than on either of the two coasts. It has been historically associated with white Protestant males of the lower and middle classes, the least fashionable element in the American political mix today.

Although there are many learned and thoughtful Jacksonians, including some who have made distinguished careers in public service, it is certainly true that Jacksonian philosophy is embraced by large numbers of people who know very little about the wider world in which the United States finds itself. Jacksonian political philosophy is often an instinct rather than an ideology, a culturally shaped outlook that the individual may not have worked out intellectually, a set of beliefs and emotions rather than a set of ideas. However, ideas and policy proposals that resonate with Jacksonian values and instincts enjoy wide support and can usually find influential supporters in the policy process. So influential is Jacksonian opinion in the formation of American foreign policy that anyone lacking an ear for this popular feeling will find much of American foreign policy baffling and opaque. Foreigners in particular have alternately over- and underestimated American determination because they failed to grasp the structure of Jacksonian opinion and influence. Yet Jacksonian views on foreign affairs are relatively straightforward; once they are understood, American foreign policy becomes much less mysterious.

Realism

To begin with, although the other schools often congratulate themselves on their superior sophistication and appreciation of complexity, Jacksonians provide the basis in American life for what many scholars and practitioners would consider the most sophisticated approach to foreign affairs: realism. While in the last analysis Jacksonian realists are American rather than Continental realists, of all the American schools they are closest to the practitioners of classic European realpolitik in their suspicion of Wilsonian and Hamiltonian enthusiasms for international law. In this they stand with Jeffersonians, deeply suspicious of the "global meliorist" elements found in both Wilsonian and Hamiltonian foreign policy ideas. Often Jeffersonians and Jacksonians will stand together in opposition to humanitarian interventions or interventions in support of Wilsonian or Hamiltonian world-order initiatives. However, while Jeffersonians espouse a minimalist realism under which the United States seeks to define its interests as narrowly as possible and to defend those interests with an absolute minimum of force, Jacksonians approach foreign policy in a very different spirit, one in which honor, concern for reputation, and faith in military institutions play a much greater role.

Jacksonian realism is based on the very sharp distinction in popular feeling between the inside of the folk community and the dark world without. Jacksonian patriotism is an emotion, like love of one's family, not a doctrine. The nation is an extension of the family. Members of the American folk are bound together by history, culture, and a common morality. At a very basic level a feeling of kinship exists among Americans.

We have one set of rules for dealing with one another; very different rules apply in the outside world. Unlike Wilsonians, who hope ultimately to convert the Hobbesian world of international relations into a Lockean political community, Jacksonians believe that it is natural and inevitable that national politics and national life will work on different principles from those that prevail in international affairs. For Jacksonians the world community Wilsonians want to build is a moral impossibility, even a moral monstrosity. An American foreign policy that, for example, takes tax money from middle-class Americans to give to a corrupt and incompetent dictatorship overseas would remind those Jacksonians who have read *Bleak House* of Mrs. Jellyby, the character in the novel who neglects her own children in a constant frenzy of activity on behalf of the poor people of Borrioboola-Gha. It is nonsense; it hurts Americans and does little for Borrioboola-Gha. Countries, like families, should take care of their own; if everybody did that, we would all be better off. Charity, meanwhile, should be left to private initiatives and private funds; Jacksonian America is not ungenerous, but it lacks all confidence in the government's ability to administer charity at home as well as abroad.

Given the moral gap between the folk community and the rest of the world, and given that the world's other countries are believed to have patriotic and communal feelings of their own—feelings that similarly change once the boundary of the folk community is reached—Jacksonians believe that international life is and will remain both

violent and anarchic. The United States must be vigilant, strongly armed.
Our diplomacy must be cunning, forceful, and no more scrupulous than
any other country's. At times we must fight preemptive wars. There is
absolutely nothing wrong with subverting foreign governments or assas-
sinating foreign leaders whose bad intentions are clear. Indeed, Jacksonians are more likely to tax political leaders with a failure to employ
vigorous measures than to worry about the niceties of international law.
Of all the major currents in American society, Jacksonians have the least
regard for international law and international practice. In general Jacksonians prefer the rule of custom to the written law, and that is as true in
the international sphere as it is in personal relations at home. Jacksonians
believe that there is an honor code in international life, as there was in
clan warfare in the borderlands of England, and those who live by the
code will be treated under it. But those who violate the code, who commit terrorist acts against innocent civilians in peacetime, for example,
forfeit its protection and deserve no more consideration than rats.

Many students of American foreign policy, both here and abroad, dismiss Jacksonians as ignorant isolationists, but this misses the complexity
of the Jacksonian worldview. Their approach to war is more closely
grounded in classical realism than many recognize. Jacksonians do not
believe that the United States must have an unambiguous moral reason
for fighting. In fact they tend to separate the issues of morality and war
more clearly than do many members of the foreign policy establishment.
The Gulf War was a popular war in Jacksonian circles because the
defense of the nation's oil supply struck a chord with Jacksonian opinion.
That opinion, which has not forgotten the oil shortages and price hikes of
the 1970s, clearly considers stability of the oil supply a vital national
interest, and it is prepared to fight to defend it. The propaganda about
alleged Iraqi barbarism in Kuwait did not inspire Jacksonians to war,
and neither did legalistic arguments about American obligations under
the UN Charter to defend a member state from aggression. Those are
arguments to screw Wilsonian courage to the sticking place. Jacksonians
don't care. Had there been no UN Charter and had Kuwait been even
more corrupt and repressive than it was, Jacksonian opinion would still
have supported the Gulf War. It would have supported a full-scale war
with Iran over the 1980 hostage crisis, and it will take an equally hawkish stance toward any future threat to perceived American interests in
the Persian Gulf region.

In the absence of a clearly defined threat to the national interest, Jacksonian opinion is much less aggressive. It has not, for example, been enthusiastic about the American intervention in the former Yugoslavia. There the evidence for unspeakable atrocities was much greater than in Kuwait, and the legal case for intervention in Bosnia was strong. Yet Jacksonian opinion saw no threat to the interests, as it understood them, of the United States, and Wilsonians were the only segment of the population that was actively eager for war.

In World War I it took the Zimmermann telegram—a German offer to Mexico to regain territory lost in the Mexican War in return for helping Germany against the United States—and the repeated sinking of American ships in defiance of American warnings to convince Jacksonian opinion that war was necessary. In the years 1937–1941 neither the Rape of Nanking nor Nazi atrocities in Europe drew the United States into World War II. The attack on Pearl Harbor did.

To engage Jacksonian support for the Cold War it was necessary to persuade Jacksonians that Moscow was engaged in a systematic, far-reaching campaign for world domination, and that this campaign would succeed unless the United States engaged in a long-term defensive effort with the help of allies around the world. (That that involved a certain overstatement of both Soviet intentions and their capabilities is beside the present point.) Once Jacksonians were convinced that the Soviet threat was real and that the Cold War was necessary, they stayed convinced. Populist American opinion backed the Cold War, accepted conscription, lived with an unprecedented tax burden, and worried only that the government would fail to prosecute the Cold War with the necessary vigor.

No one should mistake the importance of this strong and constant support. Despite the frequent complaints by commentators and policy makers that the American people are "isolationist" and "uninterested in foreign affairs," Americans have made and will make enormous financial and personal sacrifices if they believe that these are in the nation's vital interests as they understand them.

This mass popular patriotism, and the martial spirit behind it, give the United States immense advantages in international affairs. Since the two world wars no European nation has shown the same willingness to pay the price in blood and treasure for a global presence. Most of the "developed" nations find it difficult to maintain large, high-quality fighting forces. Though not all the martial patriotism in the United States comes out of the world of Jacksonian populism, without the Jacksonian tradition the United States would be hard-pressed to maintain the kind of international military presence it now has.

Pessimism

While in many ways Jacksonians have an optimistic outlook, there is a large and important sense in which they are pessimistic. Whatever the theological views of individual Jacksonians, their culture believes in original sin and does not accept the Enlightenment's belief in the perfectibility of human nature.

As a corollary Jacksonians are premillennialist; they do not believe that utopia is just around the corner. In fact they tend to believe the opposite: that the Antichrist will get here before Jesus does, and that human history will end in catastrophe and flames, followed by the Day of Judgment.

This is no idle theological concept. Belief in the approach of the "end times" and the "great tribulation," concepts rooted in certain interpretations of Jewish and Christian prophetic texts, has been a powerful force in American life from colonial times. Today tens of millions of Americans believe that the establishment of the State of Israel began the countdown toward Armageddon. Tens of millions more may not share this specific interpretation of the Holy Books, but they accept the general historical framework: that neither Wilsonians nor Hamiltonians nor anybody else will ever succeed in building a peaceful world order, and that the only world order we are likely to get will be bad.

This has many implications. It deepens the skepticism with which much of the American public receives proposals for do-gooding foreign aid grants to international financial agencies and developing countries. No matter how much money we ship overseas, and how cleverly the development bureaucrats spend it, it won't create peace on earth. Plans for universal disarmament and world courts of justice founder on the same rock of historical skepticism. Jacksonians just tend to think none of these things will do any good.

In fact they think they may do harm. Linked to the skepticism about human imitations of the Kingdom of God is a deep apprehension about the rise of an evil world order. In theological terms, this is expressed as a fear of the Antichrist, who, many commentators affirm, is envisaged in Scripture as coming with the appearance of an angel of light—perhaps a charismatic political figure who offers what looks like a plan for world peace and order but is actually a satanic snare.

For most of its history Jacksonian America believed that the Roman Catholic Church was the chief emissary of Satan on earth. Rooted in the bloody struggles of the British Reformation, the Scotch-Irish border people came to believe that the bishop of Rome was the conscious head of a vast conspiracy. For two hundred years plots and rumors of plots roiled British society. Catholics tried to blow up King James I and both houses of Parliament in the Guy Fawkes plot. Mary Queen of Scots schemed with the French to overthrow Elizabeth I and bring back the Inquisition, with Protestant martyrs burned at the stake. The later Stuarts participated in papist plots against the liberties of Britain. True and false accusations stirred public opinion to a fever pitch, while a steady stream of propaganda reinforced popular fear of the cruelty, the cleverness, and the utter ruthlessness of the Vatican and its vast and far flung army of conspiratorial secret allies.

Fear of Catholicism has gradually subsided, but during the Cold War, the Kremlin replaced the Vatican as the principal object of American fears about the forces of evil in the world. The international communist conspiracy captured the old-stock American popular imagination because it fitted cultural templates established in the days of the Long Parliament and the English Civil War, when fears of the Antichrist or of global conspiracies, along with hostility to strong government, were fixed in the imaginations of the Scotch-Irish ancestors of American Jacksonians. Descendants of immigrants from eastern Europe had their own cultural dispositions toward conspiracy thinking, plus in many cases, deep hatred and fear of Russia.

The fear of a ruthless, powerful enemy abroad that possesses a powerful fifth column within the United States—including high-ranking officials who serve it out of either greed or misguided ideological zeal—is older than the Republic.

During the Cold War this "paranoid tradition" in American life focused mostly on the Kremlin, though organizations like the John Birch Society saw ominous links between the Kremlin and the American establishment. Though generally helpful in sustaining popular support for Cold War strategy, the paranoid streak has proved more difficult to integrate into effective American policy since the Cold War. To some degree the chief object of popular concern in post–Cold War America is the Hamiltonian dream of a fully integrated global economy, combined with the Wilsonian dream of global political order. To the Jacksonian ear, the senior George Bush's call for a "new world order" had distinctly Orwellian overtones. Christian Coalition founder Pat Robertson traces the call for a new world order to a satanic conspiracy consciously being implemented by the pillars of the American establishment.[22]

The fear that the Establishment, linked to its counterpart in Britain and, through Britain, to all the corrupt movements and elites of the Old World, is relentlessly plotting to destroy American liberty is an old and potent one. Should seriously bad economic times arrive, there is always the prospect that, with effective leadership, the paranoid element in the Jacksonian world could ride popular anger and panic into power.

Code of Honor

Another aspect of Jacksonian foreign policy is a deep sense of national honor and a corresponding need to live up to, and be seen to live up to, the demands of an honor code. Some things are so disgusting and cowardly that we can't do them, and some indignities so demeaning that we can't suffer them at the hands of others. Honor compels us to undertake some difficult and dirty jobs, however much we would like to avoid them. The political importance of this code should not be underestimated; Americans are capable of going to war over issues of national honor. The War of 1812 is an example of Jacksonian sentiment forcing a war out of resentment over continual national humiliations at Britain's hands. (However, those who suffered directly from British interference with American shipping, the merchants, opposed the war.) The power of the honor code has not faded since then. In the twenty-first century, national honor would require the United States to fulfill its commitment to protect Taiwan from invasion.

The perception of national honor as a vital interest that we must be quick to protect has always been a wedge issue driving Jacksonians and Jeffersonians apart. The Jeffersonian peace policy in the Napoleonic Wars became impossible as the war hawks grew stronger. The same pattern recurred in the Carter administration, when gathering Jacksonian fury and impatience at Carter's Jeffersonian approaches to the Soviet Union, Panama, Iran, and Nicaragua ignited a Jacksonian reaction that forced Carter to reverse his basic policy orientation and ended by helping to drive him from office. What Jeffersonian diplomacy welcomes as measures to head off war often look to Jacksonians like pusillanimous weakness. You can deal with a bully only by standing up to him. Anything else is appeasement, which is both dishonorable and futile.

The honor code also requires that we live up to our commitments. We have obligations to those we have promised to protect. Once the United States extends a security guarantee or makes a promise, we must fulfill that promise, come what may. Jacksonians, who had the least faith that South Vietnam could build democracy or that there was anything about Vietnam of interest to the average American, were steadfast in support of the war, though not of the strategy, because we had given our word to defend South Vietnam. Jeffersonian opponents of the war, who believed that fighting a bloody war in support of a corrupt and incompetent government was a dishonorable act, battled against Jacksonians, whose honor code taught them that fighting is honorable and that to abandon South Vietnam would be a craven betrayal.

We must also follow through. Jacksonian opinion was resolutely against the 1999 war in Kosovo at its outset. However, once American honor was engaged, Jacksonians like Senator McCain began to urge a stronger fighting strategy: There was a great consensus among them not to exclude the option of ground troops. It is a bad thing to fight an unnecessary war, but it is inexcusable and dishonorable to lose one once it has begun.

Reputation is as important in international life as it is to the domestic honor of individual Jacksonians. Honor in the Jacksonian imagination is not simply what one feels oneself to be on the inside; it is also a question of the respect and dignity one commands in the world at large. Jacksonian opinion is sympathetic to the idea that our reputation, whether for fair dealing, cheating, toughness, or weakness, will shape the way others treat us. Therefore, at stake in any crisis is not simply whether we satisfy our own ideas of what is due our honor; our behavior in the crisis and the resolution we obtain must preserve our reputation—our prestige—in the world at large.

War Doctrine

Jacksonian America has clear ideas about how wars should be fought, how enemies should be treated, and what should happen when wars are over. Jacksonians recognize two kinds of enemy and two kinds of fighting: Honorable enemies fight a clean fight and are entitled to be opposed in the same way; dishonorable enemies fight dirty wars and in that case rules don't apply.

An honorable enemy is one that declares war before beginning combat; fights according to recognized rules of war, honoring such traditions as the flag of truce; treats civilians in occupied territory with due consideration, and—a crucial point—refrains from the mistreatment of prisoners of war. Those who surrender should be treated with generosity; an enemy that surrenders, then at a convenient opportunity launches a sneak attack, has passed beyond the pale. Adversaries that observe the code will benefit from its protections; those that want a dirty fight will get one.

This pattern was very clearly illustrated in the Civil War. The Army of the Potomac and the Army of Northern Virginia faced each other throughout the war, and fought some of the bloodiest battles of the nineteenth century, including long bouts of trench warfare. Yet Robert E. Lee and his men were permitted an honorable surrender and returned unmolested to their homes with their horses and personal sidearms. One Confederate, however, Capt. Henry Wirz, was executed after the war, convicted of mistreating Union prisoners of war in Andersonville, Georgia.

Although American Indians often won respect for their extraordinary personal courage, Jacksonian opinion generally considered them to be dishonorable opponents. American Indian warrior codes (also honor-based) permitted surprise attacks, the murder of civilians, and the torture of prisoners of war. This was all part of a complex system of limited warfare among the tribal nations, but Jacksonian frontier-dwellers neither were nor wanted to be students of multicultural diversity. In Jacksonian terms, Indian war tactics comprised a dishonorable, unscrupulous, and cowardly form of combat. Anger at such tactics led Jacksonians to abandon the restraints imposed by their own war codes, and the ugly conflicts along the frontier spiraled into a series of genocidal conflicts in which each side felt the other was violating every standard of humane conduct.

The Japanese, another people with a highly developed war code based on personal honor, had the misfortune to create the same kind of impression on Jacksonians. The "sneak" attack on Pearl Harbor—actually, a clerical error prevented Japan from presenting a declaration of war before the attack—enraged Jacksonians, already suspicious of Japan on racial grounds and inflamed by years of missionary-based reporting on Japanese atrocities in China. The gross mistreatment of American prisoners of war (the Bataan death march, for example) further stoked a terrible rage. Japanese fighting tactics—again, fully in accordance with Japanese cultural notions of honor—only confirmed American ideas of the Pacific enemy as ruthless, dishonorable, and inhuman. This contributed to the vitriolic intensity of combat in the Pacific theater so chillingly detailed in John Dower's magisterial history *War Without Mercy*.[23]

Popular fury against Japan briefly became the dominant force in American politics. By the summer of 1945, American popular opinion was fully prepared, if it had come to that, for invasions of the Japanese home islands, even if these were defended with the tenacity (and indifference to civilian lives) that marked the fighting on Okinawa.[24]

Given this background, the Americans who decided to use the atomic bomb may have been correct that the use of the weapons saved lives, and not only those of American soldiers. Had the invasion of the home islands gone forward, and hostilities continued for another six to twelve months, millions of Japanese civilians would have died in the conventional bombing raids that would swiftly have mounted in intensity as more forces from the European theater were concentrated against Japan, and as the full weight of American aircraft and munitions production was devoted to the task of wearing down Japanese resistance and punishing Japanese temerity. Millions of additional civilian casualties would have resulted from starvation, disease, and exposure as American forces systematically went about the task of, in the words of Strategic Bombing Commander (and, subsequently, 1968 running mate of Jacksonian populist third-party candidate George Wallace) Gen. Curtis E. LeMay, bombing them back into the Stone Age. "I'll tell you what war is about," said LeMay in an interview. "You've got to kill people, and when you've killed enough they stop fighting."[25]

By contrast, although the Germans committed terrible crimes against civilians and against prisoners of war (especially Soviet prisoners of war) during the conflict, their behavior (with certain exceptions, especially in the treatment of downed fliers) toward the armed forces of the United States was more in accordance with American ideas about military honor. Germany delivered a formal declaration of war; with certain exceptions it honored international agreements in the treatment of American prisoners of war; its soldiers fought fiercely but in accordance with what American soldiers and officers recognized as the codes of war. As a result, despite the bottomless criminality of the Nazi regime, the German army that served it so well and so long won a measure of respect from the Americans (and their British cousins). Gen. Erwin Rommel is considered something of a military hero among Jacksonians—an honorable enemy. No Japanese warrior achieved this status, despite the considerable personal courage of their soldiers, the audacity of their commanders, and their sometimes brilliant performance in the face of overwhelming American material supremacy.

If the Germans avoided exposure to the utmost fury of an aroused American people at war, they were nevertheless subjected to the full, ferocious scope of the violence a fully aroused American public opinion will sustain, and even insist on, in the course of an honorable war.

Jacksonian opinion has strong convictions on the subject of the use of force. Many of these date from well before the Revolution, and were on display as early as King Philip's War, between the settlers and the Indians in seventeenth-century Massachusetts.

The first rule of war is that wars must be fought with all available force. Jacksonian opinion finds the use of limited force deeply repugnant, and considers the phrase "limited war" to be oxymoronic. There is only one way to fight: You must hit them as hard as you can as fast as you can with as much as you can. Nothing else makes sense. That was Oliver Cromwell's strategy in Ireland; it was Andrew Jackson's strategy in the Creek wars against the Indians. It was Douglas MacArthur's strategy in Korea, and it was what Jacksonians desperately wanted to do in Vietnam. It was the repeated failure of political authorities to fight this way in Vietnam that ultimately eroded Jacksonian support for the war. While the other three schools, for different reasons, embrace the idea of limits on both one's objectives in war and the degree of force one is prepared to employ, Jacksonians see war as a switch that is either on or off. They don't like the idea of violence on a dimmer switch. Either the stakes are important enough to fight for, in which case you should fight with everything you have, or they aren't important enough to fight for, in which case you should mind your own business and stay home. To engage in a limited war is one of the costliest political decisions an American president can make; neither Truman nor Johnson survived it.

The second key Jacksonian concept about war is that the strategic and tactical objective of American forces is to impose our will on the enemy with as few American casualties as possible. The code of military honor does not turn war into sport; it is deadly earnest business. This is not the chivalry of a medieval joust or of the orderly battlefields of eighteenth-century Europe, on which it was considered bad form to attack one's opponents by surprise or at night. One does not take risks with one's soldiers' lives to fight fair. Some sectors of opinion in the United States and abroad were both shocked and appalled during the Gulf and Kosovo wars by the way in which American forces attacked the enemy from the air without engaging in much ground combat. The turkey shoot quality of the closing moments of the war against Iraq made a particularly painful impression.

Jacksonians dismiss such thoughts out of hand. Since foreign evil-doers have forced us into war, whatever casualties the other side suffers are self-evidently the fault of their own leaders rather than of the United States. Furthermore it is the obvious duty of American leaders to crush the forces arrayed against us as quickly, thoroughly, and professionally as possible. It is also their duty to accomplish these objectives with the smallest loss of American lives they can manage. Victory must be a commander's first concern; the well-being of his troops is the second. A reputation for avoiding casualties on the enemy side wherever possible would not enhance the popular reputation of an American general.

The history of the more than 1,250 armed conflicts between U.S. forces and the tribal peoples of North America reveals many instances in which American forces enjoyed superiority in technology and firepower comparable to those in the Gulf War.[26] The records routinely show enormous disparities in the casualties of United States and tribal forces. There was never any doubt in the minds of American commanders that achieving such overwhelming superiority and exploiting it to the fullest to secure total victory was what they were supposed to do. To perish like George Armstrong Custer was more foolish than brave.

Jacksonian opinion takes a broad view of the permissible targets in war. Again reflecting a very old cultural heritage, Jacksonians believe that the enemy's will to fight is a legitimate target of war, even if this involves American forces in attacks on civilian lives, establishments, and property. The colonial wars, the Revolution, and the Indian wars all give ample evidence of this view. The conflict between pro- and antislavery elements in Kansas prior to the Civil War was fought in this spirit as well. Sherman's march to the sea showed the degree to which the targeting of civilian morale, through systematic violence and destruction, could to widespread popular applause, become an acknowledged fighting strategy.

Probably as a result of frontier warfare, Jacksonian opinion came to believe that it was the spirit of the enemy nation, rather than the fighting power of the enemy's armies, that was the chief object of warfare. It was not enough to *defeat* a tribe in battle; one had to "pacify" the tribe, to convince it utterly and totally that resistance was and always would be futile and destructive. For this to happen, the war had to go to the enemy's home: The villages had to be burned, food supplies destroyed, civilians killed. From the tiniest child to the most revered of the elderly sages, everyone in the enemy nation had to understand that further armed resistance to the will of the American people, whatever that might be, was simply not an option. The tribal leadership had to maintain an iron discipline over its hotheaded young men; half a dozen teenagers banding together on a raiding party would bring instant, terrible, and implacable retribution down on the entire community, and perhaps endanger the very existence of the people.

With the development of air power and, later, of nuclear weapons, this long-standing cultural acceptance of civilian targeting assumed new importance. Wilsonians and Jeffersonians protested against the deliberate terror bombing of civilian targets in World War II; since 1945 there has been much agonized review of the American decision to use atom bombs against Hiroshima and Nagasaki. None of this hand-wringing has made the slightest impression on the Jacksonian view that the bombings were justified and right. During both the Vietnam and Korea conflicts there were serious proposals in Jacksonian quarters to use nuclear weapons; why else have them? The only reason Jacksonians have ever found persuasive for not using nuclear weapons is the fear of retaliation.

Jacksonians also have strong ideas about how wars should end. "There is no substitute for victory," as General MacArthur said; the only sure sign of victory is the unconditional surrender of enemy forces. Just as Jacksonian opinion resents limits on American weapons and tactics, it also resents stopping short of victory.

Unconditional surrender is not always a literal and absolute demand. The Japanese, for example, were assured after the Potsdam Declaration that while the United States insisted on unconditional surrender and acceptance of the terms, the Japanese could keep the "emperor system" after the war. However, there is only so much give in the idea—all resistance must cease, United States forces must make an unopposed entry into and occupation of the surrendering country, and the political objectives of the war must be conceded in toto.

When combined with the fury and hatred of the kind that animated American public opinion in 1945, political leaders understood that they did not have the flexibility to approve conditional surrenders or compromise solutions to the war, even in the face of the appalling costs of an invasion of the Japanese home islands at a time of growing apprehension about Soviet intentions. When the Joint Chiefs of Staff discussed the prospect of an invasion of Kyushu, the southernmost of the major Japanese home islands, Adm. William Leahy projected that 268,000 Americans would be killed or wounded out of an invasion force of 766,000.[27] The invasion of the chief island of Honshu, tentatively planned for the spring of 1946, would have been significantly more costly.

While projected casualty figures like these led a number of American officials to argue for modification of the unconditional surrender formula, Secretary of State James F. Byrnes told Truman that he would be "crucified" if he retreated from this formula, a formula that had gotten a standing ovation when Truman reported on it to Congress in his first address as president. Truman, wisely, agreed.[28] Untested as a national leader, he lacked the stature to challenge Roosevelt's wildly popular and often restated demand for unconditional surrender. Not only did limited war, in Korea and Vietnam respectively, eventually cost Presidents Truman and Johnson their jobs, but Jimmy Carter's inability to resolve the Iranian hostage crisis with a clear-cut victory destroyed any hope he had of winning the 1980 election. And the senior George Bush's refusal to insist on an unconditional surrender in Iraq may have cost him the 1992 presidential election. For American presidents, in sum, MacArthur has been proved right: "There is no substitute for victory."

To be sure, once the enemy has made an unconditional surrender, the honor code demands that it be treated magnanimously. Grant fed Lee's men from Union supplies. Sherman's initial agreement with Gen. Joseph Johnston's Confederate army was so generous that it was overruled in Washington. American occupation troops in both Germany and Japan very quickly lost their rancor against the defeated foes; not always disinterestedly, in Europe GIs were passing out chocolate bars, cigarettes, and nylon stockings even before the guns fell silent. The bitter racial antagonism that colored the Pacific war rapidly faded after it. Defeated countries under foreign occupation are always chaotic places, and battle-hardened young men thousands of miles from their homes and families are seldom the tamest of houseguests, but in neither Japan nor Germany did American occupiers behave like the Soviet occupation forces in eastern Germany, where looting, rape, and murder were still widespread months after the surrender.

In both Germany and Japan, the United States had originally envisioned a harsh occupation strategy with masses of war crimes trials and strict economic controls, somewhat akin to the original radical Republican program in the post–Civil War South. But in all three cases the victorious Americans quickly lost the appetite for vengeance against all but the most egregious offenders against the code. Nowhere did the United States insist on economic reparations on its own account, and there was no significant popular support for long-term punitive measures. Whatever was said in the heat of battle, even the most radical Reconstructionists envisioned the South's ultimate return to its old political status and rights. In the same way, soon after the shooting stopped in World War II, American public opinion simply assumed that the ultimate goal was for Germany and Japan to resume their places in the community of nations.

Not everybody qualifies for such lenient treatment under the code. In particular, repeat offenders will suffer increasingly severe penalties. Although many Americans were revolted by the harsh and greedy peace forced on Mexico after the Mexican War of 1848 (Ulysses Grant felt that the Civil War was in part God's punishment for American crimes against Mexico), Santa Anna's long record of perfidy and cruelty built popular support both for the war and for the peace. The pattern of frontier warfare in which factions in a particular tribe might renew hostilities in violation of an agreement helped solidify the Jacksonian belief that there was no point in making or keeping treaties with "savages."

It is noteworthy that in the international conflicts of the twentieth century, there were no major populist backlashes calling for harsher treatment of defeated enemies. American diplomats largely enjoyed a free hand in rebuilding relations with enemies who passed under the yoke. There was no popular cry for reparations after either of the world wars, nor did the United States present the Soviet Union with a bill for the costs of the Cold War. This should not necessarily be taken as a sign of moral superiority; the French, the British, and above all the Soviets suffered far more at German hands than Americans did. Still, the tendency toward generous treatment of a beaten foe has been and remains an element of Jacksonian feeling toward war.

On the other hand, when foreign enemies lack the good taste to surrender, Jacksonians carry grudges that last for decades. Some of the roots of anti-Chinese feeling in the United States today date back to Chinese and North Korean mistreatment of captured Americans during the

Korean War. American food and energy aid to North Korea, indeed any engagement with that defiant regime, remains unpopular with Jacksonians for the same reason. Neither the mullahs of Iran, the assassins of Libya, nor Fidel Castro have ever been forgiven by Jacksonian opinion for their crimes against and defiance of the United States—nor will they be, until they acknowledge their sins.

The failure of the Soviet Union to make a formal surrender, or for the Cold War to end in any way that could be marked as V-USSR day, greatly complicated American policy toward post–Cold War Russia. The Soviet Union lost the Cold War absolutely and unconditionally, and Russia has suffered economic and social devastation comparable to that sustained by any losing power in the great wars of the century. But because it never surrendered, Jacksonian opinion never quite shifted into magnanimity mode. Wilsonians, Hamiltonians, and Jeffersonians all favored reconstruction support and aid, but without Jacksonian concurrence the American effort was sharply limited. Advice was doled out with a free and generous hand; aid was extended more grudgingly.

This is far from a complete account of Jacksonian values and beliefs as they affect the United States. In economic as well as defense policy, for example, Jacksonian ideas are both influential and unique. Convinced that the prime purpose of government is to defend the living standards of the middle class, Jacksonian opinion is instinctively protectionist, seeking trade privileges for American goods abroad and hoping to withhold those privileges from foreign exports. Jacksonians were once farmers; today they tend to be service and industrial workers. They see the preservation of American jobs, even at the cost of some unspecified degree of "economic efficiency," as the natural and obvious task of the federal government's trade policy. Jacksonians can be persuaded that a particular trade agreement operates to the benefit of American workers, but they need to be persuaded over and over again. Jacksonians are also skeptical, on both cultural and economic grounds, of the benefits of immigration. Immigration is seen as endangering the cohesion of the folk community and introducing new, low-wage competition for jobs. Neither result strikes Jacksonian opinion as desirable government policy.

Assessment of the Jacksonian School

Jacksonian influence in American history has been, and remains, enormous. The United States cannot wage a major international war

without Jacksonian support; once engaged, politicians cannot safely end
the war except on Jacksonian terms. From the perspective of members of
other schools and many foreign observers, when Jacksonian sentiment
favors a given course of action, the United States will move too far, too
fast, and too unilaterally in pursuit of its goals. When Jacksonian sentiment is strongly opposed, the United States will be seen to move too
slowly or not at all. For both foreign and domestic observers, to antici-
pate the course of American policy it is important to understand the
structure of Jacksonian beliefs and values.

It would be an understatement to say that the Jacksonian approach to
foreign policy is controversial. This approach has certainly contributed
its share to the headaches of American policy makers throughout history.
It has also played a role in creating a constituency for the idea that the
United States is addicted to crude cowboy diplomacy, an idea that—by
reducing international faith in the judgment and predictability of the
United States—represents a serious and real liability for American foreign policy.

However, despite their undoubted limitations and liabilities, Jacksonian policy and politics are indispensable elements of American strength.
Although Wilsonians, Jeffersonians, and the more delicately constructed
Hamiltonians don't like to admit it, every American school needs Jacksonians to get what it wants. If the American people had exhibited the
fighting qualities of, say, the French, in World War II, neither Hamiltonians, Jeffersonians, nor Wilsonians would have had much to do with
shaping the postwar international order.

Moreover, as folk cultures go, Jacksonian America is actually open
and liberal. Non-Jacksonians at home and abroad are fond of sneering at
what must be acknowledged to be the deeply regrettable Jacksonian
record of racism, and its commitment to forms of Christian belief that
strike many as both unorthodox and bigoted. And certainly Jacksonian
America has not been in the forefront of the fight for minority rights, nor
is it necessarily the place to go searching for avant-garde artistic styles or
cutting-edge philosophical reflections on the death of God. But folk cultural change is measured in decades and generations, not electoral cycles,
and on this clock, Jacksonian America is moving very rapidly. The military institutions have moved from strict segregation to a serious attack
on racism in fifty years. In civilian life the belief that color is no bar to
membership in the Jacksonian community of honor is rapidly replacing
earlier beliefs. Just as southerners whose grandfathers burned crosses

against the Catholic Church now work very well with Catholics on all kinds of social, cultural, and even religious endeavors, so we are seeing a steady erosion of the racial barriers.

Jacksonian America performs an additional service by making a major, if unheralded, contribution to America's vaunted "soft power." It is not simply the Jeffersonian commitment to liberty and equality; the Wilsonian record of benevolence, anticolonialism, and support for democracy; or even the commercial success that follows Hamiltonian policies, that attracts people to the United States. Perhaps beyond all these it is the spectacle of a country that is good for average people to live in, a place where ordinary people can and do express themselves culturally, economically, and spiritually without any inhibition. The consumer lifestyle of the United States, and the consequences of a federal policy that enriches the middle class and makes it a class of homeowners and automobile drivers, wins the country many admirers abroad. The popular culture, the result, for the first time in human history, of millions of ordinary people having enough money in their pockets and time on their hands to support a popular culture that has more resources than the high culture of the aristocracy and elite, is what hundreds of millions of foreigners love most about the United States, and its dissemination makes scores of millions of foreigners feel somehow connected to or even part of the United States. The cultural, social, and religious vibrancy and unorthodoxy of Jacksonian America—not excluding its fondness for such pastimes as professional wrestling—is one of the country's most important foreign policy assets.

It may also be worth noting that the images of American propensity to violence and of the capabilities of American military and intelligence forces and operatives that are so widely distributed in the media probably also increase international respect for American strength, and discourage attempts to test it.

This basically positive assessment would be incomplete without a description of the two most serious problems that the Jacksonian school perennially poses for American policy makers. Both of them spring from the wide ideological and cultural differences that divide the Jacksonian outlook from the other schools.

The first problem is the gap between Hamiltonian and Wilsonian promises and Jacksonian performance. The globally oriented, order-building schools see American power as a resource to be expended in pursuit of their far-reaching goals. Many of the commitments they wish to make, the institutions they wish to build, and the social and economic policies they wish to promote do not enjoy Jacksonian support; in some cases they elicit violent Jacksonian disagreement. This repeatedly puts Hamiltonians and Wilsonians in an awkward position. At best they are trying to push treaties, laws, and appropriations through a sulky and reluctant Congress. At worst they find themselves committed to military confrontations without Jacksonian support. More often than not the military activities they wish to pursue are multilateral, involving limited warfare or peacekeeping forces. These are often unpopular both inside the military and in the country at large. Caught between their commitments (and the well-organized Hamiltonian and Wilsonian lobbies and pressure groups whose political clout is often at least partially responsible for these commitments) and the manifest unpopularity of the actions required to fulfill them, American policy makers dither, tack from side to side, and generally make an unimpressive show. This is one of the structural problems of American foreign policy, and it is exacerbated by the divided structure of the American government and Senate customs and rules that give a determined opposition many opportunities to block action of which it disapproves.

The second problem has a similar origin but a different structure. Jacksonian opinion is slow to focus on a particular foreign policy issue, and slower still to make a long-term commitment to pursue a given policy vigorously. Once that commitment has been made, it is even harder to build Jacksonian sentiment for a change. This is particularly true when change involves overcoming one of the ingrained mental preferences in Jacksonian culture: It is, for example, much harder to shift a settled hawkish consensus in a dovish direction than vice versa. The hardest task of all is to maintain support for a policy that eschews appealing but perhaps inappropriate simple answers in the interest of more "complex" approaches. Having gotten Jacksonians into a war in Vietnam or the Persian Gulf, it is very hard to get them out again without satisfying total-victory conditions. Once Red China or Vietnam has been accepted as an enemy nation, it is very difficult to build support for normalizing relations or, worse still, extending foreign aid.

These problems, which are responsible for many of the recurring system crashes and unhappy stalemates in American foreign policy, cannot be fully solved. They reflect profound differences in outlook and interests in American society, and it is the job of our institutions to adjudicate these disputes and force compromise rather than to eliminate them.

Efforts by policy makers in the other three schools to finesse these issues often exacerbate the basic problem, which is the cultural, political, and class distance between Jacksonian America and the representatives of the other schools. Attempts to mask Hamiltonian or Wilsonian policies in Jacksonian rhetoric, or otherwise to misrepresent or hide unpopular policies, may serve in the short run, but ultimately they can lead to a collapse of popular confidence in an administration and the stiffening of resistance to any and all policies deemed suspect. When misguided political advisers persuaded the distinctively unmilitary Massachusetts governor Michael Dukakis to put on a helmet and get in a tank for a television commercial during his 1988 presidential campaign, they only advertised how far out of touch with Jacksonian America they were.

Chapter Eight

THE RISE AND RETREAT OF THE NEW WORLD ORDER

With the end of the Cold War, the four traditional schools have become more relevant than ever. The Cold War was a long era of relative stability, both in world politics generally and in the politics of the American foreign policy debate. While major changes took place during the forty years between 1949 and 1989, including the final collapse of the European empires and the emergence of newly independent states around the world, the structure of world politics changed only slowly. The defection of Yugoslavia from the Soviet camp was virtually the only change in European power politics between the Berlin airlift of 1948 and the fall of the Berlin Wall.

During this long period of stasis, the politics of American foreign policy also changed relatively little. Within the United States the elements of the broad-consensus Cold War coalition disagreed over particular policies and strategies, but generally agreed that international Communism, led by the Soviet Union, constituted a fundamental threat to the vital interests, even the survival, of the United States, and that a policy of global containment was the best means of meeting the challenge. Cold War hawks sometimes challenged the containment strategy as defensive and defeatist, calling for "rollback" rather than containment.

Cold War doves sometimes hoped to replace containment, at least partially, with engagement. Though the Vietnam War and its aftermath severely tested the Cold War consensus, generally speaking, it survived from the 1940s to the 1980s.

Partly because the Cold War consensus was so deep and so durable, and partly because American historical memory was so drastically curtailed by the myth of the Cold War, the struggle against the Soviet Union generated its own language to describe the various debates over American foreign policy. The history of the years between the two world wars was revised to create a satisfying if only partially accurate morality play. In this drama courageous and far-sighted "interventionists" who understood the nature of the new and dangerous world grew from small beginnings to defeat the traditionally entrenched "isolationists." Following that defeat a new dichotomy developed in American politics, almost entirely unrelated to anything that had come before: the Cold War dichotomy of "realist" hawks and "idealist" doves.

Realists or hawks—that is, virtually all Jacksonians together with many Hamiltonians and such Cold War Wilsonians as Washington senator Henry "Scoop" Jackson—favored an activist, even an aggressive, no-holds-barred approach to the Soviet Union, one in which our use of military forces, intelligence operatives, and alliances with unsavory characters was required given Soviet unscrupulousness. Idealists or doves, many Wilsonians and virtually all Jeffersonians, favored a more high-minded approach to the Cold War, aiming to defeat the Soviet Union by setting a better and more compelling example to the nations of the earth. Idealists also tended to prefer economic aid to military aid, multilateral institutions to unilateral action, and wanted to use the exigencies of the Cold War to support domestic programs ranging from teaching more science in American schools (after *Sputnik*) to domestic desegregation as a way to demonstrate the essential justice of market democracy to the developing world. Idealists, one could say, wanted the United States to lead by example; realists wanted it to lead by leading.

With hindsight it seems clear that neither "realism" nor "idealism" provided an infallible guide to the perplexities of the Cold War. Realists' support for apartheid South Africa, the generals of South Vietnam, and Cuban exiles at the Bay of Pigs did not bring the United States much joy. Realists often scoffed at cultural exchanges and other programs of "engagement" during the Cold War, on the very rational ground that Communist governments narrowly restricted participation in such activities to hard-core regime loyalists. As it turned out, however, exposing the Communist faithful to Western societies, artists, and scholars played a significant role in weakening the grip of communist ideology on the Communist elite.

On the other hand, idealistic arguments that men like Ho Chi Minh and Fidel Castro were aspiring nationalists who could be saved from communism by American friendship have not held up well. During the Cold War some doves argued that American hostility helped spark the Cold War by forcing the Soviets to adopt defensive behavior; these assertions, too, have been somewhat undermined by the documentary records emerging from the formerly Communist world.

Be all that as it may, the end of the Cold War opened a new era in American foreign policy. As late as 1989 it seemed as if the Cold War division between hawks and doves was enduring and monolithic. The debates over United States policy in Central America featured a cast of characters little changed from the Vietnam-era debates or, for that matter, from the great debates of the 1950s. The politics of disarmament—with hawks favoring caution and warning of the problems of verifiability, and with doves arguing for bolder steps—also reflected positions that went back many years. Over the decades these positions had frozen into solid political blocs, and individuals mostly espoused very predictable views. Those like journalist and author Victor Navasky, who had thought Alger Hiss innocent in 1952, were likely to oppose American military engagement in Central America, to turn against the Vietnam War early rather than late, to support sanctions against the apartheid regime in South Africa, and to oppose the embargo against Castro's Cuba. Those like Sen. Strom Thurmond, who thought Hiss guilty, could generally be counted on to take opposing stands in each of these cases.

It took time for the new politics of the new era to manifest itself fully, but by the end of the twentieth century, it was becoming clear that the old Cold War language no longer described the politics of American foreign policy. Issues like China policy and trade produced new coalitions, splitting both the old hawk and dove camps in unexpected ways. Vietnam-era doves flocked with neoconservative hawks to denounce China's human rights record and to demand trade sanctions against Beijing. Mixed flocks of doves and hawks also took to the media during the controversies over American policy in Bosnia and Kosovo during the 1990s. Some of the most inveterate Cold War hawks wanted nothing to do with the interventions in the wars of the Yugoslav succession, while some of the Cold War's most predictable doves sounded more like Theodore Roosevelt on San Juan Hill than George McGovern as they argued for American action against the Serbs.

Groping for new ways of describing the emerging political alignments, commentators and policy makers turned increasingly toward the older, pre–Cold War language to use words like "internationalist" and "isolationist" to describe the new politics of American foreign policy. Other polarities that increasingly figured in discussions included the contest between "multilateralist" and "unilateralist" approaches to intervention, and the approaches to regional and world trade issues called free trade and protectionist.

All this was a sign that the Cold War typologies and classifications were no longer useful; coalitions were dissolving into their constituent schools. As the Cold War coalitions broke up, the four traditional schools reasserted themselves. Hamiltonians, Wilsonians, Jeffersonians, and Jacksonians each interpreted the end of the Cold War in a different way, drew their own lessons from events, and set out to shape post–Cold War American foreign policy in the light of their values and hopes. As a result the Cold War alliances between Hamiltonians and Jacksonians on the one hand and Wilsonians and Jeffersonians on the other broke up, and new coalitions struggled to cohere in response to new international conditions.

The Quest for a New World Order

In U.S. politics at the end of the twentieth century, the foreign policy establishment was divided, but the overwhelming preponderance of elite opinion was either Hamiltonian, Wilsonian, or an uneasy amalgam of the two. The corporate sector, prominent think tanks like the Institute for International Economics, and most of the economics profession in the universities united behind the Hamiltonian program of free trade and globalization; the increasingly influential community of nongovernmental organizations (NGOs) and the foundations who supported them were largely Wilsonian; the intellectuals and professors who alternate between think tanks and government posts were largely divided between these two viewpoints as well. Jeffersonians could also be found; some were libertarian intellectuals like Ted Galen Carpenter at the Cato Institute; others were academics whose views on the limits and uses of American power had been formed during the Vietnam era or who saw what Yale historian Paul Kennedy called the dangers of "imperial overstretch" to American national interests. Jacksonian strength lay among military intellectuals; a group of influential commentators, intellectuals, and columnists; political scientists reviving the realist tradition in international relations; conservative think tanks like the Heritage Foundation; and the Congress, where key senators like Jesse Helms, a Republican from North Carolina, became chairman of the Senate Committee on Foreign Relations following the Republican victory in the 1994 elections.

With the end of the Cold War, the four schools shifted into a new configuration closer to the 1919–41 alignment than to the Cold War pattern. Hamiltonians and Wilsonians were what we can call globalist, believing that the construction of a global order was the fundamental task of American foreign policy. The two globalist schools thought in 1989 as in 1919 and 1945 that the end of a major international conflict created a valuable opportunity to build a new world order. For these schools the collapse of the Soviet Union meant an unparalleled opportunity to achieve long-held key American goals, and the end of the Cold War was the signal for a vast and systematic intensification of American political and economic efforts around the world. For Wilsonians this had to do with promoting the rule of law, the spread of democracy, and the construction of a genuine international consensus against aggression and for the protection of human rights by international police actions, and even the creation of a permanent armed body at the disposal of the UN Security Council. For Hamiltonians it meant a unique opportunity to develop a worldwide trading and finance system based on the unchallenged might of America's military forces and on the dynamism of its economy.

The other two schools, Jeffersonians and Jacksonians, opposed each other on many issues but united behind the belief that globalism went too far. These nationalist schools also interpreted 1989 the way they had interpreted 1919 and 1945: The end of the global conflict meant that the United States had the opportunity to reduce its international commitments. This was not a full return to the isolationism of the twenties and thirties; most participants in the foreign policy debate agreed that the United States has vital interests beyond its hemisphere. However, the nationalist camp believed that the national interest was best served by pursuing less ambitious and far-reaching projects than the glittering globalist visions of a new world order. Some, particularly those opposed to the ambitious trade liberalization agenda, worried that the globalist quest for a new world order would lead to a situation in which Hamiltonian and Wilsonian policy makers were willing to sacrifice the interests of the American people for the sake of that order.

As the Cold War ended, the globalists were in the ascendant; both the first Bush and the Clinton presidencies were staunchly globalist. The globalist coalition weakened through the 1990s, however, and the election of 2000 saw the second Bush court Jacksonian and even Jeffersonian support for a modified Hamiltonian international agenda that stepped back from the ambitious Wilsonian goals of the post–Cold War decade. The story of the rise and fall of the globalist coalition, and of the waning American commitment to a Hamiltonian and Wilsonian "new world order," is the story of the 1990s.

In the euphoria that followed the Soviet defeat, the globalist establishment believed that the ambitious Hamiltonian and Wilsonian international programs were largely compatible and reasonably easy to accomplish. The Gulf War reinforced the perception that the two programs could be simultaneously achieved with little expenditure of money, blood, or political capital. Hamiltonians could see the Gulf War as a preventive war against an aspiring nuclear power in a region of vital national interest; Wilsonians could call it a war for international law, with the UN Security Council acting as Wilsonians had always hoped it would. Everyone could note with some satisfaction that allies like Japan had been forced to contribute money toward the cost of the war.

The domestic and international Gulf War coalitions were so broad and so easily assembled that many concluded that the politics of foreign policy in the United States would not be excessively difficult. The overwhelming military power demonstrated by the United States in the conflict suggested that building the new world order would not greatly test the willingness of the American people to absorb large losses in combat. For some years after 1989, most of the foreign policy establishment saw few obstacles, either external or internal, to using American power to build a world order that satisfied the key criteria of Wilsonians and Hamiltonians alike.

As the nineties wore on, this sunny picture began to darken, even as continuing economic growth in the United States strengthened the country's technological and military lead in the world. The aftermath of the Gulf War was not as satisfactory as the war itself. The war ended with Saddam still in power and the United States trapped in the very uncomfortable position of seeking, long-term, the double containment of both Iran and Iraq. This was the beginning of a decade-long process of education for Hamiltonians and Wilsonians, in which both groups slowly learned that while there were few abstract limits on American power in the post–Cold War world, there were sharp and even crippling limits on the foreign policy establishment's ability to command public and congressional support at home. As the costs and complexities of the Hamiltonian and Wilsonian agendas were more clearly understood, wide gaps began to open within the globalist consensus, further reducing the ability of either school to pursue a vigorous and consistent agenda.

Crown of Thorns I: Hamiltonian Struggles

Hamiltonians began the 1990s in a state close to euphoria, launched into an extraordinary and creative period of policy initiatives and institution building, and then spent the decade learning the limits of their ability to achieve their most cherished goals. Although some of the Hamiltonian optimism in 1990 may, in hindsight, look premature or excessive, there is no doubt that the post–Cold War world was far more favorable to basic Hamiltonian hopes than the world had been in many years.

Looking across the world in 1990, Hamiltonians very naturally felt that their hour had come. The Communist world had collapsed. The developing world was more open than ever before to the gospels of free trade and free markets. The social democratic alternative to liberal capitalism was clearly bogging down; Anglo-American capitalism and capitalist order enjoyed a degree of economic, cultural, and intellectual hegemony without any real precedent around the world.

Surely the time was ripe for the creation of a Hamiltonian world order based on open trade, fiscal responsibility, and liberal finance. The World Bank and the IMF could be strengthened and invigorated; the gaps remaining in the old Bretton Woods framework of international institutions—chief among them, the absence of a permanent international trade organization—could finally be filled in. The creation of a market-oriented international system of commerce, finance, and trade became the keystone of Hamiltonian policy. Regional trade agreements like NAFTA and global institutions like the World Trade Organization would be central to this policy. In the 1990s Hamiltonians sought to seize the hour and attempted to achieve something that American statesmen had wanted since John Adams drafted a model treaty to guide the diplomats of the infant American republic: a worldwide trade system based on enforceable guarantees, giving American products equal access into all the major markets of the world.[1]

This ambitious and stirring trade agenda, dating back to the Reagan administration, and consistently backed by both the Bush (Senior) and the Clinton administration, duly and regularly endorsed by the overwhelming majority of economic experts, took enormous strides and made significant institutional gains during the 1990s. NAFTA and the WTO came into being. A summit of Latin American heads of state endorsed the concept of the Free Trade Area of the Americas (FTAA). Country after country across the developing world opened its financial system to international competition, and international capital flows achieved unprecedented volumes and flexibility, while increases in world trade continued to drive growth in rich and poor countries alike.

In the midst of this general, worldwide flowering, the United States, as Hamiltonians had both assumed and predicted, flourished as never before. As a global trading nation, the United States was uniquely positioned to benefit from liberalization and growth in every quarter of the world. As Asia, Latin America, and Europe embraced market-opening measures, American industries and states received important new stimuli. The extraordinarily flexible capital markets of the United States, combined with its entrepreneurial culture, its educated workforce, its continental markets, and its advanced infrastructure, allowed American entrepreneurs and business quickly to identify, and exploit, new opportunities.

The successes of Hamiltonian trade and development policy during the 1990s did not, however, succeed in winning widespread popularity for the Hamiltonian agenda. Indeed, inside the United States that agenda gradually lost steam during the decade. On the Left, labor unions, environmentalists, and other civil society groups blamed the Hamiltonian trade strategy for everything from falling wages in the United States to poor labor and environmental standards abroad. On the Right, conservative groups, with support in Congress, denounced the trade agenda as a moral sellout of American principles to countries like China and, in terms once heard only on the Left, as an attack on the living standards of the American people. Both Left and Right also joined to attack such pillars of the Hamiltonian economic agenda as the IMF and the World Bank.

The failure of Hamiltonian policy to gain more popular support in the United States is, at first glance, inexplicable. From 1982 through 2000 the United States witnessed, back to back, two of the three longest economic expansions in its history, punctuated only by the very short and mild recession of 1990–91 (blamed on an oil price jump following Iraq's invasion of Kuwait).[2] In inflation-adjusted (1996) dollars, real GDP grew from $4.9 trillion to $9.1 trillion between 1982 and 1999;[3] the total financial assets of American households grew from $12.6 trillion to $29 trillion[4] in those years. The rise in American exports during the 1990s played a major role in keeping the expansion healthy; so too did the reduction in inflation made possible by open trade. In the past many analysts noted that other economic expansions were curtailed when economic demand taxed American factories and labor markets to the breaking point; uncontrollable, demand-driven price increases generated inflationary pressures that ultimately brought the expansions to a halt. In the 1990s, however, overseas goods took the pressure off the American economy, allowing a blistering pace of economic growth to continue without the price pressures that had proved so costly in the past.

Under the circumstances, one might have expected American parents to be naming their children Nafta and Gatt rather than participating in protest marches against international trade agreements. But the profound political problems of the Hamiltonian trade agenda reflect both the economic transition through which the country has passed in the last generation and the effects of that transition on the views and goals of American business—on the structure of Hamiltonian opinion.

The wrenching transition from an industrial to a post-industrial economy was the most important development in American society between 1970 and the end of the twentieth century. This economic revolution created a difficult political context for Hamiltonian policy makers, and brought fundamental changes to the attitudes of the American corporate sector. Unfortunately for those policy makers, many of these changes served to reduce public support for Hamiltonian policy on the one hand, and on the other to weaken the ties between American business and the national government that had long been the central concern of Hamiltonian thinking.

Popular opposition to Hamiltonian trade policy has been widely noted, and the story behind it is relatively straightforward. From the New Deal through the 1960s, the manufacturing economy had provided stable employment and rising living standards for millions of American blue-collar workers. When real weekly wages peaked in 1973, 20 million Americans, or 26 percent[5] of the civilian labor force, held manufacturing jobs. With little meaningful economic competition from overseas, oligopolistic American firms enjoyed stable income and shared rents and productivity gains with their workers, who often organized into powerful unions.

To many Americans this was the best economic system seen in the history of the world. It combined security, affluence, and opportunity to an unprecedented degree. Blue-collar workers enjoyed steadily rising standards of living, could buy their own houses and cars, and had little fear of unemployment. Their children, should they show the talent or inclination, had every opportunity for college and university education and finding a place in the professional world.

This system could not endure. The Pax Americana gave other countries—initially Germany and Japan, later the developing world—the peace and order they needed to recover and/or to develop. Detroit's automobile companies and its unionized work force faced competition from efficient international rivals. At the low end of the skills market, the textile companies that had earlier migrated from New England to Dixie continued their migration—to Taiwan, Korea, and ultimately Vietnam, Bangladesh, and the rest of the Pacific Rim. In attempting to respond to this new competition, American companies could either transfer production abroad or automate at home; neither course did much for the wages or job security of low and semi-skilled workers.

As the markets for goods became more tumultuous and competitive, financial markets also lost their postwar calm. International capital movements, almost frozen from the depression until the European recovery of the 1950s, picked up once again. The Eurodollar market created an offshore pool of funds exempt from the careful regulatory structures that had tamed national capital markets following the upheavals of the depression and World War II. Crisis prone and destabilizing as these markets were, corporations struggling to adapt to newly competitive goods markets (and to the destabilizing inflationary and currency shocks of the post–Bretton Woods period) needed all the flexibility they could get.

During this period the apparent interests of major corporations and many ordinary citizens diverged sharply. Real weekly wages fell sharply: In 1993 they were 11 percent[6] lower than twenty years previously, even though business sector productivity in those years rose 34 percent.[7] Unemployment had averaged 4.8 percent in the 1960s; 6.21 percent in the 1970s; and 7.27 percent in the 1980s.[8] Inflation was also up sharply—it averaged 1.8 percent in the 1950s; 7.86 percent in the 1970s; and 6.85 percent in the first half of the 1980s.[9]

Other costs to working families of the new and more flexible economy were harder to measure, but no less real. Although more than 17.1 million more Americans were receiving Medicare and Medicaid in 2000 than 1973,[10] the number of Americans not covered by any health plan fell by only 6 million during those years,[11] reflecting a dramatic increase in the number of working people not covered by health insurance. Additionally many working Americans paid a larger share of their health care costs and enjoyed less freedom in choosing physicians and treatments as corporations sought to reduce costs and turned to HMOs. A shift from defined benefit to defined contribution pension plans shifted the risks of future economic problems from companies to workers. As male wages fell, millions of married women entered the labor force, leaving many families feeling both financially stretched and emotionally exhausted.

The biggest losers were found among poorly educated young white men. In 1998 dollars, the average hourly wages for young white men with only a high school education stood at $12.15 in 1973; in 1998 that income was only $8.86.[12] Workers with less than a college education also suffered the most severe decreases in health coverage. [13] This reflected a major social change. In 1973, American society provided a sort of social guarantee for most of its young white men: If they finished high school, they would get a steady job that would allow them to support a family on a modest but sufficient income. It was necessary, perhaps desirable, in the great scheme of things for that guarantee to die so that better things could take its place in a more productive and high-technology post-industrial economy. But the social and personal costs of this change in the structure of our society were very great, and by the end of the century many families and individuals had still not adjusted.

Finally, and perhaps most important, the changes that swept through national and international markets after 1973 powerfully increased the sense of insecurity among many Americans. The new and more flexible firms that emerged in the 1980s and 1990s no longer believed in lifetime employment or in lifetime commitments to communities and regions. This was inevitable; flexibility and opportunism were the characteristics that made them successful.

Downsizing, restructuring, and merger-linked layoffs throughout the economy spread unease even among those whose incomes continued to rise. For the millions of workers whose incomes dropped as their feelings of insecurity rose, the economic changes of the era remained profoundly unpopular, and the motives of the business community that so enthusiastically celebrated the new breed of cutthroat companies and ruthless CEOs were deeply suspect.

A series of international financial crises contributed to the broad (though by no means universal) public unease about the merits of the new economy. More Americans heard about the $50 billion bailout of Mexico following the 1994–95 peso crisis than heard about Mexico's rapid but gradual recovery and repayment of the debt. The international financial crisis of 1997–98, which at its height posed a genuine threat to the stability of the world economy, helped cement in many minds the equation of free markets with dangerous turmoil.

Increasingly, many Americans came to associate these negative changes with Hamiltonian policy, and especially the effort to create an open, rule-based global trading system. The old and deep-seated fear of cheap foreign-labor competition had been a chief mainstay and support of Hamiltonian politics during the 150 years when Hamiltonians stood for protective tariffs. In 1896 William McKinley's presidential campaign reminded voters that they had the opportunity to vote for "Bill McKinley, author of the McKinley Bill," one of the stiffest tariff measures ever passed by an American Congress. The McKinley tariff was given credit for "the full dinner pail," the 1896 equivalent of a chicken in every pot. Since then, the American corporate establishment has dramatically revised its views of free trade, but popular opinion has remained skeptical.

Did the Hamiltonian support for free trade simply reflect the desire of a greedy and immoral corporate elite to raise profits by exporting American jobs to low-wage third-world sweatshops? This suspicion gained credibility during the 1992 presidential campaign, when revelations that American taxpayer money had gone to help companies in El Salvador advertise the availability of cheap labor to American factories damaged the Bush campaign in many blue-collar households.

"Rosa Martinez produces apparel for U.S. markets on her sewing

"GOODS WILL BE SO MUCH CHEAPER"

Our contemporary debates over trade policy have deep roots in American history. Fear of floods of cheap imports from low-wage manufacturers in Europe led many workers as well as industrialists to favor high tariffs in the nineteenth century. Advocates of free trade pointed out then what they still say now—that free trade will benefit consumers.
Library of Congress, Prints and Photographs Division, LC-USZ62-99407

machine in El Salvador," read the cheerful, taxpayer-subsidized ad in a trade magazine. "You can hire her for 33 cents an hour. Rosa is more than just colorful. She and her co-workers are known for their industriousness, reliability and quick learning. They make El Salvador one of the best buys."[14]

The use of taxpayer funds to export jobs to low-wage developing countries struck many Jacksonians as a terrifying perversion of the basic functions of government. To Hamiltonians, by contrast, this was a natural part of the country's strategy for growth.

The domestic political situation was further complicated by the differential impacts of Hamiltonian trade policy on various regions and economic sectors in the United States. Manufacturing was, of course, a heavy loser, and so were states and regions historically most dependent on those industries. From 1900 to 1970, the percentage of the American workforce engaged in manufacturing increased by roughly a third;[15] after 1970, all these gains were lost, and by April 2001 the percentage of the workforce engaged in manufacturing was one-third *less* than it had been in 1900.[16]

Workers, of course, suffered the consequences, but there was also a major shift of power and wealth away from old-style heavy-metal manufacturing companies. A comparison of the *Fortune* 500 list of the largest American corporations in 1972 and 2000 illustrates the shift. In 1972 LTV Steel Company, Inc., ranked 21 on the list; by 2000 it had fallen to 384; and by the end of that year it had filed for Chapter 11 bankruptcy. US Steel ranked 13 in 1972; its successor, USX, was 51 in 2000. Bethlehem Steel fell from 30 to 412; Reynolds Metals from 123 to 335.[17] The declines of these companies and industries had a counterpart in regional economies; while California and the Sun Belt enjoyed population growth and rising incomes during the period, midwestern and northeastern cities and states faced much more difficult conditions. Not surprisingly those difficulties were reflected in the attitudes of many elected representatives toward economic changes and those deemed responsible for them.

U.S. trade policy in the 1990s was not simply about market opening across the board. International trade negotiations involve trade-offs and priorities. For the United States in the late 1980s and 1990s, this meant offering most foreign manufacturers and certain commodity producers increased access to American markets in exchange for greater opportunities abroad for American financial firms, service companies, and the entertainment industry. At the same time the United States acquiesced in continuing subsidies, export promotion schemes, and other interference in agricultural trade from the European Union (EU) and Japan. These policy decisions had clear regional and social consequences. Despite the long American economic expansion, corn and wheat prices in the late 1990s sank in real terms to levels last seen in the 1840s.[18] European opposition to genetically modified agricultural products threatened American farmers with a choice between lower productivity and diminished access to key foreign markets.

Hamiltonians could and did argue that U.S. trade policy was sound.

Services are the cutting edge of the new economy, while both manufacturing and agriculture have less capacity for long-term growth. Certainly the American economy was bigger, stronger, and better positioned for the future in 2000 than it had been ten years earlier. Even so, the differential impact of the policy on different regions and on workers with different levels of education still helps explain why political opposition to U.S. trade policy remained so strong during the long economic expansion of the 1990s. Thus a Pew Center survey on public opinion in February 2000 showed that while 64 percent of respondents supported American efforts in support of "free trade with other countries," 78 percent felt that "protecting the jobs of American workers" should be the top priority in these efforts.[19]

By 2000, globalization had become politically unpopular in the United States, yet further regional and world progress toward an open, law-based international economic system would require continuing strong American leadership. Hamiltonians were passionately committed to the need for American leadership but encountered enormous and apparently growing difficulties in gaining the necessary congressional and political support for core Hamiltonian initiatives.

An additional problem for Hamiltonians during the last third of the twentieth century came from the impact of economic change on the business leadership of the United States. The midcentury business elite, made up of relatively stable large corporations, believed that it was natural and necessary for its leadership to exercise civic and political leadership as well. At the local level, corporate philanthropy underwrote symphony orchestras and other worthy cultural endeavors; nationally business worked closely with the federal government.

But as the economic and financial turmoil of the last third of the century increasingly made itself felt, business leadership changed. Managers were no longer secure on their perches in a new world of hostile corporate takeovers. Many companies and their CEOs no longer felt able to play the same kind of leadership role in society; corporate philanthropy survived, and total giving in some cases grew, but giving had now to be linked more directly to specific concerns and interests of a given company. Patterns of corporate employment changed as well; managers increasingly saw themselves as individuals rather than as members of a broader corporate community.

All this made business leadership less able and willing to look at policy from the perspective of society as a whole; the policy focus of the

CEOs even of leading companies progressively narrowed to the economic interests of the corporation for which they worked.

Most important of all, the relationship between corporate leadership and the federal government changed profoundly, and it changed in ways that challenged some of the core tenets of Hamiltonian thinking. By the 1970s the regulatory structures of the New Deal state, once accepted by most of the business world as providing an organizing and stabilizing framework for profitable business activity, had become obstacles to corporations struggling to reinvent themselves and redefine their businesses. Business needed flexible access to capital. The Federal Reserve wanted to maintain regulatory control over interest rates and financial markets. Business wanted freedom to set its own rates and to slash unprofitable activities. Federal regulators wanted to preserve archaic systems of regulation.

Beginning in the 1970s and accelerating in the 1980s, the federal government, long seen by Hamiltonian business interests as the natural and inevitable partner and agent of the business community, came to be seen as the enemy of business. Federal taxes were destroying entrepreneurial spirit; federal regulations were strangling business.

These war cries were not new in American history, but the loudest attacks on federal strength had generally come from Jeffersonian and Jacksonian enemies of big business. Hamiltonian industrialists had pushed for the Banks of the United States and the tariff; they had supported the grants to the railroads and the assertion of federal authority over the states in interstate commerce; above all they had supported the federal government in the long and bitter contest over states' rights that climaxed in the Civil War.

Laissez-faire was once the cry of small proprietors and businesses too weak to gain federal patronage and support. During the last third of the twentieth century it reigned, temporarily, as the priority of the cutting edge of corporate America—an ideology appropriate to new businesses struggling to grow into major corporate leaders, and to old businesses struggling to reinvent themselves and to adjust to the new and more dynamic market conditions of the era.

What all this meant was that, apart from trade and international policy, American business was losing faith in the core Hamiltonian belief that American business needed a strong and effective government. The natural constituents of Hamiltonian policy were abandoning the cause.

One important mark of the weakness of traditional Hamiltonian politics was the eclipse of the liberal wing of the Republican Party and of the progressive Republican tradition. The old northeastern Republicanism had been the expression of a self-confident corporate elite that enjoyed a comfortable and stable partnership with the national government and, since the Civil War, had been the chief vessel of the Hamiltonian message; its virtual disappearance from the commanding heights of national politics during the 1980s and early 1990s testified to the complexity and importance of the changes taking place in the American corporate world.

The gap between business and the national government manifested itself in another and potentially even more damaging way. By the 1980s many large companies had sought to reinvent themselves as true multinational companies. They had an American origin, but they were world companies, equally committed to their customers and their stockholders wherever they might live. Corporations were becoming citizens of the world, cosmopolitan organizations with no special loyalty to any government or society. This development too undermined the historic support for Hamiltonian thinking.

There was increasing talk among business leaders of a new, "postnational" corporation. Could the multinational corporation of the 1980s really be considered a national corporation anymore? If General Motors bought equity in Japanese car companies while Japanese companies opened production facilities in the United States, could one convincingly say anymore that what was good for General Motors was good for the United States?

The idea, widespread in the 1990s, that globalization weakens the power of the nation-state posed an even deeper challenge to the Hamiltonian tradition and to the political power of American business. From Alexander Hamilton on down, Hamiltonians have believed that pro-business policies would strengthen the American state and therefore render the nation more secure and more powerful. If that assumption no longer holds, and the evolution of modern business means that the American state loses the ability to defend American interests, then the Hamiltonian tradition as we know it has come to an end, and Hamiltonians will have to choose between either strengthening business or defending the state.

American business interests have been accused of many things over two hundred years of history: greed, indifference to the plight of the poor, the use of illegal means to crush the small farmer and the independent business. A generic public loss of confidence in the essential patriotism of the American business community would be devastating. If big business is no longer American in any real sense, what right does it have to influence the formation of American foreign policy, or domestic policy for that matter?

What Hamiltonians failed to grasp was the degree to which Jacksonian opinion saw the multinational corporation as a suspect agent. If corporations, or rather the people running them, lose that basic gut sense of loyalty to the American people and the American state, then they cross an important line. They are no longer trusted and esteemed members of the American folk; they are aliens whose intentions cannot be trusted. Jacksonian suspicions that American financiers and industrialists were hireling lackeys of Britain created many political problems for Hamiltonians in the nineteenth and twentieth centuries; a new suspicion that the corporate world has fallen under the sway of foreign interests and alien loyalties can have long-term consequences in American politics.

The alienation between Jacksonian America and the corporate elite that grew up after 1973 could be the most significant development in American politics since the civil rights movement. There were clear signs in the 1990s that popular opinion was turning against the business elite. Large jury awards to plaintiffs in civil suits with corporate defendants were one result of this alienation; a growing disgust with the way corporate political contributions were affecting the political process was another. Campaign finance reform initiatives were passed into law through referendums in Maine, Missouri, Arkansas, California, Colorado, Montana, and Nevada. Jacksonian political insurgents like Perot, McCain, and Ventura found campaign finance to be a hot-button issue with an audience that went far beyond the traditional left-wing critics of the corporate sectors.

The economic upturn of the 1990s began to reduce the social tension and polarization of the previous two decades, but at the turn of the century the Hamiltonian international agenda was still constrained by an inchoate but strong opposition based on deep-seated questions about both the consequences of the Hamiltonian agenda for ordinary people and the degree to which large corporations could still be considered part of the American national community. Whether the issue was fast-track authority for the president or support for the World Bank and the IMF in the event that new financial crises demanded new bailouts, Hamiltonians lived with an uneasy sense that, despite more than a decade of unrivaled economic success, they could no longer count on congressional backing.

While Hamiltonians still often won key legislative battles, such as the 2000 vote on permanent normal trading relations with China, every battle over trade policy became an exhausting, all-consuming struggle. Almost two-thirds of the Democrats in the House of Representatives broke ranks with their party's president and presidential candidate over the 2000 China trade vote, and organized labor waged one of its bitterest campaigns in modern memory against the normalization vote.

Meanwhile the international climate for Hamiltonian policy was also becoming more difficult. Japanese paralysis and European assertiveness were reducing the ability of American diplomats to set a global trade agenda. The developing countries that originally welcomed the WTO agreement had become disillusioned with what they saw as a trade system still skewed against them. It would take strong and confident American leadership to keep the world trading system moving in ways that served core national interests; that leadership was harder for Hamiltonians to provide in 2001 than it had been in 1989.

Crown of Thorns II: The Wilsonian Agony

The other half of the dominant globalist coalition in post–Cold War American foreign policy underwent a triumph-and-tragedy experience during the 1990s similar in some ways to the Hamiltonian fate. Like Hamiltonians, Wilsonians in the first flush of joy following the collapse of European Communism believed that their deepest dreams were closer than ever to realization. As the nineties wore on, however, Wilsonians increasingly came to appreciate the difficulties that lay in their path.

If the collapse of the Soviet Union, with the spread of free markets, brought joy to Hamiltonians, Wilsonians were thrilled at an even wider and potentially more profound change in global society: the rise of free peoples. With the collapse of the Soviet Union, democratic regimes sprang up throughout the old Warsaw Pact states. When Boris Yeltsin led the democratic resistance to a Communist/military coup, when a "velvet revolution" brought peaceful change to Czechoslovakia, and East German democrats drove the Communists from power through peaceful street demonstrations, Wilsonians rejoiced. When military regimes yielded to democracies across Latin America; when Nelson Mandela achieved a peaceful, negotiated end to the apartheid state in South Africa and went on to win free and fair elections there; when Beijing students built a model of the Statue of Liberty; as Taiwan moved toward genuine multiparty democracy—Wilsonians celebrated a springtime of the peoples more widespread and far more promising than the European revolutionary movements of 1830, 1848, or 1918.

Fascism and Communism alike had collapsed. Free political systems were spreading across the world. International institutions paralyzed by the Cold War began to revive: A democratic Russia took the Soviet Union's old seat on the Security Council, and initially showed signs of joining a democratic bloc on that body.

There had never been anything quite like this worldwide flowering of freedom. The United States, the victor in the Cold War, had seen its principles triumph once again over a dictatorial enemy; the prestige of American democracy had never been higher. To Wilsonians the meaning was clear: The time had come for the United States to advance resolutely toward the establishment and consolidation of a democratic peace in a democratic world.

As free markets and free governments spread through the world, brought in by the spontaneous free choices of more and more of the world's peoples, Wilsonians believed that they and the Hamiltonians could, should, and would work hand in hand to extend the domain of freedom. Providing technical assistance, economic aid, and, occasionally, diplomatic support, the United States would lead this worldwide revolution, subdue the occasional rogue state, and consolidate what Francis Fukuyama, following the German philosopher G. W. F. Hegel, called the end of history.

Inspired and challenged by this historical opportunity, Wilsonians set out to take full advantage of the democratic opening. While continuing long-term efforts to increase American foreign aid to developing countries and to improve the lot of refugees, Wilsonians responded to the end of the Cold War with a sevenfold program aimed at a transformation of international life even more sweeping and revolutionary than the program Wilson himself had brought to Paris decades before.

First, they wanted to assist the transition of the old Soviet Union and its former European satellites toward full, stable democracy. Second, they wanted to complete the rout of communism and see the growth of democratic regimes in Asia, starting with China. Third, they sought to consolidate the shift in Latin America away from military regimes toward at least formal democracy, and they wanted to deepen democratic institutions in the region. Fourth, Wilsonians hoped to assist South Africa's transition toward multiracial, multiparty democracy, and subsequently to spread democratic values and practices to other sub-Saharan countries in Africa.

The remaining three goals were thematic rather than geographic. Wilsonians wanted to use the historical window of the "democratic spring" to strengthen the role of international judicial and political institutions, to usher in an era of law-based international relations. Strengthening the UN and the World Court, putting dictators on trial for human rights abuses, and developing the use of multilateral sanctions as an instrument of international policy were some of the goals of this ambitious agenda. Wilsonians worked to extend the sway of international law to new topics—in particular, to develop a law-based approach to global environmental problems. They also worked to revive such documents as the Universal Declaration of Human Rights. Treated with derision and cynicism by many nations since it was signed in 1948, the declaration was dusted off in the 1990s.

Next, Wilsonians worked to give a greater voice both internationally and within countries to something called "civil society," generally taken to mean NGOs, though as commentator David Rieff points out, Wilsonians often look very selectively at civil society. The National Rifle Association (NRA), fundamentalist churches, and pro-life protest movements are not, for example, what Wilsonians in America or elsewhere mean by civil society. Building on their earlier work, NGOs like Amnesty International, Human Rights Watch, Freedom House, Doctors Without Borders, and Greenpeace achieved great international prominence during the 1990s. At the same time a host of NGOs in developing and transitional postcommunist countries emerged and, at times, played significant roles in political events in their home countries. Wilsonians sought to bring United States policy into harmony with the values and goals of the leading international NGOs, and also sought financial support for hard-pressed NGOs in poor countries, some of them dictatorships.

Finally, Wilsonian opinion was significantly more feminist in 1990 than in 1945 or 1919. From missionary times forward, there had always been a feminist component of Wilsonian politics, but in the post–Cold War era, Wilsonians would for the first time make serious and largely successful attempts to enlist the power and prestige of the United States for a systematic program to improve the lot of women around the world. Increasingly, both public and private aid agencies as well as diplomats and officials would be pressed to focus on issues like the role of women in development and education and opportunities for women in developing (and Islamic) countries.

This was a vast and ambitious agenda. Nothing quite like it had ever been put into play. Visibly rooted in traditional Wilsonian values, it committed the United States to nothing short of a revolutionary foreign policy. It sought to overturn one of the hardiest, most durable elements in modern international life: the tradition dating from the seventeenth century that each sovereign state has a free hand when it comes to domestic policy. Moreover, it committed the United States to support, in many countries, political groups that sought the overthrow of existing regimes. Organizations like the privately managed, but U.S.-funded, National Endowment for Democracy made grants to activists and groups being persecuted by their governments.[20]

The Wilsonian agenda was not utterly unprecedented, however. The nineteenth-century British efforts to suppress the slave trade, the interventions of various powers to protect the Christian subjects of the Ottoman sultans, Allied policies toward Germany and Japan, and American interventions in various countries aimed at preventing the spread of communism during the Cold War were all examples of political interventions in defiance of strict Westphalian principles. Nevertheless the Wilsonian agenda of the 1990s was uniquely far-reaching and systematic. Unlike American political interventions during the Cold War, it was also divorced from traditional power politics. "Friendly" dictators would be the targets of subversion as well as hostile ones.

The dramatic Wilsonian agenda had significant successes. No doubt partly because of the influence and example of the world's most powerful country, democratic institutions and elections spread rapidly during the 1990s. According to Freedom House, which pioneered efforts to measure the presence or absence of democratic freedoms throughout the world, the number of "free" or "partly" free countries rose from 105 in 1989 to 145 ten years later, while the number of "not free" countries fell from 62 to 47 during the same period.[21] Except for some of the former Soviet republics and Serbia, virtually every former Communist country in Europe made substantial strides toward the institutionalization of democracy. Poland, the Baltic republics, Hungary, the Czech Republic, Slovakia, Bulgaria, Slovenia, and Croatia surprised the skeptics by the strength and vigor of their democratic institutions.

Only one Latin American country—Cuba—entered the twenty-first century under a formally dictatorial regime, and Brazil, Argentina, and Chile enjoyed unprecedented levels of democratic stability. A process of peaceful transition from one-party rule in Mexico was well under way, and the strife-torn republics of Central America also seemed to be emerging from a decade of civil war and dictatorship.

In the Far East, Taiwan witnessed the first peaceful transfer of power from one party to another in the history of Chinese politics. South Korea also witnessed a peaceful transfer of power through elections. The pattern of coup and dictatorship seemed broken forever in Thailand. A democratic revolution brought dramatic change to Indonesia. A democratic opposition survived the transfer of power in Hong Kong, and strong democratic movements for change were visible in Malaysia and Myanmar.

While the African record was more checkered, the stability of South Africa's multiracial democracy continued to point the way to a brighter future for the continent. Mandela's growing stature as an international leader and elder statesman gave Africa a democratic hero of the stature of Washington and Gandhi, and forever demolished the canard that democracy was contrary to the genius of African society.

The list of new and emerging democracies only hints at the scope of Wilsonian progress during the 1990s. Despite the tensions that developed later between Russia, China, and the United States, the Security Council was a far more effective institution in the 1990s than during the Cold War. The rising influence in many countries of civil society both internationally and in national politics could not be ignored. The status of women and its importance in rural development, poverty reduction, and population control became a fixed and perhaps permanent feature of the international development agenda. Britain's arrest and detention of Pinochet set a new and important precedent in international law, even if he ultimately escaped trial in Spain on grounds of poor health.

This brief summary, which only touches on Wilsonian achievement in the post–Cold War period, is still enough to establish that Wilsonian activism in the nineties contributed to important and lasting change. It was, by any reasonable measure, a stunning achievement and a major triumph.

Nevertheless the end of the century saw Wilsonians in a period of retrenchment, reconsideration, and even retreat. As with Hamiltonians, the successes of Wilsonian policy abroad did not strengthen Wilsonian influence at home. There seem to be three major reasons for this. In the first place, exhilarated Wilsonians overestimated their ability to achieve rapid, sweeping change with minimal American investments. A decade of American advice and aid in Russia ended with Russian public opinion much more profoundly alienated from, and suspicious of, the United States than it had been in 1989. In retrospect the Wilsonian belief that Russia could be quickly and easily remodeled into a Western-style democracy seems based on a misreading of history. Germany and Japan became democracies after 1945, but those countries had been defeated and occupied. Russia in 1989 was more like the Germany of 1919 than the Germany of 1945. The broad failure of American policy to create a stable, friendly democratic Russia told heavily against the Wilsonians, who had argued that precisely this outcome was possible.

Wilsonians similarly overestimated the strength of democratic forces in China, and the ability of the United States to influence Chinese behavior by either promises or threats. The enthusiasm of 1989 induced many Wilsonians to think that the student democracy movement in China had a realistic chance of taking power and leading that country in a democratic direction. Wilsonian misreading of China was nothing new. Wilsonians had hailed Sun Yat-sen's revolution in the belief that he and his backers had the capacity to lead China toward a democratic future. Chiang Kai-shek benefited from a similar illusion.

Once the Chinese government had suppressed the student movement, Wilsonians hoped that American threats and sanctions would force China to change course. This hope quickly proved unfounded, as the United States was forced to abandon the use of trade sanctions to force human rights improvements in China. After a decade of economic growth, student opinion in China had moved away from democratic ideals toward a prickly, anti-American nationalism. When, in the course of the Wilsonian-supported war against Yugoslavia, the United States bombed China's embassy in Belgrade, the student-worker coalition that once marched for democracy marched on the U.S. Embassy in Beijing.

This again was probably a question of misjudging the timing and underestimating the complexity of change in China rather than misreading the overall direction of the country. With hundreds of thousands of Chinese students returning from studies in the United States, the long-term impact of American values in China will be extensive and deep. Yet it does not follow that China is moving quickly or smoothly toward a democratic order today, any more than the presence of American-educated Chinese among the revolutionary elite of 1911 implied it then.

That Wilsonian initiatives and ideas contributed to policy failures in Russia and China outweighed the fact that in many smaller, less important countries the Wilsonian agenda had been crowned with success. Much of the damage was self-inflicted. If Wilsonians had not oversold their ability to bring change to Russia and China, the outcomes there might not have been held against them. But the failures and the damage were real. Both Jacksonians and Hamiltonians lost confidence in the ability of Wilsonian-inspired diplomats and policy makers to handle American relations with the world's great powers and hard cases, and Jeffersonian concerns about the possible consequences of Wilsonian overstretch deepened. Russia and China policy became effective issues in George W. Bush's 2000 presidential campaign.

This damage was compounded by the second factor that undermined Wilsonian achievements: the degree to which the logic of Wilsonian policy pulled the United States toward profoundly unpopular interventions abroad.

Defending human rights abroad ranks very low on the list of public priorities for American foreign policy. According to the February 2000 Pew poll, only 39 percent of the American people believe that defending human rights abroad should be a "very important" goal of the United States.[22] Yet more than once in the nineties, Wilsonians found themselves urging the American people to fight overseas wars for precisely this goal.

There were bruising battles over interventions in Somalia, Haiti, and Rwanda during the nineties, but the definitive battles on the issue took place over U.S. policy in the wars of the Yugoslav succession. The long and depressing series of battles in the United States over appropriate policy in the Balkans served to introduce Wilsonians to the dismal perplexities of American foreign policy in the absence of the Cold War.

The appalling atrocities of those wars brought many Wilsonians to the conclusion that military intervention was a moral duty. This feeling was particularly strong among those who looked back with regret and shame on the U.S. failure to take stronger, more effective, and earlier steps against the Nazi persecution of the Jews. These "holocaust Wilsonians" saw the prevention of future atrocities of this kind as the central and inescapable moral duty of the United States, and believed that "Never again" should become one of the basic principles of the American state.

Yet Wilsonians found, to their great chagrin and surprise, that popular enthusiasm for military intervention was limited. Revulsion against atrocities did not quickly or universally translate into the political will to put American forces in harm's way. The military was profoundly suspicious of open-ended, ill-defined humanitarian interventions, and the political establishment showed little interest in sending American troops against hostile fire. Television pictures on the evening news made Americans angry, and created a general sentiment that "something ought to be done," but the "something" that most people had in mind never seemed to include ground troops with a combat mission.

In one of history's many ironic twists, as the killing went on in Bosnia Wilsonians were left to lobby for—well—war. The Cold War doves had discovered a hitherto unsuspected taste for blood.

From a broader historical perspective, Wilsonian blood thirst was less unexpected. It is often the most ideologically committed who urge their government to the strongest, most confrontational policies. It was the strict Catholics, not the slackers and backsliders, who wanted to massacre French Protestants on St. Bartholomew's Day in 1572; it was the fanatical Peter the Hermit, not corrupt and lazy clerics in it only for the money, who preached the First Crusade beginning in 1096; it was the fervent and messianic Russian Slavophiles who dragged the weak government of Nicholas II into the assertive Balkan policy that ultimately forced the Russian Empire into what became World War I. When God closes the books on Judgment Day, one of the great questions to be answered will be whether zeal and idealism were responsible for more human suffering than were sloth and greed.

The Wilsonians, of course, have a far more benign worldview than some of the ideologies cited above. It is also true that the advice of ideological activists sometimes has good results, but it is still clear that it is the true believers who often lead great powers into confrontational policies.

While Wilsonians were ultimately successful in getting the United States to start and fight an air war against Yugoslavia in 1999, the events of the nineties only underlined the extent to which American public opinion was unwilling to follow the Wilsonian lead into one humanitarian war after another. The genocide in Rwanda, the civil conflicts in Sudan and Somalia, the horrifying breakdown of order and civilization in failed states like Sierra Leone, the Russian war against the Chechens, and the international war in the Congo did not persuade American public opinion to back a consistent strategy of humanitarian intervention, either alone or with the UN. The very plenitude of occasions for such intervention was the most powerful argument against humanitarian interventions; Americans could see no limit to the calls on their purse or their troops if Wilsonian interventionism became the cornerstone of American policy.

Faced with American opposition to humanitarian interventions, but still committed to the use of force to end horrific human rights violations, Wilsonians proposed the formation of an international police force of some kind, perhaps under UN control. From a Wilsonian standpoint, such an approach seemed simple, obvious, and entirely benign. The United States would not have to supply bodies to the front lines of the world's conflict zones: It would merely pay a reasonable share of the expenses of training, maintaining, and deploying an international force.

But this approach brings us to the third factor limiting Wilsonian success and influence in the battle over American foreign policy. The Wilsonian support for international police forces, law courts, and other instruments of coercion runs headlong up against a strong and widespread feeling against any institutions or policies that infringe on the sovereignty of the United States.

The decade following the Cold War provided growing evidence that the old American reluctance to pool sovereignty with other countries for a common purpose was still strong and, with the Soviet menace out of the way, playing an increasing role in the politics of American foreign policy. Reagan's 1982 rejection of the Law of the Sea, a 132–country agreement on property rights and other issues relating to seabed resources and navigation, was part of a larger and longstanding determination not to make any sacrifices of sovereignty for the sake of international law.

The Kyoto protocols, the International Criminal Court, the Comprehensive Test Ban Treaty, and the Land Mine Treaty were examples of initiatives dear to the Wilsonian dream of a world of international law at which the United States balked. More important in the long term was the growing movement in the United States to abandon the entire network of arms control arrangements so painstakingly negotiated with the Soviet Union in the last half of the Cold War. For Wilsonians the growing support for a national missile defense system, which would upset the balance of nuclear weapons widely credited with preventing nuclear attacks in the two generations since Nagasaki, was a disaster. Wilsonians worried about a new arms race, about the dangerous temptations for the United States if it achieved nuclear invulnerability, about the effects of a missile defense system on relations with allies in Asia and Europe, and about the collapse of the entire multilateral system of disarmament and arms control.

They worried, but there seemed precious little they could do. Not only did the Senate at least temporarily reject the Comprehensive Test Ban Treaty in the fall of 1999, but progress toward development of a national missile defense system ground on relentlessly, despite the failure of key tests.

Wilsonians were coming up against a thorny conceptual problem with their own agenda. On the one hand Wilsonians have always been powerfully drawn to the idea of a supernational authority, a legal system that binds sovereign nations to accept its dictates. This requires more than an international judicial system; it requires international policemen with the ability to enforce those judicial decrees. It is an appealing idea, and some Wilsonians have compared this system to the American federal system, in which the independent states joined together to create a common federal authority to keep the peace.

Politically this idea inspires deep, even fanatical opposition from many quarters. While interested in international law with respect to commerce, and while accepting the usefulness in certain circumstances of international agreements on subjects like arms control, Hamiltonians remain viscerally wedded to the sovereign power of the United States as the final safeguard for the property and well-being of American citizens. Jacksonians are even more deeply committed to national sovereignty. Jeffersonians fear, with some reason, that since no currently feasible international authority can be truly democratic, then Americans lose liberties when international authorities assume powers over American courts and legislatures.

One solution to this problem is for the United States to act as the arbiter and enforcer of international law. Hamiltonians and Jacksonians do not object to this idea in principle, but in practice both are unwilling to see the United States act as vigorously or as impartially as such a role would require. Wilsonians in moments of frustration with the weakness or sloth of international institutions often call on the U.S. government to act as the enforcer of Wilsonian order. But the theory behind it makes most Wilsonians uncomfortable. Are Wilsonians working to build the empire of law or the empire of America?

Moreover, making the United States the judge, jury, and executioner of a global justice system strikes many as a dangerous step. Not only Jeffersonians worry that this would involve the United States in endless quarrels and wars; additionally this idea is so radically unacceptable to countries like China and Russia that to proceed far down this course risks serious international trouble.

In the waning years of the Clinton administration, Wilsonian diplomats worked to address their growing isolation. Secretary of State Madeleine Albright launched a charm offensive in the direction of Jesse Helms, the Jacksonian/Jeffersonian North Carolinian then serving as chair of the Senate Foreign Relations Committee. She met with little success, however, in altering Helms's policy views. UN Ambassador Richard Holbrooke went further and accomplished more, seeking to accommodate Helms's views while advancing Wilsonian causes. Holbrooke's greatest success was to win Helms's support for the repayment of overdue U.S. dues to the United Nations following a negotiation that was almost as difficult as the Balkan peace process that led to the Dayton Accords.

By the end of the twentieth century, Wilsonians were coming to realize that the key constraints on their ability to build the global order they had long sought did not come from hostile external powers but from their limited political resources inside the United States. The limits on Wilsonian policy were neither fixed nor absolute. Under favorable circumstances, Wilsonians could bounce the United States into the occasional humanitarian war; when the sun, the moon, the planets, and all the stars lined up right, the Senate might even ratify an occasional treaty.

Failing war, there was pork. On smaller matters Wilsonians were consistently able to develop and fund a network of initiatives through such organizations as the National Endowment for Democracy and the National Democratic Institute, which acted to promote democratic movements and institutions abroad. They were also able to win significant funding, often channeled through Wilsonian NGOs, for humanitarian relief efforts outside the United States, although support for most forms of American foreign aid steadily declined.

Yet it was abundantly clear that Wilsonians lacked the domestic political strength consistently to implement their foreign policy. The same forces that blocked United States membership in Wilson's League and that kept the United States out of the Permanent Court of Justice in the 1920s were still capable of blocking crucial Wilsonian initiatives early in the twenty-first century. Too powerful to be ignored, Wilsonians were too weak to impose their ideas on the policy process in a consistent, effective way.

The Partnership Sags

Even as both Hamiltonians and Wilsonians discovered the limits of their political power within the United States, they also increasingly began to discover the conflicts and fissure points within their common globalist agenda. Wilsonians and Hamiltonians were closer to an effective consensus in 1990 than they were ten years later.

Much of the problem came from the growing Wilsonian doubts about two core features of the Hamiltonian project. First, the growing environmental movement began to see Hamiltonian plans for unrestricted free trade as subversive of environmental efforts both at home and abroad. At home, environmentalists felt that the WTO and NAFTA undercut American efforts to ensure, for example, better fishing practices—requiring that tuna and shrimp fishermen used, respectively, only dolphin- and turtle-safe nets in their operations. Abroad and more generally, environmentalists saw Hamiltonian trade and investment policy as facilitating a laissez-faire development strategy that placed few or no obstacles in the path of those who wished to sacrifice environmental prudence for the sake of immediate profits and jobs.

An additional element of opposition developed around the consequences of the Hamiltonian agenda on labor rights. A slow and generally unnoticed movement during the nineties saw a number of prominent human rights organizations raise labor rights to the level of primary human rights. In particular, the right of free association had long been seen as a fundamental human right, permitting, for example, the free establishment of political parties. In the 1990s human rights organizations came to feel the force of arguments that the right of free association also includes the right to form free trade unions, and such groups as Human Rights Watch, Freedom House, and Amnesty International added certain labor rights to their list of key rights whose violation should trigger a response by international civil society.

Characteristically, the human rights groups as well as the environmental groups wanted international practice and law to sanction those who violated core labor and environmental standards. This was a direct challenge to the heart of the Hamiltonian agenda. The WTO rules defining fair trade practices scrupulously omitted any provisions for sanctions linked to labor and environmental practices. The idea that labor unions, environmental groups, and human rights organizations would use their power in international civil society to impose labor and environmental standards horrified both Hamiltonians in the United States and their partners overseas. At best, such complicated and divisive new issues would make further progress toward a Hamiltonian world economic order far more difficult; at worst, the entire WTO system would explode as civil society placed heavier and heavier demands on its fragile rules and procedures.

Yet as the decade moved forward, it was clear that the issues between Hamiltonians and Wilsonians would not go away. Repeated clashes over China policy demonstrated that while they still agreed on the need for strong global policy by the United States, their differences over the direction and priorities of that policy threatened to end in deadlock and throw power by default toward those who opposed most if not all global engagement by the United States. Protectionists openly gloated over the Wilsonian and Hamiltonian disagreement over China trade, much as the irreconcilables like William Borah had gloated eighty years earlier over the deadlock between Wilson and the Hamiltonian Senator Lodge over the League of Nations.

The WTO system created additional problems for Wilsonians. Given the sensitivities of many of the member governments, negotiators had established high standards of privacy and confidentiality for dispute resolution and adjudication panels. Meetings were not open to the press; the records of proceedings would be kept secret; civil society groups were not able to present *amicus curiae* briefs in WTO proceedings.

Wilsonians could not let these issues go. The governance of "international space," the area of international agreements and institutions, is of vital interest to Wilsonian thinkers. Originally international space was dominated by governments and large corporations. The democratization of international space—the growing presence of NGOs, trade unions, political parties, and other noncorporate interests—was seen by Wilsonians as essential to the healthy growth and development of international order and law. With the extension of international space—a key goal of Wilsonians—the question of the "democratic deficit" in international governance came increasingly to the fore.

As more civil society groups came to see the relevance to their domestic priorities of decisions made by international institutions, and as new technologies like the Internet reduced the costs and increased the means for international cooperation among civil society groups, powerful coalitions grew up, capable of mounting international campaigns over trade policy and other international issues.

The gradual Wilsonian secession from the Hamiltonian trade agenda helped bring progress on that agenda to a halt. The collapse of the 1999 ministerial meeting of the WTO, held in Seattle amid bitter street protests, confirmed a trend already clearly present: The Hamiltonian agenda of the early 1990s had lost political momentum. The ability of the United States to achieve key Hamiltonian goals was in doubt—again, less because of foreign opposition to those designs than because of internal dissension within the United States.

Meanwhile Hamiltonians found themselves increasingly alienated from core elements of the Wilsonian agenda. Economic sanctions, and especially unilateral economic sanctions, were anathema both to Hamiltonian principles and, often, to specific and powerful Hamiltonian interests. For Wilsonians sanctions were a relatively cheap tool to use against peccant governments abroad. Were the Chinese arresting dissidents and persecuting the Tibetans? Sanction their trade. Was Myanmar's human rights record an affront to all decent people? Block American companies from investing there. Did Castro arrest independent journalists? Tighten the embargo.

Hamiltonians saw this as self-defeating madness. Wilsonians saw it as our simple moral duty. Hamiltonians somewhat reluctantly conceded that multilateral trade sanctions could be useful and appropriate. The concession came partly because multilateral sanctions clearly had a greater chance of being effective than unilateral ones; it also came because Hamiltonians well understood that effective multilateral sanctions would rarely be proclaimed. Wilsonians freely conceded that multilateral sanctions were preferable to the unilateral kind, but they continued to argue that there were times when U.S. principles demanded that Americans take a stand, whatever others did.

The question of humanitarian wars also divided the schools. The apparent enthusiasm of Wilsonians for these interventions increasingly dismayed Hamiltonians as the 1990s slipped by. Wilsonian interventions appeared to have high costs, higher risks, and very low or uncertain returns. How much more democratic was Haiti after the American invasion than before, how much closer to a durable political or economic order? How long, Hamiltonians wanted to know, would American troops be bogged down in the former Yugoslav republics before they could come home? What, exactly, was the policy outcome Wilsonians aimed at in these cases? What risks—of conflict with countries like China and Russia, or of tensions with American allies—were Wilsonians ready to run in pursuit of their aims?

Jacksonians oppose limited warfare at all times. Hamiltonians are more flexible but still want much clearer answers than Wilsonians could give about American interventions abroad. Furthermore Hamiltonians tend to be far more tolerant of moral shortcomings at home and abroad than are their Wilsonian colleagues. Ethnic oppression has gone on for a very long time, Hamiltonians reasoned, though they did not often say so in public; ethnic cleansing has been rather commonplace in twentieth-century Europe. Ugly, wicked, and distasteful though it is, is it really a crime that *requires* armed opposition from the United States?

Hamiltonians viewed the Wilsonian aspects of Clinton administration policy with increasing dismay, sharing a quiet sense that Secretary of State Madeleine Albright's Wilsonian convictions were taking the country in a dangerous direction, committing it to risky ventures, and unnecessarily drawing hostility and jealousy from other great powers.

This dismay deepened dramatically in 1999 when the United States and its NATO allies mounted an air war against Yugoslavia. Aside from widespread unhappiness with the Clinton administration's negotiation strategy, its lack of clear goals, and apparent miscalculations along the road to war, Hamiltonian realists were taken aback by the revolutionary nature of the legal theories used to justify the war. Hamiltonians do not as a rule make a fetish of international law, but Hamiltonians see the United States as a conservative, status quo power on security issues. Hamiltonians do not as a rule like precedents that undermine the importance of national sovereignty.

Additionally the arrest of Pinochet alarmed Hamiltonians about the degree to which American Wilsonians, in league with their colleagues abroad, were eroding legal doctrines whose protection American diplomats and presidents might well need someday. As in 1919, the Wilsonian desire for an international legal system higher than national sovereigns clashed with the Hamiltonian belief that no earthly power should be greater than the government of the United States.

Early in the twenty-first century the deepening tensions between Hamiltonians and Wilsonians were splitting the globalist coalition into its constituent parts.

The Opposition Coalition

Even as their partnership faltered and their agendas stalled, the globalist schools dominated American foreign policy after the Cold War. But

Jeffersonians and Jacksonians did not surrender. With increasing energy and resourcefulness they began to chip away at the dominant policy constructs and institutions, and their efforts enjoyed increasing success as the Cold War faded into the past.

Jeffersonians and Jacksonians saw the end of the Cold War very differently than the globalists. After the two world wars, Jeffersonians and Jacksonians had seen the outbreak of peace as providing an opportunity for the United States to scale back on its international commitments and to concentrate more attention on domestic matters. They both believed that with the end of the Soviet threat it was possible for the United States similarly to scale back its military and political commitments overseas. Although there were frankly isolationist figures in this coalition—like Pat Buchanan, whose 1999 book *A Republic, Not an Empire* attacked Franklin Roosevelt's decision to enter World War II—as a whole the coalition was less isolationist than nationalist. That is, unlike the globalists, nationalists did not see the creation of a favorable world order as the first priority of American foreign policy; rather, they believed that American national interests could be adequately defended with something less than an American commitment to a total world order, that the United States should concentrate on particular issues, regions, and problems rather than attempt to build a universal order.

Most of the Jacksonians and Jeffersonians of the 1990s were anything but naive. There were military dangers out there, ranging from nuclear weapons to terrorists; there were economic dangers to ordinary Americans from predatory trading nations; there were moral and political dangers in the concept of world order itself, a concept that threatened to undermine American sovereignty in various ways. Globalists believed that only a new world order could adequately safeguard key American interests; nationalists believed that certain aspects of that order themselves constituted threats to key national interests.

Yet the Jeffersonian and Jacksonian ideas about national strategy remained far apart. Jeffersonians talked about a "peace dividend," sought to reduce the size of the armed forces and of the intelligence services, to declassify material from the Cold War, and to scale down or end American troop commitments in Europe and the Far East. Jacksonians were not particularly eager for military cutbacks but looked to reduce the number of political and economic concessions the United States made for the sake of its Cold War strategies. Jeffersonians thought that the end of the Cold War hastened the day when the United States could cut back on its military commitments to South Korea and Japan; Jacksonians believed that the end of the Cold War reduced the need for trade and economic policy concessions to Asian export powers like Korea and Japan.

Jeffersonian dissent alone would not have slowed the globalist juggernaut. The American foreign policy process was relatively comfortable with Jeffersonian dissent. As Cold War doves, Jeffersonians had continually sought to limit the nation's foreign commitments, promote multilateral over unilateral approaches, and substitute patience and diplomacy for the resort to arms. Jeffersonians had not been uninfluential during the Cold War, but generally their influence was felt at the margin of policy and manifested by relatively subtle changes in emphasis and design.

Had Jeffersonians been the only school to dissent from the post–Cold War globalist coalition, the effect on U.S. policy would have been small. However, the gradual but ultimately steep and sustained decline in Jacksonian support for the political and economic underpinnings of the U.S.-sponsored world order represented a much more serious challenge to the globalists.

From the standpoint of American history, the most unusual and significant feature of the Cold War consensus was that the traditionally nationalist, if not isolationist, Jacksonian school spent forty years endorsing and supporting an ambitious global agenda. After 1989 that support began to dwindle.

This was by no means a return to the isolationism of the interwar period. It did not represent a lack of support for either a strong military or military alliances seen as enhancing national security. However, when it came to such matters as UN dues, foreign aid, signing or ratifying international conventions on such issues as land mine bans, child-soldier recruiting, the Comprehensive Test Ban Treaty and various International Labour Organisation labor rights conventions, proponents suddenly faced enormous congressional obstacles. Trade liberalization also proved problematic; after striking victories on ratification of NAFTA and the Uruguay Round trade agreement, establishing the World Trade Organization, the Clinton administration was unable to win fast-track authority for future trade negotiations, and both polling and political data pointed to falling support for free trade.

For different reasons both of the opposition schools were in a poor position to shape American foreign policy in the early nineties. Jeffersonians had warned that Reagan's policy of ideological confrontation with the Soviet Union would lead to a new and unending Cold War. In the late 1980s many Jeffersonians had convinced themselves that American power was fated to decline. The obvious upsurge in American international standing and economic power of the 1990s took them aback. Largely isolated in opposing the Gulf War, Jeffersonians took another blow when the war ended in an easy victory with neither the heavy casualties nor the political problems that many Jeffersonians had predicted. When the Balkan interventions did not end in unmitigated, clear disasters, Jeffersonian croaking about the dangers of intervention, the arrogance of power, and the costs of imperial overreach had lost most of their credibility. Jeffersonians continued to cry wolf in the 1990s, but fewer and fewer people listened.

Jacksonians gained power and self-assurance during the period. Early in the 1990s they were still ensorcelled by the Cold War, when any assertion of American ideals or interests abroad was seen as a move against a rival superpower in a zero-sum competition. For several years after the end of the Cold War, Jacksonians were swayed by the idea that where the United States had once contained communism, it was now our job to contain chaos. If disorder broke out in one part of the globe, malefactors in other continents would be encouraged by its spread. If Saddam's aggression went unpunished in Kuwait, someone might try the same thing in Africa or Asia.

Jacksonians realized only gradually that they didn't really care if chaos spread in central Africa. An unpunished genocide in Rwanda might encourage ethnic slaughter in Assam or Liberia, but Jacksonians awoke from the fever dream of the Cold War and found that they could live with these outcomes more easily than they had thought. While these ethnic slaughters were all very sad, from the standpoint of the American folk it might be better to have half a dozen slaughters in progress than to have American troops in harm's way in half a dozen festering world trouble spots.

What went for troops also went for money. When corrupt third-world governments could threaten to turn to the Soviets if we denied their requests for foreign aid, Jacksonian opinion sighed, but paid up. Take away the Soviets, however, and there was no longer a threat. What would an African republic do if the United States turned it down? Turn to France? *Tant pis,* said Jacksonian America: So much the better. With the Cold War over, Jacksonians saw no particular value in buying influence with soldiers, money or trade concessions. Let Europe police the Balkans, and if they fail, so much the worse for them. Let Japan bail out the Thais. Let the IMF go its own way.

Of course, Jacksonians saw direct threats to national security differently. There was little opposition to programs aimed at financing Russia's dismantling of its nuclear weapons. Jacksonians criticized the administrations of George H. Bush and Bill Clinton for cutting the defense budget. There was a great deal of popular unease about potential nuclear and biological terrorist threats to the homeland, and a willingness to spend far more money on these threats than the Bush and Clinton administrations asked for.

Over the course of the 1990s, Jacksonian opinion became steadily more aware of the gulf between its priorities and those of the globalist establishment. It also became more self-confidently assertive about fighting for its positions in policy debates.

Jeffersonians and Jacksonian nationalists, though united in skepticism about the new world order, were at least as deeply divided as the globalists. Jeffersonians generally opposed NATO expansion and national missile defense; Jacksonians supported these initiatives and, in contrast to Jeffersonians, also supported higher military budgets. Nevertheless both Jeffersonians and Jacksonians shared a strong belief that the globalist agenda in both its Hamiltonian and Wilsonian forms exposed the United States to unnecessary risks and costs. But Jeffersonians and Jacksonians failed to articulate, much less to unite behind, a coherent alternative to the globalist national strategy of the George H. Bush and Clinton years.

As a result the United States went from its Cold War political structure, in which two strong and stable coalitions debated the implementation of a consensus national strategy, to a new and less stable configuration in which two weak coalitions argued against each other and within themselves over the basic strategic architecture. The new globalist and nationalist coalitions were weak and divided; certain wedge issues split them completely and, in one spectacular case, the issue of national missile defense, the old Cold War coalitions came back to a kind of ghostly, single-issue half-life.

Jacksonians supported the idea of national missile defense with great passion, and considered irrelevant the technical criticisms of the system's feasibility. Missile defense was a vital question; if we couldn't build a good one now, that was all the more reason to get started in a hurry. What better way to learn than by doing? Moreover, the threat of missile defense under Reagan had, Jacksonians argued, forced the Soviet Union

PEACE INSECURE AND PEACE SECURE

These Nast cartoons reflect the long nineteenth-century debate over the
need for coastal defenses for American cities against European navies. This
controversy reflected a widespread awareness that America's major cities
then lay dangerously exposed to attack by powerful European war fleets.
There was here a definite resemblance to the twentieth- and twenty-first-
century battle over missile defense. Opponents said that the proposed
coastal defense systems were expensive and unworkable; supporters believed that the systems could work and could make a difference. History's
verdict on the coastal defense debate is mixed. What should be clear, however, is that Americans in the nineteenth century saw their homes and
families as vulnerable to devastating foreign attack. Only in the twentieth
century would historians and diplomats come to believe that eighteenth-
and nineteenth-century Americans felt secure behind their oceans against
security threats from abroad. *Thomas Nast. Library of Congress, Prints and Photographs Division*, Harper's Weekly, *February 13, 1875, page 136*

to concede American strategic supremacy; why not a new round to force
countries like China to accept their inability to match American might?

Hamiltonians were more easily swayed by technical concerns, but in general Hamiltonians also supported missile defense. If the system worked, fine; if not, at least it was a politically popular way to raise massive federal funding for high-tech research and development. In particular, throwing money at the software challenges facing any effective missile system might never stop an enemy missile, but it would almost certainly give American software firms major advantages in designing and developing new and complex programs.

Thus for the system's proponents, its feasibility was a secondary concern. They hoped it would work but were committed to try, whatever the outcome.

The old doves reunited to oppose missile defense. Jeffersonians gagged at the expense. Hundreds of billions of dollars for a system that could not be shown to work was bad enough. Worse still, the system seemed uniquely exposed to cheap countermeasures. It would be cheaper for enemies to confuse and defeat a missile defense system than for us to keep upgrading it to meet new tactics and challenges. For Jeffersonians this was the ultimate military-industrial boondoggle: a Maginot Line in the sky, erected at ruinous expense with no promise of long-term success.

Jeffersonian opposition to national missile defense was strong and passionate but not absolute. If a cost-effective missile defense system could ever be built, it is likely that many Jeffersonians would come to support its development and deployment as part of a broader pullback of American forces from the rest of the world. A missile defense system that replaced worldwide American troop deployments and reduced the need for entangling alliances would strike many Jeffersonians as preferable to the status quo. Nevertheless the habitual Jeffersonian suspicion of Pentagon and defense contractor claims about the costs and qualities of expensive new weapons systems kept Jeffersonian opinion largely united.

Many Wilsonians, uniquely, tended to oppose national missile defense even if it could be shown to work. A bitter hatred of arms races and armaments, deeply rooted in the long historical experience of Wilsonian politics, played a part in this opposition. More fundamentally, Wilsonians feared that an effective national missile defense would encourage American (read: Jacksonian and Jeffersonian) isolationism by uncoupling the nation's fate from that of the rest of the world. Why care about people in other places if, come what may, they couldn't even bomb us? At the same time the incompatibility of a national missile defense system with existing arms control treaties gravely endangered the fragile fabric of arms control and nonproliferation agreements that Wilsonians hoped could one day lead to the abolition of nuclear weapons.

Although rarely discussed, the offensive potential of a national missile defense system played an important role behind the scenes of the debate. Any system capable of defending both itself and the United States from missiles and space-based weapons would constitute an impregnable space-based weapons platform that would provide the United States with an unprecedented ability to project force anywhere in the world. Conventional armies, navies, factories, bases, power plants, and cities are much easier targets to find and hit than small, rapidly moving missiles. A space-based missile system could give an American government the ability to universalize Richard Olney's statement and assert that the "United States is practically sovereign on this planet and its fiat is law upon the subjects to which it confines its interposition."

It takes some heroic assumptions to reach a point where a global Olney Doctrine would be a practical possibility. The space weapons system would have to work and to survive the inevitable countermeasures attempted by other states. If other countries took the obvious and perhaps inevitable step of developing new and unconventional biological, chemical, and other counter-weapons, the United States would have to develop effective countermeasures against these also. This may seem unlikely, expensive, and difficult, but for Jacksonians in particular the idea of a global Olney Doctrine is such a glittering prize that no effort should be spared to achieve it. It is the Holy Grail of Jacksonian foreign policy: a weapons system that defends this nation while intimidating all others, and that would allow the United States to control events around the world without risking the lives of its citizen soldiers. This vision, more sweeping even than the vision of an umbrella in space protecting us from hostile missiles, lies just under the surface of the national missile defense debate, and it is one reason for the continuing and, to many, deeply and painfully surprising ability of the passion for missile defense to survive the repeated disappointments that the technologies proposed to implement it have so far consistently delivered.

Deeply divided on many issues, and liable to split completely on missile defense, neither the globalists nor the nationalists could create an effective and consistent policy for the post–Cold War era. American foreign policy makers in the coming years must try to move the country past this deadlock. If they don't, the United States will simply drift indecisively, unable to respond effectively to changes and challenges. Of all approaches to foreign policy, drift is the least likely to achieve the benefits that any of the schools seek, and it raises the probability of developments that none of the schools would welcome—perhaps a military challenge from a country like China, perhaps a new global financial crisis more threatening and catastrophic than the events of 1997–98, perhaps the horrible consequences of a leap too far into a quagmire in the Balkans or elsewhere.

Divided We Coast

By the closing months of the Clinton administration, American foreign policy could have been compared to a car. In the front seat the Wilsonian and Hamiltonian schools agreed that the car should go as fast as possible, but they disagreed on the best course. Their feet were together in pressing on the accelerator, but they wrestled for the wheel. Jeffersonians, meanwhile, sat in the back and exercised the classic privilege of the backseat driver: They complained loudly and irritatingly that the car was going too fast, and that it was taking wrong turns.

The three schools were so busy fighting that at first none of them noticed that the engine—the Jacksonians, whose support gave the car its real power and drive—were no longer responding. Hamiltonians and Wilsonians pumped the accelerator, but to no avail: The car continued to slow.

The car hadn't stopped, though. It still had momentum from the past, when the Jacksonian engine gave its all for the Cold War. When the car was headed downhill, when the foreign policy going was easy, it could still achieve a respectable speed. Sometimes the drivers managed to tweak a response from the engine, and a new burst of energy powered the car a little farther and faster.

But over time the car was clearly slowing down. And it was becoming harder and harder for the administration to get the car to climb hills. Increasingly, both Hamiltonians and Wilsonians had to look for the line of least resistance, the downhill path, when steering the car, because taking the car uphill—doing something difficult, like returning Elián González to his biological father or getting fast-track authority—looked harder and harder.

Institutionally, the struggle between globalists and nationalists took the form of a political struggle between the executive and legislative branches of the government, and, to some degree, between the civilian and military departments of the executive branch. Hamiltonians and Wilsonians dominated the civilian offices in the executive branch.

In the military institutions and the Congress, the political balance was different. Within the military, the historical memory of Vietnam still runs deep; overreaching—engaging in a military confrontation that the American people may not support over the long term—remained a real fear in the Pentagon. Additionally, there was an institutional resistance to the new structures and procedures required for humanitarian interventions. The skills and attitudes needed to take a hill are not the same as those needed for civilian crowd control and law enforcement. Should the Pentagon be training soldiers or international policemen?

Given these considerations, the Pentagon has become something of a center for Jeffersonian and Jacksonian thinking. The United States should make the smallest number of interventions consistent with national safety, and both humanitarian interventions and interventions with limited force should be made rarely if at all.[23]

At the same time, the Jacksonian and Jeffersonian opposition took refuge in the Congress and its arcane, minority-friendly rules. The classic institutional struggle between the executive and legislative branches in American politics was exacerbated and embittered when insurgent Republicans, many with strong Jacksonian leanings, took control of Congress in 1994.

Bill Clinton quickly found himself in the classic position of the head of an administration attempting to execute its foreign policy without congressional support. In the short run this isn't impossible or even particularly difficult to do. Under the American system presidents have substantial leeway to conduct policy from day to day without congressional mandates or accountability. The ordinary business of responding to events abroad, initiating negotiations, signing agreements, receiving ambassadors, exchanging state visits, conducting intelligence operations, arranging economic bailouts, and directing military diplomacy does not require congressional approval; the president has broad power to carry out the foreign relations of the United States. The Senate may refuse to ratify a treaty like the Comprehensive Test Ban Treaty, but then the president can nevertheless announce that the United States will abide by its limits, and Congress has little more to do or say. These powers should not be underestimated: Clinton waged war against Yugoslavia without the slightest shadow of a fig leaf of congressional consent.

Over the long run, however, without congressional support, the car begins to slow. Presidents lose much of their power to accomplish anything important. The president can make speeches about the UN or the

IMF Fund, but without congressional votes on appropriations, he cannot deliver the substance to back up his words. The president can proclaim American acceptance of the "three no's" of Taiwan policy (no independence for Taiwan, no U.S. recognition of Taiwan as one of two Chinas, and no Taiwanese membership as a sovereign nation in any international organization) when visiting China, but congressional resolutions and the slow passage through the legislative machine of proposals like the Taiwan Security Enhancement bill make a mockery of his claim to lay down permanent, fixed American policy on this issue.

In the end a president without congressional backing must govern like a Stuart king: He confines his objectives as far as possible to the narrow set of actions that require neither new money nor an affirmative congressional vote. In extremis, like the Stuart kings who often took money from France to support government expenses that Parliament wouldn't support, presidents without congressional support may look to foreign countries to support their foreign policies—as Reagan sought to raise money for the Nicaraguan contras.

Faced with an executive using every resource at hand to frustrate congressional mandates and counter congressional wishes, legislators search for opportunities to exert control over executive policy. The Congress attaches riders to unrelated bills, holds up ambassadorial nominations, requires annual reviews and reports, and uses all of its considerable powers of obstruction and delay to force the executive to terms.

Foreign Policy and the George W. Bush Administration

The presidential election of 2000, the closest and most controversial American election in more than a century, was largely determined by foreign policy questions. In 1996 Clinton won 240,000 votes from Cuban Americans, or 43 percent of the total.[24] Angered by Clinton's return of six-year-old Cuban refugee Elián González to his father's custody in Cuba, following a highly publicized battle in the courts and the media, and unappeased by both Vice President Gore's ineffectual efforts to disassociate himself from the administration position and Sen. Joseph Lieberman's desperate election-eve pilgrimage to, literally, pray at the tomb of Jose Mas Canosa, controversial founder and long-time leader of the anti-Castro Cuban American National Foundation, Cuban Americans shifted decisively into the Republican column. Gore received less than 50 percent of Clinton's 1996 share of the Cuban American vote, garnering just 18 percent.[25] This shift precluded what might otherwise have been an undisputed Gore victory in Florida. Additionally, controversial decisions to delay and ultimately to stop manual vote recounts by nominally Democratic Cuban American officials in Dade County effectively frustrated Gore's hopes.

But foreign policy played an even larger role in the 2000 campaign. Widespread public doubts about the NAFTA and WTO trade agreements and the political and economic agenda behind them largely fueled Green Party candidate Ralph Nader's presidential campaign. Opposition to trade agreements seen as neglecting labor and environmental issues became a major preoccupation of student activists, environmentalists, and the labor left, enabling the Nader campaign to attract enough votes to deny Gore the presidency.

George W. Bush, by contrast, stressed the differences between his foreign policy and the alleged excesses of Clintonian globalism. He cited the Clinton intervention in Haiti as an example of the unnecessary use of American forces, and his campaign both hinted that a Bush administration would seek to withdraw American forces from Kosovo and fulminated against the Clinton administration's support for unpopular international financial institutions like the IMF and the World Bank.

Behind these effective attacks lay two very different approaches to foreign policy, and the struggles between them would dominate the early months of the new administration. Many in the new civilian leadership of the Pentagon wanted an assertive, unilateral foreign policy and sought to present this approach as a Jacksonian foreign policy for a post–Cold War superpower. The ultimate goal of American foreign policy should be, they believed, to convert the present American hegemony into a more durable system. Strengthening the U.S. military lead, and especially the creation of a massive, space-based weapons system, was the means they envisaged to achieve this goal. The United States, these Jacksonians argued, was powerful enough to defy the hesitations of its allies—and rich enough to scorn warnings from countries like Russia and China that a U.S. missile defense system would set off a new arms race. This was the hour, these Jacksonians believed, in which the United States could and should make its bid for true global supremacy.

Jeffersonians in the administration—led by Secretary of State Colin Powell—read the national interest differently. The United States was, these officials believed, essentially a status quo power with few demands to place on the international system. We should be conserving our present power and alliances while avoiding unnecessary conflicts with potentially hostile countries like China. They had objected to Wilsonian overreaching in the Clinton administration; Jacksonian overreaching under Bush would please them no better. The status quo works pretty well for the United States, they believed, and there was no reason for the U.S., of all countries, to needlessly destabilize international politics—or to run great risks for uncertain rewards.

The early months of the Bush administration saw the followers of these two schools wrestling for control of American foreign policy. Jacksonians wanted a hard line with China and North Korea, a quick decision to deploy a missile defense system without extended negotiations with either Russia or the allies, and U.S. withdrawal from such Wilsonian international initiatives as the Kyoto Protocol on global warming and the establishment of a permanent international criminal court. Some of these battles they won and some they lost, but the Jacksonian attempt to recast American foreign policy as an exercise in unilateral hegemony is both dramatic and ambitious.

The American foreign policy process rarely satisfies the expectations of the doctrinally pure, however, and it seems at least likely that the Jacksonian defense intellectuals now attempting to set the national agenda will find the limits placed by events on their initiatives unusually chafing. By August 2001, the new team had already had to return to the bargaining table with North Korea, seek Russian understanding on missile defense, turn the other cheek to Chinese provocations following the forced landing of an American spy plane on Hainan Island, accept the indefinite extension of the U.S. military presence in the Balkans, and turn to the IMF to bail out key American allies like Turkey, Argentina, and Brazil. A divided Congress, with a narrowly Republican House and a razor-thin Democratic majority in the Senate, ensures that the partisans of all four schools will be well placed to influence American foreign policy on the issues that matter most to them. Within the Republican coalition, Jacksonian support for a strong military (and a well-stocked military pork barrel) clashes with Jeffersonian zeal for lower taxes, balanced budgets, and smaller government. Congressional elections in 2002 and the approach of the presidential contest of 2004 will force American foreign policy makers toward policies that can command broad public support—a dynamic that often undercuts supporters of a clear but controversial foreign policy direction.

The George W. Bush administration, like so many of its predecessors, seems fated to discover something Fisher Ames knew: in this democratic republic you can pull at the tiller as hard as you like, but the raft of state responds only sluggishly and partially to your commands—and your feet will always be wet.

This is frustrating to statesmen and especially to intellectuals with sharp and well-honed views, but after more than two centuries on often stormy seas, it is beginning to look as if the very sluggishness and unresponsiveness of the old unwieldy raft helps keep it afloat.

Chapter Nine

THE FUTURE OF AMERICAN FOREIGN POLICY

An Anatomy of Providence

Earlier I suggested that the special providence shaping American foreign policy for success bore the fingerprints of Adam Smith's invisible hand. The endless, unplanned struggle among the schools and lobbies to shape American foreign policy ended up producing over the long run a foreign policy that more closely approximated the true needs and interests of American society than could any conscious design. Fisher Ames's metaphor works for foreign policy as well as domestic; the republican raft wallows ahead even as the superbly fitted monarchical and aristocratic merchant ships sail on magnificently—until they strike a rock and sink.

This is a structural argument about democratic governance, suggesting that the advantages of democratic government apply in international affairs as well as in domestic ones. It is as true for countries like Germany and Japan as it is for the United States, and certainly in both those cases and many others a shift to democracy at home has produced much happier results in foreign affairs.

But the good luck or, for those who prefer, the providential blessings of the United States go further. We are fortunate not just in having a democratic form of government and federal and constitutional structures ensuring that many voices are heard in our process; we are fortunate in the political culture that informs our democratic society. Each of the four schools that together represent the American foreign policy debate makes distinct contributions to national power, and each is well matched with the others—capable of complementing one another and of flexibly combining in many ways to meet changing circumstances.

Each of the four schools has made distinct contributions to national power, both by building up the power and cohesion of American society and by providing the nation with both hard and soft power abroad. Admirable as each of the schools is, however, all of them are limited. We are better off with four of them than we would be with any one of them on its own. Left to itself, each school would press its insights too far, alienating important domestic interest groups and either missing opportunities or taking unnecessary risks abroad.

As it is, one of the chief advantages of having four dominant schools rather than one is that American foreign policy tends to be pragmatic and results driven. Students of international relations are fond of dogmatic statements. Realist theoreticians make assertions about the inevitability of international conflict; idealists anathematize the realist dogmas and proclaim their own faith in the ultimate compatibility, if not perfectibility, of humankind.

These doctrines are interesting and, on their own terms, compelling, but policy makers are often better off treating doctrinal assertions of this kind with respectful skepticism. For one thing it seems unlikely that these controversies will ever be settled to the satisfaction of all parties; unlike disputes in the natural sciences, disputes in philosophy and the social sciences have a way of lingering unresolved, sometimes for thousands of years. For another thing it may not matter that much to policy makers whether the idealists or realists will someday, somehow, be proved to have been right all along. We may in fact live in a world in which realist logic ultimately governs international relations; nevertheless, today, this week, this year, on this issue or with respect to this country, it may well behoove the United States to act as if the opposite, idealistic logic prevailed. Or vice versa. It is, to use one of the most dreaded epithets in foreign policy writing, a little naive to suppose that the key to successful foreign policy is first to derive a correct account of the eternal principles that guide the political life of nations, and then religiously and dutifully seek to apply these eternal principles in one's daily life.

The competition among four schools, affected in different ways and to different degrees by the philosophical doctrines of political idealism or realism, ensures that American foreign policy over the long term tends to be pragmatic rather than doctrinal. When and where grand Wilsonian or Hamiltonian proposals for international cooperation are widely and broadly seen to advance the interests of the United States, American policy moves in that direction. When, on the contrary, a political consensus builds that some particular proposal risks sacrificing concrete American interests to vague, impractical, do-gooding international designs, Jacksonian opinion rebels. American foreign policy tends to follow the evidence; it is not wholly committed to either realist or idealist principles *a priori,* and, in the confused and ambiguous world in which we live, that is probably a good thing.

We can also be grateful that our four schools are promiscuous. That is, any of the schools is able to coalesce with any of the others depending on circumstance. Rigid regional, class, confessional, or ethnic loyalties give some countries relatively rigid systems of political competition. This limits their political options and increases the chances that these countries will be unable to find effective solutions to foreign policy problems.

While the American system is far from perfect, each of the four schools is able to combine effectively with the others, in broad or narrow coalitions for large goals or small. While in some ways Hamiltonians are the least populist, and Jacksonians the most, their common concern for national strength and assertion allows them to combine effectively. Wilsonians and Jeffersonians deeply disagree about the purposes and limits of American power, but they can and do cooperate effectively on such measures as disarmament proposals to reduce the threat of war. As the kaleidoscope of American foreign policy turns through the years, the schools combine and recombine in one new coalition after another.

The ability of the four schools to form varying coalitions in response to external or internal pressures reinforces the pragmatism and flexibility of American foreign policy. It also helps that individual Americans are rarely passionately attached to one school and only one school, but are, rather, responsive to the appeals and logic of the different schools to different degrees at different times.

A final factor contributing to flexibility is the pragmatic character of the schools themselves. While all the schools are based on ideas and values, none of the schools is totalitarian or even a closed system. The American polity is, in the broadest sense of the word, liberal, and so is each of the schools. The Wilsonians are not Jacobins, much less Bolsheviks. Jacksonians, representatives of popular folk culture, do not link that culture indissolubly with a single religious hierarchy or sect. The Jeffersonian ideal of the nation as a "pure city upon a hill" is not linked to an ideal of ethnic purity. The Hamiltonian commercial party is not the possession and plaything of a hereditary caste. An underlying common grounding in liberal values among all four schools facilitates their cooperation and helps keep conflict between schools within bounds.

The Misfit

If the American foreign policy process has many strengths, it has at least one serious weakness, and on more than one occasion in American history that weakness has created serious crises for the United States.

This weakness is a consequence of the peculiar relationship of the United States to world order. As we have seen, the chief international concern of the American people through the centuries has been the relationship of the United States to the growing and changing global economic and political order. The historical periods when that relationship is clear and reasonably satisfactory are periods when the American foreign policy system works well. The years of the Monroe system were one such era, and the roughly forty years of the Cold War were another. During those years Americans disagreed about many things, but they broadly agreed on the relationship of the United States to the world. From 1823 to World War I, they agreed that the basic interests of the United States were better served by a world system under British leadership than by any feasible alternative. From 1947 to 1989 there was an equally clear consensus that the fall of the British Empire and the rise of the Soviet Union left the United States with no reasonable alternative but to lead a global coalition against the Soviets.

In other eras, however, the United States has lacked a clear consensus about its relationship to the global system, and different schools have stood for fundamentally different strategic approaches to the core issues of American foreign policy. These periods have historically been much more difficult for the United States, and our foreign policy has been much less effective.

The two great historic examples of such times in the American foreign policy system are the period between American independence and the promulgation of the Monroe Doctrine in 1823, and the period between World War I and the 1947 promulgation of the Truman Doctrine. Both were periods when great Continental powers challenged the British-based maritime world order, and both were eras in which Americans were basically divided over their attitudes toward both Britain itself and the larger order it had built.

In these situations, American foreign policy was subject to many of the ills that its critics describe. Foreign policy doesn't go away in the absence of a strategic consensus; it proliferates. The United States has policies from each of the four schools, but no strategy. Lobbies, sometimes unrelated to any of the major schools, also seize hold. Ethnic lobbies entrench themselves in certain niches; arms lobbies take hold elsewhere; various government bureaucracies and private interests take control over decisions that directly affect their key interests. Various executive departments and both houses of Congress freelance, developing points of view of their own.

Perhaps the most striking example of gridlock and policy proliferation came in the interwar years, 1919–41, an unhappy period in the history of American foreign policy that unfortunately looks increasingly similar to our own. Then as now the period of drift began when Hamiltonians and Wilsonians saw the end of a great world conflict as a time for greatly expanded American activity abroad, while Jeffersonians and Jacksonians believed that, with the danger ended, the United States should pull in its horns.

Then as now a globalist coalition of Hamiltonians and Wilsonians fell out among themselves. The issue then was the Treaty of Versailles. With Hamiltonians and Wilsonians unable or unwilling to compromise, the Senate rejected the Treaty of Versailles, and the United States failed to join the League of Nations.

Nothing, however, was settled. After the fight over the ratification of the treaty, each of the four schools went off on its own, enacting laws and conducting policies that furthered sometimes incompatible goals. Politicians did what they could to keep all the strong currents of political feeling as happy as possible; everybody got something, but American foreign policy as a whole was distracted and unfocused.

The four schools kept busy in the interwar years, but they accomplished very little of real value. With arch-Hamiltonian Andrew Mellon safely ensconced in the Treasury Department, and with Hamilton's dream of a national bank revived in the form of the Federal Reserve system,

Hamiltonians were in a position to pursue their economic goals even though Lodge's version of the treaty failed. In particular Mellon and New York Fed chairman Benjamin Strong systematically committed the United States to a new and central role in the global economic system.

Although the global financial disruption was not as great in 1919 as it would be after 1945, still the United States had new opportunities and new responsibilities in the postwar world. Britain had been forced off the gold standard during World War I and needed American help to return to that standard in 1925. The return was not a success, but it was classically Hamiltonian to believe in sound money, and to act in cooperation with other countries to restore the gold standard as quickly as possible after the war.

Meanwhile Hamiltonians addressed themselves to the problems of postwar financial reconstruction in Germany. No other nation could do this effectively because the Allied war debts to the United States were an essential part of the German reparations puzzle: Britain, Belgium, and France needed reparations from Germany to service their war debts to the United States. The two reparations plans that set the stage for the economic recovery of the 1920s were designed by Americans and implemented with the help of American banks and the Federal Reserve; this was a degree of American participation in European financial matters that would have astounded earlier generations, and can hardly be called isolationist. Throughout the world American financial leadership was strongly felt after 1919; no longer an indebted, developing nation, the United States had the world's largest economy and the world's largest gold reserves, and had become the world's most important net creditor.

Yet this Hamiltonian policy, accompanied by the traditional Hamiltonian high tariffs, did not amount to effective national strategy. The American diplomats and financiers who were active in fostering international economic cooperation, had only very limited authority. What Europe really needed, as many contemporary financial experts fully understood, was a complete write-down of the wartime debts. The United States needed to write off the debts owed it by Britain, France, and the minor Allied powers; Germany in turn needed release from the intolerable burden of reparations.

British and French statesmen made clear that these problems were linked, but it was politically impossible in the United States to consider debt forgiveness. "They hired the money, didn't they?" asked Calvin Coolidge. Jacksonian opinion was not about to write off nearly $13 billion in hard-earned taxpayer money.¹ As Sen. Hiram Johnson wrote to his sons, explaining his opposition to Hoover's proposed moratorium on war-debt repayments during the depression, "The ordinary man . . . like myself . . . resents in this time of stress being saddled with unusual and harsh taxation, and paying $250,000,000 this year, which should have been collected from Europe."² Raising the taxes of American citizens to subsidize debt relief for foreign countries was no more popular then than it would be now.

Jeffersonian arguments focused on the hypocrisy of the debtor nations and noted that they claimed to be unable to pay their debts to the United States but found no difficulty in raising the money to oppress the inhabitants of their vast colonial empires. For the United States to forgive the war debts would simply feed militarism and imperialism abroad. "Every dollar we deduct from this legitimate claim will feed the militaristic maw of that country [France]," Senator Borah wrote in 1923.³

William Jennings Bryan proposed linking debt forgiveness to "satisfactory" disarmament agreements,⁴ but such potentially constructive approaches were overshadowed by fierce resistance to the idea of expensive foreign giveaways. Rep. Louis McFadden of Pennsylvania saw Britain's interest in a moratorium and forgiveness as part of a wider British plot against the United States. "As soon as the Hoover Moratorium was announced," he thundered, "Great Britain moved to consolidate her gains. After the treacherous signing away of American rights at the 7–power conference at London in July, 1931, which put the Fed under the control of the Bank of International Settlements, Great Britain began to tighten the hangman's noose around the neck of the United States."⁵

This opposition made real progress on the debt issue impossible, and the result was unsatisfactory from every point of view. With government encouragement American bankers lent Germany money to repay the Allies. Ultimately the financial instability of this system helped precipitate the German financial collapse of 1932,⁶ deepening the depression in the United States and assisting Hitler's rise to power in Germany. The United States never recovered the war debts; of the nearly $12 billion owed, only $2.6 billion was ever repaid.⁷ (Finland was the only country to pay its debt to the U.S. in full, its last debt installment coming in the U.S. bicentennial year of 1976.⁸) The Allies got precious little out of Germany as well, with only 2.5 billion gold marks paid out of the total bill of 132 billion in reparations.

American financial policy in Europe could operate only within narrow limits—and though within those limits it was remarkably successful, those limits doomed it to failure in the end. Brilliant tactics could not overcome the lack of a coherent strategy in American economic policy between the wars. The costs were high. Bad feeling over war debts helped divide Britain and France from the United States, while bitterness over reparations inflamed German opinion and gave Hitler one of his best issues. Perhaps even worse, from the standpoint of American Hamiltonians, the instability of the European financial system helped undermine the health of the major banks in the United States. The 1932–33 banking crisis was the worst in American history, shutting the doors of every bank in the United States for a period and immeasurably worsening the depression.

The Wilsonians fared no better. The failure of the Treaty of Versailles and the repudiation and death of Wilson did not kill the Wilsonian impulse in American foreign policy. On the contrary: The 1920s saw a sustained burst of Wilsonian policy initiatives. In particular, in the 1920s the United States led the most sustained program of international disarmament in history. In 1922 the Washington Naval Conference committed the world's leading naval powers—Britain, Japan, and the United States—to strict limits on their naval strength;[9] net reductions of 82, 83, and 81 percent respectively. Though talks on disarmament by land and air were less conclusive, important conventions on arms trade limits were nevertheless negotiated in 1919 and 1925; the second was ultimately ratified by the United States in 1934, by which time, unfortunately, the convention was a dead letter.[10]

In addition to unprecedented progress in international disarmament, the twenties saw the appearance at least of significant progress toward a major Wilsonian goal: the abolition of war. On a bilateral basis American opposition to compulsory arbitration agreements disappeared; Secretary of State Frank Kellogg negotiated nineteen arbitration and thirteen conciliation agreements during four years in office.[11] Before leaving to serve as a judge at the Permanent Court of International Justice in the Hague, Kellogg won the Nobel Peace Prize for the crowning achievement of his career, and perhaps of the American peace movement: the Kellogg-Briand Pact of 1928.[12] Ratified by the Senate and technically still in force,[13] this treaty committed signatory nations to renounce war forever; the treaty was ultimately signed by all the major powers and virtually every independent state in existence at the time.

The 1920s saw continuing Wilsonian influence over American policy toward China. The Nine-Power Treaty committed the major powers in the Pacific to respect Chinese territorial integrity and to continue to observe the restrictions of the open door.[14] As movements for independence began to develop in the European empires, Wilsonians continued to show strong American support for figures like Gandhi and to vilify old-fashioned British imperialists.

Yet Wilsonians, like Hamiltonians, were running on a short leash. The keystone of the Wilsonian vision remained American participation in the League of Nations, and that dream faded ever farther into the distance. Wilsonians also made a major effort to persuade the Coolidge administration to accept the jurisdiction of the Permanent Court of International Justice, the forerunner of today's World Court. Here again they were defeated.

Without a real commitment by the United States to an effective policy in support of international law and collective security, the flimsy network of disarmament, arbitration agreements, and the Kellogg-Briand Pact fell apart in the harsher international conditions of the 1930s. The result demonstrated the unhappy principle that success is sometimes the most wounding form of failure. Wilsonians got what they wanted, skeptics pointed out: a solemn international treaty banning war. The result was the greatest war in world history, in which the precious pact played no role at all. Right up to the present day, the collapse of the ambitious peace and disarmament movement of the 1920s has been used by realist critics of Wilsonian idealism to show the futility of using paper agreements to stop wars.

The other two schools also enjoyed hollow victories during the interwar years. Jacksonians rolled their eyes at arbitration treaties and Kellogg-Briand, acquiescing in them because they judged, correctly, that there was no point in wasting political capital on a last-ditch opposition to something so feeble and pointless. Jeffersonians hailed these agreements and used them to support their contention that the United States could get all the benefits Wilsonians attributed to the League of Nations and the international court without actually joining the dreaded organization. We saw earlier how Jeffersonians were also able to apply the lessons of history they derived from World War I, and pass a series of strict neutrality acts during the 1930s.[15] Long-standing Jeffersonian suspicions of international bankers and corporations were further gratified in 1933 when Franklin Roosevelt withdrew from the London

Economic Conference, unilaterally devalued the dollar, and, to the great satisfaction of the old Bryanite wing of the Democratic Party, ultimately issued silver certificates of the Federal Reserve as legal tender in the United States. The "cross of gold" was gone.

Jacksonians also had their victories, enjoying an effective veto over American policy in these years. In some ways the early years saw the realization of the Jacksonian ideal in foreign policy: Great Britain had disappeared as either a creditor or a hemispheric power rival. The United States was also able to block the one international development that could have posed serious dangers to American interests in the 1920s and in fact posed problems for American military planners: the specter of an Anglo-Japanese alliance in the Far East. But here again the achievement was limited and negative, the United States managed to prevent the creation of a security system in Asia that it didn't like, but was unable to set up a viable alternative because of internal weakness and division rather than foreign opposition.

Otherwise, from a national security point of view, the interwar period was a time in which American prestige stood high. Through the 1920s and most of the 1930s, few foreign powers dared oppose the United States or insult its flag. Annoying or obstreperous Latin American regimes could be swatted at will, yet the United States was spared the necessity of maintaining large and expensive armed forces.

For Jacksonians this happy situation was reinforced by a powerful position in the politics of foreign policy. Jacksonian opposition was decisive in scuppering Hamiltonian debt cancellation initiatives and Wilsonian efforts to join the League of Nations or the World Court. Wilsonians, Hamiltonians, and Jeffersonians all effectively conceded Jacksonian sentiment a veto over the conduct of American foreign policy and catered to Jacksonian sensibilities. It was not a bad world, if only it could have lasted.

The interwar period remains a paradoxical and haunting episode in the history of American foreign policy. It witnessed the most dramatic examples of American peacetime leadership in Europe and Asia—and is usually labeled a period of rampant isolationism. It was an era of an unrestrained probusiness policy at home and abroad that ended in the greatest business depression in American history. It was an era of unprecedented American activity in support of international law, disarmament, and arbitration—and it ended in the most brutal and wicked war in the history of mankind. It was also an era in which each of the four schools was able to achieve a substantial portion of its agenda—but the period ended with what all the schools had most wished to avoid: a world war. The paradoxes don't stop there. While the war was the disaster that every policy school had hoped to prevent, the outcome of the war was even more favorable for the United States than that of World War I. Moreover, with the end of World War II it soon became clear that the four schools had learned something from the interwar period; the passive consensus of the twenties and thirties yielded to the united and activist Cold War consensus of the next generation.

Stalemated by the evenly balanced schools, each capable of exercising a veto, none capable of leadership, the American government worked harder than ever before at foreign policy after 1919 but had less than ever before to show for it. The domestic stalemate prevented the United States from acting effectively, and forced it to wait passively on events. As the threat to American security became more real and focused, the country began to come together, and by the time Japan attacked Pearl Harbor, the four schools united to successfully prosecute the resulting war. The United States was ineffective and divided in the absence of danger, united and potent in the face of it.

These are, to some degree, consoling reflections, but even so, it seems clear that Americans would have been better off if their foreign policy process had prevented the Second World War, rather than helping them win it and then pick up the pieces. Furthermore the world of the twenty-first century is, potentially, much more dangerous than that of fifty years ago. It is unclear that the United States could emerge today as nearly unscathed from a great-power war. It is therefore not a promising sign that after 1989, as in 1919, the American foreign policy debate appears to be subsiding again into a standoff, while policies proliferate in the absence of strategy.

In 1941 and again after World War II, it was an external challenge that inspired Americans to develop a consensus strategy. Throughout the Cold War, the Soviet Union gave American schools a focus. Now comes a moment of truth: Can the United States develop a strategic consensus for a global role in the absence of the kind of challenge once posed by Germany, Japan, and the Soviet Union, or are we like the grandmother in Flannery O'Connor's short story "A Good Man Is Hard to Find," unable to behave well unless faced with a life-and-death threat?

"She would of been a good woman," her killer, The Misfit, remarked in the end, "if [there] had been somebody there to shoot her every minute of her life."[16]

The Challenge

The United States now faces a truly momentous turning point in its history, and we must do something we have never done before: develop a coherent, politically sustainable strategy for American world leadership in peacetime. While the United States has been the world's greatest power for almost a century, from World War I to the present, building a peacetime consensus on what that power is for and how it should be used is something new. From 1919 to 1941 there was no consensus; from 1941 to 1989 there was no peace; after 1989 it has been clear once again that there is no effective consensus in the American political system.

There is, unfortunately, no automatic force that will create a new consensus on demand. As the experience of the twenties and thirties shows, political deadlock over foreign policy can be a very durable arrangement. One could well envision the United States moving through a decade or more without a coherent consensus—longer, if no external events forced the country to respond. This is not ideal, even though in some ways it meets the basic test of democratic politics: All the interest groups get a substantial share of what they value most.

Until the day when American bumbling and lack of focus permits a real threat to arise, or until misguided policy once again lands the United States in a Vietnam-style quagmire, many groups in the United States would be largely satisfied by foreign policy gridlock. Ethnic lobbies would reign happily over the matters that mean most to each of them. Economic lobbies would also prosper. Defense companies would help shape arms export policies, with ample credits available for key clients. Military bases with powerful congressional patrons would continue to flourish regardless of military need; the Pentagon would continue to be forced by powerful political constituencies to procure weapons even if these purchases crowded out some necessary and useful new systems. Farmers, financiers, pharmaceutical companies, and filmmakers would continue to receive strong government backing in international trade negotiations. Sugar producers would have the satisfaction of forcing American consumers to pay two, three, and four times the world price for sugar even as the development prospects of neighboring countries were stunted by lack of access to U.S. markets.

Foreign policy would probably be partitioned among the schools. Hamiltonians would gravitate to Treasury, the Fed, and the Office of the United States Trade Representative. Wilsonians in such sanctuaries as the State Department would get to promote civil society; provide technical assistance to aspiring democracies; condemn some, though not all, foreign evildoers; and engineer the occasional humanitarian interventions and wars. Jeffersonians would declassify Civil War documents; harass the military establishment; and slow, if not halt, such developments as the continued expansion of NATO. Jacksonians would build a defensive missile system whether it made sense or not, block the ratification of goody-two-shoes treaties brought in by Wilsonian secretaries of state, and yank the purse strings when Hamiltonians showed signs of excessive generosity to international financial institutions or when Wilsonians pressed too hard for intervention in some godforsaken hellhole far from the beaten track of obvious American security interests.

The system would more or less work; unhappiness would be more or less evenly distributed across the political spectrum, and most of the people would be at least somewhat satisfied most of the time with most of the policy outcomes on most of the issues they cared most about. The car would coast along slowly as far as it could.

To some degree this will happen whether or not the United States develops an effective foreign policy consensus for the future. A consensus strategy is never monolithic; there were bitter disputes over American foreign policy during both the Cold War and World War II. Democratic political systems adjudicate issues on the basis of compromise and accommodation, lubricating any unpleasant friction with generous applications of pork; that tendency won't and shouldn't disappear. But neither will it, by itself, be enough for effective foreign policy. The United States will be expected to provide vigorous, farsighted leadership; our continued power and security will depend in very large measure on the wisdom, courage, and resolution that the country shows in both choosing and pursuing its goals. As in the 1920s and 1930s the world needs more effective, thoughtful, and committed American leadership than it seems likely to get; as in those years the problem is less that Americans are isolated from the rest of the world than that our engagement is incoherent, contradictory, and ultimately less effective than it needs to be.

The Gyroscope of World Order

In order to rebuild an effective strategic consensus among the four schools, we must take the step that the original Cold Warriors decided to skip. We must take on the old myth of virtuous isolation buried beneath the old myth of the Cold War, and replace both myths with a new picture of the United States as a nation uniquely concerned from its earliest days with the growth and development of world order—with the moral, social, economic, and political as well as the security dimensions of that order.

I do not expect that we will, or even that we should, arrive at some kind of uniform consensus about what kind of order (if any) we should be trying to build, or about what policies are most likely to bring us success. Continuing debate over those issues is an inevitable consequence of the different interests and values found in our complex society; the four major schools and many other voices can, should, and will have their say in broad discussion over the proper aims, methods, and limits of American foreign policy.

Nevertheless we can and should be able to reach a national consensus about the need for the United States to play the role of, in Colonel House's phrase, "the gyroscope of world order." As the dominant global power for most of the twentieth century, the United States entered the twenty-first as a global hegemonic power on a novel scale. The British world hegemony of the nineteenth century was neither as intensive or as extensive as the American system became at the end of the Cold War. The Spanish hegemony of the sixteenth and early seventeenth centuries scarcely touched China, India, and Japan, while the Ottoman sultans met Holy Roman Emperor Charles V and King Philip II of Spain on at least equal terms. Before that, no empire stretched across the Atlantic or simultaneously incorporated the heartlands of Europe and Asia.

The American hegemony today is militarily supreme, culturally pervasive, technologically dominant, and economically dynamic. Its allies and enemies alike fear being swallowed up in it; it is the basic fact of international life.

Surprisingly, however, there is little discussion and less consensus in the United States about what some might call our hegemony but others—perhaps skeptical Jeffersonians—might call our empire. Is it good for the American people? What is its structure? Where are its vulnerabilities and strong points? Should American foreign policy consciously seek to strengthen the system's hold on the world, be indifferent to the system, or actively seek to reduce the nation's world role? How, if at all, should the system be changed or reformed? How valuable is it to the American people? What price is worth paying to defend it? Assuming that global hegemony is desirable from the standpoint of the American people, how can it be defended? Should that hegemony be deepened and widened?

The British hegemony was brilliant but short-lived. What are the prospects for ours? Will the twenty-first century also be an American century, and should we care?

What kind of hegemony do we want, and why? What policies on our part will best conserve what is good in it, and minimize the risks and costs associated with the maintenance of a worldwide dominion? What is the point of our "empire"—to make us rich, or to make us safe, or to build a better world?

Any effort to develop a serious national foreign policy consensus must take up these issues and more. Without a clearer public understanding of the American hegemony as a system and as a power phenomenon, it is difficult to have meaningful public discussion about security policy, much less develop a serious and deep public consensus about military strategies and deployments. Questions about the relative merits of multilateral and unilateral approaches can also be effectively discussed only in the light of an understanding of the dynamics and requirements of hegemony. Fundamentally, Jacksonian hesitations and misgivings about globally oriented economic and political initiatives can be addressed only when the American people have reflected on, and absorbed the realities of, the hegemony and come to a considered public judgment about its value to the country.

The near-total absence of this absolutely central question from American public discussion may be the greatest price we pay today for our historical amnesia. The question of world order and of the U.S. relation to it was, as we saw, the central problem of American foreign policy from 1776 to the present day. With the collapse of the British Empire and the American move to pick up the fallen pieces of the British world order, the care and maintenance of world order became our major national task. Virtually everything that happens in American foreign policy is in some way related to this overarching—and sometimes overwhelming—national responsibility, but candid discussion of this reality is largely absent from our national political discourse.

In the late 1940s the United States began running a global system, but we told ourselves that we were only fighting the Cold War. Substantial sections of American public opinion accepted the idea that a definite threat from the Soviet Union required a defensive, worldwide response from the United States. While it was widely acknowledged that both the threat and the defensive response had economic and social dimensions, the chief focus of the contest was widely seen as military security.

When the Cold War ended, we were still running a world system, but substantial elements of American public opinion didn't know that, and didn't understand to what degree much of our Cold War policy had actually been shaped by the necessities of the world system rather than simply by the conflict with the Soviet Union.

The reality today is that our national security and prosperity depend on the health of the world system—and the health of that system depends on the wisdom, strength, and foresight of American foreign policy— and on the willingness of the American people to back up their government's policies. To avoid another era of potentially very dangerous strategic gridlock, we will need a debate over the American hegemony and its meaning for the national interest.

This debate is all the more important because of changes that have taken place in the world since early in the twentieth century. The United States enjoyed a luxury in the 1920s and 1930s that it doesn't have today: the opportunity to respond late to ominous international developments. Weapons fired from Europe and Asia were incapable of reaching the North American mainland; moreover, Britain and France, once great and powerful states, still stood like scarecrows in world politics—they could not move, but the crows didn't know that, and such restless powers as the Soviet Union, Germany, Italy, and Japan proceeded more cautiously than they might have. Now the United States is alone in the field; no one doubts that we must be on the front lines in any response to world problems, whether military, political, social, or economic in origin.

Static

In launching this debate, the American elite faces a somewhat skeptical public, especially among Jacksonians. To a much greater extent than it likes to acknowledge, the American elite has a long way to go to regain the confidence of the American people. Hamiltonian trade policy looks to many Americans like a scheme to drive Americans' wages down for the sake of corporate profits. Wilsonian support for humanitarian interventions looks like the road to a never-ending series of expensive, morally ambiguous, and potentially bloody engagements. As always, the young women and men on the front lines in these interventions will not be drawn primarily from the homes of the elite, and Jacksonians are smart enough to know that the children of Wilsonian war hawks will generally stay far, far away from the slaughterhouses of our future wars. Jeffersonian squeamishness about American power and the use of force strikes Jacksonian sensibilities as weak and muddleheaded, while the Jeffersonian critiques of the motives and morals of American foreign policy seem almost anti-American.

Unfortunately the lawyers, academics, policy makers, and business leaders who make up so much of the American foreign policy leadership are poorly prepared to overcome these handicaps. While there has been much talk lately about the decline of the foreign policy elite and the spread of foreign policy interest to new, nontraditional groups, the reality is a little different. It is true that the old, focused foreign policy elite—located in a handful of northeastern blue-chip banks, white-shoe law firms, and the very highest reaches of what was once a small cadre of professional military men—has lost influence. But its place has not been taken by the masses. Rather, a diversified neoelite of educated upper-middle-class professionals and academics has taken its place. Drawn largely from perhaps 10 or even 15 percent of the country's population rather than the 1 or 2 percent traditionally involved in directing foreign policy, the new elite is both ethnically and geographically diverse by comparison with the old. Jews and Catholics compete in the neo-elite on equal terms with white Protestants; California, Texas, Florida, and Georgia are heard from as much as New York, Massachusetts, and Connecticut. Women are far better represented than ever before. Furthermore the neo-elite is far more permeable than the old elite ever was—African Americans, Hispanics, and Asian Americans are scaling its heights with great and welcome speed.

The neo-elite is not, however, socially diverse: That is, it still occupies a lofty and narrow slice of the American social pyramid. To some degree this is both inevitable and unexceptionable. The problem is that the neo-elite has not yet acquired all the characteristics of a viable leadership class—in particular the capacity to represent and lead the rest of society.

Precisely because the neo-elite is much larger than traditional elites, its members increasingly grow up having little direct contact with or knowledge of their non-elite fellow citizens. Economic segregation in the American system of suburbs means that most upper-middle-class people usually end up living and attending school with other members of their class.

Members of the neo-elite increasingly owe their positions in life to long years passed in academia—the closest thing in American life to a sanctuary from the non-elite. Today's National Security Council, Treasury Department, or State Department staffer is less likely than his or her predecessor of fifty years ago to have served in the armed forces; to have passed a significant part of life outside the cloistered walls of the academy; or to have much contact with the 250 million Americans who fall below the economic and social standards of the upper middle class.

This growing social gap in American life is partly a result of broad social changes such as the rise of two-income households, and partly a result of the changes in the national economy. Since people of the same educational level tend to marry one another, and since income inequality is highly correlated with differences in educational levels, the rise of a large class of professional women has tended to widen the economic and social differences between professional and nonprofessional families. Combined with a marked increase in income inequality generally, the United States now has a large group of people—I have called it the "super middle class"—with household incomes in excess of $100,000. Many have incomes three, four, and five times the 1998 median household income of $38,885.[17]

Paradoxically, the old elite in some ways had more contact with ordinary Americans than many members of the neo-elite can claim. Because the old elite was such a small group of people, its members—and especially the boys, from whose ranks the foreign policy leadership would emerge—could not as a practical matter grow up isolated from the rest of society. In addition, leading members of the elite placed an enormous value on ensuring that their sons and pupils had a taste of "real life" with "real people." Teddy Roosevelt, an early apostle of the strenuous life, lived and worked with cowboys in Montana. Endicott Peabody, who, as the headmaster of Groton, prepared Franklin Roosevelt, Dean Acheson, Joseph Alsop, and McGeorge Bundy for national leadership, prepared for his school responsibilities by serving as a mission priest in Tombstone, Arizona, during its frontier days. Books like Kipling's *Captains Courageous* instructed generations of privileged young men that they would not mature until they left the cocoon of upper-class privilege.

The story is told that one summer Calvin Coolidge ordered his son Calvin junior to work in the tobacco fields of the Connecticut Valley. "If my father was President," said the astonished farm worker next to him when he discovered the young man's identity, "I wouldn't be working in a tobacco field."

"You would if your father were my father,"[18] said the presidential scion. Few of today's pampered offspring of the neo-elite could make a similar claim.

Today the sons and the daughters of influential Americans are more likely to spend their summers working as interns at prestigious media companies than doing physical labor, or even working as waiters or check-out clerks.

There is no need to romanticize the bygone era of privilege and *noblesse oblige.* (Acheson, for example, was not noted for his common touch.) Still, the old tradition of doing manual labor among the working classes, plus the experience of two world wars and conscription from 1940 through 1973 (with a gap of a few months in 1947–48),[19] gave previous generations of the foreign policy elite a more intuitive understanding of their fellow Americans than that possessed by many of their neo-elite successors. This problem is getting worse as time goes by; each new generation of the neo-elite is farther from its roots among the American people. Not only did the older generation share the experiences of conscription and war, but vast social mobility in the post-1945 United States brought millions of formerly blue-collar families into the middle class. Where today's professors and professionals are often second-generation middle and upper middle class, the postwar generation of intellectuals often had strong blue-collar roots.

Perhaps the rarest thing in the United States today is to find a well-educated young American who sees earning the respect of ordinary Americans on an ordinary job as the necessary foundation to a strong personal character and valuable career. Plenty of young Americans study abroad, precisely to acquire a sympathetic understanding of people different from themselves, but few venture from the citadels of privilege to learn about their fellow citizens at home: Tibet, yes; Peoria, no.

We still see some slumming—volunteer work among economically disadvantaged subcultures considered picturesque or fashionable in some way—but there is almost no sense in our educational system or among the parents of the neo-elite that living and working on equal terms among ordinary middle- and lower-middle-class Americans is an important and necessary part of a first-class education. It is therefore not surprising that when the neo-elite comes to think about the national interest, it has problems understanding the views, values, and priorities of non-elite Americans, and even greater difficulty in communicating its own views to general audiences.

Compounding this problem is a serious deficiency in the American academy: an almost complete neglect of the arts of rational persuasion. Bright young Americans simply don't get much training in learning to speak and, above all, to write in ways that their average, less-privileged fellow citizens find convincing. Indeed, it is generally true in the United States today that the "better" the schools one attends, and the longer one stays in them, the less ability or desire one has to speak or write in ways that will be persuasive to the great majority of one's fellow citizens.

This is an odd model of education for a democratic society, and one result is that the neo-elite, whether Jeffersonian, Wilsonian, or Hamiltonian by inclination and instinct, almost universally produces foreign policy concepts that do not immediately speak to the basic interests and needs of ordinary citizens. To make matters worse, its far-from-silvertongued representatives are then extremely poor at presenting and defending these awkward and perhaps ill-conceived ideas.

This is no way to run either the foreign or the domestic policies of a great nation. Sooner or later, unless these problems can be addressed, the United States will come to grief as the governed increasingly—and justifiably—tune out the governors.

Yet the need for genuine leadership in our politics cannot be emphasized enough. The importance of leadership in the formation of foreign policy and in building a popular consensus behind it can perhaps best be illustrated by the career of Andrew Jackson. Jackson was a widely read, thoughtful, and farsighted man; he also passed all the cultural tests of Jacksonian America. As a hero in two wars against Britain, a victor in Indian wars, and someone widely admired for his no-nonsense approach to Spanish weakness and misrule in Florida, Jackson enjoyed an enormous degree of trust among ordinary American citizens. He possessed virtues that they understood; without ever descending to the degrading status of a career politician, he had demonstrated his commitment to the nation and the common good through a long and visible life of public service.

Yet Jackson was in no way limited by the views of the popular culture out of which he emerged and on which his political strength chiefly depended. College-educated at a time when university education was rare, he became a rich and successful planter. He was enormously well read, and such hostile observers as Mrs. Daniel Webster were agreeably surprised by his polished manners and cultivated small talk.

In office, his foreign policy was nicely judged. He was sometimes flexible and sometimes firm. In a controversy with France over reparations due American citizens as a result of illegal French actions during the Napoleonic Wars, he sometimes hinted at force but ultimately accepted a sound compromise settlement. Because the country backed him, his threats were credible and alarming; because the country trusted him, he could afford to compromise. In disputes with Great Britain, he had an assurance that weaker figures could not match; having been wounded by a British saber as a young prisoner in the Revolution, and then having defeated the British at New Orleans, he could not credibly be called soft on England. He was therefore free, to an unusual degree among American presidents, to make foreign policy on the merits, and to let the chips fall where they may.

The freedom that comes from winning the trust of Jacksonian America was an important asset for a number of other American presidents. Had Lincoln lived, his personal prestige would probably have carried Reconstruction through with less suffering, and perhaps even with a better final result for the freedmen. The two Roosevelts and Eisenhower were three presidents who were able to harness public trust to the task of carrying out an effective foreign policy. It was Nixon's anticommunist credentials with Jacksonian America that made his opening to China possible; Reagan's Jacksonian backing enabled him to make the most sweeping disarmament proposals of any American president during the Cold War.

Presidents who lack such personal respect and dignity have suffered enormously. Their options are often narrow precisely because they do not enjoy public trust. It would have been much easier for Reagan to return the Panama Canal than it was for Jimmy Carter. A President Hubert Humphrey probably could not have negotiated an opening to China. A son or daughter of a Teamsters family would have an easier time selling a trade agreement than the pampered St. Albans–bred son of a senator; someone who can speak directly and convincingly to the American people, regardless of background, can win broad public support for difficult but necessary steps in foreign and domestic policy.

If our leadership class continues to produce politicians who have only weak claims on the respect of Jacksonian America, then the nation's ability to follow an effective foreign policy will be seriously diminished. In the meantime, the task facing serious students of American policy and those who aspire to lead the nation is to find within each of the enduring traditions of American statesmanship ways to speak to the aspirations

and values of the American people in order to win their firm and enduring support—and to create policies that deserve the sacrifices that people
may someday have to make to see that they are carried out.

Envoi

It would take us far beyond the scope of this book to attempt to
describe a national grand strategy for a post–Cold War world. Nevertheless I believe I owe it to readers to declare my preference among the
schools: Which one is best suited to take the lead in defining a new
American foreign policy?

This is harder to do now than it was when I began my research. The
more I have come to understand each of the schools, the more I value
their contributions, and the more I believe that the American foreign
policy system works best when all the schools are strongly and wisely
led.

There is no school whose perspectives we can afford to lose, but in
looking at the tasks we now face, it seems to me that the voice of the Jeffersonian school is the one that currently most needs to be heard.

Jeffersonians believe that the greatest danger facing the United States
is the consequences of international overreaching. We can press our hegemony too far; we can insist too hard that our principles, whether Wilsonian ideals or Hamiltonian commercial values, be universalized into the
practice of other countries. Our power can grow so great, and our use of
it seem so unpredictable to others, that in self-defense the rest of the
world can unite to limit our power and perhaps to undermine our security. Jeffersonians would rather that our power remain within limits that
we Americans choose for ourselves than to find it one day confined within
limits that others choose for us.

Potentially, Jeffersonians have the ability to determine the strategic
future of the United States for many years to come. On the other hand,
they may sink into continuing marginalization and irrelevance.

The key question will be whether they can replicate the kind of
strategic thinking exemplified by John Quincy Adams when he proposed
what subsequently became known as the Monroe Doctrine. Adams looked
at the broad range of genuine American interests and found the least
risky, most economical, and most dignified method of securing them
under the conditions of the day. The combination of Jeffersonian reluc-

tance to engage in unnecessary risks and wars, and a clear-sighted vision of key national interests, resulted in the most elegant solution possible—the policy that did the most and cost the least.

To achieve that result the Jeffersonians of the Adams era had to overcome many of their own dearest beliefs. They had to accept that an arrangement with Britain was in the best interests of the United States—a direct reversal of the foreign policy ideas that Jefferson had advocated as far back as the Washington administration. The Monroe Doctrine was part and parcel of a larger Jeffersonian retrenchment; it was the party of Jefferson that chartered the Second Bank of the United States, passed a protective tariff, and developed a program for national infrastructure development that could almost have come from the pen of Hamilton.

In all this the Jeffersonians were not so much disavowing their ideals as adapting them to the real world. The United States could never prosper without manufacturing and trade. It could never be secure without some kind of arrangement with Britain. Given that, the question became: How could the country accommodate necessity with the least possible risk and cost?

This approach to foreign policy will be critical for American success in the future. The United States has global interests and duties; Hamiltonians and Wilsonians are right about this. Yet the policies they propose are sometimes impractical and sometimes unwise. Furthermore Hamiltonian and Wilsonian proposals for international cooperation raise profound and difficult questions. Just how far should the United States go in pooling sovereignty with other countries for the sake of various economic or political objectives? How much of a world criminal court do we need? How much power should the WTO have over acts of Congress and state legislatures?

Often questions like these take the forms of trade-offs. How much authority over NATO decisions must the United States share in order to get more help out of the allies? How much money does the United States need to contribute to the IMF or the World Bank, and how much decision-making power must we share with other countries in these institutions so that they are able to act most effectively to stabilize the international economy and promote rapid economic growth in developing nations?

Americans do not need and probably cannot get a permanent consensus about these and dozens of other, similar questions, but we do need more agreement on the way we evaluate answers to these questions.

What kind of world is the United States trying to create? What is the shape of the ultimate trade-off between a unilateral hegemony in which the United States dominates all other countries to the full extent possible but then finds itself largely alone when threats arise, and a kind of multilateral world system in which the United States gives up some control but gets more help?

The problems and needs of the world are almost infinite. So too are the potential challenges to American interests. Given the need for Wilsonian and Hamiltonian global policies, and given also the real constraints, internal and external, political and economic, on American power, the United States needs "strategic elegance"—a grand national strategy that distinguishes between the vital and the secondary interests of the country, and secures all of the vital interests and as many of the secondary interests as can reasonably be achieved with the fewest risks and costs.

Strategic elegance was the mark of the Monroe Doctrine; it permeates Walter Lippmann's best work and it profoundly informs the concept of containment as proposed by George Kennan. Strategic elegance is the highest quality of the Jeffersonian mind and the supreme gift of the Jeffersonian tradition. It is perhaps the single most-needed quality now in American foreign policy.

It is this approach that can best bring about a basic strategic consensus for the United States. A clear statement of national interests and an elegant grand strategy, plainly expressed and clearly reasoned, will in good time win the support of the American people. Jeffersonian grand strategists can and should harness sometimes inflated Hamiltonian and Wilsonian eagerness for new world orders and grand legal and political structures, while persuading Jacksonians of the real importance of pared-down, simplified, and streamlined forms of American international engagement. That job has to be done in the light of a commonsense approach to American security and sovereignty, and to the very real linkages and dependencies that engage Americans, whether we like it or not, with the destinies of all the other people on the planet.

If Jeffersonian strategists rise to the occasion, they have the opportunity to build the foreign policy of the American future, much as John Quincy Adams set us on a course that lasted well into the twentieth century.

The alternative is less appealing, both to the nation and to Jeffersonian interests. Jeffersonians can do as they did in the 1930s and as some of them continued to do into the 1940s: rest in denial concerning the true extent of the nation's vital interests. More than in the middle of the twentieth century, the United States is now inextricably tied to events that take place elsewhere in the world. The spread of weapons of mass destruction, the environmental dangers and consequences of worldwide industrial development, the potential for pandemic diseases arising in overpopulated and medically underserved portions of the world, and the ever closer bonds linking world finance and trade all make American leadership in world politics a required course, not an elective.

If Jeffersonians blind themselves to this reality, and confine themselves to sniping at the moral inconsistencies, blunders, and costs of American foreign policy, and attempt to revive a contemporary version of the myth of virtuous isolation, they will achieve, perhaps, an illusion of the purity sought by their Pilgrim forebears, but they will betray the values they cherish. That would be a pity, because the Republic needs Jeffersonian caution, Jeffersonian conservation of such precious resources as liberty and lives, and the Jeffersonian passion for limits.

If Jeffersonians retreat into sterile opposition to all military and economic leadership, they will merely deprive the country of the counsel of those whose insight, turned to the purposes of constructive statesmanship, can best protect the country's inner values while shaping its external engagements.

The United States today needs exactly what John Quincy Adams and James Monroe gave it in 1823: a grand strategy that is rooted in the concrete interests of the American people, that respects and serves their moral values, and that at the lowest possible cost in blood, treasure, and political concentration of power secures their lives, their fortunes, and their sacred honor.

Afterword

Since the first edition of this book appeared, the world of American foreign policy has changed. On September 11, 2001, more than 3,000 people perished in hijacked airliners and in terror attacks on New York and the Pentagon. Since then, American forces have overthrown the Taliban regime in Afghanistan as what President George W. Bush called a first step in America's new war—a war on terror. U.S. forces have moved into Georgia, the Philippines, and Yemen, and the Pentagon has begun to plan an attack on Iraq. As of June 2002, it seemed possible, though by no means certain, that the war on terror would become, like the Cold War, the central organizing idea of American foreign policy for a generation or more.

These dramatic changes, however, did not alter the underlying structure of the American foreign policy system. The four schools continued to play a vital role in American foreign policy as the nation struggled to cope with the aftermath of the September attacks.

The strong and immediate Jacksonian response to the attacks made a deep impression on both domestic and foreign observers. Osama bin Laden and his aides appear to have made a common mistake about the United States. They had noted the hesitation in American foreign policy during the 1990s, when presidents were slow to commit U.S. forces overseas and quick to withdraw them in the absence of strong Jacksonian support, and they concluded that when faced by a resolute adversary capable of inflicting casualties, the United States would back down. This is precisely what the Japanese authorities hoped for when they sought to dishearten the United States by knocking out the Pacific Fleet in December 1941.

Neither the Japanese nor Al-Qaeda understood what can be called the "Pearl Harbor effect," the transformation of American opinion which takes place following a peacetime attack on the United States. The Pearl Harbor effect galvanizes Jacksonian opinion throughout the country, creating deep support for the determined prosecution of a war. The British attack on the Lexington militia in 1776, the Confederacy's attack on Fort Sumter in 1861, real or alleged Native American atrocities, and the attack on Pearl Harbor itself united most Americans behind support for major wars. When American forces go abroad in search of monsters to destroy—in Beirut under Ronald Reagan, in Somalia under the first President Bush and Bill Clinton—public opinion can turn violently against policy and force a withdrawal. Fear of such failure imposes caution on presidents dispatching forces on what Jacksonians would regard as optional interventions. But when peaceful Americans minding their own business are attacked at home, this is war. The whole hive swarms out to sting the intruder to death. As an imperial power, even and perhaps especially when engaged in projects of humanitarian intervention, the United States can be irresolute and divided; in self-defense it is focused and ruthless.

From a Jacksonian standpoint, the attacks of September 2001 were if anything more cowardly and less justified than the Japanese attack at Pearl Harbor, and Americans of every political party and in every region of the country united to express their support for the most vigorous possible retaliation. Jacksonians old and new (and the events of September 11 brought many Americans in touch with the Jacksonian element of their own makeup for the first time) wanted the United States to take all possible steps against this monstrous evil, and they were prepared to grant the president unlimited funds and virtually unlimited authority to prosecute the war on terror until total victory was achieved.

In pursuit of this victory, Jacksonians were not troubled by issues of international law. Terrorists who kill thousands of innocent people do not deserve the protection of the Geneva Convention, Jacksonians argued, and they supported the internment of captured Taliban and Al Qaeda fighters on the U.S. naval base in Guantanamo, Cuba. Foreign criminals who stage sneak attacks on American civilians in peacetime do not, Jacksonians believe, have any rights that the United States is bound to observe. Jacksonians were not particularly troubled by reports that U.S. forces were responsible for damage to civilian targets during the bombings in Afghanistan and were prepared to support further action against Saddam Hussein in Iraq.

As always, Jacksonian support is a mixed blessing for a wartime president. On the one hand, a roused Jacksonian public is ready to pay any price and bear any burden to win what it regards as a just and necessary war. On the other hand, Jacksonians want results and they hold presidents accountable. When they lost confidence that Presidents Truman, Johnson, and Nixon had viable strategies to win the Korean and Vietnam wars, Jacksonians withdrew their support from these embattled leaders. As he surveys the complex landscape of the modern Middle East, President George W. Bush knows that the enormous support he received in the first year of the war will remain with him only as long as he can demonstrate concrete progress in the war—or at least formulate and communicate a war strategy that Jacksonian America can understand and accept.

The Jacksonian response may have been the most dramatic, but the other schools were also represented in the debates and policy-making as the new war took shape. Jeffersonians responded to the attack by arguing for a reduced American presence in the Middle East. American alliances with questionable Arab regimes plus one-sided support for Israel had, Jeffersonian critics suggested, inflamed opinion against the United States and made the country a target. Jeffersonian critics were also quick to turn against what they perceived as heavy-handed Justice Department tactics in the war on terror. Was it really necessary, Jeffersonians asked, to abridge the civil liberties of resident aliens? When the U.S. government rounded up an undisclosed number of aliens and held them for months without disclosing their names, Jeffersonians saw violations of precisely the values that made the United States worth fighting for. As the Bush administration prepared to use the September attacks as a justification for rolling back a host of Vietnam-era restrictions on the activities of the CIA and other U.S. agencies, Jeffersonians warned that these rash steps would lead to new excesses in the future.

Wilsonians were generally ready to support a vigorous prosecution of the war on terror, but they urged the administration to do so as far as possible through international institutions and with due respect for international law. They argued that since capturing and controlling terrorists would require close intelligence cooperation and the exchange of financial information with many countries, the nature of the new security threat made wholehearted support from allies more necessary than ever. This, Wilsonians said, should force the Bush administration to see the importance of cooperation with the international community. The goodwill of allies cannot be taken for granted; the United States can only retain the support of its allies by observing international law and helping to build international institutions.

From a Hamiltonian perspective, the war was a dangerous challenge to the basic elements of American power. The attacks on the World Trade Center were more than an attack on a New York City landmark; they were an attack on the citadel of international business. The attacks and their aftershocks had a measurable effect on the U.S. economy, but they also called into question the security of the entire international economic system that the U.S. had built. Would the need to improve security slow the passage of vital goods across national frontiers? Would important industries like civil aviation and tourism recover? Would U.S. companies and travelers around the world become the targets of terrorist action? Would the oil monarchies of the Middle East collapse as the war progressed, and would the vital oil trade be disrupted?

From a Hamiltonian point of view, the new war needs to be waged with great vigor, but also great strategy. There are many fronts in the war. The point is not simply to hunt down and punish the mass murderers who planned the attack; it is to ensure that the international American system emerges from the war stronger and richer than ever. Hamiltonians looked for ways to prosecute the war that would strengthen U.S. ties with key allies in Europe and Asia.

News, for example, that no links between Saddam Hussein, Iraq, and the terrorists of September 11 could be established did not diminish the Hamiltonian case for overthrowing the Iraqi dictator. Whether or not he was involved in the attacks on the United States, Saddam Hussein's support for terrorism and his evident determination to build weapons of mass destruction posed serious threats to what Hamiltonians see as vital national interests.

In summary, although the attacks of September 11 represented a new kind of warfare and a new threat to American security, the subsequent debates over American foreign policy fell into patterns as old as the republic itself. As ever, no single school was fully satisfied by American foreign policy, and a chorus of criticism attended each step the Bush administration took. Jacksonians wanted faster progress toward an invasion of Iraq, protested what they saw as "moral ambiguity" in the Bush administration's efforts to restrain Israeli reactions to Palestinian suicide bombers, and resented the limits and delays placed on American action by the need to sustain key U.S. alliances in the war. Jeffersonians felt that the administration response was too fast, too far reaching, and too indiscriminate. Wilsonians were concerned that the administration was avoiding vital, necessary tasks like nation-building in Afghanistan. Hamiltonians fretted that rash Jacksonian action would alienate allies and complicate the always difficult task of preserving the U.S. position in the Middle East. Yet despite or perhaps in part because of this creative tension and perpetual quarrel, in the opening months of the war the Bush administration astonished the skeptics as it overthrew the Taliban government in Afghanistan, dealt Al-Qaeda a series of devastating blows, strengthened security cooperation with Russia, ensured China's cooperation in some key fields and, despite rising popular anti-American and anti-Israeli feeling in Europe, held the Western alliance together through the first phase of the new challenge.

This was not yet victory, but it could not be called failure.

World power does not come with a guarantee. Great powers rise and fall. New technologies, new weapons, and new ideologies have repeatedly overturned existing orders, bringing small peoples out of obscurity into empire and sending great empires crashing down into ruins.

The events of September 11, 2001, reminded Americans that the world remains a dangerous and unpredictable place. The special providence that brought the United States through the eighteenth, nineteenth, and twentieth centuries may be needed more than ever in the twenty-first. Fortunately, the combination of patriotic unity and vigorous debate which sprang up as the nation entered this strange new war provides at least some assurance that the United States will face its new challenges with all the strengths that have made it so formidable in the past.

Notes

Chapter One

The American Foreign Policy Tradition

1. James Bryce, *The American Commonwealth* (New York: Macmillan Company, 1927), vol. 2, p. 565.

2. Finley Peter Dunne, "The Philippine Peace," *Observations by Mr. Dooley* (New York: R. H. Russell, 1906), p. 116. Mr. Dooley's language was translated into "standard speech" by Philip Dunne, the columnist's son, and reprinted in Karl Meyer, ed., *Pundits, Poets & Wits: An Omnibus of American Newspaper Columns* (New York: Oxford University Press, 1990), p. 124.

3. Quoted in Samuel Eliot Morison, Henry Steele Commager, and William E. Leuchtenburg, *The Growth of the American Republic* (New York: Oxford University Press, 1980), vol. 2, pp. 241–42.

4. James Morris, *Pax Britannica* (New York: Harcourt Brace & Company, 1968), p. 28.

5. Henry Kissinger, *Diplomacy* (New York: Simon & Schuster, 1994), p. 18.

6. George P. Shultz, *Turmoil and Triumph: My Years as Secretary of State* (New York: Charles Scribner's Sons, 1993).

7. James A. Baker III, *The Politics of Diplomacy: Revolution, War & Peace, 1989–1992* (New York: G.P. Putnam's Sons, 1995).

8. Richard Nixon, *Beyond Peace* (New York: Random House, 1994), p. 30.

9. Cited in Adrienne Koch and William Peden, eds., *The Life and Selected Writings of Thomas Jefferson* (New York: Random House, 1944), "Third Annual Message, October 17, 1803," pp. 334–35; and "To the President of the United States (James Monroe), Monticello, October 24, 1923," pp. 709–10. Robert V. Remini, *The Life of Andrew Jackson* (New York: Penguin Books, 1988), pp. 56–57, 309. For Polk on Oregon see Donald Bruce Johnson, *National Party Platforms, vol. 1: 1840–1956* (Urbana: University of Illinois Press, 1956), "Resolved, that our title to the whole of the Territory of Oregon is clear and unquestionable; that no portion of the same ought to be ceded to England or any other power, and that the re-occupation of Oregon and the re-annexation of Texas at the earliest practicable period are great American measures, which this Convention recommends to the cordial support of the Democracy of the Union," p. 4. See also his inaugural address, March 4, 1845, in J. D. Richardson, *Messages and Papers of the Presidents* (Washington, D.C.: Bureau of National Literature, 1897), vol. 4, p. 381. For the Mexican War, see Polk's address in ibid., vol. 4, p. 442. For Buchanan on Ostend Manifesto,

see *House Ex. Docs.*, 33d Cong., 2d sess., no. 93, pp. 129–31, quoted in Thomas A. Bailey, *A Diplomatic History of the American People* (New York: Meredith Publishing, 1964), p. 295. For Grant's obsession with Santo Domingo, see C. C. Tansill, *The United States and Santo Domingo, 1798–1873: A Chapter in Caribbean Diplomacy* (Baltimore, Md.: Johns Hopkins University Press, 1938). Also see William Javier Nelson, *Almost a Territory: America's Attempt to Annex the Dominican Republic* (Newark: University of Delaware Press, 1990). For the Isthmian canal see David McCullough, *The Path Between the Seas: The Creation of the Panama Canal, 1870–1914* (New York: Simon & Schuster, 1977), pp. 26–27. (Orig. cit. for Grant quotation, *North American Review*, Feb. 1881.) There were seven Grant expeditions to Central America between 1870 and 1875. In addition to Andrew Johnson, Ulysses S. Grant, and numerous other functionaries and politicians, Theodore Roosevelt was also a vocal advocate of annexing Canada. In 1887 he wrote:

> It would have been well for all America if we had insisted even more than we did upon the extension northward of our boundaries. Not only the Columbia but also the Red River of the North—and the Saskatchewan and Frazer as well—should lie wholly within our limits, less for our own sake than for the sake of the men who dwell along their banks. Columbia, Saskatchewan and Manitoba would, as States of the American Union, hold positions incomparably more important, grander, and more dignified than they can ever hope to reach either as independent communities or as provincial dependencies of a foreign power that regards them with a kindly tolerance somewhat akin to contemptuous indifference. Of course no one would wish to see these, or any other settled communities, now added to our domain by force; we want no unwilling citizens to enter our Union; the time to have taken the lands was before the settlers came into them.

(Theodore Roosevelt, *Thomas Hart Benton*, nat. ed. [New York: Charles Scribner's Sons, 1926], pp. 170–71.) On June 24, 1864, a *New York Herald* editorial declared that "four hundred thousand thoroughly disciplined troops will ask no better occupation than to destroy the last vestiges of British rule on the American continent and annex Canada to the United States."

10. Warren Christopher, *In the Stream of History: Shaping Foreign Policy for a New Era* (Stanford, Calif.: Stanford University Press, 1998), pp. 54, 61.

11. *Conference on the Limitation of Armament Report* (Washington, D.C.: U.S. Government Printing Office, 1922), "Appendix–Treaty 1, a treaty between the United States of America, the British Empire, France, Italy, and Japan, limiting naval armament," chap. 1, articles 1–4, pp. 872–73.

12. All can be found in *Merriam-Webster's Biographical Dictionary* (Springfield, Mass.: Merriam-Webster, 1995). Washington Irving (1783–1859) was on the staff of the U.S. Embassy, Madrid (1826–29), secretary of the U.S. legation in London (1829–32), and U.S. minister to Spain (1842–46); Edward Everett (1794–1865) was U.S. minister to Great Britain (1841–45); George Bancroft (1800–91) served as U.S. minister to Great Britain (1846–49) and U.S. minister to Germany (1867–74); Nathaniel Hawthorne (1804–64) was U.S. consul in Liverpool, England (1853–58); John Lothrop Motley (1814–77), author of *The Rise of the Dutch Republic* (1856), *History of the United Netherlands* (1860–67), *The Causes of the American Civil War* (1861), and other works, served as secretary of the U.S. legation at St. Petersburg (1841) and as U.S. minister to Austria (1861–67) and to Great Britain (1869–70); George Washington Williams (1849–91)

was the author of *History of the Negro Race in America* (1883) and *History of the Negro Troops in the War of the Rebellion* (1888) and served as U.S. minister to Haiti (1885–96).

13. Sidney Ratner, James H. Soltow, and Richard Sylla, *The Evolution of the American Economy: Growth, Welfare and Decision Making* (New York: Basic Books, 1979), pp. 211–12; *Statistical Abstract of the United States 1998* (Washington, D.C.: U.S. Bureau of the Census, 1998), p. 786; B. R. Mitchell, *International Historical Statistics: The Americas, 1750–1993*, 4th ed. (London: Macmillan Reference Ltd., 1998), pp. 761–74.

14. U.S. Department of Commerce, Bureau of the Census, *Historical Statistics of the United States: Colonial Times to 1957* (Washington, D.C.: U.S. Government Printing Office, 1957), p. 542.

15. Paul W. Gates, *The Economic History of the United States,* vol. 3, *The Farmer's Age: Agriculture 1815–1860* (New York: Holt, Rinehart, and Winston, 1960), p. 152.

16. U.S. Department of Commerce, Bureau of the Census, *Historical Statistics of the United States, Colonial Times to 1970* (Washington, D.C.: U.S. Government Printing Office, 1975), part 2, series U 274–294, pp. 898–99.

17. Robert E. Lipsey, *Price and Quality Trends in the Foreign Trade of the United States* (Princeton, N.J.: Princeton University Press, 1963), pp. 45–52.

18. U.S. Department of Commerce, Bureau of the Census, *Historical Statistics of the United States, Colonial Times to 1970,* part 1, series K-18, p. 457.

19. Morton Rothstein, "The American West and Foreign Markets, 1850–1900," in David M. Ellis, ed., *The Frontier in American Development: Essays in Honor of Paul Wallace Gates* (Ithaca, N.Y.: Cornell University Press, 1969), p. 386.

20. Ron Chernow, *The House of Morgan: An American Banking Dynasty and the Rise of Modern Finance* (New York: Atlantic Monthly Press, 1990), p. 5. (Originally cited in Robert Sobel, *Panic on Wall Street: A Classic History of America's Financial Disasters with a New Exploration of the Crash of 1987* [London: Macmillan, 1968], p. 42.)

21. Bray Hammond, *Banks and Politics in America: From the Revolution to the Civil War* (Princeton, N.J.: Princeton University Press, 1957), pp. 457–59.

22. Kenneth M. Stampp, *America in 1857: A Nation on the Brink* (New York: Oxford University Press, 1990), p. 221.

23. Mira Wilkins, *The History of Foreign Investment in the United States to 1914* (Cambridge, Mass.: Harvard University Press, 1989), p. 194.

24. M. St. Clair Clarke and D. A. Hall, *Legislative and Documentary History of the Bank of the United States: Including the Original Bank of North America* (Washington, D.C.: Gales and Seaton, 1832), p. 417

25. Douglass C. North, *The Economic Growth of the United States, 1790–1860* (Englewood Cliffs, N.J.: Prentice-Hall, Inc., 1961), p. 143 (on canals and railroads). See also Harry H. Pierce, "Foreign Investment in American Enterprise," in *Economic Change in the Civil War Era*, David T. Gilchrist and W. David Lewis, eds. (Greenville, Del.: Eleutherian Mills–Hagley Foundation, 1965), pp. 41–42 (railroads specifically), pp. 41–53 (on foreign investment more generally).

26. Pierce, "Foreign Investment in American Enterprise," pp. 48–49.

27. Ibid.

28. Alan Bell, *Sydney Smith* (Oxford, England: Clarendon Press, 1980), p. 211.

29. Cited in Richard Hofstadter, ed., *Great Issues in American History,* vol. 1, *From the Revolution to the Civil War, 1765–1865* (New York: Random House, 1958), "Andrew Jackson, Bank Veto Message," pp. 291–92.

30. Cited in ibid., vol. 2, *From Reconstruction to the Present Day, 1864–1981* (New York: Random House, 1982), "Populist Party Platform," pp. 143–44.

31. Wilkins, *The History of Foreign Investment,* p. 579.

32. Ibid., p. 566.

33. Ibid., p. 567.

34. Ibid., p. 569

35. Chernow, *The House of Morgan,* p. 76.

36. *Financing Anglo-American Trade,* p. 146.

37. Chernow, *The House of Morgan,* p. 6.

38. See L. M. Sears, *Jefferson and the Embargo* (Durham, N.C.: 1927); see also Bailey, *Diplomatic History,* pp. 125–29.

39. For a great many citations of public opinion on war scares and various territorial conflicts with Great Britain, see index entry in Bailey, *Diplomatic History,* under "Public Opinion." He cites newspaper editorials on almost every major issue.

40. Cited in Robert S. Browning III, *Two If By Sea: The Development of American Coastal Defense Policy* (Westpoint, Conn.: Greenwood Press, 1983), p. 148.

41. Ulysses S. Grant, *Personal Memoirs of U. S. Grant* (New York: Library of America, 1990), p. 776.

42. Browning, *Two If By Sea,* p. 168.

43. See Bailey, *Diplomatic History,* pp. 242–43.

44. Ibid., p. 385; see also pp. 327–30 (On the *Trent* Affair), pp. 342–45 (on Confederate raiders and warships); and pp. 376–78.

45. Grant, *Personal Memoirs,* p. 774.

46. House Committee on International Relations [now Foreign Affairs], Subcommittee on International Security and Scientific Affairs, *Background Information on the Use of U.S. Armed Forces in Foreign Countries, 1975 Revision.* Committee Print, 94th Congress, Ist session, 1995, prepared by the Foreign Affairs Division, Congressional Research Service, Library of Congress, p. 84.

47. Capt. Harry Allanson Ellsworth, USMC, *One Hundred Eighty Landings of United States Marines, 1800–1934* (Washington, D.C.: History and Museums Division Headquarters, U.S. Marine Corps, 1974).

48. Grant, *Personal Memoirs,* pp. 773–80.

49. For first U.S. relations with China (1844) and Japan (1854), see Arthur Power Dudden, *The American Pacific: From the Old China Trade to the Present* (New York: Oxford University Press, 1992), pp. 7, 19.

50. For all these incidents see Ellen C. Collier, "Instances of Use of United States Forces Abroad, 1798–1993" (Washington, D.C.: Congressional Research Service, Library of Congress, 1993), and Ellsworth, *One Hundred Eighty Landings.*

51. Bailey, *Diplomatic History,* pp. 422–28.

52. From a letter to John Blair written in Paris on August 13, 1787, in Julian P. Boyd, ed., *The Papers of Thomas Jefferson,* vol. 12 (Princeton, N.J.: Princeton University Press, 1955), p. 28.

53. Don E. Fehrenbacher, ed., *Abraham Lincoln: Speeches and Writings 1859–1865* (New York: Library of America, 1989), "Reply to Chicago Emancipation Memorial, Washington, D.C., September 13, 1862," p. 364.

54. Richard Hofstadter and Beatrice K. Hofstadter, eds., *Great Issues in American History,* 2nd ed., vol. 3, *From Reconstruction to the Present Day, 1864–1981* (New York: Vintage Books, 1982), p. 165.

Chapter Two

The Kaleidoscope of American Foreign Policy

1. Walter Lippmann, *The Public Philosophy* (Boston: Little, Brown, 1955), p. 20.

2. Governor Ronald Reagan gave the Panama Canal issue special prominence during the 1976 presidential primaries. He accused the Ford Administration of maintaining a "mouselike silence" in the face of "blackmail" from Panama's "dictator." He repeatedly used a line guaranteed to get applause: "When it comes to the Canal, we built it, we paid for it, it's ours, and we should tell Torrijos and Company that we are going to keep it!" Reagan's position appealed to many Americans, because he presented the issue, simplistically, as a test of our nation's power and greatness. Ford later believed he lost several primaries to Reagan over Panama. (Jimmy Carter, *Keeping Faith: Memoirs of a President* [New York: Bantam Books, 1982], p. 154.)

3. Anthony Lewis, "Abroad at Home; We Did It Right," *New York Times*, September 30, 1994, sec. A, p. 31.

4. Instead of Nicaragua: *Strategic Trends Towards the 21st Century: Economic and Political Challenges* (Kuala Lumpur: Malaysian Strategic Research Centre, 1995), p. 13.

5. Ibid., p. 9

6. Ibid., p. 6

7. Eric Alterman, *Who Speaks for America?: Why Democracy Matters in Foreign Policy* (Ithaca, N.Y.: Cornell University Press, 1998).

8. Pat Robertson, *The New World Order* (Dallas, Texas: Word Publishing, 1991), p. 6.

9. Noam Chomsky, *"Human Rights" and American Foreign Policy* (Nottingham, England: Spokesman Books, 1978), p. 10.

10. Ibid., p. 78.

11. Remarks by John J. Sweeney, January 22, 1998, delivered at the National University of Mexico, Ciudad Universitaria, Mexico.

12. Stephen E. Ambrose, ed., *Nixon: The Triumph of a Politician 1962–1972* (New York: Simon & Schuster, 1989), p. 259.

13. Irving Kristol, *Reflections of a NeoConservative: Looking Back, Looking Ahead* (New York: Basic Books, 1983), p. 227.

14. Muhammad Mahathir and Shintaro Ishihara, *"No" to ieru Ajia (The Asia that can say "no")* (Tokyo: Koubunsha, 1994).

15. Jean-Jacques Servan-Schreiber, *The American Challenge (Le Défi américain)* (New York: Atheneum, 1968).

16. Conrad Black, "Britain's Atlantic Option—and America's Stake," *National Interest* 55 (Spring 1999), pp. 21–22.

17. Cited in at least three places: Derek H. Davis, *Dallas Morning News*, November 11, 1995, p. 4G; James Warren, *Chicago Tribune*, September 16, 1993, p. 2.; essay by Robert Stone, "Uncle Sam Doesn't Want You!" *New York Review of Books*, September 23, 1999, p. 22.

18. Richard M. Nixon to H. R. Haldeman (audiotape, June 23, 1972). Also cited in *1,911 Best Things Anybody Ever Said*, Robert Byrne, ed. (New York, N.Y.: Fawcett-Columbine, 1988).

19. According to the Boston Historical Society and Museum, the tea was a blend of Darjeeling and Ceylon black teas from Sri Lanka.

20. Ralph Waldo Emerson, "Essay VII: Politics" in *Essays* (New York: Thomas Y. Crowell Company, 1926), p. 412.

21. As the Austrian minister of foreign affairs, of course.

22. See, for example, Gore Vidal, *The American Presidency* (Chicago, IL: Odonian Press, Common Courage Press/LPC Group, 1996), pp. 53–54.

23. *Appendix to the Congressional Globe of the 24th Congress,* 1st Session, vol. 2. (Washington, D.C.: Blair and Rives, eds., 1836), p. 434.

24. The exact citations are:

> When a state increases in wealth and luxury, men indulge in ambitious projects and are eager for high dignities. Each feels ashamed that any of his fellow men should surpass him. The common people feel themselves oppressed by the grasping of some, and their vanity is flattered by others. Fired by evil passions, they are no longer willing to submit to control, but demand that everything be subject to their authority. The invariable result is that the government assumes the noble names of free and popular, but becomes in fact that most inexecrable thing, mob rule.
> (Polybius [*Histories 6, c.* 125 B.C.])

> "Democracy is more cruel than wars or tyrants." (Seneca [*Epistulæ morales ad Lucilium, 104, c.* A.D. 63]).

25. Alexis de Tocqueville, *Democracy in America,* vol. 1 (New York: Vintage Books, 1990), p. 234.

26. Benjamin Disraeli, *Wit and Wisdom of Benjamin Disraeli, Earl of Beaconsfield* (New York: Appleton, 1881), p. 95.

27. The Oregon boundary question agitated public opinion in the 1840s, with American opinion rallying behind the cry "Fifty-four Forty or Fight!" This would have given the United States most of what is now British Columbia. The *Trent* affair came in 1861. A U.S. ship stopped a British vessel in international waters, searched it, and removed two Confederate commissioners who were traveling to Britain to represent the interests of the South in the Civil War. Britain demanded their return; war was narrowly averted when Lincoln accepted the British position. Paradoxically, the American act was legal under British law, while the British protest reflected the longtime American position.

28. According to the National Commission on Excellence in Education, in 1983 only 16 percent of high school graduates completed a geography course. (National Commission on Excellence in Education, *A Nation at Risk: The Imperative for Educational Reform* [Washington, D.C.: National Commission on Excellence in Education, 1983], pp. 18–19.

29. Charles Francis Adams, ed., *The Works of John Adams,* vol. 9 (Boston: Little, Brown, 1854), p. 277.

30. George Washington, "The Farewell Address." In Saul K. Padover, ed., *The Washington Papers* (New York: Harper & Brothers, 1955), p. 321.

ChapterThree

Changing the Paradigms

1. Will L. Clayton, "Memorandum for the Under Secretary for Economic Affairs," May 27, 1947, reprinted in Meredith Hindley, "How the Marshall Plan Came About," *Humanities* (November/December 1998).

2. James Chace, *Acheson: The Secretary of State Who Created the American World* (Cambridge, Mass.: Harvard University Press, 1999).

3. Lippmann discusses the alliance at length in Walter Lippmann, *U.S. Foreign Policy: Shield of the Republic* (Boston: Little, Brown, 1943).

4. Franklin D. Roosevelt, "Fireside Chat on National Security," in *The Public Papers and Addresses of Franklin D. Roosevelt* (New York: Macmillan Company, 1941), p. 635.

5. Henry Kissinger, *Diplomacy* (New York.: Simon & Schuster, 1994), pp. 39–40.

6. 1 Cor. 13 (KJV).

7. Bruce W. Jentleson and Thomas G. Paterson, eds., *Encyclopedia of U.S. Foreign Relations*, vol. 2 (New York: Oxford University Press, 1997), p. 243.

8. From a footnote in Milton Friedman and Anna Jacobson Schwartz, *A Monetary History of the United States 1867–1960* (Princeton, N.J.: Princeton University Press, 1963).

9. Winston S. Churchill, *The Gathering Storm* (Boston, Mass.: Houghton Mifflin Company, 1948), p. 135.

10. U.S. Department of Commerce, *Statistical Abstract of the United States, 1998* (Washington, D.C.: U.S. Department of Commerce, 1998), pp. 31, 71.

11. David Hackett Fischer, *Albion's Seed: Four British Folkways in America* (New York: Oxford University Press, 1989).

Chapter Four

The Serpent and the Dove

1. Henry Adams, *The Education of Henry Adams* (Boston: Houghton Mifflin Company, 1974), p. 172. (Dispatch from Charles Francis Adams to Earl Russell, 5 September 1863.)

2. Gorton Carruth, ed., *Encyclopedia of American Facts and Dates*, 9th ed. (New York: HarperCollins, 1993), p. 652.

3. Joseph Bucklin Bishop, *Theodore Roosevelt and His Time Shown in His Own Letters*, vol. 1 (New York: Charles Scribner's Sons, 1920), p. 431.

4. Quote from Dudden, *The American Pacific*, p. 4.

5. Bureau of the Census, *Historical Statistics of the United States: Colonial Times to 1970*, vol. 2 (Washington, D.C.: U.S. Department of Commerce, 1975), pp. 904–5.

6. Ibid.

7. G. J. Younghusband, *The Philippines and Round About* (London: Macmillan Company, 1899), p. 148.

Chapter Five

The Connecticut Yankee in the Court of King Arthur

1. Dana L. Robert, *American Women in Mission: A Social History of Their Thought and Practice* (Macon, Ga.: Mercer University Press, 1996), pp. 129–30.

2. Gordon Langley Hall, *Golden Boats from Burma: The Life of Ann Hasseltine Judson, the First American Woman in Burma* (Philadelphia, Penn.: Macrae Smith Co. 1961), p. 123.

3. Charles W. Forman, "The Americans," in Martin E. Marty, ed., *Modern American Protestantism and Its World*, vol. 13, *Missions and Ecumenical Expressions* (Munich: K.G. Saur, 1993), p. 39.

4. See also Samuel Wilson, ed., *Mission Handbook: North American Protestant Ministries Overseas* (Monrovia, Calif.: Missions Advanced Research and Communication Center, 1979), p. 25.

5. Direct correspondence with Randy Pearson, Director of Mobilization, Wycleffe Bible Translators.

6. United Bible Societies, "2000 Scripture Language Report" (Service Center, New York: January 21, 2001), p. 1

7. Direct correspondence with W. W. Vardell, Special Services Manager, Gideons International, February 16, 2001.

8. Dana L. Robert, *American Women in Mission: A Social History of Their Thought and Practice*, Chap. 3.

9. Patrick French, "The Horror," *Sunday Times* (London), April 18, 1999, p. 4.

10. Wang Xiaoqiu, "Dr. Yung Wing: The First Chinese Student in America," *China 2000*, June 1998.

11. Samuel Eliot Morison, *The Oxford History of the American People* (New York: Oxford University Press, 1965), p. 805.

12. U.S. Census Bureau, *Statistical Abstract of the United States: 2000* (Washington, D.C.: U.S. Department of Commerce, 2000), p. 186.

13. William R. Hutchison, *Errand to the World: American Protestant Thought and Foreign Missions* (Chicago: University of Chicago Press, 1987), pp. 1–2.

14. *The Far East and Australia 2000, Thirty-First Edition* (London: Europa Publications, 2000), pp. 613, 622.

15. Eddie C. Y. Kuo and Tong Chee Kiong, *Religion in Singapore, Census of Population, 1990 monograph no. 2* (Singapore: National University of Singapore, 1995), pp. 8, 10.

16. Christians now constitute 3.6 percent, 8 percent, and 1 percent, respectively, of the Taiwan, Hong Kong, and Thailand populations. (*The Far East and Australia 2000, Thirty-First Edition* [London: Europa Publications, 2000]), pp. 307–12, 361, 1204, 1212; U.S. Department of State, Bureau of Democracy, Human Rights, and Labor, *2000 Annual Report on International Religious Freedom*.

17. Unofficial sources estimate that the total Christian population in China alone in 1998 was as high as 90 million. *The Far East and Australia 2000*, p. 279.

18. ". . . the network of Catholic and Protestant 'house churches' in China, which serve an estimated 30 million to 40 million believers who worship illegally in private homes . . . ," John Pomfret, *International Herald Tribune*, January 11, 2000, p. 1.

19. Michael Prior and William Taylor, eds., *Christians in the Holy Land* (London: World of Islam Festival Trust, 1994), p. 33.

20. Nancy Mitford, *Madame de Pompadour* (New York: Harper & Row, 1968), p. 284.

Chapter Six

"Vindicator Only of Her Own"

1. Noam Chomsky, "The Demolition of World Order," *Harper's Magazine*, June 1999, p. 15.

2. John Quincy Adams, "An Address Delivered at the Request of the Committee of Arrangements for Celebrating the Anniversary of Independence, at the City of Washington on the Fourth of July 1821 upon the Occasion of Reading the Declaration of Independence" (Cambridge, Mass: Hilliard and Metcalf, 1821), p. 5.

3. 1 Sam. 8:14–18 (RSV).

4. John Quincy Adams, "An Address Delivered at the Request of the Committee of Arrangements," p. 32.

5. William E. Borah, "Speech on the League of Nations," November 19, 1919, quoted in Richard Hofstadter, ed., *Great Issues in American History From Reconstruction to the Present Day, 1864–1991* (New York: Vintage Books, 1982), p. 229.

6. Thomas Jefferson, "Lucerne and Potatoes," May 1, 1794, letter to Tench Coxe, in Merrill D. Peterson, ed., *Jefferson: Writings* (New York: Library of America, 1984), p. 1014.

7. Bureau of the Census, *Historical Statistics of the United States: Colonial Times to 1970* (Washington, D.C.: U.S. Department of Commerce, 1975), p. 1104.

8. Thomas Jefferson, "Last Trial for Peace," January 28, 1809, letter to James Monroe, in Peterson, *Jefferson: Writings*, pp. 1199–1200.

9. Andrew Johnson, "4th Annual Message" presented in written form to Congress, December 9, 1868.

10. George W. Norris, "Speech Against Declaration of War," April 4, 1917, in Hofstadter and Hofstadter, *Great Issues in American History*, p. 214.

11. *Historical Statistics of the United States*, p. 1141.

12. Ibid., p. 1114.

13. State Department: Bureau of Personnel.

14. "Combined Statement of Receipts, Expenditures, and Balances of the United States for the Fiscal Year Ending July 30, 1935," U.S. Department of the Treasury.

15. Business Executives for National Security, "The Defense Finance and Accounting Service—All Roads Lead to DFAS," *Update #3*, September 11, 1997.

16. "Statement by the Director of Central Intelligence Regarding the Disclosure of the Aggregate Intelligence Budget for Fiscal Year 1998," press release, no. 03–98, March 20, 1998.

17. Robert R. Newlen, "Fifty Years of Silent Service: A Peek Inside the CIA Library," *American Libraries*, vol. 29, no. 4, April 1998, p. 62.

18. *Historical Statistics of the United States*, p. 1104.

19. *Statistical Abstract of the United States 1996* (Washington, D.C.: U.S. Bureau of the Census, 1996), p. 297.

20. M. Tulli Ciceronis, *Pro Milone,* edited by A. B. Poynton (Oxford: Clarendon Press, 1852), p. 4.

21. Richard Morris, ed., *Encyclopedia of American History* (New York: Harper & Row, 1982), p. 205.

22. Thomas Jefferson, to the Emperor Alexander, Washington, D.C., April 19, 1806, in Peterson, *Jefferson: Writings,* p. 1161.

23. Almanac Singers, "Billy Boy," *Songs for John Doe,* Almanac Records, March 1941:

> Don't you want a silver medal, Billy boy, Billy boy?
> Don't you want a silver medal, charlin' {sic} Billy?
> No desire do I feel to defend Republic Steel. . . .
> Don't you want to see the world, Billy boy, Billy boy?
> Don't you want to see the world, charmin' Billy?
> No, it wouldn't be much thrill to die for DuPont in Brazil. . . .

24. Gore Vidal, *The American Presidency* (Chicago: Odonian Press, Common Courage Press/LPC Group, 1996), p. 39.

25. Adams, "An Address Delivered at the Request of the Committee of Arrangements," p. 32.

26. Mark Derr, *The Frontiersman: The Real Life and the Many Legends of Davy Crockett* (New York: William Morrow, 1993), p. 169.

27. Charles Sumner, "The True Grandeur of Nations" (a speech delivered on July 4, 1845) (New York, N.Y.: John B. Alden, 1899), p. 39.

28. Bruce Catton, *U.S. Grant and the American Military Tradition* (Boston: Little, Brown, 1954), p. 17.

29. James A. Field, Jr., *America and the Mediterranean World, 1776–1882* (Princeton, N.J.: Princeton University Press, 1969), pp. 234–36.

30. The first minister was appointed in 1778 (Franklin), and the title of ambassador was first used in 1893 (Thomas Bayard). *Merriam-Webster's Biographical Dictionary,* p. 380, and Beckles Willson, *America's Ambassadors to England (1785–1929): A Narrative of Anglo-American Diplomatic Relations* (London: John Murray, 1928), p. 402.

31. See Willson, *America's Ambassadors to England,* p. 282.

32. Ibid., p. 147.

33. Ibid., p. 184.

34. *Historical Statistics of the United States: Colonial Times to 1970,* p. 1115.

35. August 7, 1999, from staff and wire reports (CNN).

36. Based on author's interviews.

37. "The day that France takes possession of N. Orleans fixes the sentence which is to restrain her forever within her low water mark. It seals the union of two nations who in conjunction can maintain exclusive possession of the ocean. From that moment we must marry ourselves to the British fleet and nation." Thomas Jefferson, "The Affair of Louisiana," April 18, 1802, letter to the U.S. Minister to France, Robert R. Livingston, in Peterson, *Jefferson: Writings,* p. 1105.

38. Gorton Carruth et al., eds., *Encyclopedia of American Facts and Dates*, 6th ed. (New York, N.Y.: Thomas Y. Crowell Company, 1972), p. 124.

39. Thomas Jefferson, "The Monroe Doctrine," October 24, 1823, letter written to the president of the United States, James Monroe, in Peterson, *Jefferson: Writings,* p. 1482.

40. Thomas Jefferson, "The Spirit of Manufacture," June 28, 1809, letter to P. S. Dupont de Nemours, in ibid., p. 1209.

41. *Historical Statistics of the United States: Colonial Times to 1970,* p. 1142.

42. Chris Cook and Brendan Keith, *British Historical Facts, 1830–1900* (London: Macmillan Press, Ltd., 1975), p. 185.

43. Joel David Singer, *The Wages of War, 1816–1965* (New York: John Wiley & Sons, Inc., 1972), pp. 61–62. Statistics for France and Austria are from 1859; Prussia, from 1864; and Russia, from 1856.

44. *Historical Statistics of the United States: Colonial Times to 1970,* p. 1142.

45. This was largely based on Chile's readiness to deploy ironclads vis-à-vis the U.S. Navy's reversion to an all wooden fleet. Michael Clodfelter, *Warfare and Armed Conflicts,* vol. 1 (Jefferson, N.C.: McFarland & Company, 1992), pp. 578–81; Clark G. Reynolds, *Navies in History* (Annapolis, Md.: Naval Institute Press, 1998), pp. 120–36.

46. *Encyclopedia of U.S. Foreign Relations,* pp. 34–35.

47. Eric Solsten, ed., *Germany: A Country Study* (Washington, D.C.: Library of Congress, 1995), p. 50, fig. 5.

48. *Historical Statistics of the United States: Colonial Times to 1970,* p. 1141.

49. George W. Norris, "Speech Against Declaration of War," April 4, 1917, in Hofstadter and Hofstadter, *Great Issues in American History,* pp. 212–15.

50. Bruce W. Jentleson and Thomas G. Paterson, eds., *Encyclopedia of U.S. Foreign Relations,* vol. 4 (New York: Oxford University Press, 1997), p. 339.

51. *Encyclopedia of U.S. Foreign Relations,* vol. 3, pp. 231–33.

Chapter Seven

Tiger! Tiger! Burning Bright

1. David M. Kennedy, *Freedom from Fear* (Oxford, England: Oxford University Press, 1999), p. 847. See Richard B. Frank, *Downfall: The End of the Imperial Japanese Empire* (New York: Penguin Books, 1999), for lower casualty estimates.

2.

War	*Combat Deaths*
American Revolution (1775–83)	6,824
Indian Wars (1789–1879)	3,577
War of 1812 (1812–15)	2,260
Mexican-American War (1846–48)	1,733
Civil War (1861–65)	234,414
Spanish-American War (1898)	385
World War I (1917–18)	53,513
World War II (1941–45)	292,131
Korean War (1950–53)	33,870
Vietnam War (1964–73)	47,072
Persian Gulf War (1990–91)	148
Kosovo War (1999)	0
TOTAL	675,927

Sources (partial list): Howard Peckham, *The Toll of Independence;* Clodfelter, *Warfare and Armed Conflicts.*

3. Clodfelter, *Warfare and Armed Conflicts,* pp. 952–53.

4. Ibid., pp. 1216, 1311.

5. Ibid., p. 886.

6. Ibid., p. 1216; and "Age and Sex Distribution of the World's Population" (New York, N.Y.: United Nations, 1996).

7. There were 6,162,000 tons dropped in Vietnam vs. 2,150,000 in World War II. Clodfelter, *Warfare and Armed Conflicts,* vol. 2, p. 1288.

8. Note that the large number of civilians killed in "free-fire" zones were counted as military casualties. (Stanley I. Kutler, ed., *Encyclopedia of the Vietnam Conflict* [New York: Charles Scribner's Sons, 1996], p. 103.)

9. A ratio of 47,072:365,000, or 1:8.

10. Clodfelter, *Warfare and Armed Conflicts,* vol. 2, p. 956.

11. Capt. Arthur R. Moore, *A Careless Word . . . A Needless Sinking* (Kings Point, N.Y.: American Merchant Marine Museum), passim.

12. Clodfelter, *Warfare and Armed Conflicts,* vol. 2, p. 901.

13. For their work on the Pacific war, I am deeply indebted to John Dower and David Kennedy.

14. *Defense Spending (1999; $ billion)*

NATO Allies	$188.2
Pacific Allies	$53.7
Gulf Cooperation Council	$28.4
China (1998)	$11.2
Russia	$4.7
Total	$286.2
United States	$283.1

In 1999 NATO included Belgium, Canada, Czech Republic, Denmark, France, Germany, Greece, Hungary, Italy, Luxembourg, the Netherlands, Norway, Poland, Portugal, Spain, Turkey, and the United Kingdom. Pacific allies included Japan and the Republic of Korea. Gulf Cooperation Council included Bahrain, Kuwait, Oman, Qatar, Saudi Arabia, and the United Arab Emirates. ("Report on Allied Contributions to the Common Defense: A Report to the United States Congress by the Secretary of Defense" [March 2000].) Chinese and Russian expenditure figures are from International Monetary Fund, *Government Finance Statistics Yearbook* (Washington, D.C.: IMF, 2000), pp. 99, 353. Chinese expenditure is for 1998.

15. Hofstadter and Hofstadter, "The Klan's Fight for Americanism," *Great Issues in American History,* p. 319.

16. Idem., 321

17. Theodore Roosevelt, "The Puritan Spirit and the Regulation of Corporations" (Speech of August 20, 1907), in *The Works of Theodore Roosevelt: National Edition,* vol. 16: *American Problems* (New York, 1926), p. 84.

18. Magnus Magnusson, ed., *Cambridge Biographical Dictionary* (Cambridge, England: Cambridge University Press, 1990), p. 1222.

19. Sarah. Morgan, *The Civil War Diary of a Southern Woman* (New York: Simon & Schuster, 1991), p. 24.

20. Fanny Trollope, *Domestic Manners of the Americans* (London: Penguin Books, 1997), pp. 95–96.

21. Ibid., p. 100.

22. Pat Robertson, *The New World Order* (Dallas, Tex.: Word Publishing, 1991), passim; especially part 2: "Threats to Freedom"; chap. 5: "The Establishment."

23. John W. Dower, *War Without Mercy: Race and Power in the Pacific War* (New York: Pantheon Books, 1987).

24. The United States killed one hundred thousand Japanese here *(Encyclopaedia Britannica).*

25. Richard Rhodes, "The General and World War II," *The New Yorker,* June 19, 1995, p. 47ff.

26. Clodfelter, *Warfare and Armed Conflicts: A Statistical Reference,* vol. 2, p. 460.

27. Douglas J. MacEachin, "The Final Months of the War with Japan: Signals Intelligence, U.S. Invasion Planning, and the A-Bomb Decision" (Washington, D.C.: Center for the Study of Intelligence, 1998). *Encyclopaedia Britannica* estimates that 2,000,000 Japanese would have been killed in an invasion.

28. David M. Kennedy, *Freedom from Fear: The American People in Depression and War 1929–45* (New York: Oxford University Press, 1999), pp. 834–35 and 844–45.

Chapter Eight

The Rise and Retreat of the New World Order

1. Bruce W. Jentleson and Thomas G. Paterson, eds., *Encyclopedia of U.S. Foreign Relations,* vol. 1 (New York: Oxford University Press, 1997), p. 11.

2. Associated Press (from wires), February 1, 2000, p.m. cycle.

3. *Economic Report of the President, 2000* (Washington, D.C.: U.S. Government Printing Office, 2000), p. 321.

4. U.S. Bureau of the Census, *Statistical Abstract of the United States, 1999* (Washington, D.C.: U.S. Department of Commerce, 1999). Consumer Price Index calculation done with index in *Economic Report of the President, 2000,* p. 373.

5. U.S. Bureau of the Census, *Statistical Abstract of the United States, 1975* (Washington, D.C.: U.S. Department of Commerce, 1975), p. 355.

6. Bureau of Labor Statistics, *National Employment, Hours and Earnings,* series ID: EEU30000051.

7. *Economic Report of the President,* February 1996 (Washington, D.C.: United States Government Printing Office, 1996), p. 332.

8. Bureau of Labor Statistics, *Labor Force Statistics from the Current Population Survey,* series ID: LFS21000000.

9. *Economic Report of the President,* 2000, p. 373.

10. The 1973 figure for Medicaid recipients (23.5 million) is from the *New York Times,* July 2, 1973. The current number (40.6 million) is from Health Care Financing Administration (HCFA), CMSO, HCFA-2082 Report, January 27, 2000.

11. *Statistical Abstract of the United States: 1975,* pp. 72–73; and William J. Clinton, State of the Union Address, January 27, 2000.

12. Lawrence Mishel et al., eds., *The State of Working America 1998–99* (Washington, D.C.: Economic Policy Institute, 1999), p. 161.

13. In a September 27, 1994, speech "Toward a New Social Compact: The Role of Business," Robert B. Reich and G. Scott Thomas, "America's Most Educated Places," *American Demographics,* October 1995.

14. International Confederation of Free Trade Unions, "Trade Union Campaign for a Social Clause: Anti-Union Repression in the Export Processing Zones," April 1996.

15. B. R. Mitchell, *International Historical Statistics: The Americas, 1750–1993,* 4th ed. (London: Macmillan Reference Ltd., 1998), p. 107.

16. Bureau of Labor Statistics Fax On Demand Service Series 3020, "Establishment Data," received 5/7/01.

17. "Fortune 500 Largest U.S. Corporations," *Fortune,* April 17, 2000, pp. F-15, F-3, F-17, F-13; *Fortune,* May 1973, pp. 246–47.

18. Prices inflation-adjusted for 1967 dollars. Steven J. Taff, "Crop Data Don't Reveal Much about Farmer Prosperity," *Minnesota Agricultural Economist Newsletter* 697 (Summer 1999).

19. Pew Research Center for People and the Press, "Doubts About China, Concerns About Jobs: Post-Seattle Support For WTO," *February 2000 News Interest Index,* Final Topline, February 9–14, 2000.

20. See, for example, *National Endowment for Democracy Annual Report 1998* (Washington, D.C.: NED, 1998).

21. Adrian Karatnycky, ed., *Freedom in the World: The Annual Survey of Political Rights and Civil Liberties, 1999–2000* (New York: Freedom House, 2000), p. 7.

22. Pew Research Centers, "Doubts About China, Concerns About Jobs: Post-Seattle Support For WTO," p. 16.

23. This is not to say that there are no Wilsonians in foxholes. Some military intellectuals see the proliferation of humanitarian interventions as both necessary and manageable. It is likely that over time the influence of these thinkers will grow. Humanitarian interventions and peacekeeping missions provide new missions and new constituencies for military institutions—and new career tracks for officers who embrace the possibilities and responsibilities the new roles present.

24. James A. Forrest, Ph.D., Research Director of Hispanic Trends, Coral Gables, Fla. Estimate formulated using archived Miami-Dade election data and Census population information.

25. Eric Green, "Hispanics Vote 2–1 for Gore Over Bush in U.S. Presidential Elec-

tion," U.S. Department of State, International Information Systems, November 14, 2000.

Chapter Nine
The Future of American Foreign Policy

1. Bruce W. Jentleson and Thomas G. Paterson, eds., *Encyclopedia of U.S. Foreign Relations*, vol. 4 (New York, N.Y.: Oxford University Press, 1997), p. 291.

2. Hiram Johnson, *The Diary Letters of Hiram Johnson 1917–1945*, ed. Robert E. Burke, vol. 5 (New York: Garland Publishing, Inc., 1983), facsimile of letter of December 27, 1931, p. 3.

3. LeRoy Ashby, *The Spearless Leader; Senator Borah and the Progressive Movement in the 1920's* (Urbana: University of Illinois Press, 1972), p. 106.

4. Ibid.

5. Rep. Louis T. McFadden, Pennsylvania, remarks in Congress, May 23, 1933, on the Federal Reserve Corporation.

6. William L. Langer, ed., *Encyclopedia of World History* (London: George G. Harrap & Co. Ltd., 1968), p. 1007–10.

7. Jentleson and Paterson, *Encyclopedia of U.S. Foreign Relations*, vol. 4, p. 291.

8. Ibid.

9. The tonnage limits required Britain to cut back 2,455,371 tons; Japan, 1,529,268; and the United States 2,252,838. According to the U.S. Navy's general board, the displacement in metric tons in 1921 was:

	Great Britain	United States	Japan
Total constructed warships:	1,781,596	1,302,441	641,852
Constructed capital ships:	1,015,825	728,390	494,528
Under construction (all types):	182,950	747,007	707,888
Total	2,980,371	2,777,838	1,844,268

Under the terms of the Five-Power Treaty, Great Britain and the United States were each allowed 525,000 tons, Japan 315,000.

Sources: Richard Dean Burns, *Encyclopedia of Arms Control and Disarmament*, vol. 2 (New York, N.Y.: Charles Scribner's Sons, 1993), p. 640. See also Clark G. Reynolds, *Navies in History* (Annapolis, Md.: Naval Institute Press, 1998), p. 176.

10. *Encyclopedia of Arms Control and Disarmament*, vol. 2, pp. 714–17.

11. Jentleson and Paterson, *Encyclopedia of U.S. Foreign Relations*, vol. 3, p. 2.

12. Ibid., vol. 3, pp. 2–3.

13. Malcolm Shaw, *International Law*, 2nd ed. (Cambridge, England: Cambridge University Press, 1986), p. 543.

14. *Encyclopedia of World History*, p. 1122.

15. These included the Neutrality Act of 1935 (banning shipments of weapons to belligerent countries), 1936 (banning war loans), 1937 (making the other two acts into law, and forbidding American citizens from traveling on oceanfaring vessels of belligerent nations), and 1939 (revising the 1935 act to allow "cash and carry" purchases). (Jentleson and Paterson, *Encyclopedia of U.S. Foreign Relations*, vol. 3, pp. 231–33.)

16. Flannery O'Connor, *A Good Man Is Hard to Find and Other Stories* (New York: Harcourt, Brace & World, Inc., 1953), p. 29.

17. In constant (1998) dollars (Bureau of the Census, 2000 *Statistical Abstract of the United States* [Washington, D.C.: U.S. Department of Commerce, 2000], p. 466.)

18. Richard Norton Smith, "Calvin, We Hardly Knew Ye," July 30, 1998, keynote address at the John Fitzgerald Kennedy Library, Boston, Mass.

19. George Q. Flynn, *The Draft: 1940–1973* (Lawrence: University Press of Kansas, 1993), p. 107.

Acknowledgments

In working on this book I have been blessed by a special providence of my own: the friendship and assistance of a large group of remarkable people.

First and foremost, I wish to thank Richard C. Leone and the board of directors of The Century Foundation. Their courageous and generous support and guidance to a young and struggling writer made this book possible, and they never lost hope in the many years it took until a somewhat older and more weatherbeaten writer delivered the final manuscript. There were years in between when it looked as if the book would never be done; I am more grateful than I can say to Dick and the board for their continuing faith.

The World Policy Institute at the New School University provided me with an institutional home and both intellectual and financial support during much of the research for this book. I am especially indebted to James Chace for his editorial assistance and his willingness to let me try out early versions of these ideas in the pages of the *World Policy Journal*. Jonathan Fanton, the president of the university, did me the great honor of appointing me president's fellow at the World Policy Institute, and I am grateful for his friendship and support. I am also grateful to Peter Schmuhl, Adam Feibelman, Noah Sternthal, and Tomas Matza for research assistance in my years at the New School.

In 1997 Leslie Gelb invited me to join the Council on Foreign Relations as senior fellow for United States foreign policy, and since then I have benefited from Les's friendship and intellectual leadership and from the financial support of the council. Sharing in the life of this community of scholars, policy makers, and brilliant lay readers and thinkers has widened my outlook, sharpened my mind, and brightened my life.

Gary Hufbauer and Lawrence Korb served as directors of studies at the council during my tenure; I thank both of them for their personal kindness and their commitment to helping the fellows get on with their work. Michael Peters and Jan Murray have done everything in their power to make the council a place where fellows can work peacefully and without distraction. I am grateful to them, and also to other friends who have done so much to make my council experience one of the happiest and most fulfilling of my life. In particular, Judith Adams, Frank Alvarez, Nancy Bodurtha, Esther Burnham, Charles Day, Patricia Lee Dorff, Irina Faskianos, Theophilos Gemelas, Rossana Ivanova, David Kellogg, Elizabeth Kurdys, Cristy Lemperle, Elise Carlson Lewis, Anne Luzatto, Elva Murphy, April Palmerlee, Russell Pomeranz, Carol Rath, Jeffery Reinke, Bettina Schaeffer, Jacqui Selbst Schein, Lisa Shields, and Marie Strauss have made working here a real joy.

In my years at the council I have been supported by some of the most talented and dedicated young professionals it has ever been my privilege to know. Rebecca O'Brien,

E. Benjamin Skinner, Derek Lundy, and Laurence Reszetar threw themselves into this project with an almost terrifying enthusiasm, and much that is valuable in this book is the result of their dedication and skill.

One of the greatest treasures of the Council on Foreign Relations is its staff of librarians. Leigh V. Gusts, Marcia L. Sprules, Michelle McKowen, Connie Stagnaro, Barbara Miller, and Ming Er Qiu went far beyond the call of duty; I simply could not have finished this book without their help.

Thanks to the support of the Council on Foreign Relations, the good offices of the New America Foundation, and the hospitality of Abe Lowenthal and the Pacific Council for International Policy, I had the rare privilege of submitting draft chapters of the manuscript to study-group sessions in New York, Washington, and Los Angeles that were attended by some of the most formidable and accomplished women and men in the fields of American history and foreign policy. I would like to express my appreciation for their valuable comments to all of the study group members, who among others included: Richard Betts, Rachel Bronson, David Callahan, Ted G. Carpenter, Anne Carruth, John Cavanagh, James Chace, Steven Clemons, Alberto Coll, Kyle Crichton, Robert DeVecchi, David Duffie, Daniel W. Fisk, Alton Frye, Arch Gillies, Michael Green, Ted Halstead, Owen Harries, Paul Heer, Jim Hoge, Morton Holbrook, Chris Isham, Adrian Karatnycky, Judith Kipper, Radha Kumar, Charles Lemert, Michael E. Lind, Bette Bao Lord, Michael Mandelbaum, James Mann, Robert A. Manning, Ann Markusen, Stanley McChrystal, Shoon Murray, Kimber McKenzie, Janne E. Nolan, Jonathan Paris, David Rieff, William D. Rogers, Gideon Rose, Stanley Sheinbaum, Elisabeth Sifton, Jessica E. Stern, Bruce Stokes, Julia E. Sweig, David Victor, Ruth Wedgewood, and Fareed Zakaria. I am particularly grateful to Arthur Schlesinger, Jr., for the unfailing patience and courtesy with which he labored to prevent me from committing grievous crimes against the memory of Andrew Jackson. Almost every page of the final draft shows the influence of the thoughtful comments and helpful suggestions of the study group readers; the responsibility for any remaining errors of fact or interpretation is, of course, my own.

I would also like to thank Haleh Nazeri and Jonathan Tepperman for arranging a "shadow study group" consisting of junior staff members of the Council on Foreign Relations. Submitting one's work to the sharp eyes and candid judgment of a group of brilliant young people just out of college and university is both bracing and sobering; I recommend it highly, and I thank Haleh, Jonathan, and their associates for allowing me to have this valuable experience.

In addition to the unstinting support of friends and colleagues at the World Policy Institute at the New School and the Council on Foreign Relations, I have also been the beneficiary of the generosity of a group of donors who helped underwrite my salary and expenses in both places. Allen Adler, Henry Arnholdt, Stanley S. Arkin, Robert J. Chaves, Kimball Chen, Mary van Evera, Joachim Gfoeller, Jr., Wade Green, John H. and Susan Gutfreund (through the Gutfreund Foundation), John H. J. Guth (through the Woodcock P. Foundation), J. Tomilson Hill, Frank W. Hoch, Robert M. McKinney, Winthrop R. Munyan, and Robert Rosenkranz have all been extremely generous in the support of my work. The financial support was welcome and badly needed; the friendship was and is beyond price.

Sherle Schwenninger played an immense role in this project, as he has done in virtually all of my major intellectual activities for fifteen years. Alison Silver, my longtime editor at the *Los Angeles Times,* has done wonders for my writing style and taught me the importance of grounding contemporary commentary on foreign affairs in American history. John Koten and Jim Jubak, my principal editors at *Worth* magazine, Mark Warren at *Esquire,* and Marty Beiser at *GQ* have steadfastly supported my work through this long process. Owen Harries at the *National Interest* published a version of my chapter on the Jacksonian foreign policy tradition. The enormous response generated by that publication is a testimony to the strong grip that the *National Interest* has on the attention of its readers. Jonathan Segal at Alfred A. Knopf has been as patient as Richard Leone. My literary agent and dear friend, Geri Thoma, has been there for me every step of the way; meeting her was one of the great turning points of my life. Andrea Barrett has been endlessly patient with my whining. My parents, Loren and Polly Mead, spent countless hours reviewing the manuscript of this book, as they did of my first. I am, as always, grateful for their love and support.

Index

Page numbers in *italics* indicate illustrations.

About the Author

Walter Russell Mead is Senior Fellow for U.S. Foreign Policy at the Council on Foreign Relations. A contributing editor at the *Los Angeles Times* and a senior contributing editor of *Worth* magazine, he has also written for the *New York Times,* the *Washington Post, The Wall Street Journal, The New Yorker, Harper's,* and *Foreign Affairs.* He is the author of **Mortal Splendor: The American Empire in Transition.** He lives in Jackson Heights, New York.

This is the book every parent should read
to ensure that their children become blessings to the world.
—Dr. Laura Schlessinger
Internationally Syndicated Talk-Show Host, Author of *Bad Childhood—Good Life*

RAISING
RESPECTFUL
CHILDREN
IN A
DISRESPECTFUL
WORLD

Jill Rigby
AUTHOR OF *MANNERS OF THE HEART*

P9-DNT-468

HOWARD BOOKS
A DIVISION OF SIMON & SCHUSTER
NEW YORK LONDON TORONTO SIDNEY

Published by Howard Books, a division of Simon & Schuster
1230 Avenue of the Americas, New York, NY 10020

Raising Respectful Children in a Disrespectful World © 2006 by Jill Rigby

All rights reserved, including the right to reproduce this book or portions thereof in any form whatsoever. For information, address Howard Books, 3117 North 7th Street, West Monroe, Louisiana 71291-2227
www.howardpublishing.com

Library of Congress Cataloging-in-Publication Data

Rigby, Jill M.
   Raising respectful children in a disrespectful world / Jill Rigby.
      p. cm.
   Includes bibliographical references.
   ISBN-13: 978-1-58229-574-9
   ISBN-10: 1-58229-574-3
   1. Child rearing. 2. Parenting. 3. Moral development. 4. Respect. 5. Mass media and children. I. Title.

HQ769.R554 2006
649'.7—dc22
                                                                    200604357

10 9 8 7 6 5 4 3 2 1

HOWARD is a registered trademark of Simon & Schuster, Inc.

Manufactured in the United States of America

For information regarding special discounts for bulk purchases, please contact Simon & Schuster Special Sales at 1-800-456-6798 or business@simonandschuster.com.

Edited by Liz Heaney
Interior design by Stephanie D. Walker
Cover design by Carlos Lerma and Stephanie D. Walker.

Scripture quotations not otherwise marked are taken from the *Holy Bible, New International Version*®. NIV®. Copyright © 1973, 1978, 1984 by International Bible Society. Used by permission of Zondervan. All rights reserved. Scripture quotations marked KJV are taken from the *King James Version*. Scripture quotations marked MSG are taken from *The Message*. Copyright © by Eugene H. Peterson 1993, 1994, 1995. Used by permission of NavPress Publishing Group. Scriptures marked NKJV are taken from the *New King James Version*. Copyright © 1982 by Thomas Nelson, Inc. Used by permission. All rights reserved. Scriptures marked CEV are taken from the *Contemporary English Version*. Copyright © 1991, 1992, 1995 by American Bible Society. Used by permission. Scriptures marked NASB are taken from the *New American Standard Bible*®. Copyright © The Lockman Foundation 1960, 1962, 1963, 1968, 1971, 1972, 1973, 1975, 1977. Used by permission. (www.Lockman.org).

To Chad and Boyce, my grown sons.
In spite of my mistakes, in spite of my faults,
you have become men of great respect,
who will one day lead with humble hearts
families of your own.
I love you dearly.

contents

acknowledgments

I MUST BEGIN WITH MY MOTHER, Omer Evelyn Shea McDonald, also known as Miss Evelyn, MeMe, MomMeme, and Momma Mac. At seventy-eight, you're the most amazing woman I have ever known, living to serve others—the perfection of unselfishness. You walk your talk—"Give till you got nothing left to give, then God will give you more to give."

My precious daddy, Claiborne Lamar McDonald, who passed to heaven when I was eighteen years old. He was a grizzly bear with a teddy bear's heart. A one-of-a-kind father who proved to be irreplaceable. He taught me how to love because I want to, not because I have to.

Danielle Nienaber, more than an assistant, more than a friend. You've listened to story after story while completing grueling assignments, all without grumbling. You've never refused even my most outrageous request. Not only have you walked every step with me, you've even walked in Wilbur's shoes.

Mike and Lisa Conn, more than friends, more than business partners. You've stood by me through the trials and struggles of building The Community of Manners, never faltering in your commitment to Manners of the Heart. It is an honor to welcome your words of wisdom to these pages.

Coach Payton Jordan, more than a legend, more than a coach, more than a friend. How thankful I am for your willingness to share your years of experience in working with youth to reinforce the principles of this book. Your years on earth may be many, but your heart beats as strong as the athletes who ran in the Olympics under your leadership.

Jean Rohloff, more than a friend, more than a sister, more than an English professor. You're the one who sees what I miss. You're the one who never tires of my lack of knowledge, who is always ready to answer "just one more question," knowing that I'll probably call back in fifteen minutes with another.

Donna Munson, more than a friend, more than a sister. You've been there to soothe my hurts, share my joys, and encourage my writing. You've dreamed my dreams and never given up on me, even though at times I gave up on myself.

B. J. Giles, more than a friend, more than a once-upon-a-time sister. When others walked away, you drew closer. You're the one who knows your nephews all too well and still seeks my advice with the raising of your children.

Barb Stiegler, more than a friend, more than a sister. You fed my body and soul in the final days of completion. Your belief in this book kept me going when the going got tough.

Liz Heaney, more than an editor, more than a master wordsmith. Your unending patience in working through the pages of this book with me, word by rewritten word, was nothing short of a miracle, a true gift from above.

Steve Laube, more than an agent, more than a supporter. Your encouragement and counsel made this book a reality. You steered me in the right direction, when I didn't know which direction to take.

Chrys Howard and Philis Boultinghouse, more than publishers, now dear friends. I can't believe you listened to the ramblings of a woman with plenty of passion, but little writing experience, and still decided to take a chance.

Everyone at Howard Books, much more than a publishing house. I fell in love with each of you the first day I visited your offices. My love and respect have deepened in the months since. You've become more than colaborers; you've become family.

The dear children who took part in our research study—more precious than silver, more priceless than gold. Know that Miss Jill has prayed for each of you since the day we met.

To the Manners of the Heart board members, kids, parents, teachers, and businesses who share my passion and support our efforts to bring a return of civility and respect to our country.

From the bottom of my heart,

I thank you.

introduction

A CLASSIC TOMBOY STOOD IN FRONT OF ME. Long burnished hair with rippling waves that fell on her shoulders, looking unwashed and unkempt. Suzie's eyes looked away, then down as she stood at the table. But never into mine.

She was one of many kids being interviewed for a special study we were conducting among children ages four to fourteen. Taller than most, she stooped to avoid towering over the other girls.

Halfway through the survey I asked a question that revealed her pain: "What's the nicest thing your parents could ever say to you? What would really make your heart feel good?"

"Be a lady."

Her answer confused me. Why would she want her parents to tell her to be a lady? Her demeanor proclaimed that she was anything but. I saw no indication that this was her deepest desire. As I'd watched her enter the room, I suspected Suzie was angry, but I didn't know why.

So I asked her, "Do you usually listen to your parents?"

Her reply was an abrupt and emphatic "No!"

"Why not?"

She leaned over the table to make her point, looking directly in my eyes, "Because I'm in rebellion."

1

"What are you rebelling against?"

"I've already told you!"

Wiggling in my seat, I tried to remember answers she had already given. I knew Suzie desperately needed to know I had been listening to her. She didn't need another adult who seemed not to care enough to pay attention.

"Let me see, Suzie," I muttered, stalling.

When I looked up at her, she gave me a look of disgust, as if to say, "Don't you get it?"

I got it. Her stance gave it away. "You're rebelling because you really want to be a lady and nobody's helping you. Is that it?"

She nodded her head as she shifted hips and re-crossed her arms. "Yeah."

I was looking at the face of rebellion. Suzie wasn't angry about what was right; she was angry about what was wrong.

I suspect she's like many other kids on this score. Today's kids are angry and rebellious at rates higher than any other generation. They are the first generation to do worse psychologically, socially, and economically than their parents. But they're not rebelling against rigidity and rules as the hippies of the sixties did; they are rebelling against the lack of structure and adult guidance.

At a much deeper level, today's kids are seeking revenge. The adults in their lives say one thing and live another; and the kids see through their parents' phoniness, lostness, and insecurities. These kids want to get even. They're lashing out at a society that has not given them what they really need . . . security within boundaries. They want to inflict on others the pain that has been inflicted on them. What they can't see is that their revenge will destroy them.

Our children, from ghettos to gated communities, are desperate, searching for someone who will tell them the truth.

You, parent, should be that person.

Suzie desperately wants someone to teach her how to be a lady. She doesn't want to be an angry, insecure, awkward girl. She wants to become a confident young woman, but no one seems to care or even notice, so she's going to scream until they do. Not with an audible scream, but with an insidious moaning from the depths of her soul.

As the next group of kids came to the table, Suzie turned to leave, but I couldn't let her just walk away. "Suzie, I need a hug. It's been a long morning."

She hesitated but walked back when I stretched open my arms and added, "You're the only one tall enough around here to hug me." (Her stooping had told me that she was self-conscience about her height.) As we embraced, I whispered in her ear, "Be a lady, the beautiful lady that I see inside." Her lips quivered, but I can't say I saw a smile.

I'm hoping and praying that Suzie's parents will wake up and help her. If they don't, I'm afraid that within two years their daughter's rebellion will only intensify and she'll end up hurting those around her and herself.

You picked up this book because you want to raise respectful children in today's disrespectful world. This is an achievable goal, and you can succeed, even if at the moment it seems like an impossible task. But to do so, you must be willing to:

- Be the person you want your children to become

- Abandon old notions of building self-esteem, and enroll your family in the School of Respect

- Help your children find their purpose and use perseverance to fulfill that purpose

- Use encouragement to motivate your children

- Set boundaries without building walls between you and your children

- Use discipline to instill righteousness in your children

- Do all you can to protect and shield your children from the garbage of our culture

- Engage your children in meaningful activities, not useless entertainment

- Find contentment so your children can be filled with gratefulness

- Listen with your heart to your children's needs

Do you believe you can do it?

I believe you can . . . if you follow God's principles. His principles are so broad that they transcend both culture and time yet so practical that they will equip you with every tool needed to school your children in manners of the heart.

I invite you to come with me and explore how you can help undo the damage in our children from a culture gone awry. It would be my honor to be your guide as you raise respectful children in the midst of our disrespectful world.

What Went Wrong?

WHEN I WAS GROWING UP, people weren't perfect, but society was certainly more civil. The lines between right and wrong were clear. There was a sense of law and order.

Teachers were teachers. So teachers taught.

Parents were parents. So parents trained.

Kids were kids. So kids obeyed.

Respect for authority was paramount. Service to others and respect for property were natural elements of community. Teaching manners and instilling character were the cornerstones of public education. Parents looked at the right side of the report card (conduct) before they looked at the left (grades). Kids got in a lot more trouble if they were disrespectful to a teacher than if they made a B minus.

Times past weren't perfect, but they certainly had an attitude of respectfulness that's now missing.

Today we live in a society where:

- An elderly woman can push a grocery cart filled with a week's supply of groceries across a parking lot, and instead of offering to help, other shoppers hurry past her, leaving her to handle the heavy bags alone.

- A high-school student who has been caught cheating on an exam can truthfully tell the teacher, "No big deal. My dad will handle you."

- Kids would rather eat alone in their room, listening to music on their headphones, than join the family conversation at the dinner table.

I could fill this book with one example after another of disrespectful behavior. How did this happen? How did our respectful world become so disrespectful? We've substituted self-esteem for self-respect, and in the process we lost our manners.

We Replaced Self-Respect with Self-Esteem

Fifteen years ago when I began visiting my twin sons' school cafeteria to teach table manners, I had no concept that a volunteer project for a local school would grow into a full program that is now being used in schools and homes across the country. Since then *Manners of the Heart* (curriculum for schools) and *Manners of the Heart at Home* (a parents' guide to the school curriculum) have been changing the lives of children, families, and communities.

My experience of working with children and parents has convinced me that the troubles of today can be traced back to the early seventies, when a group of psychologists began theorizing why the rebellion of the sixties had taken place. Some experts concluded that the fifties were a time of such rigidity that teenagers who grew up in the "era of rules" were destined to revolt.

The overwhelming majority of professionals, however, agreed that the reason teenagers rebelled was because of a deep need to be someone, not just Americans, but individuals. Not members of a corporate body, but individuals making their own decisions based on personal beliefs, not the beliefs of parents or society. "Believe in yourself" became the mantra of the day.

Specialists began telling parents that the secret to raising healthy children was to build their self-esteem. Books on the subject of self-esteem skyrocketed to the top of bestseller lists, encouraging parents to be friends, not authority figures, with their kids. Discipline was out. Experts said that children needed to make their own decisions. Slowly, but surely, children became the center of the universe.

Parents today are still being told that the secret to raising healthy children is to build their self-esteem—praise 'em in the morning, praise 'em in the noontime, praise 'em when the sun goes down. We've been told to never deny our children anything and to stand against anyone who dares to correct our little ones—all with the goal of helping our kids feel good about themselves.

I received the following letter from parents who did all they were told to do in raising their fourteen-year-old son:

> He has very low self-esteem and very little motivation or desire to succeed in play or academics. We try to use positive reinforcement and praise him for completing projects or whatever we see him do well or put effort into. We make a point not to compare him to other children, but he tries hard to be like others (*he really doesn't know what he likes or even who he is*). He is in trouble at school almost every day for disrespect, and we know that he can do better . . . he just needs to know that he *can*, and he has to want to try to do better. Please help! Any suggestions?

These parents had followed the advice of the day. But rather than help their son, they had unwittingly hurt him.

One of my favorite no-nonsense parenting experts, John Rosemond, agrees that by emphasizing self-esteem, we've lost something of great value:

> Character development has been de-emphasized and psychological development has become the focus. As this babble rose to a din, our collective perceptions of children began to change. We began to view them not as fairly durable little people who needed to be taught respect, responsibility, good manners, and the like, but as fragile little containers of something called self-esteem, which could be irreparably damaged with a harsh word.[1]

As a result of this emphasis on self-esteem, twenty-somethings are returning home rather than facing the world on their own. College kids are flunking out because they don't know how to manage their schedules. Kids are growing up without problem-solving skills because their parents think love means solving all their problems for them. Many adolescents have no respect for authority because their parents didn't command their respect. Instead, these parents gave too much and expected too little.

In our attempt to build self-esteem in children, we have reared a generation of young people who are failing at life, haven't a clue who they are, and are struggling to find a reason for living. These kids fall for the latest craze, healthy or unhealthy. It doesn't matter, as long as they're in the middle of it. They would rather die than give up their cell phones. And they feel that others have an obligation to serve them.

Roy F. Baumeister, professor of psychology at Florida State University, was a proponent of self-esteem in the early seventies, but he has since changed his views. Thirty years later Baumeister now recommends, "Forget about self-esteem and concentrate more on self-control and self-discipline. Recent work suggests this would be good for the individual and good for society—and might even be able to fill some of those promises that self-esteem once made but could not keep."[2] I agree. Rather than seeking to build self-esteem in our children, we need to focus on building self-control and self-discipline, which will develop self-respect.

Many people use the words *self-esteem* and *self-respect* synonymously, but I believe the two are worlds apart. When we seek to help kids feel good about themselves (the goal of self-esteem), we teach them to focus on *themselves* and how *they* feel and what *they* want. I believe this perspective keeps children from participating in the world; it encourages them to see everything as if looking into a mirror, so that they grow up believing, "It's all about me."

Kids raised with a focus on self-esteem have an unbalanced view of the world. They live by the motto: "I want it, and I want it now." Kids with this attitude aren't exhibiting self-confidence. They are exhibiting self-conceit, a view of themselves that says they are superior to others.

But when we help kids respect themselves, we teach them to focus on *others* and how *others* feel and what *others* need. This perspective, in turn, leads children to see everything through a window, seeing their own images reflected against the world beyond the glass, rather than in a mirror, and to grow up believing, "It's more about others and less about me."

So what's the bottom-line difference between self-esteem and self-respect? Self-esteem is "me centered," while self-respect is "others centered."

The quest for self-esteem has turned the world upside down. Shifting to the pursuit of self-respect will turn the world rightside up again. Why?

Because kids with self-respect put others ahead of themselves. They feel an obligation to others and a responsibility to society. Bullies can't rock their foundation because kids who have self-respect know who they are and what they stand for. They have a balanced view of the world. Their confidence is balanced with humility; they exhibit humble confidence.

If you are parenting to build self-respect in your children, you'll focus on who your kids are becoming rather than on how much you give to them. You'll teach them how to serve others rather than to expect to be served. You'll teach them to contribute to the world rather than to expect the world to give to them. You'll teach your kids to do their best, whether that means being number one or not, and to work toward goals so they can experience the satisfaction and confidence that a job well done brings.

Self-respect is the fruit of discipline;
the sense of dignity grows with the ability to say no to oneself.
ABRAHAM J. HESCHEL

Let's sum up the different results of these two parenting goals:

Self-Esteem	Self-Respect
Happiness (which is fleeting)	Joy (which is lasting)
Greed	Gratitude
Arrogance	Humility
Insecurity	Confidence
Discontentment	Contentment
Futility	Perseverance
Self-centeredness	Others-centeredness
Ill-mannered	Well-mannered

The result of parenting to build self-esteem? Undisciplined, rude, greedy, disrespectful, and ill-mannered children. The result of parenting to develop self-respect? Disciplined, caring, productive, respectful, and well-mannered children.

Unfortunately, because our society for the past four decades has emphasized self-esteem rather than self-respect in kids, we have far more disrespectful children than respectful children. Old-fashioned courtesies have become unimportant, and we've lost our moral foundation.

We Lost Our Manners and Therefore Lost Our Morals

Today, it's the rare child who says:

"Please."

"May I help you?"

"Yes sir" and "Yes ma'am." (Yes, I'm from the Deep South. Frankly, just this once I wish the rest of the country would follow us. There is no better vehicle for teaching young children respect than through the use of "sir" and "ma'am.")

"May I get your chair?"

"Excuse me."

"Thank you."

"I'm sorry."

In the quest for self-esteem, such courtesies have become uncommon, at least for the members of the new royalty. Little princes and princesses are not expected to humble themselves before others by extending common courtesies.

Judith Martin, better known as syndicated columnist "Miss Manners," offers this insightful explanation of the critical importance of manners:

> The attitude that the wishes of others do not matter is exactly what manners are intended to counter. And no one has yet come up with a satisfactory substitute for family etiquette training in the earliest years of life to foster the development of the child in such principles of manners as consideration, cooperation, loyalty, respect. . . . As a result of the ever-wider abandonment of home etiquette training, schools have become increasingly stymied by problems they identify as lack of discipline and commitment to moral behavior. . . . A society can hope to function virtuously only when it also recognizes the legitimacy of manners.[3]

Respect lies at the heart of manners and morals. A person's respect for authority, respect for others, and respect for self go a long way toward determining the moral decisions that person makes. Manners instilled in the early years become the foundation for moral behavior in the later years.

Scripture affirms the relationship of morals and manners—the morals in the heart are the basis for outward behavior.

> The good man brings good things out of the good stored up in his heart, and the evil man brings evil things out of the evil stored up in his heart. For out of the overflow of his heart his mouth speaks.[4]

> Good people do good things because of the good in their hearts. Bad people do bad things because of the evil in their hearts. Your words show what is in your heart.[5]

> It's who you are, not what you say and do, that counts. Your true being brims over into true words and deeds.[6]

In other words, the respectful child produces good deeds from a good heart, and a disrespectful child produces bad deeds from a corrupted heart. Whatever is in your child's heart determines what your child will say and do.

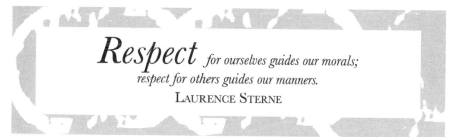

Respect for ourselves guides our morals;
respect for others guides our manners.
LAURENCE STERNE

If you want to raise respectful children in a disrespectful world, you must command their respect through a balance of love and discipline, even in the little things. When it comes to working with kids, the little things *are* the big things. And the younger the child, the more important the little things. When your children respect you, they will more easily respect God, and in the process respect others and themselves.

Is it possible to fill the hearts of our children with the "right stuff"? Can we raise respectful children in a disrespectful world? You better believe it. It's not as hard as you might think. It just takes spiritual muscle and emotional fortitude. Both are within reach, if you know where to turn.

The next generation is ready for the absolute truth. They want and need the world to be turned rightside up again. It's our duty to develop the spiritual muscle needed to help them.

Your Charge

Jesus asked the Father not to take His disciples out of the world, but to protect them from the evil in the world.[7] Our charge as parents is to prepare our children to be in the world and not of the world. We must train them to stand on their own two feet. With loving guidance our children can affect the world without becoming infected by it.

You can equip your children with humble confidence so that they can handle whatever comes at them. It's not your children's minds that will help them do that, but their hearts.

Let the disrespectful world throw its best shot. You *can still* raise respectful children in this disrespectful world.

Reality Check

Before moving on to the next chapter, consider your answers to these questions as you strengthen your resolve to raise respectful children in this disrespectful world:

1. Which category best describes your current parenting style?

   - Befriending your kids

   - Letting your kids make their own decisions

   - Never refusing your children anything

   - Training your children's hearts

2. Do you allow your children to get away with *little* things that may be disrespectful?

3. What have you tried to develop in your children?

    -   Self-respect

    -   Self-esteem

4. Has your parenting style reaped the desired results?

5. How are your children's manners reflected in their behavior?

    -   In school

    -   At home

6. Which is more important to you, that your children . . . ?

    -   Be number one

    -   Do their best

7. Do you insist that your children say the following?

    -   "Yes, ma'am" and "No, sir"

    -   "May I get your chair?"

    -   "Excuse me."

    -   "I'm sorry."

8. Are you praying regularly for wisdom to raise your children to be respectful?

Where Have All the Parents Gone?

MY EYES COULDN'T FIND THEIR WAY BACK to the pages of my book because my heart was tied to the image on the TV screen. A young girl stood in the middle of an empty street in the early morning hours, looking more like a prostitute than a lost child. Smoke from her cigarette swirled around her face. An investigative reporter stepped into the frame to begin his interview.

"How long have you been on the streets?" he questioned.

The coldness of her heart poured out in her words as she revealed that she had been on the streets for five years, since the age of eleven.

What could possibly have driven her to the streets at eleven years old? I wondered. *Why had her parents not come to her rescue? Are they dead?*

The reporter continued his conversation with the misplaced teenager, "You don't want to live like this, do you? Don't you want out of this existence?"

For a moment her shoulders fell and the hardness in her eyes softened. Looking beyond the reporter into the obscurity of the street, she replied with a broken whisper, "Yeah . . . but I can't find the door."

While this young woman's situation may be extreme, far too many children, even those living at home with their parents, are "unable to find the door." In a less dramatic but no less damaging way, these kids are raising themselves. Journalist David Brooks agrees. He visited several high schools a few years ago, spending time with students, listening to their dreams and listening to their hearts. He reported his conclusions in an article for the *Atlantic Monthly.* Here is an excerpt from that article:

> When it comes to character and virtue, these young people have been left on their own. Today's go-getter parents and today's educational institutions work frantically to cultivate neural synapses, to foster good study skills, to promote musical talents. . . . We spend huge amounts of money on safety equipment and sports coaching. We sermonize about the evils of drunk driving. We expend enormous energy guiding and regulating their lives. But when it comes to character and virtue, the most mysterious area of all, suddenly the laissez-faire ethic rules: You're on your own, Jack and Jill; go figure out what is true and just for yourselves.[1]

In this chapter we are going to examine the three different styles of parenting—*parent-centered, child-centered,* and *character-centered.* Parent-centered parents are more concerned with their own agenda than their child's best interests. Child-centered parents are more concerned with their child's approval than their child's well-being. Character-centered parents are more concerned with their child's character than their child's comfort. Only character-centered parents truly parent and, as a result, raise respectful children.

Let's take a closer look at each of these so you can determine if your parenting style may be inadvertently harming your child and what you need to do to raise a healthy, respectful child instead.

Parent-Centered Parents

A few years ago a student in my sixth-grade Sunday-school class raised her hand to share a story I've never forgotten. With tears streaming down her cheeks, she sobbed, "Miss Jill, I don't know what to do. I asked God to forgive me, but I can't forget what I saw and heard last night."

Before I could embrace her, she continued, "I thought if I asked God to forgive me, I wouldn't see the pictures any more . . . and I'd forget the words, but they won't go away."

I moved next to her and wrapped my arms around this child as she wept uncontrollably, beyond consolation. One of her closest friends sat on the other side to hold her hand. I suggested we go to a quiet place to talk, but the little girl insisted on telling the class her story.

Saturday night she had plans to meet friends at the movies. Her dad agreed to take her, because there was a film he wanted to see playing at the same time. When they arrived at the theater, the movie she was to see with friends was sold out. Rather than take her home, her father took her into the movie of his choice, which was a raunchy, violent film filled with everything a twelve-year-old shouldn't see or hear.

Consequently, she had not been able to sleep. She tossed and turned as the images replayed in her head all night. Why? Because her father put his own agenda before his daughter's best interests.

While this father's selfish motivation is easily seen, the motivations of many parent-centered parents are not so obvious. One mom explained it this way, "It all starts with a natural and normal desire to be a good parent. We all want to correct the mistakes we think our parents made." Another adds, "There is an element of being afraid, of not doing something that seemingly everyone else is advocating as being good for children."[2]

Still, it's not difficult to detect the motivation behind comments such as these:

- "We'll do whatever it takes to make the team."

- "My six-year-old is headed for Harvard."

- "We were rejected from the only nursery school that can guarantee acceptance into the best grade school."

- "I'm worried. My four-year-old can't read a chapter book yet. She'll never be able to compete."

All of these parents are trying to fill their own emptiness through their children's achievements. That's usually the case with parents who have an intense need for their children to be "perfect." As a result their parenting choices are not about helping their children become all they are meant to be, but about filling the parent's own need for recognition. Parent-centered parents often persist in pushing their children to be number one in every endeavor, whether in the classroom or on the sports field. Their motto?

"Nobody cares who comes in second."

With this attitude in place, pregnant women are enrolling their unborn children in *the* nursery school. Preschoolers have portfolios of artwork and videos of dance recitals to enhance their applications to elementary school. Commercial tutoring has become a $3 billion industry in the United States, partly because students who already get good grades are now expected to polish their skills even further. Scholastic Aptitude Test (SAT) tutors talk of students as young as thirteen bursting into tears because of the pressure to get into a good college.[3]

Enrid Norris, a marriage and family counselor, has observed "an increasing proliferation of antidepressants for children, in part due to the increasing pressure they are in to perform, at younger and younger ages. Children are no longer allowed to be children, more symbols of their parents' prosperity and of their parents' worth."[4]

When we insist that our children become who *we* need them to be, rather than who God intends them to be, we're not parenting, we're pushing. Our efforts become about us, not our children—and our children know it. One of two things usually happens: either we push them right out of our lives, or we push them right out of living, as vividly illustrated in the film *Dead Poets Society.*

In the movie, John Keating, played by Robin Williams, is an instructor at an elite boarding school for boys. He's determined to reach the hearts of his students through the education of their souls. He befriends them outside the classroom and challenges them within the classroom. He makes them think. He makes them hungry for more knowledge.

The father of Neil Perry, one of Keating's favorite students, cares only about his son's academic accomplishments. He can't see his son; all he sees is his own image in his son. He views education as a necessary means for his son to become the man he needs him to be—the next great physician. But Neil has an extraordinary gift for the stage, not medicine. His classmates are awed by his talent and encourage his interest in drama.

When Neil confronts his father, his dad uses guilt to manipulate Neil: "I've made a great many sacrifices to have you here, Neil, and you will not let me down."

"But, you've never asked me what I want."

"You have opportunities that I never even dreamed of. I am not going to let you—"

"But I've got to tell you what I feel," Neil interrupts.

In a low, firm voice his father replies, "If it's more of that acting business, you can forget that."

Knowing all too well that tone of voice, Neil concedes, "Yes, sir."

His father ends the conversation with a satisfying smile and a pat on the back, as he walks past his son, "Well, let's go to bed."

"But I was good. I was really good," Neil whispers to himself as he ambles down the hallway in despair.

If you've seen the film, you know the tragic ending: a young man pushed to suicide by his parent-centered father.

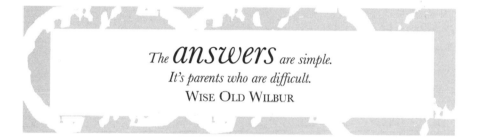

The ansωers are simple.
It's parents who are difficult.
WISE OLD WILBUR

Child-Centered Parents

Children raised in child-centered homes don't fare any better than those raised in parent-centered homes. Just ask TJ.

TJ was a handsome boy who had grown up in the church. He had everything a child could hope for: parents who loved each other, nice clothes, the latest gadgets, doting grandparents, a beautiful home in a wonderful neighborhood, and enrollment in a private Christian school.

But in eighth grade, signs of trouble began surfacing: a skirmish with a classmate at school, then an incident of mouthing off to a teacher, followed by suspicion of drug use . . . all with a rapidly declining attitude at home.

When he was in ninth grade, TJ was asked not to return to his school. For the next two years he moved from one school to another. Even so, when he turned sixteen, his parents gave him a new SUV. Somehow he graduated from high school. With the freedom of college came the real trouble. TJ was out of control—lost in a world of drugs.

I talked with him a few days after I had received a distraught phone call from his mom, "He's gone again. We don't know where he is. I'm terrified we've lost him forever this time." When I asked TJ about his life and his troubles, this is what he told me:

> I just wish my parents had told me what to do. They never did. It was always whatever I wanted to do. I know they were just trying to make me happy, but I made all the decisions. I hated that . . . what does a kid do with that? When they didn't know what to do, they gave me toys. All that stuff was just garbage. They piled it on till I couldn't take it anymore.

TJ needed parents, not indulgent gift givers. So did Robert.

Robert, a second grader, came home with my sons one Friday to spend the night. Shortly after they arrived, we headed for a nearby pond to fish from the pier, as we knew this was not an everyday occurrence for Robert. After ten minutes he announced, "This is boring. What can you do with a fish if you do catch it? My dad gave me money; let's go buy something."

We stopped fishing, but we didn't go to Wal-Mart; we headed home.

When I called the boys to supper, Robert came in with a decorated plastic container. When I asked the reason, he replied, "My mom sent it because she knows I won't eat anything else." Inside the container—a peanut butter and jelly sandwich with the edges sliced off, cut on the diagonal. I replaced his prepared plate with an empty plate. He requested a certain fruit drink that I didn't have, so he opted for no drink.

Don't get me started on Robert's bad manners, but it wasn't his fault; he had child-centered parents. Robert needed his parents to treat him as their son, rather than acting like one of his subjects. He was a classic example of what I affectionately call "aristobrats"—children treated like royalty.

Kids in a child-centered home are allowed to make decisions their parents should be making, the parents being more concerned with their kids' approval than their well-being. Child-centered parents often get caught in the indulgence trap: "If I just give my children enough, they will appreciate all that I've done and in return become wonderful, respectful children, because I've satisfied their desires." Unfortunately, the indulgence trap sucks you and your children in, leaving you drained and your children empty.

Regrettably, many parents seem caught in this trap. Take a look at the results from two questions in a recent poll by Time/CNN:

1. Are today's children more or less spoiled than children 10 or 15 years ago? Eighty percent of those who responded said *more.*

2. Are your own children spoiled or not spoiled? Sixty-eight percent of those who responded said *very/somewhat spoiled.*[5]

Our materialistic society makes it difficult not to spoil children, but regardless, if children are spoiled, their parents are the only ones to blame. The media and other parents may tell us that our children *need* a cell phone by age nine or that they *need* a television in their rooms (70 percent of third graders have a television in their rooms[6]), but ultimately the decision of what comes into our homes is up to us. Or at least it should be.

Parents who are overworked and overtired are often tempted to fall into the trap of buying things for their kids to make up for not being there. But this never works. The overindulgence of child-centered parents offers things rather than relationship, and this only makes matters worse. Just ask King Midas. Remember his story?

Midas was a hard-working, honest king who adored his daughter, Marygold, who loved nothing more than to spend time in the rose garden. In years past her father had shared his appreciation of the garden, teaching his daughter the complicated process of tending roses. But the more the king loved his daughter, the more he wanted to bequeath her all the gold in the world. He spent all his time thinking about how he could amass more gold rather than spending time with his daughter, all the while proclaiming it was for her he was working so hard.

One day a stranger offered to grant King Midas one request. The king requested that everything he touched would turn to gold. The next morning King Midas arose to find his wish had come true. Everything he touched turned to gold. *What can I do for Marygold with this gift?* he thought. The king ran to the garden and transformed his daughter's beloved flowers into pure gold. Soon the entire garden sparkled in the morning sun.

King Midas returned to the palace for breakfast. He seated himself at the table and waited for his daughter to join him. Suddenly, Marygold entered the dining hall, weeping uncontrollably.

"What is the matter?" cried her father.

As she held a golden flower before him, Marygold said, "This is the ugliest flower that ever grew! I ran to the garden to gather some roses for you this morning; all the beautiful roses that smelled so sweetly and were all the colors of the rainbow have turned this horrible golden-brown color."

Not able to stand her sorrow, King Midas embraced her before he realized what would happen when he touched her. "Marygold," he cried. But Marygold could not answer. She had become a golden statue, the victim of her father's desire for wealth.

Unlike what happens in real life, this children's tale ends well. The stranger returned and told Midas how he could rid himself of the "golden touch." Midas followed the instructions and restored his daughter and her garden to their fragile beauty. The only gold that King Midas ever desired to see again was the golden strands of his daughter's hair.

Like King Midas, indulgent parents fool themselves into believing their obsession with things is for the good of their children. But providing for your kids is much more than providing them with the latest electronic devices, name-brand clothes, and a car at sixteen. Children don't want *things* from their parents. They don't need the gold; they need you.

Keep in mind that overindulgence isn't just buying toys and things; it's also doing for kids what they should be doing for themselves.

Case in point. A one-sided "conversation" with an exasperated friend went something like this: "I don't know what I'm going to do with Maggie. I can't take her anymore, and I don't understand why she's the way she is." Without taking a breath, my friend continued, "I've done everything for this child. She's never had to do anything around here. I don't feel like I expect too much. Last night when I asked her to put her wet towels in the basket, not on the carpet, you would have thought I asked her to scrub the toilet! But the new problem is homework. She's decided it's too hard and doesn't want to try. She's in middle school . . . I can't do her homework for her anymore."

Can't do her homework *anymore?*

Kids need parents who will teach them age-appropriate life skills, whether it be tying their shoes, cleaning their rooms, or doing their homework. They need parents who will teach and watch and wait, parents who have the patience to allow their children to struggle just enough to learn a new skill.

The more we give our kids, the less they appreciate *us*, which leads to disrespect. To respect means to hold in high regard. We can't respect someone we do not appreciate. This was brought home to me several years ago when my sons were in elementary school. I found myself fussing at them for not being appreciative, after I had foolishly indulged them. One of the boys stopped me in my tracks: "Mom, when I grow up . . . I think my kids will love me more if I give them less."

When we give too much and expect too little, we end up with kids who are selfish and unappreciative. We're not training them to be independent; we're training them to be dependent on us. If we're not giving them the tools they need to stand on their own two feet, they'll soon need a crutch. What they choose to lean on varies greatly from one child to the next. TJ, a "good boy" from a "good home," found his crutch through a dependency on drugs. His rebellion against his parents was a loud, long "Stop, I can't take anymore!" Indulgence produces resentment, which leads to rebellion.

Neither the parent-centered parent nor the child-centered parent gives children what they need; they have, in fact, relinquished their responsibility to parent well. When parents carefully take on their parenting responsibility and focus on producing character in their children, their children flourish. Let's explore what's different about this third parenting style.

Character-Centered Parents

Mike and Lisa Conn are some of the most character-centered parents I know. The effectiveness of this parenting style can be seen in the lives of their three children.

Ali and her older sister, Ashley, both graduated from high school with top honors, earning scholarships to a great university. They don't drink or smoke, and they don't date boys who do.

Ali just returned from a dream trip for a college sophomore—six weeks in Europe. In order to afford the trip, she worked summers, vacations, and every chance in-between since she entered high school. Her parents helped with a small gift, but Ali paid her own way.

Both girls are popular, even though they're different from their peers. Their closets aren't filled with seldom-worn clothes. They don't own expensive sports cars or have the latest gadgets. Still they never complain—quite the contrary.

> *Many well-bred people* **neglect** *laying down any rules for the guidance of their children. . . . Parents owe it to their children and to society to instruct them how to be gentle, courteous, and above all, self-denying. Teach them to respect each other's rights, to enjoy their merry romp and innocent fun without hurting each other's feelings, or playing upon some weakness.*
> YOUTH'S EDUCATOR FOR HOME AND SOCIETY (1896)

Both girls have goals and a work ethic to reach those goals. They don't have to be entertained to be content. They command respect without trying because they're always ready to help a friend, regardless of inconvenience.

I've never witnessed girls who love their father the way these girls do. They not only love him, but they also respect his word. And their mother? She's best friend to both.

And Aimee, who's still at home? She's following in her older sisters' footsteps—destined to become another daughter who returns tenfold blessings to her parents.

What do character-centered parents do that is so different from parent-centered and child-centered parents? They have their priorities in the proper order. See if you don't agree.

1. *Character-centered parents parent with the end in mind.* They make decisions that are focused on the desired end result—children who respect God, others, and themselves. Stephen Covey, author of *The 7 Habits of Highly Effective People*, explains this concept well:

   > The *end* represents the *purpose* of your life. Until you can say what that purpose is, with assurance, then you just cannot direct your life in the manner that would bring you the greatest satisfaction. There are no shortcuts here. To engage in this habit, you need to

have a dream, define your own vision, and get into the practice of setting goals which will allow you to make measurable progress toward the dream . . . to re-align your efforts so that you will ultimately achieve your heart's desire.[7]

Character-centered parents accept the dream and challenge of raising respectful children, and they define that vision by choosing to focus on building their children's character above all other endeavors. Parenting with the end in mind is intentional, not accidental.

Mike and Lisa have done a beautiful job of establishing their home with the end in mind. Their two older girls have proven it.

2. *Character-centered parents look to God's principles for their instructions on how to parent.* They know they can't trust their own wits to raise their children, nor can they trust the so-called "child experts," since these "experts" have gotten our culture into parenting trouble in the first place. So they rely on the wisdom that comes from biblical teaching, not the knowledge from secular psychology books. (Our society has changed parenting approaches numerous times in the past two hundred years, but the Bible has remained unchanged for two thousand years.)

3. *Character-centered parents keep their promises.* I'm convinced that Matthew, the author of the first book in the New Testament, was talking to parents when he said, "Do not swear by your head, for you cannot make even one hair white or black. [Your children will do this for you.] Simply let your 'Yes' be 'Yes,' and your 'No,' 'No.'"[8] If our children trust us, they will obey us. This, in turn, leads them to respect us and, ultimately, God.

Keep in mind that kids make no distinction between a semiaffirmative answer and a promise. In other words:

* You say, "We'll see."

  Child hears: "It'll probably be OK. Sure."
  You meant: "Probably no, but I'll take another look at it."

* You say, "Honey, I'll have to think about it."

  Child hears: "Keep asking me; I'll probably give in."

25

You meant: "I can't decide now; I'm uncomfortable with the idea, but I need a good reason to say no."

A child cannot distinguish the gray in our answers because their world is black and white, right or wrong. As it should be. If you mean no, say, "No."

4. *Character-centered parents put God first, then their marriage, children, others, and finally themselves.* We all have our priorities, whether we're conscious of them or not. The decisions you make reveal your priorities. The consequences of your decisions either bring the devastation or preservation of your family.

The Character-Centered Parents' Priority List

God

Husband/Wife

Children

Others

Self

Most of us want to put ourselves first, but to do so guarantees disaster for our kids. Selfishness is at the root of our most disastrous parenting decisions. Take a moment to reflect back on the parent-centered dad who stole his daughter's innocence by taking her to that R-rated movie. This father put himself on top of the list rather than God, who would not have exposed a twelve-year-old to an R-rated movie. A character-centered dad would have taken his daughter home with the promise that he'd take her to see the children's movie she wanted to see another time.

Why do character-centered parents put their marriage before their kids? Because children need to know that their parents' love for each other is the foundation of their love for their children. Kids who know this grow up feeling secure. But when a parent claims to no longer love the other parent, the children lose the foundation of the parents' love for them. That's why divorce can be so destructive for children. Character-centered parents keep the marriage ahead of the children, others, and, above all, ahead of self!

Character-centered parents don't put other people's needs ahead of their children's. They understand that even good activities can be wrong if children suffer as a result of Mom or Dad's involvement. If supper comes from McDonald's three nights a week because of Mom's meetings, her priority list has gotten out of order. "Others" have moved above the children.

The list of priorities shown on the previous page must not be rearranged, or the family will suffer. When *God* is the head of the home, and you honor each other as *husband and wife*, the rest of the priority list will play out.

- You will be able to work together to train your *children*.

- You can reach out to *others* as a family.

- God will take care of each of *you*, for God honors the family that honors Him.

Your Child's Heart

A wounded twenty-year-old summarized the pitfalls of parent-centered and child-centered parenting better than I ever could. When asked what makes teenagers more miserable today than in past generations, she gave the following reply:

> Teenagers don't know who they are. They don't know what to believe in because their parents say one thing, but live another. You know, most parents today don't have good answers; they just put you off when you ask the big questions because they're still trying to figure out what's really important.
>
> Parents think their kids really want a lot of stuff. Maybe we do, but it's just a substitute for the real thing. Teenagers have to know they're number one with somebody. Most of the time my parents were so caught up in their own world, they didn't see how much I needed them. I wanted to be more important to Dad than his work. I wanted to be more important to Mom than her church friends. It's not so much time, as it is a heart thing. You know if it's there, and you know if it's not there. If you don't feel it from your parents, you're going to keep looking till you find it somewhere.

She nailed the truth, didn't she?

When I speak, I often draw the outline of a heart on a chalkboard as I pose the following question to my audience: "Today you have the opportunity to fill the empty heart of a child. What will you place in that heart?"

Regardless of the makeup of the audience, the answers are the same. We seem to agree, regardless of faith, socioeconomic standing, or race, that children need the following qualities:

Did you notice that respect is at the center of the heart? Just as it should be.

Now, take a long, hard look at the diagram. Why don't we see more young people filled with these attitudes and attributes? I believe it's because too many parents don't parent. They have neglected the education of their children's hearts.

If you choose to be a character-centered parent, you can fill your children's hearts with all they need to become all they were created to be. Helen Keller's words remind us that "Character cannot be developed in ease and quiet. Only through experience of trial and suffering can the soul be strengthened, vision cleared, ambition inspired, and success achieved."[9]

I'm not going to tell you it's easy, because it's not. But I want you to know it can be done.

Reality Check

Before moving on to the next chapter, consider your answers to these questions as you strengthen your resolve to raise respectful children in this disrespectful world:

1. What category of parenting best describes you?

   • Parent centered

   • Child centered

   • Character centered

2. Are your expectations for your children attainable?

3. What motivations are behind your dreams and aspirations for your children?

4. Do you sometimes find yourself pressuring your children to achieve a certain "success"?

5. Do you spend a lot of time and effort developing character in your children?

6. Have you made the firm decision that, no matter what, you will do your best to raise respectful children in this disrespectful world?

7. Are you optimistic, doubtful, or pessimistic about your decision?

8. How does your list of priorities compare to the one on page 26?

RAISING RESPECTFUL CHILDREN

Enroll in the School of Respect

MY TEN-YEAR-OLD SON, Boyce, folded his report card in half as he held it before my eyes. "Look, Mom, I made all As."

"Yes, you did!" I agreed. But when I unfolded the card to look at the right side, my glowing quickly turned to gloom. More than half of those little squares on the right were filled with ugly Us and even a U- rather than beautiful Ss. His card looked something like this:

Rigby						
Last Name						

Boyce	
First Name	

ACADEMICS							**CONDUCT/PERSONAL DEVELOPMENT**				
QUARTERS	1	2	AVG	3	4	AVG	QUARTERS	1	2	3	4
Reading	A						Practices Self-Disipline	U-			
Language	A						Respects Rights of Peers	U			
Spelling	A-						Is Respectful to Authority	U			
Social Studies	A						Observes School Rules	U			
Mathematics	A						Is Courteous	U			
Science	A						Is Dependable	U			
French	A-						Is Neat and Orderly	S			
Penmanship	A-						Conduct	U			

GRADING SCALE:
A=100–94 B=93–86 C=85-77 D=76-70 F=69–Below

REPORTING CODE:
S–Satisfactory N=Needs Improvement U=Unsatisfactory

When I flipped the card over, I found his teacher's comments: "Report card is wonderful . . . however, I want that conduct to improve. He says things without thinking. Sometimes his words hurt other people's feelings." Needless to say, Mrs. Manners was devastated.

The wise words of an educator I'd heard speak years before rang in my ears, "You can make all As and still flunk the school of life." If I didn't do something drastic, my son would flunk the school of life. Neither of my sons was going to learn respect or manners at school alone. They needed to learn these lessons first at home. I decided right then to enroll them in the School of Respect.

The best way to raise respectful kids is to enroll them in the School of Respect as soon as they are born. Babies come into this world with a need to be taught and trained. Their first understanding of respect comes from their interaction with their parents, even in the first months of life. Even if unspoken, they have questions that must be answered, and they naturally look to their parents for those answers.

The book of Proverbs instructs parents to: "Train a child in the way he should go."[1] The original Hebrew word for "train" is *chanak,* which means to initiate or discipline or dedicate.[2] "Way," or *derek,* means a course of life or mode of action.[3] So the original intent of this passage is: "Discipline a child for his course of life and the actions he should take."

Noah Webster understood this verse's true meaning. Peek into the pages of *Webster's* 1828 edition with me to find an excellent definition for *education*:

> The bringing up of a child with instruction . . . formation of manners. Education comprehends all that series of instruction and discipline which is intended to enlighten the understanding, correct the temper, and form the manners and habits of youth, and fit them for usefulness in their future stations.[4]

Parents who enroll their children in the School of Respect are undergirding their children's formal education, because respect lies at the foundation of success. In an interesting study a few years ago, Albert Siegel, a noted researcher at Stanford University concluded:

When it comes to rearing children, every society is only twenty years away from barbarism. Twenty years is all we have to accomplish the task of civilizing the infants who are born into our midst each year. These savages know nothing of our language, our culture, our religion, our values, our customs of interpersonal relations. The infant is totally ignorant about . . . respect, decency, honesty, customs, conventions, and manners.[5]

A bit harsh, perhaps, but a point well taken. God has given us twenty years to educate our children's hearts and to train them to respect God, others, and self so that they can become respectful members of society who help, rather than hurt, the world.

The School of Respect

The School of Respect has four distinct stages, according to age: *Tots* (birth to two), *Tykes* (ages three to five), *Tweens* (ages six to twelve), and *Teens* (ages thirteen to nineteen). Each stage has a different developmental goal, and parents need to utilize specific training methods to help their children meet each of those goals. During each stage, children have two critical questions, which the parents need to answer. Parents who successfully answer these two questions give their kids a vital part of the preparation they need to become respectful, responsible young adults.

The School of Respect		
Stage	**Goal**	**Training**
Tots: Birth to two	Trust	Routine
Tykes: Three to five	Security	Recognition
Tweens: Six to twelve	Obedience	Relationship
Teens: Thirteen to nineteen	Self-Respect	Responsibility

Let's take a closer look at each of these four stages.

Stage 1: Building Trust in Tots through Routine

Babies come into the world totally dependent on their parents to meet their every need—physical, mental, social, and emotional. We meet our babies' physical needs by feeding, bathing, and clothing them; their mental needs by providing a stimulating environment; and their social needs through providing safe interaction with others. We meet their emotional needs by answering two key questions.

Question 1: Can I Trust You?

During this stage your tot is striving to learn trust, his first developmental goal. What training method will help you answer this question for your child? *Routine.* If you provide a routine for your tot, you will be answering this critical question with a resounding yes. Your tot learns to trust you when you put him on a schedule for feeding and sleeping.

I realize that feeding and sleeping schedules are sometimes criticized as being parent centered, but look at it from your baby's perspective. If he knows that he will be fed and put to bed at the same time every day, your baby doesn't have to become distressed before someone feeds him or cranky before someone puts him down for a nap. He learns he can trust you to meet his needs, and he can relax in his environment.

My own experience has convinced me that this is so. When our twin sons were born, I was fortunate to have an old-fashioned pediatrician who stressed the importance of scheduled feedings, and with his help I had the boys on a four-hour feeding schedule six weeks after they were born.

Outings were a treat for all of us because the boys were content; they knew their needs would be met. Each day we followed a routine, and this made their lives secure and our lives serene. (Well, most days—don't think there weren't difficult days.)

The day began with breakfast, a nap, then playtime. After they ate lunch, I put them down for an extended nap, then took them on an afternoon stroll. When we arrived back home, they had more playtime. The day closed with supper, baths (which became playtime when they were toddlers), down time, and bedtime. As much as possible we did these things at the same time every day.

When we provide routines for our kids and follow that routine day by day, we are slowly answering the first critical question of this stage in the School of Respect. Through our routines we are showing our children that, yes, they can trust us to take care of their needs—and we are helping them take their first step toward respecting authority.

Parents also build trust by answering this next question.

Question 2: Who's in Charge?

As I mentioned earlier, I've often wondered if the writer who penned the words, "Let your 'Yes' be 'Yes,' and your 'No,' 'No'" was thinking of parents—more specifically, parents of a toddler. Tots want to know, "Who's in charge?" (And they are hoping you are, because they know they don't have a clue what to do.) That's why they say the word *no* so often. They want to know if you are in charge and will tell them what they have to do.

This is why I disagree with the notion of removing accessories from tabletops when couples start having kids. Accessories provide parents opportunities to teach their kids that the parent—not the child—is in charge, that the parents' "no" overrides the children's "no." If you'll patiently take on this battle at home, your child will be welcome in anyone's home, because she'll know not to touch.

Establishing that you are in charge will go a long way toward making bedtime a more enjoyable experience when your tot turns two. Bedtime is one of the early testing grounds of your authority. But if you have already demonstrated that your "no" means no, your child will be less likely to wage a major battle with you every night when you try to put her to bed.

Your tot's bedtime routine aids in answering this "Who's in charge?" question. Every night when you put her to bed—read her a bedtime story, snuggle, give plenty of good-night kisses and hugs, and pray with her as you tuck her in, safe and sound. No exceptions. Such a routine will make it far less likely that she will get up fifteen times during the night or end up sleeping in the hallway outside your door.

If we could decode what our tots mean when they are wailing, we might hear, "Daddy, I'm going to see if you *really* mean what you say" or "Mommy, I'm going to scream, just to see if you really love me." This is why I cannot stress strongly enough the importance of establishing routines during the first two years of your children's lives. Routines build trust, and if your children trust you as infants, they'll feel more secure as tykes.

Stage 2: Developing Security in Tykes through Recognition

Justin stood on top of the giant slide at Bayberry Park as a confident five-year-old superhero preparing for a death-defying feat. Scanning the area, he spotted his heroine who was engaged in a deep conversation with a friend.

"Moooooommmm," he shouted. No response.

He tried again, "Mom, Mom, Mooooooooooooommmmm . . . watch this!"

"OK, honey, I'm watching," Mom yelled back, continuing her conversation.

Still not satisfied, he tried one more time, "Mom, you're not watching!"

"Honey, I'm watching, I'm watching," she fired back in exasperation.

Justin finally made the big leap down the slide, hoping Mom was watching. When he reached the bottom, he looked at Mom, who wasn't watching. Instead of running to her, he ran from her.

Please . . . don't make the mistake of this mom.

In this second stage kids discover the world—people, places, and things. They don't want to miss any of it, but they need a sense of security to be able to engage with their exciting new world.

How do we help our tykes develop a sense of security? Through the training method of *recognition*. Parents can use recognition to answer the two key questions of this stage.

Question 1: Are You Watching Me?

Between the ages of three and five, your tyke needs to know you're watching him. If he discovers you are watching, his trust in you will grow. But if he discovers you are not watching him, whatever trust has been established up to this point will erode. He needs to know that you will be there to protect him if he needs protection. If you watch him now, in time, he will stop asking you to watch him because he will have developed the security he needs to explore the world unafraid.

When one of my sons was four, he managed to escape the watchful eyes of his parents and grandparents and wander through the halls of the American Museum of Natural History in New York. We found him clinging to a handrail, mesmerized by a display of prehistoric creatures. When I knelt down beside him, he looked at me with tear filled eyes of gratitude, and said, "I'm OK, Mom; I wasn't scared. I knew you would find me." At that moment I knew my son felt secure . . . maybe a little bit too secure!

When children know we are watching out for them, they feel protected. This frees them to be more giving to others. For instance, a four-year-old who knows her parents are there for her has the security to be unselfish, to share with her playmates, and to help them. She has the freedom to show concern for others because she's not consumed with watching out for herself—a beautiful by-product of security.

Recognition also helps you answer the second question of this stage.

Question 2: Who Do I Belong To?

Pointing to her chest, four-year-old Rebecca asked her mom, "Who am I?"

"You're Rebecca. Rebecca Thompson."

"Not my name. Who am I on the inside?" Rebecca questioned.

Her mom answered, "You're God's child. He placed you in our family to be loved and cared for."

When her daughter asked, "Who am I?" Rebecca's mom seized a teachable moment, an opportunity to recognize who her daughter was, thus giving her security. She went on to tell her daughter about the day she was born, as well as other anecdotes from her days as an infant.

This wise mom was answering her daughter's real question: *who do I belong to?* Children have a deep need to belong, to fit in. They need to be recognized as part of the family circle, and when they are recognized as such, they develop security.

Because children this age need to be accepted—to belong—they're eager to please. Hasn't your young child asked, "Can I help?" I know it's easier to unload the dishwasher yourself than to allow a four-year-old to help, but when you let your child help with chores, you are giving her an opportunity to feel a part of the family. Kids this age can do simple household chores, such as helping with dinner, hanging up clothes, putting wet towels in the laundry basket, and picking up their toys. When they accomplish such tasks, they begin to feel a sense of value and worth. They begin to think:

- "My family needs me to do my part."

- "They can't make it without me."

- "I want to help my family as much as they help me."

When children know they're valued members of the family, it gives them a deep sense of security. When they reach adolescence, this security creates a firm foundation for them to stand on as they branch out from the family during the tumultuous tween years.

Stage 3: Helping Tweens Learn Obedience through Relationship

Children who have developed trust in their early years and gained a sense of security in their tyke years are in a position to master the developmental goal of the tween years: obedience. Obedience, which is critical at this stage when children are extending beyond the boundaries of the family, is a learned response. We aren't born with a natural inclination to obey. Quite the contrary, we're born with an inclination to disobey.

What, then, causes children to obey their parents? What training method will help your children learn obedience? Your *relationship* with them. During this stage your children want to know if you really love them, and they will test you on this question, over and over again.

Question 1: Do You Really Love Me?

Tweens desperately need to be loved. This is an extension of needing to belong. You must be the one to satisfy the need behind this question, because kids obey the person who loves them. If your tween doesn't know you love him, he will search in the wrong places for someone who does.

Keep in mind that a tween's disobedience is often a test of your love. A ten-year-old is most likely not going to ask in words, "Do you really love me?" Instead, he asks through his actions. How can you let your children know you *really* love them during the tween years, cultivating obedience rather than disobedience? By:

1. *Listening to your tweens.* Think of the E. F. Hutton commercial—when your children talk, you'd better listen. Just as your three-year-

old needed you to watch him, your nine-year-old needs you to listen when he speaks to you. And I don't mean the "Uh-huh" kind of listening. Listen to your tweens with all your being. Listen with your eyes. Listen with your ears. Listen with your heart. When you're too tired to listen, listen anyway. If you will listen to tweens when they're nine, they'll obey you when they're sixteen.

2. *Telling your tweens no when no is better than yes.* Scripture teaches that discipline shows children they are loved. When you love enough to say no, you are showing your kids you care about who they are and who they become.

   Here are some ways to discipline with love:

   * *Speak in a firm voice without sarcasm.* Sarcasm conveys disgust, not love. Use of sarcasm teaches your child to use the same tone with you in the teen years.

   * *Say to your child, "I love you too much to allow you to* (go to the late show with friends, go to a party without parents present, or be disrespectful of your sister)."

   * *Don't berate your child, but correct the misdeed.* You know those words that still haunt you from your childhood, "Why aren't you smart enough to listen?" and "I don't care what you think." Instead, say, "I know you're smart, so I know you can choose to listen. When you choose to listen, we'll talk." "I hear your viewpoint, but I will not allow you to spend the night at your friend's house without my calling her mom or dad. It's your choice."

   * *Don't lose your temper.* Instead, count—to five hundred if necessary. Don't laugh . . . I started counting one afternoon when I lost my patience with my sons during a long car ride. When I reached one hundred, the boys asked how high I was going to count. When I said to five hundred, they promised to settle down if I would just stop counting!

   * *Turn a negative situation into a positive one.* Remind your child that she is too smart or too talented or too old to act in an

inappropriate way. Acknowledge your tween's value, and she'll live up to your expectations. When your tween forgets to do her chores, say, "I'm counting on you to do your chores, because I know you're old enough to handle the responsibility."

Your tweens will be assured of your love when you listen to their ramblings. They will accept your discipline when it comes from your heart.

Not only do tweens need to know their parents love them, they also need to know their parents are real.

Question 2: Are You Real?

Just as tweens will obey the person who truly loves them, they'll obey the person they can look up to. If we expect obedience from our tweens, we must be authentic persons our children can trust above all others.

Your tween daughter is growing up in a time when there are few worthy role models. In fact, very few people in your tween's world are real—they're not who they're pretending to be. Musicians are lip-synching, fashion models are airbrushed, and sports stars are cheating. Your tween is looking for authenticity in someone—and that someone needs to be you.

Keep in mind that children learn more from what we do than from what we say. This is particularly true during the tween years, when we parents can no longer fool our kids. (Not that we really ever could.)

They're watching our every move and seeing if our actions match our words. An Old Testament passage gives parents instruction in this area, "Be careful, and watch yourselves closely so that you do not forget the things your eyes have seen or let them slip from your heart as long as you live. Teach them to your children and to their children after them."[6]

If you're not authentic, your children will rebel in disrespect toward you and, often, toward society. Children respect parents who are respectable. If you expect from yourself that which you expect from your children, you'll all pass this test. Be the person you want your child to become. We teach what we know, but we reproduce who we are.

What should your authenticity look like to your tween?

1. *Be the same on the inside as you appear on the outside.* In other words, you can't be one person out in the world and another person behind the doors of your home.

2. *Don't say one thing and do another.* Drinking one too many on Saturday nights disqualifies you in the eyes of your tween to discuss the hazards of drinking.

3. *Be honest in your business dealings.* Children in this age bracket listen and watch you more intently than your supervisor at work. They need you to be the most honest person they know.

4. *Don't show any hypocrisy.* This will lose your tween's respect faster than any other weakness. Are you in church when the doors open, but never open the Bible for study? Do you pray in public, but not with your family?

Your tweens are more likely to obey when you meet their need for love and authenticity. If your tween is being disobedient, revisit these two questions and check your heart to see if you've given your child satisfying answers. It could be that you've let your guard down in an area. It's not too late; kids are more than willing to give parents another chance. They want us to succeed in raising them to be respectful. They need us to succeed.

A tween who turns thirteen with an obedient heart is ready for the final stage in the parenting process, the development of self-respect.

Stage 4: Teaching Self-Respect through Responsibility

Teens are searching—for truth, for answers to life, and for themselves. During this final stage the disrespectful world can thwart you in your goal of raising a respectful teenager.

Your challenge is to help your teenager develop self-respect, because in so doing his questions will be answered and his search will end in success. Teens with healthy self-respect discover that the secret to finding themselves is to find satisfaction in making wise choices and in offering respect to others.

If you want to help your teenagers develop self-respect, you must instill the understanding that:

- The reasons we do what we do are more important than what we do

- We were put here to serve, not to be served

- What we give is more important than what we are given

- Through humility we gain confidence

What's the training method that can help you teach your teen self-respect? *Responsibility.* During this stage you need to begin moving the responsibility for your teen's development from your shoulders to his. The more responsibility you give your teen, the more opportunities he'll have for success and the building of self-respect. With each accomplishment your teen's self-respect grows. George Bernard Shaw understood this principle of building self-respect when he said, "No man who is occupied in doing a very difficult thing, and doing it very well, ever loses his self-respect."[7] Teens with self-respect know there are consequences for their choices and are ready to accept the challenge of being in charge.

Let's look at the first question we need to help our teens answer.

Question 1: Who Am I?

More than eleven thousand teenagers, ages twelve to seventeen, were surveyed as part of the National Longitudinal Study of Adolescent Health to determine which factors were most helpful in preventing risky behavior, such as substance abuse, early sexual involvement, teen pregnancy, violence, and suicide.[8] The findings reinforced a fundamental belief of character-centered parents: teenagers who have the presence of a parent before school, after school, at dinnertime, and bedtime were less likely to engage in risky behaviors than those without parental connectedness.

In a radio interview about the study, lead researcher, Dr. Michael Resnick, commented:

> I think that fundamentally what the study did is to challenge a widespread myth that we have in the United States, which is that once a child has moved from early childhood into adolescence, what parents say or think or do or hope or dream for their child, somehow no longer makes a difference. And many parents in this country . . . feel that once a kid has reached

adolescence, they must surrender that child to the peer group—and in fact that is not the case. We found that across the board in aggregate for our kids that sense of closeness and caring with parents, including for older adolescents, was a very important determinant of health and well being.[9]

Larry Crabb calls this "connecting"[10] and says that parents must make a heart connection to enable their children to find themselves. Your teen's greatest hope of answering the question, "Who am I?" comes from her connection with you. Her teen years are the time in her life when she must know there's nothing she can do to make you love her more and nothing she can do to make you love her less. Your unconditional love and faith in her enables her to become confident in knowing herself.

I know the attitudes you see in teens may lead you to believe that your teen doesn't need you anymore, but it's just the opposite. Your teen needs your presence now more than ever. Teens have so much to discover about themselves, and you need to be the one to guide your teen and be there for him when she makes mistakes. Your goal is to enable your teen to face the world with enough self-respect to thrive in it!

Help your child answer the question of who he is by emphasizing that the choices we make determine who we become. For example:

1. *Allow your child to experience consequences of poor choices.* For example, rather than insisting your sixteen-year-old go to bed at 10:00 on Friday night before a big Saturday-morning soccer game, allow him to choose his own bedtime. When he lets his team down because he's too tired to play his best, he'll learn how to set priorities.

2. *Allow mistakes to mold character.* For example, let's say your seventeen-year-old son decides to mud ride with friends on private property. You find out about it, and you know he destroyed the grass that was just beginning to sprout. Talk with him about this, and require that he apologize to the neighbor and make restitution. Go with him to apologize to the owners of the property and to inform the owner that he will pay for the damaged sod to be replaced. (You will need to work with your teen for how he will come up with the funds for this, of course!)

3. *Ask thought-provoking questions.* These can help you transfer the responsibility for your teen's maturing to him.

- What do you believe about premarital sex? (Teens know your opinion, but have you asked their opinion?)

- What are your goals for yourself . . . I know what Mom and Dad would like to see you accomplish, but what do *you* want to accomplish?

- What's more important to you, character or money?

Thirty-Six Ways to Cultivate a House of Respect

1. Pray together.
2. Say, "You're precious."
3. Tuck 'em in bed.
4. Hug, hug, and hug.
5. Say, "I love your eyes."
6. Sing, "Good morning."
7. Sing, "Good night."
8. Cut toast into heart shapes.
9. Say, "I love seeing your face every morning."
10. Tuck a love note in a lunchbox or a briefcase.
11. Have patience, patience, patience.
12. Look, learn, and love.
13. Put yourself in the other fellow's shoes.
14. Speak as respectfully to your spouse as you do to your boss.
15. Fly a kite together.
16. Love your kids enough to discipline.
17. Listen with your heart.
18. Show your kids how much you love your wife.
19. Show your kids how much you love your husband.
20. Draw a smiley face with syrup on your child's pancakes.
21. Give a backrub without being asked.
22. Polish your spouse's shoes.
23. Pray together.
24. Give something to every person who asks for help.
25. Preach less; love more.
26. Offer to read your child a book before you're asked.
27. Listen with your eyes.
28. Call just to say, "I love you."
29. Answer questions.
30. Say, "I'm sorry."
31. Clean your spouse's car.
32. Polish your child's bicycle.
33. Write a letter to your child, and send it through the mail.
34. Say, "Thank you."
35. Watch *their* favorite TV show.
36. Pray together.

- How's your relationship with God? (The journey of self-discovery for your teen begins with you and ends with God. Ultimately, your teen must decide for himself if he will receive God's reconciliation through Jesus Christ. You can show the way by your own walk of faith.)

This list could go on forever. See that this kind of dialogue between you and your child never stops. As your relationship role shifts from authority figure to friend, these conversations can continue to deepen.

I can't overemphasize the need to stay connected to your teen. You must be available to listen when your teens need to talk to you, not just when you need to talk to them. Talking is easy; listening is hard. If you'll wait until teens ask you for your opinion, they're more likely to hear your answer. During this time of their self-discovery, your opinions can have a greater impact on their self-image and building of their self-respect than our society wants you to believe.

Now let's look at the second question of this stage.

Question 2: Can I Be in Charge?

Our culture no longer offers absolute truth. Instead, it says that whatever feels good is good and right. While *we* may know that just because something feels good doesn't mean it's right, ultimately our kids need to learn this lesson for themselves.

It's hard for parents to give teenagers responsibility for dealing with their own problems, because often the consequences of their behavior might be embarrassing or uncomfortable. But this is another great gift you can give your teen—the gift of growing up. As Henry Ward Beecher once said, "You cannot teach a child to take care of himself unless you will let him take care of himself."[11] So give your teen more responsibility; just be careful not to give too much too soon. Giving a teen too much responsibility too fast is as dangerous as giving a two-year-old a butcher knife and saying, "Now, don't cut yourself." When parents give teens too much responsibility, they set kids up to fail and perhaps to put them in danger. So give teens appropriate responsibility, and give it one step at a time.

Here are some ideas for how you can help your teen succeed at being in charge of his life:

1. *Put teens in charge of developing their own talents.* Up until now you have controlled the practice schedule; now it's time to relinquish that control so your teen reaps the rewards of a job well done, as he develops the self-discipline to practice.

2. *If you haven't given cooking lessons yet, this is the time to start.* Build your teen's confidence in the kitchen by having him prepare supper one night a week. (Teens need to learn this life skill before they leave home.)

3. *Ask your teen's opinion on current events.* Engage in conversations about politics. Discuss the candidates and the issues during election season. Prepare your teen for the day she will cast a ballot.

4. *Encourage decision making.* Rather than telling your fifteen-year-old that it's time to do homework, remind him that the rule of the house is no television before homework is completed. Let him make the decision as to when he'll do his homework. Enforce the rule, but let him choose to skip his favorite TV show because he chose not to do his homework before the program started.

5. *When mistakes are made, don't rescue your teen; instead, help your child resolve the problem.* Discuss options to rectify a mistake. She'll never be able to take charge of her own life until she learns to resolve conflicts and solve problems on her own.

6. *Help teens develop goals, and determine a method to accomplish those goals, and then step back and watch.* Set aside a Saturday at the beginning of ninth grade to discuss your child's goals for high school. Write down the goals regarding such things as: grade point average, class emphasis, extracurricular activities, and church and community involvement. Assess how much time it will take to participate in each activity. Point out that to do one thing well is much better than to just participate in several things. Encourage your teen to use the goal sheet as a guide for decision making.

7. *Wait to be asked your opinion.* Don't offer unsolicited advice, unless there's danger.

8. *Remind your teens that God is in charge of us all.* I did this by having my sons read a few verses from the book of Proverbs every day before they left for high school. Yes, it was hard to do this every day, but the practical words found in God's Word helped to guide the boys' thinking during the day.

Graduation from the School of Respect

Your child's teen years are the culmination of all you've worked hard to accomplish until now. If there's trouble in the teen years, the breakdown probably started years earlier. Disrespectfulness comes from disappointment— not because a teen didn't get the things he wanted, but because he didn't get the things he needed to fill his heart with wisdom and respect.

Our children need us to have strong relationships with them, and they need us to be role models they can trust. If we understand the questions our children are asking, we can give the guidance they need to enter the world.

The School of Respect		
Stage	**Goal**	**Training**
Tots: Birth to two Can I trust you? Who's in charge?	*Trust*	*Establish Routines* Set a schedule Be the parent
Tykes: Three to five Are you watching me? Who do I belong to?	*Security*	*Offer Recognition* Pay attention Show ownership
Tweens: Six to twelve Do you really love me? Are you real?	*Obedience*	*Build Relationship* Be a good listener Be authentic
Teens: Thirteen to nineteen Who am I? Can I be in charge?	*Self-Respect*	*Give Responsibility* Enable self-discovery Transfer accountability

While there are no guarantees with parenting—for children ultimately make their own choices—don't ever forget that your children will benefit from your example as much as from your training:

- If you treat your spouse with respect, your children are more likely to respect each of you and follow that pattern in their relationships.

- If you manage your money well, your children will learn the value of a dollar.

- If you appreciate people of all races, your children will be more likely to grow up without prejudice.

- If you handle losing well, your children will be equipped to lose well too.

- If you can laugh at your own mistakes, your children will better be able to laugh at their imperfections.

- If you accept tough jobs as a challenge to be overcome, your children will be better equipped to fight their way through to complete their assignments.

- If you choose not to drink and drive, your children will most likely model your behavior.

Respect for parents, God, and others becomes respect for self and results in a respectful young adult. Are you doubtful you can do it? Don't be. Keep reading . . . you can raise children who graduate with honors from the School of Respect . . . you just need to be a willing coach!

Reality Check

Before moving on to the next chapter, consider your answers to these questions as you strengthen your resolve to raise respectful children in this disrespectful world:

1. What is more valuable to you?

   - Your children's character

   - Your children's grades

2. Have you answered the questions for your children in each stage of the School of Respect?

3. Do you sometimes brush your children off when they're trying to get your attention, especially when you're busy? How do you think they interpret this?

4. Are chores around the house just something to do (an option), or are they necessary responsibilities for your children as members of the family?

5. If your children viewed God's love through you, would it be unconditional, patient, always trusting, slow to anger (1 Corinthians 13:4–7)? What do they see in you?

6. In the past, has your "no" meant an absolute no, or "sometimes," "maybe," "depends," or even "yes"?

7. Are you giving your children opportunities to serve others?

8. Have you been attempting to demand respect from your children rather than commanding respect from them? Are you ready to change your ways if needed?

Stress Purpose, Not Performance

IN 2003 A STORY OUT OF PARIS shocked the sports world. Colonel Christophe Fauviau, a demanding military father, "aided" his sixteen-year-old son, Maxime, on the tennis court by spiking the water bottles of his son's opponents with tranquilizers. One opponent lost his life in a car accident following his match because he fell asleep at the wheel; another was hospitalized. The colonel's son was a good tennis player, but he was not headed for international fame, while his younger sister was set for stardom as one of the most talented young players in France; her career was now in serious jeopardy because of the charges against her father.

A friend of Maxime's told a reporter, "I don't think it prejudges the colonel's case to say he is a stubborn man, convinced that officialdom was getting in the way of his children's future. He couldn't accept that Maxime was just a nice boy and not much more than an average regional player."[1]

This is an extreme example, but every week thousands of parents sit on the sidelines or at the dinner table, pushing their children to be Number One, no matter the cost. Sadly, these parents are not concerned about who their children will become; they are only concerned about their own dreams being fulfilled through their kids.

Janine Bempechat, associate professor of human development at

Wheelock College, has done extensive work in the area of adolescent development. She has concluded that:

> The overriding concern parents have in setting expectations is their children's future success. But those expectations can have a negative effect if parents don't teach children the lessons they need to negotiate life. It's those life lessons—not academic knowledge or recreational skills, but qualities like diligence, perseverance, and responsibility—that will have the greatest effect on their lives. Parents need to remember that making sure their children acquire those skills is more important in the long run than whether a child gets an A on a report card or wins a swimming meet.[2]

Parents who want to raise respectful children need to pay attention to these words. Before we attempt to help our kids in their endeavors, we need to step back and examine our motives. We've got a tough question to ask ourselves that will determine if we are inspiring our kids out of a heart of love or if we are pushing them out of a heart filled with selfish ambition.

> *It's not about* ***winning***;
> *it's the joy of competition and being blessed*
> *with the opportunity to do what I love.*
> *I've never been one to project myself as Number One—*
> *I just go out and do the best that I can with what God has given me.*
> COACH PAYTON JORDAN

Define Your Goal

Ask yourself these defining questions: Do I want my child to be Number One? Or do I want my child to be the best he can be? In other words, don't ask what you want your child to do; instead, ask who you want your child to become. The answers to these questions will determine in which direction you'll lead and how you'll lead.

There's a stark contrast between the choices. One is about performance; the other, purpose. Take a look at the chart below as you ponder your answer:

Number One	vs.	The Best You Can Be
Success		Significance
Short-term		Long-term
Room for compromise		No room for compromise
Covers mistakes		Rectifies mistakes
Gives up		Perseveres
Competes with others		Competes with self
Self-centered		Others-centered
Receives awards		Receives rewards

Parents who want their kids to be Number One focus on what their kids do, on their performance. The goal is short-term—win this match, win first place, be class valedictorian—with little thought for what kind of adults the children will become. Parents who push their kids to be Number One often push so intensely that some kids are willing to cover up their mistakes and compromise to ensure they make it to the top. Others burn out or give up.

According to Dr. Michelle Kees of the University of Michigan:

We see middle-school children who are already worrying if their grades are good enough for college, and teens entering high school whose primary focus is their college application. It's no longer about volunteering in order to make a difference, it's volunteering so that their college application looks different. It's no longer about taking achievement tests to show what you know; it's to show where you are in the class. And this emphasis certainly has to have an impact on children.

The drive to succeed should be in balance with a child's capabilities. We see some adolescents who are burning out. In the middle of their sophomore, junior, or senior year, their interest in school dissipates, their focus and concentration and drive start to fade. We see average students who are pressured to achieve above and beyond what they're capable of, or where their best interest lies.[3]

Those kids who don't drop out often grow up looking at life as a competition that they *have* to win. Worst of all, kids who grow up being told that winning is the only thing are more likely to grow up to become driven, self-centered adults. Sure, they may win awards, but these are fleeting, as their hearts are not full of the qualities needed to negotiate life—diligence, perseverance, respect for self and others, and responsibility, to name a few.

But character-centered parents who want their children to be the best they can be are concerned about helping their children live up to their purpose. What's their purpose? Living up to their God-given potential. As we've discussed earlier, who your children become should be more important than what they do.

Jesus is the greatest example of someone who lived with purpose, who reached His potential. In the Garden of Gethsemane He reached His potential to become the Savior of the world when He confessed, "Not my will, but thine, be done."[4] He reached the pinnacle of His purpose for walking among us when He went to the cross to save us from eternal separation from God. Jesus lived with the end in mind.

Character-centered parents make decisions with the end in mind— raising their children to become respectful adults who reach their God-given potential—so they encourage their children to correct their mistakes and rectify their wrongs. They inspire their kids to keep striving to reach their full potential and to persevere in the face of setbacks.

Kids raised with this kind of parenting are more likely to grow up to become adults who reach out to the world and make a difference in the lives of others. Their hearts are full of the "right stuff"—a long-lasting reward.

Never forget that your children are a part of you. They know the real you. They know your motives. They know if you're proud they tried their best, even though they weren't the best player on the team, or if you're disappointed because they're not like "Jimmy," who's faster and quicker. They know if winning matters more to you than their best effort.

"Winning isn't everything; it's the only thing" may have worked on the football field for the Green Bay Packers and Vince Lombardi, but it's a poor philosophy of life—and it certainly doesn't belong in the home. If winning is the only thing that matters to you, you may produce winners on the field but lose them off the field.

An Important Life Lesson

Several years ago I watched with great interest a high-school track coach at a state meet. The incident I witnessed serves as a reminder of the importance of keeping your focus on competing with yourself, not on your competition. The state championship rested on the outcome of the final race. As the runners neared the finish line, the lead runner made the serious mistake of glancing over his left shoulder and then his right. As he turned his head back to look ahead, the runner in the left lane leaned into the rope to take the race. The second-place finisher was devastated. Afterward the coach took him aside to have a private chat, which is impossible in the middle of a track stadium. The conversation went something like this:

COACH: Son, how many times have I told you, never take your eye off the mark. It doesn't matter what the other runners are doing. You're out there to run your best, regardless of what anyone else is doing.

RUNNER: But, Coach, I needed to know where my competition was.

COACH: Why?

RUNNER: Why? 'Cause . . . um . . . um . . . I don't know why.

COACH: Exactly . . . that's because it doesn't matter. It only matters how well you're running. If you concentrate on beating yourself, you don't have to worry about the competition.

Everyone present that day learned a life lesson—it doesn't matter what anyone else is doing. You're not competing with your neighbors. Your children aren't competing with the other kids in their class. Motivational speaker Zig Ziglar urges, "What you get by achieving your goals is not as important as what you become by achieving your goals."[5]

If you've raised your kids to be the best they can be, they are on their way to fulfilling their purpose, which is the ultimate way to help them "feel good about themselves," as we so often hear today. Rather than stressing performance, stress purpose. Help your children discover the reason they're here so that they can live up to their God-given potential.

How to Stress Purpose, Not Performance

God created each of your children with talents, abilities, and a unique personality to form a one-of-a-kind human being who can make a difference in this world. Your job as parent is to help your kids become their best selves, so they can fulfill their God-given purpose. Here are some suggestions to get you started.

Help Kids Uncover Their Strengths and Weaknesses

It's not always easy to uncover the strengths and weaknesses of your children. Make an effort in the early years to offer opportunities for exploration of the gifts that God has given your children. They can't always identify their strengths—that's why you must be intentional in looking for opportunities that enable them to find their interests:

- *Expand your children's world as much as possible.* The more your children visit museums, the better. We lived in New York City when the boys were four years old. There were days we stayed in the Metropolitan Museum from opening to closing. My sons have an appreciation of art that far exceeds most of my friends' interest or knowledge.

- *Expose them to good books.* Read a long classic, little by little, when your children are young. You'll fill their minds with possibilities and dreams of other places.

- *Read biographies* of people from many walks of life, from great artists to statesmen to missionaries to military generals, folks that made a difference in their fields and in the world.

- *Spend time in the great outdoors.* Watch how your children react. Are they comfortable sleeping under the stars or fearful? At home with the sounds of the woods or ready to go home as soon as you get there?

- *Encourage your kids to get a taste of many different activities before they settle into one or two.* It's OK for elementary-school children to try all the sports their school offers or to try playing a variety of musical instruments. Once they reach fourth or fifth grade, they begin to zero in on their areas of greatest interest. It's now time to settle on one or two activities per school year.

- *Involve them in craft activities and art projects.* Such activities will reveal any hidden artistic talent. Does your child enjoy the easy projects, or does she prefer a challenge? Does she become easily frustrated, or does she have an abundance of patience to complete a project?

- *Support their interests.* If your child enjoys art, set up an art corner in your home to encourage the budding artist. If your child enjoys nature, enroll him in programs that offer outdoor activities.

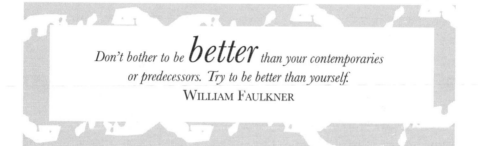

*Don't bother to be **better** than your contemporaries or predecessors. Try to be better than yourself.*
WILLIAM FAULKNER

As you provide your kids with opportunities like the ones above, look for a pattern to emerge. What kinds of things is each child interested in? In what areas does each excel? What things give each child joy?

Although it is never a good idea to compare your children, looking at their differences can reveal their individual strengths. I was blessed with an ongoing study in my home through my identical twin sons. It was fascinating to watch Chad's leadership skills as he tended to overpower Boyce much of the time. Boyce, on the other hand, displayed the qualities of a good negotiator as he was willing to compromise for the sake of peace. Chad had a strong eye for color and proportion along with a keen mathematical sense. Boyce was a highly creative thinker and problem solver.

Because I had observed these qualities in my sons, I steered Chad toward architecture, which would allow him to use his sense of design and analysis. I encouraged Boyce to pursue entrepreneurship so he could enjoy his gift of creative thinking.

So what fields did they choose in college? Chad earned a degree in economics and obtained a commercial real-estate license. Boyce earned a business degree in entrepreneurship. Good matches for both.

God has blessed your kids with specific talents and gifts to fulfill a specific purpose. When you help them identify those talents, you help them find their purpose.

Encourage Stickability by Helping Your Kids Keep the Big Picture in Mind

The *American Heritage Dictionary* defines *perseverance* as to "persist in or remain constant to a purpose, idea, or task in the face of obstacles or discouragement; steadfastness."[6] Using this definition as a basis, would you agree that perseverance can be defined as stubbornness with a purpose? It's not just refusing to give up; rather, it's refusing to give up *for a reason*. People who persevere have a passion behind their persistence. They have a dream, and when they bolster that dream through discipline, they persevere. Perseverance happens when dreams meet discipline. It's working not for gain, but for reward. Perseverance enables your child to succeed for the right reasons.

> *Let us not grow weary while doing good,*
> *for in due season we shall reap if we do not lose heart.*
> GALATIANS 6:9 NKJV

My mother believed you could reach your goals if you "use your abilities and stick to the task at hand." She taught us to set a goal and let nothing deter us from reaching that goal. We called her brand of perseverance "stickability."

"Don't quit," she would say. "Victory is within reach. Just keep reaching." Her words were powerful because she lived what she preached.

Mother began working as a sales clerk in a downtown store to supplement her family's income when she was eleven years old. (I know, I know . . . but this was long before child-labor laws, and I'm not so certain Mother was truthful about her age.) Even though she was poor, she made a wise decision with her first wage of fifty cents that became a lifelong habit. She gave a nickel to the church, saved ten cents, and used the rest for necessities.

She encouraged my brother, sisters, and I to do the same. When we received our first allowance of twenty-five cents a week, each of us saved a nickel, gave a nickel to the church, spent ten cents on necessities, and spent the last nickel for fun. (Mother *was* reasonable.) Every time we saved a dollar in coins, we could cash them in for a crisp, green dollar bill. When we approached Mother with a handful of coins, she would say, "See . . . money *does* grow on trees, if you plant the right seeds."

Money Tree

You'll need Mod-Podge®, Plaster of Paris.®, a bundle of paper money, medium-size sponge brushes, 4-inch pots and 6-inch saucers. Pour Mod-Podge in a small plastic bowl.

Help your children glue pieces of paper money to the pot using the sponge brush and glue until covered. Let dry. Paint the entire pot with a thin layer of Mod-Podge and let dry again. Mix Plaster of Paris according to directions. Fill each pot to the bottom of the rim. Allow to stand for 20–30 minutes. Push a small branch into the pot and allow to harden overnight. Cover top of plaster with a little sheet moss or Easter grass.

Tell the children my mother's story of saving money. Encourage them to put the tree in their room and place their coins in the saucer until they save a dollar. When they cash in their coins for a crisp bill, hang the money on the tree.

Money really does grow on trees when you plant the right seeds!

Mother had a purpose in mind for the money she earned—to give it away. She didn't earn money in order to buy for herself, but in order to buy for others. She didn't have "wants" like the rest of us. She met her needs and then looked for ways to help meet the needs of others. (At the tender age of seventy-eight, my mother now gives away more money than she keeps.)

You can teach your kids a similar lesson by having them make a money tree. Not only is this a great way to teach stickability, it can also be a lesson in priorities and money management. As your children collect their coins, remind them they're planting valuable seeds. Discuss the importance of keeping their priorities straight. Help them establish a budget for the money they save. If they spend their change on trivial things, children learn quickly that they won't be able to "grow" the big dollars. When they come to you with a dollar in coins, use my mother's phrase, "Money does grow on trees when you plant the right seeds." It's all about setting your priorities with a bigger purpose in mind.

It will take all the perseverance you can muster to teach your children stickability. But if they are going to grow up to fulfill their potential, they'll need stickability and perseverance. So encourage and persuade, all the while being careful that in encouraging perseverance, you don't cross the line by expecting perfection.

Guard against Perfectionism

Seeking perfection is not the same as seeking perseverance. Perseverance is striving to do the best you can do, even while knowing you can never be perfect. Why do we insist on perfection in our children when we ourselves will never be perfect?

You've witnessed the mom who says to her ten-year-old, average-size daughter, "No snacks for you. You're getting a little plump around the edges." Or the father who says to his son, "You'll get it right next time," after his son placed second in a race. Often parents who aggressively push their children propel them right into perfectionism. Perfectionism can actually keep children from achieving their potential. The message that comes through loud and clear to kids is that nothing less than perfect is of any value.

Have you caught yourself "helping" your son do an art project? Do you remake your daughter's bed after she has made it up? Do you wipe the counter again after the kids cleaned the kitchen? I can ask you these things because I committed these wrongs against my sons. I'm a classic perfectionist who has to work daily to overcome the irrational expectations I have of myself and others.

Your child could be headed down the destructive path of perfectionism if he or she:

- Has unreasonable personal expectations

- Is never satisfied with projects

- Is critical of others

- Has trouble making decisions

- Falls apart when criticized

- Procrastinates out of fear of failure

- Is critical of himself

If you recognize your child in this list, you can prevent perfectionism from becoming a lifelong malady by offering your child unconditional, accepting love.

In addition:

- Stop the "nothing is ever quite good enough" attitude.

- Accept your child for who he is, and help him grow into his potential.

- Remember what it was like to be your child's age. So what if the juice is spilled or there's misspelled words in your first-grader's paper. Mishaps and mistakes are part of growing up.

- When your child is disappointed by her shortcomings, share stories of times when you "messed up."

- Don't compare your child with siblings or classmates.

- Encourage your child to be his best, and let him know that's good enough for you.

One of the most obvious characteristics of perfectionists is the lack of downtime in their lives. Most perfectionists are serious-minded, driven folks who've forgotten the value of just playing around. Kids can get caught in this self-defeating trap. It's your job to make sure that doesn't happen.

Allow for Play

Twelve-year-old Stephanie collapsed when she walked through the back door of her home one afternoon. She couldn't take it anymore. Tears filled her eyes. Mom's attempts at consoling her daughter were in vain. Stephanie finally picked herself up and headed for her bedroom. A half-hour later Mom found her fast asleep, cradling a stuffed bunny from her toddler days.

Between dance, volleyball, study group, and school, Stephanie was exhausted. How did her schedule get so out of control? Because her mom forgot the importance of unstructured playtime, even for older children.

For young children, play is their work. Attributes that lead to success, such as patience, getting along with others, and problem solving are best learned while kids are just being kids. Have you ever watched how a group of kids on the playground interact? Stock traders could learn a lot about the art of negotiation by watching the give-and-take of eight-year-olds as they play a game of kickball.

The job of a football coach *is to make men do what they don't want to do, in order to achieve what they've always wanted to be.*
Tom Landry

Children at play feel safer trying new things around peers rather than parents because the level of expectation is lower, and as a result, it heightens their curiosity and creativity. Children who can't seem to focus in structured settings are able to concentrate when it comes to play. Kids who play hard on the playground may transfer that energy into seeking their potential later in life.

Some additional life skills gained during playtime include:

- Ability to make choices and decisions based on what's best for all

- Perseverance

- Ability to encourage others

- Ability to find joy in other's accomplishments (which is too often lost in the classroom or sports field)

- Strategic planning

- Ability to express ideas

Parents who allow their kids lots of time for free play are equipping them with important skill sets they need to succeed and fulfill their potential. When children play name games, sing songs, and recite jump-rope rhymes, they're developing language skills. When they construct a block tower, follow directions to a game, and figure out pieces to a puzzle, they're developing thinking skills. When they string beads, make clay figures, and cut with scissors, they're developing small-muscle skills; and they develop large-muscle skills when they play ball, roller skate, and run relay races. When they make up stories, put on a puppet show, and play dress-up, they are nurturing skills in creativity. When they team up to play ball games, discuss rules for a card game, and decide who will play what part in a dramatic play, they are developing their social skills.

The value of play is priceless. When they are being silly and laughing, children receive the refueling they need to meet the challenges of growing up.

Encourage a Close Relationship with God

When our children develop a close relationship with God, they begin on their own to want to please Him. In so doing, they'll naturally desire and work toward fulfilling God's call on their lives and reaching their full potential. How can you help your children cultivate a relationship with God? In large part by showing the power of prayer.

Teaching children to pray is easy if you are a praying parent. Your children will discover the joy of prayer through your prayers, so:

- *Pray before every meal.* If you do, by the time they're three, your kids will be asking you if they can pray before you have a chance to ask them—and they will embrace this habit for themselves. It doesn't matter where we are or who's with us, before we begin a meal, one of my grown sons reaches across the table to take the hand of whoever he's with to offer grace. And it's not a rote prayer, but words from the heart. "Saying grace" is the most basic of all prayers.

- *Allow your kids to "catch" you talking to God during the day.* If they do, they will learn to rely on prayer not just for the big things, but the little things too.

- *Let them see you on your knees in prayer.* This will help them understand God's majesty and holiness.

- *Let them hear you tell others that you'll pray for them.* Your kids will be more likely to develop a desire to pray for others too.

- *Talk with them about answers to prayer for your family.* This teaches your children that God does answer prayer.

You're probably familiar with the classic book *Goodnight Moon* by Margaret Wise Brown. For more than fifty years, this book has encouraged children to find comfort in telling the moon goodnight. I'd like to encourage you to instill another "Goodnight" habit in your children. When your kids are young, encourage them to say, "Goodnight, Lord" as you tuck them in bed after night-night prayers. When they awaken, kiss them, and remind them to say, "Good morning, Lord." This is a beautiful, holy habit that teaches children to talk to God before the day begins and as it comes to a close.

If you fail at all other points but accomplish the task of instilling a desire to talk to God in your children, you will have still equipped them with the best tool to discover their purpose.

(The search for purpose in your child's life starts with you and ends with God.)

Reality Check

Before moving on to the next chapter, consider your answers to these questions as you strengthen your resolve to raise respectful children in this disrespectful world:

1. How do you deal with your child's losing a competition?

2. Do the chores you assign your children teach them duty and responsibility?

3. Do you find it easier to give up or stick things out?

4. Do you encourage your children to set goals?

5. Do you push your children toward perfectionism?

6. Are you a perfectionist?

7. Do you pray as a family? Do your kids see you praying?

8. Do you set the following goals?
   - Family goals
   - Career goals
   - Financial goals

Coach; Don't Cheerlead

CONSIDER THESE TWO SCENARIOS:

Scenario 1: The game's over. Johnny leaves his outfield position with his head so low you can see the button on the crown of his baseball cap. He'd struck out twice and missed a fly ball. He isn't sure which hurts more, his pride or his backside, from tripping over his own two feet when he went for the fly ball.

His mother is waiting for him as he mopes off the field. "Oh, Johnny, I'm so proud of you. You're the best player on the team. If all the guys could play like you, well . . . we'd be the state champions!"

"Momma, don't . . . don't say that."

But Momma continues, "Oh, Johnny, don't ever forget . . . you're the best!"

Scenario 2: The game's over. Johnny struck out twice and missed a fly ball because he tripped over his own two feet . . . in front of the coaches, parents, spectators, and his teammates. It was a crucial play—the win-or-lose moment—and he had blown it.

He can barely walk, much less hold his head up. His brain is telling his little bird legs to run—get out of there—but they don't want to move. His heart is aching, and his ego is wounded.

Momma greets Johnny as he finally makes it to the sidelines, the last player off the field. Squatting down to get eye-to-eye with her son, Momma says, "Oh, Johnny, tough game today. My heart hurt with yours when you struck out. And that fly ball, ugh . . . your feet just didn't cooperate, did they?"

Johnny looks into his mother's eyes and reaches for the warmth of her embrace as she continues, "I tell you what, Johnny. How about if this weekend I make some lemonade and those cookies everybody likes. We'll invite some of the older guys over and between Dad and the guys, you can work on your hitting and fly balls," Momma says with great empathy.

Johnny nods his head in agreement.

Then his mother adds, "If you keep working at it . . . you'll get it. It just takes practice. I know you can get it. Dad and I will help you."

In the first scenario, Mom functions as a cheerleader. How do you think her words affected her son? At ten years old, Johnny knew he wasn't the best player on his team, and he knew he hadn't played well during the game. And unless his mother had left the game or somehow missed most of it, she had to know it too.

Here are a few possible responses that her words of false praise might have elicited in her son:

- *Mom lied to me. How could she do that?* (Mom's words of false praise damaged his trust in her.)

- *I messed up. Why didn't she care that I had a bad game?* (Mom's refusal to acknowledge what had really happened makes Johnny feel worse than he feels about how he played the game. Doesn't she even care about him or even see him?)

- *I know I'm not the best player on the team, but I love baseball. Why isn't it OK to just be part of the team?* (Mom's false praise gives Johnny the impression you have to be the best. Anything less is not good enough.)

- *I'll never be the best player on the team, so what's the use in trying?* (Since Johnny knows he'll never be the best, he gives up trying to improve.)

In the second scenario, Mom serves as Johnny's coach. She doesn't use false praise to try to make him feel better. Instead, she lets him know she understands how bad he feels and encourages him by telling him she's going to see he gets help to improve his game. She doesn't deny reality but offers Johnny hope that he will perform better in the future.

As a result her son likely had one or more of the following responses:

- *Mom's the best. She really loves me.* (Mom sealed the bond with her son by joining in his disappointment. Her words told him his number one fan felt his pain.)

- *I messed up, but Mom still loves me.* (Because she didn't sugarcoat his mistakes, Johnny knows his mom's love for him is not based on his performance.)

- *I'm glad Mom and Dad will help me. Maybe I can be a good player.* (Mom's offer to provide help gives Johnny hope that he can improve.)

- *I won't give up. I'll play better next week.* (Mom's encouragement gave Johnny the motivation to persevere, even in the face of disappointment.)

Cheerleader vs.	Coach
Offers false praise	Offers genuine praise
Doesn't/can't offer instruction	Provides expertise
Uses external motivation	Uses internal motivation
Applauds mediocrity	Expects excellence

In the rest of this chapter we are going to take a closer look at why it's so important that parents not take on the role of cheerleader, and then we'll discuss how you can be the coach your kids need in order to grow up to become respectful adults.

Don't Cheerlead

Perhaps you're still wondering what's so bad about being a cheerleader parent. After all, what's so bad about telling kids they're great?

If you think about it, the reason will quickly become evident. Cheerleaders can't help their team win. All cheerleaders do is keep yelling about how great their team is—even when the scoreboard and stat sheet paint a very different picture. Cheerleader moms try to boost their children's flagging spirits in the face of an athletic defeat, a low test score, or a disappointing placement in a contest, but they don't do anything to equip their children to do better next time.

When a parent praises a child who has done nothing to earn that praise, the praise is false because it's not based upon fact. Consider these examples:

- A ten-year-old wants to take drum lessons. His mom says: "Oh, sweetheart, you're so talented, you don't need lessons."

- A sixteen-year-old is in tears because of her acne. Mom tells her, "Your face is beautiful."

- A high-school freshman hands her mom her report card, which is filled with Cs. Mom smiles and says, "Honey, it's OK. We know you're the smartest kid in your class."

- After hearing his seven-year-old play the piano after just one lesson, Dad says, "I can't imagine you could play any better."

- After attending a speech contest in which his daughter stumbled over words and forgot her closing, Dad tells his daughter, "You're the very best I've ever heard."

Parents who say things like these to their kids may be well intentioned, but their words hurt rather than help. Let me show you why.

False Praise Diminishes Trust

Kids know when they have done well and when they haven't. We cannot erase the pain of defeat by telling them they did well. We also lose an opportunity to strengthen our relationship with them, because our disingenuousness shakes their trust in us. When we acknowledge they didn't do well, we are telling our children we feel their pain, and we gain a deeper level of trust because they know they can count on us to tell them the truth about themselves, but with love.

We all have friends who flatter us. You know the kind I'm talking about—female friends who tell you your new hairstyle is the best one you've ever had, your new hair color takes ten years off your face, or you look slimmer in the dress that's a size too small. Men do it too—Tom might tell Jim his tie is "right in style" even though the tie doesn't match his shirt. While these friends may mean well, you likely don't go to them when you want an honest answer.

When I really want to know the truth, good or bad, I turn to my friend Jean. Why? Because experience has taught me that she'll tell me the truth, the whole truth, and nothing but the truth . . . even when it's hard to take. So Jean's the one I turn to when I need an honest opinion about matters more important than my hairstyle. I trust her and her judgment of me. She has never offered false praise; she always offers help.

Here's the tough truth: false praise (I like to call it junk praise) is a lie. Telling your children they're the best when they're not is a lie, plain and simple. Remember, a child's world is black and white, there's no gray. Your words are either true or they are false—there are no half-truths. So when cheerleader parents offer unwarranted praise to their children, the kids will hear it as a lie. Instead of helping the child feel better, false praise causes kids to lose their trust in their parents because they wonder, *what else are my parents lying to me about?*

You were meant to be the one your child turns to when she needs someone she can really trust. Whether she's five years old and just lost her best friend on the playground or fifteen and feeling like a failure because she wasn't chosen for the homecoming court, she needs to know she can trust you to tell her the truth about herself. She needs you to acknowledge something painful has happened and that you understand how she feels.

For example:

- With your five-year-old, you might say, "I know how much it hurts when you lose a friend. Let's talk about what happened and see if both of you might need to say, 'I'm sorry.' Come on, I'll push you on the swing while we talk."

- When your fifteen-year-old's ego is bruised, you might say, "Not every girl in your class can be on the homecoming court. Maybe Cindy just knows more of the kids than you do—she *is* dating a football player. And you're trying out for the play in the spring, aren't you?"

But loss of trust isn't the only consequence when parents give kids false praise.

False Praise Undermines Ambition

Dr. Jean Twenge, an assistant professor of psychology at San Diego State University, reports, "This generation has given up. We're looking at 'Generation Whatever,' with many kids feeling like they can't make a difference."[1] In our quest to help our children feel good about themselves (gain self-esteem), we shower them with false praise because we don't want them to feel bad. But for words of praise to inspire and motivate, they must be warranted.

False praise stifles motivation to improve. After all, if we tell our children, "You're the best," what's to improve? False praise can lead to a false confidence, causing a child not to get the help or instruction needed to reach his or her potential. Somewhere along the line these kids will find out the truth about themselves.

Parents destroy their children's ambition when they shower them with false praise and then make excuses for their lack of achievement. That's what Billy's mom did. She told him his singing was fabulous and that he was going to be a star. He quit his voice lessons because he was tired of the voice exercises and felt his instructor was too rigid. A few months later when Billy tried out for the spring musical and didn't receive a part, his mom played the blame game, telling people:

"Joey beat Billy for the lead because his dad works with the director . . . that has to be the reason."

"Billy's voice was scratchy from all the singing he's been doing at church."

"This play is small potatoes for Billy. He's trying out for a part in the community theater next month anyway."

If children lack ambition, they won't keep striving to become more than they are today. As a result they won't develop self-respect, because they haven't experienced the confidence that comes from setting a goal and achieving it through hard work and perseverance.

If parents only tell their kids how wonderful and beautiful and smart they are, their children will grow up believing it and also expecting the world to tell them the same thing. Rather than doing things out of a healthy, internal motivation of self-respect or concern for others, these kids are motivated by what others think of them. They want to be in the limelight, and when they aren't, they get confused and don't know what to do.

I saw this when my sons graduated from high school. Several of their peers, who had excelled in high school, suddenly seemed to fall by the wayside. When they no longer received weekly accolades telling them how great they were, they didn't know what to do. They didn't go to college or pursue careers. They were left without support or direction because the false motivating praise that got them through high school had never been internalized and transformed into self-respect.

False Praise Fails to Offer Guidance

Cheerleader parents tend to feel good about themselves as parents because they are saying nice things to their kids, trying to make them feel good about themselves; but they stop short of offering what their children really need: guidance. For example, they say things like:

- "It's not your fault you failed."

- "I don't know why your coach won't let you start. You're his best player."

- "Oh, darling, you're so beautiful. You can't win them all."

- "Forget about it; you'll make the goal next week."

While encouraging words like these may affirm kids when they are disappointed in themselves, they miss the mark because they fail to offer guidance, which is what the kids really need. Cheering won't ensure our children's victories—only hard work does that. Victory in sports, and in life, grows out of how prepared we are. Victory grows out of training.

It's not enough to tell our kids we believe in them and that they can do anything they want. They need us to guide them, to show them how to do what they want or need to do. This was brought home to me when my sons turned twelve and were old enough to mow our lawn. One day I announced that I believed they were now mature enough, smart enough, strong enough, and tough enough to handle the job. After this ego-building speech we headed for Sears to purchase a power mower. When we got back home, I helped them fill the tank, started it up, and told them to start mowing. I went back in the house and left them in the backyard. Thirty minutes later Chad came bounding in the house, "Mom, aren't you going to show us how to do it?"

"Darling, I gave you instructions. I know you can do it; you're smart enough," I replied.

Chad came right back at me, "But, Mom, you can't just tell us; you have to show us."

Once again my son stopped me dead in my tracks with truth. Telling our children isn't enough; we have to show them, which is why kids need parents who are coaches rather than cheerleaders.

Good coaches do two things: they offer encouragement, and they coach by example.

Offer Encouragement

Coach Payton Jordan, the former Olympic track coach who led the 1968 United States team to the gold in the Mexico City Olympics and coached Stanford's national championship teams for thirty years, is a great role model for parents who want to effectively coach their kids. Jordan's peers and team members refer to him as a "teacher, mentor, friend, hero, role model, leader, motivator, a master at creating self-respect, a man of rectitude, discipline, and integrity, and a national treasure."[2]

As I was researching this book, I contacted Coach Jordan, and we became good friends. As we talked about his training philosophy, he told me that encouragement lay at the heart of his coaching. Bob Moore, a former team member, agrees. "Coach Jordan had a talent for making you feel better about yourself and more confident in your ability to take on any challenge. He could look you straight in the eye and make you feel like you would climb mountains and swim through shark infested waters to meet his expectations of you . . . and then, the miracle of it all, was that those expectations became your expectations!"[3]

Your encouragement or lack of encouragement can make or break your child's self-respect. What follows are concepts I've adapted from Payton Jordan's coaching philosophy. These concepts can aid parents in their efforts to raise respectful children.

Words of Encouragement

Admonish, exhort, move, prompt, urge, incite, induce, persuade, gladden, brighten, hearten, pick up, inspire, elevate one's mood, give a lift, put one on top of the world, exhilarate, rejoice, do the heart good, enliven, console, give comfort, reassure, pat on the back, embolden, bolster, support, foster, nurture, and we could keep going . . .

I urge you to read through these words several times before you move on. Let each one sink into your heart.

Speak Words of Genuine Praise

We all need a little praise, a pat on the back, for a job well done. When you acknowledge your children's accomplishments, you help build their self-image. Nothing feels better than knowing you did something well that was noticed, especially by someone you love and trust.

False praise can destroy motivation, but genuine praise can bolster it. When children receive genuine praise from their parents, they'll want to try harder; they'll long to live up to the expectations laid before them. So praise your kids when they accomplish a task. Encourage them to keep going with comments such as, "Boy, you're going to feel good when your teacher sees how hard you've worked on this science project," rather than saying, "I'm going to be so proud of you when you turn in this science project." Phrase your comments to focus on how the child will feel. This lets your child know your encouragement is for his or her good, not for your ego.

When your children do extra chores to earn money to buy a present for a grandparent, give away their favorite toy to a child who doesn't have a toy, or help a friend who's upset rather than going to the "party of the decade," remind them God is watching what they do, not to catch them doing something wrong, but to smile at them when they do something right. I call such moments "God Winks." By the time they're teenagers, kids won't be doing a good job just for you; they'll be motivated by their desire to honor God.

Your goal is to move your child from depending on your encouragement for motivation to being self-motivated, and when parents provide genuine praise, they help their children make this move.

Build Their Character

"I don't want it," eight-year-old Boyce complained, as he threw his baseball trophy on the floorboard of the car. "I hate baseball. I hate my coach. I hate this trophy."

When I got over the shock, I scolded Boyce with not-so-wise words, "Boyce, that's no way to talk about your coach and no way to treat your trophy. You should be grateful to your coach and proud of your trophy."

"Mom, you don't get it, do you?" he came back with a disrespectful pitch.

Obviously I was missing something. "Boyce, you better explain in a hurry, or we're going to have to do something about that rotten attitude," I answered in my most motherly tone.

"Mom, everybody gets one. It's no big deal," Boyce said as he slumped down on the seat with that pitiful little-boy look of disappointment.

He was right. It *was* no big deal. It didn't matter if he tried or not, if he ever hit the ball or not, because everybody on the team got a trophy for participation. No one was singled out for excellence. Don't misunderstand. Boyce wasn't upset because he thought he was the best player and deserved special recognition. Quite the contrary. He didn't feel he had earned the trophy, so he couldn't be thankful for it.

Participation in Little League sports used to be a character-building experience. Too often in today's sports programs we're more focused on coddling children than coaching them to excellence. We try to make all things equal by stroking our kids, but this ruins their ability to be grateful for their achievements. Here are some ways to help your kids develop character, which is what they really need:

- *Don't make excuses for your child.* Rather than making excuses for your child's less-than-stellar performance, let him know you believe he can do better.

- *Raise your expectations.* Don't lower them to accommodate your child. Our kids will live up to our expectations when they're challenging, but reasonable. Don't set your expectation on last-chair trumpet in the high-school band, when you know your child is capable of moving up. Encourage your child with extra lessons and your willingness to sit and listen to him practice.

- *Dream big with your child.* Help your child understand it doesn't matter where she is today; what matters is where she's going to be tomorrow. A great conversation starter with your child is to ask, "Who do you want to become one day?" If the response is "the most famous inventor in the world," tell your child stories of famous inventors, such as Thomas Edison, who once said, "If I find 10,000 ways something won't work, I haven't failed. I am not discouraged, because every wrong attempt discarded is often a step forward."[4]

Let your children know nothing worth achieving ever comes easily.

Another coach whose philosophies can offer us helpful insights into training our children fascinated me and most of America during a career that spanned almost thirty years. He showed us all how to lead by example with integrity and consistency.

Coach by Example

When I was in high school, the Dallas Cowboys dominated the NFL, as did their coach, Tom Landry. Wearing his signature felt fedora, he commanded his team from the sidelines with confidence and cool that set the mark for other coaches in the league. Landry was known as a man of few words, but the words he spoke were important.

Known as "America's coach," Landry built the Dallas franchise from the ground up, never deviating from his own priority list: God, family, and football. (Sound familiar?) He wrote it on every training-camp blackboard for twenty-nine years. I believe part of his long-term success came from keeping his priority list in order.

Coach Tom Landry's demeanor exuded confidence under pressure. He commanded control of his team because he had earned their respect. At Landry's memorial service in February 2000, one of his most successful players, Roger Staubach, with tear-filled eyes said, "He was our rock, our hope, our inspiration. He was our coach."[5]

What a great description of what it means to be your kid's coach! Be their rock, hope, and inspiration.

Be Their Rock

Roger Staubach wasn't the first to refer to Coach Landry as a rock. The media frequently called him the "Rock of Gibraltar." Why? Because Tom Landry was a man of character who never compromised his integrity. What a lesson for us as we seek to instill respect in our children: we must be the rock upon which their character is built.

I've said it before, and I'll say it throughout this book because it is so important: *kids follow their parents' example.* If you want to raise respectful kids, you need to be their rock. They need you to live a life of integrity born out of character that has been shaped by the principles found in God's Word.

Jesus said, "I will show you what he is like who comes to me and hears my words and puts them into practice. He is like a man building a house, who dug down deep and laid the foundation on rock. When a flood came, the torrent struck that house but could not shake it, because it was well-built."[6] Is your life a solid rock upon which your kids can build their belief system?

Someone once said, "A man who stands for nothing will fall for anything." Quite a contrast to Jesus's exhortation to build your life on the solid foundation of God's Word. What do you believe in? What do you stand behind? If you're not building your life on the solid foundation of God's Word, then you are standing on shifting sand, and so are your kids. Everyone's talking about spirituality today, having faith in something. I tire of hearing "all that matters is that you believe in something." Not true. What matters is whether what we believe in is true.

A highly educated man once told me he had a recurring dream of being thrown into the ocean. The waves violently tossed him back and forth until he finally went under. Just when all hope was gone, he resurfaced for a saving breath of air, only to begin the torment again. I tried to help him see that this recurring dream represented the lack of a foundation of faith in his life. With all his education and worldly success, his soul was not anchored.

Scripture tells us that when we turn our hearts and minds to God, the sure foundation, "we will no longer be infants, *tossed back and forth* by the waves, and blown here and there by every wind of teaching and by the cunning and craftiness of men in their deceitful scheming."[7]

Your children need you to provide them with a solid foundation of trust in God and their parents. Your children need to know your character and integrity are rock solid. They need to know that you:

- Are not deceived by every new teaching that comes along

- Are not persuaded to accept a contract from a company of questionable ethics, even though your partners don't have a problem with it

- Are the one to dissent when your child's elementary school wants to sell alcoholic beverages at the fall carnival to make more money, because it sends a mixed message to the children about alcohol consumption

- Run in the other direction when temptation comes in the form of another who is not your spouse, no matter the difficulties you're experiencing within your marriage

When parents don't compromise their integrity, they give their children the rock-solid foundation they need. Such parents provide a model for how their kids can develop a rock-solid foundation of their own.

A good coach also exemplifies hope.

Hang On to Hope

Coach Landry racked up four losing seasons in a row during his first years with the Cowboys. Even so, he was offered a ten-year contract to continue with the team because of his attitude and his determination to build a winning team. When asked about his unending optimism, he commented,

"I've learned that something constructive comes from every defeat."[8] This perspective allowed him to offer hope to his team, and that hope enabled them to persevere. Hope provided the Cowboys with the motivation to keep on trying, and their efforts eventually took them to the top of the NFL, winning two Super Bowl championships, five NFC championships, and 270 victories.

Do your kids see hope in you when times get tough? Do you persevere, expecting a positive outcome? I'm not advocating naiveté; I'm talking about mature hope that stems from a rock-solid foundation of hope and trust in a sovereign God.

I learned a great lesson in hope when I decided to write *Manners of the Heart*. After I'd sent off a proposal to numerous publishers, a writer friend told me, "It takes twenty-five rejections before you'll get an acceptance." I had a choice to make every time I found a rejection letter in the mailbox. I could see each rejection letter as a crushing blow to my hope that one day I would be published, or I could see each rejection as bringing me one step closer to my goal. I chose the latter option. Together, the boys and I began celebrating each rejection letter as it arrived.

If you exemplify hope in the midst of difficulties and challenges, your daughter won't quit the first time she's humiliated on the soccer field or the fifth time she has to sit on the bench. Your son will keep trying for first

Love . . . *always protects, always trusts, always hopes, always perseveres.*
1 CORINTHIANS 13:6–7

chair in the school band and will spend more time practicing so he can one day achieve that goal. When our kids see us not giving up when we face defeat or rejection, we teach them to persist toward their own goals, to keep working toward mastery.

Nothing is more gratifying to a parent than seeing evidence that our kids have "caught" what we have been trying to teach them. I worked hard to exemplify hope to my sons. That's why I was so excited the day Chad's own hope was rewarded.

Chad loved football and started playing in fourth grade, determined to one day become an outstanding player. But I knew he had little chance of this because his body simply refused to grow at the rate of his teammates. He was the kid who followed every play up and down the field, patting every player as he came back to the sidelines. He played with his heart, continuing to go out for the team in hopes that one day he would turn into the player of his dreams.

When summer football training started up each year, I'd tell Chad that maybe this year he was going to "pump up." I found "little" guys who had made it big in the NFL to use as examples of those who succeeded despite their size. I reminded Chad that his teammates appreciated his enthusiasm and needed his encouragement. I emphasized his contribution in each game, pointing out that even though his shining moment had not come yet, he was already an important member of the team because he gave so unselfishly while he continued to hope for the chance to prove himself.

In seventh grade, Chad's coach put him in the game. The opposing quarterback threw a long pass, and Chad caught the ball, right in front of the intended receiver! I was so proud of my son at that moment that I lost all dignity! But I wasn't the only one. The bench cleared. The whole team celebrated Chad's moment of glory. Why? Because they knew he had given his all to his team. Chad played with his heart, a heart filled with hope, and they wanted to rejoice with him when his hope did not return void.

Hope is the heartbeat of the family. Love your family enough to give them hope, no matter how difficult the circumstances.

And . . .

Be Their Inspiration

In one of our "Business of Manners" training sessions, I ask the participants to record ten attributes they would like to see in an employee, and then we compile their answers into one list. Next, I ask if anyone in the room is the perfect employee in the company. When no one says yes, I challenge the attendees to make their lists a personal goal for themselves.

Let me challenge you to do something similar. What would the perfect parent coach look like to you? And more important, what qualities in you do you want your children to emulate? Answer that question, and then with God's help strive to live up to those qualities!

- Do you want them to be the best they can be? Then expect nothing less of yourself.

- Do you want your kids to respect your word? Then keep your word.

- Do you want them to tell the truth? Then always tell the truth. Don't sugarcoat it or tell half-truths.

- Do you want your children to be unselfish? Then give generously to those in need.

- Do you want them to persevere? Then don't give up when the going gets tough.

- Do you want your kids to be faithful? Then keep your commitments.

- Do you want them to have self-control? Then don't lose your control.

- Do you want your children to be patient? Then endure irritations with grace.

- Do you want them to respect others? Then show respect for others, beginning with your spouse. Fathers should teach their children to respect their mother. Mothers should teach their children to respect their father. Together you teach your children how to respect others.

If you live out the qualities on your list, you will inspire your kids to live that way, as well. No one can be perfect, but we all can try to be a little better today than we were yesterday.

Do the Best You Can!

Coach Jordan said it best: "[Being a coach] means going out and doing the best you can with what God's given you."

If you take your coaching position with your children seriously, one day your children will say of you what one of Jordan's former teammates said about him: "He is an outspoken proponent of old-fashioned values: a man of principle, of character, and of courage and determination."[9]

Reality Check

Before moving on to the next chapter, consider your answers to these questions as you strengthen your resolve to raise respectful children in this disrespectful world:

1. Are you a parent who refuses to give up in spite of all odds?

2. Do you find yourself coaching—or cheering—your children?

3. Do you sometimes give false praise to your children in order for them to feel good about themselves?

4. Do you let your children know your expectations for them?

5. Do you tell your children the truth about their performances in sports or music or academics?

6. Do you offer guidance in words and actions to help your children achieve their goals?

7. Do your priorities match Coach Landry's: God, family, football (or whatever the task at hand)?

8. If your children followed in your footsteps, would they walk in the right direction?

6

Set Boundaries
without
Building Walls

SOME JUNIOR-HIGH STUDENTS HUDDLED around the inside perimeter of a schoolyard fence. A passing psychologist from the local university noted this and subsequently suggested that the fences represented unwelcome limitations, and that children would do better with an unrestricted schoolyard. Thus the fences all came down. The result? The children began to huddle in the middle of the playground, because they did not know where the boundaries were.[1]

The boundaries we'll visit in this chapter are the rules for behavior that protect our children from disaster and communicate that someone in authority cares enough about them to provide direction and guidance. Kids need firm boundaries so they can get on with the task of growing up to be respectful and responsible.

When God created the Garden of Eden, He put boundaries in place for Adam and Eve's protection. God gave the Israelites the Ten Commandments so they would know what He expected in terms of their behavior—not for His good, but for the good of His children. As our heavenly Parent, He knows what's best for us—what will bring joy or sorrow, happiness or despair, blessing or burden. God wants us to provide the same guidance and protection for our children by setting boundaries, not for our comfort, but for our children's security.

Boundaries can help children to:

- Develop self-control and a sense of responsibility for their own behavior

- Resist peer pressure and every new fad that comes along, dangerous or not

- Understand that wrong behavior has negative consequences

- Feel secure under the protection of parental authority

- Know what's expected of them

- Gain wisdom, knowledge, and guidance in a complicated world

Without a doubt, boundaries go a long way to help children develop the qualities they need to become respectful adults. So in this chapter we'll explore how you can set boundaries that help rather than hinder your children and that do not create walls between you and them, beginning with the importance of a unified front.

Present a Unified Front

After twenty-two years of parenting, Mike and Lisa Conn, the character-centered parents you met in chapter 2, have learned the importance of presenting a unified front to their kids, particularly when it comes to establishing and enforcing boundaries. This hasn't always been easy, though, because Mike and Lisa are opposite in almost every aspect of temperament and personality. They see life from different perspectives and have not always agreed on what's best for their daughters, Ali, Ashley, and Aimee. Through the years they've argued about whether or not the baby should wear a cap, how short their daughters' skirts should be, when to set curfews, and issues ranging from baby formulas to restaurant choices.

But in spite of their differences in parental philosophies, Mike and Lisa have been able to maintain a united front in the family. This has required compromise and patience, but the efforts have paid great dividends. For one thing, their kids can't play one parent against the other, thus dividing Mom and Dad and weakening the idea of the family as a team.

So be proactive and talk with your spouse about the boundaries you want to set before they become issues with your kids. Don't wait until they get older. Work out as many disagreements you and your spouse may have before you need to implement any boundaries.

If unforeseen conflicts come up later, resolve them in private. Never argue in front of the kids. Make sure they hear you both saying the same thing. When parents are always disagreeing about what's best for their kids, their children begin to wonder if the family is in danger of falling apart. Your kids need to know you are together when it comes to family values and boundaries and consequences. When they do, they will feel secure, knowing that you love and respect each other. They will also be more likely to accept your boundaries without much resistance.

Agree on which few, well-chosen issues will not be open for discussion—period—and then stick to your word. Some parents falter in attempting to make every rule nonnegotiable; others falter in not having any nonnegotiables. Too many rules, and children will rebel; not enough rules, and children will rebel.

One of the nonnegotiable rules in our home is saying "please" and "thank you." I still remember waiting in the grocery store for fifteen minutes one day until one of my sons finally said "thank you" to the storekeeper who offered him a cookie.

If Mom and Dad are united on the nonnegotiables and enforce them when the kids are young, the teen years will go much smoother for all concerned. You'll be able to keep your cool under pressure because the decision has already been made. You can lower your voice to a whisper, even when your child is bellowing to negotiate.

Here's a case in point:

I didn't think much about it when the phone rang one Friday night, until it hit me that the boys were at a spend-the-night, twelve-year-old birthday party. I reached for the receiver to hear, "Jill, I'm having a problem with your boys."

Like an army sergeant who just received word of an infraction of one of his men, I responded, "I'm on my way."

"Wait a minute . . . let me explain," Diane quickly said to stop the onslaught of the military. "We were getting ready to watch a movie, when the boys told me they weren't allowed to watch PG-13 movies."

My heart stopped pounding and now swelled in my proud chest, "Oh, really? Well, that *is* true."

I told this mom the issue wasn't up for discussion because one of our nonnegotiable house rules was no PG-13 movies until the boys were thirteen. So I offered to rent a couple of movies and bring them so the boys could watch a movie I deemed more appropriate. The mom agreed to put the birthday party boys back in the backyard until I got there. If I had insisted the boys just come home, I would have thrown up a wall instead of preserving the boundary.

Was all that trouble worth it?

You better believe it!

Another way to ensure that boundaries don't become walls, in addition to having nonnegotiable boundaries both parents agree on, is to remember the importance of your relationship with your kids. When kids know they are loved and valued for who they are, they have a much easier time seeing boundaries as good things that are set up for their own protection.

Stay Emotionally Connected with Your Kids

It's important to note that when God gave Adam and Eve the boundary of not eating from the tree of the knowledge of good and evil, He was also "walking in the garden in the cool of the day"[2] with them. In other words, He spent time with them. He had a relationship with them. He wasn't simply dictating rules apart from His relationship with them.

I can think of no better way than this to ensure your boundaries don't become walls: spend time with your kids. Get involved in their world. For too long we've been told that children just need quality time, not quantity time. Not true. If you want to have an open and close relationship with your children, you must connect with them emotionally. I'm talking about a heart-to-heart connection. This can only happen when we're intimately involved in their lives.

Make sure your kids know you love them for who they are. If you try to establish firm boundaries outside of the context of a close relationship with them, you will likely fail. But if you maintain closeness throughout their childhood, you'll pave the way for success. When we don't take time to develop and maintain a close relationship but still expect our rules to be followed, we erect walls.

Children need quantities *of quality time.*

Here are some ways to stay emotionally connected to your children throughout their growing-up years.

Tot and Tyke Years

If you have more than one child this age, go ahead and do these things with both of them. Kids this age don't yet need to spend individual time with you.

- Have your kids lie next to you on the sofa for a back scratch following their afternoon playtime.

- Have a regular downtime before supper.

- Create a special goodnight or good morning ritual. For instance, the boys and I made up a wake-up song they heard every morning. My mother served us orange juice in bed on school mornings! (Don't worry, I never did this with my boys, but it's still a great idea.)

- Eat meals together as a family.

- Read books together at bedtime.

- Read Bible stories and God's Word together every day.

- When spending time together as a family, turn off the television, and don't answer the phone. Protect your family time.

- Play games together—catch, board games, hide-and-seek.

- Color, do crafts, and make things together.

- Cook or sew together.

Tyke and Tween Years

Kids this age need to spend time with you alone, so if you have more than one child, do your best to give each of them that much-needed, one-on-one time. Depending on their ages:

- Go on regular lunch dates.

- Volunteer as much as possible in school activities. Elementary-age children love having their parents at school. They swell with pride when *their* mom or dad walks in.

- When talking with your children, make eye contact. Give them your focused attention.

- Wash the car together.

- Cook together—teach them how to bake a cake, make cookies, cook simple meals.

- Do crafts together . . . make a family scrapbook or a scrapbook about them.

- Watch a movie together and then discuss it.

- Be available for late-night talks.

- Share spiritual lessons you're learning.

- When appropriate, talk about your life and some the mistakes you made. They'll appreciate your vulnerability and love you for your imperfections.

Teen Years

As kids grow older, it often becomes more challenging to maintain a close relationship with them. Perhaps you have a teenager who is challenging your authority and whom you don't particularly enjoy being around. Pursue the relationship anyway. Spend time with her—just the two of you—and make sure she knows she is loved unconditionally.

Here are some additional ideas that can help you stay connected:

- If you each have a cell phone, stay in touch throughout the day.

- Send e-mails and e-cards that say, "I'm thinking of you."

- Write your children a letter at least once a month.

- Take a trip together.

- Continue to share what God is doing in your life, opening the door for deep, meaningful talks.

Even when our kids leave home to go off to college or move into a place of their own, we still need to maintain a close relationship so they know they can come to us for guidance and support should they need it. Their world is rapidly changing, and it's important for parents to be available during the disappointments and moral issues that arise.

*All I really need to know about how to live and what to do and how to be I learned in kindergarten.
These are the things I learned:
Share everything.
Play fair.
Don't hit people.
Put things back where you found them.
Clean up your own mess.
Don't take things that aren't yours.
Say you're sorry when you hurt somebody.
Take a nap every afternoon.
Flush.*[3]
ROBERT FULGHUM
ALL I REALLY NEED TO KNOW I LEARNED IN KINDERGARTEN

Again, if you maintain a united front and a close relationship with your children, you'll have a much easier time enforcing boundaries, no matter their ages.

Make Rules Age-Appropriate

Your boundaries will also be much less likely to create walls between you and your kids if you make your rules age-appropriate.

Tot and Tyke Years

During their first five years of life, one of your children's primary tasks is the development of the values that will influence them for the rest of their lives. That means you, the parent, have the opportunity to mold your child's character before the values of the disrespectful world have a chance to pull your child in the wrong direction.

One of the important values taught through boundary setting is obedience. That's why I encourage parents to require "instant obedience." Those who allow their kids, even at this early age, to break the rules a few times before doling out consequences are setting themselves up for major battles later. Don't go there. Help your kids learn the value of obedience by following through with the consequence the first time the rule or boundary is broken.

When we set and enforce rules of behavior, we are not only protecting our children from harm and teaching them to be obedient, but we are also shaping their moral values and character. So, if you want your children to grow up to become respectful, honest, kind, and compassionate and to believe in the authority of God, you need to set boundaries that reflect those values. For example:

- Instill respect for others by establishing rules such as:

  1. No hitting or biting allowed.

  2. Use good manners. Say "please," "thank you," and "excuse me."

  3. Say, "Have a good day," to employees at the grocery, bank, and so on as you exit a business. (My mother insisted on this one. I did the same with my sons. The smiles that came from the recipients were enough to teach the value of showing respect to others.)

- Instill respect for self by establishing rules, such as:

  1. Do not cross the street without an adult.

  2. Do not touch the stove when Mom is cooking.

  3. No walking away from Mom or Dad in public places.

- Teach the value of sharing by establishing rules, such as:

  1. Share your toys with your friends.

  2. Keep one and share one when candy is given out.

  3. Always let your friends go first.

Tween Years

Six- to twelve-year-olds need to be reminded of the rules and that there are consequences when they break the rules. When a boundary is broken, discipline swiftly and clearly state the reason for the consequence. Put the burden on your children's shoulders—they can handle it. You want your children to experience the reality that *their* choices determine the discipline, not your choices.

For example:

- Teach the value of honesty by establishing rules, such as:

  1. Tell the truth, the whole truth, and nothing but the truth.

  2. Do not blame others when you get in trouble. Take responsibility for your own actions.

  3. Ask before using someone else's belongings.

- Instill a sense of responsibility by setting rules, such as:

  1. Use an alarm clock to wake up, dress, and be ready for school on time.

  2. Complete homework before free time.

  3. Be ready for bed by the established bedtime, without complaining.

- Teach the value of compassion by setting rules, such as:

  1. Feed and exercise your pet on the established schedule.

  2. Don't play rough with younger siblings; use gentleness.

  3. Apologize when you hurt someone's feelings.

Give your child privileges, such as being allowed to spend the night at a friend's house when he or she demonstrates maturity in accepting your house rules.

The Year In-Between

Each September, I give a lecture to a new group of sixth-grade parents, breaking the news as gently as possible of the traumatic change that will take place in the life of their child during the upcoming school year. Children begin sixth grade agreeing with their parents' belief system. By the end of the school year, the world begins to play a more prominent role in forming who the children become.

During this year children begin forming their own opinions, making decisions about what they believe. They no longer blindly accept their parents' views, but begin to decide for themselves what is right and wrong. What they decide will be influenced by the discrepancies they can now see in adults' thinking and actions. By the end of their sixth-grade year, your kids will have become their own persons, either accepting or rejecting your views according to the authenticity they've seen in your life.

I know we've talked about the importance of your example, but it is particularly critical when your kids are in this in-between year. If you want them to "own" your values, they must see that you live by your word. They must see you living within the boundaries you have set for them, just as you expect your kids to live within those boundaries.

Early-Teen Years (ages thirteen to sixteen)

During this stage some parents back off and allow their kids more freedom than their kids are ready to handle. This is often in response to their children's moving toward independence from their parents. Yet the teen years are not the time to turn our backs. Instead, we should double our efforts to keep the relationship strong, the communication channels open, and the "rules of the house" in place.

For example:

- Teach the value of honesty by expecting your teens to:

    1. Ask permission before borrowing someone else's belongings

    2. Always tell the truth

    3. Do what they say they are going to do

- Teach the value of purity by expecting your teens to:

    1. Not view R-rated movies or play violent video games

    2. Not use coarse language or name-call

    3. Not spend time alone with the opposite sex

- Teach the value of self-respect by expecting your teens to:

    1. Attend weekly church services

    2. Dress modestly

    3. Resist peer pressure

Late-Teen Years (ages seventeen to nineteen)

Your teen believes he is now an adult. So treat him like one. Give more responsibility and more privileges accordingly. Insist on adherence to the established rules. With a strong relationship already in place, the later teen years can be a wonderful time for you and your children. They're still under your authority, but moving from dependence to interdependence.

Don't be fooled into believing there should no longer be boundaries. Boundaries are just as important at this stage as at any other. In some ways they are even more important, because this is your last opportunity to instill your values before your teens enter adulthood.

For example:

- Teach the value of self-discipline by expecting your young adults to:

    1. Be punctual

2. Practice good study habits

- Instill the value of money by requiring your young adults to:

    1. Get a summer job during high school and college

    2. Pay for their clothes, cell phones, dining out, and entertainment

- Instill a sense of responsibility by requiring young adults to:

    1. Do their own laundry

    2. Take care of their own cars

    3. Help prepare family meals

Keep in mind that your boundaries serve to help protect your children until they are mature enough to establish their own boundaries.

Good Boundaries Build Respectful Adults

Shortly before He returned to the Father, Jesus said to His disciples, "I no longer call you servants, because a servant does not know his master's business. Instead, I have called you friends, for everything that I learned from my Father I have made known to you."[4] Jesus's words deeply reflect His love for the disciples and His desire to equip them with everything they needed for their lives to be fruitful, even after He was no longer with them.

Someday we will call our sons and daughters "friend," and they will feel the same about us. While we don't stop being a parent, we will gradually move from a "parent/child relationship" to an "adult/adult relationship." Wise parents proactively plan for that day, because they know it will come sooner than they think.

Start planning today how you can use age-appropriate boundaries to help your children achieve the maturity required to successfully handle the freedoms and responsibilities of adulthood.

Reality Check

Before moving on to the next chapter, consider your answers to these questions as you strengthen your resolve to raise respectful children in this disrespectful world:

1. Do you and your spouse stand unified as a team?

2. Do your children clearly understand what is expected of them?

3. Do they obey without questioning or complaining?

4. Are you setting boundaries, not building walls?

5. Are you developing the necessary character traits in your children before they start elementary school?

6. Are you firmly instilling family values in your children that you hope will stay with them?

7. Are there "house rules" for your home that are nonnegotiable?

8. Do you spend focused time with your children?

7

Use Discipline, Not Punishment

A FATHER BATTLING HIS SEVENTEEN-YEAR-OLD son's lack of respect had reached the end of his rope. With great pride he told me about his solution to a scene that had occurred a few days earlier. "I was sick and tired of his lack of motivation. His attitude. He has never listened to me, not even when he was a little kid. He's never been interested in anything I wanted him to do with me. And that music. Have you heard that garbage? The only words I understood were the ones I use when I hope nobody's listening—and his friends were getting stranger every day.

"The final straw came last weekend. He stole two bottles of whiskey from my liquor cabinet for a party with his buddies. When I caught him red-handed, all he said was, 'You drink, Dad, and so what's the big deal?' OK, so I drink a few after work, but I'm an adult and he's a kid. I told him I wouldn't put up with his disrespect and excuses any longer. Told him enough was enough. He said he'd rather live on the street than in the house with me. So, I kicked him out. Told him to figure out life on his own. Maybe now he'll learn something."

When I asked this father how long he had been disappointed in his son's behavior, he replied, "Since the day he was born. He's just a bad apple."

A *bad apple*—from birth? What about the adage "The apple doesn't fall far from the tree"? Could that be the case with this father and son? Every child has a soul that needs to be nourished and a heart that needs to be protected. Just as a seed planted in the ground is dependent on the gardener to survive, so is a child totally dependent on a parent to thrive emotionally. How much time had this father spent in the garden of his son's heart. This father needs to understand he is reaping the fruit from the seeds *he* planted.

Children need love, and they need discipline. Parents who love their children will lovingly discipline them. By his own account, this father had not given his son the love and discipline all children need to grow up to become respectful adults.

Discipline Leads to Respect

The lack of discipline in a home is just as much a sign of neglect as not providing food and shelter. Just as every child needs to know someone loves her unconditionally and, no matter what, someone will be there for her, every child also needs to know there are limits to acceptable behavior.

Discipline comes from the Latin root, *discipere*, which means "to grasp intellectually, analyze thoroughly" from *dis*—"apart" + *capere*—"take." When parents discipline their kids, they are taking apart a problem in order to thoroughly analyze it. Discipline is meant to prevent future problems, not just solve immediate problems. It teaches, instructs, and trains. *Webster's* defines discipline as "training that corrects, molds, or perfects the mental faculties or moral character."[1] For example:

- Your two-year-old pushes her milk off the table.
  Discipline: She helps you clean it up.
  Lesson learned: We are each responsible for our own messes.

- Your ten-year-old has "forgotten" to take out the trash two weeks in a row.
  Discipline: For the next two weeks he has to do the additional chore of helping with supper.
  Lesson learned: Better to do the chores we're assigned than to neglect them. When we neglect our responsibilities, it only makes the situation worse.

Discipline is more about teaching our children what to do than about teaching them what not to do. When we discipline them, we show them the better way. Our discipline enables them to become better tomorrow than they are today. To grow. To mature. To become responsible, respectful members of society. Discipline teaches kids to *do* good rather than *feel* good.

Discipline changes an undesirable behavior, teaches a life lesson, or persuades children to think before they make a decision. It helps them become all they are intended to be.

Punishment, however, crushes children.

> *Discipline* is teaching kids to do good rather than feel good.

Punishment Leads to Rebellion

Discipline and punishment are not the same thing. *Punishment* can be defined as "retributive suffering, pain or loss; rough treatment."[2] That's a far cry from the meaning of *discipline*, "corrects, molds, or perfects the mental faculties or moral character." Punishment belittles; it doesn't motivate.

For example:

- A thirteen-year-old makes a sarcastic remark to her mom in front of a store clerk. The mom responds, "You will not embarrass me like that in public."

    Punishment: The mom makes her daughter walk behind her down the mall and out to the parked car.

    Lesson learned: My mom humiliates me. Why shouldn't I humiliate her?

- Later that day the teen doesn't come in time to help her mom put supper on the table.

    Punishment: Mom sends the daughter to her room for the night with the words, "If you're not going to help me, I don't want to see your face."

Lesson learned: My mom doesn't care about me; she just expects me to make her life easier. Why should I when she makes my life harder?

Unfortunately, the above examples really happened, and when I tried to talk to this mom about the situation with her daughter, she told me, "She is my child, and I expect her to treat me with respect. It's not about her; it's about me."

I'm afraid the handwriting is on the wall in this home. This daughter's willful disobedience is a response to her mom's inappropriate and unloving punishment. The harder parents try to demand respect from their children through punishment, the more resentment builds, which causes rebellion.

We can't demand respect from our kids; we must command it. Respect is earned. Your children will respect you if you are working on their behalf to help them reach their full potential. They'll even accept tough penalties more readily, if your motive is right. If your attempts at discipline aren't working, chances are, you're using punishment, not discipline. You are seeking to satisfy yourself, not train your child.

I have known parents who are mystified when their teen rebels, even though the parents were tough disciplinarians. They say things like: "I didn't let my kid get away with disrespect." "I insisted my kid tow the line." "My son has been working since he was fifteen." "My daughter wasn't allowed to act unladylike." But what was the motive behind these parents' toughness? I'm sure they told their children what to do, but did they train their kids through effective discipline—or did they punish them? I suspect it was the latter. Punishment for the sole purpose of forcing compliance will be ineffective. When the rules are about maintaining control rather than helping the child learn important life lessons, the child finds little respect for the rules or the rule maker.

Compare the differences between discipline and punishment in the following chart.

Discipline	vs.	Punishment
Leads to change		Leads to little change
Encourages		Discourages
Educates (teaches right from wrong)		Shames
For the child's benefit		For the parent's benefit
Comes from love		Comes from fear
Encourages respect		Encourages resentment
Leads to self-discipline		Leads to rebellion

Scripture tells us "do not exasperate your children; *instead*, bring them up in the training and instruction of the Lord."[3] In other words, use discipline, not punishment. If you punish your kids, you will exasperate (irritate, aggravate, enrage) them. Your children know your motives, even when you don't. If you want to know what your motive is . . . ask your kids; they can tell you. They see things as they are, not as we want them to be. Children know if your discipline is about you or them.

Which do you choose? Discipline or punishment? Respect or Resentment? If your goal is to raise respectful children, I urge you to try discipline and leave punishment behind. Ultimately, the goal of discipline is to help your children develop self-discipline—to be capable of policing themselves—so your penalties are no longer necessary.

"No discipline seems pleasant at the time, but painful. Later on, however, it produces a harvest of righteousness and peace for those who have been trained by it."[4] It couldn't be any clearer than that! Discipline isn't easy; it's even painful in the short term, but it leads to respectfulness.

Preventive Discipline

The summer between eleventh and twelfth grades, my sons decided to pull their first "stunt." When I called their friend's home on a Saturday morning to remind them of an early obligation, I discovered they weren't there and had not been, all night.

I spent nearly three hours on the phone, searching for the boys. When they finally drove up the driveway around noon, I was so angry I couldn't speak. They had spent the night at a forbidden home with no parents present.

Up until then their infractions of my rules had been misdemeanors. I considered this particular infraction a major crime that warranted major sentencing. It took two weeks for me to settle on an appropriate penalty, during which time my boys treated me like a queen rather than a judge. "Mom, can I help you with supper tonight?" "Mom, I thought I'd wash your car, just because . . ."

When the day of sentencing came, Judge Jill convened Court Rigby in the hallowed halls of our kitchen. "The privilege you abused was spending the night out," I began. "You decided you had a right to spend the night wherever you choose. You were wrong. You no longer have the privilege of spending the night at a friend's house. Is that understood?"

After a bit of stunned silence, Chad spoke up, "Can we go out for a couple of hours at night?"

"You can go out at night, but you are not allowed to spend the night out. That privilege has been taken away . . . that's it. Court dismissed," I said as I pounded the rubber mallet on the cutting board.

All was well until school began in the fall. Chad called right after the season's first football game, "Mom, we're going to spend the night at Matt's."

"No, I don't think so," I replied.

Spanking

I believe if all else fails, as a last resort, spanking can be an appropriate option with children from two to six who are outright defiant or in danger. A couple of swats to the rear end with a wooden spoon or switch are all that's needed to get your child's attention. But . . .

Don't spank out of anger.

Don't spank in public.

Hug and reassure your child of your love following the spanking.

I grew up in a time when spanking was part of being a good parent. I understood I was spanked occasionally because my parents loved me too much to allow me to ruin my life. And I appreciated it later. This was not abuse . . . far from it. I believe many of today's parents are more abusive to their kids because they fail to discipline than because they are using spanking as part of preventive discipline.

"Why not, Mom?" Chad questioned.

Swallowing hard before speaking again, "You lost that privilege," I said.

"But that was just for the summer," Chad retorted.

"No, the sentence was handed down without a time stipulation," I explained, "Sorry, I'll see you both at home in twenty minutes."

I hung up the phone, terrified rebellion had arrived. I was hoping the boys would drive up, but frankly, I didn't really believe they would.

I was wrong. Twenty-two minutes later Chad and Boyce walked past me in the kitchen without a word. They just looked in my eyes and nodded affirmatively.

The issue was settled.

I know you're wondering why my sons accepted this stiff discipline with such grace. After all, they were seniors in high school! I can tell you, it had very little to do with the tone of my voice or their fear of future consequences. It goes back to what we talked about in chapter 3, "Enroll in the School of Respect." The reason my sons didn't rebel against my discipline that night was because of all their years in the School of Respect, being raised with preventative discipline. My sons trusted me, and they knew I loved them unconditionally. They also recognized the decision to violate my trust came with a consequence, and they knew from experience that I would follow through.

Please don't misunderstand. I'm not saying my boys obeyed me because I was the perfect parent. I wasn't. I made plenty of mistakes, like the time I forgot to pick them up from soccer practice or the day I lost my cool and chewed them out only to find out they had done nothing wrong. There were plenty of instances when I said yes but should have said no.

But the boys understood that when I said no, the matter was not open for discussion. I tried my best to make decisions for my own life that reflected my belief system. If I expected the boys to be ready on time for school, I had to be punctual too. If I expected the boys to clean up after themselves, I had to keep the house picked up too. Most of all I tried to make discipline decisions with the big picture in mind, always asking myself, *Who do I want the boys to become?* I was concerned about their character. My aim was to help them learn to respect others, to respect rules, and to respect themselves.

My sons recognized:

- The certainty of my unconditional *love*

- The fair *consequence* for their disobedience to our house rule was deserved

- I would *follow through* on the penalty, and there was no need for further discussion

If we're doing our job as parents, our kids must know that our discipline comes from our love for them and our desire to help them become respectful, responsible adults. To achieve that end, we must administer consequences that reinforce the lessons we're teaching.

In other words, preventive discipline must be a combination of love, consequences, and follow-through. Let's take a closer look at how we can effectively implement these methods of preventive discipline.

Discipline from a Heart of Love

Paul tells us "the goal of our instruction [discipline] is love from a pure heart and a good conscience and a sincere faith."[5] This scripture can serve as our guide to ensure that our discipline is motivated by a heart of love for our child.

From a Pure Heart

Prepare your heart before the need for discipline arises by using Psalm 139 as a daily prayer: "Search me, O God, and know my heart; test me and know my anxious thoughts. See if there is an *offensive* way in me, and lead me in the way everlasting."[6] This exercise will reveal the good and the bad that resides in your heart, better preparing you to use discipline rather than punishment.

From a Good Conscience

Say what you mean, and mean what you say. The fastest way to fail at discipline is to not carry through on the demands you've made; so be careful what you say:

- "If you don't clean your room, you won't be allowed to eat for a month."

- "Timmy, if I have to ask you one more time to not slam the door, I'll lock you out for good."

Your kids will take you literally. You can't back track or expect them to second-guess you. You can't say, "Well, what I meant to say was . . ." We need to do our best to get it right the first time.

From a Sincere Faith

Let your children know you are not the final authority, but that you answer to God and His principles. Your kids will be much more willing to come under your authority when they understand you come under God's authority.

I mentioned early on that the experts have changed their minds countless times in the past two hundred years on the proper way to raise children. Scripture hasn't changed—not one word. Truth doesn't have to change with the whims of society. It stands the test of time.

For your discipline to be effective, your kids should not only know you love them and want the best for them, they must also know that with disobedience come consequences.

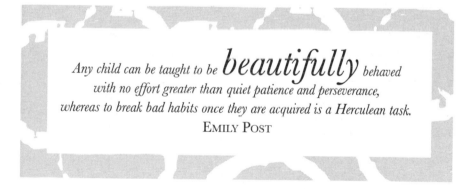

Any child can be taught to be ***beautifully*** *behaved with no effort greater than quiet patience and perseverance, whereas to break bad habits once they are acquired is a Herculean task.*
EMILY POST

Discipline through Consequences

Of the many consequences that might come to mind, I think the following are most effective.

Distraction, Time-Out, and Loss of Privileges

Infants need protection as they explore the world around them. We can train babies and toddlers to avoid danger by diverting their attention when they

Public Humiliation

Recently there's been a storm of incidents where a parent puts her child on a street corner with a sandwich board sign that tells of the child's offense. Much of the public seems to applaud the parents for getting tough with unruly teenagers.

I disagree.

Serious willful disobedience does not happen overnight. If the parent was driven to such drastic measures, there must be something missing behind the scenes. I would rather see the parents stand on the street corner with a sign confessing their failure to parent during the teenager's younger years.

Public humiliation should never be an option. Instead, deal with issues as they arise so you would never feel compelled to resort to such damaging measures.

"misbehave." A toddler's attention span is short, so the dangerous activity is quickly forgotten. If distraction doesn't work, physically move your child away from the trouble. For example, if your child refuses to stop pushing the buttons on the television when asked, pick him up and move him to another room for several minutes.

When your child is between the ages of three and six, use time-out as a consequence for misbehavior. Tell your child, "You didn't follow the rule, so you'll have to sit out until you're ready to obey." This consequence reminds me of the children's game "Simon Says." We all know the rules . . . you are only allowed to move when Simon says. If you move before he says to move, you're out of the game. If your tyke disobeys a rule, he has to sit out for a while. Use a kitchen timer set at three minutes for this age group. If your child gets up before the timer goes off, reset it, without discussion, and start over. Your child will finally give in, if you don't give up.

Time-out for tweens and teens comes in the form of the loss of privileges as a consequence of disobedience. Give an instruction once; if not followed, follow through by taking away a privilege. If your tween breaks a house rule about TV watching, take away all TV privileges for two days. As your tween grows, extend the time that the privileges is removed. For example, if your twelve-year-old daughter breaks a rule about the telephone, tell her she won't be able to use the telephone for several days. If your sixteen-year-old abuses her cell-phone privileges, she loses the phone for one month (one billing cycle!).

Natural Consequences

Painful as it may be for both of you, children must accept the consequences of their own decisions. It's tempting to rescue them, but the best discipline is self-discipline. It's through mistakes that the greatest lessons are learned. Stepping in to "fix things" will hinder, not help, the maturation process. Let your child face the consequences of poor choices.

Chad was a forgetful fourth grader until the day he found out he would have to count on his own mind rather than his mom's servant heart to remember his school work. I made the round trip from home to school to home and back to school two days in one week to help Chad cover his forgetfulness.

The following Monday morning it happened again, even after reminding the boys to check their backpacks for all needed school work. Just as Chad jumped out of the car, he remembered the papers he left on his desk. "Mom, will you pleeeeeeeeeeease go get my math sheet? I don't have class until 10:00. Thank you, Mom," he said with all the confidence in the world of my servitude. But this time I responded with a statement he had not heard before, "No, Chad, I won't do that today." It was apparent that Chad had not learned his lesson, but I had learned mine. It was time for Chad to suffer the consequences of his forgetfulness.

You would have thought by his reaction that I had told him to kiss his brother! His nine-year-old tantrum rivaled the most horrific two-year-old tantrum I had ever seen. And of course, it took place in the carpool line in front of other moms dropping off their angels. After being told to move out of the line and seeing my child pulled away from the car by an understanding teacher, I drove away with tears puddling in my lap. I circled the block wanting to return to school to ask my son to forgive me, but I knew in my heart I was doing the best thing for Chad, even though he would receive a zero on his assignment.

When I did return for the afternoon pickup, Chad had obviously surmised that his best course of action was to be quiet and non-confrontational with his mom. Finally we "kissed and made up" at supper. No apology for my decision, but a big hug with "I love you." "Yeah, I know," was Chad's reply.

You already know without my saying it, he was never forgetful again.

I have a dear friend, an English professor, who reports that more and more parents are calling to discuss their college student's grades. She is appalled at the audacity of the parents and saddened because it seems to be the students needing the most "growing up" whose parents are the ones calling her. "Counterproductive," in her words.

Repetition

This is the most effective consequence I know. It can be used no matter the age of your child—and it's almost fun! Sound too good to be true? Read on.

One night six-year-old Boyce put the last bit of macaroni and cheese in his mouth at the supper table. He jumped up from the table and headed to his room to finish his latest Lego creation.

"Now, wait a minute. Didn't you forget something?" I said just before he reached the doorway. "Remember what we do before we leave the table? Back up and give me ten."

Stomping his foot, he replied, "Aw, Mom."

With a scowl across his face, he returned to the table to finish his supper the proper way. Holding his dinner plate, he asked, "May I be excused, please?"

Too much **talk** *and you'll talk yourself into trouble and your child out of trouble.*

I replied, "Yes, you may."

He stood with dish in hand, walked to the sink, and placed it in the basin. Sighing, he reached in, picked it up again, and returned to the table and sat down.

He began again, "May I please be . . ."

Again, I replied, "Yes, you may."

The third time Boyce did this, his Dad, brother, and I began to giggle. Soon Boyce's scowl became a sheepish grin as he broke into boisterous laughter.

By the tenth repetition, I could barely stammer, "Yes, you may." The whole family was in stitches.

How many times do you think I had to remind Boyce to say, "May I be excused, please" after that night? You're right, never again. Chad, on the other hand, had to learn this lesson for himself two weeks later. A grand reminder to me that all children, even identical twins, are unique individuals with their own timetables.

Yes, it takes time and patience to use repetition as a consequence, but as you can see, this is an effective way to discipline and can be fun too. *Remember, the goal of discipline is not to punish, but to change a behavior pattern.*

Not only is repetition an effective way to correct bad manners, it can also be used to curb the use of inappropriate or bad language. If your child uses an inappropriate word, ask her to say the sentence ten times, replacing the inappropriate word with a silly word, such as, *popcorn, peanut butter,* or *stinks.* For example, if she says, "That's just stupid," have her repeat, "That's just popcorn" ten times. Next time she'll be less likely to use the word *stupid* at all.

Repetition for foul language also works on teens, but in addition to giving a silly word, I recommend giving them an appropriate alternative. For instance, if your son says something "sucks," you can ask him to say *stinks* twenty-two times. I even used *supercalifragilisticexpialidocious* on one occasion for a particularly foul word—and I requested thirty-two repetitions!

Perhaps you're thinking, *I don't have time to fool with this nonsense. Waiting for my child to repeat something thirty-two times . . .*

I beg to differ.

Disciplining through repetition will save you time, energy, and heartache in the long run. If you are willing to stand by the "give me ten" rule with gentle firmness, you can motivate your kids to change an unwanted behavior in only a few attempts. It's rare that a parent has to repeat the same exercise more than three times in order to help a child change a bad habit or instill a good one.

Why does repetition lead to behavior change? I can think of two reasons:

1. *You're offering an alternative to the wrong behavior and reinforcing it.* When you give a substitute to replace the unwanted behavior, you're training, not just doling out a penalty.

2. *It takes the sting out of the discipline.* Even the child being corrected becomes amused at the silliness of the repetition, but since our goal is to change an unwanted behavior or instill a good one, who says the discipline has to always be miserable? There are times when doing whatever it takes to help your child change is fun! And your child is motivated to change when the discipline focuses on the behavior instead of on him.

But so often in our hurriedness and tiredness we let our guards down and don't complete our mission of preventive discipline. Love and consequences will only produce change when we follow through.

Always Follow Through

A few final points to ponder about follow-through, no matter the age of your child:

- *United you stand; divided you fall.* As was pointed out in the previous chapter, you and your spouse are co-coaches on the home team. If two coaches on the same team gave opposing orders, the team would be defeated. If you disagree, do so in private. Your children will use you against each other if you're not careful to maintain a united front.

- *Be consistent.* Don't change your mind with the wind. When you're tempted to give in or tempted to bend the rules, remember you're the parent.

- *Take action.* Go over the offense and give the consequence, and then go on. We really do complicate issues of discipline by discussing and explaining. Do you really expect your child to look at you after being disciplined and say, "Oh, I understand, Dad. I get it now; you've just taken away my CD player because you love me and . . ."? Chances of that happening at that moment are slim to none.

- *Use your child's name, no matter the age.* "Jonathan, I'd like you to take out the garbage." By using your child's name, you're conveying the child's personal responsibility for the requested action. It also helps to develop his pride in a job well done. Your child is thinking, *Dad called me by name . . . I better listen.*

- *Decide ahead of time that you will win.* You're not battling your child; you're battling the wrongness of your child's behavior. For the sake of your child, you must win.

> *Discipline* is the bridge
> *between goals and accomplishments.*
> JIM ROHN

- *Stay calm.* Let a young child know by your calm demeanor that whining is absolutely, positively ineffective. You can nip whining in the bud by ignoring it. If a teen whines, explain the reason for your decision to say no, and stand by it. You can discuss alternatives, but not compromises.

- *Don't be hesitant.* Your child can hear it in your voice. Use a firm voice with confidence.

- *Expect the best.* Your children will live up to your expectations if your heart is in the right place.

- *Just say no.* When the answer needs to be no, just say so. No need to belabor an explanation. Be firm, but loving. Confident, but kind. Then let it go and move on.

- *Offer a statement, not a question.* Rather than "Would you like to go clean up your room now?" simply say, "Sally, it's time to clean your room." If you ask a question, you're giving your child the option to decide whether to obey or not.

- *Do not repeat yourself.* You want to teach your child to respond to your request the first time. If your child discovers that you'll ask repeatedly, he'll ignore you till you lose your cool, because you've programmed him to think there's more than one chance to obey.

- *Lower your voice.* When your child raises her voice, lower yours. The louder she gets, the quieter you must be. Your child will hear what you're saying, even if you think she's not listening. She wants to know what you're saying. If you're whispering, she has to calm down to hear you.

- *Never use "don't."* I believe there must be a switch at the base of a child's neck that reacts to the word *don't*. It's like having a remote control in your hand. When you say, "How many times have I told you, don't run in the house," and your child looks at you as if he's never heard you say that, believe it. He really hasn't heard you. Instead, say, "You're not allowed to run in the house. Stop in your tracks, and sit down for a while."

- *Fit the discipline to the crime.* An annoying child needs to be alone until she decides to no longer be annoying but to be helpful to others. If a child hits another child, tell her to hug that child ten times. If she leaves the yard, she loses the privilege of playing in the yard and must stay inside for the rest of the day.

- *When you do make mistakes, ask your child's forgiveness.* The level of respect your child has for you skyrockets when you're willing to humble yourself and ask for his forgiveness when you've been wrong. And following your example, your child will do the same for you.

- *Be a parent first, friend second.* During your children's teen years your relationship with them is changing from parent to friend, but you are still the parent, and teens need a parent more than another friend.

Parents who parent with a character-centered perspective use preventive discipline to meet their end goal—raising a respectful, responsible adult who is actively pursuing his or her purpose. Your children can move from your governance to self-governance if along the way you have given them ample opportunities to make their own decisions and receive the benefits of good decisions, while suffering the consequences of bad decisions.

Your reward is a close relationship with your children based on mutual trust and respect. Your child's reward is self-respect.

The Reward

Effective preventive discipline develops self-discipline in your child—the ability and desire to do the right thing because it's the right thing to do. Through instruction and discipline of moral character, your child develops respect for God, others, and self. The child who masters self-discipline is a child with self-respect who will go on to become all that you could ever hope or envision.

As wise King Solomon once said, "The corrections of discipline are the way of life."[7]

Reality Check

Before moving on to the next chapter, consider your answers to these questions as you strengthen your resolve to raise respectful children in this disrespectful world:

1. When you discipline your children, are you careful to make certain the penalty fits the disobedience?

2. Do you discipline your children to punish them or to change a wrong behavior?

3. What is the motive behind your discipline?

   - Anger

   - Fear

   - Love

4. Are your current disciplinary techniques effective?

5. When contemplating discipline, what are you more concerned with?

   - Your child doing good

   - Your child feeling good

6. Do you often yell at your children to correct them?

7. Do you find yourself correcting your children for the same things you sometimes do?

8. When you make mistakes, do you admit you're wrong and ask your child for forgiveness?

Shield Your Treasures from the Trash:
Magazines, Books, and Music

"FATHER, WHAT IS SEX SIN?" young Corrie ten Boom asked her father during a train ride as they returned home from a business trip in the city. She relates the story in her autobiography, *The Hiding Place:*

> My father turned to look at me, as he always did when answering a question, but to my surprise he said nothing. At last he stood up, lifted his traveling case from the rack over our heads, and set it on the floor. "Will you carry it off the train, Corrie?" he said. I stood up and tugged at it. It was crammed with the watches and spare parts he had purchased that morning. "It's too heavy," I said. "Yes," he said. "And it would be a pretty poor father who would ask his little girl to carry such a load. It's the same way, Corrie, with knowledge. Some knowledge is too heavy for children. When you are older and stronger you can bear it. For now you must trust me to carry it for you."[1]

How do we shield our children, our precious treasures, from the trash in a culture that bombards them with immorality at every turn? Corrie ten Boom's father had the right answer—we, as parents, must bear the burden for them. We must shield their eyes and hearts from hurtful images and wrong messages.

To protect your treasures from the trash, you must be aware of what your children are seeing and hearing. You can't protect them if you don't know they are in danger. I'm afraid your kids already know more than you think, so you need to know even more . . .

Do you know what's out there? Read on and you will. In this chapter we will look at how our kids are being exposed to disrespectful messages and images in magazines, books, and music, and what you can do to protect your kids from these messages. In the next chapter we'll do the same with movies, TV, video games, and the Internet.

Disrespectful Messages in Magazines

I recently stood in a sea of magazines at a national bookstore chain. My eyes jumped from sexual images to sexual innuendoes and back again, making me seasick. What used to be seen only inside pornographic magazines now gets blatantly displayed on the covers of mainstream publications.

Don't be mistaken, I'm not talking about magazines targeted for adult readership. Magazine moguls target girls as young as ten with periodicals that contain adult content.[2] I assure you, twelve-year-old girls know all the "hot mags." Yes, even your own daughters.

Soft porn is rampant in teen magazines—*Cosmo Girl, Elle Girl, Young Miss, Teen Vogue,* just to name a few. And that's not the only problem I have with them. The publishers of these magazines know if they can lure a ten-year-old into reading *Cosmo Girl,* she'll be reading *Cosmopolitan* by her thirteenth birthday.

And lest you think girls aren't being influenced by the images in these magazines, think again. Have you heard the new term for the young girls who dress like the models on the cover of *Cosmopolitan*? *Prostitots.* That's right . . . *Prostitots.* Bill Maher, the infamous TV host who was fired from his late-night talk show, *Politically Incorrect,* for crossing the line one too many times, was correct in his seemingly outrageous declaration, "It won't be long before there's nothing left for the prostitutes to wear." (Even more alarming is the fact that these clothes are being purchased by the parents! Young kids don't have the means to buy these clothes on their own.)

It's not only the images in these magazines that are destructive; so are the

articles, many of which aren't appropriate for adults. For example:
"Sex Special"
"Hot Tips, Toys, and More"
"How to Score Like You're on Vacation Every Day"
"Your Hot Summer Sex and Love"
"Tips That Will Make You Feel Like a Goddess in 60 Seconds"
"Sex Talk"
"10 Sex Sins Thou Shalt Not Commit Tonight"
"Ditch the Rules and Release Your Inner Sinner!"
"His Secret Sex Craving"
"I Stole My Best Friend's Boyfriend"
"Find His Dominant Sense and Send Him into Orbit"
"Make Over Your Body"
"Seven Moves to a Strong and Sexy Body"

Don't think boys are any less impressionable than girls when it comes to the magazines. When exposed to sexual images, their respect for the opposite sex diminishes greatly because the message being communicated is that girls are objects of men's pleasure.

Not only are magazines promoting sex, materialism, greed, and violence, some are going so far as to advocate the use of drugs. I would have a hard time believing this if I hadn't seen it for myself. Magazines such as *CC—Cannabis Culture* actually promote the use of marijuana, an illegal drug that threatens our youth's cognitive abilities and reasoning skills. The edition I skimmed through had numerous articles about the pleasure of smoking pot, glorifying the drug as an answer to coping with the stressed-out world. When I inquired at the customer counter if the marijuana magazine was real or a gag, the staffer informed me, "Yeah, it's real. There's about six others on the market that help 'gardeners' grow better weed, but we're sold out till next month."

How is it that magazines promoting an illegal substance are sold in national bookstore chains? I don't understand. Do you? Ask the next time you visit one of the stores.

The magazines are troubling, but at least they are easy to recognize as trouble. Books, on the other hand, can be deceiving.

Disrespectful Messages in Books

I co-host a half-hour radio broadcast, *Reality Check*, in which we discuss current trends that threaten our children. On a recent broadcast we highlighted a series of books for tween girls called the Gossip Girl series. The first book, *Gossip Girl*, opens with these words:

> Ever wondered what the lives of the chosen ones are really like? Well, I'm going to tell you, because I'm one of them. . . . I'm talking about the people who are *born to it*—those of us who have everything anyone could possibly wish for and who take it all completely for granted.
>
> Welcome to New York City's Upper East Side, where my friends and I live and go to school and play and sleep—sometimes with each other. . . . We have unlimited access to money and booze and whatever else we want, and our parents are rarely home, so we have tons of privacy. We're smart, we've inherited classic good looks, we wear fantastic clothes, and we know how to party. Our ___ still stinks, but you can't smell it because the bathroom is sprayed hourly by the maid with a refreshing scent made exclusively for us by French perfumers.[3]

Forgive me for exposing you to this, but your daughters are reading it. The books in this series are filling the slots on the New York Times Children's Books bestseller list. Upon its publication, book number eight took the number one slot. The series has sold more than 2.2 million copies with three books yet to come in the series. There's already a spin-off series titled The It Girl.

This is frightening, considering the kinds of disrespectful messages these books are broadcasting to young girls with impressionable minds:

- Lesbian sex is cool.

- Value is in your status not your character.

- There are no boundaries.

- Promiscuity is acceptable.

- With enough money you can get away with anything, and if you don't have enough money, you can pretend.

A group of readers from twelve to sixteen recently interviewed the series's author, Cecily von Ziegesar. During the interview fifteen-year-old Hanna asked von Ziegesar: "If you have teenagers, or have had teenagers, would you let them read this book? If so, would you let them read it as a "what not to do" lesson or as a "see what Mommy does in her spare time"?

Von Ziegesar replied: "I have a two-year-old daughter and a baby boy on the way—eventually they will be teenagers. I'll let them read the books when and if they're interested and just wait and see what they have to say. I don't think I'm going to be the type of parent who forbids her kids to read certain books or see certain movies or wear certain clothes or whatever. I'd rather let my kids see what's out there and make their own opinions and choices."[4]

I'd like to talk with Ms. von Ziegesar when her daughter is twelve and see if her opinion has changed. I think Samuel Taylor Coleridge, the great English poet of the Romantic period, would suggest the same thought to Ms. von Ziegesar that he once offered to a man who told him he did not believe in giving religious instruction to children. The man believed children's minds should not be prejudiced in any direction, so that when the children were able to think for themselves, they would be able to choose their religious opinions for themselves. Coleridge didn't respond, but after a while he asked his visitor if he would like to see his garden. The man said he would, and Coleridge took him out into the garden, where only weeds were growing. The man said, "Why, this is not a garden! There are nothing but weeds here!"

"Well, you see," answered Coleridge. "I did not wish to infringe upon the liberty of the garden in any way. I was just giving the garden a chance to express itself and to choose its own production."[5]

Unfortunately, Ms. von Ziegesar is not the only mom who's unwilling to protect her treasures from the trash. Many mothers are saying they're not concerned about the content in the Gossip Girl series because these books have helped their daughters develop a love for reading. (Sounds like the scheme of the enemy—enticement with legitimacy to mask the hidden immorality.)

Harry Potter and the Prisoner of Azkaban contains another type of disrespect that is permeating our children's minds through print. I'm not going to discuss whether the use of sorcery and magic is right or wrong. Instead, I'd like to point out a disturbing theme that is woven throughout the Harry Potter series. Harry Potter embraces a subjective morality. He doesn't hold to any sort of absolute truth, but instead seems to make moral decisions based upon his feelings. These books blur the line between good and evil. They tell kids that whatever it takes to come out on top is OK.

> *Books for children should contain nothing to cause fright, suggest fear, glorify mischief, excuse malice, or condone cruelty.*
> JOHNNY GRUELLE, CREATOR OF RAGGEDY ANN

Peter Chattaway, a freelance journalist and cultural critic, explains it well in his review of the book for *Christianity Today:*

The deeper problem with these books is their questionable and highly subjective morality. . . . [Harry] exhibits a flagrant disregard for the rules, even when they have been put there for his own safety, and nearly always seems to get away with it; it is also particularly disturbing to see the "heroes" of this story, including Harry himself, so eager to kill the man who betrayed Harry's parents. Harry manages to exchange his anger for mercy at the last possible moment, but his change of heart seems more like a passing whim than the result of a deeper transformation in the way he thinks and feels.[6]

When it comes to messages in the media, it's the little things that are the big things. Perhaps you think my criticism of the Harry Potter series is exaggerated, or that I'm reading into the story, but I strongly believe that as parents we must consider the subtle messages our kids are receiving through books and other media. We have to make judgment calls about the intent behind the words. The intention of *The Chronicles of Narnia* by C. S. Lewis is clear, because we know the heart of the author. Ms. Rowling, on the other hand, has chosen to keep her belief system private, leaving us with little to go on in understanding the intent of the message behind the story.

Don't make the mistake of focusing solely on the storyline in books your children read. You need to look at the messages being communicated through the actions and behaviors of the characters in these stories. We must read between the lines.

The trouble with the Gossip Girl series is obvious—blatant disrespect for society, God, and all things decent. But in some ways I find the disrespect in the Harry Potter series even more insidious, simply because it can be so easily overlooked, leaving children vulnerable and their parents unaware of any harm done.

The way I see it, the bigger the hoopla over a new release, the closer we need to examine its merits. We need to take a closer look at books our society is applauding.

And what about the music that's found alongside the books and magazines in the stores?

Disrespectful Messages in Music

My daddy's taste in music ran from classic to country. Before we kids could make our way to the living room on Christmas morning, Daddy already had the music going. His favorite Christmas tunes came from Perry Como, Johnny Cash, and Alvin and the Chipmunks.

When I was in high school, he called rock-and-roll "ya, ya, ya, racket" because he couldn't understand the words. But he was even more upset by the beat. "The rhythm makes you feel things you should only feel in the bedroom with your wife," he would say with utter disgust. I found myself echoing his disgust the day I called the music of this generation "ya, ya, ya, garbage."

Once upon a time music inspired love to blossom. Nat King Cole's "Unforgettable" touched the heart with the tender sentiment that love is a unique experience. The Carpenters' "When I Fall in Love" spoke of the one true love that lasts forever. Lyrics encouraged love with one special someone.

But along with the sweet songs, the rock-and-roll invasion took place. The biggest names found their way to the Ed Sullivan show. But behind the scenes it didn't matter who the band was—they were expected to tow the line of decency. In 1967 the Rolling Stones were asked by the Ed Sullivan show to change the lyrics of their hit song from "Let's Spend the Night Together" to "Let's Spend Some Time Together." Out of respect for Ed Sullivan, they acquiesced and were invited to return. Later that same year a controversy arose with a line from "Light My Fire" by The Doors. In contrast to The Rolling Stones, they refused to remove "Girl, we couldn't get much higher," which Sullivan felt implied drug use. The Doors never again appeared on his show.

How standards for what's acceptable in music have changed! No topic is taboo, from free sex to masturbation to sadomasochism, and whatever would be in-between. Many of today's top pop stars started out as "innocent girls" who "sexed up" their acts to increase record sales. Today's lyrics are filled with a word that begins with the letter *f*. It's even in the titles of songs by R&B crooner Eamon and the hip-hop artists OutKast.[7] Twenty years ago these folks would not have been allowed on any stage anywhere in our country. Today they perform before sold-out audiences.

In 1985 a group of United States senators' wives, believing that the decay of the nuclear family was attributable, at least in part, to the disrespectful lyrics in rock music, formed the Parents Music Resource Center to combat the problem. They demanded a method for warning parents of the dangerous material contained in the lyrics of songs of the music groups their kids were listening to. Even though the Recording Industry Association of America (RIAA) objected, along with recording artists Frank Zappa and Rage against the Machine, PMRC succeeded in their goal of requiring the labeling of records that contained "explicit lyrics or content."[8]

But the situation has continued to degenerate. Some groups originally opposed to the record labeling are beginning to admit something does need to be done.[9] We can only hope the RIAA will decide to self-police, but in the meantime we can't hold our breath waiting, because we'll all pass out, and then where will our children be?

In a recent interview about the disrespectful world, a radio commentator asked me: "So, Jill, don't you think the line has been crossed this time? I mean, really, the line has finally been crossed. Don't you think?"

"No, I don't think a line has been crossed."

"Come on, Jill, even I think this one is just too much," he said in amazement.

"The line hasn't been crossed, because no one has drawn the line. That's the problem!" I retorted, making my point.

Who is drawing the line? Society's not drawing the line. Neither is the music industry. So parents must draw the line.

> Kids are looking for an *identity*, and there is a huge mass-media machine eager to give them one—one that has nothing to do with reality. If you are a Christian, of course you want your child to have a Christ-centered identity, but you need to know that the culture-centered identity is the exact opposite.
>
> BOB JUST
> "'KILLER CULTURE': A CALL TO THE CHURCHES"

Help for Knowing When and How to Draw the Line

Blast from the Past is a delightful movie set in the sixties. Adam, a handsome young man with a heart of gold, was born in the bomb shelter of his genius inventor dad, who convinced his pregnant wife they should go underground when he thought our country had been hit by a nuclear bomb. Stocked with enough supplies to last thirty-five years, the couple raises their son, Adam, with values that were untarnished from influences of the changing world above. Adam's mother taught him manners, how to dance, and the importance of being polite. His dad taught him about baseball, science, and the pitfalls of the seedier side of life.

When Adam leaves his underground home and goes to the surface, the young man's character is tested. But rather than being changed by the world, Adam changes those he meets. His sense of duty and honor to his family superseded the temptations to indulge in the things of the world.

Granted, you and I can't raise our children in bomb shelters, nor would we want to, but we can put a shield of protection around them, keeping the bad influences from damaging their character. We can help our children become adults who change the world. How? By spending more time teaching them the "better way."

Here are a few suggestions for how you can do just that:

Model Godly Reading and Listening Choices

Don't count on that old adage—"Do as I say, not as I do." It didn't work with us, did it? Children will do what you do. What one generation condones, the next will accept, so don't read or listen to anything you don't want them to read or listen to. Do your kids see you regularly reading the bestseller of all time? More than 3,000,000,000 copies have been sold—the *Holy Bible*. And the music that's in your home . . . is it sexy or serene?

Don't Allow Free Choice in Entertainment

Make it clear that the magazines, books, and music enjoyed by members of your family will promote good values. Let your children know that if it's not fit for you to hear, then it's not fit for them to hear. If it's not fit for you to see, then it's not fit for them to see.

Open Your Children's Eyes to the Best of Culture

Expose them to images and values that show the good in our society— timeless treasures that embody the good of humankind, not the depravity. For example:

1. When you first begin reading to your children, *read Bible stories together*. Young boys enjoy hearing about David and Goliath, and the story shows that when we are armed with God's truth for protection, we can stand against giants. The story of Esther teaches girls that beauty is only skin deep, that much more important than beauty is the willingness to be courageous when given an opportunity to help others. God protected Shadrach, Meshach, and Abednego, who refused to bow in worship to false gods. They were tossed into a fiery furnace, but God walked with them, and they were not burned. What life lessons to teach your children!

2. *Visit used bookstores, and buy old children's books to read to your kids.* Look for old school readers, such as My Little Red Story Books, At Work and Play, and the Mac and Muff series. Pre-sixties readers often mingled Bible stories with stories of Dick and Jane.

3. *Introduce your children to classical music,* even if it's not your taste in music. If we don't first expose them to a better alternative, our kids will choose what others expose them to.

4. *Take your children to museums.* Fill their minds with images of fine art. When we lived in New York City, my boys were in preschool, and I often took them to museums. What a blessing this turned out to be for my sons. They learned an appreciation for art at an early age. They also learned respect for the work of others, respect for public places, and respect for rules.

5. *Use Scripture to teach middle-school children the importance of what we see and what we hear and how it affects our souls.* Your thirteen-year-old needs to know that your opinion matters, but God's opinion counts the most. Read passages such as:

   > For everything in the world—the cravings of sinful man, the lust of his eyes and the boasting of what he has and does—comes not from the Father but from the world. The world and its desires pass away, but the man who does the will of God lives forever. [10]

   > Many are the plans in a man's heart, but it is the LORD's purpose that prevails. [11]

   > "For I know the plans I have for you," declares the LORD, "plans to prosper you and not to harm you, plans to give you hope and a future." [12]

   > I urge you, brothers, to watch out for those who cause divisions and put obstacles in your way that are contrary to the teaching you have learned. Keep away from them. For such people are not serving our Lord Christ, but their own appetites. By smooth talk and flattery they deceive the minds of naive people. Everyone has

heard about your obedience, so I am full of joy over you; but I want you to be wise about what is good, and innocent about what is evil.[13]

Finally, brothers, whatever is true, whatever is noble, whatever is right, whatever is pure, whatever is lovely, whatever is admirable— if anything is excellent or praiseworthy—think about such things.[14]

6. *Encourage high-school kids to choose the better way.* High-school teens are most vulnerable to the messages of the trash, if the foundation has not been laid to understand its influence. Fortify your teens with the truth that:

- Every decision you make means choosing one thing over another.

- Teens respect other teens who stand their ground against the trash.

   Evie was a high-school student who made a decision to not become infected by the culture. She chose to live her life according to God's principles, regardless of ridicule. But rather than being alienated, she was elevated to homecoming queen by the votes of her classmates because of the great respect she commanded. Evie found that sharing God's love with fellow students without succumbing to the temptations of following the crowd was the better way.

- The friends you choose to surround yourself with today affect who you will become tomorrow.

7. *Do your part to encourage your children's school to offer only the "good stuff."* It's not enough to work hard in your home to expose your children to the good stuff; your kids need to see that your commitment goes beyond the walls of your home. They need to see that you're willing to go out on a limb in our society for their sakes. Follow my mother's lead.

   She had *Seventeen* magazine removed from our high-school library in 1972 because of an article about teenage sex. She calmly walked into the principal's office with a copy of the magazine and asked if he would want his daughter to read the article or, even worse, if he would want his daughter's date to read it. The principal agreed and had the magazine removed.

Do you want to raise respectful children in a disrespectful world? Then saturate their minds with the right stuff, the good stuff the world has to offer. By doing this, you will not only be shielding your treasure from the trash, you'll be training them to discern for themselves what is worthy of their time and interest, especially if they see you take a stand for the right against the wrong. When your kids respect you, they are on their way to becoming respectful adults.

In the next chapter, we'll take a look at how you can protect your treasures from the trash that permeates movies, TV, video games, and the Internet.

Reality Check

Before moving on to the next chapter, consider your answers to these questions as you strengthen your resolve to raise respectful children in this disrespectful world:

1. Do you allow your young daughter to buy teen magazines?

2. Do you know what your teenage children think about the latest entertainment (songs, magazines, books) the world is offering them?

3. Have you become blind to the destructive garbage the media is offering your children? Have you allowed your children to be filled with it?

4. Do you know who your children's role models are?

5. Do you know what type of music your children are listening to? What type of magazines they are reading?

6. What kinds of things do you do to help influence the culture for good? Can it impact your kids to see you doing these things?

7. Are your choices of media helping your children make wise decisions about what they read and listen to?

9

Shield Your Treasures from the Trash:
Movies, TV, Video Games, and the Internet

WANT TO KNOW A SURE SIGN your child is watching too much television? Watching too many movies? Playing too many video games? Spending too much time on the computer?

See if one of the following scenarios rings a bit too familiar:

"No! Don't . . . it's not over," cries ten-year-old Chuck.

"Darling, it's time to read," Mom says calmly.

"But I have to see _____." Or,

"But I don't wanna read a dumb old book. Books just stare at you . . . they're boring."

"I'm in a chat room . . . I gotta wait for the end of this . . . can't you see this is important?"

If you've had these kinds of arguments in your home, it's time to reassess the amount of time your child is spending in front of these screens. And just as important, what's on those screens.

Many of today's children are oversaturated with the visual images and messages they see in movies and on television and on the Web. These screens can program our youth to accept deviant behavior as normal, view violence as part of living, and believe that fantasy is reality. In this chapter we are going to examine the disrespectful messages found in movies, TV, video games, and the Internet, and then we'll discuss what you can do to protect your kids from these messages.

Disrespectful Messages in Movies

Fantasy becomes reality when characters become bigger than life on the big screen, and unfortunately, our kids often base their decisions about what's right and wrong from the movies.

Just as an addict needs more of a drug than the hit before to satisfy his habit, movie producers continue to deepen our addiction for drama and violence. With each new release the violence is more intense and the message of good versus evil becomes more blurred. Case in point: two of the top movies in the past year, *Harry Potter and the Prisoner of Azkaban* and *Revenge of the Sith* were both said to be darker than previous movies in their respective series.[1]

Bob Bloom of the *Journal and Courier* wrote, "*Revenge of the Sith* is the darkest, most tragic film in the series."[2]

George Lucas, the genius behind Star Wars, received "a lot of flak" from parents concerned about the film's rating. "A lot of people were saying, how can you do this? My children love these movies. Why can you not let them go see it?" Lucas said. "But I have to tell a story. I'm not making these, oddly enough, to be giant, successful blockbusters. I'm making them because I'm telling a story, and I have to tell the story I intended."[3]

But why did Mr. Lucas not consider his audience when making the film? Those with significant influence over children too often dismiss the responsibility that comes with their influence. It doesn't matter whether they like having the responsibility or not. They have it, and that's what matters.

The ratings in films are supposedly meant to help parents discern their appropriateness, but the ratings are flawed. A study by the Kids Risk Project at the Harvard School of Public Health found "that ratings creep has occurred over the last decade and that today's movies contain significantly more violence, sex, and profanity on average than movies of the same rating a decade ago."[4]

Could it be that in 1992 the third episode of Star Wars would have received an R rating?

Dr. Thompson of the Harvard group would argue, yes. Others agree.

The Kids-in-Mind group contends that the Motion Picture Association of America (MPAA) ratings are not accurate. Financed by the film industry, MPAA doesn't function as an independent agent but is controlled by the moviemakers, therefore making the ratings negotiable.

An additional caution to parents concerning the MPAA ratings system is that ratings are age specific, not content specific, which allows for a wide variance in opinion of what is appropriate or not. Factors beyond sex and violence are often overlooked.

Ben Jones would be the first one to tell you not to trust the ratings alone. Famous for his portrayal of mechanic Cooter in the popular eighties TV series *The Dukes of Hazzard*, Mr. Jones became a Georgia congressman following the end of the series. In a press release prior to the opening of the new movie version, Mr. Jones urged families to avoid the movie.

> Profanity and sexual content in the PG-13 film are a "sleazy insult," akin to taking *I Love Lucy* and making her a crackhead. In our show, nobody got hurt, nobody cussed, nobody bled, the good guys won, and the Duke boys were heroes because they always made the right moral choice. Don't take your kids to see it thinking you're going to see a reflection of our show.[5]

Cooter makes a good point. We can't expect that Hollywood is upholding traditional standards from the past when they remake a movie. We can't put all the blame on Hollywood when we let our kids attend remakes of old movies—or even take them ourselves.

What's a Parent to Do?

During the special study we conducted among children of varying ages, we asked a series of questions about their movie-viewing habits:

- Have you watched an R-rated film; if so, how often?

- Who allowed you to see it? Your parents, siblings, or friends?

- Have you watched a PG-13 movie; if so, how often?

- Who allowed you to see it? Your parents, siblings, or friends?

We were astonished to find kids as young as six who had watched R-rated movies. Seventy-five percent of twelve-year-olds watch R-rated movies at least once a month. Ninety percent of seven-year-olds watch PG-13 movies regularly. (Remember the PG-13 movie of today would have received an R rating just twelve years ago.) More than 65 percent said their parents were the ones who allowed them to see these movies.

As parents our first priority should be protecting our kids from the disrespectful messages in films. We all have different opinions on what is appropriate and what is not. If you trust others to make that decision for you, it could prove harmful to your child. I recommend that you see the movie you have any doubts about before you allow your children to see it. Do your homework. We can all be fooled.

I learned this lesson the hard way the night I took my sons to a PG-13 movie. (They were fourteen, and I had received reliable reports that the movie was a good choice, but I didn't check it out myself before I took them.) Without warning, a scene I deemed inappropriate appeared on the big screen. I was seated between them and reached on either side to cover their eyes. But my hands became entangled with theirs as they attempted to cover my eyes, "Mom, you shouldn't see this!" they said in unison.

"If I shouldn't see it, then you shouldn't see it . . . right?" I responded with a sixth-grade-teacher look. "Get the point?"

They nodded in agreement.

Our second priority should be to do something about the movie industry. If we parents voiced our opinions so the film industry could hear us, we could make a difference. Why do we allow the industry to dictate to us, rather than telling the industry what we would like to see? We, the consumers, hold the power. The problem is that we're not exercising our power. If we want to raise respectful children, we can make our job easier by working to change the disrespectful world . . . starting with the movie industry.

Let me offer a suggestion for how you can help transform the disrespectful world. Start in your own home. Put up your shield and don't let it down. Raise awareness that we're not helpless victims by working with those organizations involved in trying to change our culture. Here are a few of the best:

- *Citizens for Community Values (CCV):* www.ccv.org
  Phil and Vicki Burress are dedicated to the return of moral values

in our country. What began as an effort to remove the pornography industry from their city has grown into a national organization combating the entertainment industry and affecting legislation in Washington, DC.

- *Family Research Council (FRC):* www.frc.org
  Located in the heart of our capital, FRC has long been a driving force for the good of the family in our country. Under the leadership of Tony Perkins this organization has an open door to the president and uses its influence to promote sound moral principles in all areas of society.

- *State Family Policy Councils:* www.family.org/cforum/fpc/
  More than thirty states now have an established family policy council. Visit the Web site to find a council in your state or to start one! I am honored to serve on the board of the Louisiana Family Forum, the advocacy group in our state that speaks as the voice for families desiring to return our society to the moral standards of the past.

- *The Agape Press:* www.agapepress.org
  Excellent source for updates on the latest news affecting your family. Visit their Web site to sign up for a daily bulletin.

- *CitizenLink magazine:* www.family.org
  This outstanding resource for combating the entertainment industry offers a yearly subscription. The articles are insightful and from a perspective you can trust.

You'll be surprised how many folks in your local community are just waiting for someone to take the first step. You won't stand alone when you take a stand.

You'll need all the help you can get, because the movies aren't the only source of wrong messages.

Disrespectful Messages on TV and in Video Games

Disrespectfulness *is* rampant, not only on the big screen, but during prime time on the little screens (which aren't always so little anymore). Let me show you what I mean.

According to the Nielsen ratings, 6.6 million kids ages two to eleven and 7.3 million adolescents ages twelve to seventeen watched Justin Timberlake rip open Janet Jackson's bodice during the 2004 Super Bowl halftime show.[6] The incident was bad enough, but what's unforgivable is that of all those who knew what would take place that night in front of millions of innocent children, none said, "Don't do it!" How could there be such little regard for our children?

Britney and Madonna's kiss during MTV's Music Video Awards in 2003 offered another incidence of disrespectfulness. In an interview on *Access Hollywood* following the show, twenty-one-year-old Spears said Madonna's idea for shock value gave her "butterflies." She said, "[Madonna] just has this way about her, but at the same time it was very inspiring because it humbled me, and it gave me something to look up to, you know?" When asked what her mom and dad had to say, Spears responded, "Well, my mom liked it actually. . . . And my dad, weirdly enough, he thought it was fine too. I mean, come on . . . it's Madonna. If you can kiss any girl in the world, that has to be her."[7] I've often wondered how many adolescent girls kissed another girl after seeing Britney and Madonna.

Speaking of MTV . . . Nickelodeon was launched as the children's network in 1979 to offer quality children's programming. But that was nearly thirty years ago. Today Nickelodeon is a feeder station for MTV (one of the most disrespectful channels on television) as part of the Viacom empire. That's why most of the programs on Nickelodeon are unsuitable for young viewers; they're being led down the path to become MTVholics when they turn twelve. Even the couple of good shows for young children are tarnished because of the advertising that opens and closes each episode. It's an old salesman's trick . . . just get them in the front door so they'll stay awhile and buy more. Don't believe me? You don't have to take my word for it.

Leonard J. Beer, editor in chief of *Hits* magazine, a music industry trade publication, had this to say in an interview with *Frontline*:

> I'm very pro-MTV. I think MTV has probably created the best brand in television that anybody's ever created. The MTV networks make zillions of dollars. They own the kids almost from the time they come out of the fetus, you know. My kids grew up watching Nickelodeon and got moved

into the MTV networks, and you know, it's the cultural beat of their generation. And it has been since the day it went on the air. You know Tom Preston and these people, Judy McGrath, they invented one of the great art forms of our time.[8]

TV sitcoms also contain disrespectful messages. At first glance ABC's *Desperate Housewives* appeared to be the all-American dream come true— suburbia at its best. Maybe a return to *Leave It to Beaver* or *Ozzie and Harriet,* but on closer observation it turned out to be anything but. Susan is a single mom with a teenage daughter who gives her mom advice on how to seduce the "hunk" of the street. Lynette, whose husband is heading into his midlife crisis, can't relax and enjoy the gift of children. Edie, the bombshell who still acts and dresses like a lost college girl, has nothing more to offer than her body. And Gabrielle, the trophy wife married to the imprisoned husband, is more concerned with losing her figure than preparing for her baby on the way. Never satisfied, she's already had an affair with the yard boy who could be the father of her coming child.

Remember when television portrayed the best in us? No longer. Today it portrays the worst in us. You've read unsettling reports in the newspapers about teachers seducing students. *Desperate Housewives* glamorizes such deviant behavior. This is not entertainment, but sensationalism. What's even more dangerous—the characters are believable. Sad to say, we all can relate to one of these women or men in some way. That's what makes folks tune in—just enough truth to make it "real."

But a lot of folks must enjoy seeing the baser side of our personalities, because *Desperate Housewives* consistently holds the number one spot in the ratings. And it's not just adults that are making the Nielsen ratings go through the roof. This is the most popular network show with kids nine to twelve.[9] You read that correctly; kids ages nine to twelve are glued to ABC on Sunday nights.

Other shows adolescents are watching?

The top shows for twelve- to seventeen-year-old girls are: *American Idol, The O.C., Will & Grace* (this is disgraceful) and *One Tree Hill.* The top shows for twelve- to seventeen-year-old boys are: *The Simpsons, Malcom,* and *The O.C.*[10]

The new fall TV season has just begun as I'm writing this book. The Parents Television Council, a well-respected watchdog organization, rated *The O.C.* as the worst of the week due to "a violent assault, a father abandoning his family for the second time, and Marissa and Ryan having sex under highly improbable circumstances, all in one show."[11]

Many adolescents were watching; were your kids watching? If so, pay attention to these cold, hard facts:

- Eighty-three percent of the episodes of the top-twenty shows among teen viewers contained some sexual content, including 20 percent with sexual intercourse.[12] The video game "Grand Theft Auto: Vice City," rated M, was the best-selling video game among teens and preteens. In it, players can simulate having sex with a prostitute and then killing her.[13]

- On average, music videos contain ninety-three sexual situations per hour, including eleven "hard core" scenes depicting behaviors such as intercourse and oral sex.[14]

- Before the age of eighteen the average child will witness over 200,000 acts of violence on television, including 16,000 murders.[15]

- Longitudinal studies have found that eight-year-old boys who viewed the most violent programs while growing up were most likely to engage in aggressive and delinquent behavior by age eighteen.[16]

- Boys exposed to violent sex on television, including rape, are less likely to be sympathetic to female victims of sexual violence.[17]

- More than half of teens report getting some or most of their information about sex from television.[18]

- Teens who watch more sexual content on television are more likely to initiate intercourse and progress to more advanced noncoital sexual activities during the subsequent year.[19]

- Estimated number of American homes with television: 109.6 million.

- Average time American kids spend watching television each day: four hours.

- Children spend more time watching television than in any other activity except sleep.[20]

- Fifty-four percent of kids have a TV in their bedroom.[21]

I won't hit you with any more statistics. You know how bad it is. So how does all this affect our children? A noted pediatric surgeon has a strong opinion. Dr. Lorraine Day has advocated the elimination of TV viewing by children under the age of two for several years. Through her years of research she has found that:

Children watch an average of 43 hours of TV per week; that's longer than the average adult work week. While watching, they rapidly become almost hypnotized. It has been shown scientifically that within minutes of beginning to watch TV, the brain changes from the alert brain waves (beta waves) to the hypnotic waves (alpha waves) where the judgment center of the brain is bypassed. So the violence and decadence that the child sees, bypasses the judgment center in the brain and is implanted in the child's brain without any ability on the child's part to decide whether what they are seeing is right or wrong. The violence and decadence are accepted by the brain without any moral judgment being applied to it. It then becomes part of the child's permanent subconscious.[22]

I hope Dr. Day has convinced you to turn off the television. We do have control over that remote, if we will only exercise it. I regret I allowed my own sons to watch too much television when they were younger. If I had it to do over again, I would have turned it off much sooner.

*For reliable **information** on children's television, visit:*
http://www.parentstv.org.

What's a Parent to Do?

I'm always looking for the disconnect—the place where our understanding of a problem doesn't match our actions. The truth is, we don't practice what we preach. According to a recent survey by the Pew Research Center, 75 percent of adults polled would like to see tighter enforcement of government standards for broadcast content during hours children are watching.[23] *Time* magazine recently reported that 68 percent of respondents to a poll said they believe the entertainment industry has lost touch with viewers' moral standards. Fifty percent said there's too much sexual content on TV.[24]

Do you see the discrepancies between what many parents are saying and what they are actually doing? The most vulgar show on network television is number one, yet 50 percent of viewers *say* there's too much sex on TV. Seventy-five percent of adults *say* they want tighter controls to protect children's viewing, but the shows they allow their kids to watch are *Will & Grace, Desperate Housewives,* and *The O.C.*

We say one thing and do another. We still want someone else to make the hard decisions for us. I'm just as guilty as anyone else. But it's time we stood up and said, "Enough!"

Here's some ways you can say, "Enough!"

1. *Monitor your children's entertainment choices.* I'm not advocating no television at all, although I do have friends who have chosen that option and enjoy the tranquility a great deal. I am advocating the careful, systematic monitoring of every minute the box is turned on.

   For children younger than two, the questionable benefits of television don't outweigh the negative effects. Why set your kids up for attention deficit problems? It's much more important that toddlers work on cognitive and motor skills than to sit in front of a box.

2. *Practice what you preach, and turn off your television.* It's not OK for you and your spouse to watch *Desperate Housewives* with children in your home. We can't blame the media if we're watching what they give us to watch. See chapter 10 for what to do with your kids to keep them engaged and their TV watching to a bare minimum.

3. *Complain to the Federal Communications Commission (FCC) regarding the subject matter seen in television.* The regulation of obscenity, indecency, and profanity on television falls under their domain. According to their Web site. "It is a violation of federal law to air obscene programming at any time. It is also a violation of federal law to broadcast indecent or profane programming during certain hours."[25]

In an interview, Ryan Murphy, the creator of the most sexually provocative show on television, *Nip/Tuck*, said, "This year I've heard less from standards and practices than ever before. I'm surprised. I thought the climate since the election was more conservative and would turn into this big battle."[26] If we're not complaining, the FCC is not going to complain.

You can contact the FCC one of four ways:

1. U.S. Postal Service:
   FCC
   Enforcement Bureau, Investigations and Hearings Division
   445 12th Street, S.W.
   Washington, D.C. 20554

2. E-mail: fccinfo@fcc.gov

3. Toll Free: 1-888-CALL-FCC (1-888-225-5322)

4. Fax: 1-888-418-0232

The FCC promises that all complaints will be read and addressed within nine months of receipt. (We could never run our businesses this way. We would be out of business within a year.)

Last in our look at the disrespectful messages of the entertainment industry is Internet pornography. It's the most damaging of all, with repercussions that can last a lifetime.

Disrespectful Messages on the Internet

Disrespectful messages abound on the World Wide Web, but in this chapter I'm going to focus our attention on pornography because of the astounding number of pornographic Web sites and chat rooms. Sadly, many adults have been preconditioned to hard-core pornography through the soft porn on television and in the movies. The constant bombardment of sexual images has programmed many adults to accept as normal behavior what was once considered taboo.

Pornography addiction is epidemic in our society. I'll let the numbers speak for themselves:

- Porn revenue is larger than combined revenues of all professional football, baseball, and basketball franchises ($54 billion).[27] Here is a breakdown (all figures are annual):

  Adult videos .... $20 billion

  Magazines .... $7.5 billion

  Cable and Pay Per View .... $2.5 billion

  Internet .... $2.5 billion

  Child pornography .... $3 billion

In addition, another $19.5 billion is spent on everything from sex clubs to novelties.

- There are 4.2 billion pornographic Web sites.

- Daily pornographic e-mails: 2.5 billion (8% of total e-mails).

- Web sites offering illegal child pornography: 100,000

- Sexual solicitations of youth made in chat rooms: 89%

- Worldwide visitors to pornographic Web sites: 72 million annually

- Average age of first Internet exposure to pornography: eleven

- Largest consumer of Internet pornography: twelve- to seventeen-year-olds

- Fifteen- to seventeen-year-olds having multiple hard-core exposures: 80%

- Eight- to sixteen-year-olds having viewed porn online: 29%

- Seven- to seventeen-year-olds who would freely give out their e-mail address: 14%[28]

Here we are again. Discouraged by devastating information, and yet, as parents, we have no choice but to face the information and do our best to do something about it.

> *Meanwhile, even as the* Internet *has become the principle means of distributing child pornography, it has become all but undeniable that it is a significant factor in the sexual exploitation of children. For instance, the Los Angeles Police Department has conducted a ten-year study that found pornography to be a factor in 62 percent of the cases of child molestation. An FBI study of serial killers shows that 81 percent reported hard-core pornography to be their "highest sexual interest."* [28]
> KELLY PATRICIA O'MEARA

What's a Parent to Do?

In his book *The Disappearance of Childhood*, Neil Postman, one of our country's cultural critics, points out "that overexposure to adult information at a young age robs a child of his innocence."[29] Don't you agree?

Remember the girl in chapter 2 whose father took her to see an exploitive R-rated movie? Do you remember what she told me? After viewing the movie, she said, "I thought if I asked God to forgive me, I wouldn't see the pictures any more . . . and I'd forget the words, but they won't go away." This is what happens to children when they're exposed to too much too early—their innocence disappears. And it cannot be restored. And the long-term results?

Just look around. Ten-year-old girls look and act like eighteen-year-olds. Eight-year-olds use language that once only older teenagers used. Fourteen-year-olds are getting pregnant.

The National Research Council offers these tips for how parents can protect and educate children about Internet pornography:

- Allow your kids access only to Web pages that you have already checked and found safe.

- Block inappropriate material with filtering software.

- Monitor your children's Web activity, and impose a penalty if they are caught visiting unapproved sites.

- Warn your kids about explicit material and suggest they choose something better.

- Educate your children about reasons not to view explicit material, and build their sense of responsibility.[30]

But even careful monitoring and screening won't be enough if we aren't practicing what we preach. You can never protect your kids from the entertainment you take pleasure in. Are you still with me? One thing you can bank on with children from two to nineteen is that they know us— their parents—better than we know ourselves. They see straight through our deceptions.

Parents, we helped create this disrespectful world. We can't keep blaming everyone else, including the media. If we truly want to protect our children, we must start by turning our backs on the smut. It's not OK for pornographic magazines to be in your home with adolescents milling around. It's not OK to expect your children to adhere to higher standards than you hold for yourself.

If you or your spouse is struggling with pornography, there's help. Confess to a trusted friend that you're struggling. This may sound too easy, but it's not if you're the one that has to admit you're having trouble. Pornography gains a stronghold on individuals because it's the "secret addiction" until it begins to manifest itself in extramarital affairs and much worse.

Ask for help to overcome it, and with God's help and your conviction to not allow pornography to ruin your marriage and your family, you will be able to do it.

If we want to raise respectful children in this disrespectful world, our children need to see us combat the disrespectful culture rather than be a part of it. They won't desire to taste the crass side of life if we overcome an appetite for it ourselves.

Protecting Your Treasure

In the last two chapters we've taken a long, hard look at the disrespectful messages in our culture, from magazines and books to movies and the Internet. I know many days you feel helpless to combat the messages of sex for sale on every bookshelf and magazine rack. Practically any button you press on the radio or TV can lead to trouble. Images and words filled with sexual innuendoes appear from cyberspace in front of your child's innocent eyes. Billions of dollars are spent by the industry to make you feel helpless. But . . .

Remember David slew Goliath with a single stone. Like David, you just need to make certain you prepare for the battle. Read the account from 1 Samuel 17:34–37, when David convinced Saul he was capable of handling the giant:

> David said to Saul, "Your servant has been keeping his father's sheep. When a lion or a bear came and carried off a sheep from the flock, I went after it, struck it and rescued the sheep from its mouth. When it turned on me, I seized it by its hair, struck it and killed it. Your servant has killed both the lion and the bear; this uncircumcised Philistine will be like one of them, because he has defied the armies of the living God. The LORD who delivered me from the paw of the lion and the paw of the bear will deliver me from the hand of this Philistine."
>
> Saul said to David, "Go, and the LORD be with you."

If David could defeat Goliath, you can defeat the entertainment industry. "Go, and the Lord be with you."

David was willing to do whatever was necessary to protect his sheep. Are you willing to do whatever is necessary to protect your children?

Reality Check

Before moving on to the next chapter, consider your answers to these questions as you strengthen your resolve to raise respectful children in this disrespectful world:

1. Do you know how many hours a week your children watch television?

2. Are you lenient about what you allow your little ones to watch?

3. Have you allowed your children to watch the Harry Potter movies? Do you discuss the themes with them?

4. Do you know which videos your children are watching at friends' houses? Which video games they're playing?

5. Do you have safeguards in place regarding your children's use of the Internet?

6. Do you preview movies your children want to watch, even those rated PG-13?

7. Do the shows your children watch have a positive influence on them?

8. Do you sometimes watch the very things you prohibit your children from watching?

Engage;
Don't Entertain

TEACHERS WERE ASTONISHED, and I was thrilled, to see the transformation that took place during a first-time visit to an elementary school for at-risk children. When storytelling time arrived, I began by asking the children to "watch" the story with their imaginations. Before I could begin, a hand flew up. "Miss Jill, wait . . . I don't know how to do that!"

"You listen with your ears, and you look with your heart," I said as I knelt down with one hand behind my ear and the other pointing to the little girl's heart, "Do you understand?"

She shook her head from side to side.

I continued, looking at all the children, "Let's practice. Close your eyes for a minute. Imagine playing on the playground with your friends. Can you see it?" All the children nodded affirmatively, including the little girl.

"Well, that's watching with the eyes of your heart. You're not looking out the window at the playground; you're using your imagination to see the picture in your head. When you use your imagination, you're looking at the world through the eyes of your heart."

I then told them a story called "Trouble with a Capital P," a tale I wrote about twin raccoons, Peter and Penelope, who get into big trouble when they break the rules. Their all-knowing and fearless mentor, Wise Old

147

Wilbur, had told Peter and Penelope they could throw the baseball back and forth, as long as they didn't leave the backyard. They got carried away, and their neighbor, Mrs. McDonald, ended up with a broken window because of their disobedience.

During the telling of the tale, I repeatedly asked, "Do you see?" I enjoyed watching the kids as they "watched" the story. Their heads moved from side to side as if standing on the edge of the backyard as Peter and Penelope threw the ball back and forth. By the time Peter threw the ball over Penelope's head and into Mrs. McDonald's window, all the children jumped because they "heard" the glass shatter.

When Mrs. McDonald came to Peter and Penelope's house, the children "saw" the baseball in Mrs. McDonald's hand. At the conclusion of the story, our raccoon friends helped Mrs. McDonald with chores at her home to repay her for the broken window. When I asked, "What do you think Mrs. McDonald brought to our little friends when they finished doing her chores?"

The precious little girl who didn't know she had an imagination answered, "Oh, *look*, she made them homemade cookies. What a nice lady."

I winked at the teachers, who were grinning in amazement, as I hugged the little girl.

Imagination Is More Than Knowledge

It is in our imaginations that problems are solved and inventions are created. It is in our imaginations that dreams meet reality, that the impossible becomes possible. A great "imaginer," Napoleon Hill, used his imagination to find his way from a one-room cabin in the hills of Virginia in the late 1800s to become our country's first great motivational speaker. He knew the value of the imagination, "First comes thought; then organization of that thought, into ideas and plans; then transformation of those plans into reality. The beginning, as you will observe, is in your imagination."[1]

Webster's defines *imagination* as "the act of forming a mental image of something not present to the senses; creative ability; resourcefulness."[2] I think of imagination as the ability to look at the world with the eyes of your heart.

If we want our children to cure the diseases of the world one day or to create an invention that cuts our utility bills in half or to find a way to make this disrespectful world wholesome again, we must unlock their hearts. You hold the keys that will unlock those hearts. That's why you must be willing to expend the energy, time, and effort to engage your children's imaginations, rather than just offering entertainment to pacify their boredom.

One of the greatest "imaginers" of all time, Albert Einstein, once said, "Imagination is more important than knowledge. For knowledge is limited to all we now know and understand, while imagination embraces the entire world and all there ever will be to know and understand."[3]

If we want our children to become all they were created to be, we must engage their imaginations. Yes, it takes knowledge to win a game of Star Wars Battlefront II on an Xbox and skill to build a science project, but it is through imagination that the game was created and the design of the science project was conceived.

Children aren't born with knowledge, but they are born with an abundance of imagination. Observe your kids at play. Action figures aren't plastic dolls in the hands of six-year-old boys; they are superheroes saving the world with "kid general" in charge. When nine-year-old Beth puts Barbie in her pink convertible, they're off to meet Ken. Today Barbie's a famous rock star; tomorrow she'll be in the kitchen baking cookies. Yesterday she was at the beach with her little sisters, Kelly and Skipper. Don't tell these children this is fantasy . . . they'll tell you it's real!

It breaks my heart that children don't know how to use their imaginations anymore. We've robbed them of opportunities to do so. Rather than engaging children's imaginations with thought-provoking activities, we entertain them with mindless amusements.

Get Unplugged

When we surveyed a group of children and asked them, "Which do you like better: video or computer games, television and movies . . . or sports and board games? Would you rather be plugged in or unplugged?" one child replied: "I like video games; they make my mind stop. I don't think when I play them, so I don't get tired. If I'm playing outside or playing those other kind of games, I have to think too hard."

This boy just happened to prefer video games, but he could have been talking about television and movies as well. Here's my point: when children are plugged in to electronic games, gizmos, and gadgets, they are unplugged from life. They're not using their imaginations; they don't have to, the box thinks for them. Think about the time your children spend in front of a box. Rather than engaging minds and senses, the box disengages minds and desensitizes emotions. It is our duty to help our children reach their full potential, which will never happen if they spend 90 percent of their time sitting in front of a box.

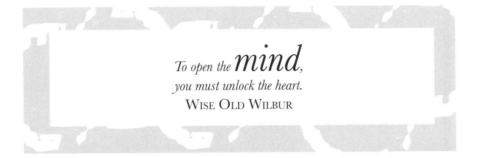

To open the **mind**,
you must unlock the heart.
WISE OLD WILBUR

Remember the adage "Necessity is the mother of invention"? You and your kids will be forced to become creative with meals, entertainment, and lighting if you will take a Saturday to unplug for real. Take this seriously. Unplug the oven. Unplug the phone. Unplug the television and computer. Unplug the lights. Unplug *all* your electrical cords. (No batteries allowed!)

When the sun goes down, gather your family, light a candle or two, and share stories from your childhood with your children. Sing a camp song. Play Go Fish or pick-up-sticks or Barrel of Monkeys. When was the last time you built a house of cards?

Try it, and I think you'll find that your kids will love "roughing it" and that the experience will bring you closer together, because you have to work as a team to figure out how to make-do without electricity.

Being plugged in keeps us from plugging in to one another. I saw this last year after Hurricane Katrina came through our city. The day after the storm, we had no electricity. Our neighbors were out in the street, not assessing damage, but visiting with one another. But as soon as the electricity came back on, the streets emptied and folks returned to their remote controls.

I realize, of course, that we can't live our lives completely unplugged. It's OK when kids use the computer for research or chatting with friends with instant messaging, and even playing games that have some redeeming quality—but we must help kids find a balance. Apart from school work, I believe the balance should be 75 percent unplugged and 25 percent plugged-in. If you want your children to engage their imaginations and use more than 10 percent of their brain power, don't allow them to be plugged-in more than fifteen minutes out of every hour.

Turn off the boxes, and turn them on to something better: real life!

The rest of this chapter is going to explore ways we parents can engage our children's imaginations by:

- Providing opportunities for creative play

- Being a kid with kids

- Getting plugged-in to reading

- Celebrating the joy of having real fun

Provide Opportunities for Creative Play

With his ordinary voice, unassuming personality, and gentle manner, Fred McFeely Rogers penetrated the hearts of his viewers on *Mr. Rogers' Neighborhood*. Despite his quiet demeanor, his love came through loud and clear. He knew exactly what children need, and he provided it: the Neighborhood of Make Believe, where children used their imaginations and creativity. Mr. Rogers engaged his young audience in play, not entertainment, because he believed in the value of creativity:

> Play does seem to open up another part of the mind that is always there, but that, since childhood, may have become closed off and hard to reach. When we treat children's play as seriously as it deserves, we are helping them feel the joy that's to be found in the creative spirit. We're helping ourselves stay in touch with that spirit too. It's the things we play with and the people who help us play that make a great difference in our lives.[4]

I couldn't agree more. When we give our kids opportunities to be creative in how they play, we enhance their ability to do creative problem-solving as they mature.

Here are some ways you can help your kids engage their imaginations through creative play:

Make an Imagination Station

My favorite Christmas gift as a child was a giant cardboard activity box that looked like a snow-covered chimney. It was filled with crayons, books, spools of yarn, scissors, and assorted "stuff" that was just stuff—until my imagination began to run wild with ideas to turn the stuff into something special.

You can get your children's creative juices flowing by gathering supplies and creating an Imagination Station. It could be a corner of the den or playroom or in a bedroom. You don't have to teach your kids how to create something from nothing; they can teach you if you provide them with the opportunity to be creative. I've never known a child who has to be coerced into creating.

What do you need for the Imagination Station? One or two of those gigantic plastic storage containers work great, because not only can they store the supplies, but your child can also work on the top, if space is tight. Don't throw away old containers from the kitchen, such as gallon jugs, oatmeal boxes, spice jars, odd-sized empty boxes, and so on. Put them in your Imagination Station. Toss in some old magazines, along with some ordinary art supplies: glue, scissors, construction paper, felt, foam sheets, buttons, pipe cleaners, yarn, markers, crayons, modeling clay, and anything else you can think of. Don't forget old grown-up clothes for dress up.

Before you know it, your kids are:

- Turning oatmeal boxes into space rockets

- Using photos from old magazines to illustrate original stories

- Molding clay into creatures-come-to-life from their imaginations

- Transforming odd-sized boxes joined with pipe cleaners into trains that can transport the clay creatures

- Turning old clothes into costumes they will use in an original play about their heroes

- Creating funny farm animals out of empty milk cartons and a little yarn, felt, scissors, and glue

The Imagination Station encourages your children to create, not vegetate. It engages their minds and even their hearts as they concoct stories and original plays. You'll be amazed at how peaceful most children play when they're using their imaginations. There's no competition between the kids, no tug-of-war, just excitement as they find the satisfaction of creating something from nothing with their own two hands.

When your kids have driven you crazy with their productions, pull out the games.

Play Games Together

Invite your neighbors, grandparents, and friends to come over one Saturday with their favorite games, favorite homemade dessert, and a card table. Pull out your favorite board games, and have a good time together.

If your gathering contains kids of varying ages, you might find the following list of age-appropriate games and activities helpful:

Three- to nine-year-olds: crayons and coloring books, Chutes and Ladders, Candy Land, wooden blocks, Duplo.

Ten- to twelve-year-olds: Silly Putty, Barrel of Monkeys, card games, Tinkertoys, Lincoln Logs, Jacks, marbles, and LEGOs.

Teenagers: dominoes, checkers, Scrabble, Clue, Life, Monopoly, and Sorry.

Don't limit yourself to table games; consider action games too. Ask your kids to come up with a list of games for all ages to enjoy together—sack race, three-legged race, relay, football toss, Frisbee, and so on—or play charades among families.

Game days provide great opportunities for the "old folks" to teach the young kids a thing or two, so get out those old board games from the attic, or scour some antique shops for old games. Children will find out in a hurry that even though seniors aren't experts at computer games, they can play a mean game of checkers or dominoes. Encourage the teenagers to join in too. And don't be surprised if this becomes an annual event in your neighborhood.

Classic Toys

Here's a list of twenty-four classic toys that are just as engaging today as the day they first came out, and even better, no electricity or batteries are needed—just your child's imagination and you.

Play-Doh
Jump rope
Matchbox cars
Airplanes
Fire trucks
Yo-yos
Mr. Potato Head
Bubbles
Building blocks
Super Balls
Candy Land
Mousetrap
Bingo
Checkers
Slinky
Silly Putty
Model cars
Science sets
Monopoly
Weebles
Radio Flyer wagons
Dollhouses
LEGOs
Kites

When the weather doesn't permit outdoor play, move the playground indoors.

Turn Your Kitchen into a Playground

We moved from a neighborhood with backyards to a thirty-six-story high-rise in Manhattan when the boys were four. I learned more about engaging children than I ever wanted to know! Talk about having to be creative! I decided to turn my kitchen into a playground for several hours each day.

Chad and Boyce loved it. I selected one bottom drawer and told them the drawer was their drawer. They could play with anything they found in the drawer. In order to keep them interested, I frequently changed the contents of the drawer, filling it with things such as: Tupperware, lids from my pots and pans, wooden spoons, and measuring spoons.

I used a lot of plastic bowls and utensils so I didn't have to worry about broken china, except when we had a nice dinner. To grownups, my kitchen looked like the utilitarian center of the house, but through the eyes of my little boys, it was their indoor playground.

I didn't have an indoor playground when I grew up, but there *was* a special place set aside for a special activity . . .

Work on Jigsaw Puzzles Together

When I was growing up, my daddy had a brown card table in the corner of the den with a puzzle-in-progress on it. Most nights after supper, Daddy would excuse himself from the dinner table "to think awhile in my corner." We knew what that meant—Daddy was going to work on a jigsaw puzzle, a complex one, at that. Even though he rarely extended a formal invitation, the rest of us understood we were always welcome at his table.

Daddy's interest in puzzles extended far beyond the challenge he found on the card table. "The tougher the puzzle, the harder you have to think," he would say when questioned about the intensity he gave his hobby. "It's about more than working a jigsaw puzzle. It's about solving everyday puzzles."

It was delightful to watch him dig with great patience through the box of a thousand cardboard cutouts, searching for the right piece. He would grumble during the search and then say, "Aha!" when he found the missing piece.

During my teen years if I needed to talk to Daddy, I often joined him at the card table after supper. I chose to talk when he was at the card table because I didn't have to look my father in the eyes if the subject was unpleasant! We enjoyed many good conversations at the puzzle table, but that wasn't the only benefit. As I watched my father work on the puzzles, I also learned how to approach life's problems: assess the situation, work through the options, and keep working at it until you solve the problem.

Don't wait any longer to set up a puzzle table at your house. You'll all learn a lot about solving problems—as a family.

Another sweet memory I have of my daddy are the times he became the human monkey bar. A virile man with great strength, he would stand erect with his arms bent at ninety-degree angles and allow us to swing back and forth on his "bars." He enjoyed being a big kid.

Be a Kid with Your Kids

With the pressures of adulthood, we often lose the pleasures of childhood. Do yourself a favor, and delight your children by being a kid in some small way. As silly as this may seem, you'll earn more respect from your children when you're willing to just enjoy being a kid with them than telling them about the big deal you closed at the office. It's as simple as the ABCs:

Always smile—Do this especially when you don't feel like it.

Blow bubbles—Walk in the house with a bottle of bubbles in hand.

Color in a coloring book—Do this rather than read one night.

Draw a self-portrait—Let the children put *your* picture on the refrigerator.

Eat a peanut butter and jelly sandwich—Invite the kids to the table for a surprise supper.

Finger paint—Yes, use your fingers, not brushes.

Goofy faces—See who can make the funniest face.

Hide and Seek—Ask your kids to play before they ask you.

Ice-cream cones for everybody—See who can eat it without getting a brain freeze.

Jump rope—Learn the Double Dutch.

Kick a can down the street with your kids—Challenge the kids to a contest.

Look up—Watch the stars at night and the clouds in the day.

Musical chairs—Rearrange the chairs after supper, and turn on the music.

No TV—Don't turn on the TV. Just don't do it!

Old-fashioned hopscotch—Draw the game board on the driveway and start hopping.

Paper airplanes—Challenge the kids to a contest.

Questions—Ask silly, silly questions.

Race around the block—Challenge the kids, even with the neighbors watching.

Scissors, Rock, Paper—Use this game to determine who goes first in the next board game.

Take a walk with the family—Walk hand-in-hand without your watch on your wrist.

Uncontrollable laughter—Start giggling for no apparent reason. Your kids will join you.

Ventriloquism—Try it; it's not as hard as it seems.

Walk barefoot in the grass—Go back to your childhood, or experience something new!

Xylophone—Kids love this instrument.

Yodel—Try it; this *is* as hard as it seems.

Zoo animal sounds—Heard a chimpanzee lately? Neither have your kids.

I must confess, I'm really just a nine-year-old kid, at least in my heart. My friends used to compliment me on being such a great mom, because I would get in the middle of whatever activity the boys were doing. Most of the time I just smiled and said, "I try."

But, just between you and me, I'll tell you the truth: I wasn't being a gallant, unselfish mom; I was participating out of total selfishness. I miss being a kid! Why just yesterday I joined in a football game with my godson and his friends. They couldn't believe this "old lady" could throw a pass!

My heart jumps for joy when I look out my front window and see the neighborhood boys playing ball in my front yard. I don't care if the ball lands in the flowers or if they even break a window. The flowers can be replanted and the glass replaced. I'm just thrilled to see those boys unplugged and plugged-in to real fun.

Plug-in to Reading

Do your children have a difficult time reading? Do they tend to put off their reading? Let me share a few suggestions to encourage your children to read:

- Keep books with you at all times. Waiting in a doctor's office is a great opportunity to read.

- Set aside a time in the evening for reading. Mom and Dad, stop your activities and read too. Show your children that reading every day is important.

- Do some research with your kids about the authors of the books they are reading. If your children know about the life of the author, they'll enjoy the books even more.

- Make a special place for reading. A quiet corner with good lighting and comfortable seating. (When I was a child, my favorite reading spot was a mimosa tree in our front yard. The limbs were strong and spread apart enough to make an inviting seat to relax and enjoy a good book.)

- Read to your children, even when they're old enough to read to themselves. Show how much fun reading can be. Make the characters of a book come alive with innovative voices and gestures.

- For every hour your child reads, allow them to stay up an extra thirty minutes on Friday and Saturday nights.

- Reward the completion of their school's summer reading list with a trip to the bookstore. Allow your child to select a book of his choice, when the "have-to-read" books are finished!

When the reading is done, it's time to get back to those seemingly unimportant activities (to you) that mean everything to your children.

Celebrate the Joy of Having Real Fun

My mother always said, "You find time to do the things you really want to do." How true. If you don't subscribe to that thought, I can assure you your children do. So, since childhood passes quickly, make the most of these years by celebrating the joy of having real fun with your children. Give them your undivided attention, unplug from the busyness, and engage your kids in conversation.

You only have one opportunity to love your kids and stimulate their imaginations, and that's today. Give hugs in abundance, get in the kitchen and bake a batch of cookies, pull out the box of "stuff," spend time doing fun, simple things with them. Your children need more of the little things and less of the big things because the little things really are the big things.

A Family That Did It

Wilmer and Betsy Mills were agricultural missionaries in remote parts of Brazil for almost nine years while their four children were growing up. Their house was equipped with an electric generator that pumped water to the house and gave them four hours of electricity at night. There was no telephone, air conditioning, computer, or television, although they did have a record player and a stack of old Walt Disney records. There was no shopping mall or playground, but the children were never bored; they never complained about having nothing to do. According to Betsy, "The children invented their own fun." They grew up bilingual, learning English and Portuguese simultaneously.

Days were filled with creative activities. Jenny and Kate loved to decorate dollhouses, built from rough board crates by their father. They spent three to four hours a day drawing in notebooks and the rest of the daylight hours playing school and store outside with their Brazilian friends who lived in mud and stick huts. John grew up as the neighborhood mascot, surrounded by his siblings' activities, enjoying cooking in the kitchen and playing with baby jungle monkeys. Wil, as oldest, enjoyed more freedom to roam with his friends, fishing in the river and hunting iguanas with his hand-made slingshot.

Reading books was a favorite ritual for the kids—an hour in the morning and afternoon accompanied nap times. Many nights they were read to for more than two hours. The children learned to read for themselves at young ages and developed exceptional comprehension skills. They were fortunate to be a part of a readers' service for missionaries, which sent boxes of children's books twice a year. Family favorites were The Bobbsey Twins, Encyclopedia Brown, The Great Brain, *The Hobbit*, and The Little House on the Prairie series. The Lord of the Rings and The Chronicles of Narnia were read aloud twice! The children enjoyed visualizing what they read and soon invented their own adventure series, illustrated in notebooks that rivaled C. S. Lewis's and J.R.R. Tolkien's works.

The children learned to play rhythm instruments, the guitar, and piano. A nightly routine often included singing four-part harmony in Portuguese as a family. Every night the family enjoyed devotions of prayer and Bible stories.

All four children are now married with their own young children, and each has excelled in various creative fields. John loves woodworking, singing, and is an award-winning cook. Jenny plays the Celtic harp and does portrait work. Kate has a masters in painting and has been a college art professor. Wil writes music, is an accomplished brick-oven bread baker, and a well-known poet. I recently listened to Wil read from his latest book of poetry at a prestigious book festival. The imagery of his words tapped the imaginations of his listeners as he shared the thoughts of his soul. Just as the room filled with heavy emotion, he picked up his guitar to amuse us with a humorous song. After receiving rousing applause, he was forced to linger well beyond his time allotment in order to answer questions from aspiring poets and to enjoy accolades from his admirers.

If you ask Betsy the secret of the phenomenal creative success of her children, she quickly says it was the blessing of the "Brazilian Wild West." Betsy says with great humility, "The kids engaged themselves. I wasn't the teacher, but the facilitator. I provided the supplies—pens, paper, paints, empty boxes, books, musical instruments. It was my great joy to sit back and watch my children tap into their imaginations. I was always astounded by the depth of creativity they found within themselves. My children had no choice but to use their imaginations to the fullest." Much to Betsy and Wilmer's credit, too, the Mills "kids" have become part of that unique group of individuals who tap in to more than 10 percent of the brain's capacity.

We can learn a great lesson from the Mills family. Preparing our children to be productive members of society is not to be found in the electronic gadgets of the new millennium but in the simple pleasures of engagement. Nights spent gathered as a family, not around the television but around the table, playing games or making music. Saturdays romping in the backyard, playing leapfrog and eating ice cream. Sunday afternoons painting the next great masterpiece on butcher paper with poster paints.

Looking at the world through the eyes of our children enriches our lives and reaches their hearts. You must unlock the hearts of your children to open their minds.

Reality Check

Before moving on to the next chapter, consider your answers to these questions as you strengthen your resolve to raise respectful children in this disrespectful world:

1. Do you help your children exercise their imaginations? Do you often use your imagination?

2. How often do you play board games or have picnics with your family?

3. Do you have dedicated time for reading to your children?

4. Can you think of some things you've been meaning to do with your child, but have been putting it off because you "haven't had any time?"

5. Can you think of many *most* memorable moments you've shared with your children?

6. How often do you sit and listen to your children to find out what's in their hearts?

7. If you woke up one morning and realized thirty years have passed and your children are all grown up, would you regret not doing certain things with or for your children?

8. Will you give your children books or another electronic device on their next birthday?

Teach Gratefulness, Not Greediness

HAVE YOU EVER SAT UNDER A LAMPPOST that resembled a giant chocolate kiss? Unless you've visited "The Sweetest Place on Earth," I doubt you've seen such a sight. When you cross the city limits of Hershey, Pennsylvania, there's something to delight the senses at every turn.

Candyland come to life.

On a recent visit I wandered into Hershey's Chocolate World to see the story behind the making of chocolate. Inside I was greeted with row upon row of candy, treats, toys, and stuffed animals of every description. Just as I decided that this was truly the land of enchantment, the magical spell was broken by a child's ear-piercing "Gimme! Gimme!" and her tired parents' "Enough! Enough!"

In the midst of this sweet paradise, I felt disheartened to see a child that was so discontent. And worse, the more she received, the more she wanted. This little girl was in the middle of Candyland, but she could not be satisfied.

Unfortunately, she has plenty of company.

Living in Candyland

Our country has become Candyland, hasn't it? Land of the free (deal) and home of the brave (shopper). Look around. We are the consumer giant, devouring every fad that comes along as if our lives depended on it. Without the latest, greatest, fastest, biggest, loudest, newest gadget, we act as if we've become nobodies. We're working longer hours than ever before to make more money so we can buy more things, even though we have no time to enjoy the things we already have, not to mention a place to store them.

We all know someone who has just bought a new car with the newest thingamabob, someone who just purchased a new home in the trendiest subdivision, or someone who's always on the cutting edge of fashion. We're bombarded with more than three-hundred thousand commercials per year on television and three million on the radio.[1] Add to that the ads in print media—magazines, newspapers, and books. As we drive on the freeways, we see more ads on billboards, in neon lights, and on the sides of trucks and buses.

We cannot escape the inundation of advertising—someone else telling us what we "need" in order to be somebody—that enters our consciousness and lodges in our subconscious, shaping our desires and wants, and deceiving us into thinking we really do need whatever it is they're selling. And so we buy.

"Everybody has too much stuff. It's the American way," said a manager of a climate-controlled storage building.[2] John Austin reports in the *Advocate*, "The insatiable race for space is fueling a $15 billion self-storage industry that dwarfs Hollywood's annual $9 billion. What was once a mom-and-pop business has become an industry with companies whose stock is traded on the New York Stock Exchange."[3]

I wonder, *Are those storage units filled with things people need? Or are they filled with things people want?* Why do we wonder that our kids want so much, when our own wants are out of control? Could it be we're passing our greediness on to our children?

Scripture reminds us: "What good is it for a man to gain the whole world, yet forfeit his soul? Or what can a man give in exchange for his soul?"[4] We're selling out, literally, and I'm afraid it's our children's hearts and souls that we're losing in the exchange. What are we teaching our kids through our own buying habits and through the things we purchase for them?

Filled, Yet Still Empty

If your children are growing up in Candyland, with their every whim granted, they'll never develop hearts of gratitude. They'll spend their lives wanting more, while missing the simple, everyday pleasures.

In chapter 2, I talked about how our kids come into our lives with empty hearts needing to be filled. When we attempt to fill those hearts with "stuff" rather than our time, our children continue to want more, because for every emotional need that's unmet, their emptiness grows deeper. A child with an empty heart has a hard time being grateful. It's not the child's fault.

Ungratefulness is epidemic among children today because parents have:

- Offered unwarranted praise, which leads children to expect rather than accept

- Given children things instead of themselves and their time

- Given too much and expected too little

When your children begin to expect "things" from you, they lose their gratitude. Think of the daughter whose father travels frequently for his job. Because Dad feels guilty for being away, he brings his daughter a gift as a token of his love. But as time passes, she stops anticipating her father's return and, instead, anticipates the gift he will bring her. When the day comes that Dad doesn't bring a gift, the daughter is unhappy—with life and with her father. Parents who overindulge their kids are nurturing ungratefulness in their children's hearts. The more things these parents give, the more things their kids want.

Is there a way to fill those empty hearts with the "right" stuff?

I believe there is!

It will take hard work, but it can be done. Cultivating a grateful heart takes time and intentional, not accidental, parenting. You must make a concerted effort to give opportunities for your children to develop gratitude. You'll need commitment, perseverance, and a bit of creativity, but you can do it!

Cultivating a Heart of Gratitude

As we discussed earlier, we need to enroll our children in the School of Respect as soon as they come into this world. If our goal is to fill our children's hearts with respect for God and others, and we succeed, our kids will grow up with grateful hearts that are focused on others and not self.

With that in mind, here are some ways to help your kids develop grateful hearts:

Train Them in Manners

Defined by an attitude of the heart that's self-giving, not self-serving, manners are much more than memorizing a set of rules. When we teach our children to be well-mannered, we are teaching them to focus on *others* and on how *others* feel and what *others* need. Manners help kids to grow up believing, *It's more about others and less about me.* So:

Tykes: Three to Five

- Encourage your kids to show concern for others. Give them a few pennies to share whenever someone asks. Drop a coin in the charity box at McDonald's. Buy an extra canned good for the food pantry, and let your child place it in the barrel.

- Say "thank you" to your kids, and gently, consistently remind them to do the same. It's better to say, "What do you need to say?" than "Say thank you."

- Say a prayer with your kids the next time you hear a siren or see an emergency. Show how to think outside themselves by praying for others in need.

- Watch for opportunities to teach service. Even young children can open car doors for the elderly or befriend the child who's left out by others.

- Teach your child how to say grace before meals.

- Begin to work on their table manners. Brush up on your own table manners, because your child is emulating every move you make. Start with holding utensils properly

- Expect "yes, ma'am" and "yes, sir." Such words teach respect for elders. Don't allow your children to call adults by their first names. You need to establish the boundary between child and adult.

Tweens: Six to Twelve

- Teach telephone etiquette: how to answer the phone, take messages, and make calls.

- Expect tweens to clean their rooms and bathroom without your assistance.

- Require them to write thank-you notes, even when they just spend the night at a friend's house.

- Teach your son to take a flower with his gift to a girl's birthday party.

- Insist that boys open doors for ladies and seat them for dinner.

- Teach girls how to graciously accept help from a gentleman.

- Accept no back talk. Use a respectful tone of voice with your children, and expect the same from them.

- Have your children practice a handshake with a firm grip while looking the recipient in the eyes.

- Begin work on the details of table manners: serving from the left and removing from the right, no reaching, asking for food to be passed to you, waiting for all to be served before you begin eating, not leaving the table till all are finished, and asking to be excused before rising.

- Ask your tweens to serve adult guests.

- Teach them to say "excuse me" when appropriate.

- Look for ways to involve them in service—helping the elderly, helping a younger child, helping Mom.

- Refer to *Manners of the Heart at Home* for more help in working with your children.

Teens: Thirteen to Nineteen

- Invite adults over for dinner, and involve your teens in your conversations.

- Remind teens not to go to a friend's house without calling first.

- Teach teens to offer to help serve and clean up when eating at a friend's house.

- Encourage teens to write a thank-you note for a meal or an overnight visit at a friend's house.

- Model being quick to say "I'm sorry" and being slow to criticize.

- Teach them that their dress tells others what they think of themselves.

- Teach your sons to be respectful of girls—to:

  1. Open car doors for them

  2. Seat their dates for dinner

  3. Not to walk in front of a girl in public places, such as restaurants and theaters, but to walk beside her or behind her

  4. Not to use inappropriate language or tell off-color jokes

- Teach your girls how to be ladies—to:

  1. Sit modestly

  2. Never use foul language, at all, ever

  3. Never pursue a boy

  4. Allow boys to treat them like ladies

- Teach the importance of responding to an RSVP invitation within twenty-four hours of receipt.

- Above all, insist that commitments be kept.

If you work on your child's manners with consistency and firmness, your child's heart will likely swell with gratefulness. When kids are grateful, they have positive attitudes and are ready to serve others rather than themselves. Grateful children grow into respectful young adults.

Of course, it's one thing to insist that your children use respectful, grateful, well-mannered speech and quite another to cultivate the attitude behind those actions. Well-groomed children who know the rules of etiquette can also be devious little troublemakers if they have been taught to "put on their manners" to impress others rather than use manners to make the lives of those around them more pleasant.

That's where the other ideas in the rest of this section can help.

Those who have good hearts find pleasure in being unselfish.
For he who does a kindness to another does a greater kindness to himself.
JOHNNY GRUELLE
"THE KIND HEARTED GINGER BREAD MAN"

Allow Your Kids to Have a Sense of Ownership

An old paint bucket sat in the cabinet under the kitchen sink in my childhood home. It wasn't a leftover from the last painting job; my parents had placed it there in order to teach us a valuable lesson in gratitude. Taped to the side of the bucket was the word *vacation*, reminding us of its purpose. Our annual summer vacation was determined by the amount of change tossed into the bucket during the year. Every time one of us washed the dishes, we had an opportunity to make a contribution to our family's vacation fund. We understood we could make a difference in the choice of destination by how much we sacrificed during the year. The year Disney World opened in Florida, my brothers and sisters and I did extra chores for months so we could put enough money in the bucket to go there on our family vacation.

I remember that vacation well—and the sense of satisfaction and gratitude I felt, in part because I had helped my family make this dream trip possible. Even though the ride in the car was long, we kids didn't argue (well, maybe just a little!). When we got there, we didn't complain about it being too hot, too cold, or being too tired, or that the lines were too long. Each of us had worked hard to earn this vacation, so we appreciated it. We weren't going to ruin "our" vacation.

Ten Simple Ideas for Instilling Gratitude

1. *Encourage the simple pleasures.* Make homemade gifts for each other. Play games rather than rent a movie. Spend the night in the backyard as an adventure at home.
2. *Teach money management:* Make sure each of your children has a piggy bank and is required to save a portion of their allowance. In addition to an allowance, allow your children to do extra chores for money to be used for "wants" they purchase themselves.
3. *Start a tradition of adopting a family* (or neighbor) throughout the year. Provide a meal you prepare and deliver together.
4. *Do not allow whining.* The best cure for whining is to ignore it totally.
5. *Don't allow idleness.* Don't let your tweens and older kids sit around doing nothing. Put them to work—outside the home and inside the home. A little hard work works wonders to change an attitude of ingratitude.
6. *Get outside with the family.* Enjoy God's creation. Appreciate the beauty. Bring back a sense of wonder that the chaos of everyday living takes away.
7. *Pray with your children* on bended knee each night.
8. *Help your children memorize* Philippians 4:8 "Finally, brothers, whatever is true, whatever is noble, whatever is right, whatever is pure, whatever is lovely, whatever is admirable—if anything is excellent or praiseworthy—think about such things."
9. *Give love and appreciation* for a job well done rather than buying a treat.
10. *Give your child age-appropriate responsibilities.* Nothing builds your child's self-respect like being held accountable for chores and decisions. Don't nag, but expect the best from your child, and you'll probably get it.

Here's the unexpected twist: Mother and Daddy gave each of us a little spending money when we arrived. Sound counterproductive? It wasn't. We'd had the privilege of helping pay for the vacation. In turn, we were given a gift of grace from our parents for our enjoyment, just because they loved us!

You can use this same principle of offering ownership with clothing, movies, and any form of "extras." For instance:

- If your daughter finds a jacket at the mall she "must have," insist she earn the money to pay for it. If she makes a concerted effort, offer to help out with part of the cost.

- Buy movie tickets for your kids, but let them earn the money for popcorn.

- Give each child a specific area of responsibility in the care of the home. Your son might be in charge of the trash. If he doesn't do his job, don't do it for him. This will give him ownership of that duty. If he won't be home the night before garbage pick up, he's responsible for getting a substitute to do his job. Or your daughter could be in charge of cleaning the hall bathroom. The same rule applies—if she can't do it, she's responsible for getting a replacement. When the kids know that if they don't do their jobs, they won't get done, they appreciate their home and feel an important part of it—they take ownership.

Teach Them That Good Things Come to Those Who Wait

I wanted to help when I saw a young mother with a tired two-year-old and a five-year-old pleading for a candy bar at the grocery store. But I knew there was little I could do to make her life easier at that moment. As I watched this desperate mother struggling to maintain her composure, I wanted to encourage her to say no to her child's pleas for a treat.

If we want to instill gratefulness in our children, we can't give in when they plead with us for a treat or present. When we do, we are rewarding them for begging. Kids who get what they want when they want it grow up to be ungrateful, impatient adults. How much better if they could learn early on that good things come to those who wait.[5]

Ideally, parents need to teach this lesson before their kids even go to school, but kids can learn this when they are older too. It works like this. Simply inform your kids that you won't be buying them any treats when you go to the grocery store or mall. Each time they ask for something, say no—and stand by it in the checkout line.

I know how difficult this is, but you can win this battle if you will stay calm and lower your voice rather than raise it as the tension mounts. Each time a child's voice is raised, lower yours, until you reach a whisper—no matter how loud the bellowing. The howling will stop because your child has to hear what you're saying. If this has been an area of struggle for you, don't give up. With persistence you can win this battle. I cannot tell you how long it will take before your child stops begging; that depends on how long your child has had the upper hand. But I can assure you that if you will stand firm, you can cure this problem.

Once you have taken back this territory, occasionally offer your kids a treat when you're out shopping. This teaches them that "good things come to those who wait," and that whining is of no benefit.

Help Them Experience the Joy of Giving

You can take this a step further by helping your kids experience the joy of giving. When you offer your child candy, place a few coins in his hand to purchase a treat to give to a friend or a sibling at home.

This simple act of benevolence will bring your child joy and can help her develop a deep desire to share with friends and siblings. This is the secret to developing a heart of gratitude—the satisfaction of giving rather than getting. Kids who learn this secret will have their focus on others rather than self, and they will grow up with self-respect.

Model Gratefulness

Parents who have grateful hearts don't have to work hard to instill gratitude in their children's hearts. They simply live what they teach. Is it really that hard? It flows naturally, if you truly believe what you're teaching.

So how do we model gratefulness for our children? Here are some ways:

- Show love and appreciation to your spouse. Say "thank you" for small kindnesses. Insist that the children respect your spouse.

- When you are contemplating a purchase, ask if the item is really something you (or a family member) need or if the item is something you simply want. In general, if the item is a want, you shouldn't buy it.

- Don't complain about minor annoyances or about wanting things you don't have.

- Say "thank you" to your children.

- Thank service providers—from clerks to bank tellers to the paper courier to those in the military.

- Show appreciation for simple pleasures: good health, creation, kindness, a good night's rest, a good meal.

- Send your child a written thank-you for an exceptional task completed.

- Display good manners.

We had just moved from New York City back to the south and the sweltering summer heat. Boxes were piled everywhere. Nothing in our temporary home had found its place yet. I was grateful to have found the box of sheets and pillows before nightfall. As the boys and I knelt by their beds, one of the boys opened our prayer time, "Now, bow your heads. Thank you, God, for mom's smile. Thank you, God, for my brother's funny face (strange thing to say since they're identical twins!). Thank you, God, for Dad. Thank you, God, for New York City. Thank you, God, for Louisiana. Thank you, God, for trees. Thank you, God, for grass. Thank you, God, for my new tennis shoes. Thank you, God . . ." and on and on and on. After quite a long dissertation, he said, "Excuse me, God, a minute"—"Mom, did I forget anything?"

You know what? He didn't forget a thing. Not because he counted his blessings one by one, but because he came to our Father with a grateful heart. It had been a long miserable day. I'm sure that's why my son was grateful for my smile. There were many moments I wanted to scream. I did lose my cool at one point in the hundred-degree weather, but my sweet son chose to forget the bad moment and remember the good.

I often share with young moms the lesson I learned from my son that day: On the bad days remember the good days. On the good days, forget the bad days. Children can do it, so why can't we? We can learn a lot about gratefulness from observing young children. They're grateful for the little things—"the sun and the moon and the stars above." They notice when we're smiling and when we're not. And at the end of the day they can always find something to be grateful for.

Proverbs reminds us that "a happy heart makes the face cheerful, but heartache crushes the spirit."[6] Do you want to instill gratefulness in your children? Remove any bitterness in your own heart, and your heart of gratitude will flood over into the hearts of your children.

Smile . . . just smile, and your children will smile back.

Reality Check

Before moving on to the next chapter, consider your answers to these questions as you strengthen your resolve to raise respectful children in this disrespectful world:

1. How is your heart?

   - Full or empty

   - Hurting or happy

   - Anxious or calm

   - Disturbed or peaceful

   - Grateful or greedy

2. Does advertising—someone else telling us what we need—have a big influence on what you consider to be your "needs"?

3. Do you find yourself giving your children things rather than spending time with them?

4. Are you more concerned with your children's comfort or character?

5. Do you often intentionally give opportunities to develop gratitude in your children?

6. Which philosophy do your actions teach and exhibit to your children?

   - Being served

   - Serving others

7. When teaching your children manners, do you emphasize the reason behind having manners, or do you just demand them to *be nice*?

8. How are your children's hearts?

   - Grateful

   - Greedy

Listen to the Children

DURING THE SUMMER OF 2005, Manners of the Heart volunteers interviewed more than four hundred children between the ages of four and fourteen for our "Listen to the Children" study. The children represented a cross section of kids from our community.

My interest in conducting this study was inspired by a book written in the seventies by Dr. Kenneth Chafin, *Is There a Family in the House?* Dr. Chafin interviewed one hundred children and asked the following ten questions, which we included in our survey:

1. What's a family?

2. Who is in your family?

3. Why do you think we live in families?

4. What would it be like if people did not live in families?

5. What are mothers like? What are fathers like?

6. What are mothers for? What do they do?

7. What are fathers for? What do they do?

8. Who is the most important person in your family to you?

9. If you could change one thing in your family, what would you change?

10. What does your family do together for fun?

To Dr. Chafin's questions, we added ten of our own:

1. Who is your hero?

2. What's the nicest thing your parents could ever tell you?

3. Are your parents always busy?

4. What's more important . . . being smart or being nice?

5. Do you do chores at home? If you don't do them, what happens?

6. Which do you like better—playing board games, sports, and outdoor stuff; or TV, movies, and video games?

7. Do your parents watch a lot of TV?

8. Do you like to read? Do/did your parents read to you?

9. When your parents tell you to do something, do you usually listen?

10. Have you ever watched PG-13 and/or R-rated movies?

We discovered, much to our surprise, that today's children responded to the questions about family just as those interviewed thirty years ago. Even though the culture has changed, the understanding of the way things should be hasn't changed. Kids seem to know instinctively what a family should be.

What's a family?

- "A group of people who love each other"

- "A group of people who never go away"

- "A mommy and daddy and brothers and sisters"

- "A man and a woman who marry and have babies together"

- "A mommy and daddy who love each other forever"

- "People who teach you right from wrong"

- "People who tie your shoes"

- "A mommy and daddy who help you when you're hurt"

- "A mom and dad who teach you how to be a mom and dad"

- "People who don't laugh at you"

- "People who play together"

- "You have to have a family, or you can't live"

What are mothers and fathers like?

- "Fathers are like big hammers. They pound people if they mess with their children."

- "Mothers are like 'a cherry on an ice-cream sundae.' Fathers are like 'the cone underneath the ice cream.'"

- "Mothers are your bestest friend."

What's more important, being smart or being nice?

- "I want to be smart, because then I would know to be nice."

- "If you're not nice, then you're not smart."

- "I know I'm smart, because I try to be nice."

- Ninety-six percent responded without hesitation, "Nice."

Children know the truth, but no one's listening. It's we adults who have gotten confused about what's right and what's wrong. We're the ones who have lost our way.

Children come into the world needing guidance to become all they were created to be. They need direction. They need examples to follow. They need someone to nurture their souls and protect their hearts. They need someone who will offer real answers. They need someone to walk beside them every step of the way with encouragement. They need more than the world has to offer.

They need parents who will parent.

We can't blame the media or Hollywood or the schools or the government or all the other institutions in the world for the way our children are turning out. They make our job much more difficult, but they are not to blame. We are. God doesn't entrust His children to the world, but to parents.

In the movie *Kramer vs. Kramer*, Dustin Hoffman plays a workaholic father, Ted Kramer, whose wife, Joanna, makes a tragic decision to leave not only her husband but also their son. Here's a man who hasn't a clue how to be a father with a young son and an all-consuming career, but he's willing to learn. Joanna resurfaces asking for custody. When Ted refuses, they wind up in a bitter battle. The most telling scene in the movie is when Ted testifies in court with great intensity that he's reduced his workload because raising a child requires so much time simply to listen.

In a moving monologue, Ted looks from the jury to the judge to his former wife and asks, "What is it that makes somebody a good parent?"

He answers his own question as he continues, "It has to do with constancy. It has to do with patience. It has to do with listening to them. Pretending to listen to them when you can't even listen anymore."[1]

Of all the skills we need to raise respectful children in this disrespectful world, the skill of listening outweighs all the rest. Listen to God's leading, listen to your heart, and listen to your children.

When you do your part, God will take care of the rest.

Arise, *cry out in the night,*
as the watches of the night begin;
pour out your heart like water in the presence of the Lord.
Lift up your hands to him for the lives of your children.
LAMENTATIONS 2:19

A Personal Note to Single Parents

I'M SURE YOU'VE NOTED there are few personal stories from our home that include my husband. Oh, how I wish there could have been. My husband left our home the first week of our sons' sixth-grade school year.

It was devastating.

No one on earth was more important to me than my husband, my college sweetheart. His life was my life. Together we had worked hard to achieve his goals. Just when I thought "one of these days" had finally come for us, he decided that rather than begin a new chapter in our family history book, our book needed to close. I begged; the boys begged, but to no avail.

I wanted you to know this book has been written from the heart of a mom who survived the devastation of rejection and the unbearable pain of broken dreams. Having lived it, I wholeheartedly agree with Dr. James Dobson that "the most difficult job in the world is that of a single mom."

But with God's help I've done it. I want you to know that you can do it too.

Stand with assurance before the throne. It *is* true that you cannot raise your children alone. But don't fret . . . you have three allies to help you—the Father, the Son, and the Holy Ghost. The Lord will bless you with an extra arsenal of protection when you're willing to allow Him to be the head of your home. Take a stand for your children, in spite of your loss and pain.

Your children can become respectful children in the midst of great disrespectfulness, if you will not allow your heart to grow bitter. Single moms or single dads, it is your own bitterness, not the actions of the wayward spouse, that will destroy your children. I know you cannot fill two roles, but you can fulfill your role. God will fill in the gaps.

Let me share a priority list with you that I've lived by for twelve years:

Priority List to Live By
God

Children

Family

Service to the church

Service to the community

The list could go on . . . with one exception. We don't belong on our own priority list. Many days I wondered and worried who would take care of me while I was taking care of my sons. Out of fear I tried to put myself on my list. But God made this truth perfectly clear to me—He would take care of me, if I kept my eyes on Him. If I had put myself on my list, I would have been telling God that I could take care of myself without Him.

Scary thought . . . I knew better. Been there and done that—it doesn't work.

Please hear me with your heart. You are on the top of God's priority list. God hates divorce. When a marriage is dissolved, a covenant with God is broken, but God will not break His covenant with you. Never forget that.

When a father abandons a child, God draws closer. He will provide the male role models your son needs and the male father figures your daughter needs. When a child is abandoned by a mother, God draws closer. He will provide the female role models your daughter needs and the female mother figures your son needs.

Hold your head high, and allow these words from Psalm 34:3–4 to penetrate your heart and give you comfort: "I sought the LORD, and he answered me; he delivered me from all my fears. Those who look to him are radiant; their faces are never covered with shame."

He did it for me; He wants to do it for you. Just ask. He's waiting to deliver you so you can lead His children back to Him.

appendix B

Family Protection Policy

Let me encourage you to pray this prayer each morning for your family. Based on Ephesians 6, it's God's insurance plan for your family.

Lord, place upon our heads the helmet of salvation,
To protect our minds.
Place upon our chests the breastplate of righteousness,
To protect our hearts.
Buckle around us the belt of Truth,
That we would know the Truth and speak the Truth,
That we would not be deceived, nor would we deceive.
Lord, we will carry the sword of the Spirit,
Your Word, as an offensive weapon.
Enable us to walk in the path of peace
You lay before us this day,
Not stepping to the left or to the right,
But walking in its narrow way.
And now, with the Holy Spirit dwelling within,
With Jesus Christ, our brother, standing with us,
And with the Lord God Almighty empowering us,
We will stand and hold the shield of faith this day for
(your children's names),
Until each can carry it in their own faith.
Amen.

Must-Read Books for Parents

Dietrich Bonhoffer, *The Cost of Discipleship*

S. Truett Cathy, *It's Better to Build Boys Than Mend Men*

John Eldredge, *Waking the Dead: The Glory of a Heart Fully Alive*

John Eldredge, *Wild at Heart: Discovering the Secret of a Man's Soul* (for dads)

Staci Eldredge, *Captivating: Unveiling the Mystery of a Woman's Soul* (for moms)

Elisabeth Elliot, *Discipline: The Glad Surrender*

Eva Marie and Jessica Everson, *Sex, Lies, and the Media*

Richard Foster, *Devotional Classics*

Cheri Fuller, *The Mom You're Meant to Be: Loving Your Kids While Leaning on God*

Ellie Kay, *Money Doesn't Grow on Trees—Teaching Kids the Value of a Buck*

Thomas à Kempis, *The Imitation of Christ*

Walt Larimore, *The Highly Healthy Child*

Brother Lawrence, *The Practice of the Presence of God*

Kevin Leman, *When Your Best Isn't Good Enough*

——, *Sex Begins in the Kitchen: Because Love Is an All-Day Affair*

C. S. Lewis, *The Screwtape Letters*

——, The Chronicles of Narnia series

Max Lucado, *It's Not about Me: Rescue from the Life We Thought Would Make Us Happy*

Brennan Manning, *The Ragamuffin Gospel*

Calvin Miller, *Into the Depths of God*

Norman Vincent Peale, *The Power of Positive Thinking*

Fred Rogers, *The World According to Mister Rogers*

——, *You Are Special: Neighborly Wisdom from Mister Rogers*

Jill Rigby, *Manners of the Heart at Home*

John Rosemond, *John Rosemond's New Parent Power*

John Rosemond, *Family Building: The Five Fundamentals of Effective Parenting*

Hannah Whitall Smith, *The Christian's Secret of a Happy Life*

J. R. R. Tolkien, The Lord of the Rings

A. W. Tozer, *Keys to the Deeper Life*

——, *The Knowledge of the Holy*

——, *The Pursuit of God*

Rick Warren, *The Purpose-Driven Life: What on Earth Am I Here For?*

Dallas Willard, *Renovation of the Heart: Putting on the Character of Christ*

notes

Chapter 1: What Went Wrong?

1. John Rosemond, "From Spock to Rosemond," Syndicated column, July 25, 2000. Found online at http://www.rosemond.com/ EditorialEExprint.LASSO?-token.editorialcall=91501.112113.

2. Interview with Roy F. Baumeister, Florida State University, http://www.fsu.edu/profiles/baumeister/ (accessed April 12, 2006).

3. Judith Martin, "The World's Oldest Virtue," *First Things* 33 (May 1993): 22–25.

4. Luke 6:45.

5. Luke 6:45 CEV.

6. Luke 6:45 MSG.

7. See John 17:15.

Chapter 2: Where Have All the Parents Gone?

1. David Brooks, "The Organization Kid," *Atlantic Monthly*, April 2001, http://www.theatlantic.com.

2. Camilla A. Herrera, "Too Much Parenting Might Be Damaging," *Stamford Advocate*, July 23, 2005.

3. Marjorie Coeyman, "Childhood Achievement Test," *Christian Science Monitor*, December 17, 2002, http://www.csmonitor.com/2002/1217/

p11s02-lehl.html (accessed April 13, 2006).

4. Camellia A. Herrera, "For 'Alpha Parents' Only the Best Will Do," *Stamford Advocate*, July 18, 2005.

5. Nancy Gibbs, "Do Kids Have Too Much Power?" July 17–18, 2001, http://www.time.com/time/covers/1101010806/cover.html (accessed April 13, 2006).

6. Krista Conger, "TV in Bedrooms Linked to Lower Test Scores," *Stanford Report*, July 13, 2005, http://news-service.stanford.edu/news/2005/july13/med-tv-071305.html (accessed April 13, 2006).

7. Will Edwards, "The 7 Habits," http://www.whitedovebooks.co.uk/7-habits/7-habits.htm (accessed April 13, 2006).

8. Matthew 5:36–37.

9. Josephson Institute of Ethics, http://www.josephsoninstitute.org/quotes/quotecharacter.htm (accessed April 13, 2006).

Chapter 3: Enroll in the School of Respect

1. Proverbs 22:6.

2. James Strong, *The Exhaustive Concordance of the Bible: Showing Every Word of the Text of the Common English Version of the Canonical Books, and Every Occurrence of Each Word in Regular Order*, electronic ed. (Ontario: Woodside Bible Fellowship, 1996), 2596.

3. Strong, *Exhaustive Concordance*, 1870.

4. Noah Webster's 1828 Dictionary.

5. Dr. Albert Siegel, professor of psychology at Stanford University. *Stanford Observer*, October, 1973, 4.

6. Deuteronomy 4:9.

7. George Bernard Shaw, www.thinkexist.com.

8. Michael Resnick, et al., "Protecting Adolescents from Harm," Findings from the National Longitudinal Study on Adolescent Health, *Journal of the American Medical Association* 278, no. 10 (September 10, 1997), http://jama.ama-assn.org/cgi/content/abstract/278/10/823?maxtoshow=&HITS=10&hits=10&RESULTFORMAT=&fulltext=%22protecting+adolescents+from+harm%22&searchid=1139432338669_8489&FIRSTINDEX=0&journalcode=jama (accessed April 13, 2006.)

9. Michael Resnick, interview by Norman Swan, "Adolescent Health," *The Health Report: ABC Radio National*, September 22, 1997.

10. Larry Crabb, *Connecting* (Nashville: Word, 1997).

11. Henry Ward Beecher, "Wellness, Academics, and You," http://i4learning.com/way/parent_portal/talking.asp (accessed April 13, 2006).

Chapter 4: Stress Purpose, Not Performance

1. "A Tennis Dad and a Court Mystery," *The Observer*, August 10, 2003, http://observer.guardian.co.uk/europe/story/0,11363,1015753,00.html (accessed April 13, 2006).

2. Janine Bempechat, https://www.pta.org/parentinvolvement/helpchild/oc_greatexpect.asp.

3. Michelle Kees, "Is Your Child Overscheduled and Overstressed?" *Children's Mental Health News*, July 29, 2005.

4. Luke 22:42 KJV.

5. ThinkExist.com, http://en.thinkexist.com/quotes/zig_ziglar/3.html (accessed April 13, 2006).

6. *American Heritage Dictionary*, s.v. "perseverance."

Chapter 5: Coach; Don't Cheerlead

1. Jean Twenge, L. Zhang, and C. Im, "It's Beyond My Control: a Cross-temporal Meta-analysis of Increasing Externality in Locus of Control, 1960–2002," *Personality and Social Psychology Review* 8 (2004): 308–19.

2. Mike Tymn, "Third Wind," *National Masters News*, February 2005, http://fairmodel.econ.yale.edu/aging/tymn.pdf, accessed April 13, 2006.

3. John B. Scott and James S. Ward, *Champions for Life* (Columbus, Ohio: Nicholas Ward, 2004), 166.

4. Thomas Edison Quotes, http://www.thomasedison.com/edquote.htm (accessed April 13, 2006).

5. "Landry Remembered at Services," CBS News, http://www.cbsnews.com/stories/2000/02/17/archive/main161898.shtml (accessed April 13, 2006).

6. Matthew 7:24–25.

7. Ephesians 4:14, emphasis mine.

8. Coaching Quotes, http://www.coachqte.com/landry.html (accessed April 13, 2006).

9. Scott and Ward, *Champions for Life,* 166.

Chapter 6: Set Boundaries without Building Walls

1. Gary and Anne Marie Ezzo, "Toddlers—The Neurological Boundaries of Learning," http://www.gfi.org/java/jsp/article40.htm (accessed April 13, 2006).

2. Genesis 3:8.

3. Robert Fulghum, *All I Really Need to Know I Learned in Kindergarten,* (New York: Villard, 1990), 6.

4. John 15:15.

Chapter 7: Use Discipline, Not Punishment

1. *Miriam-Webster* OnLine, http://www.m-w.com/dictionary/discipline (accessed April 13, 2006).

2. *Webster's Desk Dictionary*, 1995, s.v. "punishment."

3. Ephesians 6:4, italics mine.

4. Hebrews 12:11.

5. 1 Timothy 1:5 NASB.

6. Psalm 139:23–24, italics mine.

7. Proverbs 6:23.

Chapter 8: Shield Your Treasures from the Trash: Magazines, Books, and Music

1. Corrie ten Boom, *The Hiding Place* (Uhrichsville, Ohio: Barbour, 1971).

2. Media Awareness Network, "How Marketers Target Kids," http://www.media-awareness.ca/english/parents/marketing/marketers_target_kids.cfm (accessed April 13, 2006).

3. Cecily von Ziegesar, *Gossip Girl* (New York: Little, Brown, 2002), 3.

4. Sarah Webb Quest, "The Gossip Girl Speaks," October 17, 2004, http://www.suite101.com/article.cfm/professional_writing/111559 (accessed April 13, 2006).

5. James C. Humes, *Speaker's Treasury of Anecdotes about the Famous* (New York: Harper & Row, 1978), 154.

6. Peter Chattaway, "Harry Potter and the Prisoner of Azkaban,"

Christianity Today, April 24, 2004, http://www.christianitytoday.com/movies/reviews/harrypotter3.html (accessed April 13, 2006).

7. LYRICS007, http://www.lyrics007.com/Eamon%20Lyrics/Finally%20Lyrics.html (accessed April 13, 2006).

8. Answers.com, "Parents Music Resource Center," http://www.answers.com/topic/parents-music-resource-center (accessed April 13, 2006).

9. Bob Smithouser, "Mind over Media," Focus on the Family, www.family.org/fofmag/pf/a0026144.cfm (accessed April 13, 2006).

10. 1 John 2:16–17.

11. Proverbs 19:21.

12. Jeremiah 29:11.

13. Romans 16:17–19.

14. Philippians 4:8.

Chapter 9: Shield Your Treasures from the Trash: Movies, TV, Video Games, and the Internet

1. Michael Elliott, "A Movie Parable," http://www.christiancritic.com/mov2004/hpotter3.asp (accessed April 13, 2006).

2. Bob Bloom, Movie review in *Journal and Courier*, http://www.rottentomatoes.com/click/movie-1146058/reviews.php?critic=columns&sortby=default&page=3&rid=1394248 (accessed April 13, 2006).

3. BBC News, "New Star Wars Movie a Bloodbath," May 4, 2005, http://news.bbc.co.uk/2/hi/entertainment/4513837.stm (accessed April 13, 2006).

4. Kimberly Thompson, "Violence, Sex, and Profanity in Films: Correlation of Movie Ratings with Content," *Medscape General Medicine*, July 2004, http://www.medscape.com/viewarticle/505766.

5. MSNBC News, "Breaker! Breaker! Ben Jones Says Movie Trashes the TV Version," July 15, 2005, http://www.msnbc.msn.com/id/8573374 (accessed April 13, 2006).

6. Parents Television Council, "It's Just Harmless Entertainment," http://www.parentstv.org/PTC/facts/mediafacts.asp (accessed April 13, 2006).

7. "Spears Says Mom Approved of Madonna Kiss." Found online at http://www.talk.livedaily.com/showthread.php?t=35239.

8. *Frontline*, May 24, 2004, http://www.pbs.org/wgbh/pages/frontline/shows/music/interviews/ (accessed April 13, 2006).

9. Nielsen Ratings, January 2005.

10. Ibid.

11. Parents Television Council, "Headlines and Highlights," October 2005, http://www.parentstv.org/PTC/publications/bw/2005/0926worst.asp.

12. Kaiser Family Foundation, "Sex and the Media," 2003, http://kff .org/entmedia/upload/Sex-on-TV-3-Content-and-Context.pdf (accessed April 13, 2006).

13. Mike Snider, "Video Games: Grand Theft Auto: Vice City," *USA Today*, December 27, 2002, 8D.

14. S. R. Lichter, *Sexual Imagery in Pop Culture* (Washington, D.C. Center for Media and Popular Policy).

15. American Psychiatric Association report, 2004.

16. Parents Television Council report, 2004.

17. American Psychological Association, *Violence and Youth: Psychology's Response, Volume 1*, (Washington, D.C. American Psychological Association), 32.

18. M. J. Sutton, et al., "Shaking the Tree of Knowledge for Forbidden Fruit," *Sexual Teens, Sexual Media: Investigating the Media's Influence on Adolescent Sexuality*, ed. Jane Brown, Jeanne Steele, and Kim Walsh-Childers (New York: Erlbaum), 25–55.

19. Rebecca L. Collins, et al., "Watching sex on television predicts adolescent initiation of sexual behavior," *Pediatrics* 114, no. 3 (2004): 280–89.

20. A. C. Huston and J. C. Wright, "Television and socialization of young children," in T. MacBeth, ed., *Tuning in to Young Viewers* (Thousand Oaks, Calif.: Sage), 37–60.

21. Huston and Wright, "Television."

22. Dimitri A. Christakis, et al., "Early Television Exposure and Subsequent Attentional Problems in Children," *Pediatrics* 113 (2004): 708–13.

23. Pew Research Center, "Support for Tougher Indecency Measures, but Worries about Government Intrusiveness," April 19, 2005.

24. *Time* magazine poll, March 3, 2005.

25. Federal Communications Commission, http://www.fcc.gov/.

26. *Entertainment Weekly*, September 16, 2005.

27. C. R. Jayachandran, "Porn rules Net revenue charts," Times News Network, September 26, 2003. Found online at http://economictimes .indiatimes.com/articleshow/msid-203421.

28. Kelly Patricia O'Meara, "Free Speech Trumps 'Virtual' Child Porn," *Insight on the News*, May 27, 2002.

29. Neil Postman, *The Disappearance of Childhood* (New York: Delacorte, 1982).

30. As reported by CBS News on May 2, 2002. For more information on the full report, "Youth, Pornography, and the Internet," from the National Research Council, visit www.nationalacademies.org.

Chapter 10: Engage; Don't Entertain

1. ThinkExist.com, http://en.thinkexist.com/.

2. ThinkExist.com, http://en.thinkexist.com/.

3. Fred Rogers, *The World According to Mister Rogers* (New York: Hyperion, 2003), 183.

Chapter 11: Teach Gratefulness, Not Greediness

1. Parent page, "Blow up Your TV!??" http://www.lausd.k12.ca.us/ Haskell_EL/parent%20information/tv2.htm (accessed April 13, 2006).

2. "Blow up Your TV?!!"

3. John Austin, "Americans' race for space fuels boom in self-storage," the *Advocate*, November 13, 2005, H1.

4. Mark 8:36–37.

5. See Acts 20:35.

6. Proverbs 15:13.

Chapter 12: Listen to the Children

1. *Kramer vs. Kramer*, DVD, directed by Robert Benton (1979, Columbia Pictures Home Entertainment , 2001).

About the Author

JILL RIGBY is an accomplished speaker, columnist, television personality, family advocate, and founder of Manners of the Heart Community Fund, a nonprofit organization bringing a return of civility and respect to our society. Whether equipping parents to raise responsible children, encouraging the education of the heart, or training executives in effective communication skills, Jill's definition of manners remains the same—an attitude of the heart that is self-giving, not self-serving. She is the proud mother of twin sons who testify to her contagious passion.

Manners of the Heart Community Fund

Manners of the Heart is a nonprofit organization working to bring a return of respect and civility to our society through curricula for K-12 students, parenting seminars, and high-impact training for corporations and communities.

Manners of the Heart Curriculum

Can you imagine how different our society would be if every child had self-respect and showed respect for others? Our elementary school curriculum makes it possible. Through the use of creative materials, intensive training for educators and parents, and support from volunteers, *Manners of the Heart* brings schools, homes, and communities together to prepare young people with not only head knowledge but heart knowledge to lead in the right direction.

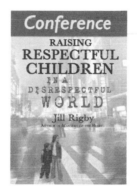